A Guide to World Money and Capital Markets

A Guide to
World Money and
Capital Markets

L. J. Kemp

McGRAW-HILL Book Company (UK) Limited

London · New York · St Louis · San Francisco · Auckland · Bogotá · Guatemala
Hamburg · Johannesburg · Lisbon · Madrid · Mexico · Montreal · New Delhi
Panama · Paris · San Juan · São Paulo · Singapore · Sydney · Tokyo · Toronto

Published by
McGRAW-HILL Book Company (UK) Limited
Maidenhead · Berkshire · England

British Library Cataloguing in Publication Data

Kemp, L. J.
  A guide to world money and capital markets.
  1. Banks and banking, International
  2. Money market
  I. Title
  332   HG3881
  ISBN 0-07-084566-2

Library of Congress Cataloging in Publication Data

Kemp, L. J. (Lynette J.)
  A guide to world money and capital markets.

  Includes index.
  1. Investments—Handbooks, manuals, etc.
  2. Investments, Foreign—Handbooks, manuals, etc.
  3. Money market—Handbooks, manuals, etc.
  4. Capital market—Handbooks, manuals, etc.
  I. Title.
  HG4527.K45   332.6'73'0202   81-8149
  ISBN 0-07-084566-2   AACR2

Typeset by Santype International Limited and
Printed in Great Britain at the Alden Press, Oxford

Contents

Preface

I found it essential to write this book in order to do my job more effectively. Being involved in the investment decisions of a multinational company which accounts in eighteen currencies and earns revenues also in a number of others, I required a knowledge of the many alternative options. One course of action, which was obligatory under previously enforced exchange controls, was to convert all repatriated earnings to the base currency—in this case, sterling. Another strategy, which in the case of the UK has only recently become possible, is to seek the best return on surplus earnings subject to certain constraints such as risk, liquidity, volatility, availability etc.

Despite being based in the City of London, which by many criteria is the major financial centre in the world, the necessary information required to formulate a multicurrency portfolio strategy has not been readily available. Certainly it has not been available from a single source. This book represents a considerable amount of research in order to bring together a description of all the investment opportunities in 25 different markets. For an international company such as the Sedgwick Group it would have been anyway necessary to compile most of the information presented here. It is certain that the same information is also vital for other multinational companies and international investors of all categories—hence the publication of this book.

Moreover, in researching the information for the book, the differences between various markets and the similarity in domestic government objectives have presented an interesting dichotomy. It is my belief that, due to a number of factors such as increasing communications and decreasing economic insularity between nations, world financial markets are moving towards a common base. This process has certainly been developing rapidly during the 1970s and will continue during the 1980s and beyond. The dynamism experienced in recent years makes it difficult for any investor to keep abreast of the changes and innovations in financial markets. It is intended, therefore, to regularly update this book through future editions in order to fulfil that essential function and to maintain its value as a work of reference.

In compiling this book, the Sedgwick Group has undoubtedly been a major contributor—not least for the tolerance shown to me for the time it has taken. In addition, I could not have written this without all the assistance and time contributed by many others.

In particular, I would like to thank the following people who have helped in checking certain chapters or who have assisted in providing material: Victor Abrams, Chris Burton, Magne Fosheim, Dr Edmund Goldberger, Janet Harris, Werner Hauger, Andrew Goodwin, André Marini, Anthony Maynard, Antonio Profico, Anthony Reymond, Dr Raimund Solonar, Roland Stähli, Tom Tootell and Mike Wiltshire, and also Price Waterhouse & Co who have kindly given me permission to use the tables on Withholding Taxes which appear in each chapter.

I would also like to thank the long-suffering typists who didn't realize when they first volunteered quite what they were taking on, but persevered without complaining. My thanks to Liz Cooper-Mitchell, Carol Hennahane, Gillian Kemp and Linda Pawsey.

Finally, I would like to express my very great appreciation for the special contribution made by the following people: Dick Grahman, who helped right from the beginning and without whom my task would have been considerably more difficult; Michael Barnes, who provided stimulating ideas as well as copious information; Robert Forde, who assisted with the early research and who obligingly proof-read every chapter; Stephen Swift, who checked one of the chapters and supervised the checking of several others; and lastly, but not least, I would like to thank Alma Bell, my secretary, for keeping me organized and for displaying infinite patience during this last year.

L. J. KEMP

1. Introduction

This book is designed as a comprehensive reference guide to the financial markets of 25 countries. Such a book is necessary because, with the rapid development in worldwide communications, the change from fixed- to floating-rate currency systems, and the changing attitudes of governments and monetary authorities, it is not only easier to invest in foreign markets, but the potential for greater profit (and, of course, loss) is increased by the flexibility available for informed investors to participate in foreign markets.

Markets differ, however, from country to country. The financial infrastructure, the role of financial institutions and the attitude and types of intervention by regulatory authorities largely determine what types of investment instruments are available while exchange controls and the taxation system affect the attractiveness of such instruments to foreign investors. It is difficult even for professional international investors and advisers to retain detailed knowledge of more than a few markets, particularly since financial systems are changing continuously in many respects. This book provides a thorough, but simple, description of the major markets throughout the world. It is written from the point of view of the non-resident of each country. Thus, although the author is British, the UK chapter is designed to be read by foreigners needing greater understanding of the UK system.

It is envisaged that this guide to world money and capital markets will be of use to a wide range of readers throughout the world, including: financial intermediaries, e.g., bankers, brokers, accountants; professional investors, e.g., corporate treasurers, building societies, savings associations, insurance companies, pension and superannuation funds, investments and unit trusts; international and multinational companies, e.g., financial directors requiring greater knowledge of local markets in which subsidiaries are operating; official bodies, e.g., central banks, monetary agencies, government departments; academics and students, particularly of business studies and economics; and private investors, mainly wealthy individuals.

So as to be easy to use as a reference guide, the book follows a consistent format. The chapters are arranged country by country within geographical groupings, beginning with America which includes chapters on Canada, Mexico and the USA, and ending with the Far East. The final chapter is one on international markets and covers those markets that are not peculiar to any single country, such as the Eurobond market.

Apart from Chapter 15, which is brief and Chapter 26, which follows a slightly

1

different format, each chapter is split into seven sections. Within each section each point is highlighted by a major or subordinate heading to aid reference. The major sectors and the topics covered are as follows:

1. General market environment.
2. The money market.
3. The capital market.
4. Dealing and fees.
5. Financial and monetary systems.
6. Withholding taxes.
7. Exchange controls.

1. General market environment

This is a short summary designed to give a general overview of the main financial aspects of the country in question. It particularly highlights those features of special interest or concern to the non-resident investor. The section also contains a summary table of the financial instruments available in that market.

2. The money market

This section describes all the financial instruments that are issued and traded in the money market of the country under discussion.

The term 'Money market' is used to define the network of borrowers and lenders for short-term funds. What constitutes the short term varies from country to country. Generally the short term is defined as up to one year, but in Canada, for example, the money market encompasses securities with up to three-year maturity because the Canadian Central Bank will advance credit against certain securities with a maturity of three years or less.

The advance and rediscounting facilities provided by central banks are important for ensuring that sufficient liquidity is maintained in the short-term financial system. It provides a method by which the central bank can lend to the banks either directly, or indirectly through special intermediaries such as the discount houses in London or the primary dealers in the US. Short-term lenders of funds, including the banks and other financial institutions, can continue to take up new short-term securities, thus facilitating an efficiently functioning money market. Obviously though, banks and financial intermediaries in most countries only borrow from the central bank when liquidity is tight, there being too great a demand for short-term funds relative to the available supply of funds. Under such conditions, interest rates rise as borrowers have to bid higher and higher for funds while the price of securities falls in order that buyers may be found. Interest rates fall under converse conditions when liquidity is buoyant.

As users of short-term finance, the borrowers in the money market in general are central and local governments, banks, and financial enterprises and corporations. The lenders are financial institutions, corporations, banks and financial intermediaries, and households. The major flows between participants in the money market are shown diagrammatically below. The diagram is very simple and rather general, and there exist specific variations between countries.

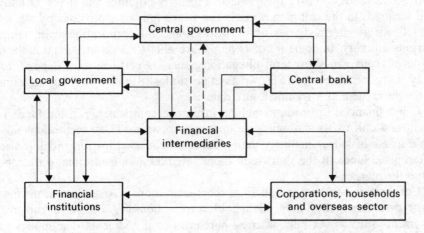

The range of securities issued and traded in the money market depend not only on the financial infrastructure and specific legislation but also on the types of borrowers. In most countries, the largest borrower is the central government which, by the issue of treasury bills or similar short-term securities, raises funds to cover temporary budget deficits.

Where the issue of treasury bills is both large and frequent the money market provides the government with a means of influencing domestic liquidity and short-term interest rates. Sustained and consistent action by the government eventually has an effect on longer-term interest rates and on other monetary aggregates, such as the growth of domestic credit and money supply. By selling treasury bills a government absorbs cash from the money market and reduces the short-term funds available to other borrowers. By varying the amount of treasury bills on sale, by buying and selling existing bills in the open market and in some cases by determining or influencing the rate of discount (interest) on new bill issues the government is thus able to manipulate trends in domestic financial markets.

Banks and other financial intermediaries are important participants in the money market. Not only do they provide the means by which funds from lenders of one group can be transferred to borrowers of another group, but they are themselves substantial borrowers of funds and also holders of assets that include short-term money market securities. It is axiomatic that they borrow short and lend long. They borrow mainly in the form of deposits that may comprise, depending on the type of bank or intermediary, sight deposits, short-term deposits at call or notice, fixed-term time deposits and savings deposits. Against their general deposit base, they grant loans and advances to the corporate and household sector. They also lend

3

directly to other banks or financial intermediaries through the interbank market and indirectly to the government and other institutions through the purchase of securities which they hold in their own asset portfolios.

Banks usually balance their books on a daily basis and often require additional short-term funds to cover their assets of security holdings and loans. Usually they bid for funds in the call money market and such funds are provided by other banks and financial intermediaries or by institutions and corporations with temporary surplus liquidity. In some markets banks are able to raise additional funds by the issue of their own short-term obligations, such as certificates of deposit, or they may sell securities out of their own asset portfolios with or without an agreement to repurchase them at a specific future date.

Other financial institutions include insurance companies, pension funds investment and unit trusts and mortgage finance companies. These institutions normally hold assets of longer maturity than most money market instruments but also they often place funds in the short-term money market and, from time to time, borrow from the market.

Corporations are major lenders of short-term money. According to the nature of their cash flows, they may often hold surplus liquidity, but have known future payments such as tax bills, salaries, purchases or investments. The money market provides them with a means of obtaining a return on temporary funds while also providing liquidity and marketability should unexpected liabilities arise. Companies may also be frequent borrowers of short-term funds. This can be arranged in the form of bank credit, or loans for specific short-term transactions against the issue of commercial bills of exchange, or through the direct issue of short-term promissory notes, such as commercial paper. The means of borrowing by companies varies from country to country and very much depends on tradition as well as on market flexibility.

Households are not major participants in the money market, which is characterized by short-term high-volume flows of funds. The minimum size in which most transactions are made tend to preclude individual borrowers or lenders. Money market mutual funds, as exist in the USA, are one method by which individuals can participate in the short-term financial market, but these funds are not yet common to most money markets.

The importance of the overseas sector depends on the circumstances specific to each country. Countries running fiscal debts or balance of payments deficits, and whose currencies are weak, generally encourage investment by foreign parties. Some with strong economies and strong currencies may restrict foreign access by temporary or permanent legislation, others may provide totally unrestricted access to foreigners but may rely upon official intervention in the markets to influence the actions of all types of investors. The openness of a particular market may determine whether or not a market in Eurocurrencies exists in that country. For example, Sweden restricts access to its markets by overseas investors and also does not provide a local Eurocurrency market. Switzerland, on the other hand, may at times restrict access to her domestic money market but actively encourages domestic banks' participation in the Euromarkets.

3. The capital market

This section describes all the securities that are issued and traded in the capital market of the country concerned.

The capital market may be defined as the network of borrowers and lenders for medium-term and long-term funds. Medium term is understood to be usually between one and five years, though one to three years is defined as short-term in some countries and the medium term may be understood to extend to 10 years in other countries. Long term is any period that is longer than the medium term and may extend to periods of 15 years, 40 years or, in some cases, have no finite term (e.g., undated government stocks).

A wider variety of borrowers and lenders make up the capital market than comprise the money market. Each has a different set of preferences as regards interest rates, maturity, liquidity and risk, so a diversity of financial instruments exists in order to satisfy the requirements of both borrowers and lenders. Not all of these instruments are available in every country. Moreover, even in the case of instruments common to most free market countries (e.g., corporate bonds) they may differ in form, trading methods, marketability, legal standing or in other respects.

Broadly defined the types of instruments within the capital market are debt securities (i.e., bonds, notes etc.), equities, commodities (including gold as a special case) and other markets (e.g., futures markets).

Debt securities debentures, or bonds, are loan issues. They may have a specified maturity or may be redeemed on a series of dates; some have no fixed redemption dates and some may be redeemed by a prearranged sinking fund or by lottery. Most have fixed rates of interest, though some may have variable or floating interest rates which have become a feature of some types of markets due to volatile interest levels experienced by many countries in recent years. Most are issued publicly and may be purchased by any investor and subsequently traded in the secondary market. Some, however, are issued by private placement (i.e., placed directly with the investor) and may not be traded in the secondary market. Some bonds issued by companies give the bondholder the right either to purchase shares of the issuing company at predetermined terms (bonds with warrants) or to convert the bond into shares of the company (convertible bonds).

Equity share issues are a common way by which companies (which are, in general, net debtors) raise funds. The use of the equity market, in preference to debt issues or direct borrowing from banks and financial institutions, depends largely on the nature of a country's particular financial infrastructure. In the UK for example, corporations tend mainly to tap the equities market for additional funds, while in France only large corporations regularly make issues in the equity market, since most French companies prefer to borrow from banks or financial institutions or to make debt issues in the bond market. In the USA both the equity and bond market are actively used as sources of corporate finance.

Other markets also exist in some countries. Gold may be traded as a commodity or may be linked to financial securities. There are 10 different ways by which to invest in gold. Some but not all of these methods are available in a number of markets throughout the world. The gold markets in each country are included in the capital market section of each chapter but, because of the unique and international nature of gold, a special section is contained in the chapter on international markets.

Other commodities are traded in specific forward or futures markets in certain countries. Some countries, such as Malaysia, provide a market in particularly local commodities (e.g., tin and rubber). Other countries such as the UK, which is a major trading country, provide a market in a wide range of commodities which tend to be those that are related to the country's traditional manufacturing industry or historic trading partners. The US commodity futures market provides the widest range of commodities which are traded on 10 different exchanges throughout the country. They range from perishable foods such as fresh eggs and frozen orange juice to grains, metals, fuels, currencies and financial instruments. Futures markets in currencies and financial instruments such as treasury bills and government bonds have been established on some US commodity exchanges during the last few years only. They allow investors to speculate or hedge against future interest-rate levels. Their popularity has encouraged similar markets to be established elsewhere such as Sydney in Australia and Toronto in Canada. A market in London is also expected in 1982.

4. Dealing and fees

This section explains how transactions in both money and capital market securities are made. In Germany, for example, the banks are multipurpose and may deal for clients on the stock exchange. In the UK stockbrokers only may deal on the stock exchange and, while a bank may act as an intermediary between client and broker, brokerage fees may be twice as high as when using a stockbroker directly. The section lists brokerage fees, commissions, other dealing fees, bond market spreads, as well as stamp duties and other relevant taxes. The terms on which settlement and delivery normally occur for all types of instruments are also given.

5. Financial and monetary systems

This section describes first the major financial institutions and second the methods by which the authorities operate their domestic monetary policies. The types of financial institutions and the way in which they interact with each other, the influence of the monetary authorities and the types of financial markets together make up the financial infrastructure of a particular country, and knowledge of this infrastructure goes a long way to providing an understanding of how and why the money and capital markets operate in a particular way.

The section on monetary policy helps to explain what are likely to be the major influences on the financial markets of each of the countries covered in the book. As an investor, it is important to understand how the markets are manipulated by the monetary authorities and the government's overall attitudes to the financial markets within its country. With such understanding the investor is better equipped to detect changes in financial trends and to be aware of the factors that are likely to produce a change in trend.

Most international investors know that, for example, the US financial markets have experienced volatile interest rates since the end of 1979, but fewer understand why. The reason is that since October 1979 the US monetary authorities have been operating a system of monetary base control. Central banks can control either the supply of money and credit or the level of interest rates, but not both at the same time. Put another way, it is not possible to control both the supply and the price of a widely traded commodity (in this case money) unless there exists complete control over everything. With this basic piece of information, the investor is thus aware that he must monitor the monetary aggregate figures (i.e., MIA, MIB, etc.) in order to estimate future interest-rate trends. This information is not enough, however. The monetary authorities back up their main policy instruments with the use of other instruments and it is thus useful to know what other tools are available and how they are used.

In addition, particular policies vary from country to country in the way they are applied. The Swiss monetary authorities use a system of monetary base control, but it differs from the system used in the USA. Most investors are aware that Switzerland has had both low and relatively stable interest rates for many years, and this may appear to conflict with the previous statement. The Swiss have been successful at controlling their monetary base and maintaining a low rate of domestic inflation, thus resulting in low interest rates. They also back up their policies with others that control the inflow of foreign capital (which tends to increase domestic money supply) and by discouraging an external market in Swiss franc securities.

The objectives of governments and authorities in determining their monetary policies are much the same but differ in emphasis. They all try to achieve monetary stability, low inflation and a stable and realistic value of their currency on the foreign exchanges with the overall objective of providing the right conditions for economic growth and the general welfare of their nationals (including near full employment). The methods by which governments attempt to achieve these objectives vary according to political philosophy and to the financial infrastructure that facilitates some methods more easily than others. Monetary and foreign exchange policies are not the only instruments. Fiscal policy is also very important in most countries and usually all types of policy instruments are used in an attempt at a co-ordinated package. It is monetary policies however that, in general, have a significant and/or immediate effect on financial markets; indeed they can only be made to work through the financial markets, and for that reason have been described for each of the countries in this book.

Monetary authorities have a choice of two broad types of monetary policy measures—direct controls and open-market operations. Greater reliance is generally placed on direct controls in less developed financial markets but have only a limited effect in more developed markets. On the other hand, market operations cannot be used efficiently in less developed markets but are more effective than direct controls in sophisticated financial markets.

Direct controls are all measures that restrict or determine aspects relating to the

7

assets and/or liabilities of banks and other financial institutions; or to the types of operations that particular institutions are permitted to engage in; or that act directly on market operants, such as interest rates. According to the country and type of policy the controls may be either statutorily imposed, mandatory, or by voluntary agreement between the monetary authorities and the financial institutions concerned. Direct controls necessarily distort the allocation of resources within an economy. Very often they are designed to do just that. For example, some 'types of controls are aimed at directing funds into the public sector or to specific economic sectors as designated by the government. If such sectors are less efficient and less profitable than other sectors then funds are directed to projects that may not have received finance under freer market conditions. On the other hand if, additionally, exchange controls also restrict the inflow of foreign capital, potentially profitable sectors may be deprived of sufficient funds so are unable to make required investments, and ultimately their profitability is reduced. Funds directed to less profitable sectors receive lower returns, which feed into the whole of the financial system, and thus result in a distorted price allocation of resources. Direct controls over interest rates have a similar effect.

Not all direct controls produce such drastic effects however. Some are applied so as to ensure that depositors' and investors' funds are protected and that a prudent level of liquidity is maintained in the financial system.

Direct controls include reserve ratios and liquidity requirements, asset ratios, qualitative and quantitative credit controls, regulations of interest rates, direct controls over specific interest rates, or restrictions on the activities of financial institutions or certain sectors.

In almost all countries, banks and, perhaps, other deposit-taking institutions are required to maintain a specified proportion of their deposit liabilities in the form of cash reserves, usually held by the central bank. These reserves may or may not earn interest. If interest is earned, then it is usually at a rate below market levels. These reserves ensure that banks are able to meet the cash withdrawals of their customers, but the ratio may also be regularly adjusted by some authorities in order to withdraw or add liquidity from or to the financial system.

With regard to liquidity controls, banks are required to maintain a given proportion of their deposit liabilities in certain specified assets. These assets are normally a mixture of money market securities which receive market rates of return, but which are highly marketable and thus 'near-cash' reserves. The monetary authorities may specify the types of assets in which liquidity must be held (e.g., government securities) and thus direct the flow of credit, and may additionally vary the ratio as an instrument of monetary policy. The higher the ratio, the lower the proportion of liabilities against which banks can extend credit (a major component of money supply). Additionally, the assets in which the banks are required to invest may provide lower returns than alternative assets and thus hold down interest rates generally throughout the financial markets.

Asset ratios require that a given proportion of the assets (as opposed to liabilities) of banks and/or other financial institutions be held in specific types of assets. The object of such direct controls is twofold. The main objective is usually to direct funds to specific economic sectors which, under market conditions, would not receive the level of investment desired by the authorities. Secondly, they hold down the volume of advances which the banks can extend to other borrowers. If an asset ratio is used as a flexible instrument of monetary policy then the monetary authorities can exercise a high degree of control over the expansion and direction of domestic credit.

Qualitative credit controls are similar to asset ratios in their objectives and effects, but are usually applied to banks only, whereas asset ratios may be readily applied to a wider range of financial institutions. Qualitative credit controls are used to specify the direction of loans and advances, i.e., the controls oblige banks to extend a specific proportion of their total lending, or to lend a minimum total amount, to special defined groups or institutions. Alternatively the controls may require the banks to extend credit to special sectors at terms more favourable than those prevailing in the market. All these methods aim not so much at controlling the rate of growth of the money supply but more at encouraging and fostering the economic growth either of developing sectors of industry or of politically preferred sectors of the economy or of the community.

Quantitative controls, on the other hand, aim at restraining the growth of credit throughout the economy and are usually general rather than selective measures. Such controls may be used flexibly, and frequently are applied in conjunction with qualitative controls. Quantitative restrictions specify that the growth of bank advances and loans should be within predetermined limits. For example, the authorities may require that bank lending for the current year should not increase in total by more than, say, 10 per cent of the previous year's level. The controls may be applied generally across the whole of the banking system where there is a high degree of co-operation between banks, or alternatively, banks may be prescribed individual limits and, in some cases, be subject to certain penalties if they exceed their limits.

Interest-rate regulations may take a variety of forms. The most common policy is direct administration of the central bank discount rate or the minimum lending rate. If either of these rates is changed by the monetary authorities then all other interest rates in the domestic financial market are consequently adjusted to a similar level. Interest rates may be held at artificially high levels with the objective of choking off demand for credit and thus slowing the growth of money supply. Alternatively, they may be held at an artificially low level in order to encourage domestic borrowing and faster economic growth. UK monetary policy in 1979 and 1980 is an example of the former method, and Malaysian monetary policy in the latter half of the 1970s is an example of the second. In well-developed or sophisticated financial markets this type of direct control has little effect, as has been demonstrated by the UK experience, because the market is flexible enough to find means of satisfying the demands of borrowers whose expectations anyway account for an eventual change in policy.

In some countries interest rate controls are applied more selectively. In Australia, for example, during the 1970s and 1980 maximum interest rates have been applied to overdrafts and advances of less than specified amounts. The objective was partly

9

to help individuals and home purchasers but also had the overall result of holding down deposit interest rates and the yields on debt securities. The controls have done little however to limit the general level of borrowing, but may have distorted the direction of credit. The Kuwait authorities impose maximum rates of interest on deposits and bank lending, though for religious rather than economic criteria. The economic effect is, however, detrimental since, in the absence of exchange controls, the policy results in large outflows of capital into foreign markets where higher returns can be earned. Some countries use interest-rate controls in conjunction with qualitative credit controls to provide cheap credit to specified sectors. France is an example, where loans to the energy, agriculture, export and other sectors are granted at favourable interest rates below other market rates.

Direct controls also include those whereby the authorities may restrict the activities of banks or financial institutions. Most countries have banking acts which specify the activities in which certain types of banks may engage. Commonly, a distinction is made between commercial banks, savings banks, investment banks, foreign banks and government owned or development banks. By differentiating in the banking act between banks and by specifying what activities each may engage in, the monetary authorities have greater flexibility to apply selective controls to particular banking groups. Similar legislation may allow the authorities to impose direct monetary controls on other financial institutions such as mortgage finance companies, insurance companies and pension funds so as to regulate, for example, the types of assets they hold.

In contrast to direct controls, market orientated policies are those whereby the monetary authorities aim to alter or influence monetary aggregates through the price mechanism by intervention in the financial markets. A government and its central bank together have the ability to use such substantial funds that they may significantly influence trends in the financial markets. In order that the authorities can operate in the open market they need both a developed financial market and one or several financial instruments with which to operate. The instrument, or instruments, used in open market intervention must represent a sufficiently large proportion of the total market such that transactions in them have an effect on the whole market. They must also be highly marketable and secure instruments so that transactions in them may easily be effected and so that major financial intermediaries are prepared to hold them in their asset portfolios.

In most countries where open market operations are used extensively treasury bills are a major market medium. The authorities issue treasury bills not only to provide short-term finance to the government but also as a means of controlling the supply of money in the financial system. Selling bills to the money market absorbs cash from the market and reduces the total amount which may be lent or borrowed in both the money and the capital market. As the supply is reduced the cost of money, or rate of interest, rises until demand for money falls and reaches an equilibrium with the available supply. As interest rates rise, money is also attracted from foreign sources (provided no inward exchange controls exist). These funds have to be converted to the domestic currency in order to benefit from the high interest rates and so compete with domestic demand, and thus tend to push interest rates still higher. This also tends to increase the value of the currency on the foreign exchanges as the demand for the currency increases, unless the authorities intervene to a sufficient degree in the foreign exchange markets so as to hold down the exchange rate. Expectations of lower interest and exchange rates together with a slackening of borrowers' demands for funds lead, eventually, to lower and more stable interest and exchange rates with a lower level of credit available in the financial system. The method produces volatility in the short term but, if the authorities are aware of what they are managing and how to measure it, can be successful in the longer term.

Problems arise however because, in large and diverse markets, the measurement of monetary aggregates is difficult and imprecise, not least because sophisticated market systems are dynamic and their major components keep changing. Psychological barriers also exist. There is no ideal interest rate except that which balances the supply and demand of money. Even that statement is polemic since objectives other than that of economic equilibrium exist. If interest rates rise to unprecedented levels the monetary authorities may reverse the policy by injecting liquidity back into the financial system (through, for example, the purchase of treasury bills) before the final stages of adjustment have been allowed to take effect. Psychological barriers however, are gradually being eroded. A decade ago, money market tables used to stop at 10 per cent because, not only was it an unprecedented rate of interest in most normal markets, but it was a nice round number and also a psychological barrier. The maximum interest rate in Kuwait which is determined on religious grounds, but to outsiders may seem purely arbitrary, is 10 per cent per annum. In recent years interest rates in some markets have gone seemingly wild. The USA is the best example. A switch in monetary policy in October 1979 resulted in the authorities placing greater reliance on open market operations. Interest rates rose to around 20 per cent in January 1980, then fell back to under 10 per cent as the Federal Reserve relaxed its restrictions, only to rise to well over 20 per cent in December 1980 as their monetary policies were again applied.

The result of restrictive measures through policies that operate on the whole market can be seen in the USA. Inflation, as measured by the consumer price index (and even that is a questionable measurement) was running at around 15 per cent in 1980. In theory an investor could earn a nominal return of 15 per cent per annum by simply buying a non-depreciable item, holding on to it for a year, and then selling it. Placing money in a financial instrument, however, involves a degree of risk for which the investor should be compensated. Certain securities are virtually credit risk free—government securities for example—and the return over and above other alternatives should reflect only the additional terms, such as the length of time the money must be 'locked in', in order to earn a return. It is not surprising therefore that during a period when the supply of money is intentionally restricted, investors (or lenders) can price their money well over the returns available from simple alternatives.

That explains a result of restrictive monetary policy, but not the reason. The authorities are concerned that not only interest rates are kept low but that inflation is both low and stable. Although inflation may be induced by a number of factors, **11** it manifests itself as too large a quantity of money chasing too limited a quantity of goods. Ideally the production of goods should be increased but this takes longer than reducing the supply of money. Also, in order that money be channelled into investments which produce more goods, returns on that type of investment need to be high enough to prevent investors from just buying and selling existing goods where the returns are both known and can be attractive. On the other hand if interest rates at high levels are sustained, manufacturers are deterred from borrowing for investment in the production of goods. It is this factor that worries the monetary authorities and leads them to reverse restrictive measures which they subsequently reimpose once interest rates have fallen. The measures do not have the desired long-term effect if applied intermittently, but the period of consistency necessary for the long-term effects to be sustained is not known.

The foregoing has illustrated the objectives and some of the results of managing the monetary base by the use of predominantly market-orientated policies. In practice fiscal policies usually also play an important role in augmenting these monetary policies. If sustained restrictive policy is applied, a government may choose to augment its monetary policy with the use of fiscal policy, in order to encourage certain types of productive investment while still reducing the overall demand for borrowing. It may, for example, introduce tax concessions or subsidies for particular industries. Often fiscal measures and direct monetary controls form the main part of a government's economic policy, with open market operations being used only to adjust temporary liquidity in the financial system in order that financial market trends are compatible with overall objectives.

Restriction of the monetary base was explained because this has been the policy adopted by many major countries in recent years. The same policies can be applied in reverse to result in expansion of the monetary base and reflation of the economy. A wider range of mechanisms, apart from the buying and selling of treasury bills, can also be used depending on the sophistication of the market. The authorities can also make minor adjustments by influencing the discount rate on treasury bills, either by the changing amount issued or by the tender rate they are prepared to accept. Although tenders from the financial market for new treasury bill issues are determined by market criteria, the authorities often have a certain degree of flexibility in accepting the tenders at the rates they prefer. Although the resultant discount rate may vary from the average of the tender rates by only a few basis points, it has wider effects on other interest rates in the money market. A change in the minimum tender rate accepted is also an indicator to the money market participants of impending further action by the authorities, perhaps in the form of increased activity in open market operations. At the close of tenders for each issue of treasury bills, most authorities announce the average tender rate, the maximum and minimum tenders and the rate accepted, together with the proportion of bidders receiving their allotment of bills. This proves an important indicator to money market participants as to the future course of interest rate and market intervention by the authorities.

6. Withholding taxes

Most countries tax interest and/or dividends earned on domestic securities. The rate of tax may be the same for residents as for non-residents, or it may differ. The tax due from non-residents is withheld at source and consequently known as withholding tax. To prevent investors in foreign markets from being unfairly taxed again in their home countries on the income or profit earned, countries have agreed double-taxation treaties between each other. Under such agreements, the withholding tax payable by the foreign investor may be reduced, or tax paid may be reclaimed.

This section lists the rates of tax payable by foreign residents on interest or dividends derived from the country concerned. Where specific exemptions for tax apply, these are listed. The table however is a general summary and intended to be used by the portfolio investor. Lower rates or exemptions may apply under certain specific circumstances but have not been identified here. It is advisable therefore to consult the specific tax treaty or professional advisers if non-portfolio types of transactions are being considered. Tax treaty countries and the special rates applicable for residents of those countries are listed in the table. Countries not listed in the table fall within the category of non-treaty countries.

7. Exchange controls

Exchange controls are crucial to the foreign investor for they determine whether, and to what extent, he has access to a particular foreign market. Exchange controls are direct controls enforced by governments to restrict or prevent the inflow and/or the outflow of capital. The object of controls is to prevent external pressure on the exchange rate, either to prevent it from falling too much or too rapidly, or to prevent it rising. Countries with balance of payments deficits often apply controls to prevent the outflow of funds, while countries with balance of payment surpluses apply controls to restrict the inflow of funds. As explained previously, an inflow of foreign capital to a country represents a demand for that country's currency which forces its value up. Outflows have the opposite effect. Governments may wish to maintain a particular value of their currency either because it is an important component of its domestic economic policy or because its currency is fixed relative to another currency, a monetary unit, or to a basket or system of currencies.

Exchange controls may be applied across the board to all types of inflows or outflows or they may be applied selectively to specific types of foreign transactions. For example many governments prevent foreigners from purchasing domestic money market securities but transactions in the domestic capital market are unrestricted.

Though not necessarily part of exchange controls, the authorities may intervene in the foreign exchange market to varying degrees. Where currencies are fixed or linked to a specified standard, they may need frequently to intervene in order to maintain a particular parity. Where the currency is freely floating on the world foreign exchange markets, the authorities generally intervene only to smooth excessive fluctuations but do not attempt to alter a trend in the value of the currency.

13

Table 1.1 Quick guide to world money and capital markets

	Australia	Austria	Bahrain	Belgium	Canada	Denmark	France	Germany	Hong Kong	Ireland	Italy	Japan	Kuwait	Luxembourg	Malaysia	Mexico	Netherlands	Norway	Singapore	South Africa	Sweden	Switzerland	UK	USA	International markets
MONEY MARKET																									
Deposits																									
Call	†	*	†	†	–	†	†	†	†	†	†	†	†	†	†	†	*	†	†	–	*	†	†	†	
Time	†	*	†	†	*	†	†	†	†	†	†	†	†	†	†	†	†	†	†	–	*	†	†	†	
Currency	–	†	†	†	†	–	†	†	†	†	–	–	†	†	†	†	†	–	†	–	–	†	†	†	†
Certificates of deposit	†	†	*	–	†	–	–	–	†	†	*	†	*	†	†	–	†	–	†	†	–	*	†	†	†
Treasury bills	†	–	–	†	†	*	–	†	–	†	†	–	*	–	†	–	†	–	–	–	†	†	–	†	†
Other short-term government securities	†	–	–	†	†	–	–	–	†	†	–	–	–	–	–	†	–	†	–	–	–	–	†	†	–
Bankers' acceptances/ commercial bills	†	–	–	–	†	–	–	–	–	†	†	–	–	–	†	–	–	–	*	†	–	–	†	†	–
Commercial paper	†	–	*	–	†	–	–	–	–	†	*	–	–	†	–	–	–	†	†	–	†	†	
CAPITAL MARKET																									
Government bonds	†	–	*	†	†	†	†	–	†	†	†	†	–	†	–	†	†	†	†	†	–	*	†	†	–
Other public sector bonds	†	–	–	†	†	†	†	–	†	†	†	*	–	–	†	–	†	*	–	†	–	*	†	†	–
Corporate bonds	†	*	–	*	†	*	†	*	–	*	*	*	*	*	†	†	*	*	†	–	†	†	†	†	
Foreign bonds	–	–	†	–	†	–	*	†	–	†	*	†	–	†	–	*	–	†	*	†	†	
Eurobonds	*	–	†	–	†	–	*	†	–	–	*	*	†	–	†	†	–	†	–	–	†	†	†	
Equities	†	†	*	*	†	†	*	†	†	†	†	†	†	†	†	†	†	†	†	†	†	†	†	†	
Options market	†	–	–	–	†	–	–	–	*	–	–	†	–	*	†	–	†	†	–	
Financial futures market	†	–	–	†	–	–	–	–	–	–	–	†	
Commodity futures market	†	–	–	†	–	†	–	*	–	–	–	†	–	–	†	†	–	
Gold market	†	*	*	–	†	–	*	†	–	*	*	–	†	–	†	*	–	†	†	†	†	
REGULATIONS																									
Withholding taxes																									
interest	†	–	–	*	†	†	†	†	†	†	*	–	*	†	†	–	–	*	*	–	†	†	†	–
dividends	†	†	–	†	†	†	†	–	†	†	†	–	†	–	†	†	†	–	†	–	†	†	†	†
Exchange controls	†	†	–	*	–	†	†	†	–	†	†	†	–	*	*	–	*	†	–	†	†	†	–	–

† Market (or regulations) exist

* Market exists but is limited; regulations exist but are lenient

– Market (or regulations) do not exist or are not available to non-residents

Intervention takes the form of the authorities buying or selling their own country's currency in the foreign exchange markets. By selling they increase the supply and thus reduce a rise in the exchange rate. By buying they increase the demand and thus support the exchange rate. To do this they use their foreign currency reserves or, where reserves are limited, they borrow foreign currencies from international sources. In most cases the currency of intervention used is the US dollar, because it is the most widely held and traded currency throughout the world. It is unsatisfactory, however, from the point of view of the US authorities since the US dollar rate can consequently fluctuate as a result of interventionist policies assumed by foreign monetary authorities. Until an acceptable alternative reserve currency can be found, however, the US dollar will continue to be used as the most marketable currency. If the new special drawing rights, or SDR (revised as from 1 January 1981), develops into a transactions currency it may help to relieve some of the responsibility imposed on the US dollar. In recent years there has anyway been a tendency for central banks to diversify their reserve asset portfolios out of the US dollar and into other currencies or currency baskets.

This section summarizes the major aspects of exchange controls such as affect portfolio investors. Special provisions as may be provided for direct investors (i.e., companies wishing to establish productive enterprises) have not been covered, and in such cases advice should be sought from the relevant authorities.

The section describes the exchange rate system and the type of market intervention adopted by the authorities. This is important to the investor who needs to be aware of the potential movements in his investment currency relative to his domestic currency. This is the most important criterion with respect to overseas investment. An investment yielding a return of 20 per cent per annum in a foreign currency may prove an effective loss to the investor if that currency depreciates by, say, 15 per cent per annum during the investment period. Conversely, an investment yielding only 5 per cent per annum in a currency which is appreciating may provide an attractive return. In addition, depending on the investor's home country's treatment of income and capital gains tax, currency gains may provide a highly profitable, if volatile, net return.

2. Canada

General market environment

Canada's financial system is based on both the US and the UK systems. However unlike those markets, the Canadian system has not developed spontaneously, but as a result of deliberate policy and encouragement by the Canadian Government during the late 1950s and 1960s. Consequently, Canada's system might be said to comprise the best of both systems, as well as incorporating some money market instruments and methods of dealing that are unique to Canada.

The money market is now highly sophisticated with an active turnover. The volume of paper issued, particularly government paper, has grown significantly during the last two or three years because of increased use of deficit financing, but the market has easily absorbed this growth.

The capital market is small relative to the size of Canada's industry. This is due to the high proportion of industry owned by US companies. The bond market is therefore dominated by Canadian Government bonds, but these, as well as corporate bonds, enjoy an active market. All bonds are traded in the over-the-counter market, and are therefore not included in statistics of stock exchange activity: yet the Canadian stock exchanges, of which there are five, record the fourth highest turnover of all world stock markets.

New markets in Canada include options trading, which commenced in 1976, and financial futures, which were established in mid-1980.

Non-residents have freedom of access to Canadian markets. There are no exchange controls, so inward and outward flows of capital are unrestricted. The major non-resident investors in the Canadian money and capital markets are US resident corporations and individuals but there is significant European participation. There is a high degree of interdependence between the USA and Canada, and in an economic sense the border exists as a formality only. The US accounts for 65 per cent of Canada's foreign trade, 70 per cent of direct investment, 65 per cent of indirect and portfolio investment and 80 per cent of foreign-owned Canadian Government bonds.

Withholding taxes are applied to both interest and dividends but recent relaxation of tax regulations has exempted from withholding tax all treasury bills, all but one of the government bonds and corporate bonds issued after 23 June 1975 with a maturity of not less than five years and one day.

16

Table 2.1 Summary of instruments

Instrument	Characteristics
MONEY MARKET	
Deposits	
call deposits	Very active. Not an interbank market
time deposits	Smaller than call market but also active and competitive
currency deposits	Market for call and time deposits in all convertible currencies
swap deposits	Unique to Canada. Available in all convertible currencies but mainly US dollar swap deposits
certificate of deposit (bearer deposit notes)	Good market in bearer deposit notes. Method of primary issues differs slightly from US and UK CDs. Some CDs not negotiable
Repurchase agreements	Used as additional method of lending and borrowing short-term funds
Treasury bills	3-, 6- and 12-month bills. Regular issues. Active secondary market
Pretender contracts	Method of forward purchasing new treasury bills
Provincial and municipal treasury bills	Issued by local government but guaranteed by central government
Bankers' acceptances	Good primary market but inactive secondary market
Commercial paper	Very active primary and secondary markets
Finance paper	Commercial discount or coupon-bearing paper issued by finance companies. Good primary market
CAPITAL MARKET	
Government bonds	Dominate domestic bond market. Issued by central and local governments. Active markets
Corporate bonds	Small market but active turnover
Foreign bonds	Negligible number of issues
Eurobonds	Good, unregulated market in Euro-Canadian bonds in Europe. In Canada, small and intermittent turnover
Equities	Highly active market
Share options	Traded on Toronto and Montreal stock exchanges. Turnover growing rapidly
Mutual funds	Traded outside stock exchanges. Growing increasingly popular
Financial futures	Small market established mid-1980
Gold	Free trading permitted in over-the-counter market. Futures and options market in Winnipeg

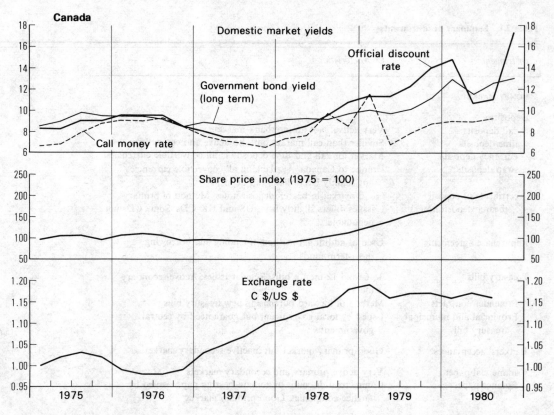

Canada

Domestic market yields

Official discount rate

Government bond yield (long term)

Call money rate

Share price index (1975 = 100)

Exchange rate C $/US $

1975   1976   1977   1978   1979   1980

The money market

Canada has one of the world's most highly developed money markets, next to the USA and the UK, mainly because of its close association with the USA. Despite Canada's small population, the size of the market is large and compares with the Eurocentres of Frankfurt and Paris. The variety of instruments available is surpassed only by markets in the US and London, the Canadian financial market being fashioned on both markets, while some of its dealing techniques are superior to both of these.

Although the majority of money market transactions are for time periods of less than one year, money market instruments may be defined as those having maturities of up to three years, since the Bank of Canada will accept paper of three years or less as collateral for advances made to the banking system.

Access to the money market is available through the commercial banks, known as chartered banks, and the authorized dealers which are equivalent to the London discount houses.

Deposits

There are active high-volume markets in both call and time deposits particularly in Canadian and US dollars. Markets also exist for deposits in all other convertible currencies, for which there are no restrictions in amounts or forms of deposit.

18

Call deposits

Money may be placed at call on a day-to-day basis and is callable by either lender or borrower, up to 12 noon for repayment the same day (i.e., by the close of business at 3.30 p.m.).

Minimum denominations for such call money are C$100 000 and US$100 000 or, if a Eurocurrency deposit, its foreign currency equivalent. As with the London discount market, call money placed with money market dealers must be fully secured by the borrower against securities issued or guaranteed by the government and other high-quality paper having maturities of up to three years. The market is highly efficient and, modelled on the London call market, it fulfils the function of giving the banking system a mechanism by which it can adjust day-to-day balances although, unlike the London market, it is not an interbank market. The banks accept call money from non-bank clients but not from other banks. Apart from requiring call money in order to balance their books, it is often propitious for the banks to borrow short-term money to finance their purchases of treasury bills.

The banks themselves lend call money to the money market dealers who require the funds to finance their purchases of money market securities. If the dealers are unable to raise sufficient cash in the call market they have direct recourse to the central bank's lender of last resort facilities by which they can sell securities with an agreement to repurchase within three months. The Bank of Canada will advance cash to the dealers, against securities offered, at a rate of $\frac{1}{4}$ per cent above three months treasury bill rate subject to a minimum rate of $\frac{3}{4}$ per cent below bank rate.

Interest on call money reflects market demand and supply and may fluctuate widely from one day to the next as a result of changes in the positions of the money market dealers and other operators in the market. In steady market conditions, yields are normally slightly below those on treasury bills thus providing the banks with a small turn between the two.

The call market is also used by the authorities for their open market operations for regulating the volume of credit.

The daily volume of the call market is on average high, and the market has no difficulty in absorbing individual transactions of between C$10 million to C$25 million. Turnover may, however, fluctuate quite widely from day to day.

Interest rates for call money tend to be fairly stable and below bank rate which acts as a ceiling on short-term interest rates. This is because chartered banks may borrow from the Bank of Canada at the bank rate, against specific securities pledged as collateral. Authorized dealers are able to borrow from the central bank usually at even lower rates as described above.

Time deposits

The market in time deposits is not as active as that for day-to-day money. This too is not an interbank market but one in which banks accept deposits from dealers and clients.

Deposits may be placed for terms of 7, 30, 60, 90 and 180 days, and for 12 months, although dealing for odd periods is also possible by negotiation with the banks.

19

Minimum denominations may be smaller than for call money, down to as little as $10 000, but large amounts can easily be accommodated by the market.

Time deposits may be placed in US and Canadian dollars and in other convertible currencies. Interest rates are based on a civil year of 365 days and are closely linked to international rates although domestic Canadian dollar interest rates are strongly influenced by domestic monetary policy and the US economy.

Swap deposits

Although sterling and other Eurocurrencies find an active market in Canada, the market in US dollars is the largest foreign currency deposit market. The US dollar is virtually a second currency in Canada and active markets existed for US dollars even before the advent of the Eurodollar market or of the development of the modern domestic market in the 1950s.

US dollar deposits may take the form of foreign currency swap deposits which are unique to Canada as a money market instrument. They are a method by which Canadian dollars are deposited and then swapped into US dollars; when the deposit matures, the US dollars are swapped back into Canadian dollars. Most deposits are made for terms of from one to six months. The investor earns the premium (or the discount) generated by the currency exchange, plus the comparable rate of interest. Thus, the dealer's quote for a swap deposit will include the interest on the foreign currency deposit plus the forward exchange premium or discount.

The Canadian banks employ the US dollars they receive in the form of call or time deposits, either in the New York money market or for on-lending in London or other Euromarket centres. Alternatively the banks may use the US dollar to swap into Canadian dollars which they can then advance to domestic customers.

The flow of US dollars into and out of the country depends to a large extent on swap rates and relative interest rates. (See graph.)

Certificates of deposit

Bearer deposit notes
Guaranteed Investment Certificates

There is a well developed market in Canadian dollar CDs, known in Canada as bearer deposit notes (BDNs) if issued by the chartered banks, and as guaranteed investment certificates (GICs) if issued by the trust companies. Apart from the names, they are identical in most other respects to CDs issued in the US and UK. The other main difference is that, in the primary market, when they are first issued, the maturity is chosen by the issuer and not by the investor. Original maturities are of 30, 60 and 90 days.

BDNs and GICs are bearer-negotiable securities. The banks also issue large-size certificates of deposit which are known as CDs rather than as BDNs. They are however non-marketable instruments and for that reason are usually issued for shorter maturities than BDNs.

Minimum denominations for BDNs and GICs are for C$100 000 but transactions are usually made in amounts of C$250 000, ranging up to as much as C$25 million.

Being negotiable instruments, yields are normally slightly lower than for time deposits of comparable terms. They may also vary slightly between themselves depending on the names of the issuing bank or trust company. The secondary market in BDNs and GICs is fairly active which allows the investor to purchase outstanding notes or certificates of odd maturities to suit his requirements.

US dollar and sterling CDs may also be purchased in the secondary market. The Canadian market is particularly used by US investors for arbitrage operations between US dollar CDs and Canadian dollar BDNs.

Repurchase agreements (RPs)

Many short-term time deposits take the form of repurchase agreements. These operate in the same way as in the USA. A borrower of funds, such as a bank or large corporation, will sell securities, usually government paper, to another party with an agreement to repurchase at a future specified date. The securities are normally bought back at the same price—their face value—plus an additional premium which represents an interest payment commensurate with prevailing market rates and the term of the loan. A reverse repurchase agreement is where the lender initiates the transaction by buying securities from another party, usually a bank, with an agreement to sell them back on prearranged terms.

Only large transactions are made in this way, usually in amounts of C$250 000 or more.

The weekly average turnover of repurchase agreements is between C$50 million and C$150 million. The maximum during any one week is about C$300 million.

Treasury bills

Treasury bills are issued by the Bank of Canada on behalf of the Treasury along the lines of UK treasury bill issues.

In the primary market, three- and six-month bills are issued by auction on a weekly basis. Twelve-month bills are sold monthly. Only banks and authorized dealers may apply, although other investors may subscribe through a bank. The bills are delivered at 3 p.m. on each Friday so tenders must be received by 12 noon on Thursday. Subscriptions must be in units of $25 000, $100 000, $1 million or over in multiples of $25 000. Subscriptions must be accompanied by a bid price, although each applicant may submit several tenders at different prices. The Bank of Canada itself normally submits two tenders, one for its own account and another for its clients. It also submits a tender to cover the whole amount of the issue both in order to underwrite the issue and also as a formality which guards against banks forming cartels to submit uniform bids at an uncompetitive price. By 2 p.m. applicants are informed of their allotments, which are made purely according to their bid prices.

Bids above the determined issue price are allotted in full. Those at the issue price are allotted proportionately and those below are unallotted. The Bank of Canada announces the highest, lowest and the average of bids received, the latter being the final issue price. At the same time, the amount of bills to be issued the following week is announced.

The bills are issued at a discount price and redeemed at par, the amount of discount representing the interest which is calculated on the basis of a civil year of 365 days.

Bills are in bearer form and issued with original maturities of either 91 or 182 days or 12 months, but 80 per cent of new issues are of 91-day terms. Unlike the UK system, the bills are not physically delivered to the successful applicants but are transmitted by wire, principally because the financial centres are separated by a considerable distance, whereas in the UK most are within walking distance of the Bank of England.

Secondary market

The secondary market in treasury bills is very active with a high average turn-over. The major participants are from the non-bank sector, largely because such investors prefer the liquidity of a treasury bill to a time deposit (for which in the past heavy penalties were applied if a deposit was broken) and also their slightly superior yields. Additionally, they offer the utmost security being guaranteed by the government. As at mid-1980 the total amount of treasury bills outstanding amounted to C$17 500 million of which at least C$4200 million were held outside the banking system. The amounts of new issues were:

C$680 million per week of 91-day treasury bills;
C$500 million per week of 182-day treasury bills;
C$500 million per month of 12-month treasury bills.

Pre-tender contracts

These facilitate a form of dealing arrangement which is not available in other financial markets. Basically, it is a very short-term forward contract between an authorized dealer and a bank or other client. The dealer will sell on his treasury bills to another such party, at an agreed price, based on the average tender price yet to be announced, plus two basis points (0.02 per cent), provided that this does not exceed the resultant highest tender price bid. This agreement enables the dealer to make a small turn on some of his bills and for the bank or client to be sure of receiving some treasury bills, albeit at a small premium.

If a dealer finds himself short of bills which he needs to resell to customers, he has the facility to borrow from the Bank of Canada, but the transaction must be reversed within 30 days though it may be extended to 90 days by special agreement with the Bank of Canada.

The dealers are also offered the facilities of daylight overdrafts by the chartered banks. That is, the banks will extend short-term overdrafts to the dealers to bridge the short time lag between their purchase of treasury bills and securities required by their customers and receipt of payment later on the same day.

Provincial and municipal treasury bills

In addition to bills issued by the central government, the major provinces and municipalities issue their own bills, known as provincial or municipal treasury bills. They are issued in smaller quantities and less frequently than government treasury bills and only with 91-day maturities.

Provincial and municipal treasury bills are issued through a branch of the central bank and may be purchased in the secondary market through banks and authorized dealers.

They are not guaranteed by the central government so yields may be slightly higher than on ordinary treasury bills.

As at March 1980 there were C$948 million provincial and municipal treasury bills outstanding. The provincial governments issue on average a net amount of about C$1500 million per quarter while municipalities issue an average net amount of C$150 million per quarter.

Bankers' acceptances

Bankers' acceptances are commercial bills issued by companies, other than finance companies, to finance trade transactions in goods which include the primary products of agriculture, fishing, forestry, oil and gas. If such bills are accepted, and thus guaranteed, by a chartered bank, they are both eligible for rediscount with the central bank and marketable between banks and private investors in the secondary market.

The acceptances (BAs) are issued at a discount with original maturities of less than 90 days and in minimum denominations of C$5000, although most interbank transactions are made in amounts of C$100 000.

As at April 1980 there were C$4693 million of BAs outstanding. During 1979 new BAs were created to the value of approximately C$350 million per quarter. The size of the market has doubled in 1980 compared with the same period in 1978.

The market in BAs was initiated in the early 1960s but the secondary market has never become very active despite the seeming advantages offered to investors of a good yield with high security and liquidity. Most bills are, therefore, accepted by a bank and held in its own portfolio until maturity.

Commercial paper

This market operates in much the same way as the US commercial paper market. The securities are promissory notes which are issued by industrial and commercial companies to finance short-term working capital, and bear the signature of the issuing name only. (They are sometimes known as corporate or industrial paper to distinguish them from finance paper, which is the same type of security, but issued by financial institutions.)

In the primary market, they are issued usually only by companies with a high credit rating who gain access to the market through an authorized dealer. Since they carry only the name of the issuer, they are secured only against the free assets of the company. Smaller companies have to ensure that the whole of the issue is covered in this way though the larger companies can often arrange unused credit lines with their bank to guarantee up to 50 per cent of the issue.

The paper may be issued for any term of from one day's notice (at the call of the issuer) up to 12 months' fixed. The paper may also be issued either at a discount or with a fixed coupon. Either way, the rate of interest is determined on the basis of a

23

365-day year. The method of calculating the discount rate differs however from methods used for other discount instruments (such as treasury bills) which makes the true effective yield higher than the discount rate of interest. For example, for a 90-day commercial paper issue of C$1 000 000 at 10 per cent rate of discount, interest is calculated first and then subtracted from the principal. The investor receives the full amount of interest even though he does not have to put up the full amount:

$$10\% \times \frac{90}{365} \times C\$1\,000\,000 = C\$24\,657$$

Investor puts up

$$C\$1\,000\,000 - C\$24\,657 = C\$975\,343$$

$$\text{True effective yield} = C\$\frac{24\,657}{975\,343} \times 4 = 10.112\%$$

Some companies may even issue notes in both discount and fixed coupon form at the same time. The amount of the issue may also be for a fixed amount or may be issued on tap.

The range of alternative terms of issue exists primarily to satisfy the investor who may, if he is purchasing a considerable quantity of commercial paper, directly negotiate his required terms, with respect to maturity, size and, sometimes, the interest or discount rate.

Some companies, such as the Canadian subsidiaries of US automobile companies, are almost permanently in the market issuing paper on a large scale, some as much as C$2 billion in a year. Such companies use the market as a permanent source of short-term capital. Others issue commercial paper in anticipation of a new bond issue, particularly when current interest rates are high but a fall in rates is expected. They thus raise short-term funds in the commercial paper market until such time that interest rates have fallen to an acceptable level.

The paper is dealt in minimum denominations of C$100 000 and above that in units of C$50 000. It may be issued publicly onto the market or it may be privately placed.

Paper issued on one day's notice is bought mainly by banks, credit institutions and corporations who want to obtain a reasonable yield on their liquid reserves. Notes issued with fixed maturities are bought by banks, other financial institutions and corporations in Canada, New York and London.

There is no secondary market in notes issued at short-term notice but there is a good market in notes bearing a fixed maturity.

Although, in the primary market, notes are sold to US and UK investors, the only secondary market place is in Canada. The secondary market is very active and is preferred by investors to bankers' acceptances, principally because, although commercial paper carries less security, its yield is much more attractive. Commercial paper is rated by the Canadian Bond Rating Service in the same way that corporate bonds are rated. This indicates the security of the paper.

Some paper is issued in US dollars and this may present good arbitrage opportunities between notes of the same company issued in both the US and Canada. Often the paper issued by the Canadian subsidiary of an American company has a higher yield than comparable US paper, particularly if the premium on forward Canadian dollars is high relative to the interest parity with the US dollar. At times, purchase of Canadian commercial paper by US investors can be of sufficient volume to effect the relative exchange rate of US and Canadian dollars.

As at April 1980 there was commercial paper outstanding to a value of C$9633 million, of which C$7572 million had been issued as Canadian dollar paper and C$2061 million had been issued denominated in other currencies, mainly US dollars. The market has grown steadily by between C$500 million and C$1000 million per annum since 1972 when total commercial paper outstanding stood at C$1013 million.

Finance paper

Finance paper is similar to commercial paper, being short-term promissory notes, but issued by finance companies. They are secured against hire purchase or other trade contracts, and thus are generally considered slightly more secure than commercial paper and consequently carry slightly lower yields.

Finance paper issued by the Canadian subsidiaries of US companies has still lower yields since it is also guaranteed by the US parent and thus commands a higher price than paper that is not guaranteed.

In the primary market the paper is normally issued with a fixed maturity but interest may be calculated either at a discount to par or by a fixed coupon rate. Discount yields are calculated in the same way as for commercial paper. The paper is purchased mainly by authorized dealers who either keep it in their own portfolios until maturity or sell it on to the banks at a small profit.

The secondary market is small and used principally by the banks. The market contracted considerably in 1965 after the collapse of a leading finance company, and confidence in the market has never since recovered. Due to its small size, brokerage fees charged by banks are twice those for commercial paper. Minimum trading amounts are C$100 000, and above that in units of C$50 000.

The amount of finance paper outstanding at mid-1980 was C$4123 million, most of which had been issued as Canadian dollar denominated paper.

The capital market

In Canada, the capital market might be defined as the market in those instruments of more than three years maturity, since the central bank will accept paper of up to three years for rediscounting to the banking system. About 50 per cent of Canadian industry is owned by US corporations, consequently the volume of private sector securities issued is not as large as would be expected with respect to the size of the country's industrial base. On the other hand, US companies with subsidiaries in Canada frequently issue bonds or shares in the Canadian market. Nevertheless, the volume of public sector bonds issued exceeds the volume of corporate bond issues by about three to one. Turnover of both types of bonds and of equities is however highly active.

Public bonds are issued by the federal and provincial governments and the municipal authorities. The federal government issues bonds throughout the maturity range, from three-year bonds, known as 'short Canadas', to bonds of 25 years' life, while the provinces and municipalities prefer longer-term bonds of up to 25 years' maturity.

Government bonds

The Government of Canada issues, through the Bank of Canada, two types of bonds, Canada savings bonds and ordinary marketable bonds. Canada savings bonds are in small denominations and of medium to long maturity, are non-marketable and issued annually to attract the savings of domestic individuals. They are not available to non-residents. Ordinary marketable bonds, that are available to non-residents, are issued almost monthly in amounts of up to C$1.5 billion, and are marketable in denominations of C$1000. They may be issued with a maturity of from three to twenty-five years. Interest is paid semiannually and capital is redeemed at par at maturity.

Table 2.2 Net new issues of government bonds (*source: Bank of Canada*)

Issuer	Year 1975 C$m	1976 C$m	1977 C$m	1978 C$m	1979 C$m	1980 C$m
Government of Canada						
Canada savings bonds	2664	754	1660	1930	−1242	−1315
Other bonds	770	1835	3878	3415	6767	7246
Total	3434	2590	5538	5345	5524	5931
Provinces						
Canada pension plan	1383	1509	1643	1663	1896	1900
Others	2532	3155	2906	3651	2955	5755
Total	3915	4664	4549	5314	4851	7655
Municipalities	641	541	922	684	709	608
Total government bonds issues	7990	7795	11009	11343	11084	14194
Government bonds as a proportion of total bond net new issues per cent	77.3	85.5	77.6	78.3	85.9	86.7

Table 2.2 shows the net new issues of both types of bonds. It shows that the volume of government marketable bonds issued per quarter has increased substantially in the last few years. Though there was a net decrease in outstanding Canada savings bonds of C$1.3 billion during 1979 (consistent with the trend over the last five years due to a change in philosophy towards marketable bonds), there was a net increase in the par value of outstanding marketable bonds of C$6.8 billion. Together with the net increase in treasury bills of C$2.1 billion, the total of C$8.9 billion was used to pay for the total Canadian dollar financing requirement

of the government, which for 1979 amounted to C$11.6 billion. The remaining C$4 billion (i.e. $11.6 billion + $1.3 billion − $8.9 billion) was met by a reduction in government-owned cash balances to leave a total of C$2.5 billion at the year end. The outstanding amount of government marketable bonds rose by C$6.7 billion in 1979. This comprised eight new public offerings and four refundings of maturing issues. Seven per cent of the total capital raised was by the issue of short-term bonds of three years maturity or less, 27 per cent was by the issue of medium-term bonds of between three and ten years maturity and the remaining 66 per cent were by long-term bonds. The average maturity of all these new issues was ten years and five months.

Provincial and municipal bonds

The provincial governments comprise Alberta, Manitoba, Ontario, Quebec, Saskatchewan, Nova Scotia, Newfoundland, New Brunswick and Prince Edward Island. They issue two types of bonds, Canada pension plan bonds and ordinary bonds. Alberta however has not made any issues since 1972 and has no outstanding direct debt. Being a mineral-rich province producing oil and gas, Alberta is a net lender rather than borrower of funds and purchases large quantities of Canadian public and private bond issues. Canada pension plan bonds are long-term bonds with net new issues amounting to an average of about C$470 million per quarter in 1979. They are designed to attract the individual saver. Ordinary bonds are also long-term bonds but are designed more for the larger investor. Both types pay interest semiannually and redeem capital in full at maturity. The money raised is used to fund the provincial governments' spending programmes. An average of about C$740 million was raised per quarter during 1979 by the issue of such bonds.

At the end of 1979 the total outstanding of both types of provincial bonds was C$11.7 billion.

The municipalities issue ordinary long-term bonds in amounts of an average of C$170 million per quarter, net. New issues have increased by C$709 million in 1979 to give a total outstanding of C$1345 million.

As with all government bonds, interest is paid semiannually and capital redeemed at par at maturity.

All bonds of the central government are issued and underwritten by the Bank of Canada. Provincial and municipal bonds are issued by separately appointed agents. Applications for new bond issues can be made through brokers and dealers, including banks. The primary market is active and new issues are normally fully subscribed. Bonds are issued at par and carry a fixed coupon rate of interest which is calculated according to a civil year of 365 days and paid semiannually. Bonds are bearer and, except for Canada savings bonds, which may be purchased in small amounts, are in minimum denominations of C$1000. All bonds are highly secure being fully guaranteed as to principal and interest by the issuing government or authority. The Canadian Bond Rating Service, which rates bonds on a scale from A + + to D, rates all central government bonds in the category A + +. Provincial

Primary market in government bonds

27

Table 2.3 **Net new issues of corporate and other bonds** (*source: Bank of Canada*)

	1975 C$m	1976 C$m	1977 C$m	1978 C$m	1979 C$m	1980 C$m
Corporate bonds	2 221	1287	3 124	3 148	1 789	1 942
Other bonds*	120	36	62	3	26	236
Total government bonds (excluding treasury bills)	7 990	7795	11 009	11 343	11 084	14 194
Total Canadian net bond issues	10 331	9118	14 195	14 494	12 899	16 372
Corporate bonds as proportion of total bonds per cent	21.5	14.1	22.0	21.7	13.9	11.7

* Other bonds include bonds issued by foreign borrowers and by miscellaneous Canadian institutions.

government bonds vary; for example, recent bond issues by the government of Ontario were rated A + + but bonds of Newfoundland and New Brunswick were rated B+ and A.

Secondary market in government bonds

Bonds, including government bonds, are dealt in the over-the-counter market made by dealers who maintain their own books and may take a position in government bonds.

The market is active and it is possible to deal in sizes of up to C$5 million or more.

Government bonds are popular because interest is paid free of tax, including withholding tax to non-residents. A few exceptions to this are federal government bonds issued prior to 20 December 1960, and all provincial and municipal bonds issued prior to 15 April 1966.

Government bonds are thus an attractive investment for non-residents. At the end of 1979 non-residents held over one-fifth of all government bonds (including treasury bills) to a value of C$5795 million compared to resident holdings of C$19 750 million. Eighty per cent of non-residents' bond holdings were held by US residents.

Corporate bonds

The market in corporate bonds is much smaller than the market in government bonds because much of Canadian industry is owned by US corporations. Between C$1000 million and C$3000 million of new Canadian dollar corporate bond issues are made each year. In 1979 C$1789 million of corporate bonds were issued compared with a total of C$11 084 million of government bond issues, including provincial and municipal issues but excluding treasury bills. At the end of 1979 there were about C$6.5 billion of corporate bonds outstanding. Although there is a smaller amount of corporate bonds outstanding, they nonetheless enjoy an active market. Once underwritten and distributed in the primary market, they are then traded in the over-the-counter market maintained by dealers who make books and hold positions in the bonds. As with government bonds corporate bonds are not traded on the stock exchanges.

Corporate bonds are bearer (but may be registered as to principal and interest), and are issued with maturities of up to 25 years in issue sizes of up to C$200 million. Minimum denominations of corporate bonds are normally C$1000 although they may sometimes be smaller. The bonds carry fixed rate coupons, payable semiannually and with interest calculated on a 365-day basis. Principal may either be redeemed in full at maturity or may be amortized through a sinking fund. Bonds with the possibility of early redemption carry a higher coupon than bonds with no such feature. The major participants in the market for corporate bonds are pension funds, mutual funds and insurance companies (which are growing institutional investors) although there are many smaller corporate and individual investors in the bonds of larger, well-known corporations. It is possible to deal in amounts of up to C$1 million.

Mortgage bonds

Mortgage bonds are issued by the National Housing Association, the trust and mortgage loan associations, the chartered banks and by other non-bank financial institutions to fund the financing of house and real estate purchase by individuals and businesses. Such bonds are considered highly secure, being issued against a pool of mortgages, and normally carry a good rating. They are not, however, as highly marketable as public sector bonds or good quality corporate bonds.

Bond rating Corporate bonds are rated by the Canadian Bond Rating Service in categories from A++ to D which indicates the creditworthiness of the issuing corporation. A++ have the highest security and their yields approximate closely to the government bond yields. Few bonds are rated as low as D, which indicates insolvency of the issuing corporation. The majority of corporate bonds, having ratings ranging from A to C, carry yields in the range of 75 to 100 basis points or more above the yields obtainable on government bonds.

Tax status Canadian corporate bonds are all attractive investments for non-resident investors since most recent issues are free of both domestic tax on interest and from withholding tax. Specifically this exemption applies to all bonds issued after 24 June 1975, having an original maturity of more than five years and a day, and where no more than 25 per cent of the issue is amortized within five years of issue.

Foreign bonds

There are very few foreign bonds issued in Canada. In 1979 the net new issue of foreign and other bonds, which include bonds of Canadian religious and charitable organizations, was only C$26 million. Such foreign bonds as are issued are usually made by US corporations with an interest in Canada, although one issue was recently made by an Australian bank. The market is completely homogeneous with the domestic corporate bond market.

Eurobonds

Eurobonds denominated in Canadian dollars have been issued since 1974. The major issuers are the Canadian provinces and municipalities, Canadian and US corporations and international agencies such as the European Coal and Steel Community.

The majority of issues are made in sizes of between C\$20 million and C\$40 million, with maturities of from five to seven years. Euro-Canadian bonds carry fixed rate coupons, with interest paid annually, free of withholding tax. The majority repay principal in full at maturity although some longer-term issues may be amortized.

There are no regulations affecting the amount of new issues or investment in Eurobonds and no official supervisory body. The number of issues depends mainly on Canadian interest and exchange rates and demand by investors for Canadian dollar securities.

In 1979 there were nine new issues and a total outstanding of about 90 Euro-Canadian bonds with a value of about C\$5 billion.

There were no issues in 1978, however, because of the weakness of the Canadian dollar and thus the absence of demand by foreign investors.

In the secondary market, trading is normally active. Bonds are issued in minimum denominations of C\$1000 but, in accordance with the rules of the Association of International Bond Dealers, transactions take place in minimum sizes of C\$10000. The market is maintained between banks and dealers in the major European financial centres. Canadian and US residents may not purchase Canadian dollar Eurobonds until six months after issue. Canadian Eurobonds are listed on either the London or Luxembourg stock exchange, but traded mainly over the counter through banks in Europe and North America.

Canadian corporations and central and local governments also issue foreign currency denominated bonds in the international markets. The government in particular tends to borrow abroad in order to support the Canadian dollar when weak.

In 1979 the government, through the Bank of Canada, made two foreign capital issues, raising the equivalent of US\$605 million from marketable securities and US\$759 million from fixed rate bank loans.

These two issues were:

1. ¥ 100 billion which comprised
   (a) ¥ 30 billion five-year bonds at 6.4 per cent coupon issued by public offering in the Japan Samurai bond market;
   (b) ¥ 35 billion syndicated loan for 10 years at 7.1 per cent interest;
   (c) ¥ 35 billion syndicated loan for 20 years at 7.5 per cent interest.
2. Sw.Fr. 1500 million which comprised
   Sw.Fr. 300 million public offering of 10-year bonds at $3\frac{5}{8}$ per cent coupon, in the Swiss foreign bond market;
   Sw.Fr. 500 million private placement of six-year non-callable note at three per cent interest;
   Sw.Fr. 700 million fixed rate bank loan for three years at $2\frac{7}{8}$ per cent per annum.

Table 2.4 Canadian equities: preference and common stock (*source: Toronto Stock Exchange*)

	1976		1977		1978		1979		1980	
	Volume, million	*Value, C$m*	*Volume, million*	*Value, C$m*	*Volume, million*	*Value, C$m*	*Volume, million*	*Value, C$m*	*Volume, million*	*Value, C$m*
CANADIAN STOCK EXCHANGES—TURNOVER										
Toronto	549.2	5093.5	679.8	6044.8	984.9	10 362.0	1390.8	18 726.0	209.1	29 514.5
Montreal	119.3	1483.6	103.6	1374.2	127.8	1 708.4	217.7	2 674.5	299.1	3 856.8
Vancouver	453.9	328.3	544.6	391.1	596.2	607.5	912.9	1 470.0	1718.0	4 420.0
Alberta	25.2	46.8	31.4	58.5	39.8	95.4	91.0	239.0	162.0	470.0
Winnipeg	0.4	1.0	0.6	0.8	2.1	17.9	0.9	1.1	1.3	1.9
Total	1148.1	6953.2	1360.0	7873.4	1750.9	12 791.2	2613.3	23 110.6	2389.5	38 263.2

	C$m	C$m	C$m	C$m	C$m
Net new issues—all exchanges	1211	3123	6 803	3 993	
Total market value of listed shares—all exchanges			71 104	109 204	
Average dividend yield—all shares*	4.5	4.8	4.5	4.2	3.66
Average P/E ratios—all shares*	9.1	8.4	8.3	8.7	8.81
STOCK PRICE INDICES					
TSE (Toronto Stock Exchange) Composite 300* (1975 = 1000)	920.8	1009.9	1 159.1	1 892.7	
Montreal SE Industrials* (1956 = 100)	187.4	159.7	190.0	275.2	

* Period averages.

Equities

The size of the market in equity shares is small relative to the size of industry because so many Canadian companies are owned by US corporations, while many of the smaller Canadian owned companies prefer to finance themselves through short-term bank borrowing. Larger companies tend to issue shares on the Toronto or Montreal stock exchanges while the Vancouver stock exchange is more often used by smaller companies which require to raise capital.

There are about one thousand companies listed on the five Canadian stock exchanges but the greatest number are listed on the Toronto stock exchange. The market value of shares listed on all the Canadian exchanges is approximately C$85 billion and net new issues of shares amounted to a nominal value of C$4 billion in 1979, C$6.8 billion in 1978 and C$3.1 billion in 1977. In terms of size, measured as the market value of listed shares, the Canadian equity market ranks eleventh in world markets and is comparable with Amsterdam and Paris. Activity, however, is much higher than its market size would suggest. In terms of turnover, the Canadian equities market ranks fourth in the world, following the USA, Japan and London, with a turnover of about C$20 billion for 1979.

Canadian companies issue both preference shares and common stock shares, but for trading purposes the market in both types of shares is homogeneous. When a company issues shares to the public its shares are normally first traded in the over-the-counter market in unlisted securities until it meets the requirements of one of the Canadian stock exchanges. Thereafter they are traded, through brokers, on the floor of one of the exchanges. Canadian companies tend to have a more conservative dividend policy than their American counterparts, having yielded an average of 4.5 per cent for the last five years, which to some extent reduces their attractiveness to investors who often prefer the US equities market.

Share options

Trading in Canadian corporate share call options began on the Toronto stock exchange in April 1976 (and subsequently on the Montreal exchange), since which time the market has grown substantially. Put options were introduced in 1979. There are more than thirty options listed, but for the year ended March 1979, the number of contracts traded was 368 490 with an average monthly trading volume of 30 700 contracts, an increase of 215 per cent over the previous year. The total value of contracts traded was C$125 million.

Options are traded through specialist dealers on the floor of the Toronto stock exchange, known as writers. They hold the shares of the quoted options on their own books but sell an option to buy (call option) or an option for an investor to sell (put option) the shares of those companies at a predetermined price known as the striking price. Options are traded in minimum lots of one hundred shares and are issued with initial expiry terms of three months. They can be bought or sold as securities in their own right through secondary market trading at any time during the life of the option. The premium or discount attaching to the option will depend on the unexpired life of the option and on how close the market value of the particular share is to the striking price attached to the option.

The following illustrates options transactions:

Seagram shares are trading at C$45 on the Toronto stock exchange.

Investor A speculates that the price of the shares will rise and wishes to purchase a call option in Seagram shares. The writer makes a three-month option price of C$1 for him to purchase the shares at the striking price of C$48. This costs him C$100 for one lot of 100 shares.

Investor B speculates that the price of the shares will fall and wishes to purchase a put option in Seagram shares. The writer makes a three-month option price of C$5 for him to sell shares, which he doesn't at present own, at the striking price of C$43.

After one month the shares have risen to a price of C$46.5. For investor A, the striking price has not yet been reached, but he could sell his option at a premium of say 50 cents (i.e., C$1.50 per option).

Investor B decides that he should sell his options to prevent further loss. He sells at a discount of C$3 per option and thus makes a loss of C$30. At the same time, he buys a new three-month put option at C$1 to purchase the shares at a striking price of C$50.

After a further month the market value of the shares has reached C$49.

Investor *A* may now exercise his option since the striking price of C$48 has been passed. However, he decides to wait until the option is due to expire. After a further month the share price is C$51.50. Investor *A* exercises his option by buying the shares at C$48 each and simultaneously sells them in the market. He has made a profit of C$3.5 per share less the C$1 spent on the purchasing of the option. For one lot of 100 shares this represents a profit of C$250 from an initial investment of C$100, less commission.

Similarly, investor *B* decides to exercise his option but makes a profit of only C$50 less his original loss of C$30 and commission.

The purpose of trading in options rather than in the shares themselves is that the investor's outlay can be much smaller while his potential profit is high. In the above example investor *A* achieved a 250 per cent return in only three months; options therefore present a highly geared form of investment while the loss is limited to the cost of the options.

The stock exchange

There are five stock exchanges in Canada, located in Toronto, Montreal, Vancouver, Winnipeg and Calgary. Toronto and Montreal together account for about 90 per cent of trading, while Toronto is eight to nine times larger than the Montreal exchange.

Only equity shares and, in the cases of Toronto and Montreal, share options, are traded on the stock exchange. All fixed-interest securities are traded in the over-the-counter market.

Each exchange is regulated by the securities commissions of each province. The stock exchanges are non-profit-making organizations whose expenses are met by the subscriptions paid by members and by companies that are quoted on the exchanges. Members are individuals, many of whom are representatives from stockbroking companies and dealers, who have bought a seat on an exchange which entitles them to deal on the floor of the exchange. The price of a seat depends on stock exchange activity and demand for membership varies between exchanges. Over the last decade, the highest price for a seat on the Toronto stock exchange was C$132 500 in 1970, the lowest price was C$12 000 in 1978. Currently (1980) the price is about C$20 000.

A member of a stock exchange may deal for his own account or for other brokers or for his own firm. The trading post system is used and, similar to the London stock exchange but unlike the US exchanges, some dealers act as jobbers, that is, they make books in specified shares and act as intermediaries between buying and selling brokers.

The monthly value of shares traded on the Toronto and Montreal stock exchanges is between C$1500 million and C$2500 million though in January 1980 it reached an all-time high of C$4091 million representing a volume of 313 million shares traded. This is about half the volume traded monthly on the New York stock exchange, although only about 11 per cent of the value of NYSE trading.

Stock exchange indices

The composite 300 index, used by the Toronto stock exchange has a base of 1975 = 1000 and tends to be very volatile (see Table 2.5 and graph). During 1980, for example, it stood at 1807 in April, rose to 2192.6 in February, fell back again to 1702.51 in March, then rose to an all-time high of 2402.2 in November and ended the year at 2200. The composite index is an index calculated from the weighted average share prices of 300 companies representing all types of companies quoted on the exchange. Separate indices also exist for each category of companies, including oil and gas, metals and minerals, utilities and services, paper and forest products, merchandising, financial services and gold. The highs and lows of these indices since 1976 are shown in Table 2.5.

The Montreal exchange uses two indices, both with a base of 1956 = 100. These indices are weighted averages of shares classified under two categories, industrials and banks.

Table 2.5 Stock exchanges indices. Highs and lows from January 1976 to June 1980 (*source: Annual Report of Toronto Stock Exchange*)

	High	Date	Low	Date
TORONTO STOCK EXCHANGE: 1975 = 1000				
Oil and gas	5155.9	Feb. 1980	950.5	Nov. 1976
Metals and minerals	2401.0	Feb. 1980	781.9	Feb. 1978
Utilities	1579.1	May 1979	1027.9	Apr. 1976
Paper and forest products	1898.3	Feb. 1980	831.1	Oct. 1976
Merchandising	1395.3	Feb. 1980	778.4	Oct. 1977
Financial services	1244.8	Aug. 1979	847.9	Dec. 1976
Golds	3535.3	Feb. 1980	736.4	Jun. 1976
Composite 300 index	2192.6	Feb. 1980	1002.1	Oct. 1977
MONTREAL STOCK EXCHANGE: 1656 = 100				
Industrial	371.6	Jan. 1980	163.2	Feb. 1980
Banks	323.5	Aug. 1979	215.0	Apr. 1977

Mutual funds

Mutual funds are growing both in size and popularity in Canada, and are now becoming a significant form of institutional investor in competition with the pension funds and insurance companies. They invest either in bonds to provide their own investors with income or in equities to provide capital growth or in a mixture of both to provide income and moderate growth. The funds also invest to some extent in foreign markets, particularly the US markets, but pension and investment funds only receive tax benefits if 90 per cent of their income derives from Canadian securities. Shares in mutual funds, more aptly described as units since their capital structure is not limited, are not listed on the stock exchanges but may be purchased directly from the fund managers. A bank or broker will normally advise a client as to the most suitable fund for his needs. Some funds specialize in achieving high income while others aim to achieve capital growth.

Financial futures markets

A financial futures market was established on the Toronto stock exchange in mid-1980. Futures contracts are available in two instruments only—bonds of the central government with a maturity of 18 years or longer and 91-day treasury bills. Contract sizes are C$100 000 for government bonds and C$1 million for treasury bills. Contracts may be traded for the current quarter up to six quarters forward. Very few transactions are made, however, beyond the second quarter forward. Dealing costs are C$80 round turn (i.e., purchase and sale) per contract.

Gold

Residents and non-residents, excluding those of communist block countries, may freely buy, sell and export gold. There is, however, no major bullion market in Canada, but transactions may be made through a bank. One gold coin, the Maple Leaf, is minted as legal tender and has a face value of C$100.

The Winnipeg Commodity Exchange provides a market in both gold futures and options trading. Indeed it was the first exchange to provide a public market in these types of transactions. There is however very little turnover in the Winnipeg market because active gold futures markets now operate in the USA and these attract almost all investor interest in North America.

There is no other public market in North America offering gold options. (The US Commodities Futures Trading Commission has so far vetoed such proposals.) The only other market exists on the European options exchange in Amsterdam.

The Winnipeg exchange trades call options in 100- and 20-ounce contracts at striking prices in multiples of US$20 per ounce.

Dealing and fees

Money market

Transactions in money market instruments may be made through any of the chartered banks. Facilities may be better and costs lower if a schedule A chartered bank is used. (See Financial and monetary system.)

For primary market subscriptions for treasury bills, a small fee may be charged at the discretion of the dealer or bank through which the application is made.

For secondary market transactions, dealing spreads charged by the dealers and banks between their bid and offer prices are 10 cents to 15 cents for treasury bills and good quality commercial paper and 10 cents to 25 cents for other instruments. Settlement and delivery occurs within three to five business days.

Capital market

Domestic bonds

All Canadian dollar government or corporate domestic and foreign bonds are traded in the over-the-counter market. This is the market maintained between investment dealers and brokers. Transactions can also be made through a chartered bank. No specific fee or commission is charged but transactions are dealt net. The dealers make a turn on the difference between their quoted bid and offer prices. For highly rated bonds, of up to 3 years maturity dealing spreads are about 20 cents. For bonds of three to five years, spreads are about 25 cents and about $\frac{1}{2}$ per cent on bonds of more than five years. For lower rated and less active bonds the spread may be as high as 1 per cent. Settlement and delivery occurs within two to five business days.

Table 2.6 Stock exchange commission rates

Transaction	Commission
All transactions basic commission	
Stock price of less than C$5	3% of consideration
of C$5 to C$15	2% of consideration + 5$ per share
of more than C$15	1% of consideration + 20$ per share
Orders over C$5000 but less than C$20 000	Basic commission $\times \left(\dfrac{\text{C\$500}}{\text{value of order}} + 0.9 \right)$
Orders over C$20 000 but less than C$40 000	Basic commission $\times \left(\dfrac{\text{C\$2500}}{\text{value of order}} + 0.8 \right)$
Orders over C$40 000 but less than C$100 000	Basic commission $\times \left(\dfrac{\text{C\$40 000}}{\text{value of order}} + 0.9 \right)$
1. with a share price of less than C$10	$+ \left(\dfrac{\text{value of order} - \text{C\$40 000}}{10} \right)$
2. with a share price more than C$10	$+ \left(\dfrac{\text{C\$40 000}}{\text{value of order}} \times 0.8625 \right)$
	$+ \left(\dfrac{\text{value of order} - \text{C\$40 000}}{10 \times \text{average price per share}} \right)$
Orders over C$100 000	Several orders amounting to a total value of more than C$100 000 and occurring within five business days may be treated as one large order for the purpose of calculating commission, in which case the lower commission for orders of over C$40 000 applies
Orders over C$500 000	Commission is calculated as for orders over C$40 000 but the portion over C$500 000 is at the discretion of the broker. Several orders occurring within five business days may count as one large order

Eurobonds

Euro-Canadian bonds may be purchased through an investment dealer or any major Canadian or foreign bank, in which case the transaction is net. Dealing spreads are $\frac{1}{2}$ to 1 per cent.

Alternatively, they may be purchased through a dealer in other Euromarket centres or through a broker on the London stock exchange or the Luxembourg stock exchange, in which case local commission rates are charged.

Equities and options

Equities are traded through a stockbroker on the floor of one of the five stock exchanges. Standard commission charges are made for all purchases and sales. Settlement and delivery occurs on the fifth business day following the transaction.

Safe custody

Non-resident investors may require securities to be held in safe custody. This service is provided by a bank or a stockbroker.

Charges vary between institutions but the following is typical.

Charges are also made by banks for receipt and delivery of securities on a scale which ranges from $\frac{1}{8}\%$ for securities to a total value of less than C$2500, to $\frac{1}{100}\%$ for securities to a total value of C$500 000. Above this amount, charges are made at the banks' discretion.

Table 2.7 Safe custody charges

Bonds	Fee	Minimum
Value of less than C$100 000	$\frac{1}{4}\%$ of par value per annum	C$3
Value of C$100 000 to C$1 000 000	$\frac{1}{8}\%$ of par value per annum	C$250
Value C$1 000 000 to C$6 000 000	$\frac{1}{16}\%$ of par value per annum	C$1250
Value of more than C$6 000 000	$\frac{1}{20}\%$ of par value per annum	C$3750
Shares		
Value of less than C$5000	5% of total annual dividend	C$3
Value C$5000 to C$50 000	$2\frac{1}{2}\%$ of total annual dividend	C$1250
Value C$50 000 to C$300 000	$1\frac{1}{4}\%$ of total annual dividend	C$1250
Value of more than C$300 000	1% of total annual dividend	C$3750

Financial and monetary systems

Financial institutions

The banks constitute the major financial institutions in Canada. All banks that operate in Canada are chartered under a Bank Act passed by Parliament and revised every ten years, when the banks' charters are reviewed. The most recent Bank Act came into effect on 1 December 1980.

Chartered banks

The chartered banks act as both commercial and savings banks. They accept deposits, provide chequing accounts and grant credit to customers for business, agriculture, consumer loans and mortgages. They also operate in the foreign exchange markets, purchase and sell securities on behalf of their customers and provide depository services.

The five largest chartered banks are the Royal Bank of Canada, the Canadian Imperial Bank of Commerce, the Bank of Montreal, the Bank of Nova Scotia and the Toronto Dominion Bank and together they account for over 90 per cent of the total assets of the banking sector.

There are ten domestic chartered banks which are privately owned, but publicly operated, with a network of over 7000 branches. These are defined as schedule A chartered banks under the rules of the new Bank Act.

Schedule B banks are all other banks, which includes those with a tightly held share capital and the 40 or so branches of foreign banks established in Canada.

The foreign banks were previously not classified as banks but as near-banks. They did not have access to the central bank for lender of last resort facilities. In order to increase competition in the banking sector, the new Bank Act has given foreign banks full bank status but under schedule B licence. Foreign and other schedule B banks are subject to the same regulations and requirements as the schedule A banks but they require approval from the Minister of Finance to operate more than one branch in Canada and are subject to specified minima for their capital and reserves. In total, foreign banks may not exceed more than eight per cent of total Canadian bank lending. Further, they may not own more than 10 per cent of the capital of a Canadian bank (the US bank, Citibank, is an exception in owning 75 per cent of the Mercantile Bank of Canada which it acquired before the new regulations came into being). Also, a foreign bank may not operate in Canada unless reciprocal arrangements exist for Canadian banks to operate in that foreign country.

Provincial savings banks

Still classified as near-bank institutions are the provincial government savings banks. These are smaller institutions owned by the local governments of each of the provinces and complement, rather than act in competition with, the commercial banks. They principally accept small savings and make loans, or guarantee loans, to local business.

Co-operative credit unions are similar to the savings banks in that they are small locally established credit institutions which accept savings deposits and grant or guarantee loans to their members. The major difference is that they are privately owned mutual associations.

Trust and mortgage companies

Trust and mortgage companies are financial intermediaries whose main purpose is to collect small savings, to act as trustees for property interest, to manage other fiduciary business and to grant mortgage finance to business and individuals. Earlier Bank Acts had prohibited the chartered banks from undertaking such business, but recent revision of the Act has widened the range of services that the chartered banks may operate, thus reducing the activities of the trust and mortgage companies to more of a secondary role.

Along with the chartered banks and the trust companies, the insurance companies also act as intermediaries in the provision of mortgage finance.

Authorized dealers

Authorized dealers act as intermediaries between the chartered banks and the central bank. They may use the Bank of Canada as lender of last resort by rediscounting treasury bills and other eligible securities, while lending to the banking system to provide liquidity in the short-term money markets. Much of the turnover in call deposits and short-term time deposits is transacted between the chartered banks and the authorized dealers. The dealers also buy and underwrite treasury bill issues which they then sell on to the chartered banks. The authorized dealers are thus similar in function to the London discount houses.

The industrial development bank and the federal business development bank

The Industrial Development Bank (IDB) and The Federal Business Development Bank (FBDB) are two crown corporations set up by acts of parliament in 1944 and 1974, respectively.

Their purpose is to provide loans or loan guarantees, and equity or leasing finance to small and medium-sized Canadian businesses at competitive market rates of interest. In such capacity, they are lenders of last resort to small businesses that are unable to obtain appropriate finance elsewhere.

These institutions also provide non-monetary assistance to small business in the form of management and legal advisory services.

The Canadian payments association

The Canadian Payments Association is a new body established together with the introduction of the new Banking Act in 1980. Membership comprises all schedule A and schedule B chartered banks and many other financial institutions, principally the trust companies and credit unions. One of the objectives of the association is to reduce the chartered banks' monopoly of the clearing system and to provide for a system of electronic fund transfer, which will facilitate same-day point of sales, debit and credit of accounts.

The central bank

The central bank is the Bank of Canada. Its headquarters are in Ottawa, although it has subsidiary dealing agents in Montreal, Toronto, Winnipeg, Vancouver and Calgary. The Bank is managed by a 12-man board of directors who are appointed by the Minister of Finance for a three-year term. In addition, a governor and deputy governor are appointed by the board for a seven-year term.

The executive committee comprises the governor, two board members and the Minister of Finance, and it helps to formulate monetary policy, though its recommendations must first be submitted to the board for a vote.

The Bank of Canada is solely responsible for the issue of notes and coins, is lender of the last resort, regulator of the banking system, implements monetary policy and supervises the currency and exchange controls.

Monetary policy

The two main objectives of monetary policy are the maintenance and stability of the currency and the management of the government debt. The two may sometimes prove mutually conflicting objectives, particularly when the bank is trying to exert downward pressure in the foreign exchange market which may reduce demand for Canadian securities but the government at the same time wishes to fund short-term debt in the money market. A balance is achieved usually through operations in the treasury bill market.

The instruments of monetary policy are reserve and liquidity ratios and open market operations in the money market, and particularly in the market for treasury bills. Bank rate policy and moral suasion of the banking system are used as supplementary tools.

Reserve ratios

All chartered banks, whether schedule A or B banks, are required to maintain specified reserve ratios. Two ratios, primary and secondary reserve ratios, are enforced.

Primary reserves are defined as the amount of cash reserves calculated as a proportion of domestic Canadian dollar demand deposits. As a result of the 1980 Bank Act the primary reserve requirements have been reduced to 10 per cent (from 12 per cent) of demand deposits, 2 per cent of the first $500 million or resident Canadian dollar notice and time deposits of less than one year, and three per cent (from 4 per cent) of other Canadian dollar deposits.

The system of reserve requirements has been revised since the new Bank Bill was enforced. This now includes a 3 per cent primary reserve requirement on foreign currency deposits of residents but for non-resident currency deposits no reserve requirements continue to apply.

Secondary reserves are defined as a proportion of total deposits and may be held in the form of cash in excess of the minimum reserve requirements, treasury bills, and overnight call deposits with authorized dealers. The secondary reserve requirement is subject to variation by the Bank of Canada to an amount between zero and 12 per cent. The Bank must give a month's notice that it intends to change the secondary reserve ratio and, if at zero, then the Bank may not increase it to more than 6 per cent in the first move.

It is this secondary reserve ratio which is used more as an instrument of monetary policy; as a fine-tuning device to aid the control of liquidity in the banking system and the growth of credit expansion. No amendments to the secondary reserve ratio was introduced with the 1980 Bank Act and, as at Spring 1981, the ratio remained at five per cent.

Reserve ratios have to be met by the banks on a fortnightly averaging basis, but the cash part of the reserves, previously held as interest-free deposits at the Bank of Canada, are now allowed to be kept as interest-earning balances with other financial institutions under the new Bank Bill.

Liquidity ratios

Allied to the minimum reserve requirements is a measure affecting minimum holdings by banks of liquid and near-liquid assets which comprise cash reserves, daylight overdrafts, treasury bills, government securities and loans to authorized dealers and brokers. The ratio of these assets to total assets is known as the 'more liquid ratio'. It is reported by banks to the Bank of Canada, though it is not determined by the central bank or enforced at a specified level. However the more liquid reserve ratio is a very good indicator of monetary policy and of economic conditions. Its highest level, when the banking system was very liquid, was 32.5 per cent, reached in 1968.

Open market operations

The Bank of Canada adopts a more passive attitude towards market intervention than the central banks of either the US or UK in that it enters the market, not so much directly to influence market interest rates and relative demand and supply of funds, but more to stabilize the market and prevent a reversal of an existing trend if it is deemed by the authorities to be of benefit to the economy.

Open market operations are used directly to raise funding of the public sector debt by the issue of treasury bills, and indirectly to influence the reserves of the banking system. If it wishes to add to the reserves of the banking system, the government buys treasury bills and other money market securities, which in turn allows the banks to increase their assets and their deposit liabilities. Conversely, the banks are forced to reduce their assets and liabilities when the government sells securities. Such open market operations thus have an indirect effect on the prices and yields of money market instruments. Sale of securities by the government will reduce prices and increase interest rates and yields while purchases will have the opposite effect.

The government effects such open market operations through a Bank of Canada but another method frequently used to influence bank cash reserves is by transfers of government deposits.

The government maintains a deposit account with the Bank of Canada, through which nearly all government receipts and payments are made. However, the government also maintains deposits with the chartered banks in order to avoid excessive fluctuation in its deposit balance held at the Bank of Canada. The government may choose to transfer the balances between the central bank and the chartered banks. This is used as an instrument of daily adjustment of the reserves of excess cash in the banking system and even of particular banks.

41

The advantage of this method of intervention is that it affects liquidity and reserves held by the banks but does not have a direct influence on prices and yields in the money market. The government may thus, in the short term, influence the expansion of credit without affecting the cost of credit.

Discount policy and bank rate

The Bank of Canada may lend short-term money to the chartered banks for a maximum period of up to six months provided the banks lodge specific securities as collateral. The minimum rate at which the central bank will grant such advances is the bank rate.

Authorized dealers alternatively are able to borrow from the Bank by discounting eligible bills or by pledging specified securities at a rate of $\frac{1}{4}\%$ above 3-month treasury bill rate according to the latest tender price, but subject to a minimum rate of $\frac{3}{4}\%$ below bank rate. The bank rate is an administered rate, fixed by the Bank of Canada, and does not fluctuate freely in response to demand and supply in the money market. It is not used as a major instrument of monetary policy but used at times in conjunction with open market operations. Bank rate is more a general indicator of government policy and intentions for the money market than a direct tool of influence.

Bank rate effectively places a ceiling on short-term money market rates since both chartered banks and authorized dealers may borrow from the Bank of Canada at a maximum cost determined by bank rate.

Moral suasion

Since, there are only a small number of schedule A chartered banks and also a high concentration of bank lending amongst a very few of these banks, the Bank of Canada is able to use moral suasion to influence the quantitative restriction of credit and the qualitative direction of credit. Therefore, without using any of the above instruments, the Bank of Canada may simply request the chartered banks to limit the amount of new credit they extend and to direct such new lending as they do undertake into specified production or needy areas of the economy.

Monetary and economic indicators

The following indicators are released at the time shown below and provide economic and monetary information which may influence the money and capital markets.

Money supply	Every Thursday
Reserve	First Monday of each month
Balance of payments	Every quarter, as soon as available
Balance of trade	Third or fourth week of each month
Gross national product	Annually, as soon as available
Industrial production	Third or fourth week of each month
Wholesale price index	Beginning of second week of each month
Unemployment	Second Tuesday of each month

Withholding taxes

Interest

Interest earned from investments in Canadian money market and capital market securities is subject to withholding tax at a rate of 25 per cent. This is reduced for residents of tax treaty countries as shown in Table 2.8. Countries marked with an asterisk are those with which Canada is currently renegotiating the terms of the various tax treaties.

Dividends

Normal portfolio dividends are taxed at a rate of 25 per cent, reduced for most treaty countries to 15 per cent. For substantial holdings of a domestic company's shareholding and where Canadian residents hold at least 25 per cent of the equity and comprise 25 per cent of the board of directors, the withholding tax rate may be lower as shown in the table.

Exemptions

The following are exempt from withholding tax on interest payments due to non-residents:

All government, provincial and municipal treasury bills.
All central government guaranteed bonds except those issued before 10 December 1960.
All provincial and municipal bonds issued after 15 April 1966 and before 1983.
All corporate bonds issued after June 1975 with maturities of more than five years and a day and with less than 25 per cent of the issue being amortized within five years of issue.
All bonds issued after 29 December 1960 where interest is not payable in, or by reference to, Canadian dollars.
Bonds of certain educational, health or government controlled institutions issued after 15 April 1966 and before 1983.

Exchange controls

Canada has free exchange markets and no restrictions on capital movements.

Exchange control authority

Since there are no exchange controls, there is no single authority, although the Bank of Canada is responsible for the monitoring of foreign exchange markets.

Currency

The currency is the Canadian dollar which is allowed to float freely with respect to other currencies. The authorities do not intervene in the exchange market to maintain specific margins against other currencies, but may operate occasionally in the spot market *vis-à-vis* the US dollar in order to stabilize excessive fluctuations.

Table 2.8 Withholding taxes

| Recipient | Interest | Dividends | |
		A	B
	%	%	%
Non-treaty countries	25	25	25
Treaty countries			
Australia	25	10	15
Austria	15	10	15
Belgium	15	10	15
Denmark	15	10	15
Dominion Republic	18	15	18
Finland	15	10	15
France	15	10	15
Germany	15	10	15
Indonesia	15	10	15
Ireland	15	10	15
Israel	15	10	15
Italy	15	10	15
Jamaica	15	10	15
Japan	15	10	15
Korea	15	10	15
Liberia	20	10	15
Malaysia	15	10	15
Morocco	15	10	15
Netherlands	15	10	15
New Zealand	25	20	25
Norway	15	10	15
Pakistan	15	10	15
Philippines	15	10	15
Rumania	15	10	15
Singapore	15	10	15
South Africa	25	20	25
Spain	15	10	15
Sweden	15	10	15
Switzerland	15	10	15
Trinidad & Tobago	15	10	15
UK	15	10	15
USA	15	10	15

Note: A For dividends from companies where Canadian residents hold at least 25% of the share capital and represent at least 25% of the board of directors.

B For dividends from companies substantially owned by foreign interests (i.e., more than 75% of share capital and/or 75% of directorial control).

Non-resident deposit

Non-residents may freely open a deposit account with a Canadian bank or any other financial institution, and may use the account to buy and sell any domestic Canadian securities, foreign securities, or real estate.

The accounts may be freely credited or debited with Canadian dollars or any other currency.

Transfer of profits and dividends

Non-residents may freely transfer the proceeds of investments in Canada without restrictions.

Gold

Non-residents may freely buy or sell gold in Canada. Gold may also be freely exported except where the gold is of US origin when a special permit is required. Additionally, permits are required for exports of gold to all communist countries.

3. Mexico

General market environment

Mexico has a free market economy. There have never been any exchange controls in force so non-residents have free access to investment markets in Mexico while residents also have free access to foreign markets.

Non-residents may purchase all descriptions of fixed interest or coupon bearing Mexican securities but interest earned is subject to withholding tax of 21 per cent which is deducted at source and cannot be reclaimed. Yields however are high by international standards because of Mexico's high relative inflation rate.

The most active securities are treasury bills, with maturities of three months and yields in 1981 well in excess of 30 per cent; and petrobonds with maturities of three years. Petrobonds are backed by specific amounts of oil reserves and their redemption value is linked to the price of oil. They therefore provide the potential of capital appreciation as well as quarterly interest payments equivalent to 10 per cent per annum net. As Mexico has the sixth largest proven reserves of oil in the world, the bonds are backed by good security. As well as being listed on the Mexican stock exchange, they are widely traded by banks in the international capital market where settlement may be made in any currency.

Non-resident investment in equities is restricted to specific types of shares and maximum foreign shareholdings by foreign investment laws. The total number of shares is anyway rather limited but demand has grown considerably since 1977. In order to facilitate greater participation in the Mexican equity market by foreigners, the Mexico Fund was launched in early 1981. This is an investment fund, managed by the Mexican Development Bank together with Mexican and US stockbrokers, with shares in the fund available through foreign stock-markets. It is expected that the fund will generate high capital growth.

The exchange rate system is managed by a controlled float. The peso has remained very stable against the US dollar between 1976 and December 1980. It is probable however that the exchange rate will become more volatile as a result of deliberate policy by the central bank. Because of the absence of exchange controls and Mexico's very open economy, the central bank finds it difficult effectively to manage the domestic money supply. The banks are subject to very high reserve ratios and some selective credit policies but otherwise the central bank undertakes very little intervention in the money market.

Table 3.1 Summary of instruments

Instrument	Characteristics
MONEY MARKET	

Deposits
  call deposits
  time deposits
  currency deposits
	Deposits can be placed with banks for overnight call up to two years or more in pesos or convertible currency. Interest rates fixed on weekly basis by central bank

Treasury bills	Issued since 1978. High yields. Very active market
Commercial paper	First issued in 1980. Issued through stock exchange by good quality companies. High yields
CAPITAL MARKET	
Petrobonds	Each issue represents specific quantity of oil. Redemption value indexed to price of oil. Fixed coupon of 10% per annum net paid quarterly. Traded internationally and settled in any currency
Telefonos de Mexico bonds	Second to treasury bills as issues of fixed interest securities. Low coupon rates but high yield to maturity. Good secondary market
Corporate bonds	Small market but becoming increasingly active. Most issued with variable coupons
Equity shares	Small market with high growth since 1978. Subject to foreign investment laws, thus limited number of shares available to foreigners
Mexico fund	Investment fund supervised by Government Development Bank. Specifically for foreigners to indirectly invest in local capital market. Listed on foreign stock exchange(s)

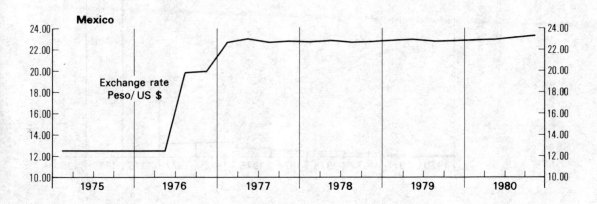

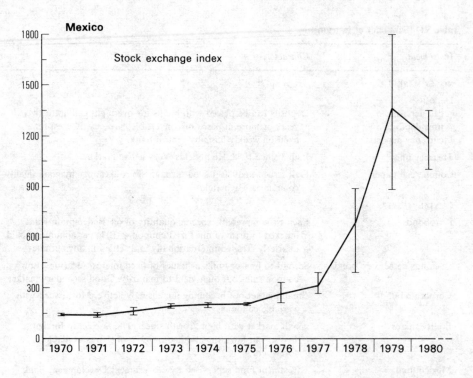

Mexico

Stock exchange index

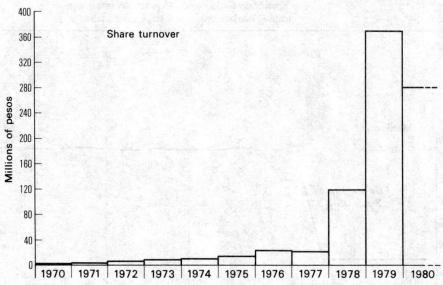

Share turnover

The money market

Deposits

Most of the banks accept deposits in both convertible currencies, predominantly US dollars, and in pesos. Since there are no exchange controls and because Mexico shares a common border with the USA, residents tend to switch their accounts between dollars and pesos depending on relative interest rates and exchange rates. Excessive switching into dollars is known as dollarization and is more prevalent when the peso is considered overvalued relative to the dollar. The banks attempt to prevent dollarization by maintaining high rates of interest on peso deposits. During 1980 peso short-term interest rates were between 20 and 30 per cent. Dollar interest rates on the other hand are kept at about $2\frac{1}{2}$ per cent below LIBOR (London Interbank offered rate) except for dollar deposits of more than $100 000 which receive competitive rates of interest.

Interest on deposits placed by non-residents in the domestic money market is subject to withholding tax. Thus while the gross rate of interest on peso deposits in the domestic market may often be at a significant premium over rates of interest on Europeso deposits, the withholding tax at 21 per cent severely reduces the attractiveness of domestic deposit rates. Withholding taxes also apply to interest earned from currency deposits placed by non-residents with banks in Mexico.

Maturities of deposits range from overnight call to two years or longer. For time deposits of more than two years' term, the banks are free to establish their own rates of interest. Rates for deposits of less than two years are determined by the central bank. The whole structure of interest rates for deposits in pesos, dollars and other major currencies is determined by the central bank once a week, and then remains fixed at those levels for the rest of the week.

The levels at which interest rates are fixed take into account the interest rates prevailing in the Eurocurrency markets because there would be an outflow of capital if domestic rates were too low relative to rates in other markets.

Certificates of deposits

There is currently no CD market in Mexico. At one time the banks did issue CDs but they were also willing to cash them on sight which negated the function of CDs as marketable fixed-term securities. They have consequently now been phased out.

Treasury bills

Treasury bills were first issued in 1978 primarily to help the government fund its considerable short-term debt, and are the only fixed interest securities publicly issued by the government. At the end of 1980 the volume of treasury bills issued since 1978 amounted to about P20 billion. They are issued onto the stock exchange by the central bank (Bank of Mexico) on behalf of the government, every Thursday with a maturity of 91 days.

They are discount-bearing notes that are redeemed at par (100 pesos per unit). The rate of discount is determined by the Bank of Mexico and announced in advance of each issue.

49

The discount is based on relative international interest rates and the differential between Mexico's rate of inflation relative to inflation in the rest of the world and in the USA in particular. Since inflation in Mexico has been high (over 30 per cent in 1980) the discount is consequently large. Treasury bills were yielding between 20 and 26 per cent per annum during 1980 and about 35 per cent in first quarter 1981.

Non-residents as well as residents of all categories may subscribe to new treasury bill issues through either a bank or a stockbroker. The bills enjoy a very active secondary market and are traded through the stock exchange. Their good marketability means that, at any time, bills may be purchased with remaining maturities as short as the current week or for any week up to thirteen weeks hence, and that their saleability makes them a highly liquid investment. Minimum trading denominations are P1000 though volumes of P100 million or more may also be absorbed by the market. For non-residents interest earned from treasury bills is, however, subject to withholding tax at 21 per cent.

Commercial paper

Commercial paper was first issued in October 1980. The paper is in the form of short-term permissory notes issued with three months maturity by large creditworthy Mexican companies. In fact only companies that are listed on the stock exchange may issue the paper and in minimum amounts of P1000 million or $50 million up to a maximum of P1500 million or $100 million per annum. The paper may be either discount notes or coupon bearing, at the option of the lender. Lenders are usually banks and corporations who purchase the paper in sizes of P1 million or more.

As with Mexican treasury bills, the interest offered on Mexican commercial paper has to be high in order to attract investors—both resident and foreign—and the early issues were yielding approximately 26 per cent per annum. Commercial paper, like treasury bills, is issued and traded on the stock exchange. It is expected that the primary market will develop successfully, but little secondary market turnover is anticipated as most investors of commercial paper hold the notes to maturity.

The capital market

The Mexican capital market is developing rapidly, with petrobonds being perhaps the investment instrument of most interest to foreigners and unique to Mexico. The stock market, which a few years ago was only of secondary importance as a means of raising capital, has now become of primary importance to companies, and over the two years between 1978 and 1980 securities to the value of more than P100 billion have been traded.

Unlike many other capital markets, the public sector does not play a dominant role in the Mexican market. Apart from treasury bills and, indirectly, petrobonds the government does not issue fixed interest securities on its own behalf, although a large number of bonds are issued by the partly government-owned Mexican Telephone Company.

Petrobonds

Petrobonds are participation certificates which represent rights to a specific quantity of Mexican oil. Mexico has the sixth largest proven reserves of oil (about 60 billion barrels) and is currently the fifth largest producer of oil, though it will probably move up in the world league table in the future.

The bonds are domestic securities but are freely available to non-residents. They were designed to offer local investors a direct stake in the country's oil reserves and, because they are participation certificates, they are effectively a direct claim on a specific number of barrels of AP1-33 light crude oil. They carry a fixed coupon rate of interest, payable quarterly, and their redemption value is indexed to the price of oil. Since the price of oil is always quoted in US dollars, the exchange risk *vis-à-vis* the dollar is small. They are also freely negotiable and enjoy a good secondary market. They thus offer the investor a liquid form of investment with a moderate fixed interest return and the prospect of a good capital gain.

Petrobonds are issued by Nacional Financiera SA (Nafinsa), the government owned development bank. They are registered securities. The registry is kept by the stock exchange commission (Comision Nacional de Valores) and the bonds are quoted on the Mexican stock exchange.

There have been six issues to date. The first was made in April 1977 and the most recent issue was made in April 1981. The first three issues were for a total of P2 billion each and the subsequent issues have been for P5 billion each. Minimum denominations are P1000 per petrobond which represents a different number of barrels per issue. In the first issue one P1000 bond represented 3.344 barrels of oil, whereas in the fifth issue one P1000 bond represented 1.438062 barrels. The oil, which the bonds represent, has not yet been extracted but is part of the country's untapped reserves that are still underground. The P16 billion of petrobonds issued to date only account, however, for some 0.05 per cent of total untapped reserves. The bonds do not therefore represent physically available oil but are securities that are technically backed by oil. The government guarantees the issues and has made an official contract with PEMEX (the state oil company) which protects the rights of the bondholders.

At issue a base price per barrel of oil, as posted by PEMEX, is specified for each bond. At redemption the price per barrel is again specified and is calculated as the average export oil price at about one month before maturity. The average export price may differ slightly from the official OPEC oil price because Mexico exports oil at different prices to different countries.

The redemption value of the bonds is calculated as the number of barrels per P1000 bond multiplied by the average export price per barrel less interest paid to the bondholders (see Table 3.2). A minimum redemption value equal to the value at issue is guaranteed.

All the petrobond issues carry a fixed rate coupon of 12.65823 per cent per annum which is payable quarterly and calculated on the basis of a 360-day year. Since interest tax paid by residents and withholding tax paid by non-residents is 21 per cent in both cases, and since the tax is deducted at source, the net coupon is 10 per cent per annum (i.e., $12.65823 \times \frac{79}{100}$ per cent). All issues also have a fixed

Table 3.2 Petrobond issues

Issue date	Redemption date	Amount issued (Value, million pesos)	Amount issued (No. of barrels)	No. of barrels per P1000 bond	Base price per barrel ($)	Base price per barrel (Pesos)	$/P exchange rate	Issue price	Interest payment dates	Coupon gross, %	Net, %
29 Apr. 1977	29 Apr. 1980	2000	6 680 000	3.3440	13.35	299.04	22.40	100%	29 Jul. / 29 Oct. / 29 Jan. / 29 Apr.	12.658 23	10.0
29 Apr. 1978	29 Apr. 1981	2000	6 592 479	3.296 24	13.40	303.38	22.64	103.75%	29 Jul. / 29 Oct. / 29 Jan. / 29 Apr.	12.658 23	10.0
22 Aug. 1979	22 Aug. 1982	2000	3 907 089	1.953 545	22.60	511.89	22.65	100%	22 Nov. / 22 Feb. / 22 May / 22 Aug.	12.658 23	10.0
22 Nov. 1979	22 Nov. 1982	5000	8 965 685	1.793 137	24.60	557.68	22.67	110%	22 Feb. / 22 May / 22 Aug. / 22 Nov.	12.658 23	10.0
29 Apr. 1980	29 Apr. 1983	5000	7 189 840	1.437 968	30.62	695.43	22.71	100%	29 Jul. / 29 Oct. / 29 Jan. / 29 Apr.	12.658 23	10.0
29 Apr. 1981	29 Apr. 1984	5000	5 514 660	1.102 932	38.50	922.84	23.97	100%	29 Jul. / 29 Oct. / 29 Jan. / 29 Apr.	12.658 23	10.0

Table 3.3

Issue price (29 Apr. 1977)	= 100% (par)
No. of barrels per P1000 bond	= 3.344
Base price per barrel	= US$13.35
(@ US$1 = P22.4)	= P299.04
Price per barrel at maturity (29 Apr. 1980)	= US$32.1
(@ US$1 = P22.7)	= P728.9
Price per barrel × No. of barrels per bond	= P2437.5
As price per certificate	= 243.75%
Minus 30 percentage points	= 213.75%
Therefore redemption value	= 213.75%

maturity of three years. The interest deducted in the redemption calculation is thus 30 percentage points (3 × 10 per cent). The redemption value can be illustrated by the April 1977 petrobond issue which has since matured, as shown in Table 3.3, from which it will be seen that an investor who bought one 1977 petrobond at issue for P1000 and held the bond to maturity would have received interest of P300 net and a capital gain of P1137.5 (2137.5 − 1000). The capital gain is subject to tax but if sold on the stock exchange up to two days prior to maturity, the capital gains tax is waived. Nafinsa guarantees to purchase on the stock exchange two days before maturity at the redemption price, so the investor does not have to forfeit any profit.

If the bonds are bought or sold during the life of the issue, the yield and price can be calculated in several ways. Four methods are as follow:

1. Profit over base price. This is a quick rule-of-thumb method of estimating the potential profit to the bondholder. It provides an estimation of whether the current bond price is justified by the current price of oil. For example:

The fourth issue of 22 November 1979 has a base price of oil of $24.60 per barrel.

The $/P exchange rate at issue was 22.67. Thus the peso base price was P557.68. At October 1980, the price of the bond was quoted at 124.125 per cent (P1241.25 per unit). To see if the price of oil justifies this quoted price, the following calculation is required.

Thirty percentage points must be added to the current price since at redemption 30 points will be deducted. This gives a price of 154.125 per cent. The present price is therefore justified by an oil price of

$$\frac{154.125}{100} \times 24.60 = \$37.91$$

$$@ \$1 = P23 \quad = P872.04$$

In October 1980 the Mexican oil price was $34.50 (P793.50) per barrel.

The quoted price of the bond was therefore at a small premium relative to the current price of oil, but given that the bond still had a remaining life of over two years to run during which the price of oil will almost certainly rise, the premium was probably justified.

53

2. Theoretical value at maturity. The method above takes the current quoted price of the petrobond into consideration in the calculation and derives the expected price of oil at maturity. This method ignores the quoted petrobond price but uses as its base the current price of oil and derives the expected value of the bond at maturity, assuming no change in the oil price. Thus, using again the fourth issue of 22 January 1979:

Number of barrels per P1000 bond	= 1.793 137
Current price of oil	= US$34.50
Peso price at exchange rate $1 = P23	= P793.50
Thus peso value of bond	= P793.5 × 1.793 137
	= P1422.85
Less interest payments (P300)	= P1122.85

Thus on the basis of the current oil price, the value at maturity would be P1122.85.

The current quoted price of the bond is P1241.25, which is a premium of 10.5 per cent over the underlying value of the bond. However as the bond (at October 1980) had more than two years' remaining life it is highly probable that the price of oil would rise sufficiently to justify such a premium. To determine what price of oil justifies the quoted price, method 1 may be used.

3. Interest adjusted. Method 2 does not, however, take into account the proportion of interest that will accrue to the bondholder. If the bond is purchased at some interval between issue and maturity the purchaser will lose 30 percentage points at redemption although he may not himself have received the whole of the interest payments. The new purchaser should therefore add to the current quoted price only the number of percentage points of interest that he will receive. From the example used in method 1, an investor purchasing the bond in October 1980 will receive the fourth quarter interest payment in November 1980 plus subsequent quarterly interest payments for two years to a total of 22.5 per cent net.

The calculation is therefore:

$$124.5 + 22.5 \quad = 146.625$$

$$\frac{146.625}{100} \times \$24.6 = \$36.07$$

$$@\ \$1 = P23 \quad = P829.6$$

His investment is therefore justified by a lower price of oil than demonstrated in method 1. Clearly the price is favourable since the current price at $34.5 per barrel is close to the required price of $36.07, yet the bond still has more than two years to maturity.

4. Yield method. Methods 1, 2 and 3 compare the price of the bond relative to the current or expected price of oil. A fourth method is based on the rate of return or yield available on a particular bond.

The investor determines that on a dollar denominated fixed interest security of similar maturity he could earn, say, 12.75 per cent per annum net. By using this rate of return as a bench-mark he can determine the implicit price of oil needed in order that he receives this return.

Assuming he purchases the same bond as in methods 1, 2 and 3 in October 1980 when it still has two years and a month to run, his required return at 12.25 per cent per annum is

$$\frac{12.75}{12} + 12.75 + 12.75 = 26.56\%$$

The quoted petrobond price is 124.125%
Required return is

$$\frac{26.56}{100} \times 124.125 = 32.97\%$$

Thus the minimum bond price at redemption must be

$$1.3297 \times 124.125 = 165.05$$

The base price of oil is $24.6 per barrel, thus the implicit price of oil at redemption is

$$\frac{165.05}{100} \times 24.6 = \$40.602$$

The interest actually received by the bondholder and the 30 percentage points deducted from the redemption value cancel each other out and have been excluded from the calculation.

If at the time of purchase the price per barrel of oil was $34.5, there is a good probability that during the remaining two years' life of the bond the oil price will reach or exceed $40.6. The investor will therefore probably receive at least his minimum required return.

Petrobonds may be purchased at issue through a Mexican stockbroker or bank. They enjoy a very active secondary market and may be traded either on the stock exchange, through a stockbroker or through major banks in the USA and Europe.

On the stock exchange turnover is high and may be as much as P20 million per day. In the first half of 1980, turnover reached a total of P18 billion compared with P2 billion in the same period of 1979. Turnover in offshore markets is not known but is believed to be substantial. If dealt locally on the stock exchange accrued interest is included gross in the price of the bonds whereas offshore banks treat accrued interest on a net 10 per cent basis. In addition, purchase and sales made through offshore banks may be settled in any currency.

Telefonos de Mexico bonds

Next to Nafinsa, which issues petrobonds, the second major issuer of domestic bonds is Telefonos de Mexico (the Mexican Telephone Company), which is 51 per cent owned by the government.

As at October 1980 there were 42 telefonos bonds outstanding in the market. They had average maturities of seven years and a net yield to maturity ranging between 17 and 25 per cent. They all, bar one, carry low coupon fixed rates of interest and thus are quoted at prices significantly below their par redemption values. The latest issue, known as the double X (XX), differs from all previous issues in that it has a variable coupon set at a premium over the one year bank deposit rate and its price is consequently closer to par than any of the other issues.

All the telefonos bonds are quoted on the Mexican stock exchange and are traded in registered form in multiples of P1000. They enjoy a fairly good secondary market though turnover is not as high as for either petrobonds or treasury bills.

Corporate bonds

Companies have in the last few years taken a greater interest in the stock exchange as a source of capital and a number of coupon bearing bonds have been issued by the larger Mexican companies. Maturities are short to medium term and the maximum remaining life of currently outstanding issues is eight years. For most issues, coupons are at variable rates set at a premium over bank deposit rates of interest which is specified at issue, but subject to maximum rates of interest as determined by the central bank.

During 1980 net yields ranged between 25 and 28 per cent with bond prices trading at 5 to 20 percentage points below par.

Corporate bonds are in registered form and are listed and traded through the stock exchange in multiples of P1000. Turnover is fairly good though less active than the market for petrobonds or treasury bills.

Eurobonds and foreign bonds

No Eurobonds have been issued denominated in Mexican pesos, nor do foreign borrowers issue bonds in the Mexican capital market. Mexican borrowers do however make substantial use of the Euromarkets. Mexican companies regularly issue Eurodollar bonds and a small number of foreign bonds have been issued by Mexican borrowers in the Yankee and Swiss foreign bond markets. More importantly, the Mexican government is a sizeable borrower in the Eurocredit market. In 1979, Mexico was the largest single borrowing country in the market, receiving US$10 455 million worth of publicized medium and long term syndicated bank loans. This was equivalent to over 13 per cent of total publicized Eurocredits for 1979. In the nine months to September 1980 Mexico borrowed $4023 million from the Eurocredit market which, although considerably less than in 1979, still represented eight per cent of total Eurocredits in the first three quarters of 1980.

The reason for this high borrowing has been mainly to support the balance of payments deficit ($4.25 billion in 1979). International banks have nonetheless regarded Mexico as a good credit risk because of the country's substantial oil reserves and have consequently been willing to extend considerable credit to the Mexican government and to other Mexican borrowers.

Equity shares

Although Mexican companies have increasingly raised equity capital through the stock exchange there are only about 100 shares traded actively on the Mexican stock exchange. Equity turnover represents only about 10 per cent of the total securities market, the rest consists of petrobonds, treasury bills and corporate bonds.

All investment in Mexican shares is subject to the 'law to promote Mexican investment and regulate foreign investment', which together with two other laws, governs investment by both residents and non-residents. In summary these laws place investors into three categories—the Mexican government, Mexican nationals and foreigners—and specify the industries and types of shares in which each category may invest.

1. Mexican government. Only the Mexican government may invest or control activities in the following industries:

   Oil extraction
   Basic petrochemicals
   Nuclear energy and radioactive minerals
   Certain other forms of mining
   Electricity
   Telegraphic and radio communications
   Railways

2. Mexican nationals. Other industries are reserved wholly for participation by Mexican nationals. These are:

   Radio and television broadcasting
   Urban and highway transportation
   Airlines and shipping
   Forestry
   Gas distribution
   Industrial holding companies (though not specifically for nationals, tax legislation precludes foreign shareholders)

3. Foreigners. Foreigners may invest in companies that undertake those activities not specifically excluded above. However there is a general rule that total foreign shareholdings should not be more than 49 per cent of total issued equity of a Mexican company and, for some industries, the maximum foreign shareholding may be less than 49 per cent. There are also certain exceptions to this general rule where, for some companies, foreign shareholdings may be greater than 49

57

per cent. These companies are Mexican subsidiaries of foreign companies such as General Motors, Volkswagen and IBM.

The areas in which foreign investment is permissible are:

Mining (except types of mining specifically reserved for nationals) up to 49 per cent, though some mining companies have a foreign shareholding limit of 36 per cent
Secondary petrochemical products—up to 40 per cent
Automobile parts—up to 40 per cent
Banking, finance and insurance—small minority holdings only allowed
All other industries up to 49 per cent

Of the roughly 100 shares that are actively traded on the stock exchange almost all are available to foreign investors. Only the Mexican Airlines, Mexicana, and the industrial holding companies such as ALFA, DESC and VISA are unavailable. However, many companies have reached their maximum foreign shareholding and in some cases (e.g., Texaco), the maximum is held by a single foreign shareholder. Such companies, with a known foreign affiliation, may split their shareholdings into A and B shares. The B shares are held by the foreign affiliated company and may be sold to other foreigners while the A shares are traded between Mexican nationals. The A and B shares are created in proportion to the maximum permissible foreign shareholding. Otherwise there is no difference between A and B shares as regards voting and dividend rights. B shares can sometimes stand at a premium relative to A shares, but principally because there is a smaller supply of B shares freely available to the foreign investor than there are A shares available to nationals.

Companies with no major foreign affiliation do not have a divided share capital. Share purchases by foreign investors must be immediately registered with the Foreign Investment Commission which keeps a record of the proportion of each company's shareholders and notifies stockbrokers when foreign shareholdings are approaching the maximum permissible limit.

The Foreign Investment Commission, comprising representatives from the major governmental ministries, supervises all foreign investment, whether direct or portfolio investment, other than investment in fixed interest securities.

Purchasing shares in companies whose foreign shareholding is at or near the legal limit may prove difficult for foreigners. The major stockbrokers therefore service their foreign clients by notifying them of any imminent availability of particular shares or purchasing shares on their clients' behalf as and when such shares become available.

Mexican quoted companies are corporations indicated by the subscript SA (Sociedad Anonima). They are subject to minimum capital structures and directorships and are also required to produce annual externally audited accounts as well as interim accounts which need not be audited.

Of the shares available to foreigners, many have low price/earnings ratios by international standards and their market prices do not, in many cases, fully reflect their underlying asset values. There is therefore believed to be substantial scope for further price rises. This is particularly so because, despite Mexico's high inflation rate (about 30 per cent in 1980). The country is expected to maintain, during the 1980s, a real rate of growth of about 8 per cent per annum. This level of growth was experienced in 1979 and 1980 and has been brought about through Mexico's increasing oil production and from which many of the companies that service the oil sector also benefit. Many companies have increased profits by more than 50 per cent in 1980. The low price of their shares relative to earnings is due to uncertainty about the effect of currently high interest rates on profits and, for foreign investors, the effect of inflation on the exchange rate (see exchange controls).

Table 3.4 lists the major companies whose shares are available to foreigners and their key statistics.

Table 3.4 Mexican shares available to foreigners (*source: Accione y Valores De Mexico SA de GV (Mexican Stockbrokers)*)

| Company | Activity | No. of shares outstanding Aug. 1980, millions | Price Aug. 1980, pesos | Price earnings ratio | | | Market value to book value ratio at Aug. 1980 |
				1979 historic	1980 est.	1981 est.	
Ahmsa	Steel	114	39	3.7	3.7	3.0	0.1
Alum B	Aluminium	12	59	4.0	3.3	2.4	1.1
Aurrera B	Retailing	360	37	15.2	9.2	6.1	3.0
Bacomer	Bank	437	32	5.7	3.9	2.7	1.3
Banamex	Bank	83	176	6.5	4.6	3.5	1.5
Campos	Steel	32	22	6.9	5.5	4.0	0.4
Carbide B	Chemicals	23	135	10.2	7.1	4.8	2.7
Cermoc	Brewery	113	44	8.8	5.5	3.6	1.1
Comrmex	Bank	85	28	4.7	3.7	2.7	1.0
Intenal	Bank	23	54	5.0	3.6	2.6	1.1
Irsa B	Chemicals	43	95	15.7	8.6	5.9	2.1
Kimber B	Paper	69	215	16.7	11.3	7.7	4.4
Livepol	Retailing	120	100	17.1	11.1	7.7	2.3
Loreto B	Paper	4	112	9.0	2.5	4.7	0.8
Moresa B	Autoparts	11	50	4.6	5.0	3.3	0.8
Nafin B	Bank	27	108	5.5	3.2	2.4	0.7
Neromex B	Chemicals	4	305	13.5	9.0	6.5	1.2
Palacio	Retailing	8	325	10.7	7.9	5.4	1.8
Paris	Retailing	17	47	9.4	6.0	4.2	1.3
Penoles	Mining	11	1920	21.9	11.6	8.0	6.4
Spicer B	Autoparts	30	146	10.9	8.6	6.3	2.8
Serfin B	Bank	16	203	6.4	4.1	2.6	1.2
Tamsa	Steel	32	180	11.4	8.6	6.4	2.5
Telmex 80A	Telephone	191	59	4.4	3.7	2.8	0.3
Termec B	Autoparts	43	42	5.4	4.2	3.0	0.6

The stock exchange

The Mexican stock exchange, now located in Mexico City, is the result of a merger in 1976 of the then three stock exchanges located in Monterry, Mexico City and Guadalajara. The stock exchange is structured as a joint stock company whose shareholders are brokers and dealers, which are the only entities authorized to do business on the floor of the exchange. At mid-1980 there were 38 shareholders of the MSE of which 31 were broking companies and seven were individuals. The National Securities Commission (Comision Nacional de Valores) supervises the stock exchange and regulates new issues and the trading of securities. Before obtaining a listing on the MSE, companies must first obtain a listing in the National Registry of Securities and Broker-Dealers. This requires that specific financial criteria are met and that the company whose shares are to be listed can prove that there exists an adequate public market for its shares. Broker-dealers are also required to be listed on the national registry in order to deal on the MSE, and are subject to specific regulations. The national registry is maintained and supervised by the National Securities Commission.

The stock exchange lists most fixed interest securities, i.e., treasury bills, petrobonds, telefonos bonds and corporate bonds and equity shares of about 340 companies. The volume both in terms of new issues and in trading turnover of both types of securities has grown enormously since the mid-1970s. Treasury bills were first introduced in 1978, petrobonds in 1977, while corporate borrowers have also sought greater amounts of capital through the issue of both bonds and equities in recent years. The market capitalization of equities is now about P350 billion, and trading volume of shares was about P280 million per day in 1980 compared to about P22 million per day in 1977. The value of turnover in fixed interest securities is larger still than equity turnover.

For equity shares, prices reflect the rapid growth in trading volume. The Mexican stock exchange index, which consists of 29 actively traded stocks, reached an all-time high in May 1979 of 1798.5, which was more than double the index for December 1978. The chart shows the change in the index and the growth of trading volume over the last decade.

The Mexico fund

The Mexico Fund (Fondo de Mexico) is a closed-end investment fund which is designed to provide foreigners free access to the Mexican capital market as well as to attract more foreign capital to the Mexican market.

The fund was launched in early 1981 with a listing on the New York stock exchange and a potential future listing on the London stock exchange. Shares are to be made available through stockbrokers and investment banks on a private placement basis in the USA, UK, France and Canada.

The fund may invest in all types of Mexican securities (apart from those areas specifically reserved for the Mexican government) without restriction. Foreigners in turn may purchase shares in the fund which have a nominal value of about US$20 per share, and have dividend rights but no voting rights. Certificates of trusts are also to be made available. These would represent rights to investment in only one share, as opposed to the ordinary shares of the fund which represent rights to investment in a wide range of shares and other securities.

The fund is held in trust by the state owned development bank, Nacional Financiera (Nafinsa) which holds all the voting rights of the shares purchased by the fund. The investment strategy and management of the fund is controlled by the management company comprising Nafinsa and 10 Mexican stockbrokers who together own 51 per cent of the management company, and three US stockbrokers, Merril Lynch, Bache Group and Solomon Brothers who together own the remaining 49 per cent. The fund, with an initial capital of about US$100 million, is hoped to provide revenues of about US$40 billion by 1985.

Dealing and fees

All Mexican securities, whether short-term money market instruments like treasury bills and commercial paper or capital market instruments like petrobonds and equities, are traded on the stock exchange.

Transactions are effected through one of the 31 stockbrokers. The largest bank, Bancomer, owns one of the brokerage houses.

Brokerage commission rates are set by the Mexican stock exchange and are standard charges made by all brokers. The commission rates are low but vary according to the price of the securities bought or sold. There are no stamp duties or additional charges made.

Since, in general, securities are in registered form it is easier, for receipt of interest and dividends, that the securities remain in Mexico and are not transferred abroad. The brokers therefore also provide safe custody services at nominal cost.

Petrobonds, as well as being traded on the stock exchange, are widely traded by banks in Europe and the USA. Such banks quote bid and offer prices for the bonds. The spread between these prices represents the banks' commission and, depending on the state of the market, may be $\frac{1}{2}$ to 1 per cent. Settlement may be made in any convertible currency.

Shares in the Mexico fund are listed on the New York stock exchange and may later also be listed on the London stock exchange. Dealing and fees thus depend on the regulations pertaining to those markets.

Financial and monetary systems

Financial institutions

The major financial institutions in Mexico are the banks, which may be classified according to four groups: savings banks, mortgage banks, investment banks and commercial banks.

The banks are regulated by the Bank of Mexico and supervised by the National Banking and Insurance Commission. All banks are subject to the banking laws,

61

which were revised in 1977 and 1978. These revisions facilitated the merging of commercial banks and investment banks, many of which were anyway already affiliated, to give rise to multipurpose banks, known as multibancos.

Most banks are privately owned but a few government owned banks have been established to provide special banking services; they may be described within the general category of investment banks. The privately owned banks are all domestic Mexican banks. Foreign banks are not permitted to establish branches in Mexico or compete for Mexican deposits. Foreign banks may establish representative offices in Mexico and are also active in providing Eurocurrency loans to Mexican companies.

Savings banks

The savings banks are small and cater for a specialized market comprising mainly individuals in regional areas. They do not provide chequing accounts and only take time deposits.

Mortgage banks

The mortgage banks also provide a limited range of services. They only provide finance in the form of mortgages to individuals and businesses. They depend mostly on other banks and institutions as a source of funds. In fact, most mortgage banks have been absorbed by other banks and have become departments of these banks.

Investment banks (financieras)

The investment banks, known as financieras, are equivalent in function to the UK merchant banks or the US and European investment banks. They do not provide chequing accounts but accept call and time deposits and provide short and medium term finance to industry and commercial enterprises. They also provide investment advice to their clients and advise on mergers and acquisitions.

Most financieras are privately owned and many have combined with commercial banks to form multibancos. Some are government owned and provide services to specialized markets. The largest government owned investment bank is Nacional Financiera S.A. This is a development bank whose aim is to encourage the development and growth of domestic industry. To this end, it provides medium and long term loans to industry and may sometimes take direct equity participation in particular companies. It also provides financial advisory services to developing industry and arranges joint ventures between foreign and Mexican companies for the production of capital goods in Mexico. It is, in addition, the main bank to lend to the government or its agencies, and borrows in the Euromarkets or in foreign capital markets on behalf of the government. Altogether Nacional Financiera is a major force in the Mexican economy. Other government owned banks, such as Banco Nacional de Comercio Exterior S.A., provide specialist services to Mexican exporters.

Commercial banks

The commercial banks provide chequing account facilities and accept savings deposits as well as call and time deposits. These banks receive most of the country's savings from the household sector and a large share from the corporate sector. They also provide most of the short-term credit extended to individuals and companies. Such loans are arranged on lines of credit terms backed by pledges against specific assets.

By merging with investment banks some of the commercial banks have become multibancos and thus provide the whole spectrum of banking services. The two largest multibancos, Banco de Commercio (Bancomer) and the Banco Nacional de Mexico (Banamex) operate an extensive branch network of over 1000 branches throughout Mexico and control about 50 per cent of all banking business. Other commercial banks, of which about six are of any significant size, operate much smaller branch networks. Next to Bancomer with an asset value in 1980 of P251 billion and Banamex (P240 billion) the other main commercial banks are Serfin (P102 billion) Comermex (P93 billion) Banco del Atlantico (P25 billion) Banpais (P22 billion) BCH (P21 billion) and Cremi (P20 billion).

The two large multibancos provide local finance of up to seven years' term but they also occasionally participate in syndications with foreign banks to provide loans to domestic industry of up to 10 years' term.

The Banco Nacional de Mexico also operates the Casa de Bolsa Banamex. Bolsa means brokerage, and so this is a banking brokerage house.

Central bank (Banco de Mexico)

The central bank, Banco de Mexico (Bank of Mexico) is wholly owned by the government. The Bank is the sole issuer of currency and is charged with regulating the banking system subject to the banking laws and in co-operation with the National Banking and Insurance Commission. On behalf of the government the Bank implements its monetary policy and supervises the floating of the Mexican peso in the foreign exchange markets.

Monetary policy

The main objective of monetary policy is to reduce inflation through control of the growth in money supply (M1) which has been growing at 32 per cent per annum in 1980, following a growth of 33.6 per cent in 1979.

The main instruments used by the central bank are qualitative and quantitative credit controls and particularly the use of legal reserve requirements. These instruments have proved only moderately effective, largely because the absence of exchange controls allow Mexican companies to borrow from foreign sources which, in the short term at least, expands the money supply. The government however recognizes that such borrowing is necessary in order to maintain the high rate of real growth in the economy and that other non-monetary policy methods are also important as a means of increasing supply to meet the inherently high demand. If supply can be increased by, for example, eliminating bottle-necks in the transport and agricultural sectors, then inflation will consequently abate.

Reserve requirements

Legal reserve requirements form the main fulcrum of monetary policy. All banks are required to deposit with the Bank of Mexico, in interest-bearing accounts, cash reserves equal to a specified proportion of their peso deposits. The reserve requirements also apply to future purchases of pesos by the banks in the forward or futures foreign exchange markets.

The reserve ratios are high—37.5 per cent in 1979 and 40.9 per cent in 1980—and are varied at the discretion of the government together with the Bank of Mexico in order to reduce the available cash against which the banks can lend. The cash reserves placed with the Bank of Mexico receive interest at rates which are commensurate with, though below, other money market rates of interest. These deposits are then used by the government to finance its budget deficit and certain other public sector expenditure.

From time to time, the Bank of Mexico may call for additional special deposits from the banks. These deposits also bear interest but are frozen at the central bank and not re-lent to the government. They therefore have an immediately restrictive effect on the money supply since special deposits remove money completely from the financial system as well as reducing the multiplier effect of bank lending against their deposit liabilities.

Interest rate policy and open market operations

Although there do exist maximum limits for interest on certain types of deposits and for coupons on corporate bonds, the authorities do not in general attempt to influence liquidity through the manipulation of interest rates. The government first issued treasury bills in 1978 and so could, in theory, influence interest rates by the amount of bills issued and/or the rate of discount attaching to the bills. In practice, however, the government needs to issue the bills to finance its budget deficit which largely determines the amount to be issued while the discount rate is determined in the market by public auction.

The Bank of Mexico is unable to use the treasury bill market for its open market operations to any great effect since while it may operate in the secondary market it cannot influence new issues in the primary market. The Bank does not undertake a large amount of open market operations in other markets to the extent that it can significantly affect interest rates or liquidity. It does undertake some operations in the spot foreign exchange market in order to stabilize fluctuations in the exchange value of the peso, particularly with respect to the US dollar. The peso, however, is a floating currency and the authorities do not attempt to maintain its value within prescribed margins or to alter an existing trend. Interest rates on bank deposits are determined once a week by the central bank but its purpose in doing so is more to maintain consistency and stability in the banking system than to influence monetary aggregates. Interest rates have to be high to compensate for Mexico's high rate of inflation, and they have to be competitive with internationally quoted rates to prevent destabilizing flows of funds into and out of the country.

The Bank of Mexico does not operate a discount window and thus cannot use discount rates of quotas to influence liquidity. The banks themselves have little need for a discount facility because they have free access to foreign markets in which they may borrow if temporarily short of funds. The interest which the banks pay on their borrowings in the Euromarkets are however subject to withholding tax at 15 per cent (reduced from 21 per cent in 1981). The tax is deducted at source and thus represents a penalty on Euromarket borrowing by Mexican banks since they are unable to claim back the tax paid.

To a large extent the additional cost of borrowing is reflected in the cost of bank lending. Unlike deposit interest rates, the central bank does not fix bank lending rates. Each bank is free to establish its own rate for lending. In the case of each bank this is determined by the average cost of funds which in late 1980 was between 25 and 30 per cent per annum, plus a spread which may be as high as 2 to 3 per cent. In addition, banks may require that its borrowers maintain compensating balances with them which may vary from bank to bank.

Selective credit controls

In addition to the reserve requirements, which in 1980 represent more than 40 per cent of the banks' deposit liabilities, a further 35 per cent of their deposits is required to be invested in public works and government sponsored projects at preferential rates of interest. This policy is designed to achieve two objectives. Firstly it provides much needed capital to developing a better industrial and manufacturing infrastructure in Mexico. Secondly it absorbs still further liquidity from the banking system and, together with the reserve requirements, ensures that the banks retain only 25 per cent of their deposits, which greatly restricts the amounts they can lend to private sector companies and households. This has not however prevented private sector companies from borrowing. Since there are no exchange controls companies can and do borrow frequently in the Euromarkets or from banks in the US. This factor is one of the major reasons why Mexican borrowers have been the most prevalent in the international capital markets.

Withholding taxes

Mexico does not maintain any tax treaties with foreign countries so all non-residents of any nationality are subject to withholding taxes at the full rate and are not able to reclaim any tax paid.

Interest on all fixed income securities is subject to withholding tax of 21 per cent. There are no securities for which interest is exempt from tax.

Cash dividends paid to non-residents are subject to withholding tax at 21 per cent, though stock dividends are exempt.

Exchange controls

Mexico is, and always has been, completely free from foreign exchange restrictions. Thus all transfers of capital, interest profits and dividends are freely transferable into and out of the country in pesos or in any other convertible currency.

Non-residents may hold accounts with Mexican banks, denominated in pesos and in other convertible currencies.

The currency is the Mexican peso which is subject to a 'controlled float' under the supervision of the central bank which may intervene in the spot foreign exchange market, using the US dollar as the currency of intervention, in order to stabilize the exchange value of the currency.

Both residents and non-residents may engage in forward foreign exchange transactions against the Mexican peso. The reserve requirements which are imposed on Mexican banks have however discouraged them from active participation in the forward market. Consequently, the majority of transactions take place with foreign banks outside Mexico.

Up until 1976 the peso had been fixed at the rate of P12.50 to the US dollar. Since September of that year, the peso was allowed to float freely against the dollar and other currencies. Since then it has stabilized, with minor fluctuations around the level of P22 to P23 to the dollar, as shown below:

Date	Exchange rate per US dollar
1 September 1976	12.50
2 September 1976—peso floated	22.50
30 December 1976	20.00
31 December 1977	22.70
31 December 1978	22.70
31 December 1979	22.80
31 December 1980	23.26

The exchange rate has remained remarkably stable considering the large inflation differential between Mexico and other countries. This is due to Mexico's high net worth as an oil producing country. It is probable that the Bank of Mexico will allow the rate to fluctuate by more than it has over the last three-and-a-half years so that trading partners and borrowers and lenders to Mexican capital markets may realize that the peso is not a fixed-rate currency. It is hoped particularly to increase the response of Mexican exporters to relative exchange rate movements.

Gold

The export of gold may only be affected by the Bank of Mexico and imports are subject to licences from the Bank of Mexico.

Residents and non-residents may freely buy, sell and hold gold within Mexico but there is a sales tax of 15 per cent applied to sales of newly mined gold.

4. United States of America

General market environment

US financial markets are the largest and most diverse in the world.

There are no exchange controls and every encouragement is made for foreigners to enter the market. This also applies to foreign borrowers. All credit facilities available to US firms are also available to foreign firms, although terms and conditions may differ.

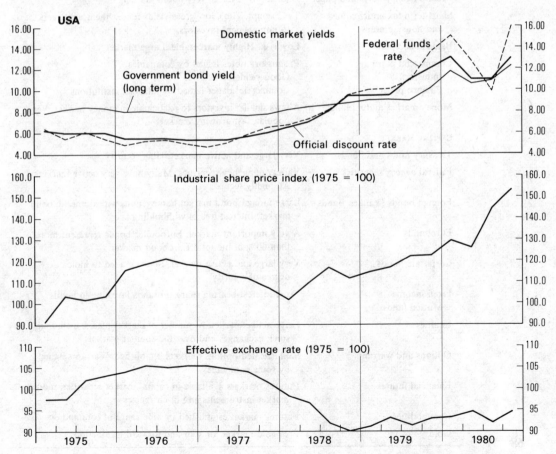

Table 4.1 Summary of instruments

Securities	Characteristics
MONEY MARKET	
Deposits	
call deposits	No call money market, but close substitutes available
time deposits	Available through wide variety of banks and savings institutions. Minimum term of 14 days
currency deposits	Market maintained in all convertible currencies. Eurodollars may be deposited with offshore subsidiaries of US banks
certificates of deposit	Large market. Active turnover. Available also in convertible currencies and with adjustable rates
Federal funds	Substitute to interbank call market. 90 % of participants are banks; remainder are financial institutions
Repurchase agreements	Substitute to call money market. Used by banks and non-bank participants
Treasury bills	A major money market instrument. Highly secure. Highly liquid
Federal agency notes and paper	High security. Large very liquid market
Short-term tax anticipation and housing notes	Tax exempt. Thus, low gross yields render them unattractice to non-resident investors.
Bankers acceptances	Low risk. Highly marketable. Large market
Commercial paper	Promissory notes issued by companies
Industrial	Good yields
Finance paper	Commercial paper issued by financial institutions
Money market mutual funds	Allows smaller investors to participate in money market. Very popular, fast growing market
CAPITAL MARKET	
Treasury notes and bonds	Very large and active market. High security
Federal agency securities	Variety of agency securities. Many have very active markets. All highly secure
Foreign bonds (Yankee Bonds)	Large foreign bond market homogenous with domestic bond market. Interest free of withholding tax
Eurobonds	A very important market. Eurodollar bonds represent more than 60 % of the total Eurobond market
Corporate bonds	Very large and active market. Bonds graded to indicate degree of security
Fixed income Mutual funds	Fixed-interest-bearing shares in funds investing in bonds
Equities	Large active market. A number of market places, including stock exchanges and over-the-counter markets.
Options and warrants	Sophisticated options markets established. Warrants issued by some companies
Financial futures	Futures markets available in capital market securities, money market instruments and in currencies
Commodities	Futures market established in wide range of commodities
Gold	Free gold market for spot and forward transactions

The financial system is complex and sophisticated so therefore requires expert advice, but it does allow the purchase of tailor-made securities to meet the requirements of the individual investor. The system is also highly dynamic, especially the short-term market which is subject to continuous change.

A large number of market-places exist. New York is the most important financial centre, but is rivalled in several major markets by Chicago and other cities. Money and capital markets throughout the States are, however, closely intertwined and banking systems are interconnected through a dense network of correspondent relationships.

Withholding taxes are deducted from interest and dividends accruing to foreign investors though capital gains are not subject to withholding taxes. The US maintains extensive double taxation treaties with a large number of countries. Through these agreements, additional taxes on interest are in many cases reduced to zero.

The money market

Deposits

Call deposits

Banks may not accept term deposits for periods of less than 14 days. Until 1 November 1980 the minimum deposit period was 30 days. In particular there is no call or overnight money market in the US. To place money for between one and fourteen days, the investor must use one of the other money market instruments. Commonly, the market in repurchase agreements is used as a substitute for very-short-term deposits. The secondary CD market, or banks' commercial paper, are also used as alternatives.

As a further alternative, the larger commercial banks with offshore banking subsidiaries in, for example, the Cayman Islands, will take short-term time or call deposits (i.e., of less than 14 days) but place them offshore. These are effectively Eurodollar deposits since the dollars do not physically enter the domestic US market. Currency deposits are accepted in minimum denominations approximately equivalent to $100 000 although occasionally, when a bank has a specific demand for a currency, it will often accept smaller amounts.

Greater flexibility exists in these offshore deposits because they are not included in the domestic banking and money supply figures and thus are not subject to the same controls as domestic deposits. Depending on the individual bank's structure, in most cases such deposits are guaranteed as to principal and interest by the full faith and credit of the holding companies of the offshore bank.

Time deposits

Yields on domestically placed time deposits depend on the general level of interest rates ruling in the money market. The yields on deposits placed offshore will depend on the individual placing bank's requirement for offshore funds at the time

69

the deposit is made, and on rates ruling in the Eurodollar market. The difference in yields between domestic and Eurodollar deposits are largely a product of US reserve requirements (see Financial and monetary systems). If US reserve requirements are high the cost of accepting domestic deposits is also high. The interest return offered to depositors is consequently lower than rates offered on Eurodollar deposits for which reserve requirements are not applicable.

The interest rates applying to Eurodollar deposits may also differ from domestic dollar deposits external (i.e., the rest of the world) demand for US dollars. Usually Eurodollar interest rates are higher than domestic rates because external demand for dollars is generated by the role of the US dollar as the currency most used for international trade.

Time deposits are usually accepted in minimum amounts of $1000 and upwards in multiples of $500.

Currency deposits

All of the larger commercial banks will accept time deposits in convertible currency. For some currencies there exists only a limited market and interest rates will vary between banks, depending on the bank's requirement to hold those particular currencies. Otherwise the market operates in a similar way to the Euro-currency market in London. For the commonly traded currencies the markets are homogenous and banks will charge common rates. These interest rates will depend on interest rates ruling in the domestic markets of each currency as well as on US banks' demands for that currency.

Currency deposits are accepted in minimum denominations approximately equivalent to $25000 although occasionally, when a bank has a specific demand for a currency, it will often accept small amounts.

Negotiable certificates of deposit

A certificate of deposit (CD) is exactly the same as a time deposit except that the investor receives a certificate from the accepting bank which confirms that bank's liability and carries the bank's guarantee of repayment of principal and interest.

CDs are first issued by banks and then bought by the investor, rather than the investor initiating the loan as with time deposits.

The special feature of a CD is that it is negotiable in the secondary market. CDs are thus a much more highly liquid form of investment than an ordinary time deposit. CDs are issued in minimum denominations of $100000 with maturities ranging from 14 days to several years. There is no legally enforced upper limit to maturities and some CDs have been issued with up to 10-year terms. However, any term greater than one year is uncommon and the majority of CDs are issued with three-month (90-day) maturity.

Yields on CDs for prime (top) name banks are lower than rates obtainable on comparable time deposits, because of their marketability. Yields are also lower than the commercial banks' prime rates which are calculated according to a formula based on the rate for 90-day CDs. CD yields of new issuers, small regional banks and overseas banks may be higher than prime rate so that such borrowers can compete for funds. For CDs issued by prime banks, rates may be up to one per cent higher than treasury bill rate, and the differential for CDs of lesser banks is higher still because the Federal Reserve does not intervene at all in the CD market and does not discount CDs or accept them as collateral, although it will adjust required reserves from time to time, thus affecting the rate and availability of CDs.

As with all time deposits interest is calculated on a 360-day year basis. A difference of between $\frac{1}{8}$ and $\frac{1}{2}$ per cent may exist between prime CDs of first-class banks, less-prime and off-prime names.

Because of their highly marketable and near-liquid nature and because they represent little or no risk, CDs are an important money market instrument. That market size is approximately $100 billion with an average daily turnover in the secondary market of approximately $2.5 billion. The CD market is dominated by institutional and corporate investors requiring a secure, short-term, liquid investment.

Eurodollar CDs

A market is made by US banks for CDs denominated in US dollars but held outside the United States, primarily in Europe. The market size is in excess of $10 billion with an average daily turnover of about $200-$300 million. Purchasers of Euro CDs tend to be US multinational corporations, bank trust departments, money market mutual funds, quasi government agencies, and non-resident commercial and institutional investors who hold dollars overseas. On 1 November 1980 the Federal Reserve introduced new reserve requirements of three per cent against the issue of all dollar denominated CDs from 14 days to 4 years and 364 days maturity. Previously, Eurodollar CDs were subject to zero-reserve requirements and were therefore cheaper for US banks to issue than were domestic CDs. As a result of the new requirements, US banks are issuing fewer Euro CDs and the yield differential between Euro and domestic CDs has narrowed.

Floating rate CDs and roly poly CDs

With high levels and volatile rates of interest becoming a growing phenomenon in major financial markets a number of floating-rate notes are being developed in order to protect the investor from rising rates of interest.

Floating-rate CDs usually have maturities of more than one year, most having two or three year terms, although CDs with maturities of five to seven years have been issued.

The pricing mechanism is on a coupon basis set every three to six months, although CDs with monthly fixes are gaining popularity. Interest is normally set at a rate of $\frac{1}{2}$ to $\frac{3}{4}$ per cent over LIBOR (London Interbank offer rate).

Roly Poly CDs are similar to floating-rate CDs except that they generally have shorter maturities (of say three months), but are rolled over at maturity when a new rate of interest is fixed.

71

Because of the new flat rate, three per cent reserve requirements FRCDs are no longer more attractive to issuing banks than straight CDs. Previously a structured system of reserve requirements had applied to CD issues. CDs of longer than six months were subject to a higher ratio than were shorter CDs. The issue of FRCDs or roly poly CDs thus gave the banks the benefit of a longer term issue but which were subject to the lower reserve requirements.

Primary and Secondary CD markets

In the primary market all the types of CDs described are usually issued by individual commercial banks and subscribed for directly by the investor.

In the secondary market an investor may buy or sell CDs of a particular bank through any bank or through a specialized dealer. There is a risk in selling CDs in a market where prevailing interest rates have risen above the rate attaching to the CD, resulting in a fall in the price of the CD, and the investor may have to accept a small capital loss or hold the CD to maturity.

A few specialized dealers provide a secondary market in CDs with less than 14 days to run to maturity. They do so by buying CDs of longer maturities and reselling via the market in repurchase agreements in such a way that they regain possession at 14 days to maturity. Alternatively, they buy CDs and hold them in their own portfolio until they have 14 days left to run. Investors may buy these 'short-term' CDs usually in minimum denominations of $1 million. This provides a method of short term investment in the absence of a call money market.

Federal funds

A simple definition of the federal (or fed) funds market is that market in which commercial banks borrow and lend excess reserve balances held at the Federal Reserve. Commercial banks that are members of the Federal Reserve hold deposits, as reserve assets, with one of the several Federal Reserve Banks (FRBs). FRBs are, in this sense, effectively banks for banks. In theory, the federal funds market is not accessible to non-bank companies and institutions. In practice, however, the market has developed such that the non-bank sector can lend and borrow fed funds through the transaction of repurchase agreements (see below).

The operation and mechanics of the federal funds market are more fully explained in the section on monetary policy.

Repurchase agreements

These instruments, called 'repos' or 'RPs', provide a method by which banks can buy temporarily idle funds from a customer by selling him US government or other securities with the contractual agreement to repurchase the same securities on a future date. The investor's capital is protected because the sale and repurchase is transacted at the same price, calculated according to the market value of the securities. An additional premium is paid which represents an interest payment. The rate of interest is determined by the prevailing demand to settle funds, the maturity of the RP, and the type of collateral used in the transaction.

The majority of RPs are issued for one business day only, although longer maturities are also common. Repurchase agreements are often made for periods of up to six months and have been negotiated for up to one year. They are, however, the only instrument issued as short as one day. RPs, therefore, provide the investor with a facility similar to the London Interbank overnight deposit market. They are a very secure, very short-term investment to the investor, and have the added advantage of prepayment if required whereas fixed-time deposits cannot generally be broken prior to maturity.

When a repurchase agreement is transacted, entitlement to the securities is physically transferred from the borrower, i.e., the bank, to the lender or the investor. This distinguishes an RP from many other types of loans which are merely secured against assets held by the borrower. Transactions are usually in units of $5 million or more.

The way in which the RP market interacts with the fed funds market and the market for immediately available funds is also further explained in the section on monetary policy.

Treasury bills

The treasury bill is the major money market instrument. About 80 per cent of Treasury debt of less than one year maturity is represented by treasury bills and these account for approximately 40 per cent of total market debt.

Treasury bills are a highly liquid short-term investment of the highest security. The majority are of three month maturity, although they are also issued with six- and twelve-month maturities.

Ninety-one- and 182-day bills (three and six months), are issued weekly. Twelve-month treasury bills are issued monthly, in each case on a Thursday. They are issued at a discount price and repaid at par at maturity. They are sold at auction through the Federal Reserve Bank of New York, at rates reflecting the conditions of the short-term money market. The bills are fully guaranteed as to capital and interest by the US Treasury. They are in bearer form and in minimum denominations of $10 000.

The discount rate on a treasury bill is not strictly comparable to the yield on an interest-bearing bond because, firstly, the discount is based on the par value of the security whereas yield is based on purchase price and, secondly, discounts issued are based on a 360-day year, compared with a 365-day year for bonds and notes.

Conversion tables are available to determine the bond equivalent yields of treasury bills. The discount rate understates the true yield.

For example, for a 91-day treasury bill quoted at a discount rate of interest of 10 per cent, the bond equivalent yield is calculated as follows:

Quoted rate	10.00
Add factor (available from money market tables) for 90 days	0.399
Interpolated from tables for extra day	0.003
Fully converted bill rate	10.402%

73

Alternatively, the bond equivalent yield may be calculated as follows:

$$\frac{\text{Quoted rate} \times 365}{360 - (\text{quoted rate} \times \text{days to maturity})} \times 100\%$$

For the same example this would be:

$$\frac{0.1 \times 365}{360 - (0.1 \times 91)} \times 100\% = 10.402\%$$

Primary market in treasury bills
Treasury bills are issued by the Federal Reserve Banks on behalf of the US Treasury Department. The market has 33 primary dealers, appointed by the Federal Reserve. Currently there are 12 bank dealers and 21 non-bank dealers. At each weekly issue of treasury bills the primary dealers purchase through a system of competitive bidding which determines the discount rate. The primary dealers purchase both for their own account and on behalf of their clients who are institutional investors, commercial banks, trust departments and individuals. Foreign investors may also participate.

Secondary market in treasury bills
The secondary market in treasury bills, with a daily trading volume in excess of $5 billion, is the largest part of the short-term money market. Transactions are in dealable lots of over several million dollars and down to $10 000. The market is highly organized and supervised by the primary dealers, who are in turn supervised by the Federal Reserve, and are charged with maintaining a smooth and efficient market in US government securities. The primary dealers meet with the New York Federal Reserve every week and return daily figures of treasury bill transactions in order that market efficiency is achieved.

Treasury bills, through the operation of the secondary market, therefore offer the investor a riskless investment, a relatively stable money market and a wide range of short maturities, coupled with near-cash liquidity.

The Federal Reserve Open Market Operations Committee uses this secondary market as one instrument to effect bank demand deposit components of the money supply.

Federal agency notes and paper

The US Treasury and the federal agencies (especially those that are government sponsored but privately owned) are heavy borrowers in the capital markets. Their bonds and notes enter the money market as they move towards maturity.

Some federal agency securities originate as short-term obligations. They have an active market at yields slightly above direct government debt but are also highly secure, highly liquid instruments, which differ from treasury bills only by a minor degree with respect to security, government guarantee and, sometimes, tax status. They also differ between themselves in some ways.

Agencies issue two types of securities:

1. Participation certificates;
2. Conventional notes, debentures and bonds.

Participation certificates represent undivided interest in pools of agency owned assets (i.e., loans or mortgages). Initially they are offered with 30-year maturities. Interest and a portion of the principal is paid on a monthly basis and, for this reason, are known as 'pass thru' securities.

Notes, debentures and bonds are secured against the general assets of the issuing agency, guaranteed as to principal and interest by the agency, and morally, though not legally, constitute an obligation of the US Government since most have a line of credit to the US Treasury.

The main features of agency securities are:

- low risk
- well-developed secondary market in some agency securities
- close substitutes for US Government securities because of their security
- higher yield—the average differential in short-term yield between agency and government securities is 15–60 basis points
- held by all sectors of the economy—the largest holders are the commercial banks, followed by the US Government, the Federal Reserve Banks, foreign governments, institutional and commercial investors and individuals.

Primary market in federal agency short-term securities

Most agency securities originate as capital market instruments although short-term notes, particularly 'farm credits' with nine-month maturities, 'fanny maes' and 'ginnie maes' with 5- to 270-day maturities, and short-term 'pass thru' securities are issued in the money market. (These instruments are further described in the Capital market section on federal agencies.)

Whether money or capital market instruments, agency securities are essentially issued in the same way that government sponsored agency securities are issued through separate fiscal agents who assemble selling groups of banks and dealers and establish offer prices. Government owned agency securities are issued both directly to the public and through syndicates.

New issues may be at a fixed rate of interest, auctioned, or negotiated.

Notes are issued at a discount and repaid at par on maturity. They are in bearer form and purchases in the primary market may be in minimum amounts of $50 000.

'Pass thru' securities pay interest and part capital monthly. Debentures and bonds are issued in coupon bearing form with interest payable semiannually. All are either registered in the name of the purchaser or ownership is recorded by book entry. Minimum denominations are usually $5000.

Primary market purchases are normally large institutional and commercial bodies who require short-term very low risk money market securities with yields higher than those obtainable on deposits, RPs and treasury bills. A large number of individuals are also active in this market, particularly for 'farm credits', because of the smaller denominations than those available in the treasury bill market.

Secondary market in federal agency short-term securities

There is an active 'over-the-counter' market in many agency issues. Quotations are found in daily newspapers, although only securities of the larger government owned agencies are regularly quoted. The secondary market is more active for the securities of some agencies than for others, but all those that issue short-term instruments enjoy a secondary market. Particularly active agencies are the Federal Home Loan Banks, Federal National Mortgage Association and the Farm Credit System. These are all further described in the Capital market section.

Dealers make books in large amounts of agency securities and their spread between bid and offer price is narrow on short-term issues. It is possible to deal in large amounts of $1 million to $5 million without upsetting the market, although individuals may deal in amounts as small as $1000 or even $500.

Dealers in US government securities are responsible for making and maintaining the market. Although many individuals also participate large financial institutions dominate in this market and acquire the bulk of agency debt, both short-term and long-term.

Municipal bonds

The highest grade municipal securities rank closely with federal agency securities but yield considerably less because of their federal tax exempt status. They therefore carry a lower gross yield and are of little interest to the foreign investor.

Short-term tax anticipation notes, project notes and housing loans of municipal governments

Tax anticipation notes are short-term tax exempt obligations issued by public bodies. They are a high-grade investment vehicle comparable in quality to treasury bills and CDs, but they too are exempt from federal tax. Although they offer the domestic investor a superior tax equivalent yield, they are of little interest to the foreign investor.

Project notes and housing loans of municipal governments are short-term paper issued by municipalities to finance short-term cash flows. Short-term housing loans have a lower credit but higher yield than project notes, unless guaranteed by the government in which case yields are about the same. Both are government guaranteed and are issued with maturities of between 30 days and one year. Again, these instruments are tax exempt and offer low yields to the non-resident investor, who cannot benefit from the tax advantage.

Bankers' acceptances

These are time drafts which are drawn on and accepted by banks. They are created to finance payments originating from letters of credit to finance shipment and storage of goods. The banks are liable for the payment of the drafts at their maturity, making the acceptances readily marketable instruments.

As an investment instrument bankers' acceptances (BAs) are discounted notes in bearer form. Interest is paid at maturity and calculated on a 360-day-year basis. The effective bond equivalent yield is probably the highest of all the money market instruments yet BAs are high quality paper because they carry a bank's guarantee.

They are negotiable through many specialized dealers who make secondary market transactions. Most common maturities range between 30 and 180 days but may sometimes be up to 270 days. The market size is approximately $50 billion with a daily turnover in excess of $1 billion.

The underlying documentation for a banker's acceptance is a letter of credit accompanied by invoices, bills of lading, etc.

For example, a shipment of Scotch whisky is to be sent to the US for delivery in six months. The respective banks of the importer (US) and the exporter (UK) check the paper work to ensure all lines of credit are satisfactory.

Either the importer or exporter may need temporary financing, but usually it is the exporter who must wait to be paid. In this case for six months. He takes his set of documents to the bank which 'accepts' it and gives funds equal to the face amount of the transaction, minus an amount to cover the bank's interest charge to the exporter.

At this point, the bank may stamp the bank draft or letter pertaining to this particular transaction, thus creating a BA by guaranteeing that they will honour the payment of the face amount at maturity. The bank then places the paper with an investor, either directly or through a securities dealer. The bank or dealer adds a small charge onto the cost of the BA to the investor. At maturity, the accepting bank redeems the paper at the face amount, giving the investor his percentage return, and starts collection proceedings with the importer or exporter.

Take, for example, a transaction for a value of $1 000 000 which is discounted by the bank. The customer (exporter) receives $950 000. The investor pays $960 000 for the six-month BA and receives $1 000 000 at maturity.

The formula for calculating the discount on a BA is:

$$\frac{\text{Quoted interest rate} \times \text{days to maturity} \times \text{face value}}{360 \text{ days}} = \text{discount}$$

To convert this discount rate into a bond (or coupon) equivalent yield, the following formula is applied:

$$\frac{\text{Quoted interest rate} \times 365}{360 - (\text{quoted rate} \times \text{days to maturity})}$$

For example, at a quoted rate of interest of 10 per cent an investor placing $1 000 000 in a coupon bearing security would receive, after six months, interest of $50 000. If he purchased the BA at 10 per cent for six months he would pay $9 950 000 and receive $1 000 000 at maturity. Since $50 000 is 5.26 per cent of $950 000 the annualized bond equivalent yield of the BA is 2 × 5.26 or 10.52 per cent.

The main purchasers of BAs in the primary market are banks, commercial companies and other financial institutions needing high-grade short-term debt instruments. They are also purchased by the federal reserve system through the Federal Reserve Bank of New York in open market operations in order to affect banks' reserves.

BAs are actively traded in the secondary market so that a particular security may have changed hands several times before reaching the investor who actually holds it at maturity. Their marketability compares with that for CDs or commercial paper. They are, therefore, a very liquid security since an investor can quickly and easily liquidate his holding at a dealer's posted bid price.

BAs are also an extremely secure form of investment since they carry the irrevocable guarantee of the issuing bank, regardless of any difficulty it may face in obtaining payment from its customer. In addition, in the highly unlikely event of default by the bank, the investment is self-liquidating in that revenue will be generated from the sale of the imported goods. The BA may either be delivered to the investor or, more commonly, the investor may purchase a depository receipt.

The receipt is a negotiable item covering a number of acceptances, with an enumeration of the specific acceptances which the receipt represents. In this case, the bank delivers the depository receipt to the investor but holds the actual acceptances in safe keeping. The depository receipt can then be traded in the open market.

Commercial paper

Commercial paper represents short-term promissory notes issued by corporations needing to raise working capital. In effect they are like CDs but issued by companies rather than banks. There are basically two types—finance paper and industrial paper.

Finance paper is issued by finance companies and some bank holding companies directly to lenders and investors. The issue and maturity dates are specified by the investor but generally the paper has a maturity of less than seven months.

Industrial paper is sold by industrial and commercial companies. The amounts and maturities are specified by the borrower so the investor is subject to market availability. Industrial paper carries a life of between 1 and 270 days.

Both types of paper are secured against a corporate IOU and guaranteed by the issuer. The return to the investor therefore depends on the financial strength and credit rating of the issuer. The security is bearer paper, is issued both in discount and coupon bearing form (often at the option of the lender) and is dealt in minimum denominations of $25 000.

Primary market in commercial paper

New issues are made on behalf of the borrowing companies by brokerage houses although recently a bank—Bankers Trust—has placed an issue in the primary market. This is the subject of a court case but it is probable that the outcome will allow banks to become primary issuers.

Currently there are about a dozen primary dealers—all brokerage houses—in the commercial paper market. These dealers buy the paper directly from the finance or industrial companies and sell to investors, charging $\frac{1}{8}$ to $\frac{1}{4}$ per cent commission. They also make a turn on the paper by receiving the interest for the period held between purchase of the paper from the issuer and resale to the investor. The major investors are banks, institutions, and large corporations who buy the paper because of its security, high yields and liquidity throughout maturities.

Secondary market in commercial paper

The primary dealers also make a secondary market in commercial paper but it is nevertheless a limited market, made mostly by and among dealers. The participants in the secondary market are generally the same as in the primary market, but usually the investors hold the paper to maturity, thus restricting availability in the secondary market.

78

Some specialized dealers make a market in providing commercial paper along with bankers' acceptances and CDs with less than 14 days to run to maturity. They buy such paper when it is issued and either hold it in their own portfolios or sell through repurchase agreements so as to regain possession at 14 days maturity. This facility provides the investor with very short-term funds (a short-term instrument not available in the deposit market and with higher yield than an RP).

Yields available on commercial paper are in general lower than those on bankers' acceptances, but higher than all other money market instruments.

Money market mutual funds

This instrument is similar to an investment or unit trust. Such funds exist primarily for the small investor with less than $10 000 and sometimes with as little as $500 to place. They allow him to participate in money market investment by means of buying shares in a mutual fund which, in turn, deposits funds in money market instruments.

Money market mutual funds have been set up only recently in the 1970s as a result of high short-term interest rates and the existence of a reverse yield curve. They developed only slowly in the early seventies, but during the period of particularly volatile short-term rates in 1979–80 they have grown rapidly from an asset value of $10 billion to over $360 billion, surpassing the size of mutual funds investing in the equity market. Their advantage to the small investor is that he can

Table 4.2 US money and capital markets—interest rates and yields (*source: OECD*)

	End 1978	1979 Jan.	Feb.	Mar.	Apr.	May	Jun.	Jul.	Aug.	Sep.	Oct.	Nov.	Dec.
Discount rate	9.50	9.50	9.50	9.50	9.50	9.80	9.50	10.00	10.50	11.00	12.00	12.00	12.00
Federal funds rate	10.03	10.07	10.06	10.09	10.01	10.24	10.29	10.47	10.94	11.43	13.77	13.18	13.78
Prime rate	11.55	11.75	11.75	11.75	11.75	11.75	11.65	11.54	11.91	12.90	14.39	15.55	15.30
3-month CDs	10.72	10.51	10.18	10.02	10.05	10.15	9.95	10.10	10.69	11.89	13.66	13.90	13.43
3-month treasury bills	9.08	9.35	9.32	9.48	9.46	9.61	9.06	9.24	9.52	10.26	11.70	11.79	12.04
6-month treasury bills	9.36	9.47	9.41	9.47	9.49	9.54	9.06	9.24	9.49	10.20	11.66	11.82	11.84
6-month prime commercial paper	10.37	10.25	9.95	9.90	9.85	9.95	9.76	9.87	10.43	11.63	13.23	13.26	12.80
6-month finance paper	10.06	10.10	9.85	9.73	9.64	9.75	9.44	9.39	9.82	10.59	11.76	12.00	11.68
5-year government notes and bonds	9.23	9.36	9.16	9.25	9.32	9.30	8.89	8.88	9.08	9.56	10.75	10.98	10.45
10-year government notes and bonds	8.36	8.43	8.43	8.45	8.44	8.55	8.32	8.35	8.42	8.65	9.44	9.60	9.59
Corporate bonds	9.49	9.65	9.63	9.76	9.81	9.96	9.81	9.69	9.74	9.93	10.71	11.37	11.35
3-month Eurodollar time deposits (in London)	7.19	11.69	10.44	10.62	10.66	10.87	10.56	10.59	11.34	12.19	12.66	15.41	14.31	14.50
3–7-year corporate Eurodollar bonds	8.46	9.56	9.89	9.77	9.86	9.67	9.80	9.66	9.86	10.19	10.61	11.80	12.02	11.93

Table 4.2 (*continued*)

	End 1978	1980 Jan.	Feb.	Mar.	Apr.	May	Jun.	Jul.	Aug.	Sep.	Oct.	Nov.	Dec.
Discount rate	9.50	12.00	13.00	13.00	13.00	12.00	11.00	10.00	10.00	11.00	11.00	12.00	13.00
Federal funds rate	10.03	13.82	14.13	17.19	17.81	10.98	9.47	9.03	9.61	10.87	12.81	15.85	18.90
Prime rate	11.55	15.25	15.63	18.31	19.77	16.57	12.63	11.48	11.12	12.23	13.76	16.06	20.35
3-month CDs	10.72	13.39	14.30	17.57	16.14	9.79	8.49	8.65	9.91	11.29	12.94	15.68	18.65
3-month treasury bills	9.08	12.00	12.86	15.20	13.20	8.58	7.07	8.06	9.13	10.21	11.62	13.73	15.49
6-month treasury bills	9.36	11.84	12.86	15.03	12.88	8.65	7.30	8.06	9.41	10.57	11.63	13.50	14.64
6-month prime commercial paper	10.37	12.06	13.60	16.50	14.93	9.29	8.03	8.29	9.61	11.04	12.32	14.73	16.49
6-month finance paper	10.06	11.79	12.39	14.70	13.68	9.01	7.42	8.03	9.08	10.29	11.15	13.07	14.78
5-year government notes and bonds	9.23	10.76	12.52	13.41	11.84	9.95	9.21	9.53	10.84	11.62	11.86	12.83	13.25
10-year government notes and bonds	8.36	10.03	11.55	11.87	10.83	9.82	9.40	9.83	10.53	10.94	11.20	9.11	9.56
Corporate bonds	9.49	11.74	12.92	13.73	13.21	12.11	11.64	11.77	12.33	12.80	13.07	13.64	14.04
3-month Eurodollar time deposits (in London)	7.19	11.69	14.41	16.97	19.94	15.00	9.75	9.75	9.81	12.50	13.94	15.25	18.31	17.75
3–7-year corporate Eurodollar bonds	8.46	9.56	12.30	13.67	14.46	14.04	11.88	10.81	10.92	11.73	12.25	12.47	13.33	13.96

participate in the high rates of return obtainable in the money market while retaining liquidity, since he may withdraw his cash at very short notice. His next best alternative is to deposit money with a bank or savings association, which are prohibited by government regulations from paying a rate of interest of more than $5\frac{3}{4}$ per cent on saving deposits, and 12 per cent on negotiable term deposit accounts. Since December 1980 maximum interest restrictions on domestic deposit accounts have been removed. All interest rate restrictions are also gradually being phased out by 1985.

The obvious attractions of such mutual funds have resulted in an outflow of small savings from the banks causing them problems of financing. The Federal Reserve consequently imposed a 15 per cent non-interest-bearing special deposit on increases in the assets of money market mutual funds from 14 March 1980. This reduced the rate of return available to the investors, but did not significantly reduce demand since the return still remained greater than from the alternative liquid investments available to the small investor. Latter in 1980 this regulation was removed.

The capital market

Although the US capital market comprises a wider range of securities than any other capital market, its apparent complexity can be simplified by grouping securities into categories of borrowers. It is because some categories of borrowers issue a variety of instruments that the market may seem initially confusing to the foreign observer.

The main types of borrowers are much the same as in most other markets. The largest single borrower is the government which issues short term notes and longer term bonds. Local government, i.e., the municipalities likewise issue notes and bonds with special tax exempt coupons. A third major category, known as Federal agencies, issue a variety of securities which are referred to collectively as agency securities. Agencies exist to finance specific economic sectors such as housing or education and raise necessary funds through the capital market by the issue of securities which best suit the needs of their funding programmes. As borrowers, all agencies represent a good credit risk but they fall into two groups—government owned and government sponsored—and the former group represents slightly better security for invested funds.

Remaining groups of borrowers, as in other markets, are corporations and foreign issuers. Additional markets, such as futures markets, are simply variations on a theme providing the investor with alternative methods of participating in already established markets.

Treasury notes and bonds

Treasury notes are coupon bearing securities with maturities of two to ten years. Treasury bonds are issued with maturities of between 10 and 30 years but are subject to a statutory limit on the coupon of $4\frac{1}{4}$ per cent, although the Treasury is currently authorized to issue up to $24 billion per annum in bonds without regard to the interest rate limit.

The market in treasury notes and bonds is large with more than $200 billion worth of issues outstanding. There is a wide range of maturities for the investor to choose from. Most older issues are available in bearer form, but all new issues are now in registered form. Interest is paid semiannually.

Primary market in treasury notes and bonds

New issues are announced by the Treasury about one or two weeks before the issue date. The price is determined at auction by competitive bidding. Participants in the primary market are usually banks, dealers and institutions although individuals also may bid. Subscriptions may be made by all types of investor directly to the Federal Reserve Bank or indirectly through a bank or brokerage house.

Minimum denominations are $1000 to $10 000 for treasury notes and $5 000 to $10 000 (though sometimes up to $50 000) for treasury bonds. The most common minimum denomination for both types of security is $5000.

Secondary market in treasury notes and bonds

Notes and bonds are traded in a large and active secondary market through banks and dealers. Minimum trading denominations are either $500 or $1000. They are traded at a price quoted to fractions of $\frac{1}{32}$ dictated by prevailing market yields, plus interest accrued on the bond or note; interest is calculated semiannually on the basis of a civil year of 365 days.

Federal agency securities

Federal agencies are government established agencies which are legally authorized to administer selected lending programmes on behalf of the US Government. The programmes are designed to attract private capital into sectors of the economy where the flow of funds is considered inadequate, including social as well as economic areas. Traditionally, funds were directed towards the agricultural and housing sectors, but more recently beneficiaries have included community development, small businesses, trade financing and universities.

Unlike other capital markets, the market in 'agencies' is not homogeneous. 'Federal agencies' is a generic term covering a number of different borrowers who are competing for capital for a variety of different purposes.

Some of the securities issued by agencies are for less than one year and thus are essentially money market securities. For simplicity they are described below according to the relevant issuing agency.

Notes, bonds, debentures, participation certificates, 'pass thru' securities

Agencies issue notes, bonds, debentures participation certificates and 'pass thru' securities, although any single agency will not issue all five types of securities.

Notes tend to be short-term (less than one year) paper issued at a discount but repaid at par at maturity. Notes are usually in bearer form.

Bonds are securities representing general loans raised by an agency and unsecured against specific assets. However they represent low risk because of the good credit rating of agencies.

Debentures are similar to bonds but usually secured against specific assets of the issuing agency. Bonds and debentures are medium- to long-term paper, generally with a life of up to 25 or 30 years. They are coupon bearing with interest payable semiannually and usually in (book entry) form.

Participation certificates represent undivided interest in pools of assets—usually mortgages and loans owned by an agency—and carry a contractual interest obligation on a specific principal amount. Interest and part principal is repaid to the investor at regular intervals—usually semiannually. Initial maturities of the certificates may be up to 30 years.

'Pass thru' securities are similar to participation certificates in that part principal and interest are repaid to the investor monthly (i.e., 30 days in arrears). Although 'pass thru' securities of the FHLB (see below) pay 45 days in arrears. They too have original maturities of up to 30 years, though because part capital is repaid ('passed thru') together with the interest payments they have a reduced average life of about 12 years. Interest and yields are calculated on the basis of the average life rather than original maturity. Interest and capital are secured against specific loans, usually mortgages.

Both participation certificates and 'pass-thrus' may be issued in bearer form but are more usually in registered form.

Government owned and government sponsored agencies

Federal agencies fall into one of two major categories. They are either government owned, or privately owned but government sponsored. The securities issued by

82

government owned agencies are fully guaranteed by the full faith and credit of the US Treasury, while government sponsored agency securities are secured only by the full faith and credit of the issuing agency. The US Government, however, assumes a moral obligation to assure that the principal and interest of all federal agency securities are protected and honoured. All new agency issues have to be first cleared with the US Treasury. Additionally, certificates of participation are effectively guaranteed directly by the US Government under the 'Sales Participation Act 1966' which provides for unlimited drawings on the US Treasury, if need be, to service the certificates.

Most of the growth in the market for agency securities is due to five agencies in particular. These are the government owned National Mortgage Association (GNMA) and the four main privately owned, government sponsored agencies whose main function is to provide loans either to the mortgage and housebuilding markets or to farming and agricultural sectors. Each of these agencies and their securities has special features which are as follows:

Privately owned, government sponsored agencies

1. Federal Home Loan Banks (FHLB)

The Federal Home Loan Bank system was created in 1932 to help finance the housing industry. The system comprises twelve regional banks which provide liquidity and home mortgage credit to its member institutions which include some federal agencies, savings and loan associations, mutual savings banks, co-operative banks, and insurance companies. Between them, the members own the equity capital of the FHLB. In order to provide credit to its members the FHLB raises additional capital from the issue of notes and bonds. Consolidated discount notes are issued on a tap basis with maturities of 30 to 270 days, at the option of the investor with interest paid at maturity. Bonds are issued every three months and carry a life of between one and 20 years, with interest being paid semi-annually.

All securities of FHLB are in bearer form, although bond ownership may be recorded by book entry. Bonds and notes carry minimum denominations of $10 000 while consolidated discount notes are issued in denominations of $100 000 and $1 million. All FHLB securities are guaranteed jointly and severally by the member banks.

2. Federal Home Loan Mortgage Corporation (FHLMC)

This government sponsored agency was established by an Act of Congress to further the development of the secondary market in home mortgages. It is wholly owned by the twelve Federal Home Loan Banks and is authorized to purchase mortgages from financial institutions whose deposits are guaranteed by an agency of the US Government, or financial institutions who are members of the FHLB.

To purchase mortgages, the FHLMC raises funds via the capital market by issuing three types of securities. Mortgage backed bonds, mortgage participation certificates and guaranteed mortgage certificates.

Mortgage backed bonds, mortgage participation certificates, guaranteed mortgage certificates

Mortgage backed bonds are guaranteed by the GNMA (see below) but yield about $\frac{1}{4}$ per cent more than GNMA securities because, in the unlikely event of default, they would take second place for repayment. The bonds carry a maturity of up to 25 years with interest paid semiannually, and are available in minimum denominations of $25 000.

Participation certificates represent undivided interest in pools of conventional mortgages. Issues have initial maturities of 30 years. Principal and interest are returned to the investor monthly and in varying amounts according to the repayment pattern of the mortgages which the loans represent.

Guaranteed mortgage certificates have a unique investment feature in that the FHLMC will, at the option of the investor, purchase the unpaid balance of the certificates at par 15 years after issuance. These certificates are issued with maturities of up to 25 years (in denominations of $100 000). Interest is payable semiannually in regular amounts according to the coupon rate and part principal repayable annually in variable amounts but subject to a specified minimum.

3. Federal National Mortgage Association (FNMA)

The FNMA is a privately owned, government sponsored agency whose function is to assist the home mortgage market by purchasing mortgages that are insured by the Federal Housing Administration and those that are guaranteed by the Veterans Administration. Additionally it deals in conventional mortgages that are not federally insured or guaranteed. To facilitate these functions, debt is issued to private investors.

Fanny maes
Securities are mainly debentures or short-term discount notes, though mortgage backed bonds are sometimes also issued. All these securities are known in the market as 'fanny maes' (a colloquialism for FNMA).

Debentures
Debentures are coupon bearing securities with interest paid semiannually. Maturities range from a few months up to 25 years for longer debentures. Capital is repaid in full at maturity. Minimum denominations are in amounts of $10 000.

Short-term discount notes
Short-term discount notes have maturities of between 30 days and one year and are offered in multiples of $5000 but with minimum trading denominations of $50 000. They are repaid at par at maturity.

Mortgage backed bonds
Additionally, the FNMA issues mortgage backed bonds which are secured against a pool of mortgages owned by the FNMA. They have medium to long maturities, are coupon bearing and repay capital at maturity. Occasionally convertible debentures are offered which may be exchanged for FNMA common stock, and also capital debentures that are not secured against mortgages. Neither of these issues carry a federal guarantee.

84

Consolidated farm credit system

The remaining three government sponsored agencies comprising the Banks for Co-operatives Federal Land Banks and the Federal Intermediate Credit Banks provide credit to the farming and agricultural sector and are part of the farm credit system, which has become a vital participant in both the money and capital markets.

This is a co-operative system which provides credit and closely related services to farmers and farm related businesses throughout the United States and Puerto Rico. The system comprises about 440 Production Credit Associations and 37 Farm Credit Banks.

Short-term funds required by these banks are obtained through the issue of Farm Credit Banks Discount Notes, which are issued with maturities of between 5 and 180 days. The notes are in bearer form and in minimum denominations of $50 000. 'Farm credits' are an instrument widely used by non-residents. For example 15 per cent are purchased by the Lloyd's Underwriting Community in London. Their popularity is due mainly to the fact that they are exempt from all state taxes and if sold up to one day before maturity the interest is taxed as capital rather than as income. On a gross basis they yield less than non-exempt agency securities but more than treasury securities. They are secured by a joint-and-several guarantee of the 37 Farm Credit Banks. *General farm credits*

The federal Farm Credit Banks collectively issue consolidated system-wide bonds in the capital market. These have maturities of five years and longer with interest payable semiannually and capital repaid at maturity. Minimum denominations are $1000 and they are registered as to principal and interest. Their guarantee is the same as for farm credits above. *Consolidated bonds*

Government owned federal agencies

Federal Finance Bank (FFB)

The Federal Financing Bank (FFB) is authorized directly by the US Government to co-ordinate and consolidate federal financing activities, thus reducing borrowing costs to participating agencies. Rather than selling to the public such agencies sell their securities to the FFB which in turn receives most of its finance from the US Treasury.

Agencies going directly to the FFB now include the Student Loan Association and the Tennessee Valley Association. They no longer offer new issues direct to the public although some outstanding securities are available in the secondary markets.

All government owned agencies are entitled to raise funds through the Federal Financing Bank and the majority now use this source in preference to offering securities directly to the public. Many issues still remain outstanding, but their importance to the investor is obviously reduced. The most significant aspect of government owned agencies securities is that the timely repayment of interest and principal is fully guaranteed by the US Government, whereas securities of government sponsored agencies carry the direct guarantee only of the issuing agency. The government owned federal agencies that are still issuing to the public, are as follows.

Government National Mortgage Association (GNMA)

'Ginnie maes'

This agency is a major issuer of securities in both the capital and the money markets. Colloquially, its securities are known as 'ginnie maes', a nickname derived from the initials 'GNMA'. The agency is a wholly owned government corporation within the Department of Housing and Urban Development. It was created in 1968 to replace the FNMA in the purchasing of mortgages which couldn't be carried out economically in the private sector. It exists to provide special assistance functions and the management and liquidation of mortgages and loans acquired from the Department of Housing and Urban Development and from certain federal agencies.

'Ginnie maes' are mortgage backed 'pass thru' securities issued with original lives of 25 to 30 years. The term 'pass thru' means that interest and part principal is returned to the investor monthly (i.e., 30 days in arrears). The principal relates to specific mortgages, and so in some ways is comparable to the way in which mortgage payments are made to a building society in the UK with the holder of 'ginnie mae pass thrus' being in the position of the building society as the lender of funds.

Yields tend to be quoted on a 12-year average life basis, rather than a 30-year-to-maturity basis, because mortgage repayments are remitted to certificate holders on a pro rata basis, as they occur, and the average life of a government backed mortgage is estimated to be 12 years. However, the yield does not take into account the repayment of interest. Tables are available from a dealer which compare the quoted yield with that on a similar semiannual coupon bearing bond. Such a conversion can show the actual yield to be up to 100 basis points higher than the apparent yield.

Farmers' Home Administration (FHDA)

The FHDA administers rural credit programmes, makes direct government loans, gives grants for housing and community facilities and insures privately funded loans.

The primary market in FHDA securities is now rather thin since relatively few new issues are offered, though about $8 billion to $9 billion of securities remain outstanding.

This agency, although at one time offering three different types of securities to the investor, now issues only 'insured notes'. These carry maturities of 10 to 15 years, but they have in the past, been issued with lives of up to 25 years. They are issued in registered form only and in varying minimum denominations. Interest and some principal are paid annually in equal amounts over the life of the loan. Interest and principal is also guaranteed by the full faith and credit of the US Government.

86

The Maritime Administration

This government owned agency is becoming increasingly active in the capital market. The volume of its issues has grown to a current level of about $15 billion, but it goes to the market for funds at irregular intervals. The agency's function is to finance commercial loans and mortgages for the reconstruction and reconditioning of merchant ships. It therefore raises funds in the market only when there is such a requirement, consequently, its new issues are in variable sizes and with differing terms. Its securities are marine bonds and notes, which are secured by ship mortgages and fully guaranteed by the government. Maturities of bonds are up to 30 years and of notes, 5 to 7 years. Both are in registered form with semiannual interest payments and usually issued in minimum denominations of $10 000, though sometimes $5000.

In the primary market, these securities are frequently handled on a private placement basis instead of a public offer basis. They usually carry relatively high yields and are therefore a good investment if held to maturity, but not so good if liquidity is an important investment criterion, since the secondary market is not particularly active.

International agencies

International agencies are privately owned by capital subscribing members who comprise the US and foreign Governments. Their prime function is the extension of loans to developing countries. There are three such international agencies, of which the best known is probably the World Bank. They raise funds by the issue of securities in both the US and other foreign financial markets. Here, the domestically issued securities are described.

The International Bank for Reconstruction and Development (World Bank)

The World Bank was established at the end of the last war to aid the post-war reconstruction and development of its member countries by providing direct loans or by guaranteeing loans made by other countries. Since reconstruction of the war-damaged countries has now been achieved, the World Bank today tends to assist developing countries.

The World Bank's capital comprises subscriptions from 125 member nations and its authorized capital now amounts to a substantial sum in excess of $80 billion. Paid-up capital subscriptions are supplemented by security offerings in the capital markets of the US, Europe and Japan. These issues are secured against the callable portion of the banks' subscribed capital. They comprise notes and bonds issued in registered form with maturities from two years up to thirty years and with interest payment semiannually. They are payable in US dollars, and minimum denominations are $1000 but are traded in units of $1000, $10 000 and $100 000.

A good secondary market exists in World Bank notes and bonds which is probably as active as the secondary market in corporate bonds.

87

The Asian Development Bank (ADB)

This bank, similar to the World Bank, was established in the 1960s to encourage economic development in Asia. Its membership comprises 41 governments whose subscriptions constitute its authorized capital, part of which is 'paid up' and part of which is callable. The latter may be called only if required to meet obligations on borrowings, and guarantees extended by the bank loans are made only for projects within the territories of developing country members. Securities of the ADB consist of 8-year notes and 25-year bonds. They are issued in the US market which it taps only at sporadic intervals. The market in ADB securities is much smaller than that in World Bank issues, there being only about $5 billion of issues outstanding. Notes and bonds are in registered form with semiannual interest payments and minimum denominations of $1000.

The Inter-American Development Bank (I-ADB)

Similarly to the ADB this bank provides assistance to member nations but specifically in Latin American countries. Its capital resources comprise subscriptions from 33 member countries, the capital being split between paid-up and callable amounts.

The I-ADB issue notes and bonds in 15 countries; usually about 50 per cent in the US and the remainder in Europe and Japan. Notes are issued with up to 10 years' maturity, and bonds with up to 25-year lives. The latter may, however, be subject to redemption prior to maturity. Both are issued in registered form with semiannual interest payments, and in $1000 minimum denominations. The I-ADB debts are secured against the callable portion of the banks' authorized capital.

Primary market in agency securities

New issues of agency securities are managed by a selling group which comprises the 33 primary dealers, banks and brokerage houses. Each agency uses its own particular selling group and, apart from the primary dealers, none of the institutions are the same for any two agencies.

Exactly how agency securities are issued depends on the type of instrument. Some issues, such as coupon bearing bonds, are announced as to size and maturity about two weeks prior to issue. The coupon is established about three days before issue and tenders invited from the public. Some discount bearing issues, such as consolidated discount notes, are issued on a tap basis, but at a predetermined price, on application by the investor. Others may be very occasionally issued by a competitive bidding process similar to that in which treasury bills are issued.

Secondary market in agency securities

The secondary market is maintained essentially by the 33 primary dealers. Although a few banks and brokerage houses do hold positions in agency securities, the majority of investors trade through the primary dealers.

Some agency securities enjoy very active secondary markets while others have relatively less liquid markets. As a rule of thumb, marketability improves as maturity shortens and even short-term discount notes are actively traded right up to maturity.

It is probably true to say that all agency securities are highly marketable by European standards but in US terms the best liquidity is enjoyed by farm credits, fanny mae notes and debentures and ginnie mae mortgage backed bonds, participation certificates and 'pass thrus'. Fanny maes are marginally more marketable than ginnie maes although the introduction of a futures market in ginnie maes (see Futures market below) has improved liquidity in the cash market.

Foreign bonds (Yankee bond market)

Bonds issued by non-residents, principally foreign governments or public authorities but also by large foreign corporations, are colloquially known as 'Yankee bonds'. Such foreign institutions, particularly those whose own domestic capital markets are poorly developed, publicly issue securities in the US to tap the huge supply of private capital.

The Yankee bond market is the largest foreign bond market in the world, in terms of issues outstanding. However, since 1978 the US Yankee bond market has fallen into second place behind the Swiss foreign bond market in terms of new issue volume. This is partly because of Switzerland's increasing importance in the international capital market but due more to the fact that foreign borrowers are displaying a growing preference for issuing dollar denominated bonds in the Euromarket rather than the US domestic market (see Tables 26.6 and 26.7). The Eurodollar market is not subject to the same regulations and restrictions as the US domestic bond market. Issuing costs are often lower for Eurobond issues compared to Yankee bond issues and, in the Euromarket, borrowers are able to tap a larger market of potential lenders. For dealing and investment purposes, the Yankee market is integrated with the domestic corporate bond market (see below). Prices and interest are quoted in dollars but interest is paid free of withholding tax.

Canadian borrowers are the largest participants in the Yankee bond market representing about half the value of total issues each year. New issues amounted to about $4.4 billion in 1979 while the outstanding volume of issues is around $50 billion.

Yankee bonds are issued in both bearer and registered form. Maturities may be as long as 20 to 25 years but more recently the bonds have been issued for shorter terms, many as short as five to seven years.

The secondary market is moderately active, with most transactions made through a bank in the over-the-counter market. Many of the Yankee bonds, particularly those of foreign governments, are considered very secure and carry triple A ratings.

Eurobonds

The Eurodollar bond market (i.e. the market in dollar denominated bonds issued and traded outside the US) is the largest of all the Eurobond markets in terms of amount annually issued, the volume of outstanding issues, and of turnover in the secondary market. Table 26.5 shows that over half of all new Eurobond issues made each year are denominated in US dollars. Both borrowers and lenders are active in the dollar bond market because it is the most widely traded of all convertible currencies. It is principally due to the fact that foreign companies earn and trade in dollars and that foreign governments hold reserves in dollars that the Euromarket originally developed. While other currencies, notably the Deutschemark, have during the 1970s gained an increasing share of the Eurobond market, US dollars remain the major currency of issue. While about 80 per cent of Eurodollar bonds are straight bonds, a variety of other forms have developed during the last few years so as to attract a wider range of investors. Straight bonds carry maturities of three to fifteen years (sometimes longer) and many redeem capital at maturity or by annuity thus reducing their average life. Convertible bonds and bonds with warrants offer the investor the opportunity respectively either to convert the bonds into shares of the issuing company or to purchase shares of the issuing company at terms specified at issue. The shares are denominated in a currency other than dollars and thus offer the investor a fixed interest return together with an equity and currency speculation. Option bonds are usually issued in other denominations apart from dollars but provide the lender with the option to receive interest and/or capital in dollars. Straight, convertible, warrant and option bonds are all bearer securities fixed interest which pay interest annually, free of withholding tax. A further type of bond carries a variable coupon. These are floating rate notes (FRNs). They have usually shorter maturities than straight bonds (5–7 years). Their special feature is that the coupon is set at some margin over LIBOR—the interest rate on Eurodollar time deposits in London. The margin is usually $\frac{1}{8}$ to $\frac{1}{4}$ per cent over six months LIBOR. The coupon is thus recalculated every six months and paid semiannually in arrears. A few FRNs, however, have interest paid and recalculated quarterly. FRN issues have become increasingly popular during 1979 and 1980 since, for the lender of funds, capital is better protected against volatile changes in yield.

In the primary market an average of about $10 billion new Eurobond issues have been made in each of the last five years, the majority of which are brought to the market by public issue rather than by private placement. New issues are managed and placed by a syndicate of international banks located in foreign financial centres. Table 26.8 lists the major primary issuers. Such banks normally lead-manage new issues though over 100 additional banks may participate in the placement of an issue. The borrowers are both US and foreign corporations, and multinationals. The market is unregulated and issues are neither registered with the SEC nor listed on the domestic stock exchanges. They are issued onto the international market and bought mainly by foreign institutions and corporations. US residents are not permitted to purchase Eurodollar bonds in the primary market, except on a private placement basis.

The secondary market is highly active. The bonds are quoted on many foreign stock exchanges in Europe and the other financial centres of the Far and Middle East. Most dealing however takes place through a bank in the over-the-counter markets in any of these financial centres. Principal centres are London, Frankfurt and Paris though Bahrain and Singapore are also developing as important trading centres.

Corporate bonds

The corporate bond market in the US, with respect to both borrowers and investors, is the largest in the world.

Corporations, which include utility companies providing gas, electricity and water, and transport companies such as the railroads, as well as commercial and financial organizations, issue bonds and notes which may vary in maturity from between 1 to 30 years. They are issued in registered form and normally provide semiannual interest payments. The majority of the corporate bonds are straight bonds so coupon rate is fixed with respect to prevailing market rates at the time of issue. With recent volatility of US interest rates therefore, the investors' capital has been exposed to a certain amount of short-term risk since, as market rates of interest fluctuate, the market price of a bond rises and falls accordingly. The redemption capital and interest payments are guaranteed by the borrowing company. The degree of credit risk is indicated by the bond-grading systems (see below). Corporate bonds are traded in the same capital markets as equity issues, i.e., on the stock exchanges and in the over-the-counter market, as described later.

The total market is extremely active but the performance and turnover of each bond depends on the type of issuer, its credit rating, the yield of the bond, marketability and other factors.

Bond grading

In order to issue bonds, a corporation (including foreign issuers) must submit its books to one of the three grading agencies for bond rating; additionally bonds already in issue are rerated annually. This is a major feature of the North American bond markets and probably a principal reason why the bond market is so successful in attracting a wide range of investors. The rating that attaches to a bond is an indicator of the issuing corporation's ability to honour its debt. This reduces uncertainty for the investor who is thus provided with an indication of how secure his capital and interest will be if invested in particular bonds. The rating agencies do not make the rating criteria public but factors analysed are a company's capital structure, gearing or leverage ratios, solvency and liquidity, earnings growth and performance of previous bond issues. Highly rated bonds needless to say carry a lower yield than lower rated bonds.

The three rating agencies are Standard and Poors, Moodies, and Fitches. All three are directly comparable. For example, Standard and Poors grade from AAA down to DDD while Moodies grade from Aaa down to ccc. In Table 4.3, Standard and Poors rating system is illustrated, but the same grading divisions also apply to both Moodies and Fitches.

Under present commercial bank regulations, bonds rated in the top four categories (AAA, AA, A, BBB), are generally regarded as eligible for bank investments and are thus known as bank quality bonds.

91

Table 4.3 Standard and Poors rating system

Bond Grade	Characteristics
AAA (triple A)	Prime grade. Triple A bonds represent the highest degree of protection of both principal and interest
AA	Highly secure. The majority differ from AAA bonds only to a small degree
A	Upper medium grade. Considerable investment strength but not entirely free from adverse changes in economic and trade conditions
BBB	Medium grade. Some speculative elements. Adequate asset cover and earnings but more responsive to business conditions than to interest rates
BB	Lower to medium grade. Interest is normally earned but deficit operations are possible
B	Speculative investment. Payment of interest cannot be assured under difficult economic conditions
CCC–CC	Outright speculation
C	Category reserved for income bonds on which no interest is being paid
DDD–D	Bonds are in default of interest payments and principal is at risk. Range between DDD and D indicates relative salvage values of the bonds

Table 4.4 Gross new issues in US capital market (US $ million)

Issuer	1975	1976	1977	1978	1979	First half 1980
BONDS ISSUED BY:						
Central government	71 699	95 900	89 445	97 351	100 101	65 232
State and local government institutions and enterprise	30 531	35 180	46 697	48 512	43 365	23 155
Central government agencies	15 559	14 742	21 107	25 899	25 181	15 389
Financial institutions	6 324	9 454	10 617	9 266	1 137	1 824
Private corporations	34 152	30 056	25 754	25 370	28 286	9 205
Total domestic bond issues	158 265	185 332	193 620	206 398	208 305	111 333
Foreign (Yankee bonds)	6 677	9 147	7 779	5 672	6 631	4 600
Total bond issues	164 942	194 479	201 399	212 070	214 936	115 933
SHARES						
Financial institutions	490	771	498	1 632	1 502	269
Non-financial companies	10 365	10 323	10 479	9 106	10 785	5 995
Total shares	10 855	11 094	11 427	10 738	12 287	6 264

Equity shares markets

The market in equity shares is split into two distinctly different markets, namely:

1. Organized securities exchange markets (stock exchanges);
2. Over-the-counter markets.

Stock exchanges

Altogether there are twelve securities or stock markets, of which the New York Stock Exchange (NYSE) is the largest and best known handling 80 per cent of total stock exchange quotation.

At present, the twelve exchanges operate separately and autonomously, but in the near future they will consolidate via a national tape—an electronic, visual and computerized communication system. This has already been directed by Congress but not yet put into effect. When operational, it will be supervised and maintained by the Stock Exchange Commission (SEC) (see below).

The relative sizes and current methods of operation of the twelve exchanges are shown below.

Table 4.5

	(Based on 1978 figures)	
Exchanges	*Volume of traded bonds and stocks, million*	*Dollar value of traded bonds and stocks, $ million*
New York	7660	210 550
Mid West	9290	10 461
America	7573	15 418
Pacific	301	7 105
Philadelphia	143	4 087
Boston	178	1 536
Detroit	20	500
Cincinnati	15	433
Spokane	14	10
National	1	0.5
Intermountain	2	0.8
Honolulu*	1	0.5

* Exchange exempted from SEC regulations.

New York stock exchange

Shares quoted on the New York stock exchange tend to be those of the larger and better known national and international companies and, as mentioned above, they account for the trading of about 80 per cent of all stock exchange quotations. Despite this, it handles only about a fifth of the volume transacted in the 'over-the-counter' market (see below).

The NYSE is an association of individuals governed by a 21-man board. There are approximately 1400 members whose functions fall into one of the six categories described below. It should be noted that trading takes place between dealer and dealer, there being no jobbing intermediary. A new member must purchase what is known as a 'seat' on the stock exchange usually from an existing member. The price of a seat on the New York stock exchange varies considerably according to market conditions. In 1929 the cost was $265 000 but by 1942 had fallen to $17 000. In 1968/69 the price had risen to $515 000 but in 1977 had again fallen to $35 000.

*Commis-
sion broker*

This is the largest category of members. A commission broker is an employee in one of about 500 commission houses (stockbrokers) devoted to handling business on the exchange and dealing in about 500 cities. He executes orders for his firm on behalf of its customers at agreed commission rates.

*Floor
broker*

He works within the exchange (on the floor) and executes orders for other exchange members who have more orders in different stocks than they can handle alone, or who wish aid in handling large orders. The floor broker takes a share in the commission received by the member firm that he is assisting.

*Registered
trader*

He is an individual who is a member in his own right and buys and sells for his own account. Alternatively, he may be a trustee who maintains membership for the convenience of dealing and for saving fees.

Specialist

He acts as both a dealer and a broker, trading in a particular or 'special' group of shares. As a broker he executes orders in stocks in which he is registered as a specialist. As a dealer he buys and sells shares in these 'special' stocks for his own account.

*Odd-lot
dealer*

Generally, amounts of 100 shares are known as a 'round lot' and amounts of less than 100 shares are known as an 'odd lot'. The odd-lot dealer buys and sells from commission firms at prices that are based on round lots, plus or minus a differential. The 'odd-lot' dealer, however, has now become virtually extinct since the NYSE acquired a computerized processing system in 1976, which made the transacting of shares in odd amounts considerably easier.

*Bond
broker*

He trades bonds or corporations on a commission basis on behalf of commission houses and also for his own account.

The American exchange (AMEX)

This securities exchange is also based in New York but provides a market for stocks and bonds of companies not large enough to qualify for the New York Stock Exchange. Its listing requirements are much less stringent and it encourages the registration of relatively young companies. Its listed quotations also include a considerable number of foreign stocks.

A special feature of AMEX is the use of associate members who are not entitled to trade on the floor, but who transmit orders through regular members at reduced commission.

The national stock exchange

This is a third exchange in New York. It opened in 1962 but is still relatively small. It has no stringent listing requirements and does not quote any stocks that are also listed on other exchanges.

The regional stock exchanges

The regional exchanges were established to provide organized markets for local securities. With the recent rapid growth in the size of companies, however, along with the growth in communications and the over-the-counter market, the importance of the regional markets has declined, such that together they represent only about 10 per cent of the total equity trading volume.

The over-the-counter market (OTC)

The majority (about 80 per cent) of all securities are not listed on any of the exchanges but are traded 'over the counter'. They represent a lower aggregate value than listed issues, but a considerably larger volume. On the stock exchanges there are about 7000 securities and about 2000 issues. On the OTC there are about 30000 securities of which about 11000 issues and 2500 bonds are regularly traded.

The estimated value of OTC share sales is about 40 per cent of total share sales across all markets, about 80 per cent of all corporate bond business, and 100 per cent of U.S. Government issues.

The following types of securities are regularly traded on the OTC:

U.S. Government and agency issues
State and local government bonds
Railroad bonds and shares
Many public utility bonds and shares
Most industrial company bonds and shares
Most banks and insurance shares

The OTC market developed because companies have been unwilling to gain listing privileges for their securities since it is not only costly but also subjects them to sometimes stringent regulations.

The market operates through dealers who are either commission houses (stockbrokers) or banks. Commission houses may deal for their own account as well as on behalf of their clients. Banks, however, are not allowed to act as principals and may only deal on behalf of clients. Securities are dealt by negotiation with the dealers or by bargaining between bid and offer prices. The quotations of unlisted shares are shown in newspapers, in the form of bid and offer prices as reported by representative dealers rather than by actual transactions. Newspapers publish a limited number of quotations, usually restricted to local issues. Comprehensive lists are available from the National Quotation Bureau Inc. in New York.

Since 1971, dealers have been able to communicate using a system of video screens known as NASDAQ (National Association of Security Dealers Automated Quotation System). This has facilitated a nationally uniform and near-perfect market. The OTC is regulated by the National Association of Security Dealers, which sets strict rules and has powers to expel unethical dealers. The organization includes all the same 3000 dealers, the 500 brokers, and most investment bankers.

The third market (off the board)

If the security exchanges comprise the first market and the OTC the second, then the third market is that trading via the OTC in stocks that are listed on a stock exchange, but between firms who are not members of an exchange and who therefore do not charge the regular listed commissions. Prices are established by negotiation and dealers have no responsibility for maintaining the market.

Increasingly individual customer orders are executed 'in house' or in the third market. Dealing takes place mostly between large institutions, such as pension funds and large insurance companies, who normally hold large blocks of shares.

The fourth market

Large block sales of securities are also arranged by private firms who link their customers together by computer terminals. Customers of these specialist firms are large institutions such as banks and pension funds. This is the 'fourth market', and the advantage to its participants, who trade in at least 500 stocks per month, is the lower commission they are required to pay and the speed of transaction.

The Securities and Exchange Commission (SEC)

All securities exchanges are controlled by the SEC. This is a government authority set up following the Securities Act of 1933, which was the result of the Wall Street crash of 1929. The commission comprises five members appointed by the President and has wide discretionary powers. Registration statements, new listing applications, and periodic reports must be prepared according to its requirements.

All exchanges have to be registered with the commission or be classified as exempted from registration. (There is only one exempt exchange—the Honolulu Stock Exchange.)

Exchanges must provide full information concerning their activities, organization, membership, and rules of procedure.

Transactions are restricted to securities officially registered with the exchange and with the commission. Companies have to keep the following current information:

- annual and quarterly reports as prescribed;
- organization;
- financial structure;

- nature of business;
- terms, position, rights and privileges of different classes of securities:
- directors, officers and underwriters;
- holders of more than five per cent of the company's equity;
- remuneration to staff in excess of $25 000;
- bonus and profit-sharing arrangements;
- management and service contracts;
- options existing to be created with respect to their securities;
- balance sheets and profit-and-loss accounts for a minimum of three preceding years as certified by accountants;
- trust indentures;
- underwriting contracts;
- articles of incorporation;
- other documents as may be required by the SEC.

All files may be inspected by the public at the offices of the SEC.

Dealers and brokers must also register with the SEC as a condition of trading across state lines. The SEC prescribes rules of trading.

Because of inside dealing, all directors, officers and holders of more than 10 per cent of a company's equity must report changes in their monthly holdings of securities.

Five types of price manipulation are specifically prohibited by the SEC:

1. Matched orders—these are fictitious transactions between two or more people, which create a price without a change of ownership;
2. Wash sales—where one person fictitiously 'prints the tape' by buying and selling a stock, thereby recording a price, but whereby no actual change of ownership has taken place;
3. Pool operations—whereby a price is raised (or lowered) by concerted activities of members of a pool;
4. Dissemination and spread of false information.
5. Short selling (i.e., selling securities before purchasing the same securities) is regulated. Short sales cannot be executed at a price lower than that established in the last preceding regular sale. Sellers have to make delivery of the securities and thus may have to borrow the securities from a commission house until he makes the purchase recession to close the transaction.

Share price indices

There are a number of indices in common use in US equity markets. Many of these are quoted daily in *The Wall Street Journal* and other financial papers, and the more common ones such as the Dow Jones Index are quoted in foreign financial press and radio. While it is true of all stock exchange indices that a rise is good and a fall is bad, the significance of a movement in either direction depends on the base of the index and method of calculation.

The Dow
Jones
index

There are four Dow Jones averages:

Industrial average
Transportation average
Utility average
Composite average

The Dow Jones industrial average is one of the most frequently quoted indices and the one which is meant when reference to the Dow Jones index is made. It is simple arithmetic average of price movements of 30 large manufacturing companies, such as General Motors and Eastman Kodak.

The transportation average is the average of price movements of twenty transport companies such as Southern Pacific and TWA. The utility average is the average of price movements of fifteen utility companies.

The composite average is a combination of the above three averages.

The Dow Jones Index is named after Charles Dow and Edward Jones, the two founders of *The Wall Street Journal*, and first devised in 1884. It is calculated as a simple average by adding all the shares together and dividing by the original number (30) but which has been adjusted over time.

Share splits and rights issued have changed the denominator which is now in the region of 1.5. This fall, from 30 in 1884, indicates the large number of share splits that have occurred over the last century. The index is published every Monday morning by *The Wall Street Journal*, although it is calculated and posted in the New York stock exchange every half-hour during the trading day.

The 30 stocks of the industrial average constitute approximately 30 per cent of the total market value of all stocks in the country. The main fault with the Dow Jones index is that shares are not weighted. Therefore the greatest weights automatically attach to the highest priced stocks.

Standard
and Poors
500 index

This index differs from the Dow Jones in that the shares are weighted by their market value. The index is calculated by taking the total market value of the 500 stocks in the index, dividing by their weighted average market value during the period 1941 to 1943, and then multiplying by 10. Therefore, if the index stands at 100, then the stocks are selling at 10 times their value in 1941–1943.

NYSE
composite
exchange

This is an index that covers all common stocks traded on the New York Stock Exchange.

As with the Standard and Poors index, each stock is weighted by its market value. In addition, the New York stock exchange also publishes specialized indices for industrial, utility, transport and financial companies.

AMEX
price level
index

This is an average of all shares traded on the American stock exchange and, as with the Standard and Poors index, the stocks are weighted by their market value.

There are a wide variety of NASDAQ indices, measuring the performance of shares traded in the over-the-counter market. They are weighted average share prices of companies within specified sectors and are posted regularly on the composite tape which runs on the national computerized system.

The NASDAQ index

Every day *The Wall Street Journal* publishes this index which is simply two figures showing the number of stocks that have gone up, and the number of stocks that have dropped in price.

Advances and declines

Of all these indices, the Standard and Poors 500 index is probably the best broad based measure of overall performance and the one probably most relied on by the market.

Options markets

The Chicago Board Options Exchange (CBOE) was established in 1973 as the first securities exchange in the world specifically for the purpose of providing a market in put and call options.

The advantages of an options exchange as a separate entity are:

1. The option contract and trading price is standardized.
2. There is a continuous reporting system.
3. Specialist market makers are appointed, whose obligation it is to maintain a fair and orderly market.
4. There is the assumption of a self-regulatory responsibility.
5. Trading is better facilitated by the provision of a specialized clearing corporation.

Options provide the investor with greater leverage since he is able to participate, without making outright purchase, in the performance of a larger number of shares with proportionately smaller funds. Thus the investor is able to speculate to a higher degree, although he may also limit his risks according to the terms of the option.

Options are sold by a 'writer' or 'maker' of the option contract at an 'exercise price' in exchange for a fee. The writers effectively act in a jobbing capacity in that they hold shares on their own books and make a market in these shares by selling the option to purchase them at specific prices. The writer's return is the price of the option, relative to the cost of those shares to the writers.

The price of an option depends on its expiration date, its 'striking price' and the market's attitude towards the underlying stock. For example the price of a particular stock option may be quoted at $2 to purchase at $25; that is the investor may pay $2 for the option to purchase the named stock at the striking price of $25. There is, of course, no obligation on behalf of the investor to exercise the option. Any time before the expiry date he may sell the option, even after it has reached or exceeded its striking price.

Once issued the option may be traded as a security in its own right at a premium (or discount) to its original issue price. The premium will depend on three factors.

99

First it depends on the general price level of the share on which the option is quoted. Secondly, the premium tends to be higher the longer the expiry date, since the odds of a share price changing in order to meet the striking price—which remains the same during the life of the option—increases with time. Therefore, the closer the striking price is to the share price when the option is purchased, the higher the premium. Thirdly, the premium tends to be higher the more volatile the price of a particular share since the volatility also increased the chance of the striking price being met.

Option prices tend to rise when interest rates are high or rising because the writers have to sacrifice income for holding shares instead of bonds and they therefore charge a higher premium to correspond with the higher opportunity cost.

Investors may also deal in 'naked options'. This is another form of short selling by which the investor sells options which he has not yet purchased. He will only do so if he believes that the price of the share concerned, and consequently the option price, will fall in the near future. He can then make a profit by buying the same options at a later date at a lower price than he has sold them. Unlike 'going short' in equities he need only deliver the securities when the option matures, unless of course, the option is called (i.e., exercised) by the new purchaser prior to maturity. In that case he will have to buy the securities in order to close the deal and make the delivery.

Warrants and rights

These, in many ways, are similar to options, but there is no specialized market place and they are purchased from the company of issue rather than from dealers or market makers.

Warrants are options to purchase ordinary shares of a particular company, and are usually purchased by bondholders who want to participate in the profit growth of that company. Warrants are often attached to new bond issues as an inducement for investors to take up the bonds. Contrary to options, which are short-term instruments with a fixed maturity date. Warrants have a longer life; indeed, some warrants never expire, though most mature within three to five years. They are sometimes very volatile and can be extremely profitable. For example, Tricontinental Inc. issued warrants at $\$\frac{1}{32}$ in 1942 which, by 1969, had risen to $76. Thus, $1000 in 1942 would have been worth $2.5 million by 1969; a simple interest return of over 90% per annum. Conversely, TWA issued warrants fell from $25 at issue to $0 within six months.

Rights unlike warrants are usually issued in connection with new share issues. They give the investor the right to purchase further shares at a given price and, in contrast to warrants, they are not normally marketable and usually have a life of only two or three weeks.

Futures markets

The USA has the largest, most sophisticated and best developed futures markets in the world. It is possible to buy futures contracts in money market instruments such as treasury bills and ginnie maes, currencies and commodities. Specialized market places have been established for the trading of different types of futures. The first such market, the 'International Monetary Market' (IMM) of the Chicago board of trade, was opened in 1972. It was conceived as a market specializing in futures contracts of monetary vehicles whether currencies, precious metals, or other financial instruments.

Financial futures

Financial futures trading began in October 1975 with futures contracts in ginnie mae mortgage backed pass through certificates. Shortly after, futures contracts for three-month treasury bills were introduced.

Since September 1978 other ginnie mae securities, 12-month treasury bills and commercial paper have been included among financial futures.

By buying financial futures the investor is essentially buying an interest-rate contract. For example, an investor may hedge the risk of capital loss resulting from a rise in interest rates and can lock in a known return. If he expects interest rates to rise to a higher level than indicated by the forward market, he may sell financial futures. So, if interest rates were to increase, the price of the securities would fall (due to the inverse relationship between price and yield). The investor would thus make a capital profit by having contracted to sell the securities at a higher price than he is later able to buy them back in the cash market.

Conversely, if the investor expects interest rates to fall below the level indicated by forward interest rates, he may choose to buy financial futures. A capital gain accrues if interest rates do fall and securities prices consequently rise. (See example on page 104.)

Three major markets provide futures in financial instruments and currencies. These markets are the Chicago Board of Trade (CBT), the International Monetary Market (IMM)—a division of the Chicago Mercantile Exchange—and the New York Futures Exchange (NYFE), the newest market, opened in August 1980, and replacing the AMEX futures exchange. The futures markets made by each exchange are as follows:

Treasury bills	90 days	CBT	IMM	NYFE
Treasury bills	1 year	IMM		
Treasury notes	4 years	CBT	IMM	
Treasury bond	20 years	CBT	NYFE	
Commercial paper		CBT		
Ginnie maes		CBT		
Currencies		IMM	NYFE	

Ninety-day treasury bill futures contracts relate to three-month bills issued on the third week of quarter-end months, i.e., March, June, September and December. A futures contract specifies a purchase of such bills in advance of their issue. Prices are quoted in terms of the IMM or NYFE index which, since treasury bills are sold

Treasury bill futures

101

at a discount, give the par value less the annualized discount rate. Thus, if the annualized discount rate is 10 per cent, the IMM quoted price will be $90 ($100 – $10). (In practice $90 is the middle price between the quoted bid and offer prices.) It should be noted that in contrast to treasury bills in the ordinary cash market, treasury bill futures prices are quoted at their term discount from par. Thus, a three-month treasury bill at an annualized discount of 10 per cent is not quoted at $97.50 ($10 × 3/12), but at $90.

On all exchanges, contracts are quoted in multiples of 0.01 points and prices are allowed to fluctuate by a minimum of 0.01 points and a maximum of 0.5 points ($25 and $1250 per contract, respectively) above or below the previous day's price.

Contracts are made in units of $1 million face (par) value. Twelve-month treasury bills are traded in the IMM futures market in exactly the same way as above.

Treasury note futures

The CBT makes a futures market in treasury notes of up to six years maturity but the IMM trades six-months to four-year treasury notes only. Contracts are traded in units of $100 000 face value at maturity on the basis of a standard seven per cent coupon. Treasury notes with different coupon rate have their redemption face value adjusted so that their prices can be quoted on a comparable basis with a seven per cent issue. For example, an eight per cent four-year treasury note would have a maturity face value of $103 440 while a six per cent four-year note would have a face value of $96 560. Prices are quoted as a percentage of par in fluctuations of $\frac{1}{64}$ ($15.625 per contract). Daily price fluctuations are limited to $\frac{3}{4}$ per cent either way of the previous day's close, except for the last day of trading (i.e., one day from cash trading) when no price limit applies. Contracts are traded for the delivery months of February, May, August and November. The last day for trading each contract is the 15th of each delivery month (or the subsequent business day if a holiday). Delivery then takes place on the 17th of the contract month.

Ginnie mae futures

The Chicago Board of Trade provides a futures market in ginnie mae modified 'pass thru' mortgage backed securities. Contracts relate to newly formed ginnie maes only and not to those already being traded in the secondary market. The contract may be agreed on a standby basis, in which case the issue may withdraw from the contract, or it may be mandatory in which case both parties must honour the contract.

Ginnie mae 'pass thrus' specify that interest and part principal is repaid monthly, so in the ordinary cash market, prices are quoted as a percentage of the unpaid principal balance and in multiples of $\frac{1}{32}$. In the futures market, contracts are traded in minimum denominations of $100 000 principal balance at a fixed rate of interest of eight per cent. Ginnie maes bearing other rates of interest are adjusted so as to be equivalent to $100 000 of ginnie mae 8s. Thus a ginnie mae seven per cent would result in a principal balance of $107 817. In the futures market prices also fluctuate in minimum amounts of $\frac{1}{32}$, which is equivalent to $31.25 per contract, but upper limits also apply at $\frac{24}{32}$ or $750 per contract, with respect to the previous day's trading price.

Ginnie mae futures are popular among the major secondary cash market participants, namely mortgage brokers and financial institutions. They use the futures market to hedge the risk of capital loss due to a rise in interest rates as well as to make additional profits if expecting a fall in interest rates. Traders are also used to dealing on a forward basis because the GNMA has a forward delivery mechanism in the cash market that is very much like the futures market: the only security to be so traded.

Commercial paper futures

Commercial paper futures are traded on the Chicago Board of Trade. Contracts are for $1 million face value of prime (AAA) commercial paper with a maximum maturity of 90 days. Prices are quoted as an annualized discount, which is the same as for the cash market. Minimum price fluctuations are one basis point, and maximum fluctuations per day are 25 basis points, per contract.

An investor in the futures commercial paper market, buying forward paper, is in effect a borrower of funds since he also undertakes to deliver commercial paper at a future date. The seller of futures commercial paper is, in effect, a lender of funds, since he pays cash to the 'long' contractors in order to receive paper. This method of operation is a reversal of the normal commodity market relationship between long and short investors.

The major participants in this futures market are the corporations which issue commercial paper and other investors in the money market. Corporations that need to borrow in the future can go long, i.e., buy commercial paper forward, to hedge against a rise in interest rates. Investors with surplus cash in the near future may go short by selling commercial paper to hedge against a potential fall in profits.

Treasury bond futures

US treasury bond futures are traded on the Chicago Board of Trade on New York futures exchange. Contracts are for new issues of bonds with minimum maturities of 15 years. The minimum trading unit is $100 000 face value with a fixed-interest rate of eight per cent. Bonds with other coupon rates are adjusted so as to be quoted in terms of treasury bond 8s. Thus, as with ginnie maes, those with a lower coupon will be quoted on the basis of a principal balance at a premium over $100 000 while those with a higher coupon than eight per cent will be quoted on the basis of a principal balance at a discount from $100 000.

Daily fluctuations are subject to minimum and maximum fluctuations of $\frac{1}{32}$ and $\frac{24}{32}$ of a point. This is equivalent to $31.25 and $750 per contract respectively.

The main participants in this futures market are banks, securities dealers, and institutions who wish to lock in a given return on bonds and to hedge against a rise in interest rate and, thus, a fall in the capital value of the bonds.

Examples of futures market transactions

1. An investor expects interest rates to fall. He therefore wishes to buy interest rate futures because the dollar price of the security will rise as interest rates fall. He chooses to buy a four-year treasury note through the IMM.

IMM quoted price	93.26 ($93\frac{23}{64}$)
Bond equivalent yield	9.00%
Four year-note price in cash market	$93 406
Bond equivalent yield subsequently falls to	8.00%
Four-year note price in cash market	$96 625
New IMM quoted price	96.40 ($96\frac{40}{64}$)
Investor sells contract and receives gain of	3.14 ($3\frac{14}{64}$)

(96.40 − 93.26), i.e., $3\frac{14}{64}$% of par or 3.218 75 × $100 000 = $3219

2. An investor expects interest rates to rise. He therefore wishes to sell interest rate futures because the dollar price of the security will fall as interest rates rise. He chooses to sell 90-day treasury bills through the NYFE.

Annual yield rate of 90-day treasury bill	4.00%
90-day bill price in cash market	$990 000
NYFE quoted price at which investor sells contract	96.00
Yield subsequently rises to	5.00%
90-day bill price in cash market	$987 500
NYFE quoted price	95.00
Investor buys back contract at	95.00
Investor's gain is	1.00

(96.00 − 95.00), i.e., 1.00% × $\frac{3}{12}$ of par or 0.25 × $100 000 = $250.00

Currency futures

The futures currency market of the IMM and New York Futures Exchange (NYFE) while similar in concept to the forward currency market, differs substantially in operational methods. These differences are shown in Table 4.8.

The main participants in this market are commercial banks that deal in the foreign exchange markets and companies that transact with foreign countries and wish to hedge against a change in the exchange rate value. Speculative traders are the most prominent participants.

Eight currencies are traded in the IMM currency futures market. The NYFE trades in five of the same currencies—sterling, Canadian dollar, Deutschemark, yen and Swiss francs—but does not trade in Mexican peso's, guilders, or French francs. Transactions must be made in specified minimum contract sizes, equivalent to between $50 000 and $100 000. The minimum daily fluctuation is one basis point, which for each contract is equal to $12.50.

Contracts are made for delivery on the third Wednesday of each quarter-end month, March, June, September and December. This is in contrast to the forward foreign exchange market, as made by banks, where forward contracts may be made for varied time periods (e.g., one, three, five months, etc.) for any date, and where contract sizes may be for odd numbers and not subject to minimum daily fluctuations.

Quotes in both the forward and futures markets are given by two prices, the first being the bid price, and the second the offer price. This is in common with all

American and continental traders, although the London market always quotes the offer price first.

The quotes will usually state whether the price is at a premium or a discount. As a rule of thumb, if the first of the two figures is larger than the second, the forward rate is at a discount. If the first figure is smaller than the second, the forward rate is at a premium. The reverse applies for London quotes.

The two numbers quoted for the forward rate will usually be the last digit of the decimal point, which should be added to or subtracted from the spot price. The futures market quote for the same time period will be the same but multiplied by ten.

For example:

	Forward market	*Futures market*
FRANCE (SPOT)	0.2337/0.2340	0.233 85
FRANCE FORWARD		
One month	3 to 4	30 to 40.234 25
Two months	9 to 9	80 to 90.234 85
Three months	13 to 14	130 to 140.235 25

The futures market always quotes currencies in terms of the US dollar, i.e., the number of US dollars per unit of currency. The British pound, deutschemark, Swiss franc, Dutch guilder and Canadian dollar are all quoted to five decimal points and the Japanese yen to four, after dropping the first two decimal points for ease of transmission.

Since each currency is quoted to a specified number of decimal places, dealers refer to 'points'. One point is defined as the last decimal place quoted. Thus for the British pound, one point means $0.0001 to the pound, whereas for the French franc, which is quoted to five decimal places, one point means $0.00001 to the franc.

Futures contracts must be made in certain specified minimum amounts. For example, for the British pound futures contracts can be made in minimum amounts of £25 000 and Japanese yen contracts in minimum amounts of Y12.5 million.

Table 4.6

	Units per contract	Decimal equivalent of minimum fluctuation	Dollar value of minimum fluctuation
British pound	25 000	× $0.000 5	= $12.50
Deutschemark	125 000	× $0.000 1	= $12.50
Swiss franc	125 000	× $0.000 1	= $12.50
Canadian dollar	100 000	× $0.000 1	= $10.00
Mexican peso	1 000 000	× $0.00001	= $10.00
Japanese yen	12 500 000	× $0.000 001	= $12.50
Dutch guilder	125 000	× $0.001	= $12.50
French franc	250 000	× $0.000 05	= $12.50

Table 4.7   Financial instruments futures contracts traded 1975–1979 (*source: Futures Industry Association*)

	Contract unit	No. of contracts traded				
		1975	1976	1977	1978	1979
Chicago Board of Trade						
GNMA mortgages, CD	$100 000	—	—	—	6 527	77 365
GNMA mortgages, CDR	—	20 125	128 568	422 421	953 161	1 371 078
Commercial paper (90 day)	$1 000 000	—	—	3 553	18 767	39 702
Commercial paper (30 day)	$3 000 000	—	—	—	—	1 292
Treasury notes (T) (4–6 year)	$100 000	—	—	—	—	11 599
Treasury bonds (T)	$100 000	—	—	32 101	555 350	2 059 594
Total		20 125	128 568	458 075	1 533 805	3 560 630
Chicago Mercantile—(IMM)						
British pound	25 000	15 015	33 465	78 701	240 099	513 682
Canadian dollar	100 000	2 677	17 068	161 139	207 654	399 885
Deutschemark	125 000	54 793	44 887	134 368	400 569	450 856
Japanese yen	12 500 000	1 790	1 449	82 261	361 731	329 645
Mexican peso	1 000 000	48 547	51 439	17 029	17 844	29 982
Swiss franc	125 000	69 933	37 246	106 968	321 451	493 944
Dutch guilder	125 000	927	392	2 812	3 585	22
US silver coins	$5 000	34 757	257	371	275	58
French franc	250 000	6 238	5 968	3 150	4 449	406
T-bills (90 day)	$1 000 000	—	110 223	321 703	768 980	1 930 482
T-bills (1 year)	$250 000	—	—	—	5 564	11 769
T-notes (4 years)	$100 000	—	—	—	—	11 072
Total	—	234 677	302 394	908 502	2 332 201	4 171 804
Commodity Exchange (COMEX)						
T-bills (90 day)	$1 000 000	—	—	—	—	27 860
GNMA mortgages, CD	$100 000	—	—	—	—	873
Total	—	—	—	—	—	28 733
AMEX Commodities Exchange (ACE)						
GNMA mortgages, CD	$100 000	—	—	—	16 671	52 493
T-bills (90 day)	$1 000 000	—	—	—	—	4 334
T-bonds	$100 000	—	—	—	—	7 492
Total	—	—	—	—	16 671	64 319
Grand total	—	254 802	430 962	1 356 577	3 882 677	7 825 485

The New York Futures Exchange did not open until August 1980.

Additionally, for ease of transaction, the value of each contract is permitted to fluctuate only in minimum amounts of $10 or $12.50 derived from the minimum permitted number of points fluctuation for each currency shown in Table 4.6.

Quotes on the forward market as operated between banks are equivalent to quotes on the futures market except that they are quoted to one fewer decimal place. Therefore, for quick comparison between forward and futures market rates,

Table 4.8 Comparison of forward market and futures market (*source: International Monetary Market*)

	Forward	Futures
Size of contract	Tailored to individual needs	Standardized
Delivery date	Tailored to individual needs	Standardized
Method of transaction	Established by the bank or broker via telephone contact with limited number of buyers and sellers	Determined by open auction among many buyers and sellers on the exchange floor
Participants	Banks, brokers and multi-national companies. Public speculation not encouraged	Banks, brokers and multi-national companies. Qualified public speculation encouraged
Commissions	Set by 'spread' between bank's buy and sell prices. Not easily determined by the customer	Published small brokerage fee and negotiated rates on block trades
Security deposit	None as such, but compensating bank balances required	Published small security deposit required
Clearing operation (financial integrity)	Handling contingent on individual banks and brokers. No separate clearing house function	Handled by exchange clearing house. Daily settlements to the market
Market-place	Over the telephone world-wide	Central exchange floor with world-wide communications
Economic justification	Facilitate world trade by hedge mechanism	Same as forward market. In addition, it provides a broader market and an alternative hedging mechanism via public participation
Accessibility	Limited to very large customers who deal in foreign trade	Open to anyone who needs hedge facilities, or has risk capital with which to speculate
Regulation	Self-regulating	April 1975—regulated under the Commodity Futures Trading Commission
Frequency of delivery	More than 90% settled by actual delivery	Theoretically, no deliveries in a perfect market. In reality, less than 1%
Price fluctuations	No daily limit	Daily limit imposed by the exchange with a rule provision for expanded daily price limits
Market liquidity	Offsetting with other banks	Public offset. Arbitrage offset

one point on the forward market is equivalent to ten points on the futures market.

Quotes on the forward market are given for standard days such as 30, 60 and 90 days and also six months and twelve months or more. In the futures market days of delivery decrease to zero, i.e., quotes are for a fixed date some time in the future rather than for standard time periods. In the futures market delivery day is the third Wednesday of the month, for all relevant delivery months. To compare futures prices with the equivalent forward prices, therefore, it is often necessary to interpolate between say 30- and 60-day forward quotes.

Commodity futures

The world's largest selection of commodities is traded in the futures market (see Table 4.9). It is possible to deal in almost any commodity ranging from agricultural and livestock products, such as wheat and pork bellies, to hard commodities like metals, including gold.

Commodities are traded on a number of exchanges of which the largest is based in New York. Trading is supervised by the 'Commodities Futures Trading Commission' (CFTF) a federal authority.

Traders can 'front' a variety of contract dates ranging from one month to one year. If the contract is held to the final month, the seller can deliver the commodity at any time during the specified month.

Participants in the commodity futures may be speculators or traders. Speculators do not generally take delivery of the commodity but hold a contract in the hope that the price of that commodity will rise so that they can subsequently sell the contract at a profit. Traders have a business reason for purchasing the commodity. Generally, traders are members of the commodity exchange and, because of their membership, can buy and sell the contract 'on the floor', and thereby pay reduced commission. Additionally, traders can execute on behalf of broking houses, for a commission.

Traders operate in the commodity futures markets to hedge their risks when purchasing raw materials for their businesses. This provides the economic justification of the futures market.

The commodity futures market is highly volatile and therefore, highly risky, but it does offer the speculative investor the opportunity of a large potential profit. When buying a futures contract a deposit of only 6 to 10 per cent of the contract price is required. The full price need only be paid when the contract is delivered. This provides a high gearing facility to the speculator, since large contracts can be purchased with relatively small funds. If the price of the commodity rises during the contract period, the speculator receives a profit according to the difference between the full price of the commodity at the date of sale and the date of purchase of the contract, and vice versa for a fall.

This differs from the options market, where a price attaches to the option itself, and profit or loss is determined according to the value placed on the option.

Table 4.9 Full list of futures contracts traded (*source: NYFE*)

CHICAGO BOARD OF TRADE	KANSAS CITY BOARD OF TRADE

CHICAGO BOARD OF TRADE
Wheat (5000 bushels)
Corn
Oats
Soybean
Soybean oil
Soybean meal
Iced broilers
Silver (5000 oz)
Gold (3 kg)
Gold (100 oz)
Plywood
GNMA mortgages, CD
GNMA mortgages, CDR
Commercial paper (90-day)
Commercial paper (30-day)
Treasury notes (4–6 years)*
Treasury bonds

MID AMERICA COMMODITY EXCHANGE
Wheat (1000 bushels)
Corn
Oats (5000 bushels)
Soybeans
Silver (1000 ozs)
Gold (old: 1 kg)
Gold (new: 33.2 oz)
Live cattle (20 000)
Live hogs (15 000)

CHICAGO MERCANTILE AND IMM
Fresh eggs
Potatoes
Live hogs (30 000)
Pork bellies, frozen
Live cattle (40 000)
Lumber
Seed lumber
Feeder cattle
British pound
Canadian dollar
Deutschemark
Japanese yen
Mexican peso
Swiss franc
Dutch guilder
US silver coins
French franc
Gold (100 oz)
Treasury bills (90-day)
Treasury bills (1 year)

KANSAS CITY BOARD OF TRADE
Wheat
Grain sorghums

MINNEAPOLIS GRAIN EXCHANGE
Wheat (5000 bushels)
Durum wheat

NEW YORK COFFEE AND SUGAR
Coffee 'c'
Sugar (11)
Sugar (12)

NEW YORK MERCANTILE EXCHANGE
Palladium
Platinum
US silver coins
Gold (1 kg)
Gold (400 oz)
British pound
Canadian dollar
Deutschemark
Japanese yen
Swiss franc
Imperial lean beef
Potatoes
No. 2 heating oil
No. 6 industrial fuel oil

NEW YORK COTTON EXCHANGE (CITRUS AND PETROLEUM)
Cotton (2)
Orange juice, frozen concentrate
Propane

NEW YORK COCOA EXCHANGE
Cocoa (30 000)
Rubber

COMMODITY EXCHANGE INC.
Copper
Zinc
Silver (5000 oz)
Gold (100 oz)

Since 7 Aug. 1980

NEW YORK FUTURES EXCHANGE
90-day treasury bills
20-year treasury bonds
British pound
Canadian dollar
Deutschemark
Japanese yen
Swiss franc

* Trading inaugurated June 1979. CDR: Collate depository receipt. CD: Certificate deliver.

Dealing and fees

The various types of investment instruments, detailed in the preceding Money market and Capital markets sections, are bought and sold through specialized institutions, and for each different category of securities different fee structures and methods of quotation apply. These are described as follows.

Money market securities

US Treasury bills

In the primary market for treasury bills, there are 33 dealers, although it is possible for anyone, including individuals, to bid for bills directly at the Federal Reserve. The Federal Reserve Bank of New York is the main issuer of treasury bills, acting as agent for the US Treasury.

Three- and six-month bills are issued weekly on a Thursday, and 12-month bills once a month. The rate of discount is determined by the market. New issues are first allotted to applicants with the highest bids and then subsequently to lower and lower bids until the issue is placed.

Treasury bills are quoted at a discount price and the difference between this discount price and the par value ($100) is the interest rate spread. For example, a 90-day bill quoted at $97\frac{1}{2}$ carries a rate of interest of $100 - 97\frac{1}{2} = 2\frac{1}{2}$ per cent for three months. Annualized, this is 10 per cent. The bond equivalent yield is $2.5/90 \times 365 = 10.14$ per cent (see Money market section). In the primary market the buyer incurs no additional fees if he applies directly to the Federal Reserve Bank. If he applies through a primary dealer, he will normally be charged a nominal sum of $25 to $40 per transaction. If he is dealing in a size of $0.25 million or more, this fee is usually waived.

In the secondary market, investors may buy or sell treasury bills through the many dealers, including the major banks and commission houses. In this market, the dealer takes a commission which is included in the difference between his bid and offer prices.

In dealing jargon, only the decimal points are normally quoted, and these are called 'basis points'. For example if a bill is quoted at 24–20 it means the dealer will buy (bid) at a discount price (against par) of say 10.24 per cent and sell (offer) at 10.20 per cent.

Minimum denominations are $10 000, although in the primary market, and any application of under $1 million is awarded on the average resultant bid price and is not bid directly.

Treasury notes and bonds. US Government and federal agency securities

The dealers in these markets are the same as those for treasury bills, although some specialist primary dealers exist for the issuing of certain agency securities.

Notes and bonds are quoted free of accrued interest, in units of $\frac{1}{32}$s. As with treasury bills, dealers tend to omit the integer and to quote only the numerator of

110

the fraction. For example, the treasury $11\frac{7}{8}$ 15 August 1983 18–22 means that the dealer will buy at say, $94\frac{18}{32}$ and sell at $94\frac{22}{32}$. If the price is quoted at $18+-22+$, it means that $\frac{1}{64}$ should be added, i.e., $94\frac{37}{64}$ to $94\frac{63}{64}$.

The addition of $\frac{1}{128}$s are quoted as '$\frac{1}{4}$s of $\frac{1}{32}$', thus $18\frac{1}{4}$–$31\frac{1}{4}$ means $94\frac{73}{128}$ to $94\frac{125}{128}$.

Specific fees are not charged by the dealers, but the difference between their bid and offer prices include some margin commission.

The minimum denominations that can be dealt in vary between securities (see Money market section). Many are $1000, but treasury notes and bonds are commonly in units of $5000 and many agency securities in units of $10 000. Any dealings in amounts of less than $100 000 however are dealt on average market prices and terms that cannot generally be negotiated.

Settlement and delivery

For all government and agency issues (including treasury bills), delivery and settlement usually occurs on the following business day. This is known as regular delivery. Other terms do exist:

Cash delivery, for settlement on the same day;
Skip day delivery, for settlement two days after transaction;
Corporate delivery, for settlement five business days after transaction, so called because of the settlement period in corporation bond market.

Market jargon

Every financial market has its own terminology and it is useful for any potential investor to have some understanding of it. The following terms are commonly used in the market for US government and federal agency securities.

A basis point is 0.01 per cent of yield, so that if the market is said to have moved by 25 basis points it has moved by $\frac{1}{4}$ per cent.

A locked market is one in which the bid and offer prices are exactly the same. This may occur at the same single dealer or between two different dealers. It represents an arbitrage situation but does not last more than a few minutes at most.

The street is a collective term for primary dealers or, effectively, for the market.

Hung up—an issue is 'hung up' if dealers have not yet managed to place the whole of the new issue.

Hung up in the street means that unplaced issues are still in the hands of primary dealers.

On a yield basis—some issues are auctioned off when only its size and maturity are known. Yield, and thus prices, are not disclosed until one or two days later.

When issued basis is similar but refers to new issues that are auctioned off before they are settled, i.e., they are traded before being issued.

Active issues list is a short list of the most recently issued bills and bonds/notes. It is used to measure market movements. For example, 'the long end is up a quarter' means that the most recently issued long (15–30 years) bonds are up one quarter of a point, or $\frac{8}{32}$nds.

111

Refunding is the issue of a new debt to replace part or all of an old debt.

Even roll is a refunding where approximately the same amount of debt is being issued for old debt.

Pay down is a refunding where less new debt is being issued.

New cash is the extra amount of new debt raised in a refunding.

Book entry form is the term used for the automatic clearing system by which most securities are issued. The majority of bonds are cleared from one custodian account to another electronically and it is therefore rare that securities are actually physically delivered.

Repurchase agreements, CDs, Bankers' acceptances, commercial paper

As with government and agency securities, dealers in other money market instruments do not charge a fee, but make their commission on the difference between the bid and the offer prices.

The primary dealers are the large commercial banks handling RPs, CDs and BAs, and commission houses dealing in commercial paper.

Transactions in the secondary market can be made through any of the large commercial US banks or through any of the major international banks. Settlement and delivery is normally for the following business day, except in the case of RPs which are always settled for cash on the same business day.

Corporate bonds

Corporate bonds may be dealt through commission houses (stockbrokers), investment banks and commercial banks who act as agents via their commercial or trust departments.

As with government and agency bonds, commission is included in the spread between bid and offer prices. In an active market, this spread is in the region of $\frac{1}{4}$ to $\frac{3}{8}$ of a point.

Settlement and delivery is for cash five business days after the transaction has taken place. Sometimes an alternative term, 'delayed delivery', operates seven or more business days after the transaction.

Equity shares (stocks) and options

Dealers in stocks are the same as those in the corporate bond market.

Investors generally use one of the commission houses to deal on one of the exchanges, and use commission houses, banks and other dealers to trade on the OTC.

When dealing on one of the stock exchanges, a complex fee structure exists. At one time brokers followed a fixed commission system, but on 1 May 1975 (May day) this was abandoned and the SEC required that all broking houses set their own commission rate structure.

Since 'May day', the cost of all transactions is now agreed by negotiation between client and broker (or dealer). In practice, only large transactions (i.e., in excess of $100 000) are usually negotiated. Smaller transactions are usually charged commissions at posted rates, which in most cases are higher than the pre-May-day rates.

As a very rough guide, the following rates give an indication of the amount of fees that might typically be payable.

Orders for 100 shares or less:

Dollar value $	Commission
Up to 162.50	10% of funds
162.50–1099.99	$13 + 2% of funds
1100.00–2499.99	$21.25 + 1.25% of funds
2500.00 +	$80.73

The maximum commission for a single round lot or odd lot is $80.73.

Orders for 100 or more shares:

Dollar value $	Commission
200–1099.99	$13 + 2% of funds
1100–2499.99	$21.25 + 1.25% of funds
2500 +	$176.364 + 0.49% of funds

Plus an additional $5 for each round lot of shares dealt.

Since 'May day' the opportunity has arisen for the development of a new type of broker, known as the discount broker. These brokers charge commission at rates of about 50 per cent of those charged by other brokers. However they offer no advice, custodial service, or any other facility apart from making the transaction.

Stocks traded 'over the counter' are sold to the client on a net price basis, that is, the price as quoted by the dealer has already taken into account the dealer's commission.

Settlement and delivery for stocks traded on stock exchanges or on the OTC is for cash five business days after the transaction is made.

Commodities and financial futures markets

These are dealt on specialized exchanges—through specialist commission houses, though also some of the larger stockbrokers—and trading takes place through a member of the particular exchange.

Commission rates are negotiable but may be on a flat fee basis, such as $100 round turn (for purchase and sale) or as a percentage of the consideration such as $\frac{1}{8}$ or $\frac{1}{4}$ per cent per transaction.

Settlement is usually for cash the following business day.

Financial and monetary systems

Financial institutions

The US has two broad categories of deposit-taking institutions, the savings institutions and the commercial banks.

Savings banks

The savings institutions may be classified into one of three types, these comprise:

1. Savings banks that are usually mutual associations with no capital structure and that accept all sizes of deposits although federally insured for deposits of up to $100 000 only.
2. Credit unions which do have a share capital structure and accept small deposits from individuals. Their deposits are insured by their own agencies.
3. Savings and loan associations, some of which have a mutual structure and others which have an equity capital structure and accept deposits of up to $100 000. These account for about 80 per cent of all savings banks' deposits.

All these types of non-commercial banks pay interest on their deposits and use the funds so obtained to grant credit and mortgages to their customers. As at January 1981 new regulations allowed them to expand their operations so they can now offer chequing account and credit card facilities.

Commercial banks

Commercial banks may also be classified according to four categories; these are:

- federally chartered banks;
- state chartered banks that are members of the Federal Reserve;
- state chartered banks that are not members of the Federal Reserve but are insured by the FDIC;
- state chartered banks that are neither members of the Federal Reserve nor insured by the FDIC.

Commercial banks may thus be federally or state chartered and subject to either federal or state regulations. Together, they account for about 40 per cent of total household savings and time deposits. The remaining 60 per cent is held by savings banks.

Federally chartered banks are subject to both sets of regulations and must also be members of the Federal Reserve System. State chartered banks are not obliged to, but may, seek membership of the Federal Reserve System. Of the 14 000 commercial banks, only about 1450 are members of the Federal Reserve although these represent about 68 per cent of all banking assets and about 80 per cent of commercial bank deposits. Banks that are members of the Federal Reserve System are insured by the Federal Deposit Insurance Corporation (FDIC).

State chartered banks that are not members of the Federal Reserve may also be insured by the FDIC provided they meet certain financial criteria. The state chartered non-member banks account for about one fifth of commercial bank assets. The state chartered banks that are neither members of the Federal Reserve nor are insured by the FDIC, account for less than one per cent of commercial banking assets. Recently passed regulations will however expand the Federal Reserve authority to cover virtually all financial institutions by 1985.

Federal reserve system

The Federal Reserve System was created in 1917 and its present authority is legally constructed under the Banking Acts of 1933 and 1935 in order to fulfil the functions of a central bank; that is to issue notes and coins, regulate the money supply, hold legal reserves of its member commercial banks, and supervise the banking regulations with respect to its member banks. The Federal Reserve, or Fed as it is commonly abbreviated, is not a single entity but a co-ordinated national system of banking authorities. There are twelve federal reserve districts, namely New York, Boston, Philadelphia, Cleveland, Richmond, Atlanta, Chicago, St. Louis, Minneapolis, Kansas City, Dallas and San Francisco. Each of these contains a federal reserve bank, although some have branches, which increases the number of banks in the Fed to 26. The Federal Reserve System has a seven-man board of governors which is appointed by the President, ratified by the Senate, and which reports to Congress. The board of governors is responsible for the supervision of the 12 main federal reserve banks, the regulations of the commercial banking system, and the exercising of monetary policy.

Members of the board of governors are also members of the open market committee, to which an additional five members are nominated by the federal reserve banks. This committee decides how open market operations should be used to achieve the government's monetary objectives and forwards directives to the Federal Reserve Banks (FRBs) who act as agents to the government, in effecting monetary policy.

Commercial banks are not legally required to be members of the Federal Reserve. The advantage of membership is the facility to discount eligible bills with the Fed, which gives member banks a source from which to borrow short-term funds when their liquidity is temporarily tight. They may do this at the discount rate which is normally below other interest rates prevailing in the money market. A further advantage is the free cheque-releasing facilities. For non-member banks, cheques are cleared by member banks for a fee. The disadvantage of membership is that member banks are required to contribute three per cent of their capital and free reserves to the capital of their local federal reserve bank, and to make available a further three per cent subject to call by the Fed. Additionally, member banks are subject to more stringent reserve requirements in that, although the ratio applied to members is the same as for non-members, the type of asset acceptable as reserves is restricted only to cash held in the banks' own vaults or held interest free at the Fed. Non-members may hold reserves in the form of interest-bearing assets such as call balances at other banks or near-cash items in the process of collection.

An increasing number of banks found that the costs of a Fed membership were outweighing the benefits and were therefore resigning their membership. This trend has now been stopped by legislation recently passed allowing the Fed to impose the requirements on all financial institutions.

Monetary policy

Since 6 October 1979, the US monetary authorities have operated a system of monetary base control. This requires controlled growth of the money supply as measured by specific monetary indicators (see Economic statistics below). The major components of all these indicators is domestic deposits, against which banks can advance credit, and it is such lending which increases the quantity of money in the economy. The monetary base can therefore be made to grow at a slower or faster rate by drawing money from, or adding it to, the deposit banking system.

The main method used by the Federal Reserve to regulate the amount of money and credit in the system is that of open market operations. By daily operating in the market, the Fed is able, through the sheer volume of its transactions, to directly influence monetary aggregates. Effectively, it alters the balance between the supply and demand for credit in the economy. However, if the Fed directs its monetary tools towards controlling the quantity of money, it cannot also control the price of money. A major consequence, therefore, is volatile interest rates in response to changes in short-term liquidity caused by the Fed's operations in the market. Additionally, because the USA is an open economy, the value of the dollar on the foreign exchange markets fluctuates sympathetically with interest-rate movements. Apart from its market oriented methods of intervention, the Fed uses few supplementary tools of monetary management. Discount policy is used only as an indirect tool, in conjunction with open market operations. Reserve requirements are an important tool, on which the Fed has recently been placing great emphasis. Also important is the method by which reserves are transferred within the banking system as this helps set the environment in which the Fed's transactions are conducted.

Reserve requirements

The Federal Reserve imposes on its members a progressive scale of reserve ratios with the actual proportion of liabilities required to be deposited as reserve assets dependent on the size and type of bank. For example different ratios apply to country banks and city banks and, as regards size, ratios depend on whether the bank's savings and time deposits are more or less than $5 million. Regulation D, introduced on 1 November 1980 applies to all banks across the board. In the past there was a graduated scale against the issue of domestic CDs and a zero rate on CDs issued in the Euromarkets. The reserve requirement is now three per cent against all types of CDs issued by all banks.

The Fed recently experimented (between October 1979 and mid 1980) in changing the emphasis of monetary control towards reserve policy and away from open market operations. The object was to limit the expansion of credit through direct control of the monetary base. Interest rates were consequently left to find their own levels, depending on demand and supply in the money market. Supply of credit in the economy was manipulated by the Fed through the imposition of reserve requirements, which, following 6 October, became more flexible and selective with respect to the types of liabilities to which they were applied. The result was a rapid rise in short-term interest rates to an unprecedented peak of more than 20 per cent. As demand at such levels abated, there subsequently followed a fall in interest rates, just as rapidly, to below 10 per cent. Such volatile reaction in interest rates has led the Fed towards moderating reserve policy and applying a more balanced mix of reserve requirements and open market operations.

The use of reserve requirements has limitations as an effective policy tool. Firstly, they are applied at present only to banks who are members of the Fed. Other banks are required to maintain minimum reserve requirements but these are set by the banking authorities of the states in which the banks are chartered. Although state reserve ratios are usually the same as those imposed by the Fed, the range of assets is broader and includes interest-bearing deposits placed at call with other banks. Thus, the cost to banks who are not members of the Fed is lower. The previous freedom of the banks to resign membership therefore imposed a constraint on the Fed in its ability to substantially increase the reserve requirements such that it affected the whole banking system. Recent proposals from the Federal Reserve recommend, however, that reserve requirements should apply to all transaction accounts, including those not previously counted in the banking system—such as savings banks—and whose balances have not been previously measured in the definition of the money supply. Secondly, the Fed itself undertakes not to increase reserve requirements by more than half of one per cent at any time. This prohibits the Fed from using reserve requirements as a fine tuning instrument.

Federal funds market

Reserve requirements must be met on a daily basis over a statement week which runs from Thursday to Wednesday (Statement Day). Excess reserves, equivalent to two per cent of required reserves, can be carried over from one reserve-averaging week to the next. However, banks tend to get rid of excess reserves (which do not earn interest) at whatever price as the reserve-averaging week approaches the end. Conversely reserve deficiencies of more than two per cent of required reserves are subject to a penalty charge by the Fed at discount rate plus two per cent. Thus, banks with reserve deficiencies borrow funds from banks with reserve surpluses. These funds are termed federal funds or fed funds.

As a consequence of the averaging week, the fed funds interest rate falls or rises sharply on a Wednesday, depending on the overall adequacy of reserves in the banking system. Federal funds, therefore, are any funds available within the Federal Reserve System, but not subject to reserve requirements. It is however the accounting concept only. Excess funds are transferred as book entries to balance deficiencies elsewhere.

Immediately available funds

Liabilities of the Federal Reserve are called 'immediately available funds', because, through a nationwide electronic communications network, these funds can be converted to cash or transferred anywhere in the US within a single day, on demand. This network is used so that any member bank may send or receive immediately available funds in the form of reserve deposits to or from any other member bank.

The transaction normally occurs within one banking day and, if the transaction is only a transfer of funds between branches of the same member bank, only book entries are involved. Effectively, therefore, the fed funds market is an overnight interest loan market.

117

The fed funds market has grown considerably since 1964 when the Federal Reserve Banks first allowed member banks to legally purchase corresponding balances from non-member banks. This encouraged the smaller banks, who are normally continual net lenders, to supply surplus funds to the larger banks, who tend to be continual net borrowers.

Further impetus to the growth of the market was given in 1970 when commercial banks that are members of the Fed were permitted to purchase the surplus balances from other non-bank institutions, such as government and federal agencies, savings and loan associations, mutual savings banks, and also branches of foreign banks established in the US.

Thus, the fed funds market is now broader than just a market in reserve balances between member banks. It is now a market in immediately available funds between all banks and non-bank financial institutions.

The fed funds rate of interest is the market equilibrium rate at which immediately available funds are cleared between the banks and financial institutions and it is closely correlated with, but normally higher than, the discount rate at which member banks may borrow from the Fed (see below).

Repurchase agreements Closely related to the fed funds market is the market in repurchase agreements (RPs). It, too, is a market in immediately available funds, and very often takes place within one business day.

The essential difference between the fed funds market and the RP market lies in the method of borrowing. While the fed funds market involves no physical transfers in the RP market, banks and financial institutions with temporary liquidity deficiencies borrow surplus funds from other institutions by transferring securities, with an agreement to buy them back at a specified date, usually the next day. The transaction may take place in one of two ways. Either the securities are sold and repurchased at the same price, with an additional charge which represents a rate of return commensurate with market levels of interest, or the repurchase price is set at a higher rate than the selling price, the difference representing the rate of return.

The securities pledged in a repurchase agreement are usually government or federal agency securities, since the funds acquired by member banks from the sale of these, rather than other, securities are free from reserve requirements.

The RP rate of interest is close to, but slightly below, the fed funds rate. Reverse RPs are exactly the same but is viewed from the side of the lender of funds. He receives securities on a short-term basis, with an agreement to sell them back at a given time for which he obtains a return on the cash he has temporarily lent.

The RP market is much broader than the fed funds market in that anyone can participate. Corporations with surplus cash may lend to the banking system, and although transactions usually occur in amounts of $1 million, or more, even individuals may, and do, also participate.

Discount policy

The Federal Reserve acts as lender of last resort to its member banks. Each of the 12 federal reserve banks has a discount window. If the banks need to borrow funds to make up their reserve positions they have a choice between using the discount windows or some other part of the money market.

In order to borrow from the discount window, banks must lodge eligible bills with the Fed which then discounts them. Federal Reserve loans to banks are direct advances in the form of promissory notes secured by government obligations or by eligible paper put forward for discounting. Maturities are up to 90 days. Notes may be paid in full or in part before maturity, in which case unearned discount is rebated. The amount due on the note is automatically charged against the borrowing bank's reserve account on the maturity date.

The rate at which the Fed discounts eligible bills (the discount rate) is not a managed rate, but a market led rate of interest, although it is usually below other rates. The discount rate alone is not, therefore, an effective tool of monetary policy but it does exert an influence on the market when co-ordinated with open market operations (see below).

The choice between using the discount window or the money market can affect the total volume of reserves in the banking system and may alter the overall credit position in the economy. If open market operations are conducted by the Fed, then reserves are affected. Trading by the banks in money market instruments such as fed funds and treasury securities involves no creation of bank reserves; existing reserves are just transferred within the banking system. In contrast, when borrowings or repayments at the discount window result in a net change in the federal reserve position, the volume of total bank reserves is affected.

Since banks can shift reserves back and forth between markets, clearly the discount rate and the fed funds rate are closely related. Prior to 1965, the discount rate had served as a ceiling on the fed funds rate because most banks borrowed in the fed funds market only occasionally, and only in relatively small amounts. The use of the discount window occurred whenever the fed funds rate approached the discount rate, the latter thus acting as a brake on the fed funds rate. The increase in lending and the need for liability management during the sixties and early seventies resulted in banks borrowing fed funds more frequently and in larger amounts to the extent that they would not be accommodated at the discount window. The increased demand for federal funds caused the (federal funds) rate of interest to exceed the discount rate, and this has been the position for most of the time since.

Another money market rate which is frequently quoted in the financial press, and which may appropriately be described here, is the prime rate. This is the rate at which commercial banks will lend to their prime customers, i.e. those with the highest credit rating. *Prime rate*

This rate is usually a couple of percentage points higher than the discount and fed funds rate and, while it follows the same trends, it is a determined rate calculated from money market rates, specifically from the 90-day CD rate.

Banks will adjust their price rate whenever they think it has got out of line with the money market. Usually one bank will announce a change ahead of the market, but other banks will very quickly follow suit. The calculation used to determine the prime rate is:

119

$$90 \text{ CD rate} \div (100 - \text{reserve ratio})$$

For example, if reserve requirement .... = 8%
and 90-day CD rate .... = 10%
then prime rate .... = $\frac{10}{92}$
.... = 10.8%
rounded to include the bank's profit margin = 11%

Open market operations

The New York Federal Reserve Bank alone transacts dealings from what is known as the Federal Reserve Open Market Desk. It uses the desk to add or subtract reserves to and from the banking system. Usually the Fed enters the market between 10.20 a.m. and 12 noon New York time, and through the 33 primary dealers carries out transactions usually in two types of instruments, namely repurchase agreements and treasury bills or notes.

It may execute RPs or purchase treasury securities when it wants to add to reserves and execute reverse RPs or sell treasury bills when it wants to drain reserves from the system.

Although RPs and treasuries are the major securities traded, the New York Fed also undertakes open market operations in other money market instruments and also in foreign currencies in order to stabilize the exchange rate.

As open market operations withdraw reserves from the market, the banks have to restore their reserves by borrowing either at the discount window or in the fed funds market. Such increased demand tends to push up the discount rate and consequently other short-term interest rates. If the policy is sustained, then long-term interest rates will follow. Thus, borrowing becomes more expensive throughout the economy resulting in a contraction of credit and a controlling influence on inflation.

If open market operations increase reserves in the system, then the existence of surplus funds in the market depresses interest rates and the reverse process applies.

Another policy at the disposal of the Fed, which has sometimes been used in conjunction with open market operations, is Regulation Q which gives the Fed the power to impose interest rate ceilings on bank time and savings deposits. This has the effect of shifting funds from the banking sector to the money market and thereby reducing the banks' deposit funds. The banks are thus obliged to bid for funds in the market which also has the effect of pushing up money market rates. Regulation Q is, however, now being phased out over the next few years.

Open market operations is the most flexibly used instrument of monetary policy and it is facilitated by large and active US money and capital markets. It is necessitated by the restrictions placed on reserve policy and because the discount rate is not used as an administered rate.

Other monetary instruments

The Federal Reserve's main aim in its use of monetary instruments is to control the money supply (see below). It does not, to any great extent, attempt to maintain a predetermined exchange value on the dollar. The assumption is that control over the domestic economy will result in a rational value of the dollar. The Fed merely attempts to stabilize excessive fluctuations in the exchange value by open market operations in the spot foreign exchange market.

The Fed may also occasionally use moral suasion to request the banks to contain their loan growth within specified limits and, conversely, it may make exceptions for loans to stimulate depressed sections of the economy.

Economic statistics

The economic statistics which influence monetary policy are released as follows:

1. *Money supply.* Several definitions of money supply are used and the information is available at different times.

   M1*a*. Currency and demand deposits at commercial banks (eliminates chequing deposits at foreign commercial banks and official institutions). Weekly release.

   M1*b*. Adds deposits at all other financial institutions that may be used to pay bills, etc. This includes savings banks, savings and loan associations, credit unions and thrift institutions. Weekly release.

   M2. Adds overnight repurchase agreements at commercial banks, overnight Eurodollar deposits held by non-bank US entities, savings accounts of less than $100 000 and funds in money market mutual funds. Mid-month release.

   M3. Adds large time deposits and term repurchase agreements (two days or longer). Mid-month release.

   L/M3. Adds term Eurodollar deposits held by US non-bank entities, bankers' acceptances, commercial paper, US savings bonds and all US treasury securities up to one year maturity. End-of-the-month release.

2. *Reserves.* Weekly from New York Fed, Friday afternoon.
3. *Reserve assets.* The fourth Tuesday or Wednesday of each month.
4. *Balance of trade.* Usually 27th of each month.
5. *Balance of payments.* Quarterly.
6. *Leading indicators.* Usually 27th of each month.
7. *Consumer price index.* Usually 22nd of each month.
8. *Real spendable earnings.* Third Thursday or Friday of each month.
9. *Wholesale price index.* End of second week in each month.
10. *GNP.* Quarterly.
11. *Productivity.* Quarterly.
12. *Industrial production.* Usually 15th of each month.
13. *Unemployment.* First Friday of each month.

Withholding taxes

Interest

Withholding taxes are chargeable on interest paid to non-resident companies and individuals. This excludes bank deposit interest paid by insurance companies. The standard rate is 30 per cent but for most countries having a tax treaty with the USA this is reduced to zero.

Table 4.10

	Interest, %	Dividends (portfolio), %	Dividends (substantial holdings), %
Non-resident corporations and individuals			
Non-treaty countries	30	30	30
Treaty countries:			
Australia	30	15	15
Austria	0	15	5
Belgium	15	15	15
Canada	15	15	15
Denmark	0	15	5
Finland	0	15	5
France	10	15	5
Germany	0	15	15
Greece	0	30	30
Iceland	0	15	5
Ireland	0	15	5
Italy	30	15	5
Japan	10	15	10
Luxembourg	0	15	5
Netherlands	0	15	5
Netherlands Antilles	0	15	5
New Zealand	30	15	5
Norway	0	15	10
Pakistan	30	30	15
Poland	0	15	5
Romania	10	10	10
South Africa	30	30	30
Sweden	0	15	5
Switzerland	5	15	5
Trinidad and Tobago	30	30	30
United Kingdom	0	15	15
United Kingdom Overseas Territories	30	15	5
USSR	30	30	30

Dividends

Dividends are subject to a withholding tax of 30 per cent but tax treaties in most cases reduce the rate to 15 per cent for portfolio dividends and 5 per cent for dividends paid by companies to non-residents having a substantial shareholding in that company. A substantial shareholding is normally 5 per cent or more.

Exemptions

Interest earned from the following securities is exempt from withholding tax:

- all securities issued at a discount to par;
- all securities having an original maturity of six months or less;
- all bonds issued in the US domestic market by foreign borrowers (Yankee bonds);
- all Eurodollar bonds which are traded outside the US domestic market.

Exchange controls

Authorities

A number of government authorities are responsible for specific sections of the exchange regulations. With respect to foreign payments and foreign inward portfolio investment, no controls apply so there are no supervisory authorities. Exceptions apply to transactions with certain specified countries (or their residents) with which the US has restricted trade, e.g. Cuba, Kampuchea, North Korea and Vietnam. Transactions involving these countries require licences from the Treasury Department.

Currency

The currency is the US dollar which floats freely with respect to all other convertible currencies. The authorities, the Federal Reserve Bank, intervene in the spot foreign exchange market, using mainly sterling, Deutschemark, Yen and Swiss francs, only to smooth out excessive fluctuations in the dollar's external value.

All residents and non-residents are freely permitted to operate in the spot and forward foreign exchange markets.

Purchase of securities

Non-residents, except those of restricted countries noted above, may freely purchase any type of US dollar denominated securities. One notable exception is the purchase of controlling interests in US banks which are subject to federal and state banking regulations.

Non-residents may repatriate all proceeds from investments, free of any restrictions.

Gold

Apart from residents of the above restricted countries, all residents and non-residents may purchase and export gold in any form.

Purchases and sales are free from licensing, tax or duty. Commercial imports of jewellery are, however, subject to import duty at 12 per cent.

5. Austria

General market environment

Austria is a small country and this is reflected in its domestic money and capital markets. It provides limited scope for the non-resident investor, there being virtually no available money market paper except for certificates of deposit issued by the major banks and only a small volume of capital market issues. Balanced against this, however, is the fact that Austria has a stable currency and a strong economy. The economy is an open one relying to a large degree on international trade, particularly with Germany to which Austria's own economy is closely linked. The government's attitude to foreign investment is generally favourable, although the central bank has authority to impose constraints on the inflow of foreign capital when the currency is subject to strong upward pressure. Apart from these policies, which are not currently in force, exchange control regulations are generally liberal.

Table 5.1   Summary of instruments

Instrument	Characteristics
MONEY MARKET	
Deposits	
call deposits	Not an interbank market. Terms available as short as overnight. Interest rates nominal
time deposits	Market becoming more competitive
eurocurrency deposits	Good market, but market more active for shorter-term deposits
Certificates of deposits	Kassenobligationen—notes issued by banks with maturities of up to five years
Other money market instruments	A few treasury bills and commercial bills issued. Virtually no market
Anonymous savings accounts	Accounts through which deposits, withdrawals and security transactions can be made but ownership is totally anonymous
CAPITAL MARKET	
Corporate bonds	Limited market. Small volume outstanding and thin secondary market
Equities	Trading limited to a few major companies. Dominated by banks and the state
Gold	Available to non-residents, but subject to VAT

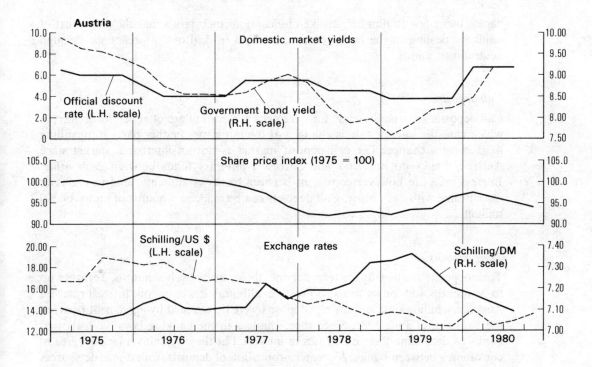

Austria

Domestic market yields

Official discount rate (L.H. scale)

Government bond yield (R.H. scale)

Share price index (1975 = 100)

Schilling/US $ (L.H. scale)

Exchange rates

Schilling/DM (R.H. scale)

1975 1976 1977 1978 1979 1980

Withholding taxes also are lenient, being applied to dividends but not to interest. Banking secrecy, as in Switzerland, is also a feature of Austrian financial markets. Anonymity of beneficial ownership of securities is also preserved.

The principal financial centre is Vienna, although the major banks have branches and provide some facilities for non-residents in other cities including Linz, Graz and Innsbruck.

The country comprises nine states and 4000 municipalities.

The money market

Deposits

Banks in Austria accept call and time deposits in Austrian schillings as well as providing a market in Eurocurrency deposits. The majority of businesses and individuals place deposits with the savings banks although all types of banks accept all forms of Austrian schilling deposits. Rates for time deposits used to be fixed by agreement between banks although the cartel has recently been broken. As from 1 July 1980 the joint stock commercial banks have been free to determine their own interest rates. Nevertheless, the Austrian money market is not yet an automatically functioning mechanism equalizing demand and supply through interest rate adjustments. An interbank market exists for the purpose of the banks balancing their accounts at the Austrian National Bank and for adjusting their liquidity but the banks, being few in number, dislike disclosing to their rivals that they are short of funds by dealing in the open market and tend to deal out of preference through neutral institutions.

Call deposits

Call deposits are usually made for overnight periods but are often left for longer, in which case the interest rate is changed at the initiative of either party if prevailing market rates change. The call deposit market is not an interbank market since Austrian banks do not lend and borrow temporary funds between each other. Interest rates are however consistent between banks as all banks tend to maintain rates in line with each other. Call deposits can be made in amounts of up to As 300 million.

Time deposits

Time deposits are usually for terms of one, three, six or twelve months. Terms of up to 36 months and longer are also possible, although less common. Interest rates on Austrian schilling time and savings deposits were determined by agreement between the banks until June 1980. Since then, changes in the banking laws have allowed banks to determine their own rates of interest, but there remains a large degree of consistency between banks. A greater proportion of deposits from domestic sources is placed in savings deposits rather than time deposits. Savings deposits have periods of notice of at least three months. The most popular are tied savings deposits, which have at least twelve months' notice of withdrawal.

Eurocurrency deposits

The Austrian banks, mainly the four largest in Vienna, also accept call and time deposits in other convertible currencies. This market has developed quite significantly during the 1970s due largely to the fact that the OPEC headquarters are in Vienna and consequently substantial sums are sometimes invested in the Euromarkets through banks in Vienna. The market, although not particularly active, is of sufficient size that deposits of up to $300 million may easily be accommodated. Most Eurocurrency deposits placed in Austria are concentrated at the shorter end of the market.

Certificates of deposit (Kassenobligationen)

Kassenobligationen are deposit certificates with maturities of from one month up to five years. They are issued only by the large banks in volumes of up to about As 2 million per year. For certificates of, for example, six months' maturity the minimum amount for which the securities are available is As 100 000. They are not very negotiable in the secondary market but may only be sold back to the issuing bank.

Other money market instruments

The central bank on behalf of the Treasury, issues treasury bills, but these may not be purchased either by the resident non-bank sector or by non-residents. They are placed exclusively with credit institutions.

Commercial bills are issued, but are not usually traded as a money market instrument between banks and are not available to the non-bank sector, either resident or non-resident. The banks tend to hold them in their own portfolios to maturity although certain types of commercial bills are also eligible for rediscounting with the central bank.

There is no other money market paper issued.

Anonymous savings book accounts

Savings accounts can be opened with the major banks in Austria which are anonymous even to the bank in which the money is placed. The savings book is issued to bearer together with a code word. The bank at no time needs to know the identity of the depositor thus the account is more secret than bank accounts in any other country—including Switzerland.

In theory a depositor must be resident in Austria for a minimum of a few months but since the accounts are completely anonymous there is no way of checking the status of the account book holder.

Austrian and foreign securities can also be bought and sold through these accounts thus preserving anonymity of beneficial ownership. At present interest earned on anonymous accounts is not taxed but the government is reviewing the possibility of introducing a withholding tax which would be in the region of 10 to 20 per cent.

The capital market

The Austrian capital market is small. One reason is that although there is a high level of savings in Austria, much has been directed in the past into the public sector through the medium of public capital markets. Private sector companies consequently have tended to go directly to banks or loan institutions for funds although corporations do also raise capital in the bond market when larger amounts are required.

The domestic capital market is constituted 80 per cent by bonds and 20 per cent by equities, measured in terms of nominal capital value, which in total is about As 322 billion outstanding. In the primary market, the number of new issues average about 50 to 70 issues per year and consist mainly of bonds issued with maturities of between 6 and 15 years. In 1979 gross new capital market public issues amounted to As 54 962 million. Only three per cent (As 32 605 million) of this was represented by new share issues, 61 per cent (As 32 605 million) were government and public sector bond issues, while 33 per cent were bonds issued by the banks and other financial institutions. In most years Austrian companies and public institutions have issued bonds abroad in foreign markets, in amounts roughly equivalent to the total volume they have issued domestically.

127

Table 5.2 New Public Issues of Bonds in millions of Austrian schillings (*source: Austrian National Bank*)

	1978		1979		1980	
	Gross	Net	Gross	Net	Gross	Net†
PUBLIC AUTHORITIES						
Federal government	21 740	17 156	26 255	18 590	24 530	
Provinces and municipalities	2 800	1 507	3 150	1 775	3 350	
Public funds	900	428	1 600	1 222	200	
Other public bodies	1 650	1 148	1 600	1 024	1 000	
Electricity supply services	2 100	−195	400	−2 101		
Industry	800	176	800	150		
Other	....	−38	....	−40		
Foreign issues	400	291	1 250	1 141	1 000	
Domestic banks	12 550	10 849	18 130	15 006	11 520	
Total bonds	42 920	31 322	53 185	36 767	41 600	
Shares						
financial institutions	329		688			
non financial institutions	2 781		1 089		1 151	

† Data not provided in 1980 Austrian National Bank Report.

Total bond issues represented As 53 185 million gross in 1979 which was a net increase over 1978 of As 36 767 million after allowing for redemptions and amortizations. Table 5.2 shows new security issues for 1978 to 1980.

The primary bond market in Austria is regulated by the Capital Market Committee which comprises representatives from Kontrolbank and other main commercial banks. The Interbank Committee—a subgroup of the Capital Market Committee—meets monthly and controls the queue of issues and coupon rates.

The secondary market is conducted mostly over-the-counter by the banks and is virtually a perfect market.

Publicly issued bonds in Austria have a maturity range of between 6 and 15 years. They may be redeemed in full at maturity or by a redemption schedule which may be either by lottery or by repurchase or redemption on the open market.

Coupon rates are determined by the general level of interest rates prevailing in the market at the time of issue, resulting from the free market interplay of supply and demand.

Publicly issued bonds are normally in bearer form in denominations of As 1000. Bearer bonds need not take the form of securities but may be deposit receipts representing a share in a global bond deposited with a bank. The holder of the deposit receipt retains exactly the same rights as if he were the holder of a physical security. In fact, the deposit receipts may also be traded on the stock exchange. For example, Bundesobligationen are global bonds issued in sizes of two to four billion schillings. The global bonds are placed with banks but deposit receipts representing a share in the bond may be purchased on the stock exchange. Non-residents may have accounts with their domestic central banks and their investments in the bond can thus be represented by deposit receipts which may be transferred to other safe custody.

Public sector bonds

The Republic of Austria is the largest single issuer of bonds. All bonds issued by the government, together with those issued by the Lander governments (provinces) are gilt-edged securities and are thus eligible for investment of trustee funds. Other bonds issued by the municipalities, public funds and other public bodies are not classified as gilt-edged securities but are nonetheless regarded as high-quality bonds.

Bank bonds

Next to the Republic of Austria, the banking sector is the second largest issuer of bonds. The banks have increasingly raised capital through the issue of bonds during the last decade. This is partly because bond issues have become more important as a means of raising capital and have been further facilitated by recent changes in the laws on issuing securities. These have increased the number of banking institutions that are entitled to issue securities.

During the 1970s roughly three-quarters of the capital raised by bank bond issues were indirect issues on behalf of the non-bank sector. The remainder was used by the banks to increase their own capital liabilities against which they can increase their direct lending.

Banks issue four types of bonds: certificates of deposit (Kassenobligationen), funded bonds, registered debentures and mortgage and municipal financing bonds. Only certain types of banks are authorized to issue these latter types of bonds.

Kassenobligationen, as previously defined, are bearer interest-bearing notes of up to 5 years' maturity. Funded bonds are defined as gilt-edged securities because they are backed by specific assets of the issuing bank. These assets, usually covering government stock, are set aside by the issuing bank to satisfy the claims of the funded bond holders, in preference to other creditors, in the event of default or liquidation of the issuing bank. The value of the bonds may not however exceed the value of the covering stock. The issuing bank may not make transactions in the covering stock except with the authorization of the government commissioner. Funded bank bonds are bearer securities.

Registered debentures are not bearer bonds but if they are marked 'order' they may be transferred by endorsement. Unlike most other bonds, they may be issued for any maturity. The debentures repay principal in full at maturity and pay interest annually during the life of the issue.

Mortgage banks and two other authorized banks (Creditandstalt and Credit Institut—a subsidiary of Länderbank) issue mortgage bonds (pfanbrief) which are secured against mortgages and municipal loans or cash claims on public institutions. As with funded bank bonds, mortgage and municipal financing bonds are classified as gilt edged securities.

129

Other bonds

Other issuers of bonds are the electricity companies, industrial companies and sometimes foreign international agencies.

Austrian companies are increasingly issuing bonds as a means of raising capital but nevertheless only represent about 1.5 per cent of total bonds issued. Foreign bonds represented 2.3 per cent of new bond issues in 1979 but these issues were on behalf of international agencies such as the World Bank and European Investment Bank. Foreign corporations do not tend to issue bonds onto the Austrian domestic market which is smaller and less active than several other European markets. A few foreign bond issues have been made in the Austrian market by international agencies, but these are neither large nor frequent. Similarly, Eurobond issues denominated in Austrian schillings are very rare. There has, as at May 1981, been only one Euroschilling bond issue, led by Ostrreichische Kontrollbank. This has now matured so there are no issues outstanding. There is a strong demand by Austrian investors for international capital issues while the Austrian banks are major participants in Eurobond issues—particularly deutschemark donominated issues.

Equity shares

The share market in Austria is very small principally because of the high rate of corporation tax charged on profit results in dividends, giving a significantly lower yield than bonds or other forms of borrowing where the interest is paid before tax. In general Austrian companies usually need only small amounts of capital, in which case they borrow from the banks, either domestically or in the Swiss market.

The amount of new equity increased by only about 700 million schillings in 1980 resulting in shares outstanding of about As 25 billion by market value compared with bonds of As 10 billion by nominal value.

The shares outstanding comprise about 55 Austrian companies and 26 foreign companies but in the secondary market, about 60 per cent of turnover takes place in shares of foreign companies.

Shares of Austrian joint stock companies have par values of 100, 500 or 1000 schillings or larger in multiples of 1000 schillings. They may be in either registered or bearer form. Most shares are ordinary shares having voting and dividend rights although preference shares, with special dividend rights but no voting rights, may also be issued.

The stock exchange

The stock exchange in Vienna uses the call-over system and lists all bonds and equities issued in the domestic market, as well as providing a floor for dealing in major convertible currencies.

Banks are authorized to deal through the exchange on behalf of their clients.

Fixed-interest securities account for by far the greater proportion of turnover but this nonetheless remains small in relation to the volume of bonds outstanding. Most trading, particularly in bonds, is effected in the interbank market and generally only the surplus trading is dealt through the stock exchange.

Gold

The Mint releases certain commemorative gold coins to authorized credit institutions which they may resell to the public, including non-residents. Three such coins are the 4 ducat Franz Joseph, the 1 ducat Franz Joseph and the 100 crown Franz Joseph. All are newly minted, but dated 1915, and consist of 13.8 g, and 30.49 g of fine gold respectively. These three coins are not legal tender and their value depends on the prevailing international gold price. An additional coin having a face value of 1000 schillings is issued as legal tender.

Sales of gold coins in Austria are subject to VAT at 18 per cent.

Dealing and fees

The commercial banks in Austria are universal banks modelled in the German fashion. They therefore act as stockbrokers and authorized repositories. Fees are as follows:

Brokerage fees for dealers

Austrian bonds	0.75% of consideration
Austrian shares	1.25% of consideration

Brokerage fees for private clients

Austrian bonds	0.4% of consideration
Austrian shares	0.7% of consideration

Eurobonds

Dealt net, Dealing spreads	about $\frac{1}{2}$% on yield
Safe custody fees	0.2% per annum on value of securities
Stamp duty	Nil

Financial and monetary systems

Financial institutions

Considering its small size and limited capital market, Austria has a large number of banks, one for every 1600 head of population.

Austrian banks now provide a universal service to their customers in much the same way as German banks. Austrian banks may still however be classified according to six groups since each type of bank was originally established to provide specialized business services. Today each type of bank still has a stronger business emphasis on its specialized function although the major banks in each group are becoming increasingly competitive in areas of activity which were once the prerogative of other types of banks. The six groups of banks are the joint stock banks, savings banks, Raiffeisen banks (agricultural credit co-operatives) Volksbanks (trade banking co-operatives), provincial mortgage banks and others, which include building societies, private banks, foreign banks and special banks.

The 10 largest banks in Austria include representatives from all but the provincial mortgage banks out of the six banking sectors. Tables 5.3 and 5.4 show the relative market shares of each group of banks in 1978 and the top 10 banks in Austria.

All banks are subject to the banking laws which were revised for the first time since 1939 and became legally effective on 1 March 1979. Apart from giving the Minister of Finance statutory powers to enforce regulations such as credit and liquidity controls on the banking system, the new laws have liberalized the banks to

Table 5.3 Relative market shares of each group of banks in 1978

	Domestic market, share of	
Bank group	Total loans	Total deposits
Savings banks	26.5	32.2
Joint stock banks	26.2	20.9
Raiffeisen banks	16.6	19.7
Volksbank	5.9	7.3
Provincial mortgage banks	9.8	2.5
Others	15.0	17.4

Table 5.4 Top ten Austrian banks

Bank	1978 balance sheet total, As billions	Classification
Creditanstalt-Bankverein (CA-BV)	142.9	Joint stock bank
Girozentrale und Bank der Österreichischen Sparkassen AG (G2)	121.0	Joint stock bank with special function as central bank for savings banks
Landerbank (LB)	86.3	Joint stock bank
Zentralsparkasse und Kommerzbank Wien (2)	75.7	Savings bank
Österreichische Postsparkasse (PSK)	61.9	Special bank
Genossenschaftliche Zentralbank AG (GZB)	61.6	Joint stock bank with special functions as central bank for the Raiffeisen banks
Österreichische Kontrollbank AG (OKB)	54.8	Special bank
Erste Österreichische Sparkasse (EO)	54.4	Savings bank
Bank für Arbeit und Wirtschaft AG (BAWAG)	51.8	Joint stock bank
Österreichischen Volksbank AG (OVAG)	23.3	Joint stock bank with special function as central bank for the trade bank co-operatives

a larger degree than previously. For example, establishment of branches by banks is no longer subject to approval by the Minister of Finance. Following demands by the banks for legally enforceable banking secrecy this has now been incorporated into the banking laws. Banks can now be sued or prosecuted for transmitting information, to which they have special access, to third parties except where such information is required for criminal proceedings or wilful fiscal offences.

The banking laws also incorporated terms by which interest rates should be reached by agreement between the banks. On 2 April 1980, however, the Association of Austrian Banks and Bankers announced that the agreement on interest rates was to be cancelled as from 1 July 1980. Since that time banks have been free to determine their own lending and borrowing rates of interest individually.

Joint stock banks

The joint stock banks provide multifarious banking services. They accept all types of deposits, grant credit to commerce and industry, issue securities on behalf of public institutions and private corporate borrowers, act as stockbrokers by dealing both on behalf of clients and for their own account, provide investment advice and portfolio management services, and provide repository services to clients. The joint stock banks also hold large shareholdings in Austrian industrial enterprises. Indeed, the two largest joint stock banks, Creditanstalt Bankverein and Landerbank, which are the first and third largest banks respectively, hold major shareholdings in most of the larger nationalized companies. These two banks are controlled by the state which holds majority shareholdings. The two banks in turn hold controlling interests in major companies such as Daimler Puch, Semperit, Chemiefaser, Lenzing and Waagner-Biro. These companies are thus indirectly nationalized companies. The two large joint stock banks also have a number of minority and majority interests in banks within the other banking sectors in Austria.

Including the two large government controlled banks there are 35 joint stock banks with about 540 branches throughout Austria.

Savings banks

Savings banks were originally established to channel small savings into mortgages and local authority loans. Since 1979 however the new banking legislation, which was designed to increase competition and encourage structural reform in the banking sector, entitled savings banks to engage in all forms of modern retail banking.

The savings bank sector comprises 164 main institutions with over 1000 branches throughout the country. The institutions are organized as an association of savings banks for which Girozentrale acts as a central bank and Steiermarkische Bank—40 per cent owned by Girozentrale—acts as a clearing house for savings banks in the province of Steiermark.

Girozentrale provide all the administrative functions of a central bank with respect to the other savings banks. That is, it supervises and manages the liquid assets and reserves of the savings banks, acts as a clearing house and refinancing house and handles certain transactions, such as export transactions, on behalf of the savings banks. Girozentrale is also the second largest bank in Austria but is not

133

government owned and unlike the two major joint stock banks does not hold significant interests in industrial enterprises. It does however conduct all forms of normal banking business on behalf of businesses and individuals both in Austria and abroad. It is structured as a joint stock company but the whole of its capital is collectively held by the other savings banks in Austria.

Raiffeisen banks

Raiffeisen banks are agricultural credit co-operatives which were originally established to provide co-operative marketing and purchasing facilities to the agricultural community. Since 1979 these banks have also been authorized to provide a full retail and commercial banking service.

The Raiffeisen banks have the largest branch network of all the banking groups with 1311 banks and over 950 branches, but they are mainly located in rural areas. Each province has an intermediate central bank for the Raiffeisen banks, known as Zentralkassen while the Genossenschaftliche Zentralbank acts as the Raiffeisen banks' central bank at a national level. This bank is Austria's sixth largest bank.

Trade banking co-operatives

This sector comprises 150 trade banking co-operatives with 308 branches. It is organized as an institution known as the Volksbank at the head of which, performing central bank functions, is the Österreichische Volksbanken. Like the Raiffeisen banks these banks were originally established to provide specialized financing services to a specific economic group, namely trading companies. They may now, however, carry out all forms of banking activities.

Provincial mortgage banks

There is one public mortgage bank in each of the nine provinces whose major function is to grant mortgages on property. Since the banking act of 1979 these banks, in common with banks in the other sectors, may now conduct universal banking activities.

Other banks

Other banks include building societies, private banks, foreign banks and special banks.

There are four building societies which compete with the provincial mortgage banks. They provide almost half of all housing loans in Austria and are the major financiers of housing construction.

There are a dozen private banks in Austria which have only a small share of the banking market. There has been a tendency in recent years for these banks to become joint stock banks.

There are almost 60 foreign banks in Austria with branches, representative offices, or equity participation in Austrian banks. Banks representing interests from Europe, USA, South America and the Far East are now established in Austria.

Special banks are those that provide a special banking function and cannot easily be classified according to any of the other banking sectors. For example, Österreichische Postsparkasse, Austria's fifth largest bank, is the post office savings bank whose main function is to collect small savings and to channel these savings into financing the government debt. Österreichische Kontrollbank, the seventh largest bank, was established to provide special banking services to the banking industry itself, such as centralized bond issues and securities repository, or the refinancing of export loans or administration of export guarantees given by the Republic of Austria.

Central bank

The central bank is the Austrian National Bank (Österreichische Nationalbank). Although several of the banking sectors have intermediary central banks, the National Bank is the ultimate central bank at state level. It is a privately owned joint stock company whose shareholders include other banks, industrial companies and other domestic interests. It provides all the functions of a central bank and is charged with the implementation and administration of monetary policy as determined by the Minister of Finance.

Monetary policy

The main aim of monetary policy is to control the expansion of credit, maintain stable interest rates, and, to a lesser degree, provide banking liquidity. Being a small and open economy, Austria is closely affected by the West German economy and also subject to the influence of inflows and outflows of foreign capital. Monetary policy thus also aims at alleviating inflationary pressures which may be caused by such capital flows. The main instruments of monetary policy are discount policy, cash reserve ratios and, of less importance, open market operations.

Discount policy

The federal treasury, using the central bank as agent, will discount treasury paper and other eligible paper—including reconstruction credits and commercial bills—which are guaranteed 80 per cent by government and 20 per cent by the issuing banks.

The discount facility is granted to all banks but access may be refused by the Austrian National Bank. As from mid-1980, the National Bank has introduced quotas for the quantity of bills the banks may discount, which may be set on a monthly basis for each type of banking institution. The system of quotas is used as a flexible policy instrument which may be applied to increase or decrease liquidity in the banking system. Due to the inadequate money market and the virtual lack of an interbank market, the volume of discounts is generally large. The largest volume of bills discounted is in reconstruction credits while the volume of commercial bills is small. By changing the discount quotas therefore, the National Bank has an expedient means of influencing monetary aggregates. There is no penalty rate of

135

interest charged to a bank that exceeds its discount quota; instead the bank may be granted a lower discount quota for the following month.

The discount rate at which the National Bank will discount eligible bills is an administered rate determined by the National Bank. Thus by establishing the discount rate the National Bank has an additional means by which to influence other interest rates in the market. For example, discount policy during 1980 has been restrictive in order to reduce inflation, which was running at six per cent per annum—high by Austrian standards—the authorities reducing the banks' discount facilities several times during the year. This succeeded in tightening liquidity and pushed money market interest rates up to about 12 per cent in the third quarter of 1980. The National Bank will also grant advances to banks against the security of government and other eligible securities, at the Lombard rate, which is normally about $\frac{1}{2}$ per cent above the discount rate.

Liquidity and reserve ratios

The National Bank supervises the liquidity in the banking system by establishing minimum cash reserves, as a percentage of total liabilities, which the banks must maintain with either their sectoral central bank, the post office savings bank, or with the National Bank. These reserves are placed in interest-bearing accounts with the relevant central bank and are designed to safeguard the interests of depositors although it is also varied by the authorities, and thus used as a flexible instrument of monetary policy.

The maximum reserve ratios are 25 per cent for sight and foreign liabilities and 15 per cent for time and savings deposits. The percentage varies however according to the type of deposit and size of bank.

Reserve ratios with respect to foreign liabilities may sometimes be used to influence external capital flows with the purpose of stabilizing the value of the currency. Though no constraints currently apply, an example of the operation of this type of policy arose during the period 1972 to 1975, when Austria suffered excessive upward pressure on its exchange rate caused by the inflow of foreign funds. The Minister of Finance thus required that banks should seek approval for all non-trade inflows of foreign capital and also that reserves equivalent to 75 per cent of foreign currency deposits should be matched by interest-free deposits at the National Bank. This successfully reduced exchange movements into Austria and while no similar regulations are currently in force, the National Bank has the facility to apply such constraints should external pressure resume.

Credit controls

The National Bank controls the expansion of credit and thus money supply growth by setting monthly limits on bank lending activities. For example, the banks may increase their loans to industry by a maximum of 1.5 per cent per month while loans to private individuals may grow by no more than 0.75 per cent per month. These limits can be changed at the discretion of the National Bank in co-operation with the Minister of Finance. New limits were set in March 1981. Banks were required to limit the growth of their non-Austrian lending through syndicated Eurocurrency loans to a maximum of 15 per cent of the 1980 volume. Restrictions on corporate lending within Austria were temporarily abolished in March 1981.

If the banking institutions fail to reach agreement on credit control the Minister of Finance, in consultation with the National Bank, has new statutory powers introduced in 1979 to set a liability credit ceiling for a period of up to 16 months. That is, he can set limits for the monthly rate by which each type of bank can increase its deposits and other liabilities. If this fails, the Minister of Finance can then set a 16-month limit on the increase of assets, i.e., loans and advances.

Open market operations

The federal treasury issues notes in units of 1 000 000 schillings to the National Bank which then uses them for open market operations, carried out partly on the stock exchange. Such notes may only be purchased by banks, so the size of the market is limited. Open market operations are also conducted in listed bonds issued by the government, the provinces and municipalities, but this policy is used as a secondary instrument of monetary control, usually in conjunction with discount policy. In spring 1981, all open market operations had been temporarily suspended.

The Minister of Finance, through the capital market committee, also exerts an influence on interest rates by controlling the issue calendar of bonds. If liquidity is tight and interest rates are high, the authorities may place a temporary moratorium on new bond issues to avoid further liquidity being absorbed from the system. Conversely, the authorities can increase bond issues if it wishes to tighten liquidity and put upward pressure on interest rates.

Withholding taxes

Withholding tax is charged on dividends but not on interest. Two exceptions are, firstly, interest earned from convertible bonds, where such interest is treated for tax purposes as dividends and, secondly, interest payable to non-residents arising from loans secured against Austrian property.

The standard withholding tax rate is 20 per cent but, for many tax treaty countries, this is reduced as shown in Table 5.5. In some cases, the reduction depends on the proportion of a company's issued share capital which is owned by the recipient.

Exchange controls

The Austrian National Bank is the relevant authority charged with implementing and administering exchange controls.

Currency

The currency is the Austrian schilling which is fully convertible. Because of economic ties, the currency is also closely linked, although informally, with the Deutschemark. The authorities attempt to maintain the exchange rate within the

Table 5.5   Withholding taxes

	Dividends, %	Shareholding required for lower rate, %
Resident corporations owning		
less than 25% of the share capital	20	
25% or more of the share capital	0	
Resident individuals	20	
Non-resident corporations and individuals	20	
Non treaty	20	
Treaty		
Belgium	15	
Brazil	15	
Denmark	10	
Finland	10	
France	15	
Germany (FR)	20	
Greece	20	
Hungary	20	
India	20	
Indonesia	20	
Ireland	10/0	25
Israel	20	
Italy	20	
Japan	20/10	50
Liechtenstein	15	
Luxembourg	15/5	25
Netherlands	15/10	25
New Zealand	20	
Norway	15	
Pakistan	20/10	25
Poland	10	
Portugal	15	
Spain	15/20	50
Sweden	10	
Switzerland	5	
Turkey	20	
United Arab Republic	10	
United Kingdom	15	
United States	10/5	95

margins determined by the EMS, although Austria is not a member and does not participate in the EMS. There is no intervention in the forward market which is influenced and determined solely by market forces.

Non-resident accounts

A non-resident may freely open an account with an Austrian bank. There are three types of such accounts.

Free schilling accounts are used to make current payments to residents or to receive proceeds from the sale of gold coin or convertible currencies. Transfers between one free schilling account and another, and balances on free schilling accounts, may be freely converted to any convertible currency.

Interim accounts are used to receive current and capital payments in Austrian schillings from residents. The transfer abroad of such proceeds requires a special licence from the National Bank but is normally granted where the foreign account holder is a resident or member of the IMF and OECD.

Blocked accounts are similar to interim accounts but are used by residents of countries that are not members of the IMF and OECD.

Purchase of securities

The purchase of fixed-interest securities by non-residents is freely permitted. The acquisition of shares or majority participation in Austrian companies is also unrestricted provided the transaction is made through an Austrian banking institution.

Proceeds of investments may be freely transferred abroad if they derive from the liquidation of foreign investment in Austria or repayment by residents of foreign loans.

Other instruments

The purchase by non-residents of Austrian land or property is subject to individual approval by the National Bank in every case. Proceeds from the sale of property already owned by non-residents may be freely repatriated.

Non-residents may freely purchase gold, but gold that is not legal tender is subject to VAT at 18 per cent.

The export of gold, including gold coin but excluding jewellery, is subject to individual approval by the National Bank.

6. Belgium

General market environment

The Belgian Government in general welcomes foreign investment. Free transfer of capital into and out of the country is allowed with only minimum regulations.

In particular a two-tier foreign exchange system is operated, the official market in convertible francs and the free market in financial francs. The authorities intervene in the official market in order to exercise some measure of control over the cross-border flows of foreign capital. Portfolio investments, however, are carried out through the free market in which no intervention occurs. The value of the financial franc is thus largely determined by market supply and demand although the authorities, having raised large loans in the Euromarkets, are able to exercise some degree of intervention in the free market too.

Table 6.1   General classification of securities markets

Instrument	Characteristics
MONEY MARKET	
Call deposits	Highly active. Participants are mostly Belgium based branches of foreign banks
Time deposits	Active but regulated market
Eurocurrency deposits	Active but restricted by lack of adequate swap market
Other money market instruments	Not available to non-bank public
CAPITAL MARKET	
Government bonds	Market of reasonable size, but financial system results in slightly restricted secondary market
Bons de caisse	Fixed interest, medium-term savings bonds issued by banks and public financial institutions
Eurobonds	Brussels is an active centre for secondary market trading. No primary market activity
Corporate bonds	Limited market. Relatively few issues outstanding and small primary market
Equity shares	Similarly limited market. About half the listed issues are those of foreign companies

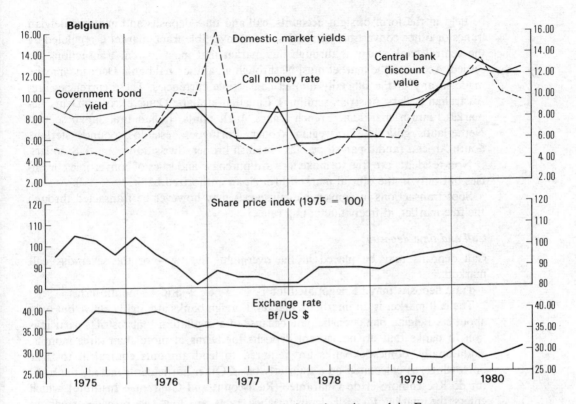

An active money market exists for call and time deposits and in Eurocurrency deposits, but the rest of the money market is not accessible either to non-bank residents or to non-residents.

The capital market is restricted principally to secondary market Eurobonds and public sector domestic bonds. Bond and equity financing by the private corporate sector is insufficient to provide a significantly large or active domestic capital market.

This is mostly due to the existence of large and powerful holding companies—a distinctive feature of the Belgian financial system—from which most corporate funds are obtained.

Apart from the two-tier foreign exchange system, other controls affecting non-resident investors are minimal. Withholding taxes are, however, applied to both interest and dividends at an effective rate of about 11 per cent for residents of those countries having a tax treaty with Belgium.

The money market

Deposits

Non-residents may open accounts for operation via either the official market or the free market. Convertible accounts, for transactions through the official market, may be held in the form of sight accounts, call and time deposits and in either Belgian francs or other convertible currencies. The convertible franc market is regulated by the central bank and it is through this market that most current transactions are settled. Access to the market must be through an authorized bank. Deposits may be made in any of the officially quoted convertible currencies. These currencies are: Australian dollars, Austrian schillings, Canadian dollars, Danish kroner, Deutschemarks, Finnish markkaa, French francs, Irish punts, Italian lira, Japanese yen, Netherlands guilders, Norwegian kroner, Portuguese escudos, pounds sterling, South African rand, Spanish pesetas, Swedish kroner, Swiss francs and US dollars.

Non-residents are free to make forward purchase and sales of convertible currencies but only in the official market through an authorized bank.

Spot transactions in convertible currencies may however be transacted through the free market, at freely fluctuating rates.

Call and time deposits

Call deposits may be placed in the overnight, the two-, or the seven-day call market.

Time deposits may be negotiated for 1-, 2-, 3-, 6-, 9- and 12-month terms.

The call market is an interbank market. Foreign banks are highly active but only about six Belgian banks participate because of a regulation that restricts participation to banks that do not accept deposits for terms of more than three months. Additionally, domestic banks are required to lend amounts equivalent to their borrowings, as calculated on a quarterly basis. Other participants include the Institut de Réescompte et de Guarantee (Rediscount and Guarantee Institute), which enters the market for call deposits when rates are low and provides credit to companies to finance exports at similarly favourable rates of interest. The Fonds des Rentes (Securities Stabilization Fund) is another important participant with the purpose of stabilizing interest rates in the call market by conducting open market operations.

Amounts dealt in the interbank call domestic currency deposit markets are usually in minimum sizes of Bf 50 million. Interest rates are constantly adjusted to those for comparable terms in the Eurocurrency market.

Time deposits may be made in smaller amounts but unlike the call market rates of interest are fixed by the Comité de Concertation des Taux d'Intérêts (the Committee on Creditor Interest Rates) which is chaired by the Governor of the Central Bank.

It is difficult to undertake interest arbitrage operations in the Brussels market because an unsatisfactory swap market exists. This is due to domestic restrictions which mean that convertible francs cannot be lent outside Belgium. The banks can sometimes take advantage of swaps if they can attract sufficiently large deposits for which they tend to pay slightly better rates of interest.

Interest on deposits placed by non-residents in Belgium is not subject to withholding tax.

Belgian franc deposits may be placed in other Eurocurrency centres, principally Luxembourg and London, usually at better rates of interest.

CDs

There is no market for Belgian franc CDs.

Other money market instruments

Although other money market instruments exist, they may not be purchased by the non-bank public. This includes residents as well as non-residents.

The instruments are briefly described below, but are used exclusively by the Belgium- and Luxembourg-based banks and financial institutions. Their purpose is as a means by which the central bank can finance the national debt and regulate the money supply. Because of the limited money market, government paper is

Table 6.2   Interest rates and yields in Belgium money and capital markets

	Money market		Capital market	
	Official discount rate	Day-to-day call money	Central government bond yields	Corporate bonds yields (non-financial companies)
End 1978	6.00	6.45	8.80	9.58
1979				
Jan.	6.00	6.33	9.08	9.34
Feb.	6.00	6.40	8.83	9.47
Mar.	6.00	5.37	8.90	9.38
Apr.	6.00	5.25	8.99	9.70
May	7.00	4.81	9.21	9.82
June	{ 8.00 { 9.00	7.64	9.42	10.13
July	9.00	9.59	9.63	10.32
Aug.	9.00	9.34	9.80	10.83
Sep.	9.00	8.91	9.90	10.92
Oct.	10.00	11.32	10.58	11.34
Nov.	10.00	10.06	11.00	11.70
Dec.	10.50	10.58	11.15	11.93
1980				
Jan.	10.50	11.74	11.42	11.82
Feb.	12.00	9.66	11.93	12.22
Mar.	14.00 .	12.59	12.45	
Apr.	14.00	14.83	12.02	
May	14.00	13.47	12.26	
June	13.00	11.96	11.84	
July	12.00	11.84	11.77	
Aug.	12.00	9.80	12.08	
Sep.	12.00	9.51	12.43	
Oct.	12.00	9.50	12.56	
Nov.	12.00	10.04	12.61	
Dec.	12.00	9.73	13.04	

sometimes hard to sell in large quantities. Major domestic banks are sometimes obliged to purchase government issues at nominal rates of interest but nevertheless the Belgian government often has to seek recourse to foreign markets for funds.

Treasury bills

These are issued by tender to the banks with 1-, 2- or 3-month maturities. Occasionally they may carry 6-, 9- or 12-month terms.

Certificats de fonds des rentes

This is paper issued by the Fond des Rentes, an autonomous body charged with the responsibility for open market operations and the regulation of the market in government securities. It finances its operations mostly through the issue of certificats de fonds des rentes which carry maturities of four months plus or minus eight days.

Bankers' acceptances

A form of bankers' acceptance is issued, which is differentiated into two categories: those that have less than 120-day maturities and those issued with between 121- and 240-day maturities.

The banks may rediscount this paper with the Institut de Réescompte et de Garantie, the discount intermediary between the central bank and the money market. To be eligible, the paper must carry at least three signatures of solvent parties.

The capital market

Government and public sector bonds

The Fonds des Rentes manages the government securities market. The government has a continuing requirement for long-term funds and thus makes frequent issues of medium- and long-term bonds, which comprise the major part of the domestic capital market.

Primary market
Government bond issues are normally made three times a year. Before a new issue, the Minister of Finance submits terms of loans to a consortium of banks for its opinion. At the same time, the coupon rate is fixed by the Committee on Creditor Interest Rates.

The banks may be asked to take the new securities 'firm', which they do when the total amount of the issue is fixed in advance. Sometimes the government issues bonds with no fixed ceiling on the total amount.

Government bonds may also be issued with a single fixed redemption date or with one or more intermediate redemption dates. They may sometimes be issued on tap depending on the network of placing agents who cover the whole country. Tap

144

issues are placed by commercial banks, private savings banks, mortgage companies and, particularly, public credit institutions.

The secondary market in government bonds is efficient and fairly active and is traded on the stock exchange through the banks or brokers. Nearly all turnover in bonds is represented by government and public sector bonds and is almost twice the turnover of the equity market. Flexibility could, however, be improved but for the fact that liquid assets of official institutions may be held only in public sector institutions and cannot be deposited with commercial banks or in private sector assets. This tends to lead to separate circuits of money within the economy. For example, savings deposited with the Office des Chèques Postaux (Post Office Savings Bank) are reinvested with the government thus representing a flow of funds direct from individuals to the government. Because such savings are not redirected to the banking system, the result is a contraction of deposits and shortage of funds in the private sector and also for placement in the money and capital markets. This is perhaps one reason why banks are obliged to lend to the private sector volumes of funds at least equivalent to the amount they borrow.

Secondary market

Bons de caisse

Bons de caisse (savings bonds) are medium-term fixed-interest bearer bonds issued by the public credit institutions and by the commercial banks. In the former case they carry maturities of between one and five years. Although terms of more than five years may be issued, they are regarded as long-term bonds. The banks usually issue bons de caisse with either three- or five-year maturities. They may be issued by public tender or private placement and the whole of the issue may be made at once or alternatively issued on tap.

Eurobonds

Brussels has become a clearing centre for Eurobonds but, although the volume of retail business handled is significant, as a Eurobond dealing centre it still ranks lower than London, Luxembourg or Frankfurt.

Issues of Eurobonds denominated in Belgian francs are not normally permitted so there is consequently no Eurobond primary market in Belgium.

Corporate bonds

There are three types of corporate bonds issued in Belgium; straight bonds, bearer receipts (to facilitate trading and possession of foreign registered securities) and convertible bonds. Securities are offered both in bearer form and in registered form, but bearer bonds are much more common.

Bond financing is not a popular method of raising funds by Belgian companies, primarily because of the predominant role of the bank holding companies (see financial system) and also the preference by companies for bank borrowing. Additionally, the supply of funds to the private sector bond market is inadequate be-

145

cause the government and public agencies tend to absorb most of the available market funds.

There are only about 325 corporate bonds quoted on the Belgian stock exchange, many of which are bonds issued by foreign companies. While, in theory, foreign companies require the approval of the Ministry of Finance in order to issue securities in the Belgian capital market, the majority of new domestic bond issues denominated in Belgian francs are made by international companies.

Equity shares

The market in equity shares is limited for the same reasons that the corporate bond market is inactive. Companies prefer to raise capital directly from the banks and, in any case, the supply of funds to the capital market is poor.

There are only about 230 Belgian companies and 150 foreign companies with

Table 6.3 Gross new security issues in Belgium capital market (billion Belgian francs) (*source: OECD*)

Securities	1975	1976	1977	1978	1979	Jan./ June 1980
PUBLIC ISSUES						
Bonds of central government	162	152	197	223	246	134
Bonds of local government	99	123	140	153	162	96
Financial institutions*	117	144	244	165		
Public enterprises	5	23	6	23		
Private companies	7	7	4			
Foreign bonds	3	.....	2			
Total public issue of bonds	393	449	593	564	408	230
PRIVATE PLACEMENTS						
Bonds of central government	4	11	28	9		
Bonds of local government	1	0.2	.....	0.7		
Financial institutions	17	12	15	13		
Public enterprises	7	7	18	10		
Private companies	16	5	5			
Foreign bonds	2	.....				
Total private placements	47	35	66	33	0	0
Total of all bond issues	440	484	659	597	408	230
SHARES						
Financial institutions	5	2	11	37		
Public enterprises	4	2				
Private companies	15	22	42			
Foreign companies	3	2	1	3		
Total	27	28	54	40	0	0

* Includes securities stabilization fund, insurance companies, banks, mortgage companies and public financial intermediaries.

quotations on the stock exchanges. Monthly trading volume is about Bf 150 million, two-thirds of which is dealing in domestic Belgian company shares.

Several types of shares may be issued—preferred shares, jouissance shares (profit-sharing certificates), and founders' shares. These each carry different dividend and voting rights. The shares most frequently traded are the jouissance shares which are similar to UK companies' ordinary shares and US companies' common stock. Non-voting and plural-voting shares are not permitted, but no-par stock can be issued. Shares are normally in bearer form although they must be deposited and registered several days before the company general meeting.

Belgian companies do not report very detailed information to the public. Many run entirely undeclared companies to handle what may be described as black market affairs.

The bank holding companies hold a large proportion of the equity shares in Belgian companies. These bank holding companies are very powerful. Regulations allow a shareholder with a shareholding of more than 25 per cent to block any move a company wants to make. In practice, the dependence of companies on the banks for working and longer-term finance, together with the apathy of the small shareholder, makes it possible to control a company with less than 20 per cent of the equity. Brufina, for example, is regarded as the holding company of the Banque de Bruxelles and yet has only 10 per cent of the equity. Nevertheless, while its own share capital is worth some Bf 5 billion, it exercises control over the bank which has a share capital worth Bf 160 billion.

The majority of Belgian companies are under the control of a holding company and, in such a financial environment, it is difficult for the independent company to survive.

The stock exchange

There are stock exchanges at Brussels, Antwerp, Ghent and Liège, but the Brussels exchange handles the largest turnover.

The market is open between 11.30 a.m. and 2.30 p.m. The call-over system is used, although the official market in ordinary shares and corporate bonds is split into three trading practices. These are:

The parquet market, the market for stocks that are traded only occasionally.

The corbeille market, the market in which the more actively traded equities are dealt and for which a flat price is quoted for immediate settlement.

Marche à Terme, the market in which the highly active stocks (i.e., the major Belgian names and the most active foreign stocks) are traded and for which there is a regular series of fluctuating quotations. Payment need only be made at the end of a fortnightly account period. The Stock Exchange Committee fixes the minimum amounts to be traded for each security, which may vary from between 5 to 100 securities according to the market value for future delivery.

147

Table 6.4 Securities listed on Brussels stock exchange

Security	1975	1976	1977	1978	1979
BONDS (Bf billion) nominal value					
Public sector	918	984	1102	1308	1440
Private sector	14	15	49	50	47
Foreign	24	26			
Total	956	1025	1151	1358	1487
SHARES (number outstanding issues)					
Belgian companies	24	17	16	14	14
Foreign companies	12	9	9	9	9
Total	36	26	25	23	23
SHARES (Bf million)					
Belgian companies total market capitalization	367	335	339	365	386

A further, over-the-counter, market exists outside the stock exchange for unlisted shares. Such shares are normally partly paid shares in larger companies and normally traded by monthly public auction with a reserve price for each issue. Transactions must be settled in cash although such public sales often lead to delays in delivery and settlement.

The stock exchanges are regulated by the Stock Exchange Committee (comprising 15 stockbrokers) which supervises the organization and running of the market and publishes daily lists of quotations and dealings.

A further committee ensures the reliability of the quotations and determines which securities should be admissible for listing.

The Brussels stock exchange handles some 231 Belgian shares, 154 foreign shares, and approximately 350 Belgian bonds. Since 1976 there have been no foreign bonds listed on the Brussels exchange.

The majority of the Belgian shares and bonds are those issued by the government or public institutions. Only about 70 Belgian and foreign shares are traded in any sizeable volume.

Table 6.5 Turnover of securities listed on Brussels stock exchange

Security	1975	1976	1977	1978	1979
(Bf million) nominal value					
Bonds	52	63	69	71	99
Shares	49	55	39	39	53
Total turnover	101	118	108	110	152

Dealing and fees

Deposits

Belgian franc deposits may be placed with a Belgian or Belgium-based commercial bank, or with a commercial bank in some other financial centre such as Luxembourg or London.

Money market

Money market instruments may not be purchased by the non-bank public or by non-residents.

Bonds and shares

These are purchased through the stock exchange and may be dealt through a stockbroker or through a bank which will use its own broker.

Settlement and delivery is either for cash or on account on a fortnightly settlement basis depending on the share and market in which it is traded.

A number of different charges are made as shown below, although the total fees are small.

Commission

1. Cash settlement

Government securities	0.3% of market value (including accrued interest)
Securities redeemable by drawings	0.4% of market value
Belgian Railway preferred stock	0.6% of market value
All other listed stocks	0.75% of market value
Minimum commission	Bf 15 per transaction.

2. On-account settlement

All shares	0.6% of market value
Minimum commission	Bf 1 per share
Carry over for following account	0.3% on market value

3. Monthly public shares

Unlisted shares	0.75% of market value
Minimum commission	Bf 1 per share or Bf 10 per transaction

Listing fees

These are paid by both buyer and seller but only half by the client, the remainder by the stockbroker

1. Cash

Government stocks	Nil
Bonds and shares	0.05% on market value

2. On account

All shares	0.02% on market value

Contract stamps

These are payable on sales and purchases of securities and on subscription to new issues

1. Cash

Government securities	0.06% of total commission or proceeds, including other expenses
All other bonds	0.12% of total commission or proceeds, including other expenses
Shares	0.30% of total commission or proceeds, including other expenses

2. On account

All shares	0.15% of total commission or proceeds, including other expenses

Settlement and delivery

Dealings in all bonds and listed stocks can be for cash. Fluctuation in the price of securities is restricted on a daily basis. Fixed-interest stocks are allowed a maximum daily fluctuation of two per cent. Stocks listed on the parquet market and corbeille markets may fluctuate by 5 and 10 per cent respectively. Some 70 or so shares listed for account settlement may fluctuate freely and the account settlement dates are fortnightly. All other securities must be settled for cash immediately.

Financial and monetary systems

Financial institutions

There are three categories of banking institutions:

1. *The commercial banks* of which 68 out of a total of 88 are foreign banks based in Brussels. All commercial banks are privately owned. Three Belgian banks (known as 'the big three') dominate, controlling about 75 per cent of deposits and representing 80 per cent of all branches of the commercial banking sector. These three are the Société Générale de Banque, Banque Bruxelles Lambert and Kredietbank.

The commercial banks, however, only account for approximately one-third of deposits and savings in the financial system.

The largest bank in Belgium is the National Savings Bank—Caisse Générale d'Epargne et de Retraite (GGER). Although not really a commercial bank it accepts current account time and savings deposits and lends funds to industry and to the mortgage market and indirectly to the government through the purchase of government securities.

2. *The national credit institutions.* The largest of these is the Société Nationale de Crédit à l'Industrie (SNCI), jointly owned by the state and the private sector. It acts as an investment bank, lending to industry and raising funds through the issue of bonds which are guaranteed by the state, and interest on which is tax free.

Other public financial credit institutions are the Caisse Nationale de Crédit Professionel (national credit funds for small and medium-sized enterprises) which lends to businesses either directly or through approved private lending intermediaries: L'Institut National de Crédit Agricole (National Farmers' Credit Institute) which lends to the agricultural sector; La Société Nationale de Logement (National Housing Society) which lends to regional housing societies, at favourable rates of interest, to promote low-cost housing; L'Office Central de Crédit Hypothécaire (Central Mortgage Loans Office) which provides mortgages and regulates the mortgage interest rate. In addition there are several other public financial intermediaries each of which is aimed at assisting low-income families or other special groups.

Altogether there are 12 public credit institutions, most of which are members of the Council of Public Credit Institutions (Conseil des Institutions Publiques de Crédit) which is headed by the governor of the central bank and also comprises representatives from the Ministry of Finance and from industry. All the member institutions are required to gain the prior approval from the council with respect to new bond issues, terms of such issues and for any change in investment of credit policies.

3. *Private savings banks.* These are privately owned and operated similarly to the National Savings Bank, except that they normally do not accept time or savings deposits for more than two years.

Apart from savings deposits, the savings banks also accept time deposits and deposits which are withdrawable at notice, mostly from individuals. Interest returns offered by savings banks are comparable with those offered by commercial banks for time deposits although they normally pay a lower rate of interest on deposits at notice. There are 31 savings banks, some of which also combine their function with that of a mortgage bank and may raise additional funds through the issue of bonds and certificates on a tap basis.

Other financial institutions

Other financial institutions include the 178 insurance companies and 52 pension funds which are substantial purchasers of government bonds in the capital market,

151

holding almost 10 per cent of central government bonds and 4 per cent of all bonds issued.

The mortgage companies and capital redemption companies collect savings from individuals and grant housing loans mainly to individuals. They too are significant investors in the bonds market and themselves issue bonds and certificates.

Central bank

The central bank is the Banque Nationale de Belgique (National Bank of Belgium) which is 50 per cent owned by the state, the remainder being held by private shareholders. It is the sole bank of issue, lender of last resort and has responsibility for some, but not all, of the supervision of the financial system. Specifically its functions are to monitor the activities of the money market and to conduct open market operations in the financial markets in order to stabilize interest rate trends and to control liquidity, to manage the foreign currency reserves of the Belgian and Luxembourg Economic Union (BLEU) and to intervene in the spot foreign exchange markets in order to stabilize the value of the currency. The National Bank also extends loans to public financial credit institutions and refinances loans to industry which have been extended by commercial banks or credit institutions. The Bank is autonomous but subject to the direction of a council that comprises representatives from all sectors of the economy. Power of veto is vested in a representative from the Ministry of Finance.

Other financial authorities

A financial supervisory role is also credited to the Commission Bancaire (Banking Commission) which has authority to set solvency requirements and liquidity ratios for the commercial banks, holding companies and savings banks.

The Fond des Rentes (Securities Stabilization Fund) undertakes open market operations on behalf of the government and is also charged with managing the market in government and other public sector securities. It also intervenes in the short-term money market for day-to-day call deposits with the purpose of stabilizing interest rates and influencing liquidity in the banking system. The funds required for it to perform this function are in part ceded direct from the Treasury, in part raised through the issue of short-term certificates to the banks by weekly tender and from borrowing in the call money market. The remainder is made available by lines of credit extended from the National Bank.

This institution is managed by a six-man committee, three of whose members are appointed by the National Bank and three by the Ministry of Finance.

The Institute de Réescompte et de Garantie (Rediscount and Guarantee Institute—IRG) is a semipublic, legally constituted discount house, charged with maintaining liquidity in the banking system by discounting eligible bills for the banks which it can itself then rediscount with the central bank.

The types of assets which the IRG will rediscount are commercial bills and acceptances which, because of their form or maturity, would not be eligible for rediscount by the National Bank. Banks, however, are only granted this facility occasionally and temporarily at the discretion of the IRG. As well as rediscounting bills and acceptances the IRG also acts as dealer for these securities and for public sector bills, and is charged with the responsibility of regulating the market.

The IRG raises the funds required for its operations through advances from the National Bank and from borrowing in the call money market. It tends to borrow only surplus short-term money from the banks and public credit institutions at consequently low interest rates enabling it then to extend loans at favourable rates of interest to industry to help finance exports.

Bank holding companies (Sociétés Financières)

The powerful holding companies, holding large equity participations in industrial and commercial companies, are a unique feature of the Belgian financial system.

Prior to 1935, Belgium had no banking regulations and the banks provided a multipurpose banking function. This included not only the accepting of deposits and lending to industry and commerce, but also facilitated the banks taking equity participation in most of the companies with which they did business. During the depression of the 1930s, these large equity holdings and the fall in the companies' market values resulted in the banks suffering substantial financial losses.

Banking regulations were consequently introduced in 1934 which separated banks into two types—deposit banks which were not allowed to hold portfolio investments on their own account, and financial holding companies which were permitted to take equity participation but were required to finance their activities through the issue of bonds and from their own share capital. The outcome of these changes was that each bank formed a separate holding company to hold shares in industry and business companies. The companies are, therefore, still influenced by the banks, but at arm's length, and banking liquidity is not jeopardized to the same degree by the potential collapse of the industrial sector.

The power of the holding companies lies in their ability with small minority holdings to influence major decisions of companies. By law a shareholder with more than 25 per cent equity has power of veto, but provided a holding company is the largest single shareholder, it very often achieves this with less than a 20 per cent shareholding.

The fact that most Belgian companies have a bank holding company as a major shareholder has inhibited the development of the domestic equity and corporate bond markets since companies tend to raise new capital through loans from the banks with which, through the holding companies, they are associated.

Monetary control

The monetary authorities have a variety of quantitative and qualitative controls at their disposal with which to control the liquidity of the banking system, the expansion of credit and the maintenance of the external value of the currency. The main instruments used are reserve ratios, discount policy, direct credit policy and to a lesser extent, open market operations.

153

Reserve ratios

Under the authority of the Commission Bancaire, banks are required to maintain reserve ratios which should not be less than 20 per cent of liabilities of less than 30 days' maturity and seven per cent of deposits of more than 30 days.

These reserves must be placed as sight deposits with the central bank or with Fonds des Rentes or in certain government securities. The commission also sets solvency ratios which are the ratio of banks' liabilities to their capital and free reserves. This is not, however, used as a policy instrument.

The reserve ratios may be changed by the Commission Bancaire and are thus used as a policy instrument. Raising the ratios effectively tightens liquidity in the banking system, thus raising interest rates while at the same time channelling funds into the public sector and to the Fonds des Rentes which can use the money to conduct further open market operations.

Discount policy

The banks may rediscount bills through the National Bank which, to be eligible, must carry three signatures, those of the transferor, the transferee and of an accepting bank, and have less than 120 days to maturity.

Bills may be discounted up to the limit of each bank's rediscount ceilings. These are set at the average amount of the previous year's Belgian franc deposits plus bonds and medium-term paper, and a bank's own free reserves. The ceilings may be adjusted by the central bank when short-term adjustments are required to regulate the cyclical trends in the market.

Raising the discount ceilings will increase liquidity since banks will have greater resources with which to extend credit by accepting commercial bills. This would also tend to result in lower interest rates in the money market though the Bank can directly influence interest rates by lowering or raising the rate at which it is prepared to discount commercial bills.

The IRG was established in 1973 in order to rediscount certain bills to the banking system which would not otherwise be eligible for rediscounting with the central bank. The discount rate charged by the IRG is slightly higher than the official discount rate charged by the National Bank but bills discounted by the IRG are not subject to the discount ceilings set by the Bank.

The official discount rate is the rate at which the central bank will discount eligible bills to the banking system, and is the rate that influences the rates of interest in the money market. Overnight call rates are usually a few basis points below the discount rate which, unless liquidity is very tight, will act as a ceiling on call rates.

Credit policy

Credit expansion may be restricted by a variety of direct measures. In 1978 these took the form of limits on the amounts of loans which could be granted by the banks for the financing of short-term foreign assets. At the same time, reinvestment requirements were imposed which obliged banks to invest part of their current

154

liabilities in official paper. These two measures were aimed at containing the growth of credit and directing funds to the domestic economy.

Credit may also be controlled by effecting changes in hire purchase conditions, and by the banks being required to limit their increase in credit to companies and households to a prescribed maximum percentage.

The commercial banks are required to lend the same amount of funds as they borrow in the form of deposits. The authorities can also influence the direction of credit by requiring that the banks lend a greater proportion of their loans and advances to particular sectors of the economy, at the expense of other sectors. The major sectors to which banks lend are the public sector, corporate sector, individuals and foreign borrowers. If the authorities wish to tighten liquidity they tend to require that banks lend to the public sector and to industry and the export sector in preference to other borrowers.

Open market operations

Open market operations are undertaken by the Fonds des Rentes. As a policy instrument, its effectiveness is restricted because of an inadequate money market in which the public are not generally permitted to participate and a capital market in which normal trading is also thin. Nevertheless, trends in both markets are influenced by such intervention, and the Fond's activities in the market are a good indicator of government policy.

Withholding taxes

Withholding taxes are chargeable on both interest and dividends.

Interest

The tax on interest to residents of non-treaty countries is 20 per cent. For most treaty countries, this is reduced to 15 per cent, but provided certain conditions are met and proper documents are filed, a further reduction is granted resulting in an effective rate of about 11 per cent.

Dividends

Dividends paid to residents of non-treaty countries are subject to a withholding tax of 20 per cent, while for most treaty countries the rate is reduced to 15 per cent.

Exemptions

No withholding taxes are chargeable to non-residents on interest and/or dividends from all deposits made with financial institutions, including notes, bonds or convertible bonds issued by these institutions.

The rates applying to residents of foreign countries are shown in Table 6.6. Where two rates are given, the lower rate applies if certain formalities are met pursuant to the individual tax treaty.

Table 6.6 Withholding taxes

Recipient	Interest,* %	Dividends, %
NON-RESIDENT CORPORATIONS AND INDIVIDUALS		
Non-treaty countries	20	20
Treaty countries		
Australia	10	15
Austria	15	15
Brazil	10–15	15
Canada	15	15
Czechoslovakia	10	15
Denmark	15	10–15
Finland	10	15
France	15	10–15
Germany	0–15	15
Greece	10	15
India	20	20
Indonesia	15	15
Ireland	15	15
Israel	15	15
Italy	15	15
Japan	15	15
Luxembourg	0–15	10–15
Malaysia	10	15
Malta	10	15
Morocco	15	15
Netherlands	0–10	5–15
Norway	15	15
Poland	10	10
Portugal	15	15
Rumania	10	15
Singapore	15	15
South Korea	15	15
Spain	15	15
Sweden	15	15
Tunisia	15	15
United Kingdom	15	15
United States	15	15

* Except for interest on deposits with financial institutions or coupon bearing and discount securities issued by financial institutions. In these cases withholding tax is zero.

Exchange controls

Belgium has a free exchange system, but has had a two-tier foreign exchange market since 1946. Payments for each type of transaction must be made through either the official market or the free market, as follows:

Official market in convertible francs

The official market is the market through which most current transactions are made. Francs bought or sold by non-residents in the official market are known as convertible francs. In general, the category of transactions made in the official market is the payment for goods and services. This includes commissions and brokerage fees.

Non-residents may open accounts in convertible francs for payments in the official market or for conversion to any of the other officially quoted currencies (see Deposits). These accounts may be held in the form of sight, call or time deposits.

Free market in financial francs

The free market is much smaller than the official market. Belgian francs bought or sold in this market are known as financial francs and may at times stand at a premium of up to two or three per cent above convertible francs. The general category of transactions made in the free market is capital transactions, including the buying of bonds and shares.

Both convertible and financial francs float freely on the foreign exchange market although the authorities intervene in the spot official market to maintain the convertible franc within the margins prescribed by the EMS.

Exchange control territory

Belgium and Luxembourg constitute a joint exchange control territory with respect to other countries. There are no controls between the two countries, which together form the Belgian-Luxembourg Economic Union (BLEU).

The authority responsible for the administration of exchange controls is the Belgo-Luxembourg Exchange Institute (IBLC), but powers for the maintenance of controls affecting capital transactions are delegated to the authorized banks.

In general, Belgium has a free exchange system. The major control enforced is through the two-tier exchange system described above. The IBLC was given the power in 1978 to prohibit the payment of interest on non-resident deposits and to impose a negative interest charge on some non-resident owned funds. This control was introduced in order to limit the inflow of speculative foreign capital, but is not being currently (May 1981) enforced.

Non-residents may deal spot or forward against the franc in all onvertible currencies through the free market.

Non-residents may freely repatriate the redemption proceeds of Belgian stocks or bonds, provided they have been held for at least six months prior to maturity.

There is no limit to the equity shareholding of a Belgium-domiciled company that may be purchased by a non-resident.

Gold

Non-residents may freely purchase and export gold in any form provided the transaction takes place in financial francs through the free market. Such transactions are free of tax and duty and licences are only required for the import of semiprocessed gold.

7. Denmark

General market environment

The Danish economy operates on the principles of free trade and free enterprise and in theory the government welcomes foreign investment.

There are, however, few opportunities for portfolio investment in Denmark. The money market is small, mainly because until recently the central government has had little need to raise short-term funds since it pursued a policy of balanced budgets. Indeed, until 1975 revenues normally exceeded expenditure. Since 1975, however, the balance of payments has suffered increasingly large deficits while the government's gross budget deficit reached 12 per cent of the gross national product in 1979. The government has consequently had to fund its deficit through the issue of debt instruments comprising treasury bills and government bonds. This has

Table 7.1 Summary of instruments

Instrument	Characteristics
MONEY MARKET	
Deposit certificates	Issued by National Bank but not available to non-residents. Three months' maturity
Deposits	Non-resident market very limited. No domestic call money market and few time deposits negotiated
Treasury bills	Issued in increasing amounts since 1975. Purchased mainly by banks and other financial institutions
CAPITAL MARKET	
Bonds	
mortgage bonds	Active market and important source of finance for companies and households. Property deeds held as security. 10–50 years' maturity
government and public sector bonds	Increasing volume of issues. Restrictions apply to purchases by non-residents. Some are lottery bonds
corporate bonds	Very limited though some issued indirectly via private mortgage market
Unit trusts	Limited funds and spread of investments
Equity shares	Poor share market. Few quotations. Company finance generally raised through banks or mortgage bonds

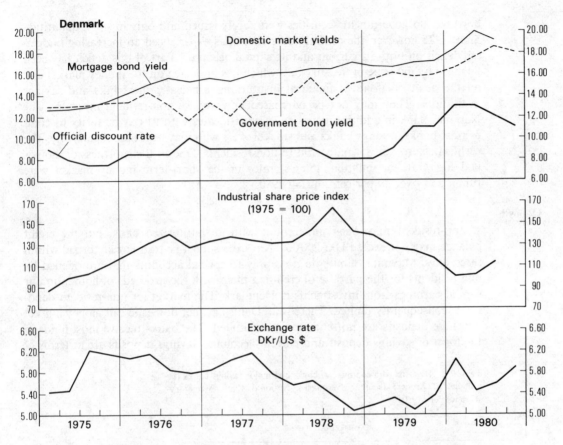

significantly increased the size of both the money and capital markets such that the volume of total government issues has risen from zero in 1974 to about kr 40 billion in 1980: while the size of the markets has grown, the range of instruments still remains small.

The capital market comprises mostly mortgage bonds in a form peculiar to Denmark. Government bonds have represented a growing share of the market in recent years because of the government's increasing funding requirements. Few other types of domestic bonds are issued and no Eurobonds are locally traded. The equity market is of little importance either to the domestic or the non-resident investor, most company finance being raised through the mortgage bond market. Exchange controls are liberal and withholding taxes minimal.

The money market

Until the late 1970s it would have been true to describe Denmark as lacking a developed money market. Few domestic short-term securities were issued and, if the government required to raise funds, it tended to do so by capital issues in foreign markets. The government in fact was generally a net lender rather than a borrower so government securities were rarely issued and only in small quantities. Since 1975 however, the central government has experienced an increasing budgetary deficit on both its current and its capital accounts. Part of this deficit has been financed by the issue of treasury bills which has impacted on the money market and on the asset portfolio of financial institutions, especially the banks and savings institutions. They may not be purchased however by non-resident investors. The National Bank in addition issues deposit certificates with 91-day maturity to commercial banks, savings banks and stockbrokers who may negotiate them freely. The certificates are not normally sold to non-residents. Due to the shortness of money, and high rate of inflation, interest rates in the short-term money market were running at over 20 per cent during 1980.

Deposits

A non-resident may open an account with an authorized bank, but the credit balance may not exceed Dkr 200 000. Any excess must be transferred abroad within three days. Maximum limits do not apply to special accounts that are opened by non-residents for the purpose of crediting them with the proceeds of liquidation or capital earnings from investments in Denmark. The market for non-resident deposits is consequently limited. There is no Danish kroner domestic call money market and time deposits are not commonly negotiated. The banks receive most funds in the form of savings deposit and current accounts. Savings deposits are at terms of

Table 7.2 **Deposits with commercial banks and major savings banks (in millions of kroner)** (source: Denmarks National Bank Monetary Review, Feb. 1980)

COMMERCIAL BANKS					
	Domestic deposits			Deposits	
End of period	Demand deposits	Time deposits	Total	from abroad	Total
1976	34 683	41 326	76 009	1878	77 887
1977	37 121	44 921	82 042	2245	84 287
1978	43 669	42 271	85 940	2643	88 583
1979	47 259	46 544	93 803	2971	96 774

MAJOR SAVINGS BANKS					
	Domestic deposits			Deposits	
End of period	Demand deposits	Time deposits	Total	from abroad	Total
1976	11 948	21 477	33 425	170	33 595
1977	13 177	24 458	37 635	232	37 867
1978	14 888	25 874	40 762	283	41 045
1979	16 145	28 787	44 932	338	45 270

either three- or six-months' notice. Banks pay interest on both, at rates determined by the discount rate and fixed by interbank agreement. This agreement is a voluntary one and not statutorily imposed. Since the beginning of 1980, when monetary conditions became particularly tight, the agreement has only been adhered to by the seven largest commercial and savings banks. Smaller banks have had to pay higher interest rates in order to bid for funds and consequently a two-tier interbank market has developed. Since 1979, however, the central bank has effectively prevented banks from competing vigorously on deposit interest rates by fixing limits on lending rates. Although the limits reflect the cost of borrowing (overdraft rates were 18 to 19 per cent in 1980) they make it unprofitable for banks to increase their deposit rates too much above those of other banks.

Table 7.2 shows domestic kroner deposits with commercial and savings banks. Non-residents are shown to have just under three per cent of deposits with commercial banks.

The capital market

Denmark's capital market displays two distinctive features. The first is the predominant role played by the bond market, in particular the market for mortgage bonds which, as a source of finance to companies and households, is as important as the commercial and savings banks put together. The second is that almost all capital demand in the bond market comes from the household sector.

Mortgage bonds

Mortgage bonds are issued by three major institutions:

1. The credit associations (Kreditforeniger) which advance first mortgage of up to 40 per cent of house values;
2. The second mortgage associations (Hypotekforeninger);
3. The mortgage loan funds (Reallaenefondes) which issue second mortgages of between 40 and 75 per cent of residential property value and up to 60 per cent for mortgages on industrial and commercial property. Exceptions are house-building where 80 per cent of the value may be raised, and social housing with a government guarantee where 90 per cent of the value is raised for up to 30 years.

The first two are legal forms of co-operatives.

There are 13 Kreditforeniger each of which is owned jointly by the borrowers and is responsible for liabilities of up to two-thirds of the principal of the loan, secured by debentures and guaranteed by the association's capital and reserves.

There are six second mortgage associations which are organized along similar lines to the credit associations.

The third group comprises three associations, owned by banks which contribute to their subsidiary associations' guarantee capital.

The sole purpose of the associations is to arrange mortgage loans. They supply mortgage bonds, in the form of debentures, to individuals wishing to raise capital

161

for house purchase. The individuals are then obliged to sell the bonds for cash on the open market via a commercial bank, savings bank or stockbroker. The banks carry the name of the issuing individual and issuing banks. The individual is therefore responsible for the interest and capital payments. The bonds are not directly guaranteed by the issuing bank or mortgage institution but are secured by mortgaged property and the capital reserves of the intermediary institution. They are considered as risk free as government bonds and to date there have been no defaults.

The bonds are irredeemable by holders but may be called in by the associations or terminated by the borrower. The total amount of mortgage bonds in circulation must be covered by mortgage deeds received as security for loans advanced.

As the loans and deeds are redeemed, corresponding amounts of bonds must be called in, usually by lot.

The market is highly efficient and both the demand and supply of funds is large. One advantage is that individuals and small companies have access to the bond market, which is open to a wide range of small lenders and borrowers, provided they have property as security.

Mortgages may similarly be obtained on ships via the Ship Credit Fund, or on farms or farming machinery via the Danish Agricultural Credit Fund.

Interest rates are subsidized for ship and house mortgages. For housing, some loans have been fixed as low as six-and-a-half per cent irrespective of bond market yields, and in addition the interest on the debt is tax deductible for individuals and businesses. A large part of the demand for funds is inelastic with respect to interest rates. Thus, another special feature of this bond market is the wide discrepancy between nominal bond rates (coupon rate) and the effective market yields, so that market bond values may differ substantially from original issue value. This occurs because the investor prefers a low coupon and a lower issue price since the capital gain arising out of redemption at par is not subject to tax, while income earned from interest is taxable. Borrowers, however, normally prefer a high coupon rate because interest payments are tax deductible from income.

Prior to 1969, mortgage bonds had original maturities of up to 60 years, but recent maturities have been for a maximum period of 50 years and a minimum of 10 years.

Government and public sector bonds

The Danish government has traditionally pursued a policy of balanced budgets, and in the past seldom had need to raise funds in the domestic capital market. On the occasions that the government did need to borrow it mostly did so by the issue of bonds on foreign markets in the form of foreign bonds or Eurobonds, or sometimes directly from the World Bank. The government still borrows in the international capital market, indeed it was the first borrower, since the abolition of UK exchange controls in October 1979, to issue a sterling denominated foreign bond (bulldog bond).

More significantly the Danish government has moved from being a net lender of funds to a net borrower and a major issuer of bonds in the domestic capital market. Table 7.3 shows that in 1974, the government issued no bonds onto the market. By

Table 7.3   Gross new issues of securities in Danish capital market (in millions of krone) (*source: OECD*)

Security	1974	1975	1976	1977	1978	1979	Jan.–Sep. 1980
Government bonds	0	6000	6941	15966	27333	34139	31370
Local government bonds	1038	905	1388	2056	2193	1495	371
Mortgage bonds	30766	33050	37075	36748	41973	47557	34333
Corporate bonds	20	99	28	0	10	83	0
Total domestic bonds	31824	40054	45432	54765	71509	83274	66074
Mortgage bonds as percentage of total	96.7	82.5	81.6	54.8	58.7	57.1	52.0
Shares	0	0	0	0	0	0	0

Table 7.4   Circulating bonds quoted on the stock exchange (in millions of krone)

End of period	Domestic government paper	Mortgage bonds	Other bonds	Total
1976	15180	204606	16686	236472
1977	27085	232195	19352	278632
1978	45121	264413	21597	231131
1979	62342	301505	22480	386327

September 1980, however, government bond issues represented almost half of all bond issues, usurping the dominance of mortgage bonds in the primary market. However, Table 7.4 shows that mortgage bonds still dominate the secondary market, since the volume of government bonds outstanding is only about one-fifth of the volume of mortgage bonds. Despite the fact that the government needs to raise funds the economy has also been suffering from inflation. In order to prevent the money supply being expanded and the exchange rate being strengthened by large capital inflows, in February 1979 the government imposed a moratorium on purchases by non-residents of government bonds issued after 1975. A similar ban had existed until 1974. Then as the volume of government paper began rapidly to increase, the government allowed purchase of its debt issues by foreigners, but closed the market to foreigners on 6 February 1979. As at May 1981 foreigners were still not permitted to purchase government paper issued since 1975; they may purchase government bonds issued before 1975 but there are so few issues outstanding that trading is extremely thin.

Some of the bonds issued by central government on the domestic market are lottery bonds. These have periodic random drawings for cash prizes.

Local authorities are making increasing recourse to the bond market but principally through the private mortgage associations and the local government credit associations.

Corporate bonds

Direct issues by companies are almost non-existent, but a considerable amount of indirect bonds are issued via the private mortgage market, partly because it is more convenient, partly because the mortgage bond market is already established and highly efficient, and partly because the cost of issues is relatively low. About 15 to 20 per cent of all bonds are issued by insurance companies and pension funds. These provide a market in the nearest thing to corporate bonds.

Unit trusts

In addition, there are five unit trusts which are open-ended investment funds. However the total size of the funds is relatively small, and the spread of their investments is limited.

Equity shares

The share market is poorly developed. Shares traded in the open market are of little importance either as a savings vehicle for investors or as a source of finance for companies. The problem, however, is more one of supply rather than of demand. The number of joint stock companies is relatively large—some 18 000 to 20 000 companies—but only a few hundred are listed on the stock exchange. Most joint stock companies are family concerns and are fairly small. Not only do the shareholders not wish to lose control, but they tend also to have an aversion to publicity with respect to their personal financial affairs. Additionally, companies are reluctant to issue shares because it is costly to do so, and also because distributed profits are subject to double taxation which is to the disadvantage of both the issuing company and the investor. Most companies are, anyway, able to raise any required finance either through the banks or through the mortgage bond markets, secured against company profit or assets. Since 1974 there have been no new issues of shares.

The stock exchange

There is one stock exchange, the Copenhagen Fondsboers.

There is almost no activity in shares and only a little in government lottery bonds and insurance company bonds. Recently an active secondary market has developed in government bonds but by far the largest turnover is in mortgage bonds. Although the banks handle the bulk of new issues, the stock exchange acts as an efficient market-place for the secondary market in mortgage bonds. Secondary market trading is largely managed by specialized stockbrokers who have the monopoly on stock exchange transactions. There is, however, no legal provision for directing all secondary market transactions through the stock exchange.

Dealing and fees

Money market

The range of money market investment mediums available to the non-resident is very restricted. Indeed, only small size time deposits and foreign exchange transactions are possible and these can be negotiated, on a net basis, through one of the seven major banks.

Capital market

Government bonds, mortgage bonds and other bonds may be dealt through a stockbroker or through one of the major banks.

Stockbrokers trade on the stock exchange which opens at 10.30. Each bond in issue is traded in turn, beginning with government bonds, followed by public sector and mortgage bonds and finishing with corporate bonds. The price for each bond is fixed as it is traded. The stock exchange is closed in the afternoon but the major banks continue to make a market throughout the day. They trade the bonds on a net basis with spreads of about $\frac{1}{2}$ per cent for government and mortgage bonds. Spreads are a little wider for some of the less actively traded corporate bonds.

Equity shares and unit trusts are not actively traded but the major banks would act on behalf of a non-resident client for a negotiated commission dependent on the size of the transaction.

Financial and monetary systems

Financial institutions

Apart from the mortgage societies, the Danish financial system is dominated by the commercial banks and savings banks. Deposits for the commercial banks come from businesses and households. There are over 100 commercial banks in Denmark and all are members of the Federation of Danish Banks which negotiates with the National Bank in the formulation of monetary policy.

Commercial banks are joint stock companies but savings banks are non-profit-making institutions. The seven largest commercial and savings banks dominate the banking system, accounting for about 80 per cent of banking business and collectively are known as 'the seven sisters'. These banks and their assets as at 1978 were:

Bank	Type	Assets (end 1978 kr billion)
Den Danske Bank Af 1981 Aktieselskab	Commercial bank	34.44
A/S Kjoben havens Handelsbank	Commercial bank	33.77
Privatbanken A/S	Commercial bank	25.09
Sparekassen SDS	Savings bank	20.44
Sparekassen Bikuben	Savings bank	13.83
Andelsbanken A/S	Commercial bank	12.03
Den Danske Provinsbank A/S	Commercial bank	10.76

165

Central bank

The central bank, the National Bank of Denmark (Danmarks National Bank), is managed by a board of directors of 25 members, a committee of directors of seven members and a three-member board of governors.

Monetary control

Despite the recent issues of treasury bills Denmark lacks a developed money market and a system of variable reserve requirements and it is therefore difficult for banking operations to be controlled by the central bank, by means of market-oriented instruments. The main instruments used are credit ceilings, the discount facility and a special deposit system.

The objective of monetary policy is to contain the rise in money supply (M2) to just below the increase in gross domestic product. Credit ceilings had been the main means of control between 1969 and September 1980, when they were relaxed in favour of a system of liquidity controls.

Credit ceilings

Aimed at restricting the supply of credit from the banking to the private sector, banks used to be set specific individual limits on the increase in their lending to corporate and personal borrowers. If banks exceeded the ceilings imposed, they were obliged to make interest-free deposits with the central bank in amounts equal to 100 per cent of any such excess. This has proved a reasonably effective method of containing the growth in bank lending. The ceilings could be raised or lowered by the central bank according to whether the government wished to encourage expansion or contraction of the money supply. Since Autumn 1980, credit ceilings controls have been applied less rigorously. Instead of each bank being set specific credit ceilings, generally agreed guidelines are established for all banks. For the nine months from 30 September 1980 to 30 June 1981, total bank advances could not be increased by more than six per cent. For the period from July 1981, new general credit ceilings will be set by the central bank. These general controls mean that the more efficient banks are able to increase their credit by more than six per cent whereas the less efficient banks are obliged to expand credit at a lower rate.

Liquidity controls

In addition to the credit ceilings, new liquidity control measures introduced stipulate that the banks should not artificially increase their deposits base (against which they can lend) by money market operations, the attraction of large time deposits from local authorities or large corporations or by the sale of securities in order to switch into direct loan assets.

Prior to September 1980 liquidity and solvency requirements did exist but could not be modified and thus were not effective as monetary policy instruments. The new liquidity controls are flexible and have a more immediate effect, especially when used in conjunction with interest rate controls.

Since March 1979 maximum limits have been placed on the interest rates which banks may charge on loans and advances. This effectively places a limit on the rates which banks can pay for deposits. While the interest rate limits have been compatible with other money market rates, they prevent banks competing aggressively for deposits, against which they can expand credit.

Discount policy

A relatively wide range of assets, including company equities, are eligible for rediscount at the National Bank at the official discount rate to which other market lending rates are directly tied. Although all banks have access to the discount facility, this is not an automatic recourse facility. The central bank can therefore control liquidity through suspension or restriction of operations through the discount window. The discount rate is determined by the board of governors of the National Bank of Denmark, and raised or lowered according to whether the authorities wish to raise the cost of money and thus to restrict the growth of credit or to whether they wish to ease monetary conditions. The discount rate has risen steadily during the 1970s from four-and-a-half per cent in 1973 to a high of 13 per cent between February and August 1980. In October 1980 it was reduced to 11 per cent.

Deposit certificates have also been issued by the National Bank to the banking system as a method of absorbing excess liquidity, although the last such issue was made in November 1976. These were issued with three-, six- and nine-month maturities at discounts fixed by the Bank, and can only be held or traded between the banks or savings banks. The certificates could be repurchased on demand by the National Bank, the price being dependent upon the original discount and the unexpired period. The system of special deposits and treasury bill issues has superseded deposit certificates as a means of controlling liquidity in the banking system.

Special deposits

In 1975, the system of special deposits was introduced after negotiation with the government and the banks. These special deposits were at three per cent of deposits held at the end of September 1975, or 24 per cent of the increase in deposits between the end of March and the end of September 1975 plus, in either case, 12 per cent of the succeeding monthly increase in deposits.

In 1977 these monetary restrictions were eased and half of the banks' special deposits were released in April.

Open market operations

In the past the National Bank has only needed to engage in open market operations to a very limited extent. It did so by buying or selling bonds in the open market with the intention of smoothing fluctuations in interest rates and bank liquidity. The major problem in recent years has been that of funding the government debt. While the bank continues to conduct a certain amount of open market operations its major operations involve the issue of government bonds and treasury bills onto the market, which has the effect of mopping up liquidity from the financial system. Government bonds, which in 1980 were yielding 19 to 20 per cent, have been providing a better return than bank deposits and many other alternative investments. As a result a large proportion of these bonds are held by investors outside the banking system. This tends to restrict the effectiveness of the National Bank's open market operations with the banking system. The issue of treasury bills—which are mainly held by banks and financial institutions rather than by the non-bank public—have in recent years provided an additional medium for the National Bank's open market operations.

Withholding taxes

There are no withholding taxes on interest or on stock dividends.

Cash dividends paid by a Danish corporation are subject to withholding tax at a standard rate of 30 per cent.

Residents of countries having a tax treaty with Denmark may reclaim some of this withholding tax by filing the relevant forms.

The reduced rate depends on the type of treaty and the shareholding held by the non-resident. This is summarized in Table 7.5.

Table 7.5 Withholding taxes

Recipient	Dividends %	% shareholding to qualify for lower rate
Non-treaty countries	30	
Treaty countries		
Group 1. Tax credit equals proportion of tax borne by the dividend income relative to the total taxable income in Denmark		
Austria	10	no minimum required
Faroe Islands	0	no minimum required
Finland	0	no minimum required
France	0	no minimum required
Germany		
Iceland	0	no minimum required
India	30	25%
Ireland	0	no minimum required
Sri Lanka	5	no minimum required
Switzerland	0	no minimum required

168   (continued)

Table 7.5 Continued

Recipient	Dividends %	% shareholding to qualify for lower rate
Group 2. As with group 1 but exempt for dividends from shipping and aviation.		
Austria	10	no minimum required
Brazil	25	no minimum required
Germany	15 or 10	25%
Israel	0	50%
Malaysia	0	no minimum required
Norway	15	no minimum required
Singapore	10	25%
Spain	10	50%
Thailand	20	25%
Group 3. Tax credit is the lower of tax paid in the foreign country and the proportion of tax borne by the dividend income relative to total taxable income in Denmark		
Belgium	15	no minimum required
Canada	15	no minimum required
Greenland	30	no minimum required
Italy	15	no minimum required
Japan	10	25%
Kenya	20	25%
Korea	5	no minimum required
Malta	5	25%
Netherlands	0	25%
Netherlands Antilles	15	25%
Nigeria	5	25%
Pakistan	15	$33\frac{1}{3}$%
Philippines	20	no minimum required
Portugal	10	25%
Rumania	10	25%
Sweden	5	25%
Tanzania	15	no minimum required
Trinidad and Tobago	10	25%
UK	5	10%
US	5	95%
Zambia	15	no minimum required

Exchange controls

Authorities

The system of exchange controls is determined by the government but administered
by the National Bank and authorized exchange dealers.

Currency

The Danish monetary area comprises Denmark, Greenland and Faroe Islands. The currency is the Danish kroner which is a participant of the EMS.

Authorized exchange dealers may engage in arbitrage, both spot and forward. Spot transactions are defined as transactions where actual delivery takes place within two banking days. Transactions taking place within three banking days or more are defined as forward transactions. Spot transactions and forward transactions for less than two years may be concluded freely. Payments to or from foreign countries may be made in any foreign currency or in Danish krone.

Non-resident accounts

Non-resident kroner accounts are fully convertible. They may be opened by authorized banks for foreign banks, insurance companies and shipping companies and for specified official institutions of the EEC. They may also be opened for other non-residents provided that the total credit balances of the accounts of an individual non-resident does not exceed 200 000 krone. Any amount in excess of this must be transferred abroad within three days.

Inward investment

Both inward and outward transfers of capital and all borrowing and lending between residents and non-residents are subject to exchange control and may be restricted. The sale to non-residents of Danish bonds listed on the stock exchange does not require a special licence, but with effect from 6 February 1979 there is a ban on foreign purchases of Danish government bonds. Bonds denominated only in Danish kroner may be resold to residents. Non-residents may freely subscribe to shares that are quoted on the Copenhagen stock exchange provided that the purchase does not represent a direct investment. Non-residents may not subscribe, however, to certificates of investment companies etc., whose latest balance sheet shows that more than 10 per cent of their assets are securities other than stock exchange securities.

Transfers of proceeds from the sale or liquidation of all types of investments and transfers of all other liquid funds in Denmark owned by non-residents are permitted freely irrespective of how the original investment was acquired.

Repatriation of profit and dividends

Interest and repayment of principal on authorized loans, credits and deposits received from persons and firms who are non-residents at the time of receipt may be paid freely, with the proviso that loans and credits obtained from a non-resident generally must not be amortized or repaid in full more than 30 days before the amortization payment, or repayment is due.

Imports and exports of securities are subject to regulations established by the National Bank. Bona fide imports of Danish securities payable only in Danish krone are permitted. Exports of Danish and foreign securities held in Denmark and belonging to non-residents may, with the principal exception of bonds denominated wholly or partly in foreign currencies, be freely sold to residents.

Foreign securities held in Denmark belonging to non-residents may with certain exceptions be sold to residents, though only with the permission of the National Bank. Foreign securities held in Denmark may be negotiated freely between residents, provided that the exchange control regulations are not circumvented.

8.   France

General market environment

Paris provides an important financial centre for the Euromarkets but the domestic French money and capital markets could be said to be still in a somewhat evolutionary stage. Until the late sixties, the financial system, being highly regulated, was not conducive to the free market interplay necessary for an efficient and effective securities market.

During the 1970s the central bank's approach to monetary policy, and changes in the banking regulations, have encouraged the growth of short-term money markets,

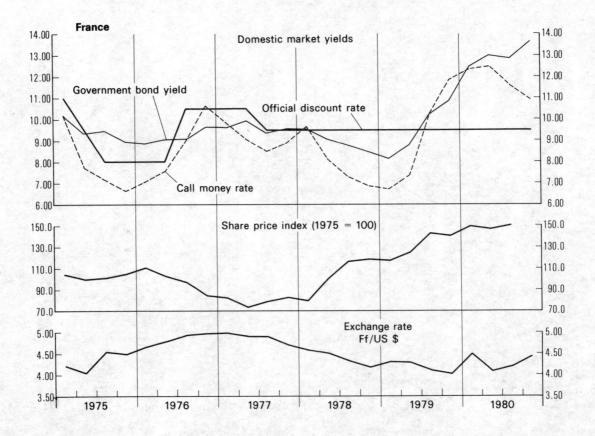

Table 8.1 Summary of instruments

Securities	Characteristics
MONEY MARKET	
Deposits	
call deposits	An active and still growing market particularly in overnight and two-day call money
time deposits	Wide range of terms available. A large and active market. Some interest rate restrictions for small amounts
Eurocurrency deposits	A major European centre for call and time deposits in Eurodollars and other currencies
Bons de caisse	The nearest instrument to a CD available. Similar terms to a CD but not marketable
Treasury bills	Available to non-residents but an inadequate secondary market
CAPITAL MARKET	
Bons du tresor	Treasury bonds of medium term maturity; three to five years
Bonds of government, local authorities and public institutions	Represent about 80 per cent of all medium- or long-term instruments issued in the domestic market
Corporate bonds	These dominate the private sector security issues and are a more important source of finance to French companies than is equity financing
Foreign bonds	A few foreign bonds but thin trading
Eurobonds	Tightly controlled new issue calendar restricting the growth of this market
Equities	Active market only for shares of major companies
Gold	May be purchased but not exported
Commodities	A wide range of commodities may be purchased through the Paris Commodity Bourse

particularly the call and time deposit markets and the Eurocurrency market, while bonds still dominate the capital markets.

Plans announced by the government indicate that the French money and capital markets will become more liberal and less regulated during the 1980s.

Although financial markets are becoming more competitive and international in outlook, the French banking system and securities market is still at present constrained by protective regulations instituted since the 1930s. The state sector still dominates the financial system. Markets are subject to a high degree of intervention by the relevant authorities, whose aims are to directly influence most aspects of the economy rather than to provide a purely stabilizing effect on markets.

Withholding taxes apply to both dividends and interest and exchange controls are rigorously enforced and may be subject to frequent change. The controls as they affect the securities market have, however, been considerably eased and only formal requirements are now applied to most transactions.

The money market

Deposits

Call deposits

This market is now a very active one with most call money placed in the franc interbank overnight market, although markets are also made in two- and seven-day call money.

The call market is a relatively recent innovation in the French financial system. It was encouraged by changes in banking regulations during the 1970s, one of which prohibited French banks from paying interest on deposits of less than 30 days. The popularity and success of the call market is evidenced by the fact that it now handles a larger volume of funds than the market for time deposits. At the end of 1979 demand deposits, of which a major proportion was money placed at call, amounted to about Ff 400 billion

The call market is primarily an interbank market, used by banks and other financial institutions to balance their books on a short-term basis by borrowing and lending liquidity between themselves. Non-bank entities may also participate by lending short-term cash to the banking system in minimum amounts of Ff 1 000 000.

Short-term deposit may take the form of ordinary deposits, both secured and unsecured, or the sale of bills with a repurchase agreement. Interest rates are freely determined by demand and supply in the market.

Time deposits

French franc time deposits may be placed for periods of seven days, or for 1, 2, 3, 6 and 12 months, or for 2 years or 30 months. Other terms are also possible and much dealing is done to the end of the month.

Short deposits of up to one month are mostly interbank transactions which are also participated in by non-bank corporate lenders. Transactions are usually arranged by the sale and repurchase of money market securities such as treasury bills. As with the call market, short-term deposits of this nature are usually negotiated in minimum sizes of Ff 1 million. Interest rates are determined by supply and demand but are influenced by the official discount rate. Table 8.2 shows that interest rates on one month interbank money correlates closely with day-to-day call money rates and during 1979 and 1980 has been about three to four per cent higher than the discount rate and sometimes even higher than the banks' prime lending rate.

This is not the normal relationship but occurs because the Banque de France has in recent years been placing greater emphasis on the use of open market operations to control liquidity in the banking system and has correspondingly reduced the amount of credit lent to the banks by means of the discount facility. Banks consequently have to bid for funds in the open market and hence pay interest rates above discount rate and sometimes above their own lending rates. It is, however, more usual for money market rates to be below the discount rate.

Table 8.2 Interest rates and yields in French money and capital markets (average rates) (*source: OECD and IMF*)

| | End 1978 | *1979* | | | | | | | | | | | |
		Jan.	*Feb.*	*Mar.*	*Apr.*	*May*	*June*	*July*	*Aug.*	*Sep.*	*Oct.*	*Nov.*	*Dec.*
RATES													
Official discount rate	9.5	9.5	9.5	9.5	9.5	9.5	9.5	9.5	9.5	9.5	9.5	9.5	9.5
Banks' prime lending rate	8.80	8.80	8.80	8.80	8.80	8.80	9.15	9.75	10.05	10.75	11.05	11.50	11.50
Overnight call money	6.67	6.64	6.68	6.77	6.82	7.20	8.01	9.34	10.44	10.99	11.47	11.95	12.47
1-month interbank deposits	6.56	6.50	6.68	6.80	6.75	7.27	8.32	9.65	10.63	11.26	11.86	12.29	12.32
1-year time deposits (amounts under Ff 100 000)	5.50	5.50	5.50	5.50	5.50	5.50	5.50	5.50	5.50	5.50	5.50	5.50	5.50
YIELDS													
Government and public sector bonds													
at issue	10.04	9.53	9.66	9.65	9.66	9.64	—	10.65	—	11.65	11.65	11.77	12.14
in secondary market	9.94	9.68	9.77	—	9.64	9.96	10.71	11.25	11.56	11.56	11.60	12.09	12.59
Corporate bonds													
at issue	10.18	—	9.86	9.90	9.88	9.83	10.99	11.01	11.80	11.93	11.85	11.96	12.42
in secondary market	10.27	10.06	10.16	—	10.01	10.30	11.12	11.54	12.03	11.85	11.84	12.33	12.92
Yield on equity shares	5.84	5.79	6.12	—	5.54	5.63	5.72	5.93	5.55	5.25	5.69	5.72	5.79

| | End 1978 | *1980* | | | | | | | | | | | |
		Jan.	*Feb.*	*Mar.*	*Apr.*	*May*	*June*	*July*	*Aug.*	*Sep.*	*Oct.*	*Nov.*	*Dec.*
RATES													
Official discount rate	9.5	9.5	9.5	9.5	9.5	9.5	9.5	9.5	9.5	9.5	9.5	9.5	9.5
Banks' prime lending rate	8.80	11.50	12.50	13.25	13.0	13.0	13.0	13.0	12.25	12.25	12.25	12.25	12.25
Overnight call money	6.67	11.99	12.17	12.96	12.40	12.61	12.43	12.04	11.32	11.37	11.22	10.74	10.88
1-month interbank deposits	6.56	12.18	12.37	13.42	12.57	12.60	12.34	11.94	11.36	11.61	11.44	10.86	11.05
1-year time deposits (amounts under Ff 100 000)	5.50	5.50	5.50	5.50	5.50	6.50	6.50	6.50	6.50	6.50	6.50	6.50	6.50
YIELDS													
Government and public sector bonds													
at issue	10.04	12.54	12.47	14.52	14.56	14.26	13.95	13.71	—	13.99	14.59	14.55	14.71
in secondary market	9.94	12.52	14.11	14.44	13.95	13.49	13.34	13.43	13.46	13.85	14.27	14.24	14.31
Corporate bonds													
at issue	10.18	13.21	12.70	14.65	14.63	14.34	14.16	13.43	13.86	14.03	14.69	14.83	15.23
in secondary market	10.27	12.91	14.57	14.80	14.42	13.87	13.88	13.77	13.84	14.05	14.57	14.61	14.68
Yield on equity shares	5.84	5.65	5.58	6.05	6.00	5.88	5.90	6.78	6.67	6.65	6.53	6.56	6.69

In the market for longer-term time deposits, amounts of less than Ff 100 000 and placed for terms of less than two years are subject to maximum rates of interest fixed by the National Credit Council. This maximum rate is normally about half the banks' prime lending rate.

Deposits of more than Ff 100 000 or of longer than two years' term are free from interest rate restrictions and rates are determined by demand and supply by borrowers and lenders in the market.

Time deposits account for about 20 per cent of all liquid or short-term savings in France. At the end of 1979 time deposits placed with all financial institutions totalled approximately Ff 145 billion.

Eurocurrency deposits

There is an active Eurocurrency money market, which preceded the development of the domestic call money market. Paris has now become one of Europe's principal markets for Eurodollar call and time deposits. Although evidently smaller than the London market, it is nevertheless of significant size.

By the end of 1979, French banks accounted for about 15 per cent of the US$666 billion Eurocurrency deposits placed with European banks. (In contrast London accounted for 42 per cent of the market.)

Foreign currency deposits with French banks comprised US$61 billion denominated in US dollars and US$38.5 billion denominated in other currencies. This compares with total domestic currency deposits of only US$6.6 billion. The Eurocurrency market is thus of significant size in relation to the local money market. Unlike the domestic market, which is hampered by regulations and controls, the Eurocurrency market is not similarly restricted, so the growth of the market has been encouraged. It has grown sixfold in the decade from 1970 to 1980.

Deposits in dollars or other convertible currencies may be placed at call, usually for a minimum of two days' notice, or on time deposit, generally for up to one year though longer terms are available for deposits denominated in major currencies. Minimum accepted sizes of call or short-term deposits are US$250 000 or foreign currency equivalent. Long deposits may be placed in minimum sizes of US$25 000 or equivalent.

Bons de caisse

There is no market for CDs in France; the nearest equivalent is bons de caisse (savings bonds). These are depository receipts issued by commercial banks with short maturities of between three months and five years. They are not, however, marketable securities though they may be accepted as collateral. Yields approximate closely to those for time deposits of comparable maturity. Their advantage over time deposits is that they can be purchased in smaller denomination (Ff 10 000), but are not subject to the maximum interest rates that apply to time deposits of less than Ff 100 000.

Treasury bills

The Banque de France issues one-, three- and six-month treasury bills which non-residents may freely purchase. They are auctioned by the Banque de France at irregular intervals. The secondary market is thin and most trading takes place between the banks and discount houses.

Other money market securities

Due to the history of the French financial system, the range of money market instruments issued is limited. French companies tend to operate with little cash in hand and a maximum of short-term debt, which results in little money from the company sector reaching the financial markets. Private drafts such as commercial or finance bills are issued by commercial banks to their customers and may be sold to third parties including non-residents. There is not, however, an adequate secondary market and such trading as does take place is very thin.

Bons du tresor

Apart from the instruments mentioned above, a possible money market security to be considered is bons du trésor (treasury bonds) which are close to maturity. These are medium-term fixed coupon paper issued by the Banque de France on behalf of the treasury and carry original maturities of one, two, three or five years.

A few semi-public institutions also issue short-term securities, but only a limited secondary market exists for this type of paper.

In particular, bonds of six-month, one-year, or two-year maturities are issued by the Caisses Régionales de Crédit Agricole (Bonds of the Regional Agricultural Loan Funds), and by the Caisses Nationales de Crédit Agricole (the National Agricultural Loan Fund) which carry original maturities of between three and five years.

The capital market

The public sector plays a dominant role in the French capital market. In the domestic market 80 per cent of all medium- and long-term financial instruments are issued either directly by the government or indirectly through government controlled institutions. Similarly, 85 per cent of domestic savings are collected by public and semipublic institutions, including banks and savings institutions, many of which are wholly or partly owned by the government.

Bonds in the public sector are issued by:

The government
Local authorities
National credit and savings institutions
Nationalized industries

Bankable bonds

The domestic bond market distinguishes between two classes of bonds—bankable and unbankable bonds. Bankable bonds comprise most issues, by both public and private sector borrowers, that have a remaining maturity of less than seven years. This includes floating rate notes which may have longer maturities but where the rollover feature makes them similar to a short maturity bond. It also includes some bonds with maturities of more than seven years where the lender has the option to redeem them within seven years. Indexed bonds and bonds that carry rights of conversion into ordinary shares of the issuing company are excluded, whether or not they have maturities of under seven years.

The maturity criterion qualifies the short-dated bonds to be held by banks in their reserve asset portfolios, hence the term 'bankable bonds'. As a result, bonds of up to seven years maturity are more marketable than other 'unbankable' bonds.

First and second category bonds

For secondary market trading purposes—principally on the stock exchange—bonds are additionally classified as first and second category. First category bonds are those issued by the state and by other public authorities, including public issues on behalf of foreign countries. Second category bonds comprise all private sector corporate issues. First category bonds are always traded before second category bonds during stock exchange trading sessions.

Government bonds

Since 1977, the French government has been trying to reduce inflation by adhering to strict control over the growth of the money supply. Within this framework the government has tried to finance a large part of its budget deficit through the issue of bonds—a method which does not create new money in the economic system. Thus, while in the early 1970s almost all of the government's receipts were derived from taxes and the central government budget remained in surplus, since 1975 it has had a recurrent deficit. This deficit has been covered by the issue of bonds on the domestic capital market. Apart from 1973 there had been no bonds issued by the central government between 1968 and 1975. In 1976 gross new issues were Ff 8.55 billion. By 1979 new issues had risen to Ff 19.95 billion (Ff 16.38 net) or just over 30 per cent of total bond issues in the French market. New issues of government bonds for 1980 were roughly double the amount raised in 1979. Table 8.3 shows gross new issues of government bonds since 1975.

Government bond issues are normally in sizes of Ff 1000 million up to Ff 2500 million and in denominations of Ff 1000.

Maturities range up to 15 years but those with an original or remaining life of seven years or less enjoy more active markets since they are the highest quality bankable bonds.

All fixed-rate straight bonds pay interest once annually. Floating rate notes pay interest twice per year. Some redeem principal in full at maturity while others are amortized during the life of the loan. Prices of straight bonds are quoted on a yield basis exclusive of acrued interest. Floating rate bonds are quoted in francs including acrued interest.

Government bonds are an attractive investment for non-residents because their coupons, particularly those of the more recently issued bonds, are at attractive

Table 8.3   Gross new public issues in French capital markets (in billions of francs) (*source: OECD*)

Securities	1975	1976	1977	1978	1979	(*Jan.–Nov.*) 1980
BONDS						
Government	....	8.55	13.47	18.25	19.95	39.60
Local government bonds	3.49	3.39	4.47	5.84	5.30	4.66
Financial institutions	13.05	21.15	22.85	23.23	25.63	60.04
Public and private non-financial enterprises	27.17	8.65	10.23	9.62	13.78	10.05
Total domestic bonds	43.71	41.74	51.01	56.95	64.65	114.35
Foreign bonds	0.15	0.25	0.30	0.87	0.83	1.10
Total bonds	43.86	41.99	51.31	57.82	65.48	115.45
SHARES						
Financial institutions	2.09	1.34	2.31	1.95	2.16	4.51
Non-financial companies	7.71	8.10	8.82	12.37	12.21	13.53
Total shares	9.80	9.44	11.13	14.31	14.37	18.04
VALUE OF ISSUES OUTSTANDING						
BONDS						
Nominal value						
government bonds	14.14	15.51	22.47	34.55	50.93	
other public sector bonds	150.64	176.17	192.71	218.66	248.35	
private sector bonds	59.68	72.66	85.17	92.48	96.21	
Total	224.46	264.34	300.35	345.68	395.49	494.15
Market value						
government bonds	30.83	34.28	47.82	66.00	108	
other public sector bonds	156.60	179.57	198.97	243.84	254	
private sector bonds	59.16	71.01	82.71	99.02	94	
Total	246.59	284.86	329.50	408.86	456.00	567.00
SHARES						
Market value—all shares	161.40	139.17	133.75	195.95	230.00	256.00

levels (Table 8.2) and interest is paid free of withholding tax. Their secondary market turnover, traded on the Paris stock exchange, is consequently quite active, and may be traded in amounts of up to Ff 10 million.

Local government bonds

The state and local governments receive finance directly from the central government and also indirectly from state owned financial institutions. They have also been consistent borrowers in the capital market through the issue of bonds, but

179

only in small volumes each year. Just under Ff 5 billion were issued in 1980 (see Table 8.3).

Like central government bonds, local authority bonds carry fixed coupon rates and maturities of up to 15 years. Bonds with less than seven years' maturity are also bankable bonds and thus are more marketable and command slightly lower yields than those with a life of more than seven years.

All bonds are guaranteed by the state but because they are not direct obligations of the government they yield between 5 and 30 basis points more than comparable government bonds.

Bond denominations are Ff 2000 and although their marketability is generally good they cannot be dealt in such large sizes as government bonds. Unlike government bonds they are not free of withholding tax with respect to annual interest payments. As with government bonds, the secondary market is made on the Paris Bourse.

Other public sector bonds

The French economic and financial system is heavily represented in all sectors by state owned institutions. In the financial sector, the three largest commercial banks are state owned, as are major savings institutions such as the Post Office Savings Bank and Caisse de Dépôts which manages the funds of the savings banks. So also are the large and influential co-operative banks such as Crédit Agricole which were designed to collect savings and grant credit to specific groups but which have become large banks in the international as well as the national market.

In industry too there are a number of large nationalized industries such as the steel and energy industries as well as a number of credit institutions designed to lend to the industry and export sectors at favourable rates.

Most of these public sector institutions issue bonds in the capital market. They are often guaranteed as to principal and interest by the government and most of them are 'bankable' bonds, having maturities of less than seven years.

Most of these public sector bonds are issued with fixed-rate coupons although a number are indexed (see Indexed bonds below). All pay interest annually and some redeem capital in full at maturity though some are amortized by the annuity principal in which equal annual repayments include interest and some capital. Maturities range up to 15 years. Public sector bonds represent 60 per cent of all outstanding bonds issued both in nominal and market value terms.

Many of these bonds enjoy very active secondary markets with daily stock exchange turnovers of Ff 10 million to Ff 20 million. For the non-resident they provide not only attractive yields but interest is not paid free of withholding tax.

Private sector corporate bonds

Bond financing is a much more important source of funds than is equity financing for French companies because higher yields available on bonds more easily attract investors. Nevertheless the private sector bond market is still underdeveloped because French domestic capital markets have historically lacked adequate funds.

This lack of funds is due partly to the traditional method of saving by French households who tend to hoard cash rather than deposit it with a savings institution or place it in the capital market but more, perhaps, to the structure of the French financial system. More than four-fifths of savings are collected by state owned institutions, which then channel funds into the public sector at the expense of the private sector and the capital market in general.

In addition the secondary market, made on the Paris Bourse, is not geared to attract either the smaller companies or the small investors, although plans are in progress for revising trading methods on the Bourse.

Consequently, companies generally first apply to the banks for loans or to government agencies for debt finance, which they will receive if their objectives coincide with those of the national economic plan. Bond issues are favoured therefore mainly by the large well-known companies who can more readily attract investors.

Corporate bonds represent approximately one-third of both the market and nominal value of bonds listed on the Bourse and about 20 per cent of new issues each year. While the volume of new corporate bond issues has remained fairly consistent their proportion relative to the total market has steadily fallen because of the increasing volume of public sector bond issues.

Maturities of new issues may range up to 20 years and occasionally longer, though most have initial lives of 10 to 15 years. Issue sizes of more than Ff 100 million have a reasonable market.

Both straight and convertible bonds are issued, though convertible bonds are only feasible for companies whose shares are well-traded in the equities market. Both types pay interest annually and, of the straight bonds, some redeem capital in full at maturity and some amortize capital on the annuity principle during the life of the loan. New issue yields of corporate bonds are close to government guaranteed bonds, with differentials of 10 to 30 basis points in the secondary market. Corporate bonds normally trade at yields which are on average $1\frac{1}{2}$ to $2\frac{1}{2}$ percentage points above comparative public sector bonds.

The majority of secondary market transactions are effected through the Paris Bourse and active markets are enjoyed for bonds of the large national and multinational French companies.

Foreign bonds

The foreign bond market in France in negligible. Very few issues have been made in the domestic market by foreign borrowers. Such issues as have been made have been on behalf of international agencies or EEC institutions and have never exceeded a total of Ff 1 billion in any one year. They are listed on the Bourse and traded in the same market as domestic bonds. (See Table 8.3.)

Indexed bonds

Indexed bonds are a special feature of the French domestic bond market.

Either the coupon rate or the redemption value may be indexed according to different criteria. Bonds currently on the market are index-linked to other currencies, fuel prices and gold.

181

All indexed bonds on the market have been issued by the public sector—private companies have been forbidden to make such issues since 1958. Though few in number, they are among the most actively traded securities on the Paris Bourse.

The gold-linked bond, the 1973 ex-Pinay $4\frac{1}{2}$ per cent state loan, is probably the most active of all securities and at times accounts for half the turnover of the Bourse. This bond has two semiannual valuations of redemption price based on a formula that takes account of the average value of the Napoleon 20 franc gold coin over the preceding 100 stock exchange quotations. Although bearing a low fixed coupon it is attractive not only because it carries the potential of capital gain through being linked to the price of gold (the Napoleon coin normally stands at a substantial and sometimes volatile premium to its gold content) but also because it is free from all taxes. It has presented a good investment opportunity for all types of investors whether resident or non-resident, but may be subject to a wealth tax in the future. Another gold-linked bond, though not tax free, is the seven per cent 1973 state loan where interest paid and principal are indexed to the value of the gold bar in Paris.

The 8.8% Emprunt Barre is linked to the value of a basket of European currencies. It therefore represents a reasonable hedge against the devaluation of the franc and is attractive to some non-residents or domestic exporters who have income in francs but liabilities spread across a number of currencies. The Caisse Nationale de l'Energie 3 per cent is linked to the revenues of the state gas and electricity utilities. This bond has proved fairly active in secondary market trading and allows investors to benefit indirectly from rising fuel prices.

Eurobonds

The French francs Eurobond market has declined in importance and activity since the mid-1970s, constrained largely by the monetary authority's concern over the exchange value and volatility of the franc. Back in 1972 the French franc Eurobond market was surpassed only by the US dollar and Deutschemark markets in terms of new issue volume. Between 1972 and 1976 the market's growth was fettered by regulations and for most of 1976 and all of 1977 was closed entirely.

It was reopened in the latter part of 1978 and has continued during 1979 and 1980, but the new issues calendar was restricted to a few select borrowers. There is still an outstanding number of borrowers wishing to raise funds through the French franc Eurobond market in preference to the domestic bond market but issues are currently being limited to about Ff 1000 million per year, or two issues per month.

The issues of all French Eurobonds are closely monitored by the French monetary authorities and the calendar and timing of new issues is subject to approval.

The bonds are in bearer form with interest payable annually, free of withholding tax. New issues vary between Ff 50 million and Ff 200 million each.

Maturities range up to 12 years but many issues operate a sinking fund which reduces the average life to between seven and nine years.

There are about 75 Eurofranc bonds outstanding that have been issued by French public and private sector companies, international institutions, Canadian and British borrowers and by sovereign states. *Secondary market*

The secondary market is maintained primarily by banks operating in the major European financial centres, although French franc Eurobonds are also listed on the London and Luxembourg Stock Exchanges.

Equities market

There are approximately 750 shares listed on the Paris Bourse, 595 of which are shares of French companies and 160 of foreign companies. They have a combined market capitalization of over Ff 250 billion. This ranks the French equity market the third largest in Europe after London, which is three times as large, and Germany which is one-and-a-half times the size of the French market.

In market value terms, equities amount to just under half the value of bonds outstanding in the domestic market though the value of turnover is approximately the same in each of the bond and equity markets.

However the share market, like the corporate bond market, is small relative to the industrial base in France. Much of industry receives capital from state institutions or from the banks, often at favourable rates of interest. This is due to the nature of banking regulations which allow the banks to lend to certain sectors of the economy subject to lower credit ceilings and thus at lower cost to the banks if ultimately to the borrowers. Although the authorities are now tightening up on these forms of credit, industries which have traditionally benefited are all those that significantly add to the productive earnings or social welfare of the country. In particular, export oriented companies, the housing sector, and energy industries have been able to take advantage of special terms of credit.

In consequence, many companies prefer private bank loans or loans from specialist state institutions (such as the Institut de Développement Industriel) which provide capital for expanding companies to raising funds directly in the market either through bonds or shares.

In addition, only a relatively small proportion of domestic savings (about four per cent) finds its way to the stock exchange. Most of the funds collected by financial and savings institutions are channelled into the public sector either directly or into government or government guaranteed securities. In general individuals shy away from the stock exchange because trading methods are both complex and perhaps anachronistic and because too little is done to make the public aware of the investment opportunities. These factors are being reviewed and changes are currently being introduced (see Stock exchange) and it is hoped that greater interest will be generated among both borrowers and lenders in the capital market.

An innovation introduced in the last few years are unit trusts (SICAVs) which are designed to attract the individual investor. They give the small investor the advantage of being able to participate in the equity market while not needing to have too great a knowledge of the market. In addition they offer some special tax concessions to residents, calculated according to the size of the investor's family. *Sicavs*

183

Table 8.4 Major French companies (*source: Société Générale Bank Ltd*)

Company	Activities	Market capitalization in millions of francs (31 Dec. 1980)
Elf Aquitaine	Oil and gas production/refining	23 384
Avions Dassault	Aerospace and defence	9 125
L'Air liquide	Industrial gas production	8 804
Elf Gabon	Oil and gas production	7 569
Française des Pétroles	Oil and gas production	6 859
Saint-Gobain	Industrial engineering	4 684
Financière de Paris (Paribas)	Financial holding company	4 003
Carrefour	Cheese and food production	3 820
Thomson–CSF	Electrical engineering	3 606
Société Générale	Bank	3 314

Of the shares listed on the Bourse, about 300 have reasonable markets but only the shares of the major national and multinational companies enjoy active markets. The top ten French companies and their market capitalization as at 31 December 1980 are shown in Table 8.4.

Dividends are paid net of tax. Residents of certain countries are eligible for a tax credit (avoir fiscal) equal to half the dividend received. The non-resident is subject to a 25 per cent withholding tax but for residents of countries that have a tax treaty with France, lower or zero rates may apply and any tax paid may be offset against domestic tax (see Withholding taxes).

La Bourse (The stock exchange)

Although there are also stock exchanges at Bordeaux, Lyon, Marseilles, Nancy, Nantes and Toulouse, the Paris Bourse handles 99 per cent of all transactions in capital market securities.

These securities include bonds, equities and gold. The size and turnover of the bond and equity market is small relative to the level of France's economic activity because less than four per cent of domestic savings are placed in the stock exchange. Consequently the market is tapped mainly by the public sector, and by the large national and international companies who dominate equity trading activity. Approximately 10 per cent of the companies quoted on the exchange account for over 60 per cent of the total market capitalization.

The methods of trading are currently being revised; the new proposals are intended to be introduced in 1982.

Up until 1980, the Paris Bourse has operated as follows:

The market opens from 11.30 a.m. to 1.30 p.m. for all bonds and from 12.30 to 2.30 p.m. for other securities. Brokers will, however, deal outside these times, particularly with the banks. It is thus often preferable for a non-resident investor to deal through his bank which in turn will use its broker.

The Bourse uses the call-over method and a restrictive trading system is operated. Prices for each of the shares in which a market is being made are fixed only twice a day at daily trading sessions. However 90 per cent of transactions are done at the opening prices. Trading outside the sessions can only be carried out at quoted prices and there are no discounts for large block trading.

Specialist dealers exist for those shares that are only seldom traded. These specialists may hold such securities on their own account but generally brokers are forbidden to take short-term position in securities for their own account, and this sometimes leads to difficulties in executing orders. However, the biggest French institutions are usually prepared to perform a jobbing function in leading equities.

There are two major markets and three trading methods operated on the Bourse. The official market comprises the cash or spot market and the marché à terme, or forward market. The unofficial market comprises the hors cote market.

On the cash market, about two thousand listed securities (bonds and equities) can be purchased in any quantity, including very small parcels of shares, but the securities and funds must be remitted as soon as transacted, within the same business day. The cash market represents 60 per cent of all transactions on the Bourse. Share price movements are restricted to four per cent of the previous day's price fixing.

Cash market

Table 8.5 Quotations and turnover on Paris Bourse (*source: London Stock Exchange*)

	1975	1976	1977	1978	1979	1980
BONDS (Ff billion)						
Nominal value of listed bonds	224.80	264.73	300.66	345.77	394.87	494.15
of which—public sector	165.06	192.00	215.44	253.27	296.61	
—private sector	59.74	72.73	85.22	92.50	98.26	
Total bond turnover (Ff billion)	26.82	28.06	26.21	38.65	48.74	64.19
Proportion of total turnover, %	46.5	51.9	55.7	46.1	51.5	60.0
SHARES						
Number of shares listed	884	845	834	792	756	748
of which—domestic	724	685	674	630	595	586
—foreign	160	160	106	162	161	162
Total market value of shares listed (Ff billion)	158.07	135.90	130.83	188.71	222.28	256.8
Turnover of shares listed (by par value) (Ff billion)	30.85	25.96	20.84	45.18	45.98	42.8
Proportion of total, %	53.5	48.1	44.3	53.9	48.5	40.0
Total turnover of bonds and shares (Ff billion)	57.67	54.02	47.05	83.83	94.72	106.99

Marché à terme (Forward market)

The market known as the 'marché à terme' is a forward market in which dealing may take place 'on account'. Two public sector indexed bonds and about 250 shares and convertible bonds are dealt in this market. Of the corporate sector only the shares and securities of the large national and international French and foreign companies may be dealt in, either for cash or for account settlement, at the option of the client. Only large parcels of securities, in lots of Ff 10 000, may be transacted in the forward market, in which share prices may be up to two per cent cheaper than those quoted in the cash market. Day to day price fluctuations are restricted to eight per cent.

Hors cote (Over the counter)

An over-the-counter market (hors cote) is operated by the stockbrokers (agents de change) and is supervised by the Chambre Syndicale des Agents de Change. They recognize prices established in the hors cote and publish daily summaries which are separate from the official price list.

The market is semiregulated and is located inside the Bourse. The securities offered in this market are mainly securities of small companies, or new issues which, after a period of successful trading, usually request admittance to the official market.

In contrast to the official market, only French securities are issued on principle although concessions are, very occasionally, made to foreign companies. Dealings may be effected within a special controlled framework for quotation. Specifically, share prices are only allowed to fluctuate by a maximum of eight per cent per trading session from 10 a.m. to 4 p.m.

New proposals

The new proposals recommend a continuous market trading system rather than the present system of two hour trading sessions. Instead of the prices being fixed on a daily basis, they will be allowed to fluctuate freely and thus facilitate a more perfect market.

While the two official markets will continue to operate as separate markets, shares that are quoted in the forward market will no longer be quoted also in the cash market. This will eliminate the two-tier pricing system that has previously operated for shares which could be dealt in either market.

A further 50 shares will be moved from the cash to the forward market to increase the size of that market and the minimum size of transaction on the forward market will be reduced to Ff 4000.

The market is also to be renamed the 'end-of-month settlement market' and will be the one on which all the major companies and securities are listed.

Modern communications systems will also aid trading and information services to investors. Screens will be made available to banks, brokers and companies both in France and abroad which will provide a continuous update of prices quoted on the Bourse. Clearing and transfer of securities are also to be improved with the use of modern electronic systems.

Costs of dealing are also to be amended. The government tax charged on investors will be abolished but brokerage charges may be increased to encourage brokers to make a market, particularly in the less active shares. One problem that has still not been resolved is that the Bourse has no jobbers, and specialists exist for only a limited range of shares. Stockbrokers will probably be encouraged to deal for their own account and to act as intermediaries by making their own books in listed shares.

Share options

Although a premium and share options market currently exists there are plans to introduce an new options market once the new proposals for trading listed shares have been effected. Initially options in about 10 of the most active shares will be available for trading on the floor of the Bourse.

Gold

There is a free gold market for bar and coin in Paris to which residents have free and anonymous access and in which no official intervention takes place. However, purchase of monetary gold by non-residents for export requires prior authorization by the Banque de France.

A 20 franc gold coin, the napoleon, is traded on the Paris Bourse.

Gold-linked bonds

Bonds that are indexed to the price of gold are a special feature of the French capital market and represent a good alternative to direct investment in gold. They can be bought in smaller amounts and provide a minimum fixed interest return. (See indexed bonds.)

Commodities

Commodities may be traded through the Paris Commodity Bourse of which foreign banks have recently become eligible to be made affiliated members.

Dealing and fees

Money market instruments

For call and time deposits, bons de trésor, and bons de caisse, dealing may be transacted through the commercial banks (banques des dépôts).

If a new client of the bank wishes to deal then French regulations require that the bank receives full financial information on the company or individual with whom it is dealing. This information usually has to be received by the bank some 48 hours before the first transaction is made.

In common with all money markets, specific fees are not charged but prices are quoted on a net basis. The dealers' commission is included in the spread between bid and offer prices. Dealing spreads are about $\frac{1}{4}$ per cent.

Domestic bonds and shares

An investor may deal either through a broker or through a bank who will use their broker. Expenses are calculated on a consideration of the deal. The bank will charge his customer according to the nature of his account but brokerage is fixed as follows.

187

FEES AND DUTIES

I. *Brokerage fees*

proportional fees (on Cash and Forward Market)

state loans and other bonds up to F 600 000	5 %
equities, rights and convertible bonds up to F 600 000	6.50%

decreasing fees (on Cash and Firm Forward Markets):
for transactions over FF 600 000, the commission rates decrease:

State loans and other bonds

From FF 600 000.01 to FF 1 100 000	3.30%
From FF 1 100 000.01 to FF 2 200 000	2.50%
Above FF 2 200 000.01	1.65%

Shares, Rights, Convertible Bonds

From FF 600 000.01 to FR 1 100 000	4.30%
From FF 1 000 000.01 to FF 2 200 000	3.25%
Above FF 2 000 000.01	2.15%

Premium or option transactions (brokerage is calculated on the amount of the option price) 4 %
In the case of premiums or options taken up, the aforementioned rates are applied to the total value of the transaction.

Contango transactions:

for contango transactions, on the contango value calculated on the basis of the settlement price including, if *such is the case*, the contango price 1.50%

for capital employed in contango transactions, on the amount of the contango transaction calculated as above 1 %

Cash deals are settled on the same day.
Account deals are settled at the end of the month.
Apart from a few specified stocks which have to be registered, securities may be taken in either bearer or registered form, at the option of the buyer.
In addition to brokerage there is a stock exchange levy of 0.3 per cent and 0.15 per cent for deals of less than or more than Ff 1 million respectively. Also there is a government value added tax of 17.65 per cent on the amount of the brokerage.*

Eurobonds

All French franc Eurobond issues are lead managed by French banks, to whom primary market applications should be made.
In the secondary market, dealing may be effected through any appropriate bank in any of the major European centres. Apart from Paris, good markets are also provided by London, Frankfurt and Switzerland.

* For most transactions the stamp duty (of 0.3%) is due to be abolished with the rationalization of the Bourse.

No fee is specifically charged on purchases in either the primary or secondary market, although some commission is accounted for in the spread between the dealer's bid and offer prices.

Dealing spreads are normally about one per cent. No other stamp duties or taxes apply.

Financial and monetary systems

Financial institutions

There are three types of banks or savings institutions in France—the savings banks, the specialist banks and the commercial and investment banks, of which the latter can be further subdivided into three categories. The functions of many banks overlap such that some may be described as belonging to more than one category.

Savings banks

These banks which include the Caisse d'Epargne (Post Office Savings Bank) and the Caisse Nationale d'Epargne, specialize in collecting household savings throughout the country. Most are state owned although Crédit Mutuel, which is regional co-operative savings banks, is privately owned by its members.

The state owned savings banks channel the savings they collect into the Caisse des Dépôts et Consignations (CDC).

CDC

The CDC is one of the most important financial institutions in France. It is a state deposit fund which also collects funds of insurance companies and social security funds and reinvests the savings in securities of public and private sector companies, in loans to municipal and local authorities, in public works projects and in the housing mortgage market.

The CDC can affect central bank policy since it is regulated under the authority of the Minister of Finance and operates both in the call money market and in the bond market.

Specialist banks

These, as their collective name implies, each performs a particular function. For example, Crédit National specializes in loans to industry for the financing of capital equipment, in mortgages for export credit finance and for the rediscounting of medium-term loans made by commercial banks to industry.

Crédit Foncier de France provides mortgage capital. Caisse Centrale de Crédit Hotelier, Commercial et Industriel, provides long-term loans to small and medium-sized businesses for the finance of capital investments. Banque Française du Commerce Extérieur provides finance for exports and for imports. The banks in this group are semipublic, i.e., part owned by the state and part owned by the private sector.

The co-operative banks might also be described as specialist banks. These are mutual associations, owned by their members, and were originally established to

189

provide credit to their members who comprised specific categories of individuals or businesses. For example Caisse de Crédit Agricole was originally established to collect savings from farmers and to grant agricultural loans. Crédit National, together with the two other major co-operative banks Crédit Populaire and Crédit Mutuel have become so large that they now assume national proportions and their range of activities is far wider than their original functions. Crédit Agricole is now more properly described as a commercial bank. Any individual or company may hold an account with Crédit Agricole and its range of activities is now so comprehensive that it has become not only the largest bank in France but, by some definitions, the largest bank in the world. It not only accepts all kinds of domestic deposits and provides all types of domestic credit, but also is an active participant in the foreign exchange market and the Euromarket.

Commercial and investment banks

This group of banks may be further subdivided into three categories, namely, commercial banks (banques de dépôts), investment banks, and medium- and long-term credit banks.

The commercial banks may undertake most forms of banking business. They accept all forms of domestic and foreign currency deposits but also grant short- and medium-term credit in the domestic market and are active in the Euromarket syndicated bank lending and bond issuing markets. The three largest commercial banks are state owned. These are the Banque Nationale de Paris, Crédit Lyonnais and Société Générale. Crédit Agricole, as mentioned above, also falls into the commercial bank category but complies with the agricultural policies of the government.

Secondly, the investment banks (banques d'affaires) also perform some commercial banking functions. The main distinction between the commercial and investment banks used to be that the former could not accept deposits of longer than two years, while the latter could not accept deposits of less than two years. This distinction ceased in 1966 and consequently the commercial banks have become the largest and most important of the banking institutions.

The third type of bank within this category is that of the medium- and long-term credit banks (banques de crédit à long et moyen terme) Sovac, Unibail, Finextel, which provide medium- and long-term loans to industry.

Central bank

The central bank is the Banque de France, which is the only bank of issue and carries, on behalf of the treasury, considerable power to regulate the French banking and financial systems.

The governor of the Banque de France alone determines the interest rate (bank rate), although the final arbiter of policy is the Minister of Finance. The governing body of the Bank is the National Credit Council (Conseil National de Crédit) which comprises representatives from banks, government agencies, labour unions, businesses and agriculture. While it was originally intended that this council should formulate and direct policy, it has now become little more significant than a formal institution. The application of monetary policy by the Banque de France is assisted by the Banking Control Commission (Commission de Contrôle des Banques). It is this commission that establishes the liquidity ratios, solvency ratios and credit ratios for all banks and financial institutions.

Monetary policy

Monetary policy in France is nearly always formulated so that it affects not only the overall economy but also particular economic objectives. For example, it may favour export orientated firms, the housing sector, or investment in energy saving equipment. Bank lending for such purposes may be exempted from bank credit ceilings, or receive subsidized interest rates.

Tight control over credit and the banking system is exercised by the Banque de France, through monetary policy which traditionally has aimed for budgetary equilibrium, but in recent years the government has suffered budget deficits caused by high energy costs and inflation.

Discount policy

Until the early 1970s the Banque de France controlled credit expansion through an elaborate system of discount ceilings and discount rates set for each bank. Plurality of discount rates existed above and below bank rate and at any time there were perhaps ten different interest rates at which the Bank of France would lend to banks. Moreover, money market intervention by the central bank was rendered ineffective because of the lack of an adequate money market largely due to the discount rate being, in general, lower than bank rate. Therefore, so long as the banks did not exceed their credit ceilings (plafond) in their lending programmes, they were able to borrow from the Banque de France at rates lower than those obtainable in the open market and relend at a considerable profit. Thus, contrary to the practice of most central banks, the Banque de France acted as lender of first resort to the banks.

Changes in central bank policy during the 1970s have resulted in a more flexible system but one that is still highly regulated and subject to fairly frequent change.

The discount rate, while it still exists, is no longer an important monetary tool. In 1971 money market rates were allowed to fall below the discount rate so that the banks would only resort to the Banque de France if unable to match their credit expansion by borrowing in the open market. At the same time, the Banque de France changed from lending to banks at fixed rates, predetermined for each bank, to a system of variable rate lending, dictated by rates prevailing in the money market. Therefore, while the official discount rate is still determined by the Banque de France, it now follows other money market rates rather than being fixed so as to influence other interest rates.

The discount rate is used for discounting the medium-term claims held by banks. Medium-term claims have a maturity of between 18 months and 7 years, and the claims that are eligible for rediscounting are those that finance exports to non EEC countries and the mobilizable parts of claims on foreign debtors to the French banking system.

Banks' prime lending rate is the rate at which banks will lend to their most creditworthy customers. It is determined in relation to the average cost of the banks' resources and overheads. The cost of bank resources is now influenced more by money market rates than by the discount rate. Any bank may make a unilateral decision to alter its prime lending rate but the other banks then usually follow by also changing their prime lending rates.

Open market operations

The Banque de France now uses open market operations more extensively. While, however, the money market is increasing in importance, such intervention is still used as a supplementary, rather than as a main regulatory, tool. The Bank's main means of intervention is the purchase or sale of bills and short-term paper through the discount houses, and the purchase from, or sale to, the specialized institutions (of medium-term paper) combined with a long-term repurchase agreement.

Additionally, the Bank may buy or sell one-, three- or six-month treasury bills or medium-term bonds, or one-month promissory notes from the banks.

Selective credit controls

The Bank still uses selective credit controls via a credit corset which is revised every six months and aims to give selective help to banking, exporting, free enterprise and competition in general.

Ceilings on bank credit expansion are still used and a system of special deposits is imposed. Smaller banks are allowed higher ceilings for credit expansion and the larger banks lower ceilings.

The existence of the credit corset system renders the use of interest rate policy ineffective as a means of controlling the money supply. The reason is that a large proportion of credit is granted to various sectors of the economy at above the normal credit ceilings and at preferential rates of interest which generally are much lower than prevailing market levels. In 1979 for example almost 45 per cent of all credit extended by the banking system was granted at preferential rates. Much of the 'cheap' loans was granted by special state owned financial institutions such as the Caisse des Dépôts and Crédit Agricole. Agriculture, French industry— particularly that which is export oriented or energy saving—and the housing sector are major areas to which cheap credit is directed although there are over 60 categories of borrowers eligible for cheap credit. As a result of this system, the money supply cannot be rationed by market oriented policy. In 1979 the growth of credit in the sectors that were rationed by the credit ceilings and market rates of interest was 9.3 per cent while credit expansion in the sectors not so rationed was 27.3 per cent.

Reserve requirements

The general level of reserve requirements are regulated. These were set at two per cent of resident demand deposits for 1975 to 1978, and subsequently increased to four per cent. In addition to this requirement there was a system of progressively scaled supplementary reserve requirements for any increase in credit of over five per cent of the average lending between the end of 1974 and mid-1975. This was modified in 1976 to a general supplementary reserve requirement of 0.5 per cent of all bank credit outstanding, which had to be deposited, interest free, with the Banque de France.

Like the credit ceilings, the reserve requirements act as an ineffective brake on credit expansion. The Banque de France does not impose penalties on banks which cannot meet their reserve requirements but, on the contrary, normally provides the banking system with extra liquidity to meet the requirements, in order that pressure on money market interest rates is prevented.

The banks' liquidity ratios are, however, controlled. There are frequent, short-term changes in the liquidity ratio (the ratio of banks' cash holdings of treasury bills and other eligible bills to domestic liabilities), and is thus actively used as a device of monetary policy.

The banks submit monthly returns to the Banque de France on the 21st of each month, showing their liquidity ratios. If the banks find that the ratio is too low as the 21st approaches, then they raise additional liquid resources by buying commercial bills from their customers. These bills are eligible for rediscounting at the Bank of France. Call deposit rates in the French franc money market also tend to rise during this period.

Withholding taxes

Dividends

For residents of non-treaty countries, withholding tax is applied to the repatriation of dividends at a rate of 25 per cent to individuals, to parent companies and to non-parent companies. Tax treaties reduce this tax to 10 per cent in the majority of cases and in many of those instances a tax credit may be granted.

Residents of those countries holding a double taxation agreement with France are able to claim the 'avoir fiscal' which is normally deducted from dividends at source. The avoir fiscal is equal to half the net dividend. The avoir fiscal may be claimed back from the French Treasury and withholding tax deducted at the reduced rate, according to the specific tax treaty. The withholding tax paid can then be offset against domestic income tax to which the investor is liable. For example, assuming a US resident investor liable to a withholding tax at the reduced rate of 15 per cent and to domestic income tax at 50 per cent

Net declared dividend	100
Avoir fiscal claimed from French Treasury	50
	150
Less 15% withholding tax	22.5
Net amount received	127.5
US income tax	63.75
Less 15% withholding tax paid	22.50
	41.25
Total net amount received	86.25
Effective tax rate	13.75%

The tax paid on dividends to foreign parent companies varies according to the country of domicile of the investor company. The proportion of equity required to be held before that company (or individual) is regarded as a 'parent' for withholding tax purposes ranges from, for example, 10 per cent for Belgium to 50 per cent for Ireland.

Interest

Withholding taxes on interest are differentiated not only by the country of domicile of the investor but also by the source of interest earnings. Different rates of tax are charged on interest arising from negotiable and non-negotiable instruments. The former are taxed at a lower rate than the latter. The non-treaty rates are 25 and 40 per cent respectively. These are reduced for treaty countries as shown in Table 8.6. Where two rates are given the lower rate applies if certain formalities are met.

Table 8.6 Withholding taxes

	Interest		Dividends (minority holdings), %
	For negotiable instruments, %	For non-negotiable instruments, %	
Non-treaty countries	25	40	25
Tax treaty countries			
Algeria	10	40	25
Australia*	10	10	15
Austria*	0	0	15
Belgium*	10	15	15
Benin	10	40	25
Brazil*	10	15	15
Cameroon	10	40	25
Canada	10	15	15
Central African Empire	10	40	25
Comoro Islands*	0	40	15
Congo	10	40	25
Czechoslovakia	0	0	10
Denmark	0	0	0
Finland*	10	10	15
Gabon*	10	40	25
Germany*	0	0	15
Greece	10	0	25
India	10	25	25
Iran	10	15	20
Ireland	0	0	15
Israel	10	15	15
Italy	10	15	15
Ivory Coast	10	40	25
Japan	10	10	15

(*continued*)

Table 8.6 (*continued*)

	Interest		Dividends (minority holdings), %
	For negotiable instruments, %	For non-negotiable instruments, %	
Lebanon	0	0	0
Luxembourg*	10	10	15
Luxembourg holding companies	25	40	25
Madagascar	10	40	25
Malaysia*	15	15	15
Mali*	10	40	25
Mountania	10	40	25
Monaco	10	40	25
Morocco	10	10	25
Netherlands*	10	10	15
Niger*	10	40	25
Norway	0	0	10
Pakistan	10	40	25
Philippines	10	15	25
Poland	15	0	15
French Polynesia	10	0	25
Portugal	10	12	15
Rumania	10	10	10
Senegal*	10	40	25
Singapore*	10	10	15
Spain*	10	10	15
Sweden*	0	0	15
Switzerland*	10	10	15
Thailand	10	10	25
Togo*	10	40	25
Tunisia	10	12	25
UK*	10	10	15
USA*	10	10	15
Upper Volta*	10	40	25
Yugoslavia	0	0	15

* Tax credit (avoir fiscal) granted.

Exemptions

Interest from most government bonds is free of withholding tax for all catagories of recipient.

Foreign states, central banks, international organisations and state financial institutions are exempt from withholding tax on interest from all domestic bonds provided they are in registered form or are deposited with a French bank.

French Franc Eurobonds are exempt from withholding tax.

Exchange controls

France exercises a strict system of exchange controls. Supervised by the Treasury Directorate of the Ministry of the Economy and depending on the condition of the country's balance of payments, restrictions on France's inward and outward investment payments may be strictly or loosely controlled at any time.

Regulation of the controls affecting indirect investments (purchase of securities etc.), but involving currency transactions, is delegated to the Bank of France.

Exchange rate system

The currency is the franc which is maintained within the limits of the European Monetary System (EMS). The monetary authorities intervene so as to smooth out fluctuations in the exchange market and maintain the exchange value of the franc within the EMS margins.

The exchange territory, apart from France, includes the islands of French Polynesia, Wallis and Futuna and New Caledonia. The currency throughout the exchange territory is the CPF franc which maintains a fixed parity with the franc of CPF 1 = Ff 0.055. Certain African countries maintain fixed parities with the French franc. Benin, Cameroon, the Central African Empire, Chad, the Congo, Gabon, Ivory coast, Niger, Senegal, Togo and Upper Volta employ the CFA franc equivalent to Ff 0.02. Mali maintains the Mali franc at a fixed parity of MF 1 = Ff 0.01.

Other overseas territories regulated by the French exchange control system are Corsica, Monaco and the French Islands of the Caribbean. All, except for Monaco, are considered as foreign countries for exchange control purposes, and do not maintain fixed currency parities with the French franc.

Non-resident accounts

A non-resident may freely open an account with a bank authorized to accept such accounts.

The proceeds of any spot or forward transactions in francs or foreign currencies may be credited or debited to that account. These may arise either in France or from a foreign country. Accounts may be freely debited for the purchase of French or foreign securities or credited with the proceeds from such securities.

Purchase and sale of securities

All movement of capital between France and foreign countries is subject to exchange control.

Non-residents may transfer abroad French and foreign securities held in France, provided the transaction takes place through the foreign dossier of an authorized bank.

Foreign securities held in France must also be deposited with an authorized bank, though French securities need not be deposited unless the non-resident wishes to execute a transaction.

Non-residents are free to purchase:

1. any short-term securities including government securities.
2. any capital market securities.
3. gold linked and other index linked securities.

The export or import of monetary gold (bars or coin) is not normally permitted. Non-residents may purchase gold as long as it is held in France.

9. West Germany

General market environment

Germany's multifacet economy is reflected in a well-developed financial market.

For the non-resident investor there are active and efficient markets in call and time deposits, both in Deutschemarks and Eurocurrencies. However, access to other money market instruments is not available because of the exchange regulation prohibiting the sale abroad of securities having less than one year's maturity.

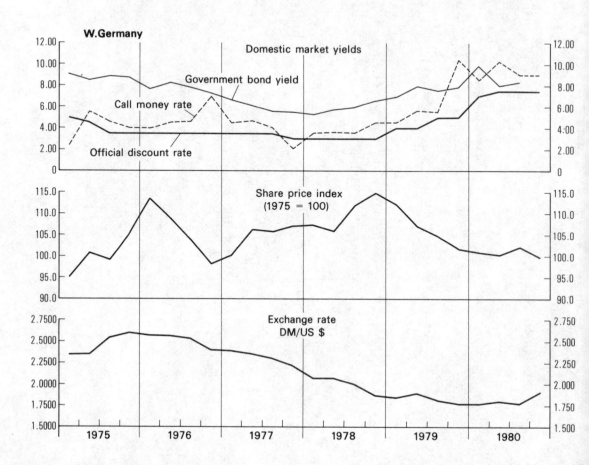

W.Germany

Domestic market yields

Government bond yield

Call money rate

Official discount rate

Share price index
(1975 = 100)

Exchange rate
DM/US $

Table 9.1 Summary of instruments

Instrument	Characteristics
MONEY MARKET	
Deposits	
call deposits	Very active interbank market. Mostly day-to-day loans
time deposits	Also active market. Terms of 7 days to 30 months
currency deposits	Call and time deposits also in Eurocurrencies
Treasury bills	Not available to non-resident investor
Treasury certificates	Not available to non-resident investor
Bankers' acceptances	Not available to non-resident investor
Commercial bills	Not available to non-resident investor
CAPITAL MARKET	
Government bonds	Major share of public sector bonds. Subject to withholding tax and coupon tax
Public authority bonds	Issued by municipalities and states. Also subject to withholding tax and coupon tax
Bonds of state enterprises	For example, railway and post office bonds. Almost identical in nature to government bonds
Bonds of financial institutions	Issued by banks and mortgage finance companies Mortgage bonds represent about $\frac{1}{3}$ of all domestic bonds. Also subject to taxes
Schuldscheindarlehen	Loans against borrowers' notes. Popular with non-residents. Free of withholding tax
Corporate bonds	Negligible market
Foreign bonds	Identical to Eurobonds except for method of issue
Eurobonds	Important market in Deutschemark Eurobonds. Free of withholding tax and other taxes
Equities	Small but reasonable active market
Unit trusts	Growing influence in domestic capital market. Designed to attract small investors
Gold	Unrestricted market in Frankfurt but subject to VAT at 13%

The capital market provides an active trade in Eurobonds and foreign bonds. The Deutschemark foreign bond market is the third largest in the world though in 1980 Germany proved the second major foreign bond issuing market. Deutschemark denominated Eurobonds undisputedly comprise the largest volume of Eurobonds after dollar denominated Eurobonds. Of domestic bonds, government, public authority and financial bonds dominate the market and there is little turnover in corporate bonds although there is a reasonable market in equity shares.

Non-residents are discouraged from holding domestic bonds by a 25 per cent coupon tax charged to non-resident investors. International bonds and Schuldscheindarlehen escape this tax. Domestic investment in companies tends to be

199

geared more to the long term. In the past shares have been tightly held by families and by the banking system, so that additional corporate financing is raised mostly through bank borrowing. Due to political pressure, however, a change in the system has already begun. Nevertheless, the banks exert considerable influence over all aspects of the German economy holding controlling interests in many areas of business and industry. In addition they provide an all-purpose function, acting as investment advisers, portfolio managers, stockbrokers as well as depositories for savings and a source of short- and long-term loans.

Apart from the ban on non-resident purchases of short-term securities exchange controls are liberal. Withholding taxes, however, are imposed on dividends and interest earned from securities.

In general, foreign investment is encouraged, although the central bank does on occasion apply monetary policies to restrict the inflow of foreign capital when the currency is subject to strong upward pressure. At the end of 1980 however, the authorities were promoting greater capital inflows from foreign sources.

The main financial centre is Frankfurt-am-Main. This is the city in which the central bank has its head office and the one in which all major banks and financial institutions are located. Dusseldorf, Munich and Hamburg can lay claims to being serious competitors but the best communications and facilities for the foreign investor are available in Frankfurt.

The money market

Deposits

The German banking system is well geared to accept all forms of deposits. The savings ratio in Germany is high (about 16 per cent of the disposable income) and the receipt of savings accounts for about two-fifths of the banking business in Germany. Household savings account for almost 80 per cent of total savings.

Consequently, there is a large deposit market in Germany for domestic lenders, which similarly accommodates the non-resident investor. Banks are free to pay interest on domestic and foreign currency deposits. Non-resident Deutschemark deposits may also be placed in any of the major European financial centres, in particular London or with the Luxembourg subsidiaries of the foreign banks. The Euro-Deutschemark market outside Germany is well integrated into the German financial system and short-term rates closely follow domestic rates.

Savings deposits, although representing a large share of domestic savings, are of little interest to the non-resident investor or those requiring liquidity. Terms of notice for savings deposits are three months for amounts of more than DM 2000 per month and are also available for terms of 12 months, 12 to 36 or more than 36 months' notice, at respectively increasing rates of interest. The markets in call and time deposits, however, are active interbank markets with large turnovers in both types of money.

Call deposits

The call market is an interbank market in which the sight deposits of banks placed with branches of the central bank are lent and borrowed without security. In this respect, it is similar to the London interbank market. Non-bank participants may also place Deutschemarks in this market through the German commercial banks in amounts of DM 100 000 up to DM 100 million. Slightly better interest rates may usually be negotiated for amounts of DM 5 million or more.

Call money (Tagesgeld) is normally day-to-day money, placed for 24-hour periods. Money may be for one day definitely and either repaid or replaced the next. The transaction may take place immediately via direct transfer from one bank account to another. Notice for repayment the next day may be given by the lender to the borrower at any time during business hours. Call deposits may also be placed for periods of seven days' notice.

As in the UK money market, the banks' requirements for day-to-day money is in order to balance their books at the close of business each day. Some banks make two-way quotes but the majority are either borrowers or lenders, although their positions may change several times during the course of a day. Rates too can fluctuate sharply during a business day in response to changing conditions of supply and demand. All money rates tend to rise at the end of a month as banks and institutions finance their stock exchange transactions, although this is becoming increasingly less significant. More usually rates may vary more widely between banks at the end of a month depending on the minimum reserve performance of the individual banks. Rates may also rise just before and after the dates that banks have to declare their liquidity position to the Bundesbank, i.e., 7th, 13th, 23rd, and the last business day of each month. Other periods of tight liquidity for the banks are the major tax payment dates—10th of March, June, September and December—and also at the end of the financial year when the banks are 'window dressing' their accounts and balances. The Bundesbank intervenes to ease liquidity at these times by providing currency swap facilities or transacting reverse repurchase agreements with the banks for periods of 10 or 20 days, at preferential interest rates.

Although interest rates are influenced by the demand and supply of funds within the banking system, call money rates are also directly influenced by official policy,

Table 9.2 Deutschemark deposits (DM million) (*source: Monthly report of the Deutsche Bundesbank, June 1980*)

End of period	Total	Domestic individuals	Domestic non-profit organization	Domestic	Domestic public authorities	Foreigners
1976	413 449	388 666	9 131	5751	6659	3242
1977	440 880	413 475	10 389	6015	7186	3815
1978	470 727	441 490	11 034	6335	7584	4284
1979	482 887	454 796	10 785	5999	6830	4477
April 1980	467 683	441 474	10 158	5546	6085	4460

both by changes in the bank rate or in the Lombard rate by official intervention in the market.

The Bundesbank announces the call interest rate whenever it changes. The rate is determined by the Bundesbank in close consultation with the three major commercial banks (the 'big three'). In theory, the Lombard rate represents a ceiling on the call rate because banks holding eligible securities are unwilling to pay higher rates in the market than they would pay if discounting these securities with the central bank. In practice, however, the Lombard facility is used only occasionally by the banks and call rates rise above the Lombard rate whenever there is a high demand from the banks for liquid resources.

Time deposits

Time deposits may be placed for fixed periods ranging from 7 days to 48 months. Specifically, the time periods are 7 days, 1, 2, 3, 6 or 12 months and, only occasionally, longer. The longer the maturity the greater is the difference between bid and offer quotations. The largest volume of time deposits is transacted for three-month periods, this being quite an important period for the banks as well as for companies, both of which are required to meet their tax liabilities on a quarterly basis.

Interest rates in this market depend on the Lombard rate which, among all the official rates, is the one to which money market rates most closely correlate.

Banks' reserve requirements for non-resident deposits may be enforced at a higher rate than for resident deposits and this affects interest rates. The central bank does not pay interest on reserves deposited with it and, if a higher ratio is imposed on non-resident deposits, the bank may quote lower interest rates for such deposits. Currently, however, the reserve requirements for non-resident liabilities are the same as for resident liabilities. Both resident and non-resident investors though, have the alternative of placing a Euro-Deutschemark deposit in foreign deposit markets. The Eurocurrency market in Luxembourg, where German banks are very active, specifically attempts to attract such deposits at rates that are very often more favourable to the investor. Interest-rate differentials are particularly noticeable for three- and six-month time deposits where they may sometimes be $\frac{1}{2}$ per cent higher than domestic rates. Rates tend to even out either side of the three- and six-month periods, with parity at one month and $\frac{1}{4}$ to $\frac{1}{2}$ per cent higher on 12-month money.

Currency deposits

Frankfurt also provides an active market in call and time deposits denominated in most convertible currencies but in particular the major Eurocurrencies such as the US dollar, Canadian dollar, Swiss, French and Belgian francs, Dutch guilder and pound sterling.

CDs

There is no market for Deutschemark CDs in Germany.

Other money market instruments

Although Germany has a fairly well-developed money market, exchange control regulations prevent non-residents from participating except in the market for call and time deposits. Specifically, non-residents are not permitted to purchase German fixed-interest securities with less than one year remaining to maturity. This legislation, therefore, precludes almost all market instruments which all carry original maturities of less than one year.

A brief description of money market instruments is given below for general information.

Treasury bills

Two types of treasury bills are issued:

1. Fixed-interest-bearing notes sold at par. These include federal railway notes and federal post office notes, as well as direct central government notes, and are issued with maturities of 6, 12, and 18 months and 2 years.
2. Non-interest-bearing bills sold at a discount.

Treasury bills are normally sold direct to banks by the Bundesbank acting as agent of the Ministry of Finance. The bills can be dealt between banks but the secondary market is limited. Non-bank institutions have to deal through the banks and cannot buy treasury bills direct.

Treasury certificates (*Finanzierungsschaetze*)

These are fixed-interest-bearing notes issued by the Bundesbank on behalf of the treasury with maturities of either one or two years. Denominations vary from a minimum of DM 1000 to a maximum of DM 100 000.

Bankers' acceptances

These are issued by German banks with short maturities of between a few days and a few months. They originated as time drafts used to finance international payments for the shipment and storage of goods, to finance payments originating from letters of credit, or for the creation of foreign exchange.

Commercial bills

First-class commercial bills of major German companies are issued with three- to six-month maturities and are endorsed by a bank. They are eligible for rediscounting at the central bank provided they bear signatures of three solvent parties and have less than three months remaining to maturity.

Table 9.3   Interest rates and yield in DM securities (*source: OECD*)

	End 1978	1979											
		Jan.	*Feb.*	*Mar.*	*Apr.*	*May*	*June*	*July*	*Aug.*	*Sep.*	*Oct.*	*Nov.*	*Dec.*
Official discount rate	3.0	3.0	3.0	4.0	4.0	4.0	4.0	5.0	5.0	5.0	5.0	6.0	6.0
Lombard rate	3.5	4.0	4.0	5.0	5.0	5.0	5.5	6.0	6.0	6.0	6.0	7.0	7.0
Day-to-day call deposits	3.56	2.99	3.81	4.32	5.24	5.16	5.60	5.73	6.36	6.50	7.87	7.86	9.02
Treasury bills	2.67	2.67	2.67	3.68	3.68	3.68	3.65	4.70	4.70	4.70	4.70	5.73	5.73
3-month domestic deposits	4.06	3.89	4.15	4.47	5.24	5.92	6.46	6.84	7.09	7.89	8.76	9.65	9.58
3-month Euro deposits	3.38	3.88	4.00	5.00	4.47	6.09	6.25	6.59	7.50	7.50	9.00	8.94	8.63
Public sector bonds													
3–7 years	6.1	6.8	6.6	6.7	6.9	7.5	7.8	7.7	7.5	7.5	7.8	8.1	8.0
7–15 years	6.7	6.8	7.1	7.2	7.3	7.8	8.0	7.9	7.6	7.6	7.8	8.0	7.9
Industrial bonds	6.8	6.8	7.0	7.0	7.3	7.6	7.9	8.0	7.8	7.8	8.0	8.4	8.2
Mortgage bonds	6.8	6.8	7.1	7.2	7.3	7.7	8.0	8.0	7.8	7.9	8.0	8.3	8.0

	1980											
	Jan.	*Feb.*	*Mar.*	*Apr.*	*May*	*June*	*July*	*Aug.*	*Sep.*	*Oct.*	*Nov.*	*Dec.*
Official discount rate	6.0	7.0	7.0	7.0	7.5	7.5	7.5	7.5	7.5	7.5	7.5	7.5
Lombard rate	7.0	8.5	8.5	8.5	9.5	9.5	9.5	9.5	9.0	9.0	9.0	9.0
Day-to-day call deposits	8.25	8.06	8.61	9.05	9.80	10.04	9.80	8.92	9.27	9.01	8.76	9.16
Treasury bills	5.73	5.76	5.76	5.76	7.28	7.28	7.28	7.28	7.28	7.28	7.28	7.28
3-month domestic deposits	8.86	8.97	9.64	10.22	10.26	10.11	9.70	8.98	8.97	9.08	9.45	10.20
3-month Euro deposits	8.47	9.19	10.19	9.31	9.13	9.44	8.38	8.63	8.81	9.00	9.69	9.13
Public Sector Bonds												
3–7 years	8.1	8.5	9.5	9.5	8.7	8.2	7.9	7.8	8.1	8.4	8.7	9.0
7–15 years	8.0	8.4	9.4	9.4	8.6	8.1	7.9	7.8	8.1	8.3	8.6	8.8
Industrial bonds	8.3	8.5	9.6	10.0	9.4	8.9	8.4	8.1	8.4	8.8	9.3	9.5
Mortgage bonds	8.2	8.6	9.6	9.6	8.9	8.3	8.1	8.0	8.3	8.6	9.1	9.2

The capital market

The German capital market is one of the world's major capital markets because of high investor demand to hold Deutschemark-denominated securities. Until 1980 non-residents have been actively discouraged from purchasing domestic securities, particularly bonds, because the authorities wished to limit the inflow of foreign capital which raises the domestic money supply and puts upward pressure on the exchange rate. In 1980 however the authorities reversed this policy and encouraged the purchase of domestic securities by non-residents in order to support the Deutschemark which has weakened as a result of Germany's balance of payments deficit.

As at December 1980, non-residents may only purchase securities with a life of more than one year to maturity. Previously, non-residents could not purchase securities with a life of less than five years and one month. Non-residents are still excluded from investing in money market instruments and from holding bonds to maturity. Secondly, non-residents are liable for a withholding tax of 25 per cent on the interest earned from domestic bonds. The tax is withheld at source and cannot be offset by tax credits. Effectively, the tax renders German domestic bonds unattractive to non-resident investors.

Schuldscheindarlehen, since they are not technically classified as securities, are exempt from withholding tax. Although they are still subject to the minimum maturity regulation, they provide a popular market among non-resident investors.

Also important to the non-resident are foreign bonds and Deutschemark Eurobonds which are free from all tax and maturity regulations attaching to domestic bonds. Since the Deutschemark has (during the 1970s) been one of the strongest of all major currencies, investor interest has also been strong so borrowers have found it a good market in which to issue bonds. Thus about 20 per cent of all new issues of international bonds (foreign bonds and Eurobonds) during the 1970s have been denominated in Deutschemarks.

Federal government and public authority bonds

Public sector bonds account for about 25 per cent of the domestic bonds issued each year, with bonds of the federal government representing the largest proportion of this.

Local authority bonds are issued by the Länder governments, municipalities and large cities.

Other public sector bonds are issued by the federal railways, the postal system, specific purpose public associations, and other public associations established under special legislation.

Public sector bonds carry the highest security being either a direct obligation of the government or indirectly guaranteed by the government. Consequently average yields tend to be 0.2 to 0.3 per cent lower than average yields obtainable on good quality corporate bonds. All bonds are issued in bearer form and for non-residents the interest is subject to withholding tax. Non-residents may not purchase bonds with less than one year remaining life.

Table 9.4 **Bond placings in domestic market** (*source: Deutsche Bundesbank*)

		Issuers			
DM million	*Total amount of issue*	*Industry commerce*	*Special institutions*	*State/local authorities*	*Foreign issuers*
1976	19 580	150	750	9 860	8 820
1977	20 920	300	300	7 850	12 470
1978	20 240	100	500	10 850	14 790
1979	22 730	....	950	11 900	9 880
1980 first half	11 155	....	....	5 200	5 955

In the primary market, a proportion of new issues of public sector bonds are left to the discretion of the central bank as regards timing. The Bank then issues them at times when it wishes to influence the capital market and mop up excess liquidity.

All government and public authority bonds are listed on one or more of the German stock exchanges and, additionally, a secondary over-the-counter market in specific issues is maintained by the German banks. The secondary market is very active. Yields react promptly to changes in market direction. Major participants are the German deposit banks. These, plus the rest of the banking system, purchase about 10 per cent of the bonds on issue. In earlier years, for example in 1975, the banks have purchased as much as 70 per cent of the federal government and public authority bonds on issue.

Bonds of financial institutions

These account for about 70 per cent of all bonds issued. Bank bonds in particular represent a large proportion of issued volume and are actively traded. Such bonds are issued and secured by the larger German banks while the funds so raised are usually to finance companies and industrial projects.

Mortgage bonds Mortgage bonds (Pfandbriefe) account for about one third of all bonds in circulation and, though now less significant in terms of new issue volume than bank bonds, are nevertheless very actively traded. They are issued with maturities of up to 15 years by private mortgage banks, including ship mortgage banks, by mortgage banks established under public law, and by the savings banks' central giro institutions. The majority are to finance first mortgages, mainly for housing.

Interest on these bonds is subject to withholding tax. The bonds are in bearer form and may not be sold to non-residents if carrying less than one year to maturity.

The major participant in the secondary market is, as with government bonds, the banking system. The large commercial banks in particular purchase financial bonds both for their own account and also to maintain a secondary market in them.

Corporate bonds

Corporate industrial bonds account for less than one per cent of gross domestic bond issue while, in net terms, issues have been negative during the 1970s. They also have a very small circulation in the secondary market. A major cause is a 25 per cent capital yield tax imposed during the 1960s on foreign holdings of German domestic bonds. At that time about 40 per cent of total bonds in issue were held by non-residents. Imposition of the tax caused foreigners to switch to other foreign bonds and resulted in the collapse of the German domestic bond market. Although the tax has since been abolished, the corporate bond market has never really recovered and industry has relied on banks for most of its capital funding. Currently direct bond financing only provides something like two per cent of finance used by industry. Indirect bond financing provides considerably more than this two per cent, since banks issue their own bonds (bank bonds) in order to raise funds to finance credit for the corporate and industrial sectors. Additionally, indirect bank financing is facilitated through the issue of Schuldscheindarlehen.

Schuldscheindarlehen

These are loan agreements which are documented in the form of a promissory letter, issued by the borrower and sometimes, though not necessarily, guaranteed by a government institution. They are issued by railways, federal government agencies, and municipal and large banks, but the ultimate borrower may be either a domestic or foreign company. This market developed when, during the 1960s, a 2.5 per cent tax was imposed on the issue of new securities. This tax applied only to industrial and foreign borrowers. It was circumvented by the banks issuing their own notes on behalf of such borrowers, secured against borrowers' promissory notes.

Under German law, the Schuldscheine is not classified as a security but evidences a loan made by the investor to the borrower for a fixed term, but which is repaid by instalments. Essentially, therefore, it is a promissory note with predetermined periodic redemption by the borrower.

Schuldscheine are a popular investment instrument for non-residents; over DM 11 billion were sold to foreigners in 1979. This popularity exists for the following reasons: firstly, interest is paid free of withholding tax, including the coupon tax payable on domestic bonds; secondly, although not traded on the stock exchanges, an active secondary market—but according to market needs and conditions—is maintained by the German banks, while they may also be purchased and traded in other European and financial centres particularly Luxembourg and London; and thirdly, yields are normally about $\frac{1}{2}$ per cent higher than on other domestic bonds of corresponding maturity.

Schuldscheine are issued with maturities of from 1 to 10 years though, as with other German domestic instruments, non-residents may not hold Schuldscheine with maturities of under one year left to run.

Although Schuldscheine are normally issued in minimum denominations of DM 1000, secondary market transactions tend to be in large amounts of up to DM 5 million.

Foreign bonds

There is little difference between foreign bonds and Deutschemark Eurobonds. The only distinction is that foreign bonds are issued in the primary market by German banks while Eurobonds are syndicated by foreign and international banks, although they are always lead managed by a German bank. Both are bearer securities and listed on the German stock exchanges as well as traded over the counter by banks in Germany and other financial centres.

The most important aspect of foreign bonds for the non-resident investor is that they are not subject to restrictions that attach to domestic bonds regarding the minimum maturities that may be held by non-residents. They are also free from coupon tax, withholding tax and also from the minimum maturity regulations. Eurobonds are automatically exempt from these restrictions also.

207

Table 9.5 **Deutschemark foreign bonds and Eurobonds in international market (in millions of US dollars)** (*source: OECD*)

	1975	1976	1977	1978	1979	Jan.–Sept. 1980
Foreign bonds issued on domestic markets						
DM foreign bonds	604.9	1 309.3	1 511.1	1 676.8	2 615.1	3 709.4
US dollar foreign bonds	6 854.6	10 631.6	7 668.2	6 354.6	2 021.4	2 021.4
Swiss franc foreign bonds	3 529.0	5 443.6	4 959.3	7 608.9	9 479.5	5 319.1
Others	1 312.3	1 558.8	2 471.6	5 901.8	3 520.4	1 824.3
Total	12 300.8	18 943.3	16 610.2	21 542.1	19 979.6	12 874.2
DM foreign bonds as percentage of total, %	4.9	6.7	9.1	7.8	13.1	28.8
Deutschemark Eurobonds in Eurobond market						
DM Eurobonds	3 099.3	2 821.4	5 215.2	6 531.2	4 769.9	2 981.7
US dollar bonds	4 922.1	9 999.2	12 336.4	7 693.4	10 214.5	9 827.2
Other Eurobonds	2 498.1	2 547.2	1 932.5	1 715.2	2 368.5	2 399.7
Total	10 519.5	15 367.8	19 484.1	15 939.8	17 352.9	15 208.6
DM Eurobonds as percentage of total non-dollar Eurobonds, %	51.7	52.6	73.0	79.2	66.8	55.3

Table 9.5 shows that the Deutschemark foreign bond market is the third largest in terms of new issues, following the Swiss foreign bond market and the US Yankee bond market. Indeed in the first nine months of 1979 new issues on the German market even surpassed new issues in the US foreign bond market and accounted for just under 30 per cent of foreign bonds issued on all markets. The DM foreign bond market behaves really as an extension of the Deutschemark foreign bond market. Borrowers tap the market because of the powerful placement power of the German banks and the moderate issuing costs while lenders are attracted by the stability and strength of the Deutschemark. Almost all Deutschemark foreign bonds, in contrast to the Swiss foreign bond market, are public issues rather than private placements.

Eurobonds

There is a very strong Deutschemark Eurobond market, second only to the US dollar Eurobond market. Deutschemark denominated bonds in the last five years have accounted for between 18 and 41 per cent of total Eurobonds issued, comprising about 320 issues with a value of DM 30.5 billion. Of the non-dollar Eurobond issues Deutschemark Eurobonds have accounted for well over 50 per cent and reached a high of 79 per cent of non-dollar issues in 1978. The annual issue of Deutschemark Eurobonds is approximately DM 9 billion, including both public issues and private placements. Monthly trading volume varies between DM 5 billion and DM 12 billion. The larger banks are the major issuers, with the Deutsche

Bank and the West-Deutsche Landesbank accounting for about two-thirds of all new issues. These two banks, together with the Dresdner Bank, the Commerzbank, the Berliner-Handels und Frankfurter Bank and Bayerische Vereinsbank comprise the members of the Capital Market Sub-committee, which meets every month to decide the calendar of new issues. This is regulated so as to ensure a digestible flow of new issues onto the market. Borrowers in the Deutschemark Eurobond market are large international corporations, foreign banks and governments, although lesser quality borrowers also have access to the market and indeed the German authorities are less stringent in their requirements of borrowers than are many other primary international bond markets. Lower quality borrowers have to pay substantially higher costs and their bonds may yield 2 to 3 per cent more than better quality issues of comparable terms. However this does not deter many borrowers who seek the status attaching to issuing an international bond and the ability to issue later bonds in other capital markets. Bonds issued include straight and convertible issues, but not some of the more sophisticated types such as droplocks, which now exist in the US dollar bond market. Deutschemark Eurobonds commonly have a fixed coupon with interest payable annually and with maturities varying from between 5 and 10 years though some are issued with original maturities as short as 3 years or as long as 15 years.

The behaviour and performance of the Euro-Deutschemark bond market is influenced by four factors:

1. The state of the US dollar bond market.
2. The effect of the lag of Deutschemark versus US dollar interest rates.
3. The strength of currency speculation in favour of the German currency.
4. The growing competition among the German banks for foreign borrowers seeking to issue Deutschemark bonds.

In the secondary market, Deutschemark foreign bonds and Eurobonds may be purchased on the Frankfurt Stock Exchange. Most are traded, however, in the over-the-counter market as maintained between the German and the international banks, both in Germany and in other major financial centres, particularly Luxembourg, London and New York.

Except on less active and low quality bonds, banks normally quote a spread of $\frac{1}{2}$ per cent between bid and offer prices.

Most Deutschemark foreign and Eurobonds are issued in minimum denominations of DM 1000 but most transactions in the secondary market occur in minimum amounts of DM 10000.

Equities

Equity financing is an even less significant source of funding for German domestic companies than is the bond market; less than 0.5 per cent of total company financing is raised through the issue of shares, and outstanding shares amount to a capital value of about DM 30 billion.

Shares are issued in bearer form and there is no restriction on the proportion of a company's equity share capital that can be owned by foreigners. Dividends, however, are subject to withholding tax.

Although there are almost 3000 public companies in Germany, the tax system makes it costly to obtain a listing and only approximately 600 have official quotes on the stock exchanges. These quoted companies account for about half of the nominal share capital of all public companies.

Some trading is limited to the shares of about 10 per cent of quoted companies. This is because some shares of public companies tend to be tightly held, either by families with an interest in the company, or by the banks. The banks play an important role in German financial markets and themselves hold a substantial slice of West German industry. Commonly they hold 25 per cent or more of the equity shareholdings of both major and smaller companies. As a result, most companies have at least one banker on their supervisory board, often in a very senior position. Due to political pressure, significant changes are now taking place and many banks are now disposing of their equity interests and selling their shares to the market. This is necessarily a gradual process so banks will continue to be major shareholders in large companies for a number of years to come.

By way of example, the Dresdner Bank has greater than a 25 per cent shareholding in more than 20 public companies. Representatives of the banks attend shareholders' meetings and not only exercise their own votes but also vote as proxies, this being given automatically by customers who have shares deposited with them. Although the banks are required by law to ask shareholders for voting instructions, this is usually done by circulating proxy voting details recommending certain action. As a consequence of this system, the majority of shares of major companies have tended to be held by a very few shareholders. It is quite usual to have 80–90 per cent of the equity represented at annual general meetings. These meetings are taken very seriously, usually last for several hours and can last as long as two days. Also, shareholders tend to take a long-term view of companies' prospects, and they are expected to hold on to shares acquired even when a company is going through difficult times.

Dividends are therefore far more important than they are with, for example, British equities. To encourage investment in German equities, the resident investor is able to benefit from a tax credit $\frac{9}{16}$ of the net dividend. This results in his obtaining a very reasonable yield. Non-residents only have a claim on the German revenue when foreign earnings are being distributed. As an example when one company, Thyssen, distributed dividends of DM 4 non-resident shareholders were entitled to claim back DM 1.19 per share compared with tax credits available to local investors of DM 2.25, resulting in a gross yield to the domestic investor of 7.23 per cent but only 5.08 per cent for the non-resident.

Unit trusts

The government is encouraging the growth of foreign and domestic unit trusts in order to attract the public to take an interest in the securities market. These unit trusts have shown a rapid growth during the last few years. They mostly comprise

Table 9.6 Gross issues of capital market securities (DM millions) (*source: OECD*)

Securities	1975	1976	1977	1978	1979	Jan.–June 1980
DOMESTIC ISSUES						
Bonds						
Central government	13 698	16 009	21 766	18 876	18 233	14 571
Municipalities and state governments	2 773	2 475	847	1 589	397	300
State enterprises	2 022	2 095	2 984	2 140	1 248	2 177
Total public sector	18 493	20 579	25 597	22 605	19 878	17 048
Bank and financial institutions (including mortgage bonds)	56 478	52 497	54 313	71 977	85 750	54 845
Corporate bonds	351	210	311	118	20	0
Schuldscheindarlehen	20 996	22 574	30 949	38 353	40 139	8 474
Total domestic fixed interest securities	96 318	95 860	111 172	133 053	145 787	80 363
Shares	6 010	6 080	4 368	5 550	5 513	4 131
INTERNATIONAL ISSUES						
Foreign bonds	1 943	1 798	2 668	2 787	3 998	3 627
Eurobonds	3 681	6 235	8 297	7 279	5 633	3 053
Total international issues	5 624	8 033	10 965	10 066	9 631	6 680

investments in fixed-interest securities and in shares of the larger quoted companies. They are traded on one or more of the stock exchanges.

The stock exchanges

There are eight stock exchanges in West Germany, at Frankfurt, Dusseldorf, Hamburg, Munich, Berlin, Bremen, Hanover and Stuttgart. The first two are the principal stock exchanges and, although Munich also represents a significant turnover, Frankfurt is by far the most important, accounting for some 46 per cent of total stock exchange turnover in West Germany. This comprises over 40 per cent of total equity market turnover and about 50 per cent of the turnover in the fixed-interest market. The Frankfurt stock exchange is also the one in which the Bundesbank carries out most of its open market operations. Within the framework of the stock exchange system, four types of market exist. These are:

1. *Amtliche Notierung.* This is the official market, under state control. Most quoted companies, and certainly the larger and well-known companies, are traded in this market as are all government and public authority bonds, financial and foreign bonds.
2. *Geregelter Freiverkehr.* This is a semi-official market whose admission regulations are less rigorous and also cheaper to comply with. Securities quoted in this market are also traded on the floor of the stock exchanges.

211

3. *Telefonhandel.* This is the telephone or 'over-the-counter' market in securities that are also quoted on the official exchange. Only the German banks can accept orders from clients and act as intermediaries in this market.
4. *Kursmakler.* This is the market created by, and dealt between, brokers who are authorized by the Minister of Finance of each province, and who fix the price of securities.

The stock exchanges use the trading post system. This is the system by which a given place on the trading floor is designated as a meeting point for transactors in specified securities. Consistent with their universal role within the financial system, the banks act as underwriters, stockbrokers, investment advisers and advisers to companies on acquisitions and mergers. Because the banks own large proportions of company equity, a new regulation was introduced in 1975 aimed at increasing security and regulation of the equity market. Banks are now not permitted to make a market among themselves for transactions of a certain size. These dealings must therefore be transacted on the stock exchange.

The equity turnover on the German stock exchanges is low, primarily because the secondary market is so restricted. Financial institutions are not big buyers and non-bank financial institutions such as insurance companies, pension funds, etc. are, compared with other foreign markets, not very important. One reason for this is that pensions are collected by employers and tend to be reinvested in the same company. Average holdings of shares as a proportion of total investment in, for example, insurance companies is only 6%. Additionally, compared with the bond market, returns from shares have been low. Yields on fixed-interest securities have for years been double the dividend yield on shares. Additionally, the capital gains tax imposed on resident investors makes the purchase of shares less attractive than the purchase of fixed-interest securities.

The tax system is another reason why companies tend not to come to the market for quotations. Certain taxes make it disadvantageous for a company to become a joint stock company (denoted by the subscript AG) and receive a public quotation. For the domestic investor, there is a property tax on wealth, including the holding of shares at 0.7 per cent of market value. There is also a turnover tax which applies to all sales and purchases of shares and debentures apart from federal and state treasury bonds. This tax, for which the buyer and the seller are jointly liable, is between 1 and 2.5‰ of sale price.

All these factors tend to inhibit the growth of the equity market. By contrast bonds, whether domestic, foreign or Eurobonds, all enjoy an active turnover.

Gold

There is a free gold market in Frankfurt accessible to both residents and non-residents and there are no restrictions on transferring gold out of the country. Purchases and sales can be effected through a commercial bank at prices which are established according to the London daily gold fix. Transactions are, however, subject to Value Added Tax at 13 per cent.

Dealing and fees

Deposits and money market instruments

Domestic Deutschemark deposits may be placed with any of the commercial banks in Frankfurt. Euro-Deutschemark deposits may be placed with a non-German national or international bank in any of the major European financial centres.

Domestic capital market

For both residents and non-residents, transactions in both fixed interest and equity securities may always be effected through a German commercial bank whose role is universal in the sense that it also provides investment advice, portfolio management and dealing services.

If the bank is a market maker or dealer in the over-the-counter market for bonds, then transactions are dealt net, with the bank's commission being included in the difference between its quoted bid and offer prices. These dealing spreads are normally $\frac{1}{2}$ to $\frac{3}{4}$ per cent. For very active bonds they may be as small as $\frac{1}{4}$ per cent, while for less active bonds they may be considerably greater. The commissions and fees shown below are for transactions carried out on the stock exchange.

Table 9.7   Brokerage and commissions on stock exchange transactions

Transactions		*Brokerage to specialist on floor of stock exchange*		*Commission to bank or stockbroker*
BONDS				
Up to nominal value	DM 50 000	0.75% minimum	DM 0.5	2.5% minimum DM 2.0
Nominal value				
DM 50 000	DM 100 000	0.50% minimum	DM 37.5	2.5% minimum DM 2.0
DM 100 000	DM 250 000	0.35% minimum	DM 50.0	2.5% minimum DM 2.0
DM 250 000	DM 500 000	0.325% minimum	DM 87.5	2.5% minimum DM 2.0
DM 500 000	DM 1 000 000	0.20% minimum	DM 162.5	2.5% minimum DM 2.0
DM 1 000 000	DM 2 000 000	0.15% minimum	DM 200.0	2.5% minimum DM 2.0
DM 2 000 000	DM 5 000 000	0.10% minimum	DM 300.0	2.5% minimum DM 2.0
more than	DM 5 000 000	0.075% minimum	DM 500.0	2.5% minimum DM 2.0
SHARES				
As proportion of market value—all accounts		1.0%		5% minimum DM 2.0
Share rights—all accounts		1.0%		5% minimum DM 1.0
Investment fund certificates		Nil		Nil

Securities turnover tax (not chargeable to banks and security dealers)

Public sector securities	1% of consideration
Other bonds	2% of consideration
Shares and promissory notes	2.5% of consideration

Settlement and delivery is effected the same day for cash.

213

Stock exchange transactions can be made for any size or amount. Banks and stockbrokers charge commission on bond price or nominal value, whichever is the larger, although the largest expense of purchasing securities is the turnover tax.

Dealings, too, are generally made in terms of the numbers of bonds or shares.

Bank shares are an exception among equities in that they are quoted not as a price but as a percentage of their nominal value.

Schuldscheindarlehen

Schuldscheindarlehen are not traded on the stock exchange but are dealt through German banks or major commercial banks in other financial centres including Luxembourg, London and New York. Commission is included in the spread between bid and offer rates, usually $\frac{1}{2}$ per cent.

Deutschemark Eurobonds

Dealing is always through a major German bank or a foreign international bank. Bonds may be purchased in Germany via the interbank market or the Stock Exchange, or through the international interbank market. Fees are included in the spread between bid and offer price and are normally of the order of $\frac{1}{2}$ per cent. Settlement and delivery is for two business days following the date of the transaction.

Financial and monetary systems

Commercial banks

The banks dominate the financial system in Germany. Among the commercial banks, more than 40 per cent of business is handled by three large branch banks, the Deutsche Bank, the Dresdner Bank and the Commerzbank, known as the 'big three'. The Landesbank has become increasingly competitive with the big three and in recent years has also gained a significant share of banking business.

Commercial banks in Germany are multipurpose banks. They act not only as repositories for savings and sources of corporate finance but also as stockbrokers, investment advisors and portfolio managers, issuers of securities in both the domestic and Euromarkets, as well as running huge portfolios on their own account. They have large shareholdings in both quoted and private companies, and are thus able directly to influence the corporate sector.

Savings banks and credit co-operatives

In addition to the commercial banks, there are over 700 savings banks, with more than 16000 branches, and approximately 2000 industrial and agricultural credit co-operatives with more than 19000 branches. Savings banks in particular channel savings into medium- and long-term loans to farmers and tradesmen. They do not issue bonds but lend out-of-deposit funds placed with them.

Mortgage banks

There are over 40 mortgage banks and building and loan associations. These are classified as specialist banks in that they provide a particular service rather than a multipurpose one; specifically they issue mortgage bonds to finance mortgage credit granted to their clients.

Central bank (*the Deutsche Bundesbank*)

The controlling authority of the banking system is the Deutsche Bundesbank in Frankfurt, although financial institutions also answer to the supervisory authorities in the Ministries of Economics and Finance in each of the federal states.

The Bundesbank is wholly owned by the government but is legally autonomous. It has the general obligation to support government economic policy but the government cannot issue it with direct instructions.

The Bundesbank is the sole issuer of currency and is charged, by legislation, with the duty of safeguarding the economy by regulating the money circulation and the supply of credit. Its head office is in Frankfurt, the centre of the financial system in Germany, but it has branches also in each of the federal states, which regulate the banking system within these states.

The Bundesbank is also lender of last resort to the banking system. Banks are able to discount eligible bills with the Bundesbank as a matter of automatic recourse, provided that the banks do not exceed their discount quotas. Quotas are set relative to each bank's capital and free reserves. Eligible bills have to carry three signatures of creditworthy parties, and be of less than three months' remaining maturity.

Monetary policy

There are a variety of controls the Bundesbank can apply to regulate the money supply and the expansion of credit. Broadly these are defined within four categories of instruments—reserve requirements, discount policy, quality and quantity controls, and open market operations.

The president of the Bundesbank in a recent statement said that German monetary policy for years has been designed 'to bring about not a given level of interest rates but, first and foremost, a given increase in the money supply'.

In setting its monetary targets the Bundesbank has the backing of the Bonn Government, the Council of Economic advisers and a wide selection of public opinion. The Bundesbank tends to stick to its longer-term objectives regarding monetary targets and does not change direction 'at the slightest wavering of the business barometer'.

In recent years the money supply reins have been manipulated elastically by the Bundesbank but the underlying policy of gradually reducing the scope for inflation step by step reached a crucial stage during 1980.

Reserve requirements

The Bundesbank sets minimum reserve requirements. These requirements may differ according to whether banks' liabilities are to resident or non-resident depositors, to the size and type of liabilities, their location, and also according to the general rate of expansion of banks' liabilities.

The percentages of liabilities specified by the Bundesbank have to be deposited as reserve balances, interest free, at the Bundesbank or its branches. Failure to observe the minimum reserve requirements results in banks being charged penal rates of interest on their reserve deficiencies. The reserve requirements thus act as a check on liquidity and as an influence on interest rates.

Reserve requirements are set at a higher rate on non-resident deposits when the Bundesbank wants to stem the inflow of foreign funds, which cause an upward pressure on the exchange rate and inflate the domestic money supply.

From October 1972 to October 1974, during the Bundesbank's Austerity Programme, penalizing constraints were placed on foreign capital. The non-resident investor was required to place a certain amount of additional cash interest free for each deposit and, for a time, an interest rate ban was also imposed. The banks at the same time were required to maintain special reserve requirements of up to 40 per cent against foreign liabilities.

Reserve requirements for resident and non-resident deposits are currently the same. The following table shows the rates applying and compares them with those applicable at the peak of the Austerity Programme in November 1973.

Selected Reserve Requirements	1977	1980	1981
Resident			
sight deposits	20.1%	9.2–14.65%	7.1–11.25%
time deposits	13.95%	6.5–10.30%	5.0–7.95%
Non-resident			
sight deposits	40.0%	9.2–14.65%	11.25%
time deposits	35.0%	6.5–10.3%	7.95%

The table shows a range of rates presently applied. Different reserve requirements apply to sight deposits and time deposits, the ratio for the former being higher than that for the latter. The ratio also depends on location. Slightly higher rates are usually applied in cities where the Bundesbank has a branch, i.e., in 'bank places' (Bankplätze). Finally smaller banks are usually subject to lower ratios and, for this purpose, banks are defined according to four size categories.

The growth of liabilities, and thus credit expansion, is also contained by the imposition of additional reserve ratios on the marginal increase in deposits. Such supplementary reserve requirements are nearly always imposed on non-resident deposits and have been (January 1978) as high as 80 per cent.

The banks report their liabilities to the Bundesbank in the middle of the month, calculated as a four-week average. At these times, the interest rates in the call money market may exhibit volatility according to the amount of liquidity in the market and whether the banks can easily meet their reserve requirements.

Discount rate policy

The banks are set quotas relative to their capital and reserves, within which limits they are able to rediscount eligible bills at the Bundesbank as a matter of direct recourse. The Bundesbank may alter the size of the quotas and the rate at which such bills are discounted (the 'discount rate').

Most bills are rediscounted directly with the Bundesbank but export bills may be discounted with the Privatsdiskont AG, which acts as an intermediary between the banks and the Bundesbank AG. It is the only bill broker and discount house in Frankfurt and is jointly owned by the commercial banks.

In addition, the Bundesbank will extend credit to the banks outside their discount quotas in order to help them satisfy short-term liquidity requirements. The rate applied to such transactions is one to two per cent higher than the discount rate and is known as the 'Lombard rate'. Lombard credits are normally granted against specific securities which are offered on a type of repurchase agreement to the central bank. Such securities may be treasury bills, non-interest-bearing treasury bonds, or fixed-interest debentures. Other money market rates are closely correlated with the Lombard rate. Bank rate, another rate frequently quoted in the financial press, is that rate at which the banks will lend to their prime credit customers. This is higher than and also moves in parallel with the Lombard rate.

The daily market rate of discount is fixed at 1 p.m. by representatives of the Bundesbank and the Privatsdiskont AG. The Bundesbank has the authority to vary the discount and Lombard rates and, by doing so, it affects not only interest rates but also credit expansion, since the banks use the discount window to augment the funds they raise through the money market. By these means, about 50 per cent of short-term lending can be controlled.

Quality and quantity controls

The Bundesbank can also establish quality and quantity requirements for different types of instruments and can publish guidelines which must be strictly followed by the commercial banks. For example, the bank may specify which investment instruments may be sold to what type of investor. Currently, non-residents are not permitted to purchase short-term securities of less than one year remaining maturity.

Open market operations

The Bundesbank is active in the money market and also sometimes in the capital market. Interest rates are influenced by the rate at which the Bundesbank is prepared to buy or sell money market paper to the banks and credit institutions. Liquidity is influenced by the extent to which the Bundesbank is prepared to make its surplus funds available to the banking system.

As far as such dealings may affect money market creditors, the Bundesbank may also enter the capital market to buy or sell long-term bonds, usually public authority bonds.

217

Economic statistics

Economic statistics are published as follows:

Reserves	Middle or end of every week
Balance of payments	First week of each month
Balance of trade	First week of each month
Cost-of-living index	Third week of each month
Wholesale price index	Fourth Tuesday of each month
Producer price index	20th of each month (or following Monday if a weekend)
Industrial production index	Third week of each month
Import and export price index	Last week of each month
Unemployment	Sixth day of each month

Withholding taxes

Withholding taxes are charged on interest earned on bonds but not on deposits. Money market instruments cannot be held by non-residents, so no provision is made for taxation on interest arising from short-term instruments.

Table 9.8   Withholding taxes

	Interest		Dividends
	Convertible or profit-sharing bonds, %	Other bonds, %	Portfolio investments, %
Non-treaty countries	25	25	25
Treaty countries:			
Argentina	15	15	15
Australia	10	10	15
Austria	25	0	25
Belgium	15	15	15
Brazil	15	15	15
Canada	25	15	15
Cyprus	10	10	15
Denmark	0	0	15
Egypt	15	15	15
Finland	25	25	25
France	0	0	15
Greece	10	10	25
Hungary	0	0	15
Iceland	0	0	15
India	25	25	25
Indonesia	10	10	15
Iran	15	15	20
Ireland	0	0	15
Israel	15	15	25
Italy	25	25	25

Table 9.8—*Continued*

	Interest		Dividends
	Convertible or profit-sharing bonds, %	Other bonds, %	Portfolio investments, %
Jamaica	12.5	12.5	15
Japan	10	10	15
Korea	15	15	15
Liberia	20	20	15
Luxembourg	0	0	15
Malaysia	15	15	15
Malta	10	10	15
Morocco	10	10	15
Netherlands	15	0	15
Norway	0	0	15
Pakistan	20	20	15
Poland	0	0	15
Rumania	10	10	15
Singapore	10	10	15
South Africa	10	10	15
Spain	10	10	15
Sri Lanka	25	25	25
Sweden	0	0	15
Switzerland	25*	0	20
Thailand	25	25	20
Trinidad and Tobago	15	15	20
Tunisia	10	10	15
UAE	15	15	15
UK	0	0	15
United States	0	0	15
Zambia	10	10	15

* Profit-sharing bonds only—other bonds are tax exempt.

Dividends are subject to a withholding tax rate of 15 per cent in most instances although, if a shareholding is greater than 25 per cent of a company's equity, then a higher rate of 25 per cent normally applies. Two exceptions are Switzerland and the USA, where the shareholding for the higher tax rate is 20 per cent and no upper limit, respectively. Additionally, the reduced rate of 15 per cent does not apply to Luxembourg holding companies.

Otherwise the tax rates are as shown in Table 9.8. Interest earned from the following securities are exempt from withholding tax:

Schuldscheindarlehen;
foreign bonds issued in German domestic market;
Deutschemark denominated Eurobonds.

Exchange controls

In general, there are few foreign exchange controls, although the regulatory bodies, comprising most of the federal ministries, have the power to impose them. Such powers have been exercised in the recent past. In 1973 measures were introduced to contain the inflow of foreign capital although they have now been almost entirely lifted.

The supervisory authority with respect to capital controls is the Bundesbank.

Exchange rate system

The currency is the Deutschemark which is a participant in the EMS (European Monetary System).

The following currencies are officially quoted on the Frankfurt foreign exchange market: Austrian schilling, Belgian and Luxembourg franc, Canadian dollar, Danish kroner, Finnish markka, French franc, Italian lire, Japanese yen, Dutch guilder, Norwegian krone, Portuguese escudo, sterling, Spanish peseta, Swedish krona, Swiss franc, and US dollar.

All banks are freely permitted to make both spot and forward foreign exchange transactions.

Money market

Money market instruments and fixed-interest securities with a remaining maturity of less than two years are not normally permitted to be sold to non-residents. Certain exceptions are sometimes made with the prior approval of the Bundesbank.

Capital market

Capital market securities may freely be sold to non-residents.

New issues of foreign and domestic bonds are subject to control of timing and terms by the Central Capital Market Committee which is a co-ordinating but voluntary body within the banking system. Otherwise, no official approval is required for bond issues.

Gold

There is a free gold market in Frankfurt to which both residents and non-residents have access. Except for the formality of a customs declaration, there is no restriction on the import or export of gold in any form.

10.   Republic of Ireland

General market environment

Ireland's financial system has grown up under the wing of the UK. Its institutions and operating methods are modelled on those of the UK and local funds have traditionally made use of the markets provided in London.

In recent years, however, particularly during the last decade, markets have been developing in Ireland in their own right. The money market, especially, has grown due to the growth of 'non-associated' banks and to positive encouragement by the government. Much money still does, however, find its way to the London market, and capital markets particularly are still very much interactive. All Irish capital market securities are quoted also in London and the Irish stock exchange is part of the UK Associated Stock Exchange.

Monetary intervention mostly takes the form of direct controls over liquidity in the banking system. Interest rates are administered by the Bank of Ireland through

Table 10.1   Summary of instruments

Instrument	Characteristics
MONEY MARKET	
Deposits	
call deposits	Active interbank market
time deposits	Most activity for up to one month money. Deposits can be placed from seven days to one year
Eurocurrency deposits	Deposits in convertible currencies accepted by banks in Dublin but usually replaced in London market
Exchequer bills	Government discount bills issued monthly by auction
CAPITAL MARKET	
Government bonds	Account for 90% of stock exchange turnover
Public sector bonds	Bonds also issued irregularly by local authorities, state bodies and public corporations
Corporate bonds	Rarely issued. Little secondary market activity
Equities	Reasonably good issuing activity. Represent only about two per cent of stock exchange turnover in secondary market. All quoted also on London stock exchange

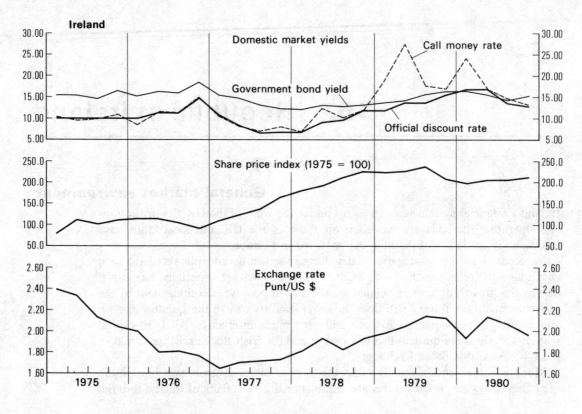

the predetermined bank rate but in general, rates are about 1½ per cent below comparable rates in London.

Exchange controls with respect to investment in Irish securities are lenient and withholding taxes for residents of tax-treaty countries are in most cases zero, for both interest and dividends.

The money market

Deposits

Most of the deposits held by the domestic commercial banks, known as Associate Banks, are small deposits at seven days' notice. The interbank market has grown spontaneously with the growth of non-associated banks. Deposits in local currency may be placed overnight or at short-term notice or for terms for up to one year or longer.

The banks also accept deposits in convertible currencies although the Eurocurrency market in Ireland is not very large.

Non-associate banks are those that do not enjoy a special relationship with the Central Bank of Ireland and comprise merchant and investment banks and branches of foreign banks. Not having a large branch network they lack the same access to the small saver, and do not enjoy the same continuity of the flow of funds as do the associate banks. This led, in the late 1960s and throughout the 1970s, to the development of the Domestic Interbank Money Market in which non-bank lenders and borrowers may also participate. As a result, moneybrokers have recently been established to help cope with the growth of the market in Dublin.

Domestic interest rates are calculated on the basis of a civil year of 365 days. Rates correlate very closely with rates in the London interbank market but are maintained at about $1\frac{1}{2}$ per cent below London rates.

Call money may be placed overnight or at two- and seven-day call in minimum sums of £Ir50 000.

Time deposits may be placed for fixed periods of one week and then monthly up to 12 months or longer. Most activity is generally concentrated in the interbank market for deposits of up to one month. Minimum sums for short-term deposits are normally £Ir50 000. Longer term deposits placed with most financial institutions can be made in sums as small as a few hundred pounds.

Eurocurrency deposits

Call and time deposits may also be placed in the interbank market in any convertible currency. Such money normally finds its way to the London money market, and the Eurocurrency market is thus not particularly active in Dublin.

Exchequer bills

Exchequer bills (the same as treasury bills) are issued on a monthly basis by the central bank on behalf of the Ministry of Finance. They are issued by auction in which individuals and the non-bank public may also bid, through a bank or stockbroker. They are bearer securities issued at a discount from par which represents the interest rate. They carry maturities of 91 days and are freely negotiable in the secondary market.

In the primary market they are bought mainly by the banks which are able to hold exchequer bills as part of their required reserves. Transactions are normally in sizes of £Ir1 million although the minimum denomination is £Ir5000. Bidders submit their tenders stating the amount and the discount price of their bid shortly before each monthly issue. The central bank determines the minimum price; those tenders above the minimum price are allotted in full, those below are not allotted, while those traders at the minimum accepted price are allotted proportionately.

The secondary market is fairly active, again mostly as an interbank market since, not only may exchequer bills be included in reserves but they are also eligible for rediscounting at the central bank.

The capital market

Government bonds

New issues of government and state sponsored institutions dominate new issues in the capital market, such that about two-thirds of the total capital raised is for financing public sector debt.

223

Table 10.2   Marketable Irish government securities (in £Ir million) (*source: Central Bank of Ireland Quarterly Bulletin*)

Held by	Nominal amount outstanding as at			
	31.12.77	31.12.78	31.12.79	31.12.80
Central bank	97.2	103.8	199.4	170.8
Associated banks	598.1	657.9	736.9	608.5
Non-associated banks	122.4	126.3	155.4	165.2
Building societies	88.6	115.9	183.6	190.4
Insurance companies	332.2	517.8	583.3	571.6
Government departments	184.6	87.7	353.2	317.1
State sponsored bodies	34.0	36.2	63.5	74.4
Other financial institutions	103.2	128.3	126.6	136.2
Other	724.6	1113.2	1323.8	1343.2
Total	2283.0	2887.1	3725.7	3577.4

The government issues bonds at irregular intervals with maturities ranging from 1 to 30 years. Bonds with less than 5-year maturities are issued by the central bank. Bonds with longer maturities are sold through the government broker.

Bonds are coupon bearing with interest calculated according to a 365-day year and paid semiannually. Coupons are usually fixed at rates that are slightly lower than for comparable British government securities. During the 1970s the public debt was additionally funded by open-ended government bonds of no fixed maturity, which are issued once a year, in the autumn.

In the secondary market, government bonds are quoted on the Irish stock exchange where they account for over 70 per cent of outstanding market value and about 90 per cent turnover for all listed securities (see Table 10.2). Approximately 55 per cent are purchased and traded by the associated banks and other financial institutions and 45 per cent by companies, individuals and foreign holders.

Irish government securities are also quoted on the London stock exchange. Only a small proportion of turnover normally occurs on the London exchange; particularly when interest rates differentials may be temporarily favourable substantial purchases are made.

Other public sector bonds

Other public sector bonds include bonds of local authorities and bonds issued by state bodies such as the Peat Board and the water authorities, and by public corporations. New issues are made at irregular intervals, perhaps every two or three years, through the government broker, and represent 10 per cent of the nominal value of the total bonds outstanding. Their maturity range is the same as for government bonds, and they also enjoy a reasonably active secondary market.

Foreign bonds

There are no foreign bonds issued or listed in Ireland, this market being centred wholly in London.

Eurobonds

Similarly there are no issues of Eurobonds denominated in Irish punts. Transactions in Eurobonds of other denominations can be made through banks in Dublin but the banks usually effect such transactions through the market in London.

Corporate bonds

Relatively few corporate bonds are issued by Irish companies which prefer to raise capital through equity issues or bank borrowing.

Those corporate bonds that are issued take the form of debentures, very often convertible debentures, with maturities of up to 10 years.

Equity shares

Equity issues represent about 30 to 40 per cent of new capital issues, including government bond issues, and amount to between 10 and 20 million punts per annum.

New issues are made through merchant banks and stockbrokers as in the London market. The banks or brokers underwrite new issues and offer them for sale in both the Irish and UK markets.

There are less than 200 quoted Irish companies listed on the Stock Exchanges of Ireland and also in London. Turnover on the Irish exchange is active in the shares of the larger, well-known companies but inactive for the many smaller companies. Movements in equity prices in general follow those of the London stock exchange, but often with a slight time lag.

Stock exchange

There are stock exchanges in Dublin and Cork, but Dublin is the major. Since 1973, they have both been members of the UK Provincial Stock Exchanges which are amalgamated with the London Stock Exchange.

Along with the provincial exchanges, the Irish exchanges are subject to rules and regulations determined by the London Stock Exchange Council although the day-to-day management and administration of each exchange is run by an autonomous committee.

The Irish stock exchanges publish their own separate official list of securities and turnover figures.

Brokers must be members of the Irish exchange in order to deal on the floor of either exchange. Currently there are over 100 members who come from more than 20 Irish firms of stockbrokers.

Unlike the London and other UK exchanges, there are no jobbers on the Irish exchanges; instead brokers deal directly with each other, but in Irish securities only. Other UK securities that are quoted on the Irish exchanges must be dealt between brokers and their agents in London or a member of a UK exchange.

Table 10.3 **Securities outstanding on Irish capital market (as at 30 June 1980)**
(*source: London Stock Exchange*)

	Number	Nominal value, £Ir million	Market value, £Ir million
Government and public sector bonds			
Short dated—up to 5 years	....	1620.1	1535.2
Medium dated—5–15 years	....	877.0	654.1
Long dated—over 15 years	....	1291.2	1095.2
Total	87	3788.3	3284.5
Corporate securities			
Corporate bonds	17	35.2	39.2
Convertible bonds and preference shares	44	13.8	8.3
Ordinary and deferred shares	78	244.5	1182.8
Total	139	293.5	1230.3

Table 10.4 **Turnover of Irish government bonds**

Period	Value, £Ir million	Number of bargains	Average value per bargain, £Ir
1974	1882.5	27 958	67 333
1975	3962.8	36 349	109 021
1976	4460.2	37 981	117 432
1977	9197.1	67 127	137 010
1978	9671.4	59 787	161 762
1979	9523.8	48 532	196 237
1980 (Jan.–June)	4218.0	28 094	150 139

Since there are no jobbers, a different trading system is used from that of the London exchange. In Ireland, the call-over system is used at two daily sessions starting at 11.45 a.m. and at 2.15 p.m.

Dealing and fees

Money market

Exchequer bills may be purchased and dealt through banks. A small discretionary fee may be charged for subscriptions to new issues.

In secondary market transactions, the spread between a dealing bank's bid and offer price is usually $\frac{1}{32}$ to $\frac{1}{8}$ per cent, which represents the bank's commission. Settlement and delivery is normally the following business day.

Capital market

All securities, including Government bonds as well as private sector equity shares, must be dealt through stockbrokers. It is possible to ask a bank to act on the investor's behalf but the bank must itself then use a broker.

Commissions are the same as those set by the London stock exchange (see Chapter 17).

Financial and monetary systems

Financial institutions

Almost three-quarters of all banking business in Ireland is controlled by the associated banks which are commercial banks, equivalent in function to the UK clearing banks, so called because they have a special relationship with the central bank. In particular they have recourse to the discount facility and the central bank's clearing facility. There are two groups of domestic associated banks, the Allied Irish Group and the Bank of Ireland Group. Both groups are the result of a series of bank mergers. Between them they have nearly 700 branches throughout Ireland.

Other banking institutions are the non-associated banks which include subsidiaries of British banks, American and other foreign banks. These non-associated banks do not have branch networks but the total number has grown quite significantly during the last decade, proving a major factor in the fostering of a domestic money market. Not having the same recourse as the associated banks to the central bank discount window, these banks needed to use the interbank market to balance their books. At one time all such business was transacted through the London market, but since the early 1970s, increasingly more business has been transacted in the domestic Irish market. This has resulted in the recent establishment of three money brokers to cope with and further aid the growth of the market.

The secondary banks in Ireland within the category of non-associated banks also include merchant banks and hire purchase finance houses. These also make use of the interbank and short-term money markets.

For savings and advances in the personal sector, the savings banks, in particular the post office savings bank and the trustee savings banks, control a large share of the market. Both are state owned and direct small savings from the public into central government.

The building societies are owned by the private sector and also collect personal savings which are directed into the house mortgage market and the government bond market.

Central bank

The central bank is the Central Bank of Ireland. It is the sole issuer of notes and coin and lender of last resort to the banking system.

227

It is responsible for the supervision of the banking system and the control of bank credit. It acts as agent to the government in conducting open market operations and the issue of short-term government securities, and also administers exchange controls.

Monetary policy

Although the bank is empowered with the full range of central bank functions, principally two instruments of monetary control are employed—liquidity ratios and discount rate policy.

Discount policy

The Central Bank of Ireland acts as lender of last resort to the associated banks. These banks may rediscount domestic commercial bills of exchange and Irish government exchequer bills.

The central bank uses this function as a major tool of monetary policy. It fixes its discount rate in order to encourage or discourage the use of the discount facility, relative to market facilities, though it does not impose ceilings on the amount of bills which may be discounted by the banks.

The discount rate is subject to bank rate which is an administered rate determined by the central bank. This is the rate on which, by agreement with the associated banks, all other interest rates are structured. As a general policy, the central bank tries to maintain interest rates at a level of $1-1\frac{1}{2}$ per cent below comparable rates pertaining in the London market. By keeping interest rates low, the government hopes to assist domestic industry, but any greater differential than $1\frac{1}{2}$ per cent would result in excessive flows of capital out of Ireland and into the London market.

Liquidity ratios

This is a major tool of monetary policy for the control of bank credit. The central bank imposes primary and secondary liquidity ratios on both the associated and non-associated banks.

Both ratios are expressed as a proportion of the banks' domestic deposits for the non-bank private sector plus net interbank deposits plus net internal liabilities. Primary liquidity must be maintained in the form of cash either in banks' own vaults or held interest free with the central bank. Secondary liquidity may be held in the form of short-term government securities.

Different ratios are applied in the case of associated or non-associated banks. For the former, the primary liquidity ratio has been in the region of a minimum 13 per cent since the early 1970s while the secondary ratio has been a minimum of 30 per cent.

Quantitative controls

Directives from the central bank to the associated and non-associated banks have, at times, been an important instrument of control. Prior to 1971 they were the principal instrument but since then, liquidity ratios coupled with the use of bank rate have become more important. Quantitative controls are still used, however, in order to supplement other policies. Such controls take the form of moral suasion from the central bank to the commercial and secondary banks regarding the direction of new bank lending and limits for such lending.

Open market operation

The central bank, on behalf of the minister of finance, undertakes open market operations, not so much to effect major changes in the financial markets, but more to stabilize the markets. The main means of such operations are the issue or selling of government securities to absorb excess liquidity and the purchase of government securities in order to ease temporarily tight liquidity in the banking system.

Withholding taxes

The standard rate of withholding tax in Ireland is 35 per cent on interest earnings, but for residents of treaty countries this is in most cases reduced to zero.

The standard rate of withholding tax on dividends is zero which applies to residents of both treaty and non-treaty countries. Dividends carry a tax credit of $\frac{35}{65}$ of the dividend payable.

Table 10.5 Withholding taxes

	Interest %	Dividends %
Non-treaty countries	35	
Tax treaty countries		
Austria	0	0
Belgium	15	0
Canada	35	0
Cyprus	0	0
Denmark	0	0
Finland	0	0
France	0	0
Germany	0	0
Italy	10	0
Japan	10	0
Luxembourg	0	0
Netherlands	0	0
Norway	0	0
Pakistan	0	0
Sweden	0	0
Switzerland	0	0
UK	0	0
USA	0	0
Zambia	0	0

Exchange controls

Authorities

The authority responsible for the administration of exchange controls is the Central Bank of Ireland, although much of the day-to-day administration is delegated to the commercial banks.

Currency

The currency is the Irish punt, denoted as £Ir. Prior to March 1979, the punt was pegged at par to the pound sterling. This relationship was discontinued when the punt became a participant in the EMS, which Britain did not join.

The authorities intervene in the spot foreign exchange market in order to maintain the value of the currency within the margins prescribed by the EMS.

Non-resident accounts

Non-residents may operate in the spot foreign exchange market through an authorized bank, but may only operate in the forward foreign exchange market if the transaction has an underlying commercial purpose.

Non-residents must hold Irish punts with Irish banks in accounts designated as external accounts. Credits to accounts in excess of £Ir100 000 require prior approval from the central bank.

Non-residents may open foreign currency accounts with authorized banks in any foreign currency without restriction.

Purchase or sale of securities

There are a number of restrictions on residents investing abroad but there are few restrictions on the inflow of foreign capital. Non-residents are free to purchase quoted Irish securities, subject only to prior notification of the central bank if transaction values exceed £Ir100 000 and provided payments are made with foreign currency or in Irish punts from an external account.

Proceeds for such investments may be freely repatriated.

Gold

Residents may freely buy, sell or hold gold in Ireland. Non-residents may also do so, provided that it is held in Ireland. The export of gold requires specific approval from the exchange control authorities.

General market environment

Italy is subject to excessive demand for funds from domestic industry and particularly from the central government and public sector while its financial markets are still developing and as yet are not sufficiently adequate to cope with such demand.

The money market has improved since the introduction, in the latter part of the 1970s, of the treasury bill and bond markets which are now proving extremely active. The capital market for long-term funds is still somewhat sluggish, however, partly due to the prominence of state controlled industries in the bond market and

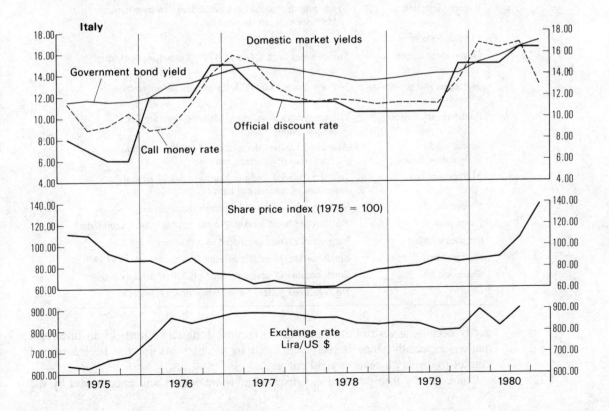

Table 11.1 Summary of instruments

Instrument	Characteristics
MONEY MARKET	
Deposits call deposits	Sight deposits treated like call deposits. Active market. Interest rates competitive with international rates
time deposits	Weakness of currency discourages long-time deposits. Most are for less than three months
certificates of deposit	Only medium-term CDs issued by savings banks. Poor marketability
repurchase agreements	Short-term loans arranged against sale and repurchase of ENEL bonds.
Treasury bills (BOTs)	Issued monthly. 3-, 6- and 12-months' maturity. Free of withholding tax
Treasury credit certificates (CCTs)	Medium-term, floating rate, government certificates. Good marketability free of withholding tax
Polyannual treasury bonds (BTPs)	Medium-term, fixed coupon government bonds. Tend to be traded in money market. Free of withholding tax
ENEL bonds	Theoretically capital market securities but attractive to money market investors because interest and principal is indexed. Free of withholding tax
Bankers' acceptances	Trade bills and promissory notes accepted by a bank. Maturities one to six months
CAPITAL MARKET	
Government bonds	Direct issues are CCTs and BTPs. Traded in short-term money market
Municipal and provincial bonds	No new issues since 1975. Finance raised indirectly
Public agency bonds	Indirect government issues. Most popular are ENEL indexed bonds.
Special credit institution bonds	Account for major share of bond market excluding short-term government securities
Mortgage bonds	Issued by special credit institutions and by special sections of commercial banks
Foreign bonds	Small number of issues by international agencies.
Eurobonds	No Eurolire bond market. No market for other Eurobonds
Corporate bonds	Very small market compared to public sector bonds
Equity shares	Small market. Normally inactive but high turnover in 1980
Share options	Small number of options traded on Milan stock exchange
Gold	No organized market for investors or speculators

partly because investors are reluctant to commit long-term funds in an uncertain market, especially since it has been usual in recent years for the Italian capital market to display a reverse yield curve.

Consequently foreign portfolio investment is welcomed and encouraged by the government largely in order to help satisfy the public sector's demand for funds. As a result, exchange controls are liberal, although withholding taxes are payable on most forms of interest and dividends—a notable exception being treasury bills and short-term government bonds. The equity market is normally inactive though it has experienced a boom during 1980. Brokerage fees are also fairly high.

Although Rome is the capital and is one of several commercial cities, Milan is the financial and economic centre of Italy.

The money market

Until the mid-1970s the money market had proved somewhat inadequate. Inflation and economic uncertainty during the 1970s and the resultant weakness of the lira resulted in a preference by domestic savers, either for liquidity or for investment in foreign markets. For similar reasons non-residents were not attracted to the Italian market. Not least because the government debt is so substantial, the Bank of Italy has tried to encourage the further development of the money market to help finance such debt. Depth has been added to the market since the introduction in 1976 of the treasury bills and, more recently, of floating rate securities.

Deposits

Call deposits

Italian banks pay interest on sight (demand) deposits and the majority of deposits made by both residents and non-residents are sight deposits. The volume of such deposits is large and turnover is quite active, such that effectively it is a call money market. Until called by the lender, deposits receive the day-to-day market rate of interest, which is a competitive rate closely linked to international rates. Interest is calculated according to a civil year of 365 days.

An interbank call deposit market also exists but for the non-bank depositor, sight deposits in excess of Lit 1 billion receive the same rate of interest as available in the interbank market.

Time deposits

The market in time deposits is smaller because of their lesser liquidity and of the weakness of the currency, a factor which discourages investors from tying their money into the Italian market for relatively long periods at fixed interest rates.

Time deposits are available for terms of up to 18 months—the maximum limit that Italian banks are allowed to accept—but very few deposits are placed for longer than three months.

The monetary authorities have played an increasingly important role in influencing short-term interest rates during 1980. This is because there has been a shift in emphasis away from direct controls towards market-oriented policies as the main means of limiting credit expansion. Interest rates are competitive with international market rates. This is necessary in order that funds that are required in the

233

domestic markets do not flow out of the country and into the Euromarkets. For non-bank depositors interest is calculated on a civil year basis of 365 days, but interbank time deposits are calculated according to a financial year of 360 days.

Certificate of deposit

There are no short-term lira CDs but the savings banks issue negotiable CDs with 18-, 24- and 36-month maturities. These are registered securities, issued at a discount, and are paid at par at maturity. No interest payments are normally paid during the life of the CD so the rate of discount is usually large.

The secondary market is not sufficiently active to provide good marketability.

Repurchase agreement

The commercial banks will undertake informal repurchase agreements whereby corporate lenders of temporarily idle funds may lend to a bank in return for long-term ENEL (electricity industry) bonds. At the same time the bank furnishes the lender with a guarantee that it will buy back the bonds at a given date, and at a given price, which is the price at which it sold the securities plus some consideration for interest. Effectively these are similar to time deposits but are normally transacted for shorter periods of only a few days. They thus guarantee the lender a particular rate of interest in contrast to interest on call deposits which is changed from day to day.

They may also be negotiated in reverse. When a corporate client wants to borrow from the bank he may sell long-term bonds to the banks with an agreement to buy them back at a specified price on a predetermined date.

Treasury bills (BOTs)

Ordinary treasury bills have been issued on a monthly basis since 1976 and their volume has grown considerably. They are now the main method by which the treasury raises funds to meet the short-term financing requirements.

Ordinary treasury bills (Buono ordinario del tesoro) are known as BOTs. The Bank of Italy offers for sale about Lit 5000 billion at the end of each month with maturities of 3, 6 and 12 months. They may not be directly subscribed for at auction by private investors, but individuals and corporations, including non-residents, may apply through a bank or stockbroker in multiple denominations of Lit 1 000 000. BOTs are issued at a discount from par calculated according to a 365-day year and at competitive bond equivalent yields. Interest earned is free of tax including withholding tax and thus, in comparison with other instruments, offers all types of investors a superior yield. As at August 1980 there were Lit 66 451 billion of BOTs outstanding.

Treasury credit certificates (CCTs)

Treasury credit certificates (certificato di credito del tesoro) are government securities issued with original maturities of up to three years, but they may be distinguished from short-term government bonds in that they carry an indexed coupon

234

payable and recalculated semiannually. As with BOTs, minimum denominations are Lit 1 000 000. The certificates are issued at par with coupons based on the weighted average yield of treasury bills over the preceding three or four months, but subject to a guaranteed minimum. The coupon rate is recalculated every six months by the same formula, and the principal is repaid in full at maturity. The certificates were first issued in 1977 and, since 1978, have been issued on a monthly basis by the Bank of Italy, which also guarantees the interest and capital repayment.

Like BOTs, CCTs are free of the tax, making their yields highly attractive to both resident and non-resident investors. Their indexed coupons enhance their popularity. Together, these two factors make them a highly marketable security that has added depth to the money market. They provide the treasury with a method of raising medium-term finance while being attractive to investors in the short-term money market.

A second type of CCT that has fixed coupons but is amortized during the life of the certificate is also issued to the banking system but is not available to the non-bank public.

Polyannual treasury bonds (BTPs)

Polyannual treasury bonds (buono del tesoro poliennali) are short- to medium-term bonds issued by the Bank of Italy on behalf of the treasury to meet extraordinary expenditure. They carry original maturities of four, five or nine years. They are issued at below par, to be redeemed at par, and carry a fixed-rate coupon. Interest is paid semiannually and calculated on the basis of a 360-day year. The majority are issued in denominations of Lit 5000 though they may be issued in larger denominations. For example, two outstanding issues have denominations of Lit 50 000 and Lit 100 000.

BTPs are called polyannuals because they are issued with a life of more than one year (i.e., four-, five-, and nine-year maturities). Four-year bonds are known as quadriennali bonds, 5- and 9-year bonds are known as quinquennali and novennali bonds respectively. They tend however to be traded with other short-term securities in the money market. Their marketability depends on yields obtainable in the market for BOTs and CCTs and thus tends to be poor when short-term interest rates are rising. Nevertheless they are an attractive medium-term investment since like BOTs and CCTs, BPTs are free from tax. About 40 per cent are held by households and companies, about 30 per cent by the banks, about 25 per cent by the Banca d'italia and the Italian Exchange Office, and the remainder by other financial institutions.

ENEL bonds

ENEL (Ente Nazionale per l'Energia Elettrica), the Italian National Electric Agency, issue straight bonds and indexed bonds. Both are guaranteed by the Republic of Italy and enjoy the same fiscal exemptions as government securities.

Although, theoretically, they are capital market securities ENEL bonds, particularly the indexed bonds, tend to be traded along with short-term securities in the money market.

The straight bonds are issued with fixed coupons with interest payed semiannually and with medium original maturities of 5 to 10 years.

The indexed bonds carry half-yearly coupons calculated on a base of a 360-day year; coupons and redemption value are both indexed. Interest is calculated on the basis of the average life yield of a selected group of 47 bonds quoted on the stock exchange, all carrying a nominal seven per cent coupon. The yield is calculated and announced by Mediobanca at the beginning of the month preceding the next interest period.

A minimum coupon is guaranteed at the rate of four per cent semiannually for the first issue and five per cent for subsequent issues.

Capital is indexed according to a premium equal to the sum of all spreads between the half-yearly coupons actually paid and the guaranteed minimum. A minimum principal repayment is guaranteed, equal to the par value of the bonds.

Secondary Markets in BOTs, CCTs, BTPs, and ENELs

The secondary market in treasury bills got off to a slow start after they were introduced in 1976. Firstly, there was little confidence in the market; secondly, the Bank of Italy initially issued only 12-months' treasury bills, many of which were left hanging on the market in considerable quantities. The issue of shorter-maturity bills and sales to the non-bank public encouraged the development of the secondary market which now has a very active turnover.

The introduction of CCTs also helped encourage the market at a time of rising interest rates and economic uncertainty.

The secondary market in treasury bills and short-term bonds is further aided by the Bank of Italy's application of reserve requirements which specify that banks may hold reserves in cash, government securities and a wide range of other bonds. Treasury bills make up a large proportion of the banking system's reserves.

Particularly, the secondary market in government bond issues and treasury bills is far more attractive than the rest of the bond market. The market has interested both private and institutional investors since the bonds and bills combine high yields free of tax with short to medium maturities. Floating-rate notes such as CCTs and ENEL indexed bonds also enjoy a good secondary market although, due to several factors such as volatile marketability, the system of indexation and only moderately high current yield when compared to government bonds, the market in floating-rate issues is greatly influenced by professional speculators, especially at times of market uncertainty.

All these securities, except the BOTs, are listed on the Milan stock exchange, but they all tend to be traded in the unofficial market made by banks and brokers. Although they may be made available in registered form, they are all nearly always traded in bearer form.

The marketability of the above securities is indicated by their daily turnover, as follows:

Table 11.2 (a) Interest rates and yields in Italian money and capital markets (average rates)

	End 1976	End 1977	End 1978	1979 Jan.	Feb.	Mar.	Apr.	May	Jun.	Jul.	Aug.	Sep.	Oct.	Nov.	Dec.
Official discount rate	15.0	11.5	10.5	10.5	10.5	10.5	10.5	10.5	10.5	10.5	10.0	10.5	10.5	12.0	15.0
Interbank sight deposits	15.68	11.91	11.31	11.27	11.41	11.41	11.43	11.37	11.74	11.27	11.29	11.31	12.23	12.56	15.52
Treasury bills (BOTs)															
3 months	......	11.80	10.88	10.66	......	11.86	11.51	10.92	11.51	11.62	11.62	11.62	12.93	13.42	16.52
6 months	......	12.81	11.74	11.74	11.62	11.86	11.51	10.92	11.51	11.62	11.62	11.62	12.93	13.05	15.62
12 months	......	12.99	12.30	12.11	12.30	12.30	12.30	12.17	12.30	12.30	12.30	12.30	12.93	12.99	14.55
Polyannual treasury bonds (BTPs)	12.66	13.35	12.92	12.77	12.70	12.72	12.74	12.70	12.75	12.88	13.05	12.16	13.36	13.51	13.93
Crediop government bonds	......	14.33	13.67	13.66	13.76	13.74	13.86	13.89	14.02	14.15	14.19	13.97	14.28	14.51	14.62
Special credit institution bonds	......	13.98	13.39	13.37	13.40	13.44	14.47	13.51	13.42	13.45	13.53	13.41	13.70	14.03	14.27
Corporate bonds	......	14.75	14.18	14.17	14.18	14.18	14.25	14.21	14.32	14.54	14.62	14.28	14.63	15.09	15.27

(b) Interest rates and yields in Italian money and capital markets (average rates)

	1980 Jan.	Feb.	Mar.	Apr.	May	Jun.	Jul.	Aug.	Sep.	Oct.	Nov.	Dec.
Official discount rate	15.0	15.0	15.0	15.0	15.0	15.0	15.0	15.0	16.5	16.5	16.5	16.5
Interbank sight deposits	16.43	12.20	17.32	16.81	16.73	16.91	16.96	17.00	17.05	18.05	17.86	17.69
Treasury bills (BOTs)												
3 months	15.00	15.80	15.80	15.36	16.04	15.56	16.04	16.04	14.84	17.00	17.00	16.52
6 months	13.74	15.62	15.87	16.12	15.75	16.12	16.25	16.12	16.00	16.87	16.87	16.87
12 months	13.64	14.55	15.01	15.54	15.54	15.54	15.54	15.54	15.54	16.55	16.55	16.14
Polyannual treasury bonds (BTPs)	13.96	16.74	14.76	14.92	15.02	15.18	15.44	15.60	15.69	16.08	16.14	16.17
Crediop government bonds	14.79	15.06	15.53	15.65	15.62	15.76	16.34	16.58	16.64	17.28	17.13	16.88
Special credit institution bonds	14.23	14.47	14.75	14.78	14.96	15.20	15.59	15.72	15.96	16.36	16.30	16.30
Corporate bonds	15.32	15.47	15.86	15.93	16.04	16.28	17.06	17.27	17.25	17.43	17.44	17.36

Treasury bills (BOTs)	up to 5 billion lire or more
BTPs and CCTs	up to 1 billion lire or more
ENEL straight bonds	up to 500 billion lire
ENEL indexed bonds	up to 100 billion lire

Good marketability is assured by a turnover of Lit 50 million or more.

As Table 11.2 shows, yields available on 12-month treasury bills and the other securities described are comparable if adjusted for their different maturities. They all compare favourably with yields on other bonds yet their interest is payable gross and free of withholding tax.

As at August 1980 there were Lit 66 451 billion BOTs outstanding and Lit 63 262 BTPs and CCTs outstanding, representing 22.9 and 21.8 per cent respectively of the total lira fixed-interest market.

Bankers' acceptances

Authorized banks now provide a secondary market in bankers' acceptances. The rules governing such acceptances were liberalized in 1978, and stamp duty paid by investors in the secondary market was reduced from 1 to 0.1 per cent. A robust secondary market is expected to develop. In 1979 (this market's first full year of trading) the volume was in excess of Lit 100 billion.

There are three types of bills which are issued in the primary market to finance trade and payments and which are also negotiable in the secondary market, particularly if endorsed (or accepted) by a bank. The bills are drawn on one trader by another with respect to future delivery of goods. The drawer may discount the bill with a bank which then 'accepts' liability for payment of the bill on maturity.

The three types of bills are:

1. Commercial drafts (tratta) issued for one month up to three months.
2. Bills of exchange (cambiale arpaghlero commerciale) issued either for less than four months or for four to six months.
3. Financial notes (paghero finanziorio) which are endorsable promissory notes and do not relate to specific trade transactions. Maturities are up to six months.

Interest is calculated on the basis of a 365-day year and comparable yields are slightly higher than for treasury bills which are the only other instrument available of similar maturity. Bankers' acceptances, unlike treasury bills, are however subject to withholding tax.

The capital market

A significant feature of the Italian financial markets is that the economy is dominated by a few state owned holding companies. Likewise most long-term finance is raised through government controlled institutions.

Household savings represent more than 50 per cent of short-term assets yet households display a high liquidity preference. There is therefore a gap between the preference by savers for short-term finance. Part of this demand is satisfied by the IMI (instituto mobilaire Italiano) created specifically to collect short-term savings and grant long-term loans. Another method, also used in Belgium, is to grant short-term credits which are constantly renewed so as to transfer short-term resources (e.g., demand deposits) into medium- and long-term credits. Banks may also be required at times to transform a certain part of their deposits into long-term bonds, particularly into bonds of the specialized credit institutions.

Domestic bonds

Issues in the domestic bonds market are dominated by the central government, public authorities and the special credit institutions (see Table 11.3). Companies do not, in general, raise capital through the bonds market but from the special credit institutions. This is because, firstly, there are few private sector companies either large or creditworthy enough to raise there own bond capital and, secondly, issues by independent companies are penalized by a higher withholding tax than is applied to issues by the public authorities or credit institutions. Since 1974 all new issues of bonds apart from government bonds have been subject to an additional 10 per cent tax on interest for bonds issued by medium- and long-term credit institutions and 20 per cent on bonds issued by corporate borrowers. An alternative to government bonds, however, could be represented by old non-government issues with a six or seven per cent face value coupon which, having been issued before 1974, also enjoy fiscal exemption. Their drawback is represented by their low relative yield and low marketability.

The bond-issuing institutions and their relative shares of the bond market in terms of outstanding par value are shown in Table 11.3.

Table 11.3 Bond issues—relative shares by borrowers

Issuer	Percentage of total bond issues
Government bonds	
treasury bonds, state railway bonds	58.7
Municipalities	0.3
Special medium- and long-term credit institutions	34.0
Public agencies	5.7
Private enterprise and other	1.3
	100.0

Government bonds

The central government sustains a permanent cash deficit and has to seek recourse to the money and capital markets to fund its debt. Table 11.3 shows that more than 50 per cent of bond issues are made by the central government. In fact, most of these issues are represented by treasury bills (BOTs), treasury credit certificates (CCTs) and polyannual treasury bonds (BTPs). These are all short- to medium-term bonds which are described in the money market section because they are mainly traded as short-term securities and are major money market instruments. They also form the largest share of the total lira fixed-interest market. As at September 1980, there were about 30 issues of government securities outstanding, worth a nominal value of Lit 104 680 billion accounting for 55.6 per cent of total 839 listed bonds in the Italian market.

Although listed on the stock exchange, they are mainly traded in the unofficial market made by banks and brokers who act as over-the-counter dealers in government securities. In the unofficial market bonds are dealt inclusive of accrued interest (tel quel). If dealt on the stock exchange they are quoted on a flat-yield basis and dealt plus or minus accrued interest.

Other funds designated for state or public expenditure are raised through the issue of bonds by the special credit institutions and public agencies. Since they are state guaranteed bonds they may be regarded as indirect government bond issues.

Municipal and provincial government bonds

Although the municipal and provincial authorities are authorized to issue their own securities directly onto the market, no new issues have been made since 1975. They derive most of their funds directly from the government or indirectly from the public agencies and special credit institutions. As at June 1980 however there were over 58 issues outstanding.

Bonds issued by the City of Naples are guaranteed directly by the government. Others are an irrevocable charge on tax revenues, thus principal and interest are guaranteed to be paid.

The state autonomous corporations may also issue their own securities but, like the local governments, most receive indirect finance from the issues made by the special credit institutions. Only the Italian state railways (ferrovie dello stato) have directly issued their own bonds. Interest and capital are indirectly guaranteed by the state.

Public agency bonds

The major public agencies are ENEL (Ente Nazionale per l'Energia Elettrica)—the National Electricity Agency; ENI (Ente Nazional Idrocarburi)—National Hydrocarbons Authority; and IRI (Istituto per la Ricostruzione Industriale)—Industrial Reconstruction Institute.

Each are statewide agencies whose responsibilities are respectively the generation and supply of electricity, the promotion and implementation of fuel and energy projects and the management of the state's industrial and financial holdings.

ENEL issues both fixed-interest bonds and indexed bonds which are described in the money market section. The indexed bonds in particular are popularly traded along with short-term securities. The other agencies issue fixed interest bonds.

Minimum denominations of public agency bonds are normally Lit 1000, though some are issued in units of Lit 100 000. Maturities may extend for up to 15 years, although a few are issued for longer than 10 years, and because the majority amortize capital during the life of the loan the average life is usually less than five years. All bonds issued by public agencies may be called by the issuer prior to redemption and the issuer also has the option to call only part or all of an outstanding loan. ENEL bonds are guaranteed as to principal and interest directly by the state. ENI and IRI bonds are guaranteed by the issuing agency. All bonds pay interest semiannually on the basis of a 365-day year. ENI, IRI and straight ENEL bonds are issued and redeemed at par. ENEL indexed bonds (indicizzato) are issued at par but redeemed according to an indexing formula described in the money market section. Together they account for about six per cent of the Italian bond market in terms of issues outstanding.

Bonds of special credit institutions

Next to the central government the major issuers of bonds are the special medium- and long-term credit institutions and, excluding BOTs, BTPs and CCTs their bonds represent the bulk of the entire Italian bond market. Together their bonds represent about 35 per cent of total bonds outstanding, but if BOTs, BTPs and CCTs are excluded, they represent 80 per cent of the market. About one-fifth of the bonds issued by these institutions are designated directly for the account of the treasury and the state autonomous corporations. The remainder are for public works and public sector enterprises as detailed below.

As at August 1980 bonds issued by the special credit institutions, excluding those on the treasury account, amounted to Lit 29 501 billion outstanding.

All the bonds are issued and redeemed at par, carry fixed-rate coupons and pay interest semiannually on the basis of a 365-day year. Units of denominations vary between Lit 500 and Lit 25 000, depending on the issuer.

The major issuers are as follows:

CCOP—Crediop bonds

The CCOP (Consorzio di Credito per la Opere Pubbliche)—the consortium of credit for public works specializes in providing the government's financing needs for special types of government works. It grants long-term loans to regional, provincial, municipal and other public agencies and also issues securities on behalf of the treasury. The treasury series of bonds are guaranteed directly by the state since they constitute an indirect form of government borrowing.

Other issues are secured against loans made to the local governments or public agencies on whose behalf the bonds are issued.

The CCOP also issues bonds against loans granted to the autonomous state corporations such as the state railways and National Road Corporation. Bonds issued by the CCOP are known as Crediop bonds.

Minimum denominations are Lit 25 000 and their average life is three to seven years, though original maturities may extend up to 25 years. As at August 1980 there were Lit 11887 billion of bonds outstanding, issued on treasury account, a large proportion of which are represented by Crediop bonds.

IMI bonds

The IMI (Istituto Mobilaire Italiano) is the most important special credit institution. It specializes in medium- and long-term credit to industry for export enterprises and for capital works projects abroad, and grants subsidized loans for productive ventures in southern Italy.

It issues bonds in denominations of Lit 1000 with maturities of from 5 to 15 years though, due to amortization, their average life is eight to nine years.

Other special credit institution bonds

Other medium- and long-term credit institutions which directly issue bonds to the market are:

1. ICIPU (Istituto di Credito per la Imprese di Pubblica Utilita);
   - issues loans to small and medium-sized businesses including commercial mortgages for the building of plant and factories
   - unit denominations of Lit 500 and Lit 25000
2. ISVEIMER (Istituto per lo Sviluppo Economico dell'italia Merdionale);
   - grants loans to ventures in southern Italy
   - unit denominations of Lit 1000
3. IRFIS (Istituto Regionale per il Finanziamento delle Imprese in Sicilia);
   - finances industrial projects in Sicily
   - unit denominations of Lit 1000
4. CIS (Credito Industriale Sordo);
   - finances industrial projects in Sardinia
   - unit denominations of Lit 1000
5. Mediocredito centrale (Central medium-term credit institution);
   - provides finance for export industries and rediscounts loans granted by the regional medium-term credit institutions
   - unit denominations of Lit 1000
6. Commercial banks
   - Some of the commercial banks have special industrial credit sections which are authorized to grant medium- and long-term credit and issue bonds on behalf of their loans to industry. They also provide funds to the deposits and loans fund which then lends to the local authorities.
   - They may also operate public works sections which grant credit to specified types of public works and which are authorized also to issue bonds against their loans to industry.

Mortgage bonds

Mortgage bonds are issued by some of the special credit institutions, which differ from those shown above, and by special sections within some of the commercial banks.

242

Both types of institutions issue mortgages to households, industry and agriculture. Mortgage bonds outstanding at August 1980 amounted to Lit 29 625 billion.

Unit denominations vary from Lit 500 to Lit 100 000. Although mortgage bonds may be issued with original maturities of up to 25 years the majority have average lives of between 5 and 10 years, due to amortization.

Foreign bonds

Apart from bonds of international agencies such as the World Bank and ECSC, there are no foreign bonds issued or listed in Italy.

The majority of bonds issued by international institutions are issued in lire although a few have been issued also in US dollars. ENI and ENEL have also issued dollar bonds.

Eurobonds

There is no primary market in Eurolire bonds, nor any secondary market in Italy for other bonds denominated in other Eurocurrencies.

Corporate bonds

As Table 11.4 shows, companies are not significant issuers in the bond market though a few of the larger companies do make direct bond issues.

Table 11.4   Gross new public security issues on Italian capital market (billion lire)

Issuer	1975	1976	1977	1978	1979	3rd qtr 1980
BONDS						
Central government	6 966	3 802	18 472	23 667	20 319	9571
Public sector enterprises	1 974	1 502	1 954	1 705	1 310	795
Financial institutions	7 813	7 091	7 734	8 372	8 394	7509
Corporate bonds	94	163	256	258	100	69
Total	17 196*	12 558	28 416	34 002	30 123	17 944
Proportion issued by						
central government, %	40.5	30.3	65.0	69.6	67.5	53.3
public sector enterprises, %	28.3	12.0	6.9	5.0	4.3	4.5
financial institutions, %	45.4	56.5	24.6	27.6	27.7	41.8
private corporations, %	5.8	1.2	0.9	0.8	0.5	0.4
SHARES						
Public sector enterprises	248	504	388	1 376	1 635	
Financial institutions	117	294	485	547	361	
Private sector companies	992	1 075	974	1 062	736	
Total	1 357	1 872	1 846	2 985	2 372	211
Proportion issued by						
financial institutions, %	8.6	15.7	26.3	18.3	13.2	
private sector companies, %	73.1	57.4	52.7	35.6	27.0	

* 1975—Lit 320 billion worth of bonds were issued by the municipalities and provinces, and Lit 30 billion worth of foreign bonds were issued. These are not shown in the table but are included in the total.

In order to make a public bond issue, companies must first seek agreement of their shareholders at an extraordinary general meeting. Bond issues may not, by law, exceed the net paid-up capital as shown in a company's balance sheet except where security can be provided against property or state guaranteed securities.

The major corporate bonds outstanding are those of Austostande, which is guaranteed by IRI, and those issued by banks, such as Efibanca and Interbanca, that also operate as special credit institutions.

Companies usually issue straight, fixed coupon bonds but if a company's issued capital is fully paid up, it may also issue convertible bonds. Existing shareholders must first be given the option to purchase new convertible bonds. Special credit institutions that specialize in loans to the corporate sector may also issue convertible bonds with respect to a third party company, provided of course, the interests of the existing shareholders have been formally protected.

Primary market for domestic bonds

The primary bond market is controlled by the CICR, an interministerial committee for credit and savings. This committee determines the timing, coupon rates and conditions attaching to the terms of the issues. Authorization is also required from the Banco d'Italian.

The commercial banks manage and underwrite the issues. Subscriptions may be tendered by non-residents and individuals through a bank or broker. The purchasers of bonds, in descending order of significance, are:

Bank of Italy
Italian Foreign Exchange Office
Banking institutions
Central Savings Bank
Post Office and Social Security Funds
Insurance companies
Private enterprise and individuals

This latter group purchases only a very small share of the market.

It is worth noting that pension funds and life assurance companies are virtually non-existent in Italy. This means that the market lacks one of the major sources of demand for long-term investments that are common in other countries.

Secondary market for domestic bonds

In the secondary market all bonds are listed and (except for government and ENEL indexed bonds) traded on the stock exchange.

Bonds are nearly always traded in bearer form although in exceptional cases, such as bonds required against a guarantee, they may be registered.

Although bonds account for the major proportion of stock exchange turnover (see Table 11.5), the market for most bonds nevertheless is not particularly active.

Equity shares

Equity finance is an unimportant source of funds for Italian companies, which tend to raise money either from the special credit institutions or from the banks. Many

Table 11.5   Value and turnover of listed securities on Milan stock exchange (billion lire)

Securities	1975	1976	1977	1978	1979
BONDS (par value listed)					
Public sector bonds	42 598	50 532	57 914	75 392	85 158
Private sector bonds	1 934	1 935	1 258	2 021	564
Foreign bonds	353	469	6 690	7	5
Total	44 883	52 936	65 772	77 420	85 727
Turnover—all bonds	567	571	569	1 158	1 155
SHARES					
Market capitalization of shares	7 328	6 958	5 352	8 147	10 355
Turnover—all shares	1 117	1 091	754	765	2 874
Number of shares listed	153	155	155	143	139

of the larger companies fall under the umbrella of the state holding companies while many of the smaller companies are tightly held family businesses. Although the number of private companies has more than doubled in the last 20 to 30 years, the number of publicly quoted companies is less than 200 and has remained virtually the same since 1950.

A small number of unlisted shares are also traded on the over-the-counter market known as the Mercato Ristretto. In order for their shares to be admitted to this market, companies must meet specified criteria, though these are not as stringent as those required for admittance to the stock exchange.

For some companies their market capitalization is below their original issue value. The inadequate equity market means that it is often difficult for companies to obtain necessary finance, while bureaucracy hampers the raising of loan capital. Very often, for Italian companies raising money is more a question of having the right contracts than of applying to the capital markets.

All listed companies are domestic companies. There are no foreign shares quoted on Italian exchanges.

Of the listed shares there are three types: common or ordinary shares; preferred shares which rank ahead of common shares for dividend payments; and savings shares which carry a fixed rate of interest but have no other shareholder privileges such as voting rights or profit-sharing dividend rights. All shares are in registered form.

For the investor, shares are generally considered to provide a poor return as compared to other capital market instruments, marketability is inadequate and dealings are dominated by insider trading, while risk is increased because reporting standards are less stringent than in many other European countries and balance sheets are not always reliable since external auditing of accounts is not yet required by law. Only companies with a share capital of more than Lit 50 billion are required to appoint external auditors.

While it is true to say, however, that the Italian equity market is normally inactive, 1980 has witnessed an unprecedented boom. New issues have almost doubled and trading turnover trebled compared with 1979. The boom is the most significant activity the market has seen for years. It is attributed to the undervalued price at which many shares had been standing for a very long time, while a number of major companies are recovering from the losses caused by inflation and world recession in recent years. Once the rise began it became self-perpetuating. Investors rushed into the equity market where returns through capital gains were becoming greater than returns on bank deposits or fixed-interest stocks. The supply of shares is not however great enough to satisfy the demand. On the Milan stock exchange, there are only 162 listed shares but only half of these are truly marketable. The remainder are tightly held by controlling interests. This limited supply thus resulted in even stronger upward pressure on the price of available shares.

The stock exchange

There are ten stock exchanges in Italy, based in Milan, Rome, Turin, Genoa, Bologna, Florence, Naples, Palermo, Trieste and Venice, but the Milan exchange is the only one of importance.

All are controlled by strict regulations and are constituted under public law. The exchanges are controlled by and supervised by the local chambers of commerce, though ultimate authority is vested in CONSOB (the national commission for companies and stock exchanges) which was established by an Act of Parliament in 1974. It comprises a president and four members nominated by decree of the President of the Republic and passed by the Council of Ministers. CONSOB is modelled partly on the SEC in the USA and partly on the commission for stock exchange operators in France.

CONSOB has authority with respect to the organization and functioning of the exchanges and with respect to the admission of stocks and shares for quotations.

All shares must be compulsorily registered as to ownership, a regulation for which Italy is unique among member countries of the EEC, and one which probably further inhibits the investment in shares by individuals.

Additionally any holdings of two per cent or more of the equity capital of a listed company by a limited company, or of more than 10 per cent of a listed company held by another listed company, must be reported to CONSOB.

If there is a cross-shareholding between the above parties that exceeds the above limits then one company must sell its excess within 12 months.

Table 11.5 shows the value of securities listed on the stock exchange. Public sector bonds account for the largest proportion of securities but the turnover figures do not adequately reflect the number or volume of transactions. By far the greater number of dealings in bonds and to a lesser extent shares, takes place in the unofficial over-the-counter market through banks.

There are eight trading posts on the Milan stock exchange, one for dealing in bonds and government securities, one for share options, one for dealing in foreign currencies, and five for dealing in shares and convertible bonds. Only stockbrokers (agenti di cambio) may deal on the floor of the exchange and these may only deal on behalf of clients and not for their own accounts. The brokers deal at the trading posts directly with each other, there being no jobbers or specialists to act as intermediaries.

The market is open from 10 a.m. to 12 noon. For bonds, options and currencies, only one price is recorded for each security traded. For shares three prices are recorded for each trading session. These take place at three stages:

– at the opening (apertura) from 10 a.m. to 10.50 a.m.;
– during the session (durante) at three trading posts only;
– at the close (chiusura) from 11 a.m. onward.

Share options

A small number of share options of the major Italian companies are listed and traded on the Milan stock exchange.

This is not a traded options market. For certain shares investors may purchase an option to buy (call option) the shares within a specified time limit and at a specified price. The option holder has the choice either to exercise the option or to allow it to lapse. The options may not, however, be traded as securities in their own right.

Gold

Residents are free to purchase gold in any form (except unrefined) but for non-residents, in practice there is no gold market in Italy. Exports of gold, except jewellery, are subject to licensing, and the import or export of coins that are legal tender in other countries is prohibited.

Dealing and fees

Money market

Transaction in money market securities may be through a commercial bank.

Ninety per cent of turnover in money market securities takes place in the unofficial interbank market. Reported daily turnover is thus often underestimated since a large number of deals may be matched orders between banks.

Payment for short-term securities must be made on the same day that the transaction takes place, but delivery may not occur for up to six months later because of inadequacies in the clearing system. Customers receive a contract note confirming ownership which may be transferred in lieu, via a bank, if the securities are sold before receipt of the certificate.

Deposits

No specific fee is charged for non-resident accounts but all currency settlement of security transactions must be effected through an authorized Italian bank. Investments may be made from special account lire or from capital account lire, both

247

deriving from the sale of convertible currencies or from foreign account lire. At present there is no substantial difference between the two classes of investments since in both cases the transfer abroad of dividends, interest and profits as well as the repatriation of capital, are unrestricted. Currency commission amounts to 0.5 per cent on disinvestment only, including amounts credited for dividends, interest and profit.

Treasury bills (BOTs) CCTs and BTPs

A commercial bank or broker charges 0.05 per cent on par value, subject to a minimum commission of Lit 4000. If however the bank is a major participant in the bond market and a market maker in treasury bills, better terms may be obtained. For example, such a bank may deal with a spread between bid and offer prices of about five cents, equivalent to a commission rate of 0.0005 per cent.

Capital market securities

Commissions charged for bonds is in the region of 0.003 per cent on par value. Share transactions are negotiable but subject to a complex scale of minimum fees charged by brokers and banks alike. Fees include brokerage, stamp duty and duty payable to the Italian exchange office. In total these expenses amount to approximately 0.7 per cent of the consideration, subject to a minimum fee of Lit 4000.

Commissions are about the same whether dealt on the stock exchange or in the over-the-counter market. Only government bonds are quoted inclusive of accrued interest (tel quel), all other bonds are quoted on a flat yield basis and dealt plus or minus accrued interest (a corso secco) calculated according to a 360-day year of twelve 30-day months.

Settlement and delivery

Settlement and delivery may either be for cash, taking place three business days following the transaction date; or forward, taking place on a particular date of each month according to a schedule drawn up by CONSOB at the beginning of each year. In general account periods run from mid-month to mid-month for settlement at the end of the month. For example, in the 1980 calendar of account periods, dealings taking place between 19 November and 19 December 1980 had to be settled by 31 December 1980.

In general bonds are dealt for cash. Consolidated and redeemable state bonds and convertible bonds may be dealt forward, but all other bonds must be dealt for cash. Shares and convertible bonds are nearly always dealt on the forward account basis but may be (though rarely are) dealt for cash.

Dealing units

Dealings on the stock exchange are transacted in round lots.

Shares are dealt in lots of numbers of shares which are specified for each share. The majority are traded in lots of 100, 500 or 1000, but the more active shares may be dealt in lots as small as 25 shares. Less active shares are dealt in larger lots which may be as large as 10 000 shares.

Bonds are dealt in lots according to their face (or par) value. The size of the round lots is also specified by type of issuer or type of bond. Most bonds of the special credit institutions and corporate bonds are dealt in lots of Lit 500 000. Others, including treasury bonds, Crediop bonds, bonds of ENEL, ENI, IRI, as well as convertible bonds, are dealt in lots of Lit 1 000 000. US dollar bonds are dealt in lots of US$1000.

Bank safe custody

A typical safe fee charged by a commercial bank is Lit 1500 per six months for every Lit 1 000 000 of securities deposited, subject to a maximum fee of Lit 150 000 per six months.

Financial and monetary systems

Financial institutions

The Italian economy is dominated by state owned holding companies which maintain large majority interests in, and exercise control over, a wide range of industry and commerce, effectively forming huge state monopolies.

The major holding companies and their interests are:

Autostrada de sole	The toll motorways
ENEL	Electricity production and distribution
Alitalia	State airline
ENI	Drilling, refining, pipeline, distribution and oil products
Finmare	The major Italian shipping line
Finmeccanica	Engineering and car production
Fincantieri	Ship building
Finsider	Steel production
RAI	Radio and television network
STET	Telephone network

Not listed above is the IRI, the Istituto per la Ricostruzione Industriale. This was established in 1933 to assist with the reorganization of the banking system which had suffered badly during the great depression. Its initial function was to take over from the banks their participation in industrial companies, on a short-term basis, with the intention of reselling in the market when conditions became more stable. In the event these interests proved difficult to resell, so the function of the IRI was changed by statute in 1937 establishing it as a permanent institution to engage in a wide range of activities but subject to directives from the government.

IRI's industrial activities are organized through its five main subsidiaries STET, Finmare, Finsider, Finmeccanica and Fincantieri (shown above). In addition the IRI has control over the financial system by having direct interests in the three largest banks.

The financial system in Italy is very clearly split into two classes of institutions—the banks which may only grant loans of up to eighteen months' maturity and the medium- and long-term credit institutions which provide all loans of longer maturity to both the public and the private sectors.

The banks comprise the ordinary credit institutions including the commercial banks, the savings banks and the co-operative banks. All, except the Post Office Savings Bank, are governed by the same banking regulations. Some of the commercial banks own special credit institutions while some banks have special departments that operate as medium- and long-term credit institutions.

The category of medium- and long-term credit institutions comprise the banks' special credit institutions which are departments or subsidiaries of certain commercial banks; the Deposits and Loans Fund which grants credit to local authorities; and the special credit institutions which consist of more than 80 institutions, but the main groups are the Fund for Southern Italy, the Industrial Management and Participation Company (GEPI), the Refinancing Institution, the Public Works and Public Utility Credit Institutions (e.g., Crediop), the Industrial Credit Institutions (e.g., IMI), the mortgage and house building credit institutions and the agricultural credit institutions.

Commercial banks

The three largest banks are the Banca Commerciale Italiana, Credito Italiana and Banca di Roma. These are commercial banks, known as banks of national interest, which is a classification for banks that are represented in at least 30 regions, and whose share capital is owned by the IRI, and thus indirectly by the state.

A second group of commercial banks is known as public charter banks. The group comprises six banks namely Banca Nazionale del Lavoro, Banco di Sardegna, Istituto Bancario San Paolo di Torino, Monte dei Paschi di Sienna, Banco di Napoli, and Banco di Sicilia. Their main distinction is that they are authorized to operate special credit sections for providing medium- and long-term finance to both state and privately owned industries, often at subsidised rates of interest.

The commercial banks may engage in most banking activities. They accept deposits (up to maximum of 18 months) advance short-term credit, and buy and sell securities on behalf of clients though not for their own accounts. Most of their credit is in the form of overdrafts since they may only make loans up to a maximum of 18 months. They may not make medium- or long-term loans, a function that is the prerogative of the medium- and long-term credit institutions. Seventy-five per cent of their lending goes to the private sector and half of this goes to small companies. The remainder of their loans are made to local authorities, autonomous government agencies, other public bodies and public enterprises. The big three, however, jointly own a bank, Mediobanca, which specializes in loans of between one and five or ten years, and borrows from savings deposits or by bond issues. Other such specialist banks are Efibanca and Centrobanca.

Loans nevertheless comprise only about half of total bank credit. Table 11.6 shows that the banking sector as a whole has steadily been increasing its investment in treasury bills at the same time as it has been losing some of its business of

Table 11.6   Trend of bank credit (percentage of total bank credit)

	1972	1973	1974	1975	1976	1977	1978
Loans	66.1	63.2	62.3	57.5	59.6	52.1	48.4
public sector undertakings	11.3	9.9	12.0	10.4	11.0	9.1	7.5
large private sector firms	18.7	15.7	15.6	13.5	12.5	11.2	10.1
other private sector firms	24.7	26.9	25.2	23.9	25.9	25.3	26.3
corporate sector total	54.7	52.5	52.8	47.8	49.4	45.6	43.9
general government	9.6	9.1	8.2	8.4	8.8	5.1	3.9
household sector	1.8	1.6	1.3	1.3	1.4	1.4	1.5
Securities	33.9	36.8	37.7	42.5	40.4	47.9	51.6
treasury bills	1.7	1.1	9.3	9.8	8.5	11.0	14.0
other securities	19.6	24.5	25.3	25.4	26.1	24.7	24.2

financing the productive system due to competition from the special credit institutions. When one considers, in addition, the banks' holding of treasury bills, their purchases of other public sector securities, and lending to the general government (which is now declining), it is clear that bank credit is being increasingly channelled into financing the public sector.

Savings bank

The savings banks, known as public charter banks, constitute the other type of banking institution. There is now little distinction between these and the commercial banks as far as their banking activities are concerned. The main difference is that the savings banks are not under direct IRI control. They are also non-profit-making, but distribute their profits to social welfare and charity organizations. The largest savings bank is the Banca Nazionale del Lavoro.

Post office savings banks

The post office savings bank is designed to collect small savings from households, which are utilized for payments to utility companies and for corporation tax due to the treasury. This is the only deposit-taking institution which is not classified as in the banking sector.

Special credit institutions

These play an important role in the Italian economy, providing most of the medium- and long-term finance required by industry and raising capital by the issue of their own bonds on the capital market, accounting for a third of the total bond issues (see Capital market).

251

The largest such institution is the Istituto Mobilaire Italiano (IMI). Its share capital is owned by the commercial and savings banks and the social security and insurance institutions. It may grant loans to companies of up to 20 years' term, may take an equity participation in Italian companies, or buy outright Italian companies which are experiencing financial difficulties. It may also undertake other special activities such as the administration of funds granted by the US EXIM bank to finance trade between the US and Italy.

Central bank

Banca d'Italia (the Bank of Italy) is the central bank. It is the sole issuer of the currency and exercises control over all the institutions under public or private law which collect savings from the public and distribute credit.

It shares its central bank functions with respect to the extension of credit to the banking system, the treasury and to foreign countries, with the Ufficio Italiano dei Cambi (the Italian exchange office). The Bank of Italy has more operating authority with respect to implementation of domestic monetary matters but the exchange office presides over exchange control regulations.

Monetary control

Monetary and exchange policy is determined by the CICR, the interministerial committee for credit and savings (Comitato Interministeriale per il Credito e il Risparmio).

The governor of the Bank of Italy participates in regular meetings of the committee which are presided over by the Treasury Minister.

Since 1973 until 1979, the authorities' main instrument of monetary policy had been the use of selective credit policy, aimed at containing monetary expansion by direct controls affecting both the growth and the direction of credit.

Since October 1979, greater emphasis has been placed on monetary base control and interest rate manipulation through the use of open market operations. The intention of the authorities seems to be a gradual change away from direct administrative controls towards more market-oriented policies.

Selective credit policy

This policy, which until October 1979 was the major means of control, has two main features. Firstly, banks are required to maintain minimum investments in bonds issued by the medium- and long-term credit institutions and bonds issued by the government and its agencies; secondly the banks are subject to limits within which they may increase their credit, based on a selected index period.

The amount of securities the banks must hold is varied as a policy instrument. When the policy was first introduced in 1973 banks were required to hold six per cent of their deposits (net of reserve and liquidity requirements) in bonds. In 1979 banks were required to transform 45 per cent of the increase in their deposits into securities. With respect to credit ceilings, banks are required to restrict their lending to specified sectors to a predetermined percentage growth for loans in excess of a specified amount. For example, the period March to September 1976 was taken as the index period and was the basis on which credit expansion was calculated. Banks were permitted to increase their loans between that period and May 1978 by 25 per cent, and between the same period and July 1978 by 30 per cent. This restriction applied only to loans in excess of Lit 30 million; loans below that amount, provided they were not to the same borrowers, were exempt. Similarly loans to the electricity industry, health services, railways or for agricultural production were also exempt.

Since July 1978, the regulations have been applied to all credit institutions, including foreign banks, with assets of over Lit 7 billion. Stage increases of up to 14 per cent for credit growth were permitted up to March 1979.

By such a policy, the authorities attempted to monitor and control all the monetary factors and to maintain an equilibrium between the demand for credit and other economic factors. It was intended as a fine tuning policy such that it might even restrict the amount of credit extended to any single borrower. Nevertheless the monetary systems came under considerable pressure because of the large demand from the public sector which virtually forced the authorities to expand credit. Despite the tight constraints, domestic credit expanded by 19 per cent in 1977, 22 per cent in 1978 and by 19 per cent in 1979. It was the failure of ceilings on bank lending which led, in the last quarter of 1979, to a greater emphasis on market-based policies through the use of the discount rate and open market operations. Limits on bank lending however continued to be tightly restrictive. In March 1980, accepting that the banks could find loopholes in the direct controls, thereby overshooting their credit ceilings, the CICR changed the rules regarding credit ceilings. It became compulsory for all banks that overshot their credit ceilings to deposit reserves in proportion to the size of their excess lending, interest free with the Banca d'Italia. It thus became expensive for banks to exceed their credit ceilings. Though this new policy does not entirely prevent quantitive increases in credit, it ensures that excessive credit is paid for at a higher rate of interest. Changes in short-term interest rates consequently now reflect the effective degree of credit restriction.

Discount policy

The Bank of Italy and the exchange office will discount commercial bills and other eligible paper at the discount rate. Control is exercised not just through administration of the discount rate but also by quantitive measures. A penalty rate, several points higher than the discount rate, is charged to banks that use the discount facility more than once each six months or that exceed their discount ceilings. The discount rate is an administered rate which is adjusted upward by the authorities when they wish to tighten credit conditions in the banking system, or downward when they wish to ease liquidity. The discount rate is used in conjunction with other policies. Formally the major additional policy was quantitive credit controls. During 1980, the issue of treasury bills and open market operations has been a more effective additional policy.

With regard to bills of exchange only those financing exports to the EEC are automatically eligible. Other bills have first to be certified as eligible by Banca d'Italia. Banks are, however, allowed to rediscount EEC trade bills in excess of their normal credit ceiling for access to central bank facilities. Aside from the discount facility Banca d'Italia will also advance loans to the banks, secured against specific fixed-interest securities at the bank rate, which is linked to the discount rate. Again limits to such borrowing are fixed for each bank and penalties are charged for borrowing in excess of these limits. The credit limits are not, however, as stringent as those for discounting bills. Since the banks are normally fully borrowed up to the limits allowed by the discount facility they tend to make considerable use of the advance facility.

Open market operations

Until 1980 the Bank of Italy undertook open market operations principally to help finance the government debt rather than directly to influence interest rates in the money market. Since early 1980, however, open market operations have been used as a major instrument, supplementing discount policy.

Treasury bills have been issued since 1976, originally to fund short-term government debt. More recently the authorities have used the quantity issued and the rate of discount attaching to the bills as a means of influencing money market interest rates. Although treasury bills are issued by auction the authorities have some autonomy in determining the discount rate of the bills by deciding the minimum tender rate they are prepared to accept. In addition, the Banca d'Italia has increasingly entered the market directly by buying or selling treasury bills and certificates in order to increase or reduce liquidity in the financial system and thereby influence a fall or rise in money market interest rates.

Reserve ratios

Until the introduction of selective credit policy in 1973, the use of reserve requirements was Italy's main policy instrument. Now, though still important, it plays a secondary role, supplementing quantitive controls and discount policy.

The objective of the reserve requirements are twofold. The policy aims at encouraging the bond market as well as the more traditional objective of managing the banking system's liquidity. The banks are required to hold a minimum proportion of their lire time savings deposits placed with them by non-bank residents and non-residents (interbank deposits are exempt) as cash reserves. The relative proportions vary between banks and credit institutions according to the size and type of institution although the maximum ratio is 22.5 per cent. Ten per cent of the difference between these deposits and their capital and free reserves must be held in cash, placed at the Bank of Italy, but on which interest may be earned. The remainder of their reserves must be kept in treasury bills and a wide range of long-term bonds. Interest may be earned on both at market rates.

Control of the banking system's foreign position

The banking system's foreign position is controlled by the Ufficio Italiano dei Cambi (Italian exchange office). Banks are required to balance, on a daily basis, their spot position with respect to non-resident accounts in both lire and foreign currencies. They must also balance on a daily basis their own foreign currency positions in US dollars, EEC currencies and all convertible other currencies.

The banks must not maintain a net foreign asset position but they have no restrictions or ceilings on their net foreign liability positions, although ceilings are set for their forward transactions against lire. The object of such a policy is to protect the value of the lire by encouraging the inflow of capital but discouraging excessive outflows. The ceilings and restrictions are subject to alteration by the authorities as a means of influencing the monetary system.

Withholding taxes

Interest

Withholding tax is payable on interest arising from lire deposits and from investment in lire bonds but excluding central government bonds and certain other bonds (see below). Interest on deposits is taxed at 15 per cent.

Interest is taxable at a rate of 10 per cent if earned from bonds issued by medium- and long-term credit institutions. All other straight bonds are taxable at a rate of 20 per cent. Interest earned on convertible bonds is taxable at 10 per cent if the bond has an expired life of up to five years from the date of issue. Thereafter convertible bond interest is taxable at 20 per cent. All convertible bonds, however, which have been issued by the medium- and long-term credit institutions are taxable at 10 per cent regardless of their expired life.

Double taxation treaties reduce the withholding tax liability as shown by Table 11.7.

Dividends

Dividends from ordinary and preferred shares are taxable at 30 per cent. Savings shares are taxed at 15 per cent. Residents of countries having double taxation agreements with Italy may reclaim up to two-thirds of the withholding tax against income tax payable in their own country of residence.

Tax treaties may reduce the withholding tax liability as shown in Table 11.7.

Exemptions

The following bonds are exempt from withholding tax:

- bonds issued by the state, regional, provincial and municipal authorities, public agencies and state administrations, e.g., BOTs, CCTs, BTPs, ENELs;
- all straight and convertible bonds issued before 1.1.74.
- issues by international agencies, e.g., World Bank, ECSC, EIB.

255

Table 11.7 **Withholding taxes**

| | Interest | | | |
Recipient	Deposits, %	Corporate bonds etc., %	Bonds of special credit institutions, %	Dividends, %
Residents of non-treaty countries	15	20	10	30
Residents of tax-treaty countries				
Austria	15	20	10	30
Belgium	10	15	10	15
Denmark	15	20	10	15
Egypt	15	20	10	30
Finland	15	20	10	15
France	10	15	10	15
Germany (West)	15	20	10	30
Greece	10	10	10	25
Ireland	10	10	10	15
Israel	10	15	10	25
Japan	10	10	10	15 or 10*
Netherlands	15	20	10	30 or 0†
Norway	15	20	10	30
Sweden	15	20	10	15 or 10‡
Trinidad and Tobago	10	10	10	20 or 10§
UK	15	20	10	15 or 5‖
USA	15	20	10	15 or 5¶

* 10% if Japanese company holds at least 25% of Italian company's ordinary shares.
† 0% if Dutch company holds at least 75% of Italian company's ordinary shares.
‡ 10% if Swedish company holds at least 51% of Italian company's ordinary shares.
§ 10% if Trinidad company holds at least 25% of Italian company's ordinary shares.
‖ 5% if British company holds at least 51% of Italian company's ordinary shares.
¶ 5% if US company holds at least 95% of Italian company's ordinary shares.

Exchange controls

Authorities

All foreign exchange transactions are subject to regulation and control by the Italian exchange office (Ufficio Italiano dei Cambi—U.I.C.) which receives directives from the Ministry of Foreign Trade. Generally, controls aim to restrict outflows of capital from residents but non-residents are encouraged to invest in the Italian financial markets and may repatriate investment proceeds freely.

Currency

The currency is the Italian lira which is fully convertible and which participates in the European Monetary System (EMS), maintaining margins of within the six per cent permissible fluctuation from its EMS par value.

The banks are allowed to engage in spot transactions in any currency and to make forward transactions for up to one year (six months if transacted with a non-bank party) in any convertible currency.

Only authorized banks are permitted to handle sales or purchases of foreign exchange. These banks are required to maintain daily balances of their spot and foreign exchange positions (see Monetary policy).

Non-resident accounts

Non-residents may open two types of accounts: lire accounts and convertible currency accounts. Foreign lire accounts may be used to credit lire arising from current and capital payments, including the sale of convertible currencies. Balances may be used to purchase convertible currencies or may be transferred to another account, known as a capital or special account, for payments due to residents.

Capital accounts may be credited with the liquidation proceeds of investments in Italy and balances may be used to purchase investments in Italy.

Special accounts are used to make payments for investment in Italy in convertible currencies.

Purchase and sale of securities

Non-residents may make investments of any kind in Italy. They may buy and sell all types of money market and capital market securities and also make direct investment in property or companies. The proceeds of such investments may be freely repatriated.

12. Luxembourg

General market environment

Luxembourg is a much larger financial centre than its geographic size suggests. It has an indigenous population of only 350 000, one-third of whom live in Luxembourg City, but has nevertheless developed as an important European principal market place for Eurobond listings and Eurocurrency deposit markets. The growth of the Luxembourg market has been encouraged by the country's liberal banking regulations, free exchange system, and the government's favourable attitude towards free enterprise. Consequently, many foreign banks have established themselves in Luxembourg which, for the above reasons, has become a refuge for foreign capital seeking a secure and efficient investment centre.

Advantageous tax legislation and the lack of restrictions on foreign ownership also provide an opportune environment for holding companies which are a special feature of the country's financial system.

Luxembourg's economy is closely linked to that of Belgium. Belgian francs are legal tender and the two countries have a common monetary and exchange control

Table 12.1 Summary of Instruments

Instrument	Characteristics
MONEY MARKET	
Deposits	
call deposits	Active market in Eurocurrency short-term deposits
time deposits	Major European market for time deposits in Eurocurrencies
certificate of deposit	Active market in Eurodollar CDs
Other money market instruments	No domestic instruments because local financing requirements of the government and business is small
CAPITAL MARKET	
Bonds	
Eurobonds	A major European centre for the listing of Eurobonds. These dominate the local capital market
foreign bonds	No distinction between foreign bonds and Eurobonds
domestic bonds	Public sector and private sector domestic bond account for only 5% of total bonds listed because local capital requirements are small
Equity shares	Small market. Equal number of foreign to domestic shares

system encompassed by the Belgium and Luxembourg Economic Union (BLEU). Thus, like Belgium, Luxembourg has a two-tier foreign exchange system. While there are no restrictions on inward investment or repatriation of interest and dividends, regulations dictate through which of the two currency markets transactions must be made.

Despite the economic association with Belgium, Luxembourg is a very nationalistic state which is proud of its independence from political affiliations and proud also of its free market financial system.

The money market

Deposits

Due largely to the growth of the Eurobond market and Luxembourg's role as a major Eurobond trading centre, an active Eurocurrency market has developed as a natural corollary. Large amounts of liquid funds are held permanently in Luxembourg to finance investment, particularly in Eurobonds. It is convenient that such funds be held in Eurodeposits. Banks too prefer to borrow Eurocurrencies in the local market to fund their operations as agents for investors in Eurobonds.

Deposits, therefore, may be placed by non-residents with any Luxembourg based bank, at call, or on a fixed time deposit in any convertible currency (see Exchange controls).

Call deposits

The call market for overnight and two-day money is an interbank market in which non-bank lenders may participate. Rates of interest depend on the liquidity in the local banking system, the banks' short-term requirements for funds in a particular currency, and the level of interest rates in the international currency markets. Because of interest arbitrage between financial centres, rates for all main convertible currencies will stabilize at levels prevailing in London and other centres.

Time deposits

Time deposits similarly may be placed with any bank for periods of a few days, a week, or from between 1 and 12 months or longer for major currencies by negotiation. This market, though not as large as the call market, provides competitive interest rates which are dependent largely on the rates pertaining in the international Eurocurrency market and also, to some extent, on local liquidity.

Interest earned on deposits may be repatriated freely by non-residents and is not subject to withholding tax.

Certificates of deposit

There is no market in domestic currency CDs although there is a large and active market in Eurodollar CDs.

259

Foreign investors in the Eurobond market often prefer the liquidity afforded by the marketability of a CD rather than placing idle funds on fixed time deposits.

Euro-CDs are issued for 3-, 6- and sometimes 9- or 12-month terms by all the Luxembourg based banks. Yields depend on prevailing levels of interest rates in the Eurodollar market, the term of the CD and the credit standing of the issuing bank.

Although the majority of CDs are issued on tap, as the issuing bank seeks to borrow from the market, tranche and floating rate CDs are also available (see Chapter 26, International markets).

Other money market instruments

Luxembourg has little need for other money market instruments mainly because the budget financing requirements of the government are low. Government securities are issued, but in small amounts and at irregular intervals. Their marketability is consequently limited and in recent years their yields have not been sufficiently attractive to the international investor.

Local companies do not issue commercial bills or paper since they are able to meet most of their short-term financing requirements through bank borrowing. Luxembourg does however provide an active secondary market in Euromarket short-term instruments such as CDs, FRNs and, more recently, Eurocommercial paper.

The capital market

Eurobonds

The principal type of security traded, and virtually the *raison d'être* for the foreign investor in the Luxembourg capital market, is the Eurobond.

Luxembourg is, after London, the second most active centre for secondary market Eurobond trading. Very little primary issuing activity is generated in Luxembourg itself, although the country is the largest centre for the listing of Eurobonds. About one thousand outstanding issues are listed and denominated in most of the major currencies.

International bonds denominated in Luxembourg francs amounted to new issues of only about Lf 55 million in the peak year of 1978. Such bonds, issued in bearer form, carry maturities of up to 10 years. The bonds most traded are Euro-Deutschemark and Swiss franc foreign bonds, as well as Eurodollar bonds for which Luxembourg represented almost 20 per cent of the total European turnover. Notably, Luxembourg accounts for more than 30 per cent of total Euro-Deutschemark dealings. As German banks are discouraged by the official reserve requirements (which inhibit the flow of capital into Germany) from developing a more active Euro-Deutschemark bond market in Frankfurt, Luxembourg has provided the major primary and secondary market for Deutschemark denominated Eurobonds.

Listed Eurobonds are quoted on the Luxembourg stock exchange but most transactions occur 'over-the-counter' through international banks. There are no restrictions on dealings by non-residents, dealing costs are minimal, and repatriation of proceeds is unrestricted and free of withholding taxes.

Foreign bonds

There is no distinction made between Luxembourg franc foreign bonds and Eurobonds, principally because the number and amounts of issues denominated in Luxembourg francs are so small, and because Luxembourg is first and foremost an international market place. Foreign bonds (including Eurobonds) listed on the Luxembourg market had a total nominal value of about Lf 1256 billion (US$45 billion), equivalent to almost 50 times the domestic bond market.

Domestic bonds

Domestic bonds are issued by the government via the State Savings Bank (Caisse d'Epargne de l'Etat) which acts as agent on behalf of the treasury.

Bonds are issued also by government-related entities such as the utilities and gas and steel companies as well as private sector companies and foreign owned holding companies. All are listed on the Luxembourg stock exchange but are commonly traded outside the floor between banks acting both on behalf of clients and for their own accounts.

The total amount of domestic bonds on issue is however very small. At the end of 1979 public sector issues amounted to about Lf 13 billion and private sector bonds to about the same; clearly this is insignificant when compared with the size of the foreign and Eurobond markets.

Interest paid to non-residents is subject to withholding tax except for interest paid by holding companies, which is free of tax. The volume of new issues in the primary market is low but secondary market trading is quite active.

Equity shares

The market in equity shares is smaller and less lively than the bond market, mainly because the domestic economy is so small. Nonetheless, a number of foreign companies seek a listing on the Luxembourg stock exchange for the following reasons.

1. The speed with which a quotation can be obtained.
2. The low expenses of obtaining a quotation.
3. The liberal and non-discriminatory controls applied by the stock exchange.

Some foreign companies seek a listing in Luxembourg because their own domestic capital markets are inadequate. Luxembourg, on the other hand, provides a healthy and active market coupled with an environment that has minimum official regulations. At the end of 1979 there were 231 domestic and 154 foreign companies with shares listed on the Luxembourg stock exchange, with a market capitalization of about Lf 50 billion (US$1.8 billion).

261

Equity shares may be purchased by non-residents and proceeds may be freely repatriated although dividends are subject to withholding tax.

The stock exchange

The stock exchange is managed and administered by the joint stock company of the Luxembourg stock exchange. The company, the Société Anonyme de la Bourse de Luxembourg, is 80 per cent owned by the state savings bank and 20 per cent by private citizens, and is supervised by a government commissioner.

The importance of the exchange as a European trading centre for European securities is increasing. Turnover and listings have grown substantially in the last two decades, not only in Eurobonds but also in equities. In 1960 there were just over 100 share and bond quotations whilst currently there are over 1000, eighty-seven per cent of which are bonds and shares of foreign companies and institutions.

Table 12.2 Securities listed on Luxembourg stock exchange (*source: London stock exchange*)

	1975	1976	1977	1978	1979
BONDS Lf billion					
Eurobonds and foreign bonds	752.3	975.9	1170.2	1139.9	1298.8
Domestic public sector bonds	11.6	12.7	13.7	12.3	13.7
Domestic private sector bonds	4.6	6.2	9.0	10.6	12.7
Total	768.5	994.8	1192.9	1162.8	1325.2
SHARES					
Domestic companies	76	73	73	68	69
Foreign companies	66	69	68	86	89
Total	142	142	141	154	158

While listing on the exchange is a requirement for companies wishing to gain access to the Luxembourg capital market, trading does not have to take place on the floor of the exchange. Most dealing occurs outside the exchange, between banks in the over-the-counter market.

The mechanics of negotiation and clearing of securities is aided by Eurex in conjunction with 69 banks from 14 countries; and also by CEDEL (Centrale de Livraison des Valeurs Mobilières), a mutual independent body set up in 1970 by 72 banks from 12 countries. Its membership has subsequently grown to, currently, about 640 institutions.

Dealing and fees

All dealing for the purchase and sale of any security traded in Luxembourg may be transacted through the banks.

For money market transactions, in particular for Eurocurrency deposits, the banks' consideration is included in their deposit bid rates.

For capital market transactions, the banks' commission is included in the difference between their bid and offer rates. For bonds this is usually between $\frac{1}{8}$ and $\frac{1}{4}$ per cent though spreads may be as large as one or two per cent for transactions in difficult markets or for less active bonds.

For transactions in equity shares a fixed commission fee is charged, but this is negligible.

Trading on the floor of the stock exchange may only be carried out by banks and stockbrokers.

Financial and monetary systems

Financial institutions

Luxembourg has monetary union with Belgium, based on an agreement dating from 1963 which constituted the Belgo-Luxembourg Economic Union (BLEU). Monetary policy is entrusted to the government and delegated to the Commissioner for the Control of the Banks. There is no central bank in Luxembourg although the Caisse d'Epargne de l'Etat (State Savings Bank) assumes some of the functions of a central bank.

Bank notes are issued by the International Bank of Luxembourg and also by the Caisse Générale de L'Etat (the General Bank of the State) which is affiliated to the State Savings Bank.

Domestic currency, however, accounts for only five per cent of currency in circulation. Belgian francs, which are legal tender and have an equivalent exchange value, are used as the main transactions currency.

The State Savings Bank is the largest of the domestic banks and it conducts most of its activities with residents only. Apart from acting as agent for the treasury in issuing bank notes and government securities, it acts as a commercial, savings, and mortgage bank to resident companies and individuals.

The remaining banks are multifacet privately owned banks providing services as commercial and investment banks. They accept deposits, deal on behalf of clients and stockbrokers and provide investment advice and portfolio management services.

The majority of the banks are branches of foreign and international banks.

Holding companies

A special feature of the Luxembourg financial system is the predominance of holding companies. These are companies whose sole purpose is the holding of equity participation in other domestic or foreign companies. They have no other

263

industrial or trading activity of their own. They may acquire, hold and manage Luxembourg or foreign securities; grant credit to companies in which they have a participation; acquire property and real estate for their own use; provide management services to companies in which they participate; and finance their activities by the issue of bonds and debentures to the public (up to a limit of 10 times paid-up capital).

Financial holding companies

Financial holding companies are holding companies formed by large group companies for the purpose of financing subsidiaries or affiliates of these groups. They need not hold a direct participation in the subsidiaries but must hold shares in part of the group. The group parent company must be shown to be the parent of both the financial holding company and the subsidiaries or affiliates.

Bank financial holding companies

Bank financial holding companies are holding companies formed by banks for the purpose of making capital funds available to industrial and commercial companies through the bank parent. To finance such lending, the bank financial holding companies may issue bonds in the Luxembourg capital market. The amount of the bonds issued may not exceed the amount required by the beneficiary companies. In the event that such bond issues do exceed the required amount of capital, surplus funds may not be held in liquid form by the holding company but must be subscribed to the purchase of treasury bonds of fixed-term or with less than 15 days left to maturity.

Investment funds

Investment funds are companies whose purpose is to create profit from investment in bonds and shares of Luxembourg and foreign based companies [Société Anonyme—(SA)] and issue share capital which may be purchased on the Luxembourg stock exchange. They have the same legal status as a holding company.

Monetary policy

The Luxembourg financial markets are mainly international and thus not influenced by domestic economic policy. Little intervention occurs in the domestic market but this is strongly influenced by domestic policy, interest and exchange rates in Belgium. The banks have no cash ratio requirements but are subject to a minimum solvency ratio with respect to their capital and free reserves, and a 30 per cent liquidity ratio with respect to their eligible liabilities.

Most of the banks' liabilities are in the form of call and time deposits denominated in currencies other than Luxembourg francs. As at December 1979 liabilities of Luxembourg banks were the equivalent of US$1 billion denominated in Luxembourg francs, US$32 billion denominated in US dollars and US$43 billion denominated in other currencies, mainly US dollars, Belgian francs, Swiss francs and Deutschemark.

Little intervention in the money or capital markets is practised by the authorities. However, some intervention is exercised in the official exchange market, though no exchange intervention occurs in the free market, in which exchange rates may freely fluctuate and through which most investment transactions are made.

Eurocurrency interest rates are determined, not by the authorities, but by demand and supply in the international currency markets. Domestic interest rates follow, very closely, those in Belgium.

Open market operations in the money market are not undertaken by the authorities in order to influence credit or interest rates.

Withholding taxes

Withholding taxes at a nominal rate of five per cent are payable on interest from domestic bonds, although to residents of countries having tax treaties with Luxembourg, this is reduced to zero in several instances. Other interest, in particular interest on Eurobonds and foreign bonds, is paid free of withholding taxes.

Portfolio dividends are subject to a withholding tax rate of 15 per cent (7.5 per cent to US residents).

Dividends arising from substantial holdings in a Luxembourg company are subject to a reduced rate of withholding tax when the recipient is a resident of a tax treaty country. A substantial holding is defined as 25 per cent, except in the case of residents of the US where it is defined at 50 per cent which may be held either by a single shareholder or together with a maximum of three other US shareholders, each of whom holds at least 10 per cent of the shares. Dividends arising from Luxembourg holding companies are free of withholding tax. Table 12.3 summarizes the withholding taxes applicable to residents of non-treaty and treaty countries.

Table 12.3 Withholding taxes

	Bond 1 interest, %	Dividends 2 (portfolio), %	Dividends (substantial holdings), %
Resident corporation and individuals	5	15	
Non-resident corporations and individuals			
Non-treaty countries	5	15	15
Treaty countries			
Austria	5	15	5
Belgium	5	15	10
France	5	15	5
Germany	0	15	10
Ireland	0	15	5
Netherlands	0	15	2.5
United Kingdom	0	15	5
United States	0	7.5	5

1. Domestic bonds only.
2. Dividends paid by holding companies are exempt from withholding tax.

Exchange controls

Luxembourg has a system of exchange controls common with Belgium which is supervised by the Institut Belgo-Luxembourg du Change (IBLC).

There is freedom of exchange for all purposes except that a two-tier foreign exchange system is enforced. This comprises, firstly, an official market in convertible francs through which commercial transactions take place and which must be carried out through an authorized bank, and secondly, the free market in financial francs through which the purely financial transactions such as the purchase or sale of securities must take place. The exchange rate in the official market is controlled by the intervention of the IBLC. Exchange rates in the free market fluctuate free of intervention and according to international supply and demand. Normally, financial francs stand at a 2–3 per cent premium over convertible francs.

The objective of the Luxembourg and Belgium exchange systems is to provide a favourable environment for international commerce while still being able to contain excessive inflows of foreign capital which might have a detrimental effect on the economy.

13. The Netherlands

General market environment

The Netherlands has an open economy and the government has traditionally welcomed foreign investment, although it prefers local financing and discourages excessive inward flows of foreign capital. Any controls however are generally

Table 13.1 Summary of instruments

Instrument	Characteristics
MONEY MARKET	
Deposits 　call deposits 　time deposits 　Eurocurrency deposits	Highly active markets; easy access with low costs. Yields depend on international interest rates and less on domestic monetary policy
Other	Other money market instruments may not be purchased by non-residents
CAPITAL MARKETS	
Eurobonds	Primary market in Euroguilder notes and secondary market in these and other Eurobonds. Efficient over-the-counter market. Issues not listed on stock exchange
Domestic bonds 　government bonds 　local government bonds 　foreign bonds 　corporate bonds 　bond investment funds	Government is the largest single issuer of bonds Bonds issued by the Bank of Municipalities (BNG) on behalf of local governments. Second largest issuer Dealt in same way as domestic bonds Issued by commercial banks, mortgage banks, other financial institutions and companies. Good market in securities of larger institutions Tailored to tax requirements of particular groups of investors
Equity shares	Equal in volume to bond market but most activity limited to shares of a few large companies
Share options	New market developed for trading share options of companies from a dozen countries
Gold	Free gold bullion market in Amsterdam plus gold options market on European option exchange

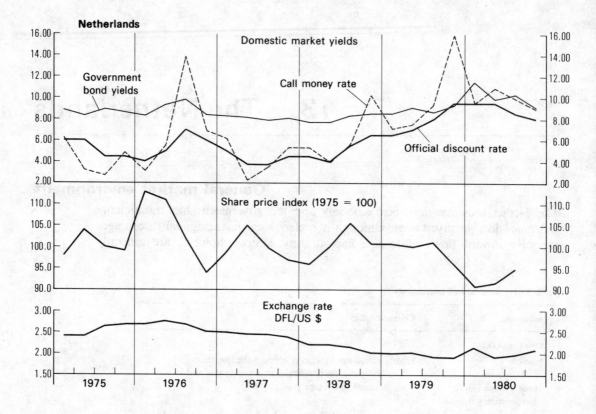

Netherlands

Domestic market yields

Government bond yields

Call money rate

Official discount rate

Share price index (1975 = 100)

Exchange rate DFL/US $

1975 1976 1977 1978 1979 1980

confined to requiring that the banking system maintains adequate domestic liquidity.

In most other respects, the Netherlands presents very few restrictions to the foreign investor, allowing free transfer of principal, profits and dividends. Exchange controls are minimal, while withholding taxes apply at moderate rates to dividends and not at all to interest.

In the money market, the opportunities for the non-resident investor are limited to call and time deposits in guilders and other Eurocurrencies. However, these markets are large and active.

The capital market provides an active market in Eurobonds and a reasonably good market in domestic bonds and equities, with easier access than similar markets in many other European financial centres.

A new market, the European Options Exchange, has recently been established in Amsterdam and, while it is still in its infancy and thus still small, it is proving to be efficient. It is intended to provide a market for options in shares of companies from about a dozen countries. Plans to introduce facilities for options trading in gold are scheduled for 1981.

Amsterdam is the principal financial centre, with Rotterdam and The Hague playing secondary roles.

The money market

Deposits

There are active interbank loan and time deposit markets, and non-residents are free to open accounts and to place funds in these markets. Interest is calculated according to a 360-day year and a 30-day month. The banks charge a small turn-over commission on bank accounts, depending on the size and utilization of the account.

Call deposits

Dutch florin deposits may be placed at call for overnight or two-day periods with any of the Dutch commercial banks or with branches of foreign banks established in the Netherlands. Dealings are usually in amount of Dfl 5 million or more. Funds may also be placed on demand deposit at one week's notice, usually in amounts of Dfl 1 million or more. In the interbank market, in which other financial institutions, corporations and local authorities may also participate, call deposits are unsecured. Bill brokers often act as intermediaries between borrowers and lenders, charging $\frac{1}{8}$ per cent commission on each transaction.

Two call rates are quoted in the market, the brokers' call rate and the bankers' call rate. The brokers' call rate is the rate for call deposits secured against treasury paper. Such call money is nearly always borrowed or lent by a stockbroker. The ceiling for the brokers' call rate is the official advance rate since brokers will tend to borrow from the central bank as soon as call market rates exceed the advance rate. In addition, since 1973, deposits with stockbroker are classified as reserve assets whereas deposits with banks are not. Thus the supply of short-term funds to the brokers is sufficient to keep the brokers' call rates close to the official discount rate.

The bankers' call rate is the rate for unsecured call deposits placed with the banking system. Banks do not always have sufficient treasury paper to provide collateral in order to claim an advance from the central bank. The bankers' call rate may thus rise significantly above the official advance rate since they may be obliged to bid for funds in the open market when liquidity in the banking system is generally tight.

For this reason yields depend on the supply and demand for funds in the money market and will also fluctuate during the course of a day, and vary between banks. Table 13.2 shows the variations that have existed between the official discount and advance rates and the brokers' call rate in the money market.

Time deposits

Time deposits may be placed for periods of one week or 1, 2, 3, 6 or 12 months, usually in minimum amounts of Dfl 100000. The local authorities, as well as the banks, are active borrowers in this market, for deposits of periods from one month to one year. The loans are unsecured against treasury paper and often yield more than Euroguilder deposits of identical terms in order to attract deposits. Loans to local authorities, including the bank for municipalities (BNG), may be placed through a billbroker.

269

Table 13.2   Structure of money market interest rates (average rate per annum per cent)

Month	Official discount rate	Official advance rate	Bankers' call rate	3-month loans to local authorities and unsecured loans to banks	3-month Euroguilder, time deposits
1978					
Jan.					
Feb. }	4.8	....	5.30	....	5.20
Mar. }					
Apr. }	4.0	....	4.40	....	4.70
May }					
Jun.	4.0	4.5	3.99	4.61	4.78
Jul.	4.5	5.0	4.10	5.51	5.4
Aug.	4.5	5.0	3.47	6.36	5.88
Sep.	5.5	6.0	5.59	6.91	6.57
Oct.	6.5	7.0	13.56	11.18	11.18
Nov.	6.5	7.0	8.76	8.93	8.93
Dec.	6.5	7.0	10.29	10.38	9.71
1979					
Jan.	6.5	7.0	8.64	8.78	8.28
Feb.	6.5	7.0	7.73	7.47	6.89
Mar.	6.5	7.0	7.14	7.46	7.10
Apr.	6.5	7.0	7.09	7.27	7.33
May	7.0	7.5	7.10	7.82	8.03
Jun.	7.0	7.5	7.57	8.73	8.71
Jul.	7.5	8.0	8.63	9.62	9.46
Aug.	8.0	8.5	8.73	9.63	9.32
Sep.	8.0	8.5	9.39	9.25	9.82
Oct.	8.0	8.5	9.28	10.20	9.86
Nov.	9.5	10.5	11.18	11.86	11.27
Dec.	9.5	10.5	15.90	14.80	13.90
1980					
Jan.	9.5	10.5	11.18	11.94	11.48
Feb.	9.5	10.5	10.99	12.07	12.05
Mar.	9.5	10.5	9.50	11.63	11.46
Apr.	9.5	10.5	10.47	10.88	10.76
May	10.0	11.0	11.14	11.23	11.14
Jun.	9.5	10.5	10.97	10.82	10.70
Jul.	9.0	10.0	10.31	10.19	10.08
Aug.	9.0	10.0	10.09	10.04	10.09
Sep.	8.5	9.5	9.89	10.45	10.50
Oct.	8.0	9.0	9.37	9.76	9.73
Nov.	8.0	9.0	9.05	9.65	9.63
Dec.	8.0	9.0	8.60	9.77	9.72

As with call deposits, yields depend on prevailing market levels of interest, but there may often be a large discrepancy between the one-week and one-month rates; the former usually approximates more closely to the call market rates and thus is dependent on the banking system's demand to settle balances.

The structure of interest rates in the market for time deposits is in theory determined by the discount rate and government monetary policy, although in recent times the strength of the guilder has been the main influence on the structure of interest rates. Though one could argue that it has been part of central government policy to protect the currency, the sensitivity of the guilder market is such that the authorities have not in the past been able to control exchange rate fluctuations when the guilder has been under pressure from the market. This pressure has now been largely relieved by newer methods of market intervention employed by the central bank.

Eurocurrency deposits

Netherlands banks are active participants in the Eurocurrency markets and accept call and time deposits in all convertible currencies at rates of interest determined by demand and supply in the international market. The banking system will accept deposits in all other convertible currencies. Such funds may be placed at call or on time deposits in amounts equivalent to Dfl 5 million and Dfl 1 million respectively.

Other money market instruments

There are no other money market instruments available to the non-resident investor.

There are no Dutch florin certificates of deposits and no other money market paper is issued apart from treasury and commercial bills. While the market in treasury bills is quite sizeable and active, it is exclusively an interbank market. Treasury bills may not be purchased by the non-bank public. Commercial bills are accepted by the banking system and are used by the central bank to influence money supply, but again, these are not dealt outside the banking system.

The capital market

Bond market

In the Netherlands, the largest part of the capital market is constituted by private loans (onderhandse leningen). The market is thus primarily a wholesale market in which mainly domestic (i.e., institutional) investors act as lenders. Borrowers are predominantly domestic, although foreign borrowers are admitted on a limited scale.

For example during 1979 the total capital raised, net of redemptions, on the Dutch domestic fixed-interest market comprised Dfl 4.5 billion in the form of publicly issued bonds and Dfl 38.2 billion in the form of private loans. Bonds

271

represent only a small proportion of the portfolio holdings by institutional investors, the largest part being private loans.

Private loans are preferred because they can be easily adapted to meet the specific requirements of both parties. They can be concluded by just a few telephone calls, are possible to arrange at any time and, although they usually bear higher interest which suits the lender, the costs of issue are lower to the borrower than would be incurred by the public issue of a bond.

There are in excess of 1500 domestic bond issues outstanding amounting to a value of approximately Dfl 70 billion. Of these, 34 per cent are issued by the government, 19 per cent by the local authorities and 47 per cent by the private sector.

Most bonds amortize capital in equal annual instalments. The bonds to be repaid are selected by drawings according to a variety of schemes that may be used. This occurs at a period of between three weeks and three months before the interest payment date.

Annual repayment may begin either one or five to ten years after issue.

Normally no outright redemption purchases are made. A few exceptions are the $2\frac{1}{2}$, 3 and $3\frac{1}{2}$ per cent perpetual loans of the state, for which some redemption in small amounts takes place gradually by central bank purchase on the stock exchange on behalf of the government. In addition, $2\frac{1}{2}$ per cent of the outstanding state loan issued in 1947 and maturing in 1987 is purchased each year on the stock exchange on 1 January.

In most cases, maturity is at par. One exception is the $8\frac{3}{4}$ per cent BNG bond maturing in 1981–83, for which redemption is specified as being in five annual instalments at 101 per cent of par, followed by five annual instalments at par. Medium- and long-term loans may be repaid in full or in part before maturity, the option on the part of the borrower beginning usually 10 years after issue. However, this option has not been exercised by any borrower in the last 30 years.

In most cases, and for all bonds issued after 1960, interest is paid annually. The majority of bonds carry a fixed coupon rate, although a few bonds issued by industrial companies have gradually increasing coupons up to a specified maximum.

Government bonds

The State of the Netherlands is the largest single borrower in the domestic bond market, issuing annually between Dfl 150 million and Dfl 800 million worth of new bonds. In the secondary market, trading in government bonds accounts for one-third of total bond turnover on the Amsterdam stock exchange.

In mid-1979 there were 84 state bonds listed with an aggregate nominal value of Dfl 20 billion, while the outstanding amount of each loan ranged from Dfl 9 million to Dfl 1200 million.

Most of these bonds are fully guaranteed as to principal and interest by the Netherlands government.

Those which are not, are:

- 80 per cent of the listed loans of the Netherland's Antilles, of which there are bonds amounting to Dfl 152 million outstanding;
- fifteen loans of the Netherlands Ontwikkelings Bank (the Netherlands Investments Bank For Developing Countries);
- sixty per cent of the listed loans of the 100 per cent state owned Netherlands railways. These bonds amount to a total outstanding of Dfl 240 million;
- one bond issued by Schiphol Airport which has an outstanding value of Dfl 42 million.

Bonds issued by the state are in bearer form and in minimum denominations of Dfl 100 000.

Local authority bonds

The local authorities and municipalities tend not to issue their own bonds on the capital market but to borrow from the BNG—the Bank voor Nederlandsche Gemeenten (the Bank for Netherlands Municipalities)—which is owned 50 per cent by the state and 50 per cent by the local authorities.

In order to finance these loans, the BNG issues its own securities. Next to the government it is the second largest issuer of bonds, and accounts for a quarter of the total bond trading turnover. Together with the Polder Boards Bank it issues bonds to the value of between Dfl 100 million and Dfl 200 million annually, in amounts per loan of between Dfl 2 million and Dfl 400 million. In mid-1980 it had about 100 issues outstanding on the market amounting to a nominal value of Dfl 12 billion.

The Netherlands Polder Boards Bank is similar to the BNG but operates on a smaller scale. It has only 10 bonds outstanding on the market with a total nominal value of Dfl 644 million. Bonds of the BNG and Polder Boards are in bearer form in minimum denominations of Dfl 50 000.

There are also 225 outstanding bonds issued directly onto the market by local provinces and municipalities. Twenty-two of these are lottery loans. The outstanding value of these bonds is Dfl 450 million and all were issued prior to December 1965. Local authorities were prohibited from issuing their own securities between 1965 and 1975 but were required to use either the BNG or Polder Boards Bank as an intermediary. The abolition of this regulation in 1975 has not subsequently resulted in any new direct issues by local authorities.

Bonds of public financial institutions

Three financial institutions, the share capitals of which are approximately 50 per cent owned by the state and 50 per cent owned by private shareholders and traded on the stock exchange, finance their activities by the issue of bonds in the capital market.

These institutions are:

- The Nationale Investerings Bank, which grants medium- and long-term loans to industry for capital investment projects;
- The Nederlandse Ontwikkelings Bank (the Netherlands investment bank for developing countries) which is wholly owned by the Investerings Bank and, as its name implies, makes loans to developing countries;
- The Export Financiering Maatschappij (the export financing company) which make loans to companies for exports or foreign capital investment.

These three institutions have 14, 15 and 4 outstanding bonds issues respectively (as at mid-1980) with a combined aggregate value of over Dfl 2000 million.

Commercial bank bonds

The outstanding volume of commercial bank bonds is over Dfl 5 billion comprising some 60 or so issues. In order to finance their medium- and long-term lending to the corporate sector, the commercial banks regularly issue bonds in one of the following three forms.

Ordinary bonds   Ordinary bonds have maturities of up to 25 years, with interest and part capital usually being repaid annually, beginning either one or five to ten years after issue. The bonds are unsecured against specific assets but guaranteed by the issuing bank.

Subordinated capital debentures   These are similar to, but rank behind, ordinary bonds in the order of creditors and thus normally carry a higher yield.

Six-year savings bonds   These bonds carry a fixed six-year maturity and are guaranteed by the issuer but unsecured against specific assets. They are usually issued on tap, while the principal and all accrued interest is repaid at redemption and not, as with other bonds, annually.

Mortgage bank bonds (pandbrieven)

Pandbrieven are bonds, issued on tap, with maturities of up to 25 years. Interest and part principal is repaid annually. The bonds are unsecured against specific assets but are guaranteed by the issuers which are mortgage banks who use the funds raised to make loans for house purchase and building. Thus the bonds are effectively secured against a pool of mortgages. Yields are higher than for other financial bonds and up to two percentage points higher than central government bonds of long maturity.

Corporate bonds

The Netherlands has a healthy corporate bond market which constitutes about 45 per cent of the total bonds issued annually.

274

The longest and most frequent issues are made by the insurance companies which raise funds on the market to finance expansion and diversification. Also prominent are the multinational companies—for example Royal Dutch/Shell, Unilever, Philips, Akzo and Estel/Hoogovers—and the large national companies, such as Nederlandse Gasunie, which is part owned by the state and part by Royal Dutch/Shell, and Pekdoed Holdings which is a conglomerate handling harbour installations, transport, pipelines, property and other interests. Further issuers include the hospitals and other health institutions.

The majority of bonds issued carry maturities of 10 years and normally repay interest and part principal annually, in 5 or 10 instalments.

Foreign bonds

Bonds denominated in Dutch guilders but issued by foreign borrowers also provide a good market. The Issuers include large foreign corporations, mostly of European origin, a few loans of foreign governments, in particular Belgium, Denmark, Austria and Australia, and some issues of international agencies such as the World Bank, the Inter-American Development Bank, the European Investment Bank and the European Coal and Steel Community.

Foreign bonds are normally issued with fixed coupons with maturities of up to 10 years and, in common with most domestic bonds, are redeemed by instalments. There are no limits on the amount of each issue and in most respects foreign bonds are managed and traded in exactly the same way as domestic bonds.

Bond investment funds

An alternative for the investor wishing to participate in the Dutch bond market, but with lower risk, might be to invest in one of the bond investment funds. These not only spread the risk to the investor but also provide experienced portfolio management. Additionally, although only a few such funds exist, the investor may choose one that suits his tax and lending requirements. Rorento, the largest of the bond investment funds, caters for the larger investor in a high tax bracket, while AMRO Oligateifonds is more appropriate for the small investor in the lower tax bracket. Returns are paid annually to the investor and include both interest and capital. The ratio of each varies according to the type of fund and the investor for which the fund is designed.

State bonds are issued by the central bank or the BNG through agent banks. They are usually for sale at a fixed price, although may sometimes be offered for sale by tender where the coupon is fixed but the amount and price are not determined until after the close of subscriptions. Subscriptions are made through members of the stock exchange which includes most of the commercial banks. These orders are then passed on to the primary issuing bank(s). When the price of state bonds is not fixed, subscriptions are allotted on the following basis:

Primary market in Dutch domestic bonds

Bids above final issue price	subscriptions fully allotted
Bids at final issue price	subscriptions partially allotted
Bids below final issue price	subscription not allotted

Corporate bonds are issued in a similar way, through a primary bank or broker, but are usually underwritten by a syndicate of banks and brokers. They are almost always issued at a fixed price. Issues are first allotted to the underwriters and other stockbrokers who subsequently make allotments to their customers, usually two to three days after the close of subscriptions. Payments and delivery subsequently takes place 30 stock exchange days after close of subscriptions.

The approximate annual new issue volume of Dutch bonds is as follows:

Issuer	Volume (Dfl million)
State of the Netherlands	150–800
BNG and polders board	100–200
National Investerings Bank / Nederlandse Ontwikkelings Bank	75–125
Commercial banks	100 +
Multinationals	100 +
Other domestic bonds	15–100
Foreign bonds	50–100

Secondary market Dutch domestic bonds

All bonds, both state and corporate, are traded on the stock exchange through a stockbroker or commercial bank. All have a reasonably good secondary market although the best markets exist for government and BNG bonds.

In general, bonds that have a new issue volume in excess of Dfl 50 million a year are assured good marketability.

The least active secondary market exists in the category 'other domestic bonds' which includes local authority bonds issued prior to 1965 and bonds of some mortgage banks and health institutions.

The total daily turnover of bonds in the secondary market is usually between Dfl 50 million and Dfl 100 million.

Foreign investors have become important participants in the secondary market, holding Dutch bonds for currency reasons as well as yield.

Market yields reflect both the security and marketability of the bonds. Government bonds carry the highest security and in general the best marketability, and thus have the lowest yield. The yield differential between government bonds and other bonds is roughly as follows:

Issuer	Average yield differential
BNG	+0.05–0.15%
Other public authorities	+0.20–0.30%
Financial institutions	+0.25–0.50%
Corporate sector	+0.25–0.75%
Mortgage banks	+0.75–1.00%
Health institutions	+1.00–1.50%

Apart from government and local authority bonds, most Dutch bonds are in bearer form and traded in minimum denominations of Dfl 1000.

Eurobonds

The Netherlands provide both a primary and secondary market in Eurobonds.

Primary market

In the primary market, Euroguilder bond new issues amount to approximately Dfl 800 million per annum, but the authorities, who fear that excessive external demand for guilders will harm the domestic economy, have limited the number of issues to one per month. New issues are managed by a syndicate of Dutch banks which may include a maximum of two foreign banks. The primary market is made by the banks in co-operation with the central bank, which is responsible for the administration and control of the market.

Each new Euroguilder loan is normally a minimum size of Dfl 175 million, and may only be issued by 'high quality' borrowers. The price of new issues depends on market demand. Since the issue price is not predetermined, there is no requirement for new Eurobonds to be underwritten. Euroguilder bonds are not listed on the stock exchange and, unlike most other Eurobonds, are not issued with a prospectus. Most are semiprivate loans in the sense that the managing syndicate of banks place the bonds with clients on a 'best efforts' basis which thus determines the issue price. Thereafter the bonds are traded freely in the public market. Euroguilder bonds are more usually called Euroguilder notes as they are generally of short maturity of five to seven years, issued in bearer form, with interest paid either annually or semiannually. The five- and six-year bonds redeem principal at maturity while seven-year bonds may repay the principal in equal amounts during the last four years of the bond's life. Full redemption may not however take place prior to maturity. Private placement Eurobonds as made by high-quality foreign borrowers are not restricted to one issue per month, but each issue is limited to a maximum of Dfl 75 million. Private placements have longer maturities than Euroguilder notes, normally of 10 to 20 years, and with average lives of up to 13 years. Redemption is not normally permitted prior to maturity.

Secondary market

The secondary market in Euroguilder notes is maintained by the many Dutch and foreign banks established in Amsterdam, as well as by banks in other Euromarkets such as London and Luxembourg. The secondary market is both active and efficient though, while non-residents may freely purchase any Euroguilder bonds, residents may only purchase Eurobonds issued by Dutch borrowers. An active secondary market is also maintained by banks in the Netherlands for Eurobonds denominated in other currencies.

Equity shares

Prior to the second world war, the Dutch market in equity issues was the world's third most important and active equity market after New York and London. The Netherlands capital market was used to float the shares of several large industrial

277

Table 13.3   New issues of securities on Dutch capital market (Dfl million) (*source: OECD*)

Securities	1975	1976	1977	1978	1979	First nine months 1980
BONDS—gross new issues						
Government bonds	1934	2735	2600	3215	3965	5220
Local authority bonds (including BNG and polders board bonds)	1193	469	998	500	300	251
Total public sector	3127	3204	3598	3715	4265	5471
Bank bonds and mortgage bonds	1201	724	2458	3031	3400	2257
Corporate bonds	1086	495	617	125	222	55
Foreign bonds	398	402	386	525	400	385
Total domestic bonds	5812	4825	7059	7396	8247	8168
EUROBONDS	1082	1589	956	767	308	448
SHARES public sector enterprises financial institutions	339	242	314	254	362	240
private sector domestic companies foreign companies	172	28	91	362	84	74
Total shares	511	270	405	616	496	314
Private bond issues (ondehandse leningen) (net issues Dfl millions)	20399	31230	37666	43037	38171	24535

companies such as Royal Dutch, Philips and Unilever, but today only 30, 50 and 60 per cent, respectively, remain in the hands of Dutch shareholders. The current market value of Dutch shares now amounts to some Dfl 60 billion, 40 per cent of which is represented by Royal Dutch/Shell. Turnover is about Dfl 5 billion per annum, but virtually no new issues are raised.

The decline in the market has been due to companies' preference for raising capital through private loans, although there are signs of a reversal in this trend.

The Amsterdam stock exchange was once a favoured market for the listing of issues by foreign companies and currently there are half as many foreign as domestic stocks quoted.

The total market capitalization of all listed shares is represented by the following sectors:

Sector	Market capitalization, Dfl billion	% of total
International companies	30	52
Trading and industry	8	14
Shipping and aviation	1	2
Banks and insurance	9	15
Investments trusts	9	15
Others	1	2
	58	100

Separate price indices may be found in the financial press for each of these sectors. Additionally, there is a general price index which is an average of all sectors. These are known as ANP-CBS indices and have a base of 1970 = 100.

Table 13.4 Average yields of Dutch securities

	Government bonds		BNG bonds	Mortgage (pand-brieven)	Corporate bonds	Eurobonds: Euroguilder notes of more than 3 years' maturity
	3 to 8 years' maturity	3 to 15 years' maturity				
1979						
Jan.	7.92	8.21	7.50	8.87	8.37	8.13
Feb.	8.12	8.35	7.70	8.78	8.41	7.99
Mar.	8.26	8.52	7.75	8.77	8.44	7.91
Apr.	8.38	8.59	7.82	8.94	8.56	7.89
May	8.56	8.79	8.22	9.30	8.88	8.18
Jun.	8.86	9.02	8.38	9.56	9.14	8.79
Jul.	8.71	9.03	8.34	9.84	9.28	8.97
Aug.	8.43	8.67	7.62	9.36	8.89	8.54
Sep.	8.49	8.69	7.83	9.47	8.86	8.62
Oct.	8.64	8.80	8.17	9.54	9.12	8.87
Nov.	9.11	9.23	8.11	10.04	9.61	9.25
Dec.	9.24	9.36	8.14	10.70	9.91	9.39
1980						
Jan.	9.33	9.43	8.00	10.62	9.89	9.42
Feb.	10.23	10.35	8.88	10.69	10.88	9.95
Mar.	11.26	11.40	9.76	12.92	12.13	11.41
Apr.	10.35	10.50	9.22	12.01	11.06	10.82
May	9.77	10.00	8.87	11.25	10.42	9.71
Jun.	9.65	9.86	8.74	11.10	10.15	9.53
Jul.	9.31	9.57	8.43	11.02	9.93	9.51
Aug.	9.30	9.50	8.29	10.76	9.76	9.56
Sep.	9.92	10.25	8.52	11.57	10.34	9.70
Oct.	9.93	10.26	8.02	11.86	10.41	9.73
Nov.	10.10	10.45	8.51	12.02	10.68	10.02
Dec.	10.26	10.51	9.03	11.92	10.87	10.13

Dutch shares are mostly in bearer form and, while there is no minimal dealing value, 40 per cent of transactions are for amounts of at least Dfl 250 000 per transaction.

The stock exchange

There are three stock exchanges located in Amsterdam, Rotterdam and The Hague, but Amsterdam has the only official exchange in which all Dutch securities are dealt. The other two exchanges are used by organizations of securities dealers, where business is done on the basis of Amsterdam prices. The Amsterdam exchange is controlled and administered by a private body, the Association pour le Marche des Titres. The market is open daily (excluding weekends) between 1 and 2.15 p.m. The auction system is used for two separate systems using specialist dealers (hockman) in particularly active shares or bonds.

The specialist acts as agent for particular issuers and is charged with maintaining the market on his specialist securities. He may also deal on his own account but is not obliged to maintain a personal book or position.

The securities for which the specialist system is used are bonds issued by the state or the BNG and a small number of active shares. The specialist fixes the price of his securities once or twice a day. He will quote an opening price at the beginning of each session, after which specialists and brokers transact in continuous and open trading.

The specialist receives commission from a bank or broker only for large block transactions which may often be at a privately negotiated price different from the official quote.

The annual stock exchange turnover is more than Dfl 40 billion, divided roughly equally between bonds and shares although, of a total of more than 2000 securities, there are three times as many bonds as shares listed.

Eurobonds are not listed on the stock exchange. The breakdown of quoted securities is as follows:

Securities	Number of issues (1979)	% of total
Dutch bonds	1396	66.3
Foreign bonds	132	6.3
Dutch shares	233	11.0
Foreign shares	282	13.4
Dutch investment trusts	32	1.5
Foreign investment trusts	32	1.5
	2107	100.0

Table 13.5 Outstanding value and turnover of securities listed on Amsterdam stock exchange (*source: London Stock Exchange*)

	1975	1976	1977	1978	1979
BONDS—issues outstanding (Dfl million)					
Public sector	28 500	30 106	32 095	33 907	36 153
Private sector	17 000	18 907	22 832	28 306	33 666
Total	45 500	49 013	54 927	62 213	69 819
Turnover (by par value)	10 930	13 370	18 067	22 070	20 487
SHARES					
Number of domestic shares	242	234	231	229	216
Number of foreign shares	323	318	318	312	300
Total	565	552	549	541	516
Market capitalization (Dfl million) of domestic shares only	48 867	50 435	50 766	52 233	58 634
TURNOVER (Dfl million)					
Domestic shares	12 776	14 423	17 777	19 587	17 839
Foreign shares	109	156	816	888	826
Total	12 885	14 579	18 593	20 475	18 665

Share options

In April 1978 a new exchange was opened in Amsterdam for the specific purpose of trading in share options. This is the European Options Exchange and is completely independent from the Amsterdam stock exchange. As the market's name implies, the options traded are foreign as well as Dutch shares. Being a new market, it is still relatively small. There are currently over 40 members but membership is continuing to expand. The exchange accommodates two types of members: associate members (usually financial institutions, including banks, who are active in dealing in securities) and ordinary members (institutions and individuals who are also members of the stock exchange).

The exchange is intended to provide a highly international market, trading share options from at least a dozen countries. However, so far only Dutch and US share options have been traded in any significant volume.

Listed on the options exchange as at August 1980 were the options of 9 Dutch companies, 13 US companies, 2 UK companies, 4 French companies, and 2 Belgian companies.

As might be expected, all are large multinational corporations. The two British companies, for example, are British Petroleum and ICI.

Call options (an option to buy) may be made in all of the quoted shares, but put options (an option to sell) may be made in only four of the listed Dutch shares, AKZO, KLM, Philips and Royal Dutch.

Option maturities are of three-month terms to January, April, July and October.

281

Turnover is running at an annual rate of about 55000 contracts with 3000 transactions per day, although dealings in Royal Dutch share options account for over 41 per cent of this business.

Gold

A market in gold options was established on the European options exchange in Spring 1981. It is hoped that the introduction of this market will add depth to the EOE and encourage the further development of the options market in Amsterdam.

There already exists a fairly active market for gold bullion in Amsterdam, though this is secondary to the markets in Zurich and London.

Dealing and fees

Deposits

Call and time deposits are accepted by any of the commercial banks in either Dutch guilders or any of the Eurocurrencies. No specific commission is charged. A small commission is charged on the turnover of bank accounts and agreed between the customer and the Dutch commercial bank concerned. This commission depends on the size and use of the bank account.

Eurobonds

These are not traded on the stock exchange but may be purchased through any of the Dutch commercial banks as well as through Dutch and foreign banks in other European financial centres. Most are listed on the Luxembourg stock exchange. No specific fee is charged but commission is included in the difference between the dealing bank's bid and offer prices.

Domestic and foreign bonds

Bonds are quoted free of accrued interest which is calculated separately on the settlement note according to a 360-day year and 30-day month. Bonds are traded ex-coupon 15 days prior to maturity. Bonds quoted on the stock exchange are dealt through a bank or a stockbroker who charge standard commission fees.

Equity shares

Equity shares are also traded on the stock exchange through a dealer. In the Netherlands the commercial banks provide a stockbroking service, although firms of stockbrokers also exist.

Standard fees are charged by banks and brokers according to fixed scales laid down by the Stock Exchange Commission Rules. These fees apply for both bonds and shares.

There are five scales; a general scale charged to most individuals and four scales of reduced fees charged to:

1. A limited group of large institutions such as insurance companies, pension funds, etc.
2. Members of foreign stock exchanges.
3. Certain government institutions.
4. Domestic correspondents.

The fees are summarized as follows (the column numbers correspond with the numbers in the above list):

Transaction amount (bonds and shares), Dfl	Fees				
	General %	1 %	2 %	3 %	4 %
Up to 20 000	1.0	1.000	0.500	0.750	0.300
20 000–200 000	0.78	0.468	0.390	0.585	0.259
Greater than 200 000	0.70	0.420	0.350	0.525	0.231

The fees are charged as a percentage of the total value of the transactions including, on bonds, the accrued interest. In addition, there is a charge of Dfl 3 per transaction and stamp duty payable at 1.2 per cent.

Delivery and settlement is for the following business day, except in the case of new issues which is up to 30 business days after the close of subscription orders.

Options

Options are traded on the European options exchange through member dealers. These are stockbrokers, who are also members of the stock exchange and the larger commercial banks such as AMRO Bank.

Commissions are charged according to a fixed scale as follows:

Transaction amount	Fees
Up to Dfl 2000	Dfl 20 + 5% of transaction amount
Dfl 2000–Dfl 10 000	Dfl 100 + 1% of transaction amount
Greater than Dfl 10 000	Dfl 200

An additional sum of Dfl 6 is charged per contract and there is a minimum commission payable of Dfl 25. Options are not subject to stamp duty.

Settlement and delivery is normally for the following business day.

Financial and monetary systems

Financial institutions

The most important financial institutions in the Netherlands are the commercial banks, since they provide a multipurpose function. There are also a number of savings banks whose purpose is to collect savings from individuals for on-lending to individuals and small businesses. Other financial institutions include mortgage banks, insurance companies and pension funds as well as a variety of specialist institutions such as billbrokers and export credit companies. Most financial institutions are privately owned although a few public sector banking institutions co-exist, but with specialized functions.

All private sector and some public sector financial institutions are supervised by the central bank or, in the case of insurance companies and other non-bank financial institutions, by the insurance supervisory authority or other relevant authority.

Commercial banks

The commercial banks are multipurpose. They accept call, time, demand and savings deposits, provide chequing account facilities, advance credit to individuals and businesses, accept commercial bills, manage new security issues, act as dealers in securities on behalf of clients and also provide portfolio management, advisory and safe custody services.

There are 75 commercial banks, all privately owned and which together control 2326 branches throughout the Netherlands. The commercial banks account for over 50 per cent of the assets of financial institutions but two commercial banks dominate the banking system. The Amsterdam-Rotterdam Bank (AMRO) and the Algemene Bank Nederland (ABN) both have a substantial branch network and together represent about 60 per cent of all commercial banking business. The third largest commercial bank is Middenstandsbank which until 1977 was a state owned bank specializing in granting credit to small businesses. Since it was sold to the private sector it has broadened its activities to encompass all the activities of a Dutch commercial bank. These three major banks together account for more than 80 per cent of all branches; only two other banks have branches in all 80 states of the Netherlands.

In addition to the domestic commercial banks there are more than 30 branches of foreign banks established in the Netherlands, most of them in Amsterdam.

Savings banks

A number of both privately and publicly owned financial institutions may be classified as savings banks. There are 80 private savings banks with 950 branches. They are non-profit-making institutions whose purpose is to accept savings and time deposits from individuals and provide medium- to long-term loans to domestic enterprises and individuals; they account for only a small proportion (about seven per cent) of total liabilities in the financial sector. The post office savings bank is the largest and only state owned savings bank with over 2600 branches; it accounts for almost half of the total liabilities of the savings banks.

The publicly owned post office also operates a postal giro service which has a higher level of deposits per head of population than similar services in any other country. The giro bank, with branches in the same offices as its savings banks service, should really be classified as a commercial bank since it provides chequing account facilities and accepts demand and time deposits as well as savings deposits. Over 90 per cent of accounts are held by individuals and represent about 14 per cent of total liabilities of the financial sector.

Mortgage banks

There are 12 mortgage banks which collect savings deposits from individuals and provide long-term loans also to individuals for house purchase. They account for almost 30 per cent of the financial sector's total liabilities. They do not generally raise additional capital through the issue of bonds on the capital market and most of the mortgage loans are classified as private debt placements (onderhandse leningen).

Public sector financial institutions

There are two major state owned co-operative banks—the banks for municipalities (Bank voor Nederlandsche Gemeenten—BNG) and the Polder Boards Bank (Nederlandse Waterschapsbank). The BNG is the larger of the two. They exist to provide medium- and long-term loans to the local authorities and municipalities, which no longer issue their own bonds in the capital market.

The BNG and Polder Boards Bank instead raise capital through the issue of securities, which can then be advanced to local governments that are in need of funds. About 95 per cent of the combined liabilities of the two banks is represented by private debt placements (onderhandse leningen) and public bond issues on the Dutch domestic market. The remaining five per cent of their liabilities is represented by call and time deposits raised in the Dutch money market.

Their total liabilities amount to about Dfl 50 billion—approximately eight per cent of liabilities of the whole financial sector.

Central bank

The central bank is the Nederlandsche Bank which is wholly owned by the state. Its president is appointed by the government but the Bank's management is completely autonomous.

Monetary policy is designed by the government in consultation with a 17-member advisory council, including four representatives from the board of the Nederlandsche Bank. The remaining members represent labour and economic interests from the major sectors of the economy and are appointed by royal decree.

The Minister of Finance takes advice from the council before making recommendations on monetary policy to the central bank. Thereafter, the Bank is free to administer the monetary policy with little interference from the government.

The central bank is required to give free banking services to the Post Office Savings Bank and other public institutions as directed by the Minister of Finance.

Monetary policy

The Nederlandsche Bank has only had statutory powers to control the credit system since the beginning of 1979. Previously, it had relied to a large extent on gentlemen's agreements and moral suasion.

The main objectives of monetary policy are to control the expansion of credit, banking liquidity and the external flows of capital to within the limits that can be accommodated by the economy. To obtain these objectives the Nederlandsche Bank uses the instruments of reserve requirements, solvency and liquidity ratios, discount policy, quantitive and qualitative credit restrictions, and open market operations.

Reserve requirements

The prime objective of controlling liquidity within the economy is attained by the use of reserve and liquidity requirements. The authorities aim to maintain total liquidity—defined as currency, call, time and savings deposits and claims on local authorities held by non-bank financial institutions—to about one-third of GNP.

Since 1973 commercial banks and agricultural co-operatives have been required to deposit, interest free with the central bank, a specified minimum percentage of their liquid assets. The reserve requirements were six per cent from 1973 to 1977 and 10.5 per cent since 1977.

Liquidity and solvency ratios

Allied to the reserve requirements, banks and other credit institutions are required to maintain specified liquidity and solvency margins. The underlying principle is that credit institutions' own resources should be sufficient to cover the risks they undertake in the course of business.

For the commercial banks liquidity reserve requirements—defined as cash, government paper, call money and rediscounted bills of exchange—were set in 1973 at eight per cent of short-term deposits, with a provision for this to be raised to 14 per cent if necessary. Additionally, the banks are set a solvency target margin of free cash liquidity against liabilities which may fluctuate between one and four per cent. During 1979 the general level of free liquidity was around three to four per cent.

During periods of moderate expansion, the liquidity and solvency requirements are sufficient to maintain adequate liquidity in the banking system. During periods of excessive credit expansion the requirements are adjusted by the central bank in order to force banks to seek recourse to the discount facility to maintain liquidity.

When used, therefore, in conjunction with discount policy, the liquidity and solvency requirements may encourage banks to maintain an adequate balance between their liquid assets and their liabilities.

Discount policy

All banks have automatic recourse to the Nederlandsche Bank to rediscount treasury paper and commercial bills of exchange of less than three months' maturity. There are quota limits, introduced in 1973, on the extent to which banks may use the discount facility, and the central bank may also specify which short-term securities it will accept for discount, or which paper it will accept on security for an advance.

The rate at which such paper is rediscounted by the central bank, the discount rate, is an administered rate and is usually adjusted in increments of $\frac{1}{2}$ per cent. It influences bank rate, the rate at which banks will lend to first-class customers, and the whole structure of interest rates, although rates in the call and short-term deposit markets are more strongly influenced by international interest rates. Table 13.2 illustrates the descrepancies which can sometimes occur between the official discount rate and short-term money market rates.

If banks exceed their quota limits when seeking credit via the discount facility, then the excess credit is charged at discount rate plus two per cent. If the quota is exceeded by more than 50 per cent then the excess interest charge is higher still. The central bank has the ability to change the supplementary interest charges as part of its policy control. Outside the discount quota, banks and other near-bank financial institutions are able to borrow from the central bank against collateral—usually treasury paper. The rate of interest at which such loans may be granted is the official advance rate, which is generally set at 0.5 per cent above the official discount rate.

Qualitative and quantitive credit restrictions

The central bank also applies certain direct credit controls aimed at maintaining a balance between domestic and foreign capital and at maintaining overall liquidity in the system. Usually the controls are not subject to variation as part of monetary policy but their application obliges the banks to increase their capital and free reserve and to ensure that their own liquidity is managed prudently. Major direct controls are as follows:

Foreign assets and liabilities

Banks are required to balance their spot and forward positions in each foreign currency in order to control excessive external capital flows in relation to domestic liquidity. They are free to borrow from foreign sources as long as such spot indebtedness does not exceed their spot foreign assets by more than Dfl 5 million at any one time. The banks are required to report to the Nederlandsche Bank, twice monthly, giving the totals of their spot assets and liabilities in guilders and in each other currency, and their spot forward position in foreign currencies with both residents and non-residents.

287

Fixed assets rule   Another direct control is the 'fixed asset rule' which requires banks and credit institutions to maintain the total value of their fixed assets (defined as free capital and reserve plus subordinated bonds) to a maximum limit of their own capital resources. This has the effect of banks' seeking recourse to the capital market to finance their expansion of business.

Credit ceiling   Annual credit ceilings are also set for bank lending to the private sector of the economy. In 1979 these ceilings were set at eight and nine per cent for the larger and smaller banks respectively. The credit ceilings apply to new lending which is not financed from borrowing from the capital market. Where, for the economy as a whole, the desired growth of credit is exceeded, the particular banks responsible are subject to a penalty non-interest-earning reserve requirement of up to 50 per cent of the amount of the excess.

This also has the effect of diverting borrowing to the capital markets. Excess demand for credit cannot be met by the banks simply printing money but must be sought in the capital markets. This tends to push up interest rates in these markets and so acts to reduce credit demand.

The central bank may similarly restrict credit to the personal sector by requiring that banks, and the Post Office Bank, restrict their consumer credit to a maximum (15 per cent in 1979) of their previous year's level.

Open market operations

The central bank also uses, as a traditional method of indirect control, the instrument of open market operations which are used in conjunction with discount policy and liquidity policy.

The Bank operates in the domestic market either to ease or to squeeze liquidity by buying or selling securities in the money and capital markets.

In the money market it trades treasury paper and commercial bills with the banking system. In the capital market it buys or sells Dutch government or government guaranteed bonds which are officially quoted on the stock exchange.

In the international market the bank makes frequent use of spot or forward currency swaps, usually in US dollars, to ease or tighten domestic liquidity when the demand for guilders or the inflow of foreign capital cannot be easily accommodated by the banking system. Because of recent experience gained with the sensitivity of the guilder in foreign exchange markets the central bank has become very proficient at intervention and has both built up a complex understanding of the market and introduced some quite original tactics.

Withholding taxes

Interest earned on Dutch domestic securities is free of withholding tax.

Dividends are subject to withholding tax at a rate of 25 per cent, which is reduced in most cases to 15 per cent to residents of countries having tax treaties with the Netherlands. If a non-resident company owns a minimum of 25 per cent of the shareholding of a Dutch company, then the withholding tax on dividends is further reduced, except in the case of Luxembourg holding companies where the reduced rate does not apply.

Withholding taxes are summarized in Table 13.6.

Table 13.6 Withholding taxes

Recipient	Interest	Dividends	Dividends on holdings of 25% or more
Residents of non-treaty countries	0	25	25
Residents of tax-treaty countries	0		
Australia		15	15
Austria		15	0
Belgium		15	5
Czechoslovakia		10	0
Canada		15	0
Denmark		15	0
Finland		15	0
France		15	5
Germany		15	10
Hungary		25	25
Indonesia		15	5
Ireland		15	0
Israel		15	5
Italy		0	0
Japan		15	5
Luxembourg		15	2.5*
Malawi		15	5
Malta		15	5
Morocco		25	10
Netherlands Antilles		15	0
Norway		15	0
Poland		15	0
Singapore		15	0
South Africa		15	5
South Korea		15	10
Spain		15	5
Surinam		15	7.5
Sweden		15	0
Switzerland		15	0
Thailand		25	5
UK		15	5
USA		15	5
Zambia		15	5
Zimbabwe		15	5

* Except for holding companies.

Exchange controls

The Netherlands has relatively few exchange restrictions.

Authorities

The relevant authority is the central bank which is responsible for administration and supervision of exchange controls on behalf of the relevant government ministries.

Territory

The exchange control territory is the Netherlands and the Netherlands Antilles which are subject to a common system.

Currency

The currency is the Netherlands guilder, otherwise known as the Dutch florin and abbreviated to Dfl. The currency of the Netherlands Antilles is the Netherlands Antilles guilder (abbreviated to NAf) which is pegged to the US dollar at the rate of $1 = NAf 1.80. The guilder participates in the European Monetary System (EMS) and the authorities intervene in the foreign exchange market in order to maintain the predescribed margins of the EMS.

Authorized banks may buy or sell convertible and non-convertible currencies in both the spot and forward markets and are also free to deal with residents and non-residents in both markets.

Non-residents' accounts

Non-residents are free to open accounts with Dutch banks in guilders or any other currency and to make or receive payments within the Netherlands and to or from any other country. This includes the receipt of interest, dividends and amortized funds.

Transaction of securities

Non-residents, including the central banks of other countries, may not purchase treasury certificates or guilder banker acceptances. Non-residents are free to purchase all other guilder securities at official market exchange rates and in unrestricted amounts.

Proceeds from securities may be freely transferred in any convertible currency to any country. The securities themselves may be freely exported and, if held in the Netherlands, do not require to be deposited with an authorized depository.

Non-residents may also freely purchase unlisted securities such as Euroguilder bonds or private placements (onderhandse leningen).

Gold

There is a free gold market in Amsterdam in which residents and non-residents may freely purchase gold in any form or amount. No licence or formal registration is required. Transactions are, however, subject to value added tax at four per cent for gold bars and other unprocessed gold and 18 per cent on other forms of gold.

14. Norway

General market environment

The Norwegian financial system is highly regulated but during the late 1970s there developed a gradual tendency towards allowing the greater influence of free market forces. Although the authorities do not intervene in the money market directly, the banks and financial institutions still have very limited flexibility because of government monetary controls which limit and direct the supply of credit and, in particular, oblige the banks to hold large quantities of low-interest-bearing assets.

Until the mid 1970s interest rates in Norway were low as a deliberate consequence of monetary policy. The objective was to help house purchasers and encourage the maintenance of full employment. Control over money supply growth has now assumed greater importance, so interest rates have been allowed to rise and banks are now allowed to determine their own interest rates instead of their being directly controlled by the authorities.

Non-residents are restricted by exchange controls principally to the placing of deposits and the purchase of financial securities. Although the whole system of

Table 14.1 Summary of instruments

Instrument	Characteristics
MONEY MARKET	
Deposits	
call deposits	Demand deposits only. No structured market for short-term deposits but flexible market available through money brokers. The market for deposits in large denominations is good
time deposits	Majority for three months. Interest very low for lesser terms
treasury bills	Low yields. Seldom purchased by non-bank investors
CAPITAL MARKET	
Domestic bonds	Growing corporate bonds market. More than 95 per cent are government or government guaranteed bonds. Non-residents require prior approval from the central bank for purchases in excess of Nkr 1 million
Eurobonds	Small market in Eurokrone issues
Equities	Small but growing market

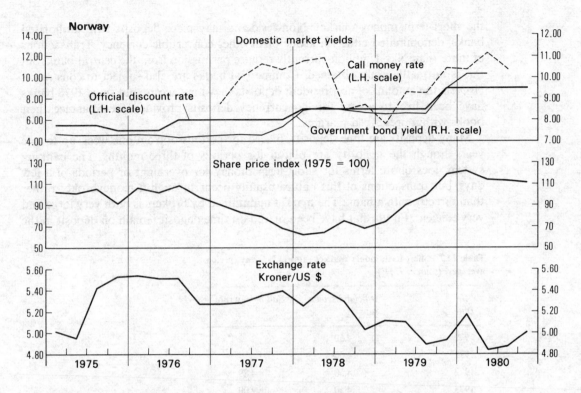

Norway

Domestic market yields

Call money rate (L.H. scale)

Official discount rate (L.H. scale)

Government bond yield (R.H. scale)

Share price index (1975 = 100)

Exchange rate Kroner/US $

1975   1976   1977   1978   1979   1980

exchange controls is likely to be revised in the near future, currently deposits or portfolio investments of Nkr 1 million or less may be made by non-residents without approval, but larger deposits require prior approval from the central bank (Norges Bank). This is normally readily granted in the case of portfolio investments of loans.

Withholding taxes apply only to dividends but not to interest.

The money market

Deposits

The market for call and time deposits is mainly an interbank market. The size of the market depends on liquidity in the domestic banking system which is affected by seasonal changes, the cost of alternative borrowing from the central bank and the level of foreign exchange transactions. The main seasonal effects are caused by the value added tax (VAT) payment dates at the end of every second month, and the oil tax payment dates semi-annually in April and October. At these times liquidity is squeezed and interest rates rise temporarily.

The domestic money market only started to gain importance in 1971, before which Norwegian financial institutions largely used facilities available in foreign money markets. Unlike the capital market, the authorities intervene very little in the short-term money market. Non-residents may place deposits with authorized banks, denominated either in krone or in other convertible currency. Transactions of more than Nkr 1 million currently require permission from the central bank, but this is normally easily obtained. Commercial banks are also subject to constraints *vis-à-vis* the amount of non-resident deposits they may accept, but since 1978 banks have been free to accept foreign currency deposits provided they balance their books within prescribed margins.

Many deposits are time deposits, placed for periods of from one week up to one year, though the majority are placed for periods of three months. The banking system does quote terms for short-term money for overnight or periods of a few days, but transactions of this nature usually occur through a moneybroker rather than directly with a bank. The market maintained by brokers is both very large and very efficient. Funds that have been placed on time deposit remain on deposit in the

Table 14.2 Short-term money market rates in Norway (period averages) (*source: IMF*)

Date	Official discount rate, %	Call money rate, %
1970	4.50	
1971	4.50	
1972	4.50	4.89
1973	4.50	7.00
1974	5.50	8.09
1975	5.0	7.53
1976	6.0	7.43
1977		
first quarter	6.0	7.50
second quarter	6.0	9.97
third quarter	6.0	11.20
fourth quarter	6.0	10.67
1978		
first quarter	7.0	11.43
second quarter	7.0	11.83
third quarter	7.0	6.87
fourth quarter	7.0	7.0
1979		
first quarter	7.0	5.60
second quarter	7.0	8.60
third quarter	7.0	8.53
fourth quarter	9.0	10.83
1980		
first quarter	9.0	10.73
second quarter	9.0	12.27
third quarter	9.0	10.16
fourth quarter	9.0	

banking system but may change hands several times through brokers acting as intermediaries between borrowers and lenders in the banking system.

Lenders of funds normally are given surety for repayment of loans in the form of either a bank guarantee or a guarantee from an insurance company. Interest rates on foreign currency deposits depend on rates prevailing in the international markets. Interest on krone time deposits now depends mainly on liquidity in the banking system. The government no longer pursues a policy of maintaining low interest rates. The commercial banks and savings banks are the only deposit taking institutions and since 1977 they have been free to set their own deposit and lending rates of interest. However, due to reserve requirements which force the banks to hold large amounts of low-interest-bearing securities, these deposit rates are lower than would otherwise be available under free market conditions. Interest rates since 1970 are shown in Table 14.2. It shows that since the interest rate agreement between banks was abolished in 1977, interest rates have risen significantly. Lending rates are generally double those for deposits.

Treasury bills

Treasury bills were introduced in 1971 primarily to be used as an instrument of the government in smoothing out temporary fluctuations in liquidity in the banking system and also as a source of short-term revenue as an alternative to borrowing from abroad.

Two types of treasury bills are issued. One type has terms that are planned to mature around the date when VAT payments are due, which occur every two months. Thus, companies may purchase the bills at issue when they have temporarily surplus funds and redeem them at maturity when liquidity becomes tighter because they are required to pay their VAT liabilities. The bills are issued at a discount with variable maturities of up to two months. Individual issues are for amounts of up to Nkr 500 million. The other type of treasury bill is issued for a fixed term of three months and with a fixed discount rate of interest. These are bought mostly by banks since they are the one instrument that yields a return and may also be included in their primary reserves.

Yields on treasury bills are relatively low, because the government obliges banks to purchase government paper through the implementation of reserve asset requirements. These low yields make them unattractive to non-bank investors. At the end of 1980 the government started to issue a new instrument known as liquidity paper, with the object of withdrawing liquidity from the banking system at times, between tax payment dates, when liquidity can be high. This paper is similar to treasury bills but carries a higher yield which, in 1980, was about 10 per cent. The issues have been readily taken up by the banks who are able to hold the bills in their reserve asset portfolios yet receive a relatively good return on their holdings.

The capital market

The Norwegian bond market is strictly regulated with respect to both the demand and the supply of bonds. On the supply side, the amounts which may be issued by the private sector and municipalities and the issue terms of bonds are stipulated by the authorities. Since September 1980 however, the corporate bond sector has been freed from some previous restrictions and has become very active. Borrowing by bond issues has increased in recent years because of the growth in lending to the private sector by state banks which is largely financed by bond issues.

The authorities also control the demand side of the bond market by requiring that the banks and financial institutions hold minimum amounts of bonds with respect to their total resources. This is known as the bond investment obligation and differs according to the type of financial institution. The ratio of bonds they are required to hold as a proportion of their total resources varies from 15 to 40 per cent. As a result of the bond investment obligation banks take up about half of all new bond issues and other financial institutions take up most of the remainder. Bond purchases that are not induced by government policy are negligible while only a very small proportion of new issues is taken up by the general public.

Corporate bonds

Private sector companies have been traditional borrowers in the bond market, attracted by regulated low interest rates. For balance of payments reasons however corporations, together with municipalities, were not allowed to borrow on the domestic bond market during 1978 and 1979 and therefore had to seek permission to borrow abroad. The bond market facility was restored to corporate and municipal borrowers in September 1980 up to a limit of Nkr 500 million with the provision that the government was able to increase its budget and reduce its net lending to the banks. Consequently Table 14.3 shows a significant decrease in the new bonds issued by municipalities and by companies that are included in the 'other bond' category for the years 1978 and 1979. The relaxed regulations resulted in a very active corporate sector new issues market at the end of 1979. Coupons were about 12 to 13 per cent, which proved attractive to both financial institutions and private investors. Initially the minimum size of corporate bond issue was Nkr 15 million but the large number of borrowers coming to the market resulted in the government raising this limit to Nkr 35 million in January 1981.

Table 14.3   Gross new issues of bonds by sector (millions of krone) (*source: Norges Bank Economic Bulletin 1980/81*)

	1974	1975	1976	1977	1978	1979
Central government	3769	4567	586	1756	6952	8624
State enterprises	125	145	245	175	60	90
Local authorities and municipalities	849	868	869	288	25	31
State banks	608	1938	1420	1194	1012	1050
Loan associations	1906	2998	4450	6110	2419	4135
Others	341	442	499	378	48	112
Total	7598	10958	8049	9901	10516	14042

The first issue of a convertible bond was made by Saga Petroleum in winter 1980. *Convertible bonds*
There are unlikely to be many convertible bond issues as the equity market is not
very active but certain companies, particularly in the oil and gas sector, do enjoy
active markets and are consequently able to attract lenders with convertible bond
issues.

Corporate bond interest rates ceased to be directly regulated by the authorities in
1977, but rates are still largely determined by the government: firstly, the government is the largest borrower in the bond market and thus the yield on government
bonds influences the yields on all other bonds; secondly, the amount and issue
terms of all new bond issues are still directly regulated by the authorities, which
ensures they continue to dominate the bond market; and thirdly, the bond investment obligation imposed by the government on banks and financial institutions
ensures that bonds are taken up regardless of unattractive yields. Nevertheless,
yields have risen in the last two or three years in line with the government's
changing attitude towards more market-determined interest levels.

The following table shows that the discount rate and government bond yield
have risen gradually over the past five years. The government no longer tries to
maintain low interest rates, though it does still attempt to maintain stability of
interest rates.

	1974	1975	1976	1977	1978	1979	1980
Discount rate	5.5	5.0	6.0	6.0	7.0	9.0	9.0
Government bond yield	7.0	7.29	7.25	7.39	8.45	8.59	10.73

The Section 15 Committee, affiliated to the Open Market Operations Committee, *Bond issuing authorities*
examines and determines, on behalf of the Ministry of Finance, the amount and
terms of all new bonds to be issued.

The central bank controls the purchase of Norwegian domestic bonds by non- *Non-resident investment*
residents. No official regulations are published, but most transactions by non-
residents seem to be limited to a maximum of Nkr 1 million, except in the case of
insurance companies or other companies that are able to demonstrate Norwegian
krone liabilities. The amount of bond investment allowed by such companies is
decided by the central bank on a case-by-case basis.

The secondary market is not very active, principally because although a large
proportion of bonds outstanding is held by financial institutions, most are held to
maturity and thus there is little turnover.

All Norwegian domestic bonds are bearer bonds.

Foreign bonds and Eurobonds

Due to the highly regulated nature of the Norwegian bond market, foreign borrowers do not seek access to the market. However Norwegian borrowers, including
the State of Norway, do issue bonds in foreign markets. Such bonds have been
issued in the domestic bond markets of the US, Luxembourg and Switzerland as

297

well as in the Eurobond market denominated in US dollars, Swiss francs, Dutch guilders, Deutschemark and Norwegian krone. There is a small market established in Norway, for the secondary trading of Norwegian krone Eurobonds, which may also be dealt through banks in other European financial centres.

At April 1981 there were eight Eurokrone issues outstanding, to a value of Nkr 720 million. The borrowers were Norwegian banks, an export credit company, a mortgage association and the City of Oslo.

As shown in Table 14.3, the central government and loan associations together account for by far the largest proportion of total bond issues. Most of the remainder are issued by public sector institutions such as the state banks and state enterprises.

Equities

The market in equity shares has been growing relative to the size of the bond market. Table 14.4 shows the value of the new issues for the last six years. In 1974 equity issues amounted to 10 per cent of all new capital raised (bond and equity issues) while by 1978 this proportion had grown to 14 per cent. For 1979 equities represented about 12 per cent of new capital raised. The secondary market, however, is not very active and only a small proportion of issues are bought by the public. The share price index has risen very little since 1975. At the end of 1980 the index had risen by only 11 per cent compared with its level at the end of 1975.

Table 14.4   New issues of shares (millions of krone) (source: Norges Bank Economic Bulletin 1980/81)

Shares	1974	1975	1976	1977	1978	1979
Mining and manufacture	480	373	251	718	526	301
Trade	110	179	134	277	187	514
Shipping	33	17	18	35	18	21
Other	253	886	969	598	971	509
Total	876	1455	1372	1624	1712	1345

However it fell substantially in 1977 and at September 1980 stood at a premium of 63 per cent relative to its level at the end of 1977. One of Norway's major industries is the oil and gas industry which is active in extraction from below the North Sea. Shares issued by companies in this sector have performed well in terms of earnings growth.

Non-residents are free to purchase Norwegian shares up to a limit of Nkr 1 million. Licences are required for larger investments in Norwegian shares: they are granted, if approved, by the central bank.

Stock exchange

There is a stock exchange at Oslo where shares and bonds are traded although bonds are also traded over-the-counter between banks and financial institutions.

Currencies are also quoted on the stock exchange in the spot market only, and particularly traded currencies are the Danish krone, Swedish krone, pound sterling, US and Canadian dollars, Deutschemark, Swiss franc, Dutch guilder, Belgian and French francs and Italian lire.

Gold

Although Norwegian residents may freely buy, sell and hold gold in any form there is no organized market for gold in Norway. The export of gold other than jewellery normally requires a special licence from the central bank: it would probably not be granted for the purpose of speculative investment.

Dealing and fees

Money market

There are no fees for placing deposits. Treasury bills may be dealt through a bank on a net basis. Dealing spreads are about $\frac{1}{8}$ per cent.

Capital market

Domestic bonds are traded on the stock exchange but transactions may be arranged through either a bank or a stockbroker. Dealing costs are the same in either case, i.e., commission charged is $\frac{1}{4}$ per cent of transacted value on both purchases and sales.

Eurobonds may only be purchased by non-residents and thus are dealt through Norwegian and other international banks. Eurobonds are dealt on a net basis with dealing spreads of about $\frac{1}{2}$ per cent.

Equities are traded on the stock exchange but may be dealt through either a bank or a stockbroker. Commission charges are $\frac{3}{4}$ per cent of transacted value for both purchases and sales.

Financial and monetary systems

Financial institutions

Considering that Norway has a population of only four million, it has a large number of banks. There are a variety of banking institutions in Norway, but only commercial banks and savings banks accept deposits. The remainder raise funds from central government and the bond market. The Banking Act makes very little distinction between commercial and savings banks, and both transact similar types of business. There is also a tendency towards mergers of the savings banks with the commercial banks.

Commercial banks

There are 25 domestic commercial banks which are structured as joint stock, privately owned companies. Three of these banks account for more than half of all

299

commercial bank resources. These banks, known as the 'big three', are Den norske Creditbank, Bergen Bank and Christiania Bank og Kreditkasse. Two of these are based in Oslo and one in Bergen. The remaining 22 are essentially regional banks based in each of the counties of Norway. There is a general trend of the regional banks merging with the big three. The commercial banks are primarily retail banks providing credit in the form of overdrafts and housing loans. By international standards, Norwegian banks are small and do not operate substantial branch networks. The commercial banks have combined assets of Nkr 80 billion but the largest of these, Den norske Creditbank, has assets of only Nkr 15 billion.

Savings banks

There are 350 savings banks with combined total assets of Nkr 60 billion. A few years ago there were over 500, but mergers and takeovers are continuously reducing the number. Some are publicly owned institutions, others are co-operatives and others are structured as joint stock companies with private shareholders. Like the commercial banks, they also accept deposits from the public, but provide generally longer-term credit than do the commercial banks. Larger in number, they are generally smaller in size than the commercial banks and provide essentially local banking facilities to individuals and small businesses.

State banks

There are nine state banks with combined assets of Nkr 93 billion. These are state owned institutions which raise money mainly through the bond market, and supply and credit to specific sectors of the economy. In this function, they are an important part of the credit market and account for half of the supply of credit from domestic sources. They represent a less significant proportion of total credit supply however, as foreign source credit is also important for the financing of major projects in Norway. Like all bond issues, the amount of funds they may raise is limited by loan commitment quotas to which they are subject.

Each of the nine state banks is responsible for supplying credit to one of the following sectors: housing, agriculture, industry, fisheries, municipalities, education, regional development, the post office and others.

The largest state bank is the Norwegian State Housing Bank which accounts for about 50 per cent of total loans from state banks and participates in 80 per cent of all new housing finance. The State Bank for Municipalities is the second largest which supplies 15 per cent of total state bank loans, and in 1978 provided Nkr 1700 million to local authorities and municipalities, compared with the Nkr 25 million which they raised directly through the bond market.

The state banks are the largest suppliers of credit to the private and local government sectors. Now accounting for over 50 per cent of domestic credit supply to these sectors they have been responsible for most of the growth of domestic credit expansion outside of the central government sector. Table 14.5 shows the change in the structure of the credit market between 1974 and 1979.

Table 14.5   Domestic credit supply to private and local government sectors
(*source: Norges Bank*)

Credit institution	1974 Credit supply (million krone)	1974 % of total	1979 Credit supply (million krone)	1979 % of total
State banks	3 937	30.6	12 150	50.8
Commercial and savings banks	4 971	38.7	5 550	23.2
Bond market and bond issuing loan associations	1 815	14.1	1 900	8.0
Other domestic credit supply	2 135	16.6	4 300	18.0
Total	12 858	100	23 900	100

Loan associations

The loan associations exercise a similar function to that of the state banks, but provide credit mainly to industry and housing. Loan associations are state owned and raise funds through the bond market, but are also subject to loan commitment quotas.

Other banks and financial institutions

In addition to the several hundred domestic banks there are almost 100 international banks in Norway offering a wide range of services. They are particularly important in supplying a large volume of credit to the Norwegian market which is

Table 14.6   Credit supply, 1976–1980, in millions of krone

	1976	1977	1978	1979	1980
Government banks	7.1	9.1	11.3	12.2	11.7
Commercial banks	4.4	5.7	2.8	2.6	3.2
Savings banks	3.5	4.1	2.9	2.4	2.6
Insurance companies	1.4	1.3	1.3	1.5	1.6
Domestic bond market	4.2	3.0	2.1	1.9	1.6
Stock market	0.9	0.7	0.8	0.8	1.1
Other	2.4	3.7	2.2	2.5	1.2
Total domestic sources	23.9	27.6	23.4	23.9	23.0
International borrowing	14.7	17.0	2.6	2.3	(2.5)
Total credit supply	38.6	44.6	26.0	26.2	20.5

too small to generate sufficient funds required for major projects such as, for example, oil rig installations. Other financial institutions include two large state owned non-deposit-taking banks, the Post Office Savings Bank and the Post Office Giro. Insurance companies and pension funds also play an important role as large holders of bonds and are subject to the government imposed bond investment obligation.

Central bank

The central bank, Norges Bank, has been established since 1816 and is a joint stock company that has been wholly owned by the government since 1949. The chairman and deputy chairman are permanent appointments made by the government. There are three other directors comprising the board which holds weekly meetings. Additionally there is a supervisory committee (comprising 15 members appointed for a six-year term) which holds quarterly meetings and is responsible for the Bank's administration.

The Norges Bank has twenty branches throughout Norway. It is the only issuer of notes and coin and advises the government on the use of policy instruments, although it is the Ministry of Finance which sets the quantitive targets for the supply of credit.

Three separate committees, which each contain members appointed by the Norges Bank, advise the Ministry on the terms and amounts of bonds to be issued; on the Norges Bank open market operations in the bond market; and on international monetary questions. These committees are the Section 15 Committee (derived from the Monetary and Credit Policy Act of 1865), the Open Market Committee and the Foreign Exchange Council.

Monetary policy

The Norges Bank, together with these three committees, comprise the monetary authorities which are directed by the Ministry of Finance. They administer the Finance Minister's credit policy which exerts an influence on all financial institutions and all markets. The Norwegian banking system is still strictly regulated in terms of both legislation and the influence of the authorities on the banks' governing bodies. Direct controls are implemented by the central bank and are obligatory for all banking institutions. Apart from the monetary instruments described below, current restrictions allow not more than one-third of the increase in the deposits of commercial banks to be lent to their customers. These constraints were introduced because the money supply has been growing too fast, caused by the fiscal deficit of the state and high bank lending to the public. In the years between the wars and the early 1970s the government was able to maintain stable economic growth and full employment by public spending during economic depressions. The depression caused by oil price increases has resulted in substantial budget deficits. The government has now realized that it cannot spend its way out of the current recession but must direct some policies to controlling the growth in the money supply. Direct restrictions inevitably put pressure on the banks' profitability which the government has attempted to alleviate by increasing new issues of treasury bills and bonds. It is intended that this will help establish a better balance on the credit market by bringing the conditions on the bond market more in line with the prevailing conditions in other sectors of the money and capital markets.

The primary objectives of monetary policy are to control the growth of total credit and to influence the quality and allocation of total credit supply to both the public and private sectors of the economy.

The main instruments of monetary policy are not market orientated, but are based on regulations and direct controls. These instruments are liquidity and reserve requirements, quotas for borrowing from the central bank, bond issue controls and the bond investment obligations.

Interest rates

Market instruments such as the discount rate and other interest rates are not used in a major way to influence monetary aggregates. This benefits the government which is the major borrower in the domestic market. Rates of interest such as the official discount rate change infrequently. The commercial banks, savings banks and life insurance companies have been allowed to set their own interest rates since 1977, but the abolition of previous direct controls has made little difference because other controls are still enforced which leave the aforementioned institutions with very little flexibility. The discount rate has little importance since the central bank does not discount securities to the banking system. It is used only as the base rate of interest for central bank lending to the banks, which is not done on an automatic recourse basis but on a controlled basis with the purpose of ironing out seasonal fluctuations in liquidity.

Liquidity and reserve ratios

The liquidity and reserve requirements are the major tool of monetary policy intended to directly influence central bank lending. There are two categories of reserve requirements—primary and secondary reserves. The primary liquidity reserves are defined as cash holdings, current account deposits with Norges Bank and with the Post Office Giro, holdings of treasury bills and, since January 1978, foreign currency loans to residents and non-residents.

These primary reserves must be held in a given proportion relative to total liabilities and apply to the commercial and savings banks but differ according to the location of the banks.

The ratio is changed frequently by the government as a major instrument of monetary policy aimed at directly influencing liquidity in the financial system. The frequency and extent of the changes is indicated below.

	Southern banks	Northern banks	Decree of
Commercial banks	3%	0%	29 June 1979
Savings banks	3%	0%	12 Oct. 1979
Commercial banks	6%	0%	14 Jan. 1979
Savings banks	10%	0%	14 Jan. 1979
Commercial banks	5%	0%	30 May 1980
Savings banks	8%	0%	30 May 1980
Commercial banks	13%	0%	1 Sep. 1980
Savings banks	10%	0%	1 Sep. 1980

Bond investment obligation

The secondary liquidity reserves are defined as holdings of government and government guaranteed bonds (which together account for more than 95 per cent of all bonds issued and outstanding) and corporate bonds. This secondary reserve requirement applies to all financial institutions which are required to hold a minimum proportion of their total liabilities in the form of such bonds. This regulation is known as the bond investment obligation. The relative obligations differ according to the type of institution and location.

BOND INVESTMENT OBLIGATION OF FINANCIAL INSTITUTIONS

	Southern	Northern	Base date	Decree of
Commercial and savings banks	60%	15%	Aug. 1979	11 Nov. 1979
Life insurance companies, municipal pension offices and pension funds	60%	30%	Mar. 1978	21 Apr. 1978

The commercial and savings banks must settle their books and make tax payments to the treasury at the end of every two-month period, while the remaining institutions settle quarterly.

Both the primary and secondary reserve requirements are subject to change as an instrument of government monetary policy. The primary reserve ratio is changed more frequently than the secondary reserve ratio which tends to be restated once a year. When there is excess liquidity in the economy, reserve requirements may be increased so that the banks and financial institutions are obliged to hold specified assets: this reduces the amount they can extend in credit and, through the bond investment obligation, directs a large proportion of bank funds into the public sector. Even when the converse applies and liquidity reserve requirements are reduced, the bond investment obligation still remains high, so credit is always directed towards the public sector at the expense of the private sector. The banks consequently complain that their flexibility with respect to their lending pro-grammes is severely restricted and that their competitive position with foreign banks for providing finance in Scandinavia is substantially reduced. The primary and secondary liquidity reserves oblige them to hold assets in low-interest-bearing securities. One effect of this is that a wide differential exists between the deposit rates and lending rates of interest charged by the commercial and savings banks. Normally, lending rates are approximately double their deposit rates.

Disclosure obligations

The commercial and savings banks, life and non-life insurance companies and the loan and mortgage associations are obliged to submit statements to the Norges Bank specifying the rates of interest and commission that they apply to their deposits and lending and any changes made. The commercial and savings banks have been free to set their own rates since 1977 and their rates are therefore higher than those of the other institutions whose rates are directly controlled by official policy.

Lending obligation

The banks experience a large inflow of funds because they are the only deposit-taking institutions. However, much of these deposits cannot be used for the advance of credit because the authorities determine ceilings for bank lending. For 1980 a ceiling of Nkr 6100 million was stipulated. This comprised a ceiling of Nkr 3250 million for the commercial banks and Nkr 2600 million for the savings banks, plus an additional Nkr 250 million for loans designed for environmental protection.

The lending of other institutions is controlled by ceilings applied to the amount of bond issues they may make. Since they do not accept deposits but raise money exclusively through bond issues, this regulation directly affects their lending programmes.

Withholding taxes

Withholding taxes are applied to dividends but not to interest. The standard rate is 25 per cent, but for residents of tax treaty countries this is reduced as shown in Table 14.7.

Exchange controls

Authorities

The Norges Bank, together with the Ministry of Commerce and Shipping, is responsible for the administration of exchange controls which, like the whole of the Norwegian financial system, is highly regulated.

Table 14.7 Withholding taxes

Recipient	Dividends %
Non-tax treaty countries	15
Tax-treaty countries	
Austria	15
Belgium	15
Brazil	25
Canada	15
Denmark	15
Egypt	15
Finland	15
France	10
Germany	15
Iceland	15
India	25
Ireland	10
Israel	15
Italy	25
Japan	15
Kenya	25
Malaysia	0
Malta	15
Morocco	15
Netherlands	15
Portugal	15
Singapore	0
Spain	15
Sri Lanka	5
Sweden	15
Switzerland	5
Tanzania	20
Thailand	25
Trinidad and Tobago	20
Turkey	25
United Kingdom	15
United States of America	15
Zambia	15

Currency

The currency is the Norwegian krone which since 12 December 1978 has been maintained against a basket of 12 currencies of Norway's major trading partners. The Foreign Exchange Committee, affiliated to the central bank, intervenes in these currencies in order to maintain the krone within defined margins.

Since November 1978 commercial banks have been required to balance their books for their spot and forward foreign exchange positions, and banks may now take covered positions in foreign currencies.

Non-resident accounts

Non-residents may open accounts in convertible krone and hold balances of up to Nkr 1 million. Except for insurance companies and selected other companies, balances greater than this amount require prior permission from the Norges Bank. Such accounts may be credited or debited with balances from or to other convertible krone accounts, with payments from or to other countries, or with proceeds from the sale of other convertible currency.

Authorized commercial banks may also accept non-resident accounts in other convertible currencies.

Purchase and sale of securities

Non-residents require approval from the Norges Bank to acquire Norwegian securities in amounts of more than Nkr 1 million. Such approval is normally easily obtained.

A licence from the central bank is also required for the transfer abroad of the proceeds from the sale of Norwegian securities. Such licences are readily granted so that in effect repatriation of capital may be freely made.

15. Sweden

Exchange controls insulate Sweden's domestic financial markets from foreign influence. The Swedish securities markets are virtually closed to non-resident borrowers and investors.

Credits to non-residents are severely restricted and domestic deposit-taking institutions are not permitted to make interest payments to non-residents.

These restrictions were originally designed for the protection of domestic monetary policy which is effected by the use of credit ceilings, interest rate controls, selective qualitative and quantitive credit controls and bond issue regulations. In recent years, however, this insularity has become increasingly necessary to combat a deteriorating balance of payments position.

Sweden's financial system comprises an unusual mix of public and private sector involvement. Its central bank, publicly owned but having all the major functions of a central bank, is the oldest central bank in the world. Sweden's largest commercial bank, the P.K. Bank, is state owned but all other commercial banks are privately owned. Similarly the National Pension Insurance Fund is state owned, but other insurance and pension funds are privately owned. The long-term credit institutions are jointly owned by the public and private sectors, but provide finance mainly to private sector industry.

Foreign institutions have severely restricted access to the Swedish market, including foreign banks which are few in number and may only establish representative offices in Sweden.

Non-residents holding Swedish krona may place these on call or time deposit with a major bank outside Sweden in one of the European financial centres such as London, Luxembourg, Switzerland or Paris. Rates of interest obtainable depend on supply and demand in the Euromarket and demand by each bank in particular to hold Swedish krona.

There also exists a small market in Euroconvertible bonds. As at May 1981 there were three issues outstanding; Aga $7\frac{3}{4}\%$ 1989, Esselte $7\frac{3}{4}\%$ 1989 and Sandvik 1988. The bonds are denominated in US dollars, in which interest is also paid, but are convertible into shares of the borrowing company at a fixed rate of exchange. Many companies listed on the Stockholm stock exchange have their shares designated into two categories—A and B shares: A shares are restricted and may only be purchased by Swedish residents; B shares are unrestricted and may be purchased by non-residents, but at a premium over the price of A shares. Swedish Eurobonds are convertible into B shares.

16. Switzerland

General market environment

Switzerland is constitutionally a confederation of states comprising 26 cantons which have sovereignty within the limits of the federal constitution. They are thus autonomous except in matters of state such as defence, communications and some aspects of the economy. Berne is the capital but Zurich is the major financial centre. Geneva and Basle are also significant financial centres, but mainly in the field of portfolio management.

The economy is based on the principle of free trade and, in general, inward and outward investment are unrestricted. Due to the strength of the economy and of the

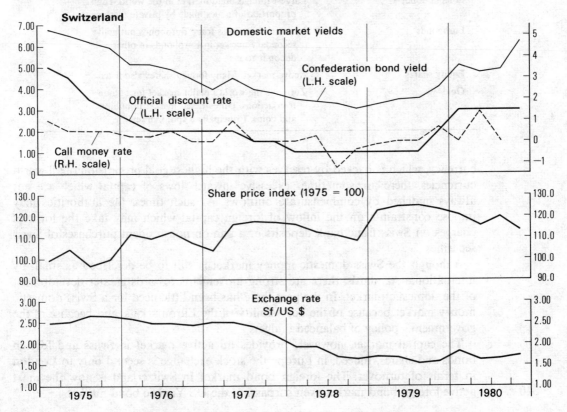

Switzerland

Domestic market yields

Confederation bond yield (L.H. scale)

Official discount rate (L.H. scale)

Call money rate (R.H. scale)

Share price index (1975 = 100)

Exchange rate Sf/US $

Table 16.1 Summary of instruments

Instrument	Characteristics
MONEY MARKET	
Deposits	
call deposits	Two-day call market in Swiss francs available in Eurocurrency market
time deposits	Interest rates low. Market subject to restrictions by authorities at times when inflow of foreign capital is excessive
fiduciary deposits	Deposits in Swiss francs or other currencies placed and managed by a Swiss bank in the Euromarkets
certificates of deposits	Non-marketable cash certificates issued. Introduction of negotiable CD market under review
CAPITAL MARKET	
Confederation bonds	Issued and guaranteed by the state
Cantonal and municipal bonds	Issued by autonomous, self-financing, local governments
Bonds of financial institutions	Issued by Swiss banks and mortgage finance houses
Corporate bonds	Active market in domestic corporate bonds
Foreign bonds	Largest foreign bond market in the world. High proportion of issues made by private placement
Eurobonds	No market in Swiss franc Eurobonds but active secondary market in Eurobonds of other denominations
Equity shares	Active market. Many foreign shares also listed
Gold	Zurich is the world's major market for bullion transactions. Unrestricted market in bullion and coins. Principally a spot market

currency, which is backed by reserves with the highest gold proportion of all world currencies, there are sometimes excessive inward flows of capital which are not always matched by commensurate outflows. At such times, the authorities may impose constraints on the inflow of foreign capital which may take the form of charges on Swiss franc bank deposits or a ban on non-resident purchases of Swiss securities.

Although the Swiss domestic money market is still to be described as small by international standards, there are strong movements towards greater development of the domestic market. In the past there has been little need for a Swiss domestic money market because of the accessibility of the Euromarkets, and because of the government's policy of balanced budgets.

The capital market, however, provides an active market in Swiss and foreign bonds and shares. Indeed, in Europe the stock exchange is second only to London in terms of turnover. The foreign bond market in Switzerland is now the most active foreign bond market even surpassing the US Yankee bond market.

Costs of dealing are minimal and comprehensive services are offered by the Swiss banks.

Withholding taxes apply to interest and dividends from domestic securities but these may be effectively reduced by double taxation treaties. Most foreign bonds are free of withholding tax to non-resident investors.

The money market

Deposits

The most important aspect of the Swiss money market is its internationalism and the dominant role of the international flows of funds which is facilitated by the banks' active participation. The domestic money market is small as compared with the money that flows to and from foreign markets. There are a number of reasons for such conditions. Firstly, the financial system is normally in a position of excess liquidity thereby reducing the need to generate domestic money market funds and often placing the banking system in the position of net lender. Secondly, the accessibility and facilities of the Euromarkets provide the Swiss banking system with suitable markets in which to lend or borrow. Thirdly, the financial requirements of the central government are small, such that the amount of paper issued is insufficient to justify the development of a domestic money market. Finally, businesses have little need to borrow by the issue of money market securities since they can adequately borrow from banks or foreign sources to meet their short-term liquidity needs.

Call deposits

As a consequence, the most important short-term market for the non-resident investor is the market for Eurocurrency call deposits.

Call deposits are usually made for periods of two or seven days. Interest rates on Eurocurrency call deposits depend on international rates determined by market supply and demand.

Since 1972 the Swiss monetary authorities have imposed restrictions during periods of excessive foreign capital inflows. These restrictions effectively prevented non-residents from placing Swiss franc call or time deposits. Such restrictions usually take the form of either an interest ban or of a negative interest rate charge on non-resident Swiss franc deposits (which has been as high as 10 per cent for deposits of less than three months). As from 31 August 1980 the last of these restrictions was abolished because, according to the Swiss Finance Minister, the Swiss economy was no longer disturbed or threatened by an excessive inflow of funds from abroad. The possibility that similar restrictions may again be imposed in the future still, however, exists. In such circumstances, the non-resident may invest Swiss francs in the Eurocurrency market or may engage in currency swap deposits.

311

Banks use Eurocurrency deposits to increase their loans and investments in Swiss francs, to increase the loans they themselves place at call with smaller Swiss banks, and to place Euro-Swissfrancs with other banks outside Switzerland. Swiss banks therefore are continuously engaging in spot and forward currency swaps.

As at December 1980 there were no restrictions on non-resident deposits in Swiss francs. When restrictions are in force it is possible for foreign institutions and individuals to engage also in currency swaps in order to invest in domestic Swiss francs. These are effected by the purchase in the first instance of Swiss francs on the foreign exchange market against, for example, US dollars. The Swiss francs are then sold in the spot market with a simultaneous repurchase forward against US dollars. Although the investor still retains US dollars, and it is the dollars that are in practice placed with a bank in Switzerland, he is deemed to be placing Swiss francs and receives the Swiss franc rate of interest. In fact, he receives the Euro-Swiss franc rate, which is higher than the domestic Swiss franc rate, because the currency swap takes place in the Eurocurrency market. Because the forward position is covered, however, he does not stand to gain or lose from changes in the relative exchange rate. Effectively, the transaction is like a repurchase agreement using currencies instead of securities. The investor sells Swiss francs with an agreement to buy these back at a future date. The price at which he buys them back is the same price at which he sold them plus a premium which represents the Euro-Swiss franc interest rate.

The Euro-Swiss franc market is one of the major Eurocurrency markets. Despite the reluctance of the Swiss authorities to encourage a market in externally held Swiss francs and despite also their wish that the Swiss franc should not be used as a

Table 16.2 Foreign currency positions of European banks (December 1980) (*source: Bank for International Settlements*)

Currency	Assets			Liabilities		
	Amount (US$) billion)	% of total	% of total non-dollar	Amount (US$) billion)	% of total	% of total non-dollar
US dollar	518.7	69.0	....	548.4	68.5	
Deutschemark	122.9	16.4	52.9	125.3	15.7	49.7
Swiss franc	49.6	6.6	21.3	51.6	6.4	20.5
Pound sterling	13.0	1.8	5.6	23.8	3.0	9.4
Dutch guilder	7.4	1.0	3.2	8.3	1.0	3.3
French franc	11.6	1.5	5.0	14.5	1.8	5.8
Yen	10.5	1.4	4.5	11.2	1.4	4.4
Belgian franc	5.9	0.8	2.5	3.7	0.5	1.5
Others	11.6	1.5	5.0	13.7	1.7	5.4
Total non-dollar	232.5	31.0	100.0	252.1	31.5	100.0
Total all currencies	751.2	100.0	....	800.5	100.0	

reserve currency, both foreign banks and non-bank investors continue to hold francs in their asset portfolios.

The Bank for International Settlements (BIS) shows that, at the end of December 1980, European banks held Swiss franc assets equivalent to US$49.6 billion and liabilities equivalent to US$51.6 billion. This represents over 20 per cent of both their non-dollar foreign currency assets and liabilities.

Next to the Deutschemark, which accounts for over 50 per cent of European banks' non-dollar external positions, the Swiss franc is the most widely held foreign currency (see Table 16.2). The Swiss franc assets and liabilities held by European banks represent over twice the volume of domestic Swiss franc assets and liabilities held by Swiss banks.

Time deposits

Swiss banks accept time deposits in Swiss francs or any other convertible currency, in periods of from one week up to one year or longer. Medium-term Swiss franc deposit rates are closely linked to the interest rate on promissory notes which are controlled by the National Bank. Domestic interest rates are fixed daily by agreement between the major banks acting in concert, while Eurocurrency time deposit interest rates depend on supply and demand in the international market. Swiss franc interest rates are traditionally low, principally because Switzerland's domestic rate of inflation is lower than that of most other countries and because of the surplus of investment funds which causes Switzerland to be a net exporter of capital. Investors have nevertheless chosen to hold Swiss francs because of the strong though volatile appreciation of the currency in recent years.

Call and time deposits are usually accepted in minimum denominations of Sfr 100 000 or its equivalent in other currencies, although for most banks a minimum of Sfr 500 000 is a more acceptable size for call deposits.

Certificates of deposits

There is as yet no secondary market in Swiss franc CDs. Short-term cash certificates of deposit have, at times, been issued by the major banks and the cantonal banks, on which interest is normally slightly higher than domestic time deposits (see Table 16.3). The certificates are, however, registered and non-transferable.

The National Bank is reviewing the possibility of establishing a market in negotiable certificates of deposit with maturities of between three months and one year. These would be issued in registered form and be subject to withholding tax.

Fiduciary deposits

Investors having a portfolio of currencies, or just one currency but not wishing to participate directly in their day-to-day management in the market, may place such funds with a Swiss bank in a fiduciary account. This is a managed account, invested by a Swiss bank in the Eurocurrency markets outside Switzerland on behalf of, and at the risk of, the client. A small commission is charged by the bank which is

313

Table 16.3 Swiss franc—interest rates and yields

	End 1976	End 1977	End 1978	1979 Jan.	Feb.	Mar.	Apr.	May	Jun.	Jul.	Aug.	Sep.	Oct.	Nov.	Dec.
Discount rate	2.00	1.50	1.00	1.00	1.00	1.00	1.00	1.00	1.00	1.00	1.00	1.0	1.0	2.0	2.0
Euro-Swiss franc two-day call deposits	.....	.....	−0.16	−6.06	−0.25	−0.13	0.25	1.25	.....	0.25	.....	.....	0.77	1.44	0.69
Euro-Swiss franc three-month time deposits	.....	.....	0.14	0.06	0.13	0.38	1.63	2.00	1.00	1.44	2.06	1.56	2.90	3.90	5.75
Domestic Swiss franc three-month time deposits	.....	.....	0.13	0.13	0.13	0.03	0.50	1.50	1.00	0.75	1.25	1.25	2.50	3.75	4.75
Cash certificates of major banks	.....	.....	2.52	2.52	2.27	2.27	2.61	3.00	3.00	3.00	3.25	3.25	3.50	3.50	3.50
Confederation bond yields	4.99	4.05	3.03	3.11	3.08	3.22	3.21	3.18	3.45	3.49	3.51	3.50	3.60	4.04	4.04
Cantonal bond yields	.....	.....	3.64	3.30	3.32	3.67	3.73	3.77	4.01	4.02	4.03	2.85	4.11	4.55	4.58

	End 1976	End 1977	End 1978	1980 Jan.	Feb.	Mar.	Apr.	May	Jun.	Jul.	Aug.	Sep.	Oct.	Nov.	Dec.
Discount rate	2.00	1.50	1.00	2.0	3.0	3.0	3.0	3.0	3.0	3.0	3.0	3.0	3.0	3.0	3.0
Euro-Swiss franc two-day call deposits	.....	.....	−0.16	.....	2.25	.....	3.25	0.13	1.38	2.75	2.25	2.50	2.50	1.00	0.10
Euro-Swiss franc three-month time deposits	.....	.....	0.14	5.44	5.63	6.94	6.00	5.50	5.63	5.38	5.81	5.94	5.44	6.06	5.50
Domestic Swiss franc three-month time deposits	.....	.....	0.13	5.00	5.00	5.75	5.50	4.75	4.75	4.75	4.75	5.00	4.75	4.75	5.75
Cash certificates of major banks	.....	.....	2.52	3.50	4.38	4.38	5.13	5.13	4.81	4.75	4.77	4.75	4.75	4.75	4.75
Confederation bond yields	4.99	4.05	3.03	4.48	4.72	5.10	4.97	4.82	4.72	4.60	4.87	4.87	4.69	4.68	4.73
Cantonal bond yields	.....	.....	3.64	4.71	4.79	5.34	5.18	4.79	4.81	4.73	4.94	5.07	5.01	4.87	4.90

usually $\frac{1}{2}$ to $\frac{5}{8}$ per cent of the amount invested. The authorities have been considering introducing a five per cent withholding tax on interest earned from fiduciary deposits but the banking system has put up stiff opposition to this proposal so that it has now been suspended.

Other money market instruments

There is virtually no other money market paper. The Swiss treasury occasionally issues three-month treasury bills but only to Swiss-based clients and banks.

The National Bank sometimes issues sterilization bonds in order to absorb excess liquidity, but they are non-marketable and are issued only to banks who have to deposit them with the National Bank for a few days over the balance sheet dates. The sterilization bonds thus provide a short-term investment alternative for the banks and temporarily reduces their operations in the foreign exchange market.

The capital market

The Swiss capital market adequately serves the country's domestic needs as well as providing considerable capital funds to foreign borrowers.

Share and bond issues represent 10 to 11 per cent of GNP, and 35 per cent of fixed capital formation. The size of the market is due to the presence of many foreign issuers who tap the market. This is because firstly the market accommodates a large inflow of funds from foreign lenders, secondly because borrowing costs are low, and thirdly because of the underwriting and placement power of the major banks and financial institutions.

The annual amount of new issues is however supervised by the Swiss Capital Market Commission, under the auspices of the Swiss National Bank, in order to prevent an excessive calendar of new issues.

Domestic bonds

Domestic bonds are issued by the federal government, the cantonal and municipal governments, financial institutions which comprise mainly banks and mortgage finance companies, and domestic companies.

Domestic bonds are issued in bearer form with minimum maturities of eight years. Units of denomination are Sfr 1000. Interest is paid semiannually and calculated on the basis of a 360-day year.

The majority of domestic bonds are brought to the market by means of public issues, though a number of private placements, particularly by financial institutions and companies, are also offered for sale.

All domestic bonds are subject to withholding tax on interest at a rate of 35 per cent except where this is reduced by double taxation treaties.

Confederation bonds

The federal government issues bonds on an irregular basis according to its requirement to fund extraordinary items of state expenditure. The state is, in most years, the smallest category of borrower, since central government debt does not play a dominant role in the economic activities of the country.

Most of the government bonds, known as confederation bonds, are issued publicly onto the market through the Swiss National Bank which acts as agent to the government in issuing and dealing in securities markets.

The bonds are issued and redeemed at par. Maturities may extend up to 15 years. Large issues may be amortized during the life of the loan, though most issues are callable by the government between two and five years prior to the final maturity date.

315

Table 16.4 Gross new securities issued on Swiss capital market (Sfr million)

Securities	1975	1976	1977	1978	1979	1980
BONDS						
Confederation bonds						
public issues	1 051	2 729	499	0	851	1 222
private placements	848	1 727	0	0	0	0
Cantonal bonds						
public issues	1 776	1 329	1 335	1 452	1 544	983
private placements	254	87	87	61	6	5
Banks and mortgage finance houses						
public issues	1 281	1 513	2 375	3 534	3 899	5 363
private placements	142	77	70	391	151	147
Companies						
public issues	3 252	2 819	2 506	4 086	3 400	1 861
private placements	504	85	264	188	163	21
Total domestic bonds						
public issues	7 361	8 390	6 714	9 072	9 694	9 429
private placements	1 747	1 976	421	641	326	173
Foreign bonds						
public issues	2 490	3 510	3 684	4 430	5 206	5 486
private placements	6 496	9 902	7 972	8 336	10 231	4 788*
Total bonds						
public issues	9 851	11 900	10 398	13 502	14 900	14 913
private placements	8 243	11 878	8 393	8 977	10 557	4 961*
SHARES						
Banks and insurance companies						
public issues	741	1 310	281	864	850	1 805
Non-financial companies						
public issues	349	224	461	226	499	463
Financial institutions and companies						
private placements	1 603	1 654	1 987	1 485	662	0
Total shares issued	2 693	3 189	2 729	2 575	2 011	2 268

* First nine months of 1980 only.

New issue sizes may be up to Sfr 500 million and the bonds enjoy a fairly good market in the first few months after issue when it is normally possible to deal in amounts of up to Sfr 1 million. After a few months, however, the bonds tend to be closely held by all types of investors and purchasing in the secondary market then becomes more difficult.

Being government securities, confederation bonds are fully guaranteed as to interest and principal by the state. Interest from confederation bonds is subject to withholding tax for non-resident investors.

Cantonal and municipal bonds

The 26 cantons are self-regulating autonomous states. The federal government is responsible principally for expenditure of a national nature, such as defence, while the cantons directly finance most of their own administrative and public welfare expenditure. Funds are raised by local taxation, augmented by bond issues on the capital market. In most years, therefore, local government bond issues are greater than confederation bond issues and, like confederation bonds, the majority are public issues. They are similar too in most other respects. Cantonal and municipal bonds have original maturities of up to 15 years though they may be redeemed up to five years prior to maturity. They are issued and redeemed at par and carry fixed-rate coupons, payable semi-annually. Their marketability also is better within the first few months of issue.

The securities are not guaranteed by the state but constitute a charge on the issuing canton or municipality. Thus, the bonds commonly yield up to one percentage point more than confederation bonds of comparable terms. In the Swiss capital market, this is quite significant, representing a return of up to 25 per cent greater than investment in confederation bonds.

Bonds of financial institutions

The bond issuing financial institutions comprise mainly the major national and international Swiss banks, the cantonal banks and the mortgage bond issuing houses. The banks issue over half of the bonds in the category issuing in recent years between Sfr 1.5 billion and Sfr 2 billion of new bonds per annum. At the end of 1980, Swiss banks together had outstanding bond issues to the value of approximately Sfr 55 billion. The Swiss banks are the major agents in the country's current role as a major European financial centre and a net exporter of capital. They are major participants in syndicated Eurocredit lending and in order to expand this business as well as to remain at the forefront of this field of international banking they issue bonds to augment their deposit liabilities, most of which are fairly short-term deposits. The banks may only issue bonds within specific limits relating to their capital and free reserves. The bonds are not secured against specific assets but constitute a charge on the general assets of the issuing bank.

One category of bonds issued by the Swiss banks are known as Kassenobliga- *Kassen-* tionen. These have original maturities of between 3 and 15 years. They are bearer *obligationen* securities, dealable in minimum denominations of Sfr 1000. While they are negotiable, they are normally sold back to the issuing bank and are not actively traded in the secondary market.

The mortgage bond issuing houses are the major sources of mortgage finance for *Pfandbrief* households and businesses in Switzerland. Though they also accept savings deposits, much of the funds they require in order to grant mortgage loans is raised through public issues of bonds, known as Pfandbrief. The bonds are secured against a general pool of mortgaged property.

317

Bonds in this category also have maturities of up to 15 years though bank bonds are generally of about 10 years' life, with normally the possibility of redemption prior to final maturity. They are issued and redeemed at par, with semiannual coupon dates, and are dealable in denominations of Sfr 1000. Yields are on average up to 50 basis points higher than those available on cantonal bonds.

Corporate bonds

The corporate sector in Switzerland is fairly small but nevertheless the annual value of bond issues by companies equals that of the financial sector. Included in the corporate sector are utilities companies which are privately owned corporations.

Companies issue three types of bonds: straight bonds, with maturities of up to 15 years; convertible bonds, with the option on the part of the holder to convert into ordinary shares or participation certificates of the issuing company on terms specified at issue; and option bonds which carry an option for the bondholder to purchase shares or participation certificates in the issuing company at a predetermined price.

Corporate bond terms are the same as for other bonds. That is, they are issued and redeemed at par, carry semiannual coupon dates, have fixed rate coupons, and are tradeable in unit denominations of Sfr 1000.

The secondary market is fairly active with most trading taking place on the floors of the stock exchanges, though some dealing also takes place in the over-the-counter market made by brokers and banks who are licensed to deal in securities. Corporate bond yields may be as much as 1.5 to 2 per cent greater than yields obtainable on confederation bonds.

Foreign bonds

The foreign bond market is the most important aspect of the Swiss capital market for the non-resident investor. Table 16.4 shows that foreign bonds are the largest component of new issues each year and that in most years the volume of foreign bonds exceeds all other issues of domestic bonds. Furthermore, Table 16.5 shows that Switzerland has now become the major market in which foreign bonds are issued, accounting for over 40 per cent of the total world market. It overtook the US yankee bond market in 1978, since when more than twice the volume of issues has been made in Switzerland than in the US.

Even so, the figures understate the importance of the Swiss capital market as an international centre. In addition to the public and private placement bonds Swiss banks grant large volumes of short-, medium- and long-term Eurocredits, denominated in Swiss francs which have grown in volume from Sfr 2.5 billion in 1975 to about Sfr 10 billion at the end of 1979.

Foreign bonds are bonds issued by foreign borrowers on the Swiss domestic capital market and are denominated in Swiss francs. The borrowers are foreign corporations, foreign sovereign states and international agencies. They originate from all over the world. For example, of the Sfr 13.1 billion foreign bonds issued in 1980, Sfr 10.5 billion were issued by borrowers from OECD countries, Sfr 0.1 billion

Table 16.5 Swiss foreign bond market—international comparison (US$ million) (*source: OECD*)

Year	Foreign bonds—country of issue					Total	Swiss foreign bond market as % of total
	Switzerland	US	Germany	Japan	All other markets		
1970	312.5	1 405.3	381.1	216.7	130.2	2 445.8	12.8
1971	867.1	1 342.7	391.7	334.3	555.0	3 490.8	24.8
1972	1014.5	1 575.1	575.6	635.8	583.6	4 384.6	23.1
1973	1535.3	1 487.5	626.9	782.4	917.7	5 349.8	28.7
1974	972.4	3 546.8	260.5	196.2	2746.9	7 722.8	12.5
1975	3529.0	6 854.6	604.9	341.5	970.8	12 300.8	28.7
1976	5443.5	10 631.6	1309.3	287.3	1271.5	18 943.3	28.7
1977	4959.3	7 668.2	1511.1	1393.5	1078.1	16 610.2	29.8
1978	7608.9	6 358.6	1676.8	4686.0	1211.8	21 542.1	35.3
1979	9479.5	4 364.6	2615.1	2655.3	865.1	19 979.6	47.4
1980	7454.7	2 796.4	4800.0	1164.6	1243.2	17 458.9	42.7

by borrowers from oil exporting countries, Sfr 0.2 billion from other developing countries, Sfr 0.3 billion from other countries and Sfr 2.0 billion by international agencies such as the World Bank, Euratom and the EIB. The largest single category of borrower on the Swiss foreign bond market is that of Japanese companies. In 1980 the Japanese issued Sfr 3.6 billion Swiss franc foreign bonds, of which about Sfr 3 billion were private placements, of which about three quarters were convertible notes and the remainder were straight bonds or notes.

Foreign borrowers come to the Swiss market because both interest rates and borrowing costs are low. The large Swiss banks, however, allow first-class borrowers only to the market. Thus issuing bonds in Switzerland can be regarded as a test for the international acceptability of a borrower. Lenders can be confident that the credit risk is good while borrowers earn considerable international prestige by being admitted to the market.

Public issues

Table 16.4 shows that about one-third of total domestic and foreign bond issues are public issues and two-thirds are private placements. Public issues are accompanied by prior advertising in the press with a detailed prospectus being printed in newspapers and circulated to potential investors. Most are straight bearer bonds with fixed-rate coupons payable annually on the basis of a 360-day year. Most maturities are medium to long with original lives of 10 to 15 years. Convertible bonds may also be offered by public issue, though these are less common. Units of denomination are Sfr 5000 or Sfr 10 000.

Individual bond issues are in sizes of up to Sfr 150 million. Issues of over Sfr 10 million must first be authorized by the Swiss National Bank and must join a queue of borrowers waiting to issue bonds. An active secondary market exists for publicly issued bonds which are all quoted and traded on the stock exchanges.

As at December 1979 there were approximately 400 bonds issued by over 350 foreign borrowers quoted on the Zurich stock exchange with a market value of about Sfr 30 billion.

Private placements

Private placements are loan issues managed by a consortium of banks who place the issues directly with their own customers. No publicity may accompany the issue which also means that no prospectus is issued. Unlike public issues, private placements may not be sold to foreign banks, central banks or states, excepting issues made by international agencies.

No secondary market exists for private placement issues, it being intended that the lenders hold the bonds to maturity. In exceptional circumstances it is possible to sell them back to the issuing banks who must then resell them to their own circle of customers. Unlike public issues, the securities are not delivered to the investors or to other non-syndicate banks but are held in custody by the managing banks on behalf of their customers. Minimum denominations of private placement issues are Sfr 50 000, which limits their attractiveness to a special category of larger investor.

Because they are held to maturity, most private placements take the form of notes. These are of shorter maturity than bonds. They must have a life of not less than three years and not more than eight. Premature repayment is allowed either after two years or after half the life of the notes has expired, whichever is the longer. Private placements are attractive to borrowers because they can be issued far more quickly than a public offering since there is no queuing procedure and preparations are a lot easier to manage. Also, because there is no advertising, costs are considerably lower. Lenders, on the other hand, receive a better yield than available on public issues reflecting the fact that private placements are non-marketable securities. Coupons are normally $\frac{1}{4}$ to $\frac{3}{8}$ per cent higher than those for comparable publicly issued bonds.

Convertible notes and bonds

A large number of convertible notes are issued by private placement, particularly by Japanese borrowers who issued more than three-quarters of their private placement notes by this method in 1978 and 1979.

Convertible notes, like convertible bonds, carry a lower coupon than straight notes or bonds but give the holder the option to convert into shares of the issuing corporation. The shares are, of course, denominated in the borrower's domestic currency and listed on the relevant domestic capital market. In the case of Swiss notes or bonds convertible into yen shares for example, in the past the investor has been able indirectly to participate in both the thriving Japanese equity market and strong appreciation of the yen, even against the Swiss franc. There is a risk, however, that the exchange rate and equity market differentials will not move in favour of the investor, in which case his convertible option becomes worthless as the price of publicly issued bonds in the secondary market reflects both exchange rate movements and the performance of the issuer's share price in his own domestic market.

Eurobonds

There is no primary market in Euro-Swissfranc bonds. The National Bank is opposed to the development of a capital market in Swiss francs outside Switzerland.

There is however an active secondary market in Eurobonds denominated in other currencies. A wide range of Eurobonds denominated in other Eurocurrencies is listed and traded on the stock exchanges. They may also be traded over-the-counter through banks and brokers licensed to deal in securities. Euroguilder notes, being of short maturity, are only traded over the counter in Switzerland.

The major Swiss banks are very active in the primary Eurobond issuing market, regularly lead managing or participating in bank syndications for the international issue of new Eurobonds.

Equity shares

There is an active market in shares quoted on the stock exchanges. There are over 200 issues outstanding, 60 per cent of which are Swiss franc issues by foreign companies and all are actively traded.

The Swiss companies listed comprise about 10 per cent banks, 20 per cent Swiss holding companies, 15 per cent insurance companies and the remainder, industrial and miscellaneous companies. The foreign companies listed include those from Australia, Belgium, Luxembourg, Germany, France, the Netherlands, the UK, Japan, Canada, South Africa, and the US, the US group representing about 20 per cent of the total equity market.

In the main equity shares are of bearer form but a few, particularly those of Swiss insurance companies, are registered. Non-residents are not generally permitted to purchase registered shares.

Swiss companies issue two types of shares—ordinary shares and participation certificates. Ordinary shares carry full dividend and voting rights.

Participation certificates

These are equity-type securities with the same property rights as equity shares but without voting rights. Dividend right certificates are similar to participation certificates allowing the holder predetermined dividend but not voting rights; these may both be purchased by non-residents.

Share purchase warrants

These are warrants issued usually to bondholders, entitling the holder to subscribe to shares of participation certificates of the issuing company. The terms are fixed at the date of issue of the warrants which normally may be held for an indefinite period, or may be sold in the market. Non-residents may also purchase share warrants but a distinction is made between warrants for bearer shares and warrants for registered shares.

Mutual funds

There are several quoted mutual funds, some of which are equity funds, and some which are property funds. An additional fund investing in bonds is not quoted but is traded 'over the counter'. The advantage of such funds is that they give the investor the opportunity to invest in a balanced portfolio. They spread risks, provide professional investment management, convenience, low cost and legal protection. The various types of funds meet an extremely wide range of investment needs. They make annual distribution of profits and dividends.

The stock exchanges

There are seven stock exchanges in Switzerland, the larger ones being based in Zurich, Basle, Geneva and Berne. Of all the European exchanges the Zurich exchange is second to London in terms of trading volume. The greatest activity is generated in the market for bonds. In terms of equity turnover, the Zurich exchange ranks third in Europe and sixth in the world. The call-over system is used whereby dealers call out their bid or offer prices and transactions are matched accordingly. The dealers who are members of the exchanges comprise both specialized stockbrokers and banks who are licensed to deal in securities. In practice, all the major banks have such licences.

The stock exchanges are controlled by the authorities of the particular canton in which each is located.

Most transactions in shares and bonds take place on the floor of the exchange. They may also be traded in the over-the-counter market since banks and brokers are permitted to deal on their own account, and usually maintain their own books in the major and more active securities. Eurobonds especially tend to be traded in this way.

Although London is the world's major price-fixing centre for gold, and New York provides the major futures market, Zurich is the home of the gold pool and the centre through which probably the largest volume of gold bullion turnover is transacted. Apart from the US dollar, the Swiss franc is the only currency in which gold is internationally quoted.

In 1980 the supply of gold to the non-communist private sector (excluding central banks' purchases of official reserves) was 1704 tonnes, of which 521 tonnes were used for fabrication. The remainder, 1183 tonnes, represented net private purchases (purchases less sales) of gold bullion. The largest proportion of this is estimated to have been transacted through banks in Switzerland.

Of the physical bullion flows estimated at 1522 tonnes in 1979, 1119 tonnes of bullion flowed into Europe from the gold-producing countries, and 360 tonnes were distributed out from Europe to other countries; the major volume of this turnover was transacted through Zurich. In 1980 private bullion flows were 942 tonnes, but due to a fall in the price of gold only 23 tonnes were distributed out from Europe.

The gold market in Zurich is open to all types of purchasers whether resident or non-resident. Gold may be bought, sold or held in any form. The Zurich market deals mainly in spot transactions. There is no futures or options market established, though it is possible to arrange forward transactions on a private basis with individual banks or bullion dealers. One bank Crédit Suisse-White Weld also offers gold options on a private basis.

Bars may be purchased in sizes as small as five grams or as large as one kilogram, all with fineness of 999.9 g per kilo. Silver bars also may be purchased in sizes of from 10 grams to one kilogram.

A wide variety of gold coins, issued by countries throughout the world, may also be purchased in Zurich. Three Swiss gold coins are widely traded—the 20-franc Vreneli (5.8 g of fine gold) which is the most popularly traded Swiss gold coin, the 20-franc Helvetia (5.8 g of fine gold) which was the first gold coin to be minted after the founding of the Swiss Confederation; and the 10-franc Vreneli (2.9 g of fine gold) which commands a price at a premium to the value of its gold content, having been minted in limited quantity.

No licences are required for the purchase or export of gold, and no customs duties or taxes of any kind are imposed on exports of gold of any kind. (Imports of manufactured gold, such as jewellery, are subject to customs duty.) Since January 1980 all sales of gold bullion have been subject to a sales tax of 5.6 per cent of the value of the sale. This has resulted in some business, which would otherwise have been conducted in Switzerland, moving to the London market.

Dealing and fees

Money market

Call and time deposits may be placed with any of the Swiss banks or foreign and international banks with branches in Switzerland.

Amounts are generally Sfr 100000 or more, or its rounded equivalent for Eurocurrency deposits (e.g., £25000, $50000).

No fee is charged but the bank's commission is included in the offered interest rate.

For fiduciary deposits, a small commission is charged of usually $\frac{1}{4}$ or $\frac{3}{8}$ per cent on amounts invested, since such deposits resemble managed portfolios.

Capital market

Domestic bonds, foreign bonds, shares and Eurobonds are all listed on the domestic stock exchanges. They may be dealt through a stockbroker but since all the major Swiss banks are also licensed members of the stock exchanges it is often simpler for a non-resident to deal through one of the Swiss banks. Brokerage and commission fees are the same whether charged by a bank or a broker.

Basic fees which are set under the Swiss Banking Convention are as follows:

BROKERAGE AND STAMP DUTY

Security	Brokerage	Federal stamp duty	Cantonal stamp duty
Swiss bonds	0.375%	0.05%	0.15%
Foreign bonds	0.500%	0.10%	0.15%
Shares			
less than Sfr 150 per share	1.00%	0.05% Swiss shares	0.15%
more than Sfr 150 per share	0.625%	0.10% foreign shares	0.15%

Notes: 1. The fees for foreign bonds include Eurobonds if traded on the stock exchange.
2. The cantonal duty shown is that for Zurich, Basle and Geneva.

Eurobonds

Though Eurobonds may be dealt on the stock exchange most transactions are effected over the counter in the market maintained by the banks. If dealt in this way no specific brokerage is charged but the dealer's commission is included in the spread between his quoted bid and offer prices. Dealing spreads are about 0.25 per cent depending on market conditions.

Gold

Gold may be bought and sold through any major Swiss bank. The bank's quoted price for dealing will include a small commission. The rate of the commission narrows as the quantity being dealt increases. For large amounts commission is $\frac{1}{16}$ to $\frac{1}{8}$ per cent of the consideration.

Commissions on gold coins are generally higher than those for gold bullion.

Settlement and delivery

Settlement and delivery of securities and of gold is normally for cash, taking place the business day following the date of the transaction.

The Zurich stock exchange does however accommodate forward settlement and delivery, dealing to the end of the month, but by negotiation.

Financial and monetary systems

Financial institutions

The major type of financial institution in Switzerland is, of course, the banks. Switzerland harbours a large number and many types of banks. There are approximately 550 banks with over 5000 branches in Switzerland. The variety of banks

324

comprise commercial, co-operative, cantonal, local, mortgage, private and foreign banks.

Most banks engage in all types of banking business though they also specialize in specific areas of banking.

Commercial banks

The commercial banks are multipurpose banks. They accept deposits, grant loans and credit to commerce and industry, manage and underwrite new security issues, deal in securities for clients and on their own account, and act as portfolio managers and investment advisors.

The major share of banking business in Switzerland (Sfr 215 billion in 1979) is controlled by the 'Big Five' banks; the Swiss Bank Corporation in Basle, the Union Bank and Crédit Suisse in Zurich, the Swiss Volksbank in Berne and the Bank Leu in Zurich. Four of these banks are joint stock companies; Swiss Volksbank is a co-operative bank. They are all international banks and not only have branches throughout Switzerland but also abroad. The largest three in particular have branches or representative offices in every financial centre of the world. They are also the major participants in the capital market, underwriting the majority of public issues floated in Switzerland.

Cantonal banks

The 29 cantonal banks provide mainly a domestic service to residents. They are publicly owned institutions whose major activities are to collect deposits and grant loans and credit to local individuals, businesses and the cantonal authorities.

Savings banks

There are 223 regional and savings banks, which likewise provide domestic banking services, and which are privately owned. In this group the mortgage banks are also included. Banks within this category primarily collect small savings and grant loans for mortgages and other domestic credit.

Private banks

Private banks are the oldest type of bank in Switzerland, though they represent a small share of the mainstream banking business. There are 25 private banks which are normally established in the form of partnerships or as limited companies with closely held equity, and deal principally with private customers. They undertake most forms of banking activities but do not advertise publicly for deposits. Their main type of business is in the field of portfolio management, but they are also very active in the private placement of foreign bond and Eurobond issues.

Foreign banks

There are a growing number of foreign banks establishing branches or representative offices in Switzerland. There are currently about 15 branches and 50 representative offices of foreign banks. Foreign bank branches may carry out most banking business but are active mainly in the capital market. Representative offices cannot transact business in Switzerland but, by maintaining a presence in Switzerland, can promote the general domestic business of their parent bank.

Other financial institutions

Other financial institutions include loan associations, financial companies and mortgage bond issuing houses.

The loan associations are co-operative banks whose function is to collect savings from their members who are individuals, farmers and small businesses in small communities throughout the country. The associations also grant credit to their members especially where such loans benefit the general welfare of local communities. There are two major groups of these co-operative banks organized as follows: 1190 within the Swiss Federation of Rauffersakassen and 14 mutual loan associations within the Federation Vaudoise.

Finance companies specialize in corporate finance and participate in the syndicated management and underwriting of public bond and share issues. They do not undertake general banking, such as providing demand deposits and chequing account facilities, but some do publicly advertise for time deposits.

There are over 70 finance companies in Switzerland. The mortgage bond issuing houses are privately owned finance companies that provide mortgage finance to individuals and businesses and obtain a major proportion of their funds through the issue of bonds in the capital market.

Central bank

The central bank, the Swiss National Bank, is a privately owned joint stock bank, although only Swiss companies and citizens are allowed to purchase its shares. It has its headquarters in Berne and Zurich and sub-branches in several principal cities.

The National Bank is the only issuer of notes and coins although, prior to 1907, there were 36 banks of issue in each of the different cantons.

The National Bank has several governing and controlling boards, each of which has government representation. The Bank Council is responsible for the broad supervision of the Bank and comprises a majority of members who are appointed by the federal government.

Another board, the Bank Committee, is responsible for the more detailed control of the Bank's operations. It helps to formulate interest-rate policy and puts forward recommendations for the selection of members and principal officers of the Directorate.

The Directorate is the Bank's highest executive and managing group. It is responsible for fixing the discount rate and other interest rates and for supervising money and capital markets. It makes policy recommendations regarding these markets at weekly meetings in Zurich.

Monetary policy

The National Bank is charged with responsibility to safeguard the gold value of the Swiss franc and to maintain the internal and external value of the currency. These objectives are commensurate with the main objectives of economic policy which are to control inflation and the money supply at a rate compatible with the growth of GNP. The main methods used to achieve these objectives are monetary regulations applied within the framework of the banking laws.

Swiss banking convention banking ordinance

There are numerous banking laws within the framework of the Swiss banking convention. Such laws are known severally as the banking ordinance.

The Banking Ordinance defines an organizational structure for the National Bank and the relationship between the National Bank and the federal government. Government representation and controlling boards of the National Bank ensure that the Bank's specific functions in the area of monetary policy are determined by the government.

The laws specify that the National Bank be responsible for implementation of the major policy instruments which are reserve requirements, control and monitoring of the commercial banks' foreign currency positions, implementation of controls with respect to non-resident funds in Switzerland, and control over the public issue of bonds.

All banks that are licensed to carry out banking business in Switzerland are governed by the Banking Ordinance and thus are responsible to the National Bank and indirectly to the federal government. For each type of financial institution, the limits of its activities are defined. Banks and financial institutions must comply with any National Bank restrictions on the extension of credit, and with special rules on savings deposits and customer protection in the event of bankruptcies.

Interest and exchange rates

Between the government, the Federal Banking Commission, the Swiss National Bank and the banks themselves, there is close co-operation. One important way in which this manifests itself is the fixing of interest and exchange rates.

Every morning of each business day, representatives from the major banks and from the National Bank meet and determine key interest rates to be charged and paid by the banks on various types of loans and deposits. Having decided on particular rates, the smaller banks (which are signatories of the convention) are obliged to follow the lead taken by the major banks.

The same procedure is adopted for the exchange value of the Swiss franc *vis-à-vis* other major currencies for transactions below $100 000 between Switzerland and the foreign exchange markets.

Banking secrecy

Another important aspect of the Swiss banking convention is strict banking secrecy. This largely had its origin at the end of the first world war when there was a flight of capital out of several European countries, particularly those with high post-war inflation. In order to attract and retain this business Swiss bankers undertook not to disclose the names of their customers and depositors, many of whom were avoiding their domestic exchange control regulations. Swiss bankers also prefer a minimum of interference from governments and regulatory authorities and for that reason also prefer not to disclose too much detail about the nature of their business. Today, Swiss bankers maintain that the relationship between a client and his banker is a professional relationship—like that with a lawyer or a doctor—and that personal details such as names of clients and the size of their accounts should not be disclosed to third parties.

Banking secrecy gives an added aspect of security and is largely responsible for Switzerland's international reputation as a safe haven for non-resident capital.

Few monetary controls are enforced by statute. Monetary policy is principally effected by close co-operation between the Swiss National Bank and the banking system. As stated before the major controls used are reserve requirements, control of the banks' foreign exchange positions and of the inflow of foreign funds and controls over new issues in the foreign market.

Reserve requirements

There are no formal reserve requirements but the banks co-operate with the National Bank with respect to reserves on non-resident deposits. This is one of the direct quantitive controls which the central bank imposes by moral suasion. Depending on economic conditions and the extent to which the currency exchange value is being inflated by the inflow of foreign funds, the banks may also be required to match any increase in non-resident deposits by holding reserves of up to 100 per cent of such additional liabilities. These reserves are required to be deposited in an interest-free special account with the Swiss National Bank. As a result, no interest can be paid to the non-resident lender of funds.

Currently, reserve requirements on non-resident deposits are zero, though until early 1980 they applied to non-resident deposits of more than three months—effectively preventing banks from accepting short-term Swiss franc deposits from foreign sources.

Discount policy

The Swiss National Bank will discount short-term claims on the federal government and federally insured export credits at the official discount rate. The National Bank also extends credit to the banks against the security of Swiss bonds, federal debt register claims, and other eligible assets.

All banks are granted access to the discount facility and official quotas are established within which limits they are able to discount bills. The banks, however, make little use of central bank credit because they are usually in positions of excess liquidity. The discount rate therefore plays more of a psychological role than that of an effective monetary instrument. Generally, the rate is considerably below other market lending rates. Rather than being an administered rate directly influencing the market, it tends to follow already established trends.

Open market operations

Although it has the authority to do so, the Swiss National Bank does not, as a rule, engage in open market operations in the domestic money or capital markets. It has little need to raise cash in the markets. This is because the government pursues a policy of balanced budgets which results in few issues of short-term government debt. The National Bank does sell a few treasury bills but these are not really used as an instrument of monetary policy. Secondly, the high degree of liquidity in the banking system means that the National Bank does not need to inject extra liquidity into the markets. The banking system reduces liquidity by itself investing and lending funds in the Euromarkets. The National Bank does at times prevent further inflows of foreign cash, but by use of reserve requirements rather than by open market operations. The National Bank's principal open market activity is in the gold and foreign exchange markets for the purpose of stabilizing the exchange value of the Swiss franc.

As an example of the close co-operation between the Swiss National Bank and the banking system, the National Bank will increase its operations in foreign markets over the balance sheet dates when the banking system is temporarily short of liquidity. This has resulted in an increasing volume of foreign exchange transactions each year between the National Bank and the commercial banks. The National Bank buys US dollars from the commercial banks on a spot basis and then engages in currency swaps for a limited period of time. The National Bank then invests these dollars in foreign markets directly, or with the Bank for International Settlements.

Other controls

Other controls include the supervision of new security issues and, in particular, public issues to ensure an orderly market. Each year a limit is set by the Banking Commission which specifies the volume of Swiss franc bonds both domestic and foreign, which may be issued each quarter. The fourth quarter 1980 limit, for example, was Sfr 2.35 billion. The banks co-operate so that borrowers wishing to tap the market may be organized into a manageable queue of issuers who have to wait their turn in order to raise capital through the Swiss market.

Other controls implemented through the system of exchange controls are designed to protect the currency, while allowing as free a flow of capital into and out of Switzerland as is possible without disturbing the economy (see Exchange controls).

Withholding taxes

Interest

Withholding tax is chargeable on interest earned from bank deposits and bonds but not on interest due from loans and advances. The standard rate is 35 per cent, but for residents of tax-treaty countries this is reduced, as shown in Table 16.6 by means of tax credit.

Table 16.6   Withholding taxes

Recipient	Interest (bonds and deposits), %	Dividends, %
Resident corporations and individuals	35	35
Non-resident corporations and individuals		
Non-treaty	35	35
Treaty		
Austria	5	5
Belgium	10	15
Canada	15	15
Denmark	Nil	Nil
Finland	Nil	5
France	10	5
Germany	Nil	15
Ireland	Nil	10
Italy	12.5	15
Japan	10	15
Malaysia	10	15
Netherlands	5	15
Norway	5	5
Pakistan	15	35
Portugal	10	15
Singapore	10	15
South Africa	35	7.5
Spain	10	15
Sweden	5	5
Trinidad and Tobago	10	20
United Kingdom	Nil	15
United States	5	15

Dividends

Dividends earned from share holdings are subject to a withholding tax of 35 per cent, but for residents of tax-treaty countries this is again reduced by means of a tax credit. The reduced rates shown in Table 16.6 are for portfolio holdings only. In some cases a lower rate applies if a shareholder owns more than 25 per cent of the shares in the company from which the dividends derive.

Fiduciary deposits

The Swiss government has put forward proposals to introduce a withholding tax of five per cent on interest earned on fiduciary deposits. A similar proposal was turned down by Parliament in 1978 and there is currently much opposition from the banking community. It seems unlikely that such a tax will be introduced in the near future.

Gold

In January 1980 a sales tax of 5.6 per cent was imposed on all sales of gold bullion in Switzerland.

Exchange controls

Switzerland has a flexible exchange control system. By tradition, Switzerland is a free trade country and in principle allows the free flow of investment both inward and outward. Its economy is one of the world's most stable and its currency has been one of the strongest. These factors have resulted in an increased demand for all types of Swiss investments. When the demand from foreigners becomes excessively strong, such that it risks the destabilization of the economy and of the currency, the authorities introduce certain protective exchange control measures in order to restrict the inflow of foreign capital.

Exchange control authority

Two government Ministries, the Federal Department of Public Economy, and the Federal Political Department determine policy but delegate administration to the Swiss Federal Council which controls imports, exports and capital payment, and also to the Swiss National Bank which controls the currency.

Currency

The currency is the Swiss franc which is fully convertible into any other convertible currency. The Swiss franc is based on the gold standard and the gold backing of the franc is fixed by law (although it can be changed by further legislation) at 0.217 59 g of fine gold. The Swiss franc has the highest gold coverage of any other currency of industrialized countries. Note issues are covered up to the full extent by gold, together with other reserves which comprise Swiss and foreign bills of exchange, sight claims on foreign countries and short-term Swiss government debt.

Bank's foreign exchange positions

The banks co-operate with the Swiss National Bank by reporting any spot or forward foreign exchange transactions they may engage in which exceed US$5 million, and by reporting daily turnover in foreign exchange transactions that involve Swiss francs where this is in excess of Sfr 15 million. They must also report their monthly forward position, must daily cover their currency exposure, and are not allowed to take net short positions.

Large industrial domestic companies also co-operate with the Swiss National Bank by also informing it of spot or forward foreign exchange transactions that they undertake in excess of US$5 million.

Non-resident accounts

Non-residents are free to open accounts in Switzerland in Swiss francs or in any other convertible currency. All settlements in Swiss francs may be made at the free market rate.

331

There is currently no special charge for non-resident accounts, although the National Bank has the authority to impose a commission charge on Swiss franc deposits—an effective negative interest rate—when external demand for Swiss francs is excessive.

Inward and outward transfer of capital

Non-residents are free to purchase Swiss securities although, when there is upward pressure on the currency, the National Bank may restrict such purchases (e.g., a ban was imposed between February 1978 and January 1979). Non-resident deposits in Swiss francs may also be restricted from time to time by the use of special reserve requirements on non-resident Swiss franc deposits held by banks in Switzerland, or by negative interest charges. Currently no such restrictions apply.

Purchase of Swiss investment property by non-residents generally requires the approval of the relevant cantonal authorities.

Bank lending in Swiss francs to non-residents requires official approval from the National Bank if such lending exceeds Sfr 10 million and has a maturity of more than 12 months. This includes the issue of foreign bonds in Switzerland and Swiss banks' participation in Eurobond issues.

Profits, dividends and principal from investment in Swiss securities may be repatriated freely.

17.   The United Kingdom

General market environment

London is arguably the world's foremost financial centre. Although it is not the largest—New York and Tokyo exceed London in terms of domestic market turnover—it has a range of investment instruments and a degree of dealing sophistication with which few markets can compare. Its financial institutions have developed through centuries of tradition and thus are unique in many ways.

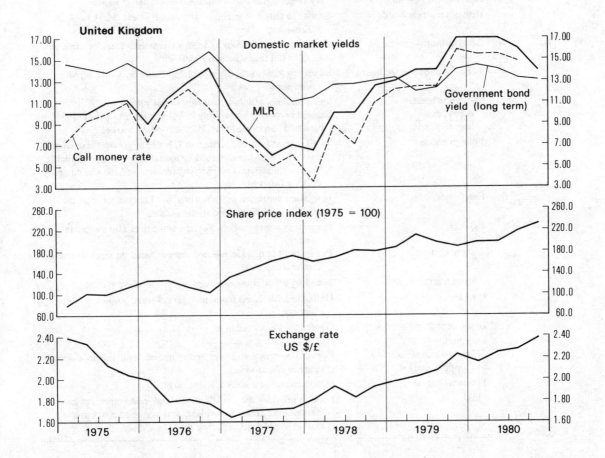

United Kingdom

Domestic market yields

Call money rate

MLR

Government bond yield (long term)

Share price index (1975 = 100)

Exchange rate US $/£

Table 17.1 Summary of instruments

Security	Characteristics
MONEY MARKET	
Deposits	
call deposits	Large active interbank market for overnight two- and seven-day call money
time deposits	Also large market for all time periods
currency deposits	Call and time deposits also accepted in all major convertible currencies
Certificates of deposit	Large markets in sterling and US dollar CDs
Repurchase agreements	Offered occasionally by discount houses and some banks as means of depositing money for unusual time periods
Treasury bills	Large, highly liquid market
Local authority securities	Bills and one-year bonds issued by local government
Commercial bills	Bills issued by companies to finance actual transactions
bank bills	Commercial bills accepted by a bank and eligible for rediscount at Bank of England
trade bills	Carry two names, only those of drawer and acceptor, but not accepted by bank
foreign currency bills	Trade bills denominated in a foreign currency
CAPITAL MARKET	
Government bonds (gilts)	Very large, highly active market. Wide range of issues
Irish government bonds	Similar to gilts, but issued by Irish government. Marketable in UK market
Local authority stocks	Long-term bonds issued by local government. Dealt in same way as gilts, but thin secondary market
Bonds of public sector boards	Similar to local authority stocks, but issued by public sector institutions
Corporate bonds	Small markets with low turnover. Usually low yields
debentures	Secured corporate loans. May be convertible into equity
loan stocks	Unsecured corporate loans. Poor secondary market
Foreign bonds	Small market for bonds issued in UK due to previous exchange controls. Some bonds issued by foreign governments available but poor turnover. Issue activity renewed in 1980 and named Bulldog Bond Market
Eurobonds	Few issues denominated in sterling, but London provides the world's major Eurobond trading centre
Equities	Large, very active market. Foreign companies also quoted in London
share options	Put and call options in selected shares offered on stock exchange. Two markets exist
share warrants	Issued by a few companies and traded on stock exchange
Unit trusts	Units available direct from managers of trust, but not on stock exchange
Investment trusts	Quoted on stock exchange
Commodities	
forward market and options market	Forward contracts and commodity options available in a diverse range of commodities
Financial futures	Establishment of a market is due in 1982
Gold	London provides the world's largest and most important gold market. Free access to residents and non-residents. Futures market established in Spring 1981

In the domestic money market a wide range of securities are available to the investor although there is no commercial paper market.

This is partly because there is a relatively small corporate bond market and thus no bond rating service in the UK, but primarily because companies have access to short-term credit through bank overdraft facilities or the issue of commercial bills.

The domestic capital market is dominated by gilts (government bonds) in terms of value of turnover, though equities dominate in terms of volume. Options and commodities represent more speculative investments while the potential of establishing a financial futures market is under review by the authorities.

London also provides the world's most important centre for the trading of gold bullion, Eurocurrencies and Eurobonds. London accounts for over 40 per cent of the Euromarket turnover and is a major centre for new issues.

Foreign investment is welcome and no distinction is made between resident and non-resident investors and borrowers, except for minor cost differences such as different rates of stamp duty.

Since October 1979 the UK has abolished all forms of exchange controls so non-residents may enter the market and repatriate any proceeds completely unrestricted.

Withholding taxes are payable on interest earnings and, while dividends are declared net of tax, residents of tax treaty countries may claim a tax credit to offset this tax.

The money market

The London money market is one of the most sophisticated and the most active in the world for both sterling and foreign currency short-term money. Major borrowers in the market are the banking system, the central government, local authorities and large corporations. Major lenders are the banks, financial institutions, corporations and, as a last resort, the Bank of England. The discount houses and moneybrokers play special roles as intermediaries and dealers in short-term money.

Deposits

The market for sterling deposits is made by banks, discount houses, finance houses and local authorities, while currency deposits are accepted predominantly by the banks. Money may be placed directly with such institutions, or through a moneybroker, who act as intermediaries between borrowers and lenders. Money may be placed, at call, for as short as overnight or as time deposits for up to several years. Interest on both types of deposits is calculated on the basis of a civil year of 365 days and is paid gross.

Call deposits

Overnight money may be placed at any time up to the close of banking hours (3 p.m.) for repayment on the morning of the following business day. Such money is required by the banks, discount houses and sometimes the local authorities to

335

balance their books between their short-term sterling assets and liabilities. The rate of interest obtainable thus depends on money market liquidity more than on the general level of interest rates prevailing in the money market. Normally, rates are higher in the morning, when many banks are in the market to borrow overnight money, and rates fall off in the afternoon when most borrowers have satisfied their requirements. When liquidity is especially tight, the Bank of England usually eases the shortage by discounting bills to the discount houses or by making advances or repurchase agreements to the banking system. If, as sometimes occurs, such help is inadequate, overnight rates may rise to phenomenal levels and on occasion have been known to reach over 200 per cent per annum, although this is very unusual.

Alternatively, money may be placed on a day-to-day basis. The funds remain on deposit until called by the lender who may do so at any time up to 12 noon for repayment on the same day. The funds receive the overnight rate of interest for each day that the money remains on deposit, but this rate is more stable than that for overnight deposits and more closely correlates with other short-term interest rates in the money market.

Finally, call money may be placed for periods of two to seven days' notice. As with day-to-day money, funds are left on deposit until called by the lender, either up to 12 noon for repayment two business days later, or up to 5 p.m. for repayment seven days later, depending on the term of the loan. Rates of interest depend on the level of interest rates prevailing in the money market, which is determined by the Bank of England's minimum lending rate, and are less volatile than overnight rates. It is up to either the borrower or lender to renegotiate the terms of the loan, subject to the same two- or seven-day periods of notice, if interest rates rise or fall significantly. Call deposits placed with discount houses are secured against specific assets—such as treasury bills and short-term government securities—of the deposit-taking institution. Those placed with banks are unsecured against specific assets.

Call deposits are transacted in sizeable amounts. The minimum acceptable deposit is usually £50 000, though in the overnight market funds are more marketable if in sizes of £1 million or more.

The total volume of sterling call money is about £8 billion to £9 billion per month, of which over 40 per cent flows through the discount houses and about 25 per cent through the London clearing banks. The market is highly active and is predominantly an interbank market whereby banking and deposit taking institutions borrow and lend between each other in order to balance their own books and thus effect the level of liquidity and the flow of funds throughout the money market. Non-bank institutions can and do participate by lending or borrowing very short-term funds to or from the money market, though less than five per cent of total call money is normally provided by the corporate sector. Participation by the corporate sector may increase or decrease according to the differential between money market rates and overdraft costs.

Time deposits

Time deposits for fixed periods of 7 days, 1, 2, 3, 6 or 12 months may be placed with the same deposit-taking institutions as accept call deposits, although the discount houses do not normally take money for more than three months. Finance houses conversely do not normally accept money for less than three months. Deposits placed with discount houses are usually secured against specific assets such as treasury bills and other short-term government securities, though discount houses also take deposits which are only secured against their general assets. Deposits placed with banks and other institutions are secured only against the general assets of the borrower. The degree of security therefore depends on the quality of the borrowing bank or institution, its assets base and reputation. All banks and licensed deposit takers are protected by the 1979 Bank Act so that deposits are guaranteed indirectly by the Bank of England for 75 per cent of the principal value.

Time deposits may be negotiated in smaller sums than for call deposits, though shorter-time deposits are not normally acceptable in sizes of less than £50000. Deposits with a bank usually obtain higher rates if made in minimum sizes of £10000, while deposits with finance houses may be made in minimum sizes of £1000, but are often not accepted for terms of less than three months.

The major participants are banks, licensed deposit takers, local authorities and financial institutions on the borrowing side, and financial institutions and companies on the lending side.

Interest rates depend on the general structure of interest rates prevailing in the money market which are greatly influenced by the Bank of England's minimum lending rate. This is an administered rate used as a major instrument of government monetary policy.

Currency deposits

London is the world's leading Eurocurrency centre and the many domestic and foreign banks based in London make a market in international bonds and notes and accept deposits in any convertible currencies. Highly active markets exist for the major Eurocurrencies, namely US dollars, Deutschemarks, Swiss francs, Dutch guilders, French francs, Belgian francs, Japanese yen, Canadian dollars, Italian lire and Asian dollars. The market for Eurocurrencies has often been referred to as the Eurodollar market because US dollars account for by far the largest single currency traded, representing even now approximately two-thirds of the total market.

Deposits in any of these currencies may be made for the same terms as are available for sterling call and time deposits; that is, money may be placed as short as overnight or as long as 12 months. Interest obtainable depends on demand and supply in the international market and fluctuates from day to day. Rates are to some extent influenced by rates prevailing in the domestic money market of a particular currency, the volume of foreign exchange transactions in that currency and, in particular, intervention by central banks to support or sell a currency.

The interest rates quoted for Eurocurrency deposits, both in London and other financial centres, are usually the London interbank Eurocurrency lending rates— known as LIBOR (London interbank lending rate). The structure of Eurocurrency interest rates is related to but independent of the domestic markets. Rates are determined purely by international supply and demand and are not regulated by any single government or monetary authority. Rates may be influenced by open market operations of particular governments in the foreign exchange market, or by certain domestic monetary or exchange control policies, but they cannot be controlled by particular governments.

The cost of deposits to a domestic bank based in the home country of a particular currency normally acts as a lower limit to the quoted Eurocurrency rate since, if Eurocurrency rates fall below domestic rates, it would be cheaper for the domestic bank to book deposits through its branch in London.

There is no similar mechanism, however, which acts to limit the upper end of the interest rate structure. If the domestic liquidity of a particular currency is tight and consequently a smaller amount of that currency is available in the Euromarket, banks operating in the Euromarket may have to pay a considerable premium for deposits of that country. Sizes of Eurocurrency deposits compare with acceptable sizes for sterling deposits. The equivalent of £50 000 is about the minimum, although the majority of transactions are in equivalent amounts of several million pounds.

Certificates of deposit

Sterling CDs are issued by domestic clearing and major commercial banks, branches of foreign banks in London and by London accepting houses. They are issued in minimum denominations of £50 000 and in multiples of £10 000 up to £500 000. Maximum denominations are £1 million. Maturities of CDs range from three months up to five years, though the majority are issued for either three or six months.

They are issued at par and carry a fixed rate of interest which is payable gross at maturity, except where the life of the CD is greater than one year, in which case interest is paid annually. Interest is calculated on the basis of a 365-day year. In the primary market, investors deal directly with the issuing bank and the CD may be drawn up and issued according to the customer's specification. CDs are bearer instruments and fully negotiable in the secondary market, which is made by London-based banks and discount houses. In the secondary market, CDs are dealt on a yield to maturity basis. Depending on how market rates of interest have moved since the issue of a CD in the primary market, the CD will sell at either a premium or a discount to its par value.

Since the CD can be sold at any time prior to maturity, it is a much more liquid instrument than a fixed time deposit and comparative yields are consequently lower. Investors in the secondary market do, however, have the possibility of taking a jobbing position by buying a longer-term CD from a dealer which may often be at better rates than are currently available in the primary market or on comparative time deposits.

The value of sterling CDs outstanding is approximately £4 billion. This is a decline from the peak volume of £6 billion reached in 1973, but still substantial enough to warrant the CD market as being one of the most active and important in the London money market.

Eurodollar certificates of deposit

Eurodollar CDs are issued by over 140 British, American and foreign banks based in London. Maturities range from between one month to five years with interest paid gross and free of withholding tax at maturity or annually if the CD life is greater than one year. Interest, however, unlike sterling CDs, is calculated on the basis of a financial year of 360 days. Issue sizes are smaller than for sterling CDs. The minimum denomination is $25 000, and thereafter in multiples of $1000. CDs of $1 million or more are, however, the most marketable. As with sterling CDs, Eurodollar CDs are bearer certificates, fully negotiable in the secondary market, which is also maintained by London-based banks and discount houses. The secondary market is extremely active, particularly in CDs which have between 1 and 12 months' remaining maturity.

The volume of the market is substantial. The amount of Eurodollar CDs outstanding by mid-1980 was approximately US$50 billion and turnover exceeds even that of the Eurobond secondary market. As with sterling CDs, Eurodollar CDs are quoted on a yield to maturity basis and available yields may often be at a premium to comparative yields obtainable on US domestic instruments. Typically, yields are $\frac{3}{8}$ to $\frac{1}{2}$ per cent higher than for comparable domestic US dollar CDs. Yields and liquidity of particular CDs depend to some extent on the name of the issuing bank, since CDs are unsecured against specific assets of the issuer. CDs of the largest London clearing banks, American banks and major international banks therefore obtain the best markets in secondary trading.

SDR CDs

Since the beginning of 1981, when the SDR (special drawing right) was simplified to a basket of five currencies, a number of international banks in London have begun to make a market in SDR denominated deposits and CDs. The interest rate is calculated as a weighted average of the Eurocurrency interest rates of the five component currencies. Payment may be made in any convertible currency, at the option of the lender, though dollars are the most usual form of payment. The exchange rate of the SDR relative to other convertible currencies is also calculated as a weighted average of its components. The interest and exchange value of an SDR deposit or CD is consequently less volatile than a single currency and provides the investor with a good average and more stable return on funds.

Repurchase agreements

Unlike the US money market, where all deposits for less than 14 days are arranged through repurchase agreements, there is no major market in repurchase agreements in the UK, although it is possible to arrange such transactions in order to make deposits in unusual sizes or time periods. For example, a corporate treasurer has a sum of money which he wishes to place in the money market for 17 days only at which date he knows he will need the money back in order to pay disbursements; he may not wish to purchase a CD or other negotiable instruments if the sum of money is not of a convenient size to purchase such paper. On the other hand, he may not conveniently be able to make a fixed time deposit for 17 days. Major banks and discount houses will, however, arrange the necessary transaction by means of a repurchase agreement whereby the bank or discount house sells securities (usually treasury bills or short-term government securities) to the treasurer at their face value which is equal to the amount that the treasurer wishes to lend. The sale of these securities is accompanied by an agreement by the borrower to repurchase the securities in 17 days' time at the same price plus a premium which represents an interest payment that is commensurate with market rates of interest for time deposits current at the time of the transaction.

The Bank of England also undertakes repurchase agreements or reverse repurchase agreements with the banking system as one method of its open market operations in order either to reduce or to increase liquidity in the market.

Treasury bills

The Bank of England issues 91-day treasury bills on behalf of the British government in order to provide the government with required short-term funds and as a means of influencing liquidity and interest rates in the money market.

The bills are fully guaranteed as to principal and interest by the government and backed by the Consolidated Fund of the United Kingdom. In the primary market, bills are issued at a discount determined by weekly tender. Each Friday the amount of bills to be issued the following Friday is announced by the Bank of England. Any institution or individual, either resident or non-resident, may subscribe, but through the intermediary of a London bank, discount house or moneybroker.

Tenders must be in minimum denomination of £50 000 or above in multiples of £5000. They must state the price offered expressed as a net amount per cent. For example, £97.50 for every £100 represents an annualized rate of interest of 10 per cent. Since treasury bills are made available on every day of the week of each tender period, the applicant must also state the date on which he wishes to take up the bills. Such bills run for 91 days from the date stated at the option of the tenderer. Tenders must be received by the Bank of England before 1 p.m. on Friday and the Bank then makes a preliminary announcement of the minimum accepted price and the number of bills to be allotted at that price. Precise results are announced at 3 p.m. when the number of tenders received, the amount allotted and at what price, the average tender price and the amount of bills to be offered at the next weekly tender are given. Tenders received at above the minimum accepted tender price are allotted in full. Tenders received at the minimum accepted price are allotted proportionately and those received at below the minimum price are unallotted.

Payment in full of amounts due in respect of accepted tenders must be made to the Bank of England not later than 1.30 p.m. on the day on which the relevant bills are to be dated. Payment must be by cash, draft or cheque drawn on the Bank of England.

The whole amount of each weekly issue is additionally underwritten by the 11 London discount houses which ensures that all treasury bills on offer will be covered. By controlling the minimum price it is prepared to accept, the Bank of England can influence rates of interest in the money market and signal changes in monetary policy. Minimum lending rate (MLR) is announced at the same time as is treasury bill rates. Until May 1978 MLR was calculated by rounding the minimum treasury bill tender rate to the nearest $\frac{1}{4}$ per cent and adding $\frac{1}{2}$ per cent.

Minimum lending rate has since been, however, an administered rate of interest and may be changed at the discretion of the Treasury in consultation with the Bank of England, irrespective of treasury bill rate.

It becomes effective immediately following its announcement at 12.30 p.m. on each Thursday. Since the present Conservative government took office in mid-1979, control of MLR has been used as the major instrument of monetary policy. It has been maintained at a high level in an attempt to reduce the growth of the money supply.

In secondary trading, treasury bills are highly marketable. Since they are highly secure and highly liquid securities, and are also fully negotiable bearer certificates, they are traded by banks, money brokers, discount houses, financial institutions, corporations and individuals. The discount houses in particular use them as security against their borrowings in the money market. Treasury bills may be bought to mature on any day within three months and are available in convenient sizes of £5000, £10 000, £25 000, £50 000, £100 000, £250 000 or £1 000 000. Because of their security, liquidity and convenience, treasury bills usually command the lowest yields of all money market instruments except, sometimes, the rate for overnight money which tends to be very volatile depending on demand and supply of money in the short end of the market.

Secondary market

The volume of the treasury bill market is substantial. Since 1979, the amount offered by weekly tender has often been £300 million per week, and as at the end of the first quarter of 1980 the amount outstanding was £4.6 billion. This is less than the amount of almost £6 billion in the third quarter of 1979, but the Bank of

Table 17.2 Holdings of British government treasury bills (£ million)

Year (end period)	Total outstanding	Official holdings	Total available to market	Banks in UK	Discount houses	Companies and financial institutions	Other*
1970	5 339	3095	2244	494	876	75	799
1971	4 677	2495	2182	504	871	72	735
1972	4 879	3160	1719	302	475	53	889
1973	6 201	4800	1401	498	321	39	543
1974	9 075	6132	2943	458	721	181	1583
1975	10 810	6320	4490	1602	1088	703	1097
1976	7 916	7916	3140	1462	652	404	622
1977	7 543	7543	3950	1523	1146	747	534
1978	6 301	6301	2813	893	1065	210	645
1979	5 368	5368	2480	1050	585	326	519
1980	3 940	1138	2804	1152	913	215	524

* Includes other public sector institutions, central monetary institutions, individuals and others.

England may buy back the bills in the secondary market as a part of its open market operations to reduce liquidity in the money market. Of the amount outstanding, over half were official holdings by the National Debt Commission. Of the remaining £2.3 billion available to the market, 40 per cent was held by banks in the UK, 11 per cent by the discount houses, 8 per cent by other financial institutions and companies and 35 per cent by foreign central banks. The remaining 6 per cent was held by other public sector institutions, individuals and other investors.

Short-dated government securities

Although the major market is the London stock exchange, an over-the-counter secondary market is maintained by money market dealers in short-dated government stock. These are gilt-edged securities with less than five years to maturity and are dealt differently from longer-dated stocks. As with all short-dated stocks prices are quoted exclusive of accrued interest, which is then added to the purchase price. Each of the 30 or so short-dated stocks have a coupon rate of interest attaching to them which is payable semiannually. All but two have fixed rate coupons which range from 3 to 15 per cent. The two have variable rate coupons which are in line with money market rates of interest and are changed every week to $\frac{1}{2}$ per cent above the tender rate for treasury bills. Short-dated gilts are dealt net of commission and settled on the same or following business day.

Banks and discount houses are active participants in this market which can reach a turnover of £9 billion per month of which one quarter may be accounted for by the discount houses alone. The discount houses purchase short gilts because their security is guaranteed by the government and they may thus be used as security against borrowings in the money market. In addition, they offer the potential of a greater profit than do many other money market securities.

Short gilts of up to one year maturity can also be used by banks as reserve assets and hence are attractive to the banking sector.

Local authority securities

Local authorities issue a number of different types of securities; specifically, bills or promissory notes, bonds, stocks and variable rate bonds and stocks. The money so raised is used to supplement money raised through rates (local taxes on property) and to finance public works, local amenities and welfare institutions.

Local authority bills

Local authority bills are also known as local government promissory notes, corporation bills, money bills or revenue bills, although they are all the same type of security.

They are similar to treasury bills, except that they are drawn on and guaranteed by one of over 500 local authorities rather than by the central government. Most bills are issued for 91 days, though some may be issued for 182 days. New issues are made on an irregular basis and require the prior approval of the Bank of England.

Once this has been granted, the local authority announces the amount of bills it is offering for sale and invites tenders from the public to be made through the local authority's appointed bank. The major proportion of bills are subscribed for by the London clearing banks and the discount houses. The latter, along with the money-brokers, also maintain a secondary market in the bills. Once the subscription is closed, bills are allotted in the same manner as treasury bills. Individuals and companies may also subscribe either directly or through a bank, discount house or moneybroker.

Normally, bills are issued in denominations of £5000, £10 000, £25 000, £50 000 and £100 000. They are bearer securities and enjoy an active secondary market. Although still considered highly secure, they do not have the benefit of a central government guarantee and thus yield slightly more than treasury bills. They are popularly held by banks and discount houses because the bills qualify as reserve assets and are eligible for rediscounting at the Bank of England. As at the end of the first quarter of 1980, there were bills amounting to £624 million outstanding representing approximately one-tenth of all local authorities' short-term debt.

Local authority bonds (*LABs*)

Local authority bonds are usually yearling bonds, having a maturity of one year and six days, though some are issued with lives of up to five years. New issues are managed and underwritten by a merchant bank, discount house or stockbroker who arranges sales direct to clients although the bonds are also quoted on the stock exchange. Terms of a new issue require the prior authority of the Bank of England which also accepts responsibility for regulating the queue of borrowers. New issues are made every Tuesday by any of over 500 local authorities. Approximately £20 million bonds are issued each week though individual issues are usually in sizes of between £250 000 and £2 000 000.

Local authority bonds are registered securities which usually carry a fixed rate of interest payable semiannually net of tax. They may, however, sometimes be issued with variable coupons which are rebased semiannually and calculated according to six months LIBOR plus an agreed margin. During 1980, variable coupons have been $\frac{7}{8}$ per cent over six months LIBOR. The highest margin was $1\frac{3}{8}$ per cent during the period when special supplementary deposits were imposed on the banking system. The lowest margin over LIBOR has been about $\frac{5}{8}$ per cent. They are transferable in minimum denominations of £1000. LABs are normally issued at par but may sometimes be issued at $\frac{1}{16}$ discount. In the first weeks after issue, the bonds are quoted by price, though thereafter they are dealt on a yield basis and bought, as with short-dated gilts, plus or minus accrued interest. A fairly good secondary market exists in these bonds, made by the merchant banks, discount houses and moneybrokers. The financial institutions such as building societies as well as industrial and commercial companies are significant investors, but many tend to hold the bonds to maturity.

Yearling bonds are growing increasingly popular because coupons are competitive with current market rates of interest and because they are dealt plus or minus accrued interest, the interest capitalized on sale may be subject to capital gains tax at 30 per cent as opposed to income tax (at 52 per cent for corporations).

As at the end of March 1981, there were over £1 billion of local authority bonds outstanding, an amount which has remained fairly constant over the past five years.

Local authority stocks

Stocks are similar to bonds in that they are consolidated issues of registered nego-tiable bonds. They differ in that they are issued directly through the stock ex-change and are underwritten by a bank, stockbroker or discount house. Stocks may be issued with maturities of up to 30 years, although two, issued by the London County Council, are undated, and one issued by Liverpool is irredeemable. In this sense they are capital market, rather than money market, securities and are described later.

Table 17.3 **Local authority short-term securities (£ million)** (*source: Central Statistical Office*)

Financial year to March	Local authority bills		Local authority bonds and stocks (less than 5 years)	
	Amount outstanding	*Net issues*	*Amount outstanding*	*Net issues*
1975	401	54	2444	208
1976	407	−7	2632	107
1977	429	14	2730	226
1978	499	55	2899	52
1979	599	100	2946	−185
1980	624	213	2814	−140

Variable rate bonds and stocks

Although some are issued with short maturities, these instruments are really capital market instruments and thus are described later. A market is maintained however, among banks, money brokers and discount houses.

Commercial bills

Commercial bills are time drafts drawn on one company or trader by another to finance the import or export or inland sale of goods or to finance stocks. Because they finance actual transactions in goods, the bills—also known as bills of exchange—are self-liquidating in that proceeds are generated by the sale of goods. The amounts for which such bills are issued vary: they may be for amounts as small as a few thousand pounds but sizes of £50 000 or more are the norm and £500 000 usually the largest size of bill issued. Bills may be issued for periods of one to six months, though three-month bills are the most common.

344

Although drawn on one company by another, the bills are payable to the bearer and thus are readily negotiable in the secondary market. This market is very active in most types of commercial bills and maintained by the clearing banks, merchant banks and discount houses. There are four types of commercial bills traded in the UK money market. These are eligible and ineligible bank bills, trade bills and foreign currency bills.

Commercial bills are issued at a discount to the par value of the bill and quoted on a yield basis. Except for foreign currency bills, the discount is calculated according to a 365-day year and will be in line with prevailing rates of interest in the money market. Eligible bank bills are the most secure and most marketable and thus yield the lowest, while conversely trade bills have the lowest security and the highest yield.

Bank bills

Bank bills are commercial bills that have been accepted by a bank. This involves the bank in accepting full liability to pay the face value of a bill on maturity through the drawing up of an acceptance credit that confirms that the terms on which bills drawn on a particular company will be honoured.

Eligible bank bills are those that have been accepted by one of a list of banks agreed by the Bank of England. These comprise 9 London and Scottish clearing banks, the 17 merchant banks that are members of the Accepting Houses Committee, 23 British and overseas Commonwealth banks, 2 Bank of England long-standing customers and 7 other banks. The bills must additionally be endorsed by one of the 11 discount houses. Eligible bank bills are so called because, having been accepted and endorsed by the requisite institutions, they are then eligible both for rediscounting at the Bank of England and as reserve assets for the banking system.

Ineligible bank bills are those which, although they have been accepted by a bank, have not been accepted by one included on the Bank of England's approved list. This list excludes many foreign banks which may nevertheless be very large and reputable banks. Yields on ineligible bank bills are consequently slightly higher than for eligible bank bills of comparable terms.

Trade bills

Trade bills carry two names only. They are not accepted by a bank, but accepted directly by a company or trader who is effectively the issuer of the bill and is party to the specific trade transaction that is stated on the face of the bill. At maturity the bill may be presented by the holder to the acceptor's bank which should also be stated on the face of the bill. The acceptor should make available to his bank the funds necessary to honour the bill, but if he has not done so then the holder has recourse to the drawer of the bill whose name is also on its face.

The rate of discount, and thus yield, attaching to a particular trade bill depends on the financial status of the acceptor by a bank. However, trade bills are considered less secure than bank bills and not only yield more but are less readily

345

negotiable in the secondary market. Only the highest quality trade bills are held by discount houses though such trade bills as are sold by the discount houses to their customers are normally accepted as the liability of the discount house.

Foreign currency bills

These are issued under the same terms as bank bills or trade bills but are denominated in a foreign currency. Normally they finance the import or export of goods between, usually, UK exporters and foreign importers. By their nature of being non-sterling bills, no foreign currency bills, may be eligible bank bills and they may not qualify either as reserve assets or for sale to the Bank of England. The most

Table 17.4 UK interest rates and yields (*source: Bank of England Quarterly Bulletin*)

	End 1976	End 1977	End 1978	Jan.	Feb.	Mar.	Apr.	May	Jun.	Jul.	Aug.	Sep.	Oct.	Nov.	Dec.
				\multicolumn{12}{c}{1979}										
Minimum lending rate	$14\frac{1}{4}$	7	$12\frac{1}{2}$	$12\frac{1}{2}$	14	13	12	12	14	14	14	14	14	17	17
Interbank overnight call money															
minimum	6	6	$10\frac{5}{8}$	$10\frac{1}{4}$	12	6	11	$11\frac{1}{2}$	5	$13\frac{7}{8}$	13	$13\frac{7}{8}$	$13\frac{3}{4}$	13	15
maximum	15	$7\frac{3}{4}$	$11\frac{1}{4}$	13	19	$13\frac{1}{8}$	$12\frac{1}{4}$	12	$14\frac{1}{2}$	14	$14\frac{1}{4}$	15	15	16	18
Treasury bill rate	13.51	6.29	11.56	12.9	12.23	11.44	11.29	11.45	13.33	13.35	13.34	13.37	13.47	16.10	15.84
3-month time deposits (interbank rate)	$14\frac{3}{8}$	$6\frac{5}{8}$	$12\frac{9}{16}$	$13\frac{1}{16}$	$13\frac{1}{16}$	$12\frac{3}{16}$	$11\frac{13}{16}$	$11\frac{7}{8}$	14	$14\frac{1}{16}$	$14\frac{1}{4}$	$14\frac{1}{4}$	$14\frac{11}{16}$	$16\frac{7}{8}$	$16\frac{15}{16}$
3-month CDs	$14\frac{3}{32}$	$6\frac{1}{4}$	$12\frac{7}{16}$	$12\frac{5}{8}$	$12\frac{7}{8}$	$12\frac{1}{16}$	$11\frac{5}{8}$	$11\frac{13}{16}$	$13\frac{3}{4}$	14	$14\frac{1}{8}$	$14\frac{1}{16}$	$14\frac{9}{16}$	$16\frac{11}{16}$	$16\frac{3}{4}$
3-month bank bills	$13\frac{5}{8}$	$6\frac{3}{8}$	$12\frac{7}{32}$	$12\frac{1}{4}$	$12\frac{7}{8}$	12	$11\frac{7}{16}$	$11\frac{5}{8}$	$13\frac{59}{64}$	$13\frac{55}{64}$	$13\frac{15}{16}$	$14\frac{4}{32}$	$14\frac{9}{32}$	$16\frac{11}{16}$	$16\frac{3}{4}$
Government gilts															
short—5 years	12.06	10.08	11.32	13.48	13.33	11.32	10.62	11.00	12.07	12.11	11.99	12.22	12.90	15.36	15.29
medium—10 years	13.61	12.02	12.12	13.61	13.80	12.07	11.41	11.70	12.56	12.24	12.25	12.54	13.17	14.85	14.96
long—20 years	14.43	12.73	12.47	13.68	13.94	12.35	11.68	11.94	12.96	12.25	12.30	12.60	13.16	14.54	14.72
Corporate bonds—20 years	15.19	13.41	12.75	13.59	14.21	13.32	12.33	12.12	12.71	12.82	12.71	12.73	13.06	14.28	14.92

	Jan.	Feb.	Mar.	Apr.	May	Jun.	Jul.	Aug.	Sep.	Oct.	Nov.	Dec.
	\multicolumn{12}{c}{1980}											
Minimum lending rate	17	17	17	17	17	17	16	16	16	16	14	14
Interbank overnight call money												
minimum	16	12	$17\frac{1}{4}$	17	$16\frac{1}{8}$	$17\frac{7}{8}$	$16\frac{7}{8}$	14	$15\frac{5}{8}$	$15\frac{1}{4}$	$11\frac{1}{2}$	$11\frac{1}{2}$
maximum	$18\frac{1}{4}$	$18\frac{1}{4}$	18	18	17	18	40	$16\frac{1}{2}$	$16\frac{3}{8}$	16	$15\frac{1}{4}$	$13\frac{3}{4}$
Treasury bill rate	15.74	16.12	16.28	16.06	16.06	15.68	14.44	14.95	14.33	14.29	13.95	13.07
3-month time deposits (interbank rate)	$17\frac{3}{8}$	$18\frac{1}{8}$	$18\frac{1}{4}$	$17\frac{3}{8}$	$17\frac{1}{16}$	$16\frac{7}{8}$	$15\frac{7}{16}$	$16\frac{3}{4}$	$15\frac{3}{4}$	16.0	15.84	14.73
3-month CDs	$17\frac{7}{16}$	$18\frac{1}{16}$	18	$17\frac{3}{16}$	$16\frac{15}{16}$	$16\frac{3}{4}$	$15\frac{5}{16}$	$16\frac{9}{16}$	$15\frac{7}{16}$	$15\frac{13}{16}$	$15\frac{3}{4}$	$14\frac{5}{8}$
3-month bank bills	$16\frac{11}{16}$	$17\frac{19}{32}$	$17\frac{13}{32}$	$16\frac{13}{16}$	$16\frac{29}{64}$	$16\frac{3}{4}$	$14\frac{27}{32}$	$15\frac{7}{8}$	15	$15\frac{1}{8}$	$14\frac{3}{4}$	$13\frac{29}{32}$
Government gilts												
short—5 years	14.87	15.22	15.21	14.58	14.07	13.45	12.67	13.55	13.10	13.20	13.14	13.29
medium—10 years	14.43	14.73	14.93	14.42	14.11	13.78	13.08	13.70	13.47	13.12	13.34	13.78
long—20 years	14.17	14.45	14.70	14.27	14.01	13.78	13.07	13.58	13.38	13.68	13.22	13.67
Corporate bonds—20 years	14.73	14.45	14.84	14.86	14.48	14.20	13.68	13.65	13.85	13.68	13.65	13.85

common currency for such bills is US dollars, which enjoy an active market in London. Bills denominated in other currencies generally do not have active secondary markets. The rate of discount attaching to foreign currency bills depends on the credit rating of the parties whose signatures are on the face of the bill and whether the bill has been accepted by a bank. It is calculated as some margin over the London interbank offer rate for comparable time deposits in that currency and is on a 360-day-year basis. The margin is small, namely, $\frac{1}{8}$ to $\frac{1}{4}$ per cent for highly rated bills.

At maturity, the bills are payable in London by the transfer of funds from the country of the currency in which the bills are denominated.

The capital market

The UK capital market is well developed and highly sophisticated. Its structure, institutions and methods of dealing date back to the seventeenth century.

In the domestic market, government securities dominate the fixed interest securities, while equities dominate the corporate sector of the market. The domestic capital market is centred in the London stock exchange which, in terms of total turnover of both fixed interest and equities—reaching £196 billion for the year to December 1980—is the third largest in the world after New York and Tokyo.

Apart from the domestic market, London also provides the world's major Euromarket. Most Eurobond issues are listed on the stock exchange and, although a significant turnover is also transacted in New York and other European financial centres, the major share of business takes place in London.

British government bonds (gilt-edged securities)

Government bonds are known as gilt-edged securities or 'gilts' because they have the utmost security, being fully guaranteed as to principal and interest by the British government. The term dates back to the nineteenth century when the bonds actually had a gold, or gilt, edge around them.

The issue of bonds is one of the major means by which the government finances its budget deficit (the public sector borrowing requirement (PSBR)).

For the year to 31 December 1980, the PSBR was £12.4 billion. Although part of the PSBR is covered by an increase in the money supply it was anyway almost covered by the increase in government securities of over £11 billion which includes refunding, but substitution, of matured (repaid) gilts. There are over 90 gilt stocks which currently comprise the market with a total nominal value of approximately £70 billion. Thirty stocks are short-dated gilts with a life of up to five years and a combined nominal value of approximately £23 billion. The medium-dated gilts have maturities between 5 and 15 years, and the undated stocks have no final redemption date. Together they have a total nominal value of approximately £47 billion.

However, the nominal value of government stocks overstates the size of the market because firstly the government gradually buys in securities as they near redemption and secondly because the market value is currently substantially below the nominal value.

347

Table 17.5   Gilt-edged securities

Maturity	Number	Nominal value 31.12.80, £ million	Market value 31.12.80, £ million
Short (under 5 years)	30	24 412	23 052
Medium (5–15 years)	37	24 923	21 481
Long (over 15 years and undated)	43	32 340	26 120
Total	110	81 675	70 653

At the extreme end of the scale the market value of irredeemable stocks is £1020 million compared with a nominal value of £2694 million.

The range and variety of gilts is such that the investor may choose one to closely fit his individual investment requirements. The range of possible maturities is from a few months up to forty years or indefinite terms, while coupons range from $2\frac{1}{2}$ to $15\frac{1}{2}$ per cent. The low coupon stocks provide for high capital growth, while the high coupon stocks provide high income. In addition, some stocks carry variable rate coupons that are changed every week to $\frac{1}{2}$ per cent above MLR in order to provide an income return in line with current market rates of interest.

Unlike floating rate notes or other securities with coupons that vary in line with current market interest levels and for which the coupon is known in advance for the period to which it relates, the coupon on variable rate stock is not known until the end of the period. Floating rate note coupons are fixed, say, every three months at a rate of, say, $\frac{1}{4}$ per cent over LIBOR to run for the preceding three-month period. In contrast, the coupon on treasury variable rate stock is determined weekly according to MLR, and the true coupon is only calculated on the ex-dividend date which is approximately 37 days prior to the dividend payment date, which occurs every six months.

The gilt-edged market is also of interest to the non-resident investor not only because the market has considerable depth and liquidity, but also because the interest payments on certain issues may be paid gross, without the deduction of withholding tax. These stocks are listed in Table 17.6. Only on War Loan however is interest paid free of withholding tax. For the other stocks, non-residents must apply to the Bank of England for tax exemption, or to a London clearing bank to which much of the administrative formality has now been delegated. The form of exemption also depends on the specific tax treaty made between the UK and the foreign country concerned. In some cases interest is paid gross, while in others it is paid net but the tax paid can be claimed back.

Gilts are referred to individually by name, coupon and redemption date, e.g., Treasury $12\frac{3}{4}\%$ 1996. Most are either exchequer or treasury stocks. Both are essentially the same, but the names denote the issuing department of central government. A small number, such as Gas 3% 1990/95 and War Loan $3\frac{1}{2}\%$ have names which specify the purpose for which they were issued.

Most have single redemption dates, though some may be redeemed between two dates (e.g., Exchequer 12% 1999/2002) at the option of the government. The majority are redeemed in full at maturity, but a few redeem capital by a sinking fund method. All stocks are redeemed at par (£100 per unit). Interest, often referred to as dividends in the case of government stock, is paid semiannually calculated from a specified date after issue. The variety of interest payment dates throughout the whole range of issues makes it possible for the investor to choose a stock with an acceptable coupon and maturity and where interest arises in a convenient month. All gilts are registered securities.

Table 17.6   Gilt-edged stocks, with interest, payable free of withholding tax

Stock	Interest payment dates	Amount outstanding, £ million
SHORT DATED		
Exchequer $12\frac{3}{4}\%$ 1981	23 May and November	600
Treasury $8\frac{1}{2}\%$ 1980/82	15 January and July	861
Treasury 3% 1982	15 February and August	400
Treasury 14% 1982	16 March and September	600
Treasury 12% 1983	17 March and September	1550
Funding $5\frac{1}{2}\%$ 1982/84	15 January and July	500
MEDIUM DATED		
Treasury $8\frac{1}{2}\%$ 1984/86	10 January and July	600
Funding $6\frac{1}{2}\%$ 1985/87	3 May and November	559
Treasury $7\frac{3}{4}\%$ 1985/88	26 January and July	500
Treasury 13% 1990	15 January and July	600
Treasury $8\frac{1}{4}\%$ 1987/90	15 June and December	600
Funding $5\frac{3}{4}\%$ 1987/91	5 April and October	400
Treasury $12\frac{3}{4}\%$ 1992	22 January and July	600
Treasury $12\frac{1}{2}\%$ 1993	14 January and July	1100
Funding 6% 1993	15 March and September	600
Treasury $13\frac{3}{4}\%$ 1993	23 May and November	1250
Treasury $14\frac{1}{2}\%$ 1994	1 March and September	600
Treasury 9% 1994	17 May and November	900
Treasury $12\frac{3}{4}\%$ 1995	15 May and November	900
Treasury 9% 1992/96	15 March and September	600
Treasury $15\frac{1}{4}\%$ 1996	3 May and November	1350
Exchequer $13\frac{1}{4}\%$ 1996	15 May and November	800
LONG DATED		
Treasury $13\frac{1}{4}\%$ 1997	22 January and July	1500
Treasury $8\frac{3}{4}\%$ 1997	1 March and September	800
Treasury $6\frac{3}{4}\%$ 1995/98	1 May and November	1000
Treasury $15\frac{1}{2}\%$ 1998	30 March and September	1100
Treasury $9\frac{1}{2}\%$ 1999	15 January and July	600
Treasury 8% 2002/06	5 April and October	600
Treasury $5\frac{1}{2}\%$ 2008/12	10 March and September	1000
Treasury $7\frac{3}{4}\%$ 2012/15	26 January and July	600
UNDATED		
War Loan $3\frac{1}{2}\%$ 1952 or after	1 June and December	1909

Short-dated gilts (i.e., maturity of five years or less) are treated and dealt differently from medium-, long- and undated gilts. Short gilts are dealt at a price plus or minus accrued interest which is calculated on a daily basis according to a 365-day year. Other gilts with maturities of more than five years are quoted at a price that is inclusive of accrued interest. For all gilts settlement and delivery takes place on the following business day. Commission charges also differ, being discretionary for short gilts and standard for medium and long gilts. Five years is a somewhat arbitrary cut-off date, but one which serves both the money and capital markets very well.

Longer-dated gilts are much more price volatile than shorter-dated gilts, while those at the very short end are much more predictable as regards price and yield in relation to the general structure of market interest rates. Thus, short-dated gilts are dealt in largely by money market participants such as discount houses, banks and financial and commercial companies, while longer-dated gilts are bought by capital market participants such as investment institutions, companies and individuals.

Primary market

In the primary market, gilts are issued by the Bank of England acting as agent of the government. New issues are announced in advance in the financial press and by notification to banks, stockbrokers and the stock exchange. Applications for new issues are invited from all members of the public who may subscribe through a bank or broker. New issues may span the whole maturity range for gilt-edged stocks and so may be short-, medium- or long-dated stocks. Undated stocks have not been issued for many years, and there are only six such stocks outstanding. Sizes of new issues range from £600 million to £1200 million and new issues may be made in one of three ways. Firstly, the whole amount of the stock may be issued at the full price which is determined on a yield basis relative to the coupon that attaches to the stock. The nominal value (par value) of all stocks is £100 per unit. Subscribers are allotted proportionate amounts of stocks once the subscription list has been closed and are then required to pay for the full amount of their allotment on the issue date.

Alternatively, stock may be issued on a partly paid basis whereby subscribers are required to pay some specified part payment on tender followed by additional payment (or payments) on specified later dates. The stocks may be traded in the market in their partly paid form, though first dividends (interest payments) reflect the lower subscription payment. For example, £1200 million Treasury $11\frac{3}{4}\%$ 1991 was issued on 10 June 1980. Subscribers were required to pay £20 per £100 nominal of stock on tender, £30 on 22 August and the balance of £44 on 26 September. Although the coupon was $11\frac{3}{4}$ per cent, the first dividend, due on 10 January 1981 was for £4.2172 per cent.

Finally, new issues may be made on a tap basis (which means that the stock is made available to the market every day over a period which may be several weeks to a few months) in response to market demand until such time as the total amount that the government wishes to issue is exhausted, i.e., the tap has run out. It is not just new stock that may be issued in this way but new issues of existing stock may

350

be made available to the market on a tap basis. The following table shows new issues of government stocks made between August 1979 and August 1980.

A secondary market in all gilt-edged stocks is maintained on the stock exchange, although an over-the-counter market in short-dated gilts is also maintained by the banks and discount houses. *Secondary market*

The secondary market is highly active. Gilts account for over 90 per cent by value of all trading in fixed-interest securities and almost 80 per cent by value of all trading in all types of securities, including equities. The average value per day of gilt trading for the year 1980 was £304.4 million for short-dated gilts and £309.8 million for other gilts, while the cumulative value for the same year was £75 177.7 million

Table 17.7 New issues of government stock, September 1979 to August 1980

Stock	Total nominal amount issued, £ million	Issue dates	Cash amount raised, £ million	Price at first issue, £	Price at exhaustion of issue, £	Date of exhaustion of tap
Treasury $11\frac{1}{2}\%$ 1984	600	12 Sep. 1979	333	$95\frac{1}{2}$	$80\frac{9}{16}$	15 Nov. 1979
Exchequer 12% 1999/2002 'A'	500	12 Sep. 1979	335	97	$81\frac{9}{16}$	15 Nov. 1979
Treasury $13\frac{3}{4}\%$ 2000/2003 'A'	1000	15 Nov. 1979	200	91		
		5 Dec. 1979	710			
Treasury 15% 1985	800	22 Nov. 1979	985	$98\frac{1}{2}$	$98\frac{1}{4}$	11 Dec. 1979
Treasury 14% 1998/2001	1000	28 Nov. 1975	200	$95\frac{1}{2}$		10 Jan. 1980
		14 Dec. 1979	400			
		9 Jan. 1980	355		$96\frac{1}{8}$	
Exchequer 14% 1984	1000	10 Jan. 1980	1062	$96\frac{1}{2}$	97	11 Jan. 1980
Exchequer $13\frac{1}{2}\%$ 1983	860	23 Jan. 1980	480	$96\frac{3}{4}$		14 Apr. 1980
		29 Feb. 1980	294		$95\frac{3}{4}$	14 Apr. 1980
Treasury $12\frac{1}{2}\%$ 2003/2005	1000	23 Jan. 1980	205	$91\frac{1}{2}$		
		15 Feb. 1980	450			
		14 Mar. 1980	215		$92\frac{1}{2}$	15 Mar. 1980
Treasury 14% 1996	800	27 Feb. 1980	160	$95\frac{1}{2}$		
		18 Mar. 1980	240			1 Apr. 1980
		1 Apr. 1980	1		$95\frac{13}{16}$	1 Apr. 1980
		11 Apr. 1980	363			

(continued)

Table 17.7 (*continued*)

Stock	Total nominal amount issued, £ million	Issue dates	Cash amount raised, £ million	Price at first issue, £	Price at exhaustion of issue, £	Date of exhaustion of tap
Treasury 13½% 2004/2008	1000	17 Apr. 1980	200	95¾	95¾	17 Apr. 1980
		16 May 1980	300			
		6 Jun. 1980	457			
Exchequer 13½% 1992	1000	8 May 1980	201	96		
		23 Jun. 1980	299		95¾	27 May 1980
		2 Jul. 1980	1			
		11 Jul. 1980	459			
Treasury 3% 1985	600	29 May 1980	414	69	69¼	4 Jul. 1980
Exchequer 13½% 1994	1000	4 Jun. 1980	400	96	40¼	16 Jun. 1980
		4 Jul. 1980	301			
		25 Jul. 1980	259			
Exchequer 12¼% 1985 'A'	600	25 Jun. 1980	240	98¼	98$\frac{7}{16}$	4 Jul. 1980
Treasury 13% 2000	1000	25 Jun. 1980	315	96	96¼	2 Jul. 1980
Treasury 12% 1987	1000	9 Jul. 1980	200	96	96⅜	16 Jul. 1980
Exchequer 3% 1983 'A'	400	17 Jul. 1980	333	83¼		
Treasury 11¾% 1991 'A'	1200	23 Jul. 1980	240	94		

and £76 520.5 million respectively. By volume, however, turnover in gilts represented only 18.5 per cent of total trading in securities. This is because the normal size of transactions is large. Although gilts may be dealt in sizes down to as little as £500, the average value per bargain in 1980 was £200 521 for short-dated gilts and £102 772 for other gilts. The depth and liquidity of the market is such that it is possible to deal in large amounts of virtually any size, particularly for short-dated gilts.

Major participants in the secondary market are the large institutional investors such as insurance companies, pension funds, building societies, banks and corporate investors. In the secondary market, gilts are traded at a price, but on a yield basis, so the price may rise above or fall below par depending on the coupon of the stocks.

As previously mentioned, short gilts are dealt at a price plus or minus accued interest, while the prices of medium and long gilts are quoted inclusive of interest.

Yields and prices are calculated daily. Three yields are usually quoted. These are flat (or income) yields, gross yields to redemption, and yields to redemption net of standard rate income tax at 30%.

Flat yields are simply calculated as coupon divided by price. Redemption yields add in the annual capital gain to maturity and are also quoted net to take account of the 30 per cent capital gains tax payable by UK residents.

Capital gains is not payable provided the stock is held for more than one year.

Irish government bonds

The Irish government issues its own fixed-interest bonds in the same manner and with similar terms to those of the British government. Since the Irish stock exchanges have amalgamated with the London and provincial stock exchanges, the securities are also quoted and dealt in the UK market. The stocks are guaranteed as to principal and interest by the Irish government and not by the British government.

In the primary market, Irish funds are issued in the same way as British government funds, but through the Bank of Ireland. Subscriptions are invited from investors in both the Irish and British markets. The size of the market is considerably smaller than for British gilts. For the year 1980, the number of new issues was 52. The total nominal amount of new issues was only £798 million for Irish government bonds, compared with £17 132 million for British government bonds.

Turnover in the secondary market is also substantially lower. For 1980, turnover for Irish funds was £7994 million compared with £151 698 million for British funds.

Yields on Irish government bonds depend on the level of interest rates prevailing in the Irish market which are generally kept slightly below those in the UK market as part of deliberate policy of the Irish government. Prices also take into account actual and anticipated exchange rate movements between the British pound which floats freely and the Irish pound which is part of the EMS.

UK local authority securities

The British local authorities issue three types of securities; bills, bonds and stocks. Bills and bonds are short-term securities, normally dealt in the money market.

Local authority stocks, alternatively known as British Corporation and County stocks, are bonds issued by local towns, boroughs or counties to finance local public works.

Issue sizes may be up to £10 million, though commonly the amount offered is £50 000 per issue. Maturities may range from short-dated (less than five years) to long-dated (up to 35 years) and a few are undated with no fixed redemption date. They are registered securities which pay interest semiannually and redeem capital at par (£100) at maturity.

In the primary market, new issues are made through the stock exchange, having first received authority from the Bank of England. Subscribers are invited to apply through a bank or a broker at a stated price based on the coupon and yield, and stocks are then allotted proportionately once the subscription has closed. New issues are normally underwritten by a bank or accepting house.

In the secondary market, the stocks are traded on the stock exchange through a stockbroker. Though they are registered securities, they are transferable in multiples of one penny. As with gilts, short-dated stocks are dealt at a price, plus or minus accrued interest, while longer-dated stocks are dealt inclusive of accrued interest.

The secondary market is particularly inactive. Although there are 779 stocks outstanding, their total nominal value is only £2700 million, while turnover for 1980 was £3820 million representing an average daily value of £15.3 million. This represents only two per cent of the total capital market turnover by value and only three per cent of the total fixed-interest market. In volume terms, i.e., by number of bargains, local authority stocks represented only 1.3 and 4.9 per cent respectively of these markets.

Yields on local authority stocks tend to be slightly higher than for gilts of comparable terms in order to compensate for their relatively lesser security. They are guaranteed as to principal and interest by the local government issuer and not by central government, though the Bank of England would support the market for any issue.

Bonds of public boards

Similar to local authority stocks, these are bonds issued by various public sector institutions such as the Metropolitan Water Board, the Agricultural Mortgage Board or Finance for Industry Limited (a state owned company that specializes in providing equity or debenture capital to British industry).

The bonds are registered securities issued and traded through the stock exchange in the same manner as for local authority stocks. There are 116 such bonds outstanding with maturities that range from short (under five years) to long (over 15 years). The aggregate nominal value of these securities is only about £450 million and secondary market trading is thin. Yields are higher than for local authority bonds by approximately one per cent for gross redemption yields not so much because of difference in security, but more because of poorer marketability.

Corporate bonds (debentures and loan stock)

Two types of bonds are issued by the corporate sector which includes UK registered companies and foreign registered companies that have also obtained a listing on the London stock exchange.

Debentures are loans secured against specific assets of the company or against the general assets of the company and rank ahead of all other capital issues, both fixed-interest and equity, in the payment of creditors in the event of a company being put into liquidation.

A second type of corporate bond, known as unsecured loan stock, is—as its name suggests—unsecured against specific assets—and ranks behind debentures but ahead of shares in the order of creditors' claims.

Debentures, like shares, are transferable in any size and in units determined by the price of the debenture. Loan stock is transferable, as are government bonds, in minimum denominations of £100 of stock or part thereof if the stock is priced below par.

Both types of bonds are registered securities and may be either straight or convertible. Straight bonds have fixed maturity dates which may extend up to 20 years (or occasionally longer). Capital may either be redeemed in full at maturity or may be amortized over the life of the loan.

Convertible bonds also carry fixed-rate coupons but also provide an option by which the holder can convert the bonds to ordinary shares of the issuing company at predetermined option dates. They carry lower coupons than comparable straight debentures but this is compensated for by the potential capital gain that may be made by conversion into shares. Both types pay interest semiannually calculated according to a 365-day year. Corporate bonds are not as popular, either with issuers or investors, as are corporate equity issues. Straight debentures and unsecured loan stocks as at 31 December 1980 amounted to a total outstanding of £13819 million nominal and £11022 million market value. This represented approximately 12 per cent of the total fixed-interest market and 3 per cent of the total capital market including equities. At the same date, convertible bonds outstanding amounted to £1737 million nominal and £1942 million market value.

In the primary market, debentures and loan stock are issued and, though not always, may also be underwritten by a bank, merchant, or stockbroker. The terms are announced in advance and applications for stock invited from the public who may tender through a bank or stockbroker. The issue price may be at a discount, at par, or at a premium depending on yield and the coupon relative to market rates of interest. If issued at a discount, the issuing company must show the amount of the discount separately in its balance sheet until written off.

Once the subscription is closed, the debentures or stock are allotted proportionately and subscribers are required to settle the full amount due for the stock they receive, having first usually paid a deposit of 5 or 10 per cent.

In the secondary market the stocks are listed on the stock exchange. Turnover is low. The average monthly value of transactions during 1980 in straight debentures and loans was £57 million with a volume of just under 15000 bargains. Covertibles had an average monthly turnover of £41 million by value and 7805 volume of bargains. Major participants in the market are insurance companies who hold just under 40 per cent by value of corporate fixed-interest securities. Other financial and public sector institutions hold most of the remaining issues, while the private sector (companies and individuals), represent about 10 per cent of the market participants. Unlike corporate bonds in some other foreign markets—notably North America and Japan—British corporate bonds are not rated as to security. Stockbrokers and other investment advisers assume the responsibility of recommending particular issues to their clients. First-class debentures of the most creditworthy companies usually yield less than comparable British government stock, not because of their greater security but because of their lesser marketability. The majority of corporate debentures are held by institutions in their long-term portfolios. This is because loan stock interest is paid by the issuing companies from their after tax profits. Institutions are able to gross up the yield by offsetting the tax paid against their

355

own tax bill. Thus, for example, a 10 per cent coupon is worth about 15 per cent to an institution, though not to an individual.

Foreign bonds

The British capital market does not provide a major market for foreign bonds. This is due to British exchange controls which were enforced for 40 years before being abolished entirely in October 1979. During this period the authorities virtually closed the market to foreign borrowers by legislating to prevent the outflow of sterling capital. Until this legislation was applied more stringently, a number of bond issues by foreign governments were made up until 1952, while bonds originating from borrowers in the overseas sterling area continued to be issued up until 1971. A total of 182 foreign bonds of these types remain outstanding.

Bulldog bonds

Since the removal of UK exchange controls, the UK bond market has once again become accessible to foreign borrowers. The first foreign bond issue on the London market was made by the kingdom of Denmark. This issue for £75 million carries a 13 per cent coupon and matures in 2005. This issue was christened by the market a 'bulldog bond'.

Although the first issue for many years, it may prove to be the pioneer in a new market which may develop in sterling foreign bonds and, as the US and Japan foreign bond markets are known as Yankee and Samurai bond markets respectively, the sterling market may become known as the Bulldog bond market.

In November 1980 the Bank of England introduced new rules for the issue of bonds in sterling by foreign borrowers. Major requirements are that no sterling denominated issues should be made in foreign capital markets, and that in the case of a foreign currency bond with an option to receive interest or capital in sterling, then the issue should be lead managed by a UK based institution, as must all sterling denominated foreign bonds or Eurobonds. Foreign borrowers issuing bulldog bonds are now also regulated as to timing by a queue operated by the Bank of England through the government broker.

Of the foreign bond issues outstanding, these may be defined in four categories—commonwealth and provincial securities, commonwealth corporation stocks, foreign stocks and bonds and foreign corporation stocks.

Commonwealth and provincial securities

These are foreign bonds issued by governments or states of the old British commonwealth countries. These were defined under the Exchange Control Act as comprising the overseas sterling areas. The last of these securities was issued by the Government of New Zealand in 1971. Commonwealth and provincial securities are similar to British government stock in that they are registered securities of consolidated issues of loan stock, issued with maturities of up to 40 years, or may even be undated. They carry fixed-rate coupons, pay interest semiannually and redeem principal at par in full at maturity. They represent fully guaranteed obligations of the issuing government or province. There are 47 such securities outstanding with a total nominal value of £252 million. Yields are higher than for comparable British government bonds but vary considerably according to the degree of risk that the market attaches to a particular foreign government. For example, as at early September 1980, South Rhodesian 6% 1978/81 bonds were being quoted at a price of £145 and yielding to redemption 27.87 per cent.

Commonwealth corporation stocks

Eight outstanding issues originate from towns or countries of old British commonwealth countries. They are similar in nature to loan stocks issued by British local authorities, in that they are registered loan stock with maturities of up to 35 years, pay interest semiannually and redeem principal at par at maturity. The eight stocks in this group have a combined nominal value of £9.7 million.

Foreign stocks and bonds/foreign corporation stocks

Foreign stocks and bonds and corporation stocks are identical in nature to the two types of commonwealth securities but have been issued by countries or local governments outside the old overseas sterling area. The last such issue was made in Norway in 1952.

There are 97 foreign stocks and bonds outstanding with a nominal value of £330 million and 31 foreign corporation stocks with a total nominal value of £50 million.

The secondary market in foreign bonds is centred on the stock exchange. Turnover is, however, extremely thin and represents less than 0.1 per cent of total market turnover by value.

Secondary market

Eurobonds

In the same way that the exchange controls prevented the development of a British foreign bond market, the primary market in sterling denominated Eurobonds was also restricted, though London provides the world's major centre for secondary market Eurobond trading.

In the primary market there have been some 20 sterling Eurobond issues. Prior to October 1979 these were issued in one of three ways which effectively made them foreign currency securities for the purposes of the Exchange Control Act. All of these carried options, excercisable by the holder, to receive interest and/or principal in a foreign currency, either US dollars or Deutschemarks. Thus, although the bonds were originally issued denominated in sterling, the liabilities of the borrower were in foreign currency and thus did not involve the export of sterling. UK residents were permitted only to purchase the bonds, as for other currency denominated bonds, with investment currency purchased at a premium.

Firstly, most issues made prior to 1973 carried options to receive interest and/or principal in Deutschemarks at a rate of exchange which was fixed for the life of the loan. Most bond issues had lives of between 10 and 15 years. At issue, the exchange rate was £1 = DM 11.11 for some of the earlier bonds.

At September 1980 the exchange rate stood at £1 = DM 4.3. Clearly such bond issues substantially increased the liability of the borrowers who have had to repay up to twice the sterling equivalent of their original debts incurred by such borrowing.

Secondly, other bonds issued up till 1974 carried options for the holder both to receive interest and principal in dollars and to convert into the US equities of the American issuers. Some of these carried options exercisable at rates of exchange fixed for the life of the issue which, as with the Deutschemark options, placed the risk on the borrower. Finally, others carried options excercisable at current exchange rates prevailing at the interest payment dates or at the conversion option dates, which placed the risk on both borrower and lender.

Because of the risks involved in Eurosterling bonds, the secondary market is somewhat illiquid. The bonds outstanding, totalling approximately £350 million, are quoted on the London and Luxembourg stock exchanges, but most trading takes place in the over-the-counter market maintained by banks in London.

Although almost a quarter of the Eurobonds listed on the London stock exchange are issued by UK companies, almost all of these issues have been denominated in US dollars.

Since the removal of exchange controls, there have been a small number of Eurosterling bonds issues. These did not need to provide currency options since the export of sterling is no longer restricted.

The first was a floating rate note issued by Scandinavian Bank. The second was a convertible bond for £15 million issued by Orient Finance at par (£100), with a maturity of 15 years and coupon at eight per cent. In August 1980, Rothschilds Investment Trust issued a third Eurosterling bond for £12 million with a maturity of 10 years and average life of 8 years. The coupon was $14\frac{1}{2}$ per cent.

The Bank of England introduced new guidelines for the issue of sterling denominated Eurobonds in November 1980. The main features of these regulations are that all sterling issues or sterling option issues must be lead managed by a UK based issuing house and while there will be no queue of borrowers, issuers of over £3 million will have to seek timing consent from the Bank of England which will ensure that no market congestion occurs.

Secondary market

Since these issues are relatively recent, it is too soon to judge their liquidity in the secondary market.

For other currency denominated Eurobonds, however, London provides a highly active primary and secondary market and, indeed, is the world's major centre for Eurobond trading. Over 400 Eurobond issues are listed on the London stock exchange, representing a nominal value of about £7 billion, although most transactions, including those in many unlisted bonds, take place in the over-the-counter market maintained by banks in London.

A full list of Eurobonds issued and traded in the London market, whether quoted on the stock exchange or otherwise, is printed in the *Financial Times* on the second Monday of each month.

At the end of 1978 the size of the Eurobond market in terms of issues outstanding was just under US$100 billion. Turnover was in the region of US$250 billion for 1980, and London is estimated to account for approximately 40 per cent of this volume.

Equities

Excluding gilts, the equity sector of the UK capital market is substantially larger and considerably more active than the market for fixed-interest securities. UK investors prefer equities for a number of reasons. Since interest rates have fluctuated significantly during the past 50 years, fixed-interest securities carry a risk of uncertain yield curves and the potential of capital loss in the short to medium term. This is augmented by increasing inflation in more recent years causing a diminution of capital in real terms which is not compensated for by adequate yields. In addition, the British tax system tends to discriminate against fixed-interest securities since interest is taxable at progressive rates of income tax. In contrast, equity shares of expanding companies can be expected to grow in capital value giving a return that is, hopefully, better than fixed coupon stock yields and in line with inflation. Capital gain is taxable at the standard rate of 30 per cent while capital losses can be offset and carried forward against capital gains tax.

Partly through tradition and partly because the equity market has now developed as a much larger and more active market than the fixed-interest market, companies too prefer to raise capital through the equities market. In recent years high interest rates anyway have placed a greater burden on companies and further deter them from issuing fixed interest stocks.

Many foreign companies also make use of the vigorous British equities market. Of the approximate 2700 companies listed, just under 400 are foreign registered companies having issued share capital directly onto the British market.

As at 31 December 1980, there were 2601 companies with ordinary shares listed on the stock exchange. The market value of these shares was £270 billion. Though shares of foreign registered companies with listings in London numbered only 396, but they accounted for £184 billion of the total market value, or 68 per cent of the total. The largest single group of foreign companies is US registered companies. One hundred and thirty-three US companies have quotations in London and represent a total market value of £117 billion. The second largest group—some 105 companies—are registered in South Africa and represented a market value of £17.9 billion. South African companies listed on the London stock exchange represent the major overseas market for South African securities and the principal means by which financial rands can be created for the purpose of portfolio investment in South Africa.

Shares are registered securities and may be ordinary or preferred shares. Ordinary shares carry full voting rights and dividend rights but rank behind holders of debentures, loan stock and preference shares as creditors to the company.

Preference shares do not carry voting rights, but they bear dividend rights in preference to the dividend rights attaching to ordinary shares. Normally such rights are for a fixed dividend. Three types of preferred shares are issued—cumulative,

359

participating and redeemable preference shares. Cumulative preference shares entitle the holder to a cumulative dividend if, for reasons of the company having made a loss or insufficient profit in previous years, the company had been unable to pay the preference dividend during that prior period. Participating preference shares entitle the holder to an agreed share of the remaining profits once the fixed portion of the preference dividend has been made and they thus enable the holder to participate in the growth of the company. Redeemable preference shares may be redeemed by either the holder or the issuing company at the option of either.

Preference shares are therefore more akin to fixed interest securities and there is a relatively small volume of such shares. They represent less than one per cent by value of the outstanding ordinary shares. Most are held by institutions.

Primary market

In the primary market, new equity issues are floated and underwritten by a merchant bank or a stockbroker. The amount and terms of an issue are announced in advance in the financial press and through the stock exchange. A full prospectus of the issuing company is also published. Subscribers are invited to apply either directly to the issuing agent or through a stockbroker. Shares are then allotted proportionately once the subscription is closed, though small shareholders requiring up to, say, 500 shares usually receive the full amount applied for even if the issue has been oversubscribed.

Companies which are issuing shares to the public for the first time have to submit their accounts to the stock exchange for approval, and must thereafter abide by the full financial disclosure and strict regulations as required by the Stock Exchange Council. Companies have to publish full sets of audited accounts annually as well as interim half-yearly accounts which need not be audited. Accounting standards in Britain are high and ensure that the true financial position of a company is made available to the investing public.

In the 12 months to December 1980, new issues of ordinary shares by companies obtaining listings for the first time raised proceeds of £356 million.

Secondary market

The secondary market is maintained on the stock exchange and transactions may only be made through stockbrokers.

There is no minimum unit in which shares may be traded. Although it is uncommon, shares may be traded in single units and in an aggregate value of just a few pounds. Similarly, there is no maximum amount or value, although very large purchases or sales may take several days to complete. Any investor purchasing more than five per cent of the issued capital of a particular company is required to disclose his shareholding to the Stock Exchange Council.

Because the stock exchange runs a two-week account period, payment for shares purchased does not require settlement until the end of the account. It is, therefore, possible to buy and sell shares within the same account period without having to actually pay for the shares, merely paying or receiving the difference between the purchase and sale price at the end of the account. If dealing within one account period the stamp duty of two per cent is not charged. Also, if a purchase and a sale is effected within the same account period commission is charged once only by the stockbroker.

It is also possible to sell shares during an account even if the seller does not possess those shares, as long as he buys the same quantity before the end of the account. This is known as selling short and is usually undertaken by an investor who speculates that the price of a particular share will fall rather than rise. If he sells the shares at, say, 100p per share and then buys at, say, 90p before the end of the account, he makes a profit of 10p per share without having advanced any principal.

Turnover in UK equities is active and most shares are readily marketable. For the year 1980, total turnover was just under £31 billion by value and 4 231 737 by volume. This represents an average transaction size of approximately £7280 per bargain and an average daily turnover of £121 million.

Turnover of specific shares or sectors of shares varies according to business and economic conditions but all shares are readily marketable because of the unique trading method used on the London stock exchange.

The activity of each sector of shares quoted on the stock exchange may be monitored by means of the *Financial Times* Actuaries Share Indices, which are calculated daily and published in the London *Financial Times*.

Share indices

The most commonly quoted index is called simply the 'FT Index'. Its full name is the Financial Times Industrial Ordinary Share Index. This is an index of the prices of 30 shares representing the 30 market leaders, or blue chip companies. The index is an arithmetic unweighted average of these share prices. Its base is 100 as at 10 April 1962. Having peaked at around 558 in early 1979, the FT Index stood at a new high of over 567 in May 1981 and was rising.

A broader based index is the FT 500 share index. This is an unweighted average of the share prices of companies representing all sectors of industry plus oil shares. The unadjusted weighting of shares, however, tends to distort this index and gives some companies, particularly oil companies, too much influence in the movement of the index. Further, price movements due to scrip and rights issues will also have a distorting effect. A still broader based index is the FT All Share Index. This includes all the shares in the 500 Index plus financial groups, commodity groups and other groups not elsewhere included. The total number of shares in the All Share Index is 750. It is calculated in the same manner as the 500 Index and subject to the same movements.

Share rights issues

One method by which already listed companies may raise new share capital is by means of a rights issue. This is an issue of shares below the current market price made available to existing shareholders in given proportion to the shares held. When the rights issue is first made, the capital is not called up immediately and, for a short period, the shares may be bought and sold in the nil-paid form which may be at a premium to the price of the shares prior to the announcement of the rights issue.

Rights issues are the most commonly used method by which companies raise new capital, partly because it is a fairly inexpensive method of obtaining finance and partly because fixed interest loans are unpopular with investors. Rights issues, however, may also be unpopular with investors because they dilute the equity of a company and thus the return to individual shareholders. The price of a share may consequently fall slightly on the announcement of a rights issue. Most issues, therefore, are made when the market is bouyant and less likely to depress share prices.

In the year to December 1980, £1060 million of new capital was raised by more than 150 companies through the issue of rights.

Share options

There are two separate markets in share options made on the London stock exchange. The first is a simple market in call options (an option to buy) and call options (an option to sell) in which the options may be either exercised or allowed to lapse. The second is the market in traded options in which the options may be traded as securities in their own right.

In the first market, over 150 market leading shares are available in option form, and call rates for some 80 or so of the most active share options are quoted daily in the share information section of the *Financial Times*. All options run for a life of three months though they may be exercised at any time during their three-month life.

In this market option prices are made by the stock exchange jobbers. Usually the price of an option is about 10 per cent of the corresponding share price. These option prices apply for dealing within a specified time period of about a week. For example, call options for Barclays Bank shares were available at 40p (the share price was 432p) for purchase any time between 17 November and 28 November 1980. The price at which the option holder may purchase the shares is the price prevailing at the date of first dealings, i.e. 17 November. The option may be exercised at any time up to three months. In this example the last declaration (or exercise date) was 26 February 1981. The investor cannot sell his option but may choose only to exercise the option or allow it to lapse. Clearly, he would only exercise the option if the market price of the share moved up by more than 10 per cent (the cost of the option). Thus if the price of Barclays shares rose within three months from 432p to, say, 500p, the investor would gain 500 − 432p = 68p less the original cost of his option. He would thus make a profit of 28p per share (less brokerage). If the investor expected the share price to fall, he could purchase a put option. This is an option to sell the shares at the specified price. If he exercises the option within the three-month period, he may purchase the shares at a lower price than he has contracted to sell them and thus make a profit equal to the difference in the share price less the cost of the original option.

For example, at the beginning of September 1980, the three-month call option for Burmah Oil was quoted at 20p per share, while the share price was being quoted at 188p, i.e., 20p on the buying price of, say, 190p (if the middle price is 188p) giving a total of 210p. Exercise including brokerage, therefore, of about 3p per share becomes the total cost represented by the option is 213p. Assuming an investor made an outlay of £100 and purchased 500 call options in Burmah Oil and within three months the shares reached 200p, the investor could exercise his option but would make a loss of £65 [500 × (213 − 200p)]. If he did not exercise the option he would make a loss of £100 plus brokerage. On the other hand, if the share price rose within three months to 220p he would make a profit of £35 [(220 − 213p) × 500] which, though small, represents 35 per cent of his original investment.

Dealing in options is a speculative investment. It gives the investor the opportunity to speculate and participate in the rise or fall of the share price with a relatively small outlay of funds.

The risk, however, is high since the share for which a particular option is purchased must rise or fall usually by a substantial margin before the option becomes exercisable. If the target, or exercise price, is not reached by the share in question, the investor looses his original outlay which he paid for the options. His potential loss, however, is limited to the cost of the original option.

It is possible for an investor to hedge his risk by buying a 'double' which is a put and a call option in the same share. His potential profit is smaller because he will lose his outlay on one of the options, but he stands to make a moderate gain if the price of the share either rises or falls. He will still lose, however, if the price does not move significantly in either direction.

The volume of options purchased is variable, but is more active if the stock market is exhibiting a strong trend either upward or downward.

The traded options market is newer and differs from the ordinary options market in several respects. As at December 1980 options of only 15 companies were available although for most of these a series of exercise prices are available for a variety of option maturities. For example on 17 November 1980, three options were available for shares of Consolidated Gold Fields Ltd. The equity price was 548p per share. Three exercise prices were quoted—588p, 638p and 688p per share. The cost of a call option differs according to the exercise price chosen and the life of the option which may be three, six or nine months. Since options in this market may be traded as securities in their own right, there is no date for first and last dealings and the option price may change from day to day depending on demand and supply. The option price is thus quoted on a daily basis until it expires. Thus for Consolidated Gold Fields, options at the exercise price of 588p were quoted on 17 November at 30p for declaration in January 1981, 55p for declaration in April 1981 and 75p for declaration in July 1981. Options at the exercise price of 688p were quoted at 9p, 22p and 35p for declaration in January, April and July 1981 respectively. Clearly, the price of the option depends on the difference between the current share price and the exercise price and on the life of the option. The farther away the exercise date, the greater chance there is of the exercise price being reached. Thus the option price for shares of the tobacco company, the Imperial Group, on 17 November 1980 was $8\frac{1}{2}$p for declaration in November 1980. This represented purely the difference between the equity price of 78p and the exercise price of 70p.

The investor in this market has the choice not only to exercise the option or allow it to lapse but he may also sell the option to a third party. If the price of the corresponding share has risen the price of the option will be at a premium compared to the price at which it was first issued and he will make a small profit. On the other hand, if the price has fallen he may sell the option at a discount to its original price but he will not lose the whole of his original investment as would happen in the other option market.

Put options may also be purchased in the traded options market since for some companies exercise prices may exist which are lower than the current prevailing equity price. At 17 November 1980, seven option contracts were available in the shares of Lonrho which then stood at 108p per share. Four call put options were available at exercise prices of between 84 and 104p. Three call options were also available at exercise prices of 110p, 114p and 120p. An investor purchasing a put option is deemed to have sold the shares at 108p and if the share price subsequently reaches the exercise price of 84p, in theory he buys them back, thus making a profit of $(108 - 84) = 24p$ less the cost of the option.

For example, for June 1980 turnover in options was fairly active, and double that of the previous two months. The number of contracts traded was 22073 for a premium value of £3 795 419 which represented an underlying market equity of £32.5 million. The average daily turnover was 1104 options traded for a total premium of £189 771 and an average value per contract of £172. Since each average contract of £172 represented an average underlying equity of £1 500, it can be seen that the potential for profit by a small outlay is significant.

Share warrants

A few companies have occasionally issued warrants, though none have been issued in recent years. These are quoted securities and give the holder the right to buy shares of the company at some date (or dates) in the future at a fixed price. Some warrants may be exercisable at any time. Most carry expiry dates, though some have no final exercise date and are thus known as perpetual warrants. The warrants may be traded separately as securities in their own right but, like options, they do not rank for dividends and can prove a risky investment. Warrants are a highly geared form of equity investment because the warrant price is usually only a fraction of the price of the equivalent share. Thus, warrant prices often stand at a considerable premium over their issue price and are strongly influenced by market conditions of supply and demand.

The stock exchange

There are 14 stock exchanges in the UK and Ireland which comprise the Associated Stock Exchange. The most important exchange and the one in which by far the major share of business is transacted is, of course, the London stock exchange.

The 13 provincial exchanges are regulated by the London Stock Exchange Council, although the day-to-day administration is delegated to local councils, and all are subject to the same dealing legislation and commission rates. The provincial exchanges specialize in the listing of local stocks and shares, though all securities listed on the London stock exchange may also be dealt through one of the provincial exchanges whose brokers are in constant communication with brokers in London.

Table 17.8 Securities traded on stock exchange (*source: London Stock Exchange Fact Book*)

	1971	1972	1973	1974	1975	1976	1977	1978	1979	1980
VALUE OF TURNOVER £ million										
Grand total—all securities	64 193	56 383	55 769	56 753	94 036	106 433	173 334	138 769	168 937	196 290
Total—fixed interest	50 816	36 317	38 690	44 137	76 490	92 270	163 166	119 554	144 831	165 489
Total—equities and convertibles	13 377	20 066	17 079	12 616	17 546	14 163	20 168	19 215	24 106	30 801
FIXED INTEREST										
British government										
short dated	22 062	15 619	20 859	20 060	41 216	47 510	78 888	62 664	65 458	75 178
medium long dated	25 335	17 124	14 552	18 202	26 028	34 414	56 871	41 015	63 492	76 521
Irish government	······	······	299	1 882	3 963	4 460	9 197	9 671	9 524	7 994
UK local authorities	1 521	1 345	1 117	2 585	3 501	4 265	5 365	4 247	4 378	3 820
Foreign government bonds	218	220	180	150	223	197	487	274	217	225
Corporate bonds	1 679	2 008	1 683	1 256	1 558	1 424	2 358	1 684	1 763	1 751
Total—fixed interest	50 816	36 317	38 690	44 137	76 490	92 270	153 166	119 554	144 831	165 489
Fixed interest as percentage of grand total, %	79.2	64.4	69.4	77.8	81.3	86.7	88.4	86.2	85.7	84.3
VOLUME OF TURNOVER										
No. of bargains, in thousands										
Grand total—all securities	6 823	7 987	6 021	5 021	6 030	4 866	6 085	5 490	5 456	5 708
Total—fixed interest	1 365	1 262	1 067	1 085	1 232	1 299	1 650	1 360	1 344	1 477
Total—equities	5 258	6 725	4 955	3 936	4 769	3 567	4 435	4 130	4 112	4 231
Fixed interest as % of grand total	12.9	15.8	17.7	21.6	20.9	26.7	27.1	24.8	24.6	25.9
Equities as % of grand total	77.1	84.2	82.3	78.4	79.1	73.3	72.9	75.2	75.4	74.1
AVERAGE SIZE OF BARGAIN, £										
Fixed interest										
British government										
short dated	153 227	133 873	144 559	115 941	138 887	158 320	217 220	172 255	198 136	212 358
long dated	65 623	51 024	44 485	50 016	66 357	73 525	92 374	88 828	115 762	118 793
Irish government	······	······	17 087	67 315	109 026	117 427	137 009	161 758	196 242	192 456
UK local authorities	16 347	22 109	13 233	29 983	42 486	51 758	50 425	42 987	58 476	57 287
Foreign government bonds	5 797	5 781	6 932	6 686	11 598	26 976	22 229	12 403	11 688	10 703
Corporate bonds	2 384	2 893	3 399	3 037	3 614	3 625	4 967	3 943	5 453	5 176
Equities	2 544	2 984	3 447	3 206	3 680	3 971	4 548	4 653	5 863	7 280

The stock exchange council comprises 36 people elected by members of the stock exchange. All new listings of securities must be first submitted to the council for approval. Very stringent requirements must be met before a quotation is given. The stock exchange is overseen by the council for the Securities Industry. The stock exchange council is responsible for regulation of the stock exchange and ensuring the protection of the public against fraudulent or doubtful companies or methods of dealing. A recent example of the council's activities in protecting the investor and ensuring the reputation of the stock exchange is the legislation against insider trading, which entered the statute book and became a criminal offence in 1980.

Full details are set out in the Stock Exchange Code of Practice. The general principle of the law is to prohibit dealing in the shares of a particular company by persons who have special knowledge, not generally available to the public, of that company. As an example, it is designed to prevent members of a company from dealing in its own shares up to two months prior to the announcement of financial results, a takeover bid or other extraordinary item and thus affecting the price of a share when the majority of shareholders have no knowledge of such information, and thus no opportunity to act in their own best interests.

Only members and their authorized clerks are allowed on the floor of the stock exchange. There are over 4000 members of the London stock exchange who comprise two types, brokers and jobbers.

Brokers Brokers are members of stockbroking firms who act as agents on behalf of their clients in the purchase and sale of securities on the floor of the exchange. There are 3537 brokers and 775 of their clerks who represent some 240 stockbroking firms and who are authorized to deal on the floor of the exchange.

Jobbers The other type of member is known as a jobber. Jobbers work on the floor of the stock exchange, acting as intermediaries between buying and selling brokers. They are dealers who act on their own account in the buying or selling of securities and who maintain their own books in particular markets of securities; each has a special pitch or post on the floor from which he conducts his business. The brokers deal directly with the jobbers and go to the pitch at which a particular jobber is located for dealing with specific types of securities.

The jobber makes the market and determines the price at which he will buy or sell securities according to the demand and supply for those securities. He stands ready at all times to buy and sell the securities for which he makes a market. He makes his profit on the difference (normally a few pence) between his bid and offer prices, though he is continually adjusting his prices either up or down depending on the volume of business and demand conditions. There are 484 jobbers and 237 of their clerks representing 19 firms of jobbers authorized to operate on the floor.

Nearly all trading of publicly issued securities is conducted on the floor of the stock exchange which is open daily between 10 a.m. and 4 p.m.

Altogether, there are almost 8000 securities listed on the London stock exchange representing a total market value of £280 328 million as at 31 March 1980. These securities are summarized in the following table together with their turnover. Fixed

Table 17.9 Securities listed on London stock exchange (31.12.80) (*source: London Stock Exchange Fact Book*)

Securities	Number	Nominal value, £ million	Market value, £ million
PUBLIC SECTOR—fixed interest			
British government securities			
short dated	30	24 412	23 052
medium dated	37	24 923	21 481
long dated	43	32 346	26 120
Total	110	81 675	70 653
Irish government securities	83	3 445	2 861
Local authority and local corporation stocks	482	2 504	2 299
Utilities and public sector bonds	110	443	325
Foreign bonds (of overseas governments)	170	669	476
Total—public sector	955	88 736	76 614
COMPANY SECTOR—fixed interest			
Loans, stocks and debentures (including convertibles)	1 799	5 348	3 796
Total—domestic fixed interest	2 754	94 084	80 410
EUROBONDS			
UK companies	85	1 932	1 513
Foreign companies	432	7 537	6 656
	517	9 469	8 169
Total—fixed interest securities	3 271	103 553	88 579
EQUITIES			
Preference shares	1 256	1 357	799
Ordinary and deferred shares	2 205	17 629	85 910
Total—all securities	6 732	122 539	175 288
British government securities as percentage of total	1.6	66.7	40.3
Total domestic fixed interest as percentage of total	40.9	80.0	45.9
Equities as percentage of total	51.4	15.5	49.5
Total company securities (equities and loans) as percentage of total	78.1	27.6	56.3

interest securities, which include mainly government gilt-edged stock, comprise only 23 per cent of total securities by market value, but represent more than 85 per cent of total turnover by value. For the year ended December 1979, turnover of all securities was £168 937 million. By volume, however, in terms of number of bargains, equities far surpassed fixed interest securities. For 1979, total turnover was 5 455 905 bargains, 75 per cent of which was accounted for by equity transactions. This apparent discrepancy is caused by fixed interest securities, particularly gilts, being dealt mainly by larger institutional investors, whereas the majority of equities

367

are dealt by individuals and small investors. For 1979 the average size of bargain in fixed interest securities was £107 750, whereas the average size of bargain in equities was £5863.

Unlisted securities market

However, the equity market was extended in order to provide an over-the-counter market in unlisted shares. This market, known as the unlisted securities market (USM), is maintained by stockbrokers and jobbers who act both as dealers on behalf of their clients and also as principals holding shares for their own account. There already existed a small number of companies whose shares were traded in this manner and which were not quoted on the stock exchange, although they suffered from a very restricted market. These shares were traded according to the rules of section 163 of the Stock Exchange Code of Practice. This market has now been superseded by the unlisted securities market (USM).

Shares in this market are offered for sale initially on a private placement method and are thereafter traded outside the floor of the stock exchange, through stockbrokers. In the initial sale, 25 per cent of the companies' shares are given to jobbers, who may then make them available to the general public through contract with stockbrokers other than the sponsoring broker who placed the major 75 per cent share.

The USM is regulated by the Stock Exchange Council despite the fact that the shares are not listed on the stock exchange. The council suggests that a company whose shares are traded in the USM should ultimately seek a full listing on the stock exchange although this is not a condition of the USM. There are no commensurate rights for a listed company to be relegated to the USM. The advantage of issuing shares in the USM is that a company may raise equity capital, which is cheaper than loan capital, while quotation costs are about half the £200 000 or more that it costs to obtain a quotation on the stock exchange. Disclosure requirements are also less stringent on the USM. A full financial prospectus and accountant's report are not required. Instead companies need only show a three-year trading record. The offer for sale must be for at least 10 per cent of a company's capital but it need not be advertised in the press as is required for listed companies.

The USM opened with quotations of 11 companies. Nine were previously quoted on the unregulated market operated under Stock Exchange rule 163, and have now transferred to the USM. The remaining two companies were not previously quoted or traded in any public market. By the end of December 1980 the number of companies on the USM had grown to 23. The activities of the companies range from oil and gas exploration to computer services.

Unit trusts and investment trusts

A holding in a unit trust represents an investment in a collective portfolio of investments. The type of investment varies between trusts. Some specialize in fixed interest investments, some in equities, and some in commodities. Each may be exclusively domestic investments or foreign investments; some may be a combination. Altogether there are over 400 such trusts and the investor chooses according to whether he requires a good income return or a good capital return at commensurately higher risk. Some trusts provide a moderate proportion of both income and capital gain.

Unit and investment trusts are established and managed by financial institutions such as merchant banks and insurance companies as well as by independent managements, and the investor is effectively purchasing both the management and expertise of the managing institution, as well as the specific type of investment, when he purchases a unit or share in a trust. Unit trusts are not quoted, nor are their units traded, on the stock exchange, but units may be purchased directly from the managers of a particular trust. A bank or stockbroker will normally advise clients of appropriate trusts in which to invest. The transaction may be made by means of a telephone call to the managers of a chosen trust, who then issue a contract note to the investor. A complete list of available unit trusts, their telephone numbers, and unit prices are published daily in the *Financial Times*.

A unit trust is a fund with no specified capital structure. In contrast, an investment trust is a limited company whose shares are quoted and traded on the stock exchange. There is, therefore, a difference in the secondary markets of the two types of trusts. The price of a unit in a unit trust is dependent upon its underlying asset value, whereas the price of a share in an investment trust is dependent not only on its underlying asset value but also on supply and demand exhibited in the equity market and for the shares of each trust. Investment trust shares may thus stand at a premium or a discount to their underlying asset value. Unit trusts expand or contract according to the number of investors and are thus sometimes known as open-ended, whereas investment trusts have a fixed capital but may borrow funds in order to increase their level of investment. The price of their shares may also, therefore, be affected by the degree of gearing, or leverage, relative to their asset value.

Managers of unit trusts make a front charge plus an annual fee whereas shares of investment trusts are liable to brokerage charges only since these are traded on the stock exchange.

The activities of unit and investment trusts are controlled by law. Unit trusts and investment trusts that have been approved for tax purposes offer an additional benefit to the resident investor in that they are subject to special tax benefits.

Net gains (i.e., gains on franked income) are subject to corporation tax at 10 per cent as against the normal 52 per cent, while management charges and expenses can be deducted from franked income prior to its becoming liable to corporation tax. Capital gains are free from tax as against the full 30 per cent normal capital gains tax. Net dividends are not subject to additional tax.

Commodities

London provides an important international centre for dealing in commodities and there are a number of commodity exchanges that specialize in the market for particular types of commodities. Commodities may be defined in two categories;

hard and soft. Hard commodities are the metals. Seven metals are traded on the London Metal Exchange (LME). These are copper, lead, zinc, tin, aluminium, nickel and silver. About 30 members of the LME, who represent dealing firms, conduct the trading in these metals by what is known as 'ring' dealing. These members meet in a room of the LME and sit round on circular benches forming a ring. Each metal is the subject of a five-minute dealing session conducted four times daily at two sessions beginning 12 noon and 3.45 p.m. At each session for each metal dealers call out their bids and offers and in that manner effect transactions between themselves, while a market clerk records all transactions. At the end of a session a bell is rung, but 'kerb' dealing may continue for 10 minutes between dealers outside the room. Dealings may be for cash (i.e., spot transactions) or for contracts three months forward or longer.

Soft commodities are mainly agricultural products which are dealt on a variety of exchanges, largely due to historical reasons. Vegetable oils and imported wheat and grain are traded on the Baltic exchange which traditionally is the exchange on which shipping space and cargoes are bought and sold. Ring trading is conducted on the Baltic exchange during two sessions—11.30 a.m. to 1 p.m. and 2.45 to 4.15 p.m. A futures market in maize and barley is also held during these sessions.

A third exchange, the London Commodity Exchange, handles transactions in most of the remaining soft commodities including cocoa, sugar, coffee, spices, vegetable oils, wool, jute and the newly established market in potatoes.

Again, the dealers congregate around a ring. In some markets—cocoa for example—the dealing session begins with a call period followed by an outcry market so that dealers with a commodity to sell can first state their quantities and prices and may then follow with their bids for the purchase of the commodity. Dealing may be for spot or for forward contracts ranging from one month up to one year.

The London Rubber Exchange is located in the same building as the London Commodity Exchange. This market is open continuously from 10 a.m. to 5 p.m. and provides the major world commodity market in rubber, although world prices are settled by a continuous process of interaction of supply and demand over the three main markets in London, Singapore and New York.

There are three ways in which an investor can speculate in the future price of particular commodities. He may, through a commodity broker, purchase either a forward contract or an option in a commodity or he may invest in a unit trust that specializes in commodities. Commodity unit trusts are subject to different trading and tax regulations than are equity unit trusts.

Forward trading

Forward trading, or futures trading, is highly speculative. To purchase a forward contract, normally only 10 per cent of the price of the commodity need be deposited, though margin calls are made by the broker on the investor if the price moves against him. Contracts must be purchased in minimum lots which vary between commodities. Dealings in copper, lead, zinc and aluminium are dealt in lots of 25 tonnes, tin in lots of 5 tonnes, and silver in lots of 10 000 ounces. Of the soft commodities, coffee is traded in lots of 5 tonnes, cocoa in lots of 10 tonnes, rubber in both 5- and 15-tonne lots, potatoes in 40-tonne lots, sugar in 50-tonne lots, and soya bean meal and grains both trade in 100-tonne lots.

Through a broker an investor may purchase a three-month forward contract in any of the hard commodities or a forward contract for any month up to 12 months into the future in any of the soft commodities by putting up a margin of 10 per cent of the value per lot. Thus, for example, if three-months' copper is quoted at £849.75 per tonne, the value of one lot (25 tonnes) is £21 243.75, but only £2124.38 (excluding commissions) need be advanced. If the price were to rise by 10 per cent within the three-month period—a moderate rise in certain market conditions—the investor could sell his contract at a profit of £2124.38, doubling his original investment. While the potential profit is high, however, the downside risk is unlimited and if the price of the commodity falls, the investor could lose all his original investment and more. Normally, the investor places a stop loss order with his broker, whereby the broker automatically sells on behalf of his client if the price falls below a certain level, thus limiting the potential loss.

The speculator, as opposed to the trader, in commodities rarely takes delivery of the physical commodity and even if he holds the contract for its full term he may sell the commodity in the cash or spot market. Alternatively, he may roll the contract over by selling his existing contract and purchasing a new three-month forward contract. He will normally purchase a forward contract when the cash price is lower than the forward price, described as a 'contango'. If the cash price is higher than the forward price, the market condition is described as 'backwardation'.

The futures market in commodities allows for forward selling as well as forward purchasing. If the investor speculates that the price of a commodity will move lower, he may sell lots of a commodity that he does not possess. This is known as 'selling short', and when the contract matures the investor may buy the same quantity in the spot market as his forward contract commits him to sell. If the price does fall between the time he first took out the forward sale contract and the time he must actually sell, he makes a profit represented by the difference between the contract value and the cash value in the spot market. If the price rises, however, his loss may be considerable since he is compelled to buy in the spot market at a price which may be substantially higher than the price at which he has sold. Under current legislation profit from commodity trading, in the hands of the individual, is treated as income rather than as capital gains. High-income resident individuals may consider therefore that they do not receive sufficient benefit to justify the high risk. Some offshore (e.g., Channel Island) registered unit trusts can turn their profits into capital gains, the benefit of which can be transferred to their investors.

An alternative method of investing in commodities, which involves less risk, although also less potential profit or loss, is the purchase of commodity options. There is no separate commodity options trading floor. The market is provided by commodity dealers, although not all commodity brokers provide this service. *Commodity options*

By paying a premium which is usually 10 per cent of the market price, the investor may purchase a call or put option to buy or sell a particular commodity in the forward market. Options may extend for up to one year in soft commodities, although the market is not yet sufficiently developed such that a 12-month option is always available in the investor's chosen commodity. Hard commodity options are usually for terms of three months.

By way of example, assume the 12-month future price of coffee is £1200 per tonne against a spot price of £1000 per tonne, but the investor speculates that the price will rise substantially higher than £1200 at some time during the coming year. He may purchase a 12-month call option for one lot (five tonnes) at a cost of £600. If the price of coffee moves up to, say, £1500 per tonne, he may exercise his option and make a profit of $5 \times (£1500 - £1200) = £1500$, less the original cost of his option. Therefore, his net profit would be £900, equivalent to 150 per cent of his original investment. The option premium is a foregone cost, but his losses are limited and he is not subject to margin calls if the price moves against him during the life of the option. Similarly, the investor may purchase a futures put option to sell a commodity if he believes the price will fall relative to the quoted futures price in the forward market.

He may also choose to hedge his risk still further by buying a double option which is both a put and a call option, allowing him either to sell or to buy the commodity depending on which way the price moves during the life of the option. The double option would cost him approximately twice as much as a single option and, since he can only exercise one, the higher cost would reduce his potential profit. In the previous example, it would have been 50 per cent of his original investment, which is nevertheless a good profit relative to other less risky forms of investments.

Financial futures

Financial futures represent an investment or speculation in the future trend in interest rates and currencies. There is currently no such market in the UK, although the possibility of establishing such a market is being reviewed, and is due to be opened in early 1982. It will be the first financial futures market in Europe. When the market opens contracts will be available in sterling and Eurodollar CDs. London will thereby provide a futures market in a Eurodollar instrument. The other financial instruments to be traded in the futures market have not yet been determined but contracts in major currencies such as dollars, Deutschemarks, yen and Swiss francs are planned.

In the US, financial futures markets have grown enormously in popularity in recent years. There it is possible to buy futures contracts in currencies and in financial money market instruments such as treasury bills and CDs, as well as longer-term securities such as 20-year treasury bonds. The market allows corporate treasurers to lock in a known return on an investment or to cover forward on a short-term loan. In addition, it allows speculative investment in the future price of money market instruments, which is effectively a speculation on the future of interest rates.

Gold

London provides the world's largest and most important market in gold. It is made by five member firms comprising two merchant banks, one subsidiary of a merchant bank, one gold broker and one metallurgical company. Representatives of these firms meet at 10.30 a.m. daily in the offices of N. M. Rothschild & Sons Limited, one of the merchant bank members. The daily 'fixing' of the gold price is made at these meetings by the five representatives who are in continuous communication with the trading rooms of their own firms and who between them match buying and selling orders at a price that equates the two. The price is always quoted in US dollars per ounce.

The trading rooms of the five member firms are also in direct communication with London banks and with gold trading centres throughout the world and, although foreign centres are active and important trading centres, it is the London daily gold fix that determines the world price of gold.

The Bank of England operates directly through the chairman of the London market who is also a member of Rothschilds Bank. The Bank of England buys or sells gold for its own account—namely the Exchange Equalization Account—which provides the gold backing to the currency and through the operation of which the Bank attempts to stabilize the value of sterling on the world foreign exchanges. The Bank also acts as agent for the South African Reserve Bank in selling some of the supply of new gold produced by South Africa, and acts also as agent for other central banks who purchase or sell gold to stabilize their own currencies.

The gold market is purely a cash or spot market and the price is determined by the laws of supply and demand. Supply is fairly steady and limited. The estimated world production in 1979 was 936 tonnes (excluding communist countries), 75 per cent of which was supplied by South Africa.

Demand depends on the strength and stability of the world economy and on confidence, particularly in the US dollar. When uncertainty is high, there is a tendency for investors to move out of assets denominated in depreciating currencies into other 'real' assets which, although they do not yield any interest, maintain their real value despite inflation or currency depreciation. Since gold is valid in all international transactions and is the asset on which ultimately all currencies are based, it is the asset most in demand when the future of alternative investments is uncertain.

Early 1980 was a period during which the world economy was in recession. There was also political instability in Iran and Afghanistan, and the US dollar was especially weak. Substantial buying of gold, particularly by the cash-rich Middle Eastern countries, as well as by European and US speculators, caused the London market price of gold to reach an all-time peak of $850 per ounce in January 1980. This represented almost a fourfold increase over the price in January 1979. The price subsequently fell steeply and stabilized at around $500 per ounce in May. This fall coincided with phenomenally high interest rates in the US markets. By September 1980 the price of gold was again rising steadily and was being quoted at over $670 per ounce.

Gold may be purchased through a bank, gold broker or bullion dealer in the form of gold bars (five grams to one kilogram) or gold coins. Gold coins minted by the Bank of England comprise the Edward VII, George V and Elizabeth II sovereigns which each contain 7.3 grams fine gold. Foreign gold coins, particularly the

South African kruggerrands, may also be purchased. The price of a coin depends on its gold content, though some dealers, particularly some of the Bureau de Change in London which offer gold coins for sale but do not buy them back, may charge a substantial premium for purchases of single gold coins. Although gold is quoted in dollars per ounce, many coins and gold bars are measured in grams or kilograms of fine gold. One ounce is equivalent to 31.1 grams of fine gold.

Gold futures

For some time it has been possible to buy forward contracts in gold bullion through either a bullion dealer or commission house (commodity broker). This is an over-the-counter market for which no public trading floor exists. Transactions are arranged through individual dealers or brokers. Terms therefore vary and the investor is required to search out the best deal. The market is, nonetheless, very large. Though its specific size is not known the forward market in London, together with the cash bullion market, has a total size which is probably the largest in the world, although the Zurich bullion market is also of comparable size.

In Spring 1981 the new London gold futures market opened. It has supplemented rather than superceded the existing forward market. The futures market has a public trading floor in Plantation House, in the City of London, where the London Metal Exchange is based. This has facilitated the standardization of forward contracts which may be purchased (or sold) in lots of 100 ounces, deliverable in London, and dealable for specific dates monthly up to six months forward (see International markets: Gold futures).

Dealing and fees

Money market

Deposits

Call deposits are dealt through a commercial bank, merchant bank, discount house or moneybroker. Time deposits of up to three months may also be placed with discount houses. Longer deposits and currency deposits are dealt through a commercial bank, merchant bank, finance house, local authority or a moneybroker. No commissions are payable but certain negotiated charges may be made by a bank according to the nature of the account.

Sterling and Eurodollar CDs

These are dealt through a commercial bank, merchant bank or discount house. The dealer's commission price is included in the difference between his quoted bid and offer prices. This dealing spread ranges from $\frac{1}{16}$ to $\frac{3}{8}$ per cent. Delivery and settlement occurs on the same or following business day.

374

Repurchase agreements

Repurchase agreements are dealt through a discount house and some banks. The premium, representing the interest payable to the lender, is in line with other deposit rates of interest prevailing in the money market. No specific commission or fee is charged.

Treasury bills, short-dated government securities, local authority bills and bonds

These are dealt through a discount house, merchant bank, commercial bank or money broker. Prices are quoted on a yield basis and bonds are dealt net, plus or minus accrued interest. The dealer's commission is included in the spread between his quoted bid and offer prices which may be as low as $\frac{1}{64}$ or $\frac{1}{32}$ per cent in the case of treasury bills and up to $\frac{1}{4}$ per cent for other securities.

Settlement and delivery takes place on the same business day if the transaction occurs before 12 noon, or the following business day if the transaction takes place in the afternoon up to 3 p.m.

Commercial bills, commercial bank bills, commercial trade bills, foreign currency bills

These are dealt through a discount house, commercial bank or merchant bank.

Commission is included in the dealing spread which is between $\frac{1}{8}$ and $\frac{1}{2}$ per cent depending on the quality of the names carried on the bills and whether the bill is an eligible bank bill or an ineligible trade bill.

Settlement and delivery occurs on the same or following business day.

Capital market

Almost all capital market securities are quoted and traded on the stock exchange. Some securities may be dealt in other markets as follows: short-dated gilts which, *Short-dated gilts* although dealt on the stock exchange, may also be dealt through money market dealers at dealing spreads of $\frac{1}{16}$ to $\frac{1}{4}$ per cent; local authority and corporation stocks may also be dealt through money market dealers, but the price and yield of *Local authority stocks* such stocks are determined and published weekly by a consortium of seven leading stockbrokers.

Unit trusts which are dealt directly through the managers of the trusts, although a *Unit trusts* bank or stockbroker will act as intermediary in advising and purchasing units in a particular trust.

Eurobonds, many of which are quoted on the stock exchange, are mainly dealt *Eurobonds* through banks and brokers at dealing spreads of $\frac{1}{4}$ to $\frac{3}{4}$ per cent depending on the currency in which the bond is denominated and Euromarket demand for securities in that currency.

Commodities Commodities are dealt through a commodity broker at fixed rates of commission which vary between the types of commodities.

375

Gold   Gold is dealt through a bank, broker or bullion dealer and their commission is included in their quoted bid and offer prices, but is smaller the larger the quantity dealt.

Stock exchange transactions

Although banks and large institutions often trade securities between each other outside the stock exchange and without the use of a broker, all stock exchange transactions must be made through a stockbroker who is a member of the stock

Table 17.10   Stock exchange commission rates

Security	Quantity	Commission on consideration for purchases and sales	
		Not divisible	*Divisible*
British and Irish government bonds			
Short dated (under 5 years)	All sizes	At discretion of broker. Normally nil for institutional and corporate investors. Typical charge for private clients is £1 per £1 000 with minimum commission of £4.	
Medium dated (5–15 years)	First £2 000	0.625%	0.7812%
	Next £2 000	0.125%	0.1562%
	Next £996 000	0.0625%	0.0782%
	Next £300 000	0.05%	0.0625%
	Next £600 000	0.025%	0.0313%
	On amount over £1 000 000	0.015%	0.0188%
Long dated (over 15 years)	First £2 000	0.625%	0.7812%
	Next £12 000	0.25%	0.3125%
	Next £986 000	0.125%	0.1563%
	Next £3 000 000	0.1%	0.125%
	Next £6 000 000	0.05%	0.0625%
	On amount over £10 000 000	0.03%	0.0375%
New issues of long-dated British government funds	First £2 000	0.625%	0.7812%
	Next £2 000	0.125%	0.1562%
	Next £996 000	0.0625%	0.0782%
	Next £9 000 000	0.05%	0.0625%
	On amount over £10 000 000	0.03%	0.0375%
Corporation and local authority stocks, Irish land bonds, Commonwealth and provincial bonds, and Other foreign bonds	First £2 000	0.625%	0.7812%
	Next £12 000	0.25%	0.3125%
	Next £986 000	0.125%	0.1563%
	Next £3 000 000	0.1%	0.125%
	Next £6 000 000	0.05%	0.0625%
	On amount over £10 000 000	0.03%	0.0375%

Table 17.10 (*continued*)

Security	Quantity	Commission on consideration for purchases and sales	
		Not divisible	*Divisible*
Eurobonds	All sizes	At discretion of broker	
Other registered fixed-interest securities including debentures, loan stocks	First £5 000	0.75%	0.75%
	Next £45 000	0.375%	0.5%
	Next £50 000	0.325%	0.45%
	Next £150 000	0.3%	0.375%
	Next £500 000	0.25%	0.3125%
	Next £1 000 000	0.2%	0.25%
	On amount over £1 750 000	0.125%	0.1563%
Bearer fixed-interest securities	First £5 000	0.5%	0.5%
	On amount over £5 000	0.25%	0.3125%
Convertible stocks and equity shares of British registered companies with London stock exchange quotations	First £7 000		1.5%
	Next £3 000		1.25%
	Next £15 000		1.00%
	Next £25 000		0.75%
	Next £70 000		0.625%
	Next £130 000		0.5%
	Next £500 000		0.4%
	Next £1 000 000		0.27%
	On amount over £1 750 000		0.17%
	First £7 000	1.5%	
	Next £93 000	0.5%	
	Next £150 000	0.4%	
	Next £500 000	0.3%	
	Next £1 000 000	0.2%	
	On amount over £1 750 000	0.125%	
American and Canadian shares and shares of other foreign companies listed on London markets	First £5 000	0.9%	0.9%
	Next £5 000	0.4%	0.8%
	On amount over £10 000	0.3%	0.375%
Investment trusts listed on stock exchange	First £7 000	1.25%	1.25%
	Next £3 000	0.5%	1.25%
	Next £15 000	0.5%	1.0%
	Next £25 000	0.5%	0.75%
	Next £50 000	0.5%	0.625%
	Next £20 000	0.4%	0.625%
	Next £130 000	0.4%	0.5%
	Next £500 000	0.3%	0.4%
	Next £1 000 000	0.2%	0.27%
	On amount over £1 750 000	0.125%	0.17%

exchange. Banks, accountants or other intermediaries may deal on behalf of their clients, but must also deal through a stockbroker. The rates of commission charged by a stockbroker are standard rates determined by the Stock Exchange Council. There are two scales of commission rates: the 'not divisible' scale that applies if transactions are made directly through a stockbroker; the 'divisible' commission rate that is charged if transactions are made through an additional intermediary such as a bank, which itself receives approximately one-quarter of the commission charged by a broker. Divisible commissions are, therefore, higher than the 'not divisible' commissions, since the stockbroker divides some commission with the additional intermediary.

Contract fee

In addition to the stockbroker's commission, a contract note fee is charged according to the following scale.

Size of transaction	Contract fee
Less than £100	Nil
More than £100 and less than £500	10p
More than £500 and less than £1500	30p
More than £1500	60p

Stamp duties

Transactions in registered stocks, bonds or shares by transfer, or other marketable securities that change hands are subject to stamp duty, payable by the purchaser as shown in Table 17.11.

Table 17.11 Stamp duties on purchases of securities

Type of security	Value of purchase	Stamp duty payable	
		By UK residents	By non-UK residents
All shares, convertible debentures and stock not included in exemptions above		2% of consideration	1% of consideration
New equity capital of listed companies where capital is newly issued onto the market or where rights issue is made. (Scrip or capitalization issues are excluded)	For each £100 or part thereof of the market value or nominal value of new shares, whichever is the greater	1% per £100	1% per £100

Certain securities are exempt from stamp duty. These exemptions are: all British or foreign government stocks or bonds; corporate debenture and loan stock (excluding convertibles); all bearer securities; unit trusts.

Settlement and delivery

Settlement and delivery for transactions in gilt-edged stocks occurs on the following business day. The remainder of securities dealt in on the stock exchange are settled on a fortnightly accounting basis, though two stock exchange account periods during the year run for three weeks.

The settlement dates are each alternate Monday. On this date the purchaser receives a stock transfer certificate—both buyer and seller having already received contract notes at the time of transaction—in return for payment of consideration, commissions and other charges. By payment of a small fee, clients may sometimes arrange through their brokers to defer payment to the next account settlement date. This is known as contango facilities. Alternatively, a client who has sold shares short and wishes to defer purchase of the same securities, may similarly arrange to defer the completion of the transaction to the next account date. This is known as backwardation facilities.

The commission charges shown above apply in most cases to quantities of shares purchased or sold during one account period. Thus, for example, two purchases of shares each of value £100 000 would be subject to the lower commission payable on transactions of £200 000.

Exceptions are medium-dated gilts for sums in excess of £300 000 and corporation and foreign stocks and bonds for amounts in excess of £300 000, for which the lower rate of commission applies only if dealings are made on the same day.

Financial and monetary systems

Financial institutions

There are many British financial institutions whose present roles have evolved through historical tradition rather than design or regulation. Most of these institutions have headquarters in the City of London which, although only one square mile in area, has the highest concentration of financial institutions in the world and is the world's leading financial centre in terms of facilities and diversification, though not perhaps in volume in which New York is a major rival.

The City contains almost 300 banks, both domestic and foreign; over 20 merchant banks; 11 discount houses; about 20 finance houses; over 200 stockbroking firms; some two dozen commodity brokers as well as licensed deposit takers, building societies, insurance companies and brokers which, besides providing important financial services, are also important institutional investors in the money and capital markets.

Commercial banks

Until October 1979, when the first Banking Act was introduced, banks in the UK were not subject to specific regulations. The act was introduced as a first step towards the harmonization of financial institutions in the EEC which requires that all member countries have a system of authorized banks. The major effect of the Banking Act has been to define banks according to two categories, those of recognized banks and of licensed deposit takers.

As at October 1980 there were 277 recognized banks which, according to the act, must have enjoyed a high reputation and standing in the financial community for a reasonable period of time. Likewise they must provide either a wide range of banking services or a highly specialized banking service and must have net assets of at least £5 million if providing a wide range of services, or £250 000 if providing a specialized service. Recognized banks only are permitted to describe themselves as banks or use that title in their names.

Also at that time there were 186 licensed deposit takers. These must be shown to be prudently and competently managed by at least two directors and to have minimum net assets of £250 000. They are not permitted to describe themselves as banks. In addition, over 130 bank-type companies were awaiting classification into one of the two categories.

The Banking Act makes no distinction between domestic and foreign banks. Foreign banks have never been placed at a competitive disadvantage with respect to domestic banks.

It is a measure of London's importance as a financial centre that every foreign bank of any consequence has a branch or representative office established in London. Foreign banks account for about 17 per cent of total domestic sterling deposits, the major share of which is represented by American banks. Foreign banks are making increasing inroads into the UK domestic market, but their main activities are in the field of corporate lending, for which they now represent about 30 per cent of the UK sterling market and Euromarket operations.

All commercial banks are owned by the private sector and, apart from the two categories defined by the Banking Act (1979), commercial banks fall into two categories by the nature of the type of business they transact. These two categories are described as retail and wholesale banking. The retail banks provide the major share of personal banking services by offering chequing account facilities, providing small short- and medium-term loans to individuals, industry and commerce and accepting call and time deposits.

The most usual method by which the retail banks advance short-term credit to individual and corporate customers is through overdraft facilities. This is one factor that negates the need for a commercial paper market, since companies needing short-term finance can draw on their bank credit facilities up to their overdraft limits.

Their role is becoming increasingly universal since they also participate in the management of syndicated loans, provide intermediary investment services and carry out transactions in the foreign exchange markets. Many of the larger banks also have subsidiaries which provide a whole range of other financial services.

These include credit card companies, hire purchase and leasing companies and merchant banks.

The largest retail banks are the UK clearing banks. The 'big four' are Barclays, National Westminster, Lloyds and the Midland. The fifth London clearing bank is Williams and Glynns Bank which is a subsidiary of one of the Scottish clearing banks, the Royal Bank of Scotland. The Bank of Scotland and Clydesdale Bank are the other two. Together, the UK clearing banks account for approximately 75 per cent of total domestic deposits. The 'big four' operate a branch network of 11 400 banks in the UK, while the other UK clearers operate a further 1869 branches.

Wholesale banks also accept deposits from the public but do not operate an extensive branch network. In general they do not make small or unsecured loans to individuals but specialize in corporate services, accepting large call and time deposits, arranging corporate loans and short-term finance and offering investment advice and intermediary services. The foreign banks mostly fall into this category although 10 American banks, such as Citibank Trust, are now offering retail banking services. The UK merchant banks also come under the classification of wholesale banks.

Merchant banks (accepting houses)

One of the major functions of merchant banks is that of accepting commercial bills of exchange. Once a bill has been accepted by a London bank, the bill not only qualifies for a lower rate of interest in the London money market, but also becomes eligible for rediscounting at the Bank of England. Because of this role as acceptors of bills, some merchant banks are otherwise known as accepting houses, although this term is only applied to the 17 merchant banks that are members of the Accepting Houses Committee. Members of this committee enjoy a closer relationship with the Bank of England and the right to rediscount bills with the Bank. The term merchant bank derives from the fact that, at one time, they were formed by groups of merchants for the purpose of financing trade. Although they have long since ceased to trade as merchants themselves, they still finance some trade through the acceptance of bills, while the remainder of their business is conducted in the corporate, rather than the personal, sector. They specialize in the management of public and privately placed new issues of all forms of corporate capital, advise corporate clients on mergers and take-overs, provide investment advice and manage pension funds and unit and investment trusts. They also accept sizeable call and time deposits in the London money market and make direct loans to businesses and, unlike the retail banks, are more prepared to provide equity or debenture capital to new ventures and higher-risk enterprises.

The four largest merchant banks in terms of net asset size are Kleinwort Benson, J. Henry Schroder Wagg, Hambros and Hill Samuel, all of which are publicly quoted companies.

Discount houses

There are 11 discount houses which are all members of the London Discount Houses Association. Their functions are as intermediaries between the Bank of

England and the banking system, providing liquidity and ensuring an efficiently operating money market. The discount houses are the only institutions to be granted lender of last resort facilities at the Bank of England. This allows them to borrow short-term money at privileged rates of interest and to lend it out for slightly longer periods at higher rates. In this way they may borrow up to 25 times their capital base. It is administratively easier for the Bank of England to control credit to the banking system, and thus influence short-term interest rates, through these 11 institutions rather than directly through the whole banking system.

The discount houses accept call money in sterling and US dollars from the banking system; the amount varies between £2000 million and £3500 million per day. In this way they are the only institutions to create additional reserve assets for the Bank, since most money placed at call with discount houses is secured against government paper and may be included in the reserve assets of the banks. Discount houses also accept deposits which are not secured against specific assets.

Another name by which discount houses are known is that of bill brokers. This is because the discount houses are the major market makers in bills of all kinds. They jointly underwrite the whole of the weekly treasury bill tender; assist local authorities by tendering for local authority bills and by buying local authority short-term bonds; and assist companies by either arranging an introduction to a bank that will offer acceptance facilities for bills of exchange or by directly discounting trade bills for companies.

They also act as dealers in buying and selling treasury bills, local authority bills and commercial bills to banks, financial institutions and large corporations. They provide also a market in other short-term money market instruments which comprise short-term gilts and sterling and dollar CDs.

The discount houses thus provide liquidity to the banking system; speed of transaction, since all transactions are agreed and confirmed by word of mouth over the telephone; a source through which the government can borrow to meet its short-term cash requirements; and a mechanism by which the Bank of England can influence short-term interest rates in the money market.

Other financial institutions

Other financial institutions such as insurance companies and building societies, post office giro and trustee savings banks are important participants in the capital market, particularly for government securities and blue chip equities.

The building societies perform a special function by collecting small personal savings and providing almost all personal mortgage finance for house purchase. They do not issue bonds on the capital market but provide mortgages as direct individual loans for 20 or 25 years from the pool of funds collected as savings. Finance houses are not banks as such, but provide loans and financial services in the form of hire purchase, leasing and factoring. Most are publicly quoted companies which also raise additional funds by accepting deposits, usually in amounts of over £50 000 and for minimum periods of three months.

The central bank

The Bank of England is the central bank and the only state owned bank in the UK. It was founded in 1694 to act as banker to the government and to manage the national debt. Apart from continuing to perform these functions, it also acts as banker to the banks—who hold large cash balances with the Bank of England ($1\frac{1}{2}$ per cent of liabilities in the case of clearing banks)—and through which the banks have cheque clearing facilities. In addition, governments and other central banks throughout the world maintain deposits with the Bank of England. The Bank also provides lender of last resort facilities to the banking system, though not directly to the banks themselves, but through the medium of the discount houses. As banker and agent to the government, the Bank maintains the Exchequer Account kept by the Treasury. This account is kept in credit by the issue of short-term treasury bills. Other government accounts such as those of the Inland Revenue and the Post Office are also maintained by the Bank. The Bank is also responsible for the issue, redemption, payment of interest and registration of other government securities.

The Bank of England also maintains the exchange equalization account through which the value of sterling is managed on the world foreign exchanges. The Bank is the sole issuer of notes and coins for England and Wales, though in Scotland and Northern Ireland certain banks are permitted to issue their own notes and coins subject to certain restrictions relating to the gold and reserve asset backing of such issues.

One of the major functions of the Bank as agent to the government is the implementation of monetary policy, primarily through interest rates, open market operations and direct controls on the banking system.

Although the Bank is subject to directives from the government in matters concerning monetary policy, it has considerable influence and works in close cooperation with the government and has a fair degree of autonomy in the day-to-day management of the banking system and its liquidity.

The Bank is controlled by a governor, deputy governor and sixteen directors who are all formally appointed by the Queen. The main office is in Threadneedle Street in the City of London and is often affectionately referred to as the 'Old Lady of Threadneedle Street'. In addition, the Bank maintains nine branches in major cities in England which manage local business and deal directly with local commercial banks.

Monetary policy

The way in which the government, through the Bank of England, controls the money supply and implements its monetary policy is currently under review. The major instruments presently used are administration of short-term interest rates, direct controls on the financial system through reserve asset and liquidity management, debt management and open market operations in the domestic money market and foreign exchange markets. The main thrust of policy has been direct control of interest rates with the object of reducing the rate of money supply growth. By a gradual change in policy which is not yet fully determined, the authorities aim to shift the emphasis to a form of monetary base control.

Reserve assets ratios, special deposits and liquidity requirements

Since 1971 until 1980 all banks were required to maintain a minimum of $12\frac{1}{2}$ per cent of their eligible liabilities in the form of reserve assets. Eligible liabilities are defined as sterling deposit liabilities of under two years' original maturity, sterling obtained by switching from foreign currencies, sterling CDs held and issued and transactions in the interbank and discount markets.

Reserve assets are defined as balances with the Bank of England, money at call with discount houses and moneybrokers, treasury bills, gilts with less than one year to maturity, local authority bills and commercial bank bills of exchange.

In 1980 it was announced that the reserve asset ratio is to be phased out and so by a series of reductions it will be gradually reduced to zero. In May 1980, the ratio was 10 per cent.

Banks are required to maintain their reserves on a daily basis. The reserve ratio is not used as a means of controlling the monetary base but, used in conjunction with special deposits, it contributes to the control of liquidity and short-term interest rates.

Special deposits were introduced as an instrument of control in 1960. They are used to require banks to deposit cash—equivalent to a given proportion of their eligible liabilities—as interest-bearing deposits with the Bank of England. At present the London clearing banks only are required to maintain special deposits equivalent to $1\frac{1}{2}$ per cent of their eligible liabilities. These deposits partly reflect the need for cash balances with the bank to cover clearing operations which the bank facilitates. It is also used, however, as a fulcrum by which the bank effects changes in short-term interest rates since an increase in the special deposits would reduce liquidity in the banking system and thus apply an upward pressure to interest rates.

Supplementary special deposits were introduced in 1973 and used intermittently up until June 1980 when they were abolished as a monetary instrument. Under the supplementary special deposit scheme, otherwise known as the corset, the authorities set guidelines for the rate of growth of the banks' interest-bearing eligible liabilities. The rate of growth could be no more than a given percentage over the average level in a specified base period. Growth in excess of these levels required the offending banks to place non-interest-bearing supplementary special deposits (SSDs) with the Bank of England. The amount of SSDs rose progressively with the amount of the excess growth of liabilities. Growth of over five per cent in excess of the limits was subject to SSDs equivalent to 50 per cent of the excess. The effect was to increase the borrowing costs to banks which were over the prescribed limit. In extreme cases, this was 2.5 times market rates of interest. The SSD scheme encouraged banks to manage their assets rather than their liabilities. With the special deposit system alone, a call on special deposits encourages banks to practise liability management since they meet the reduction in their reserves by bidding for funds in the money market, thereby increasing their liabilities in order to obtain more reserve assets. Interest rates in the interbank money market would be pushed up in consequence. The SSD scheme, in contrast, placed a limit on the degree to which banks could increase their liabilities. Banks therefore tended to

384

manage their assets by switching from non-reserve assets. The sale of these non-reserve assets depressed their prices and thus pushed up interest rates.

The authorities have already abolished the corset or supplementary special deposit scheme on the grounds that it produces disintermediation in the financial system. In other words, it reduces competition in the controlled sector—comprising banks that are subject to Bank of England controls—and lending is shifted to the uncontrolled sector, comprising banks and financial institutions which are not subject to Bank of England controls.

Proposed revisions

The banking figures for the first month following the removal of the corset, July 1980, showed a marked increase in bank lending. This was largely due not to a dramatic increase in the money supply, but to liabilities and bank credit which had previously been operating outside the controlled banking system, and which had subsequently shifted back into the system.

The special deposit system is intended to remain in order that the Bank of England can retain some control over liquidity in the banking system as a whole.

On the basis that it is neither necessary as a means through which interest rates can be influenced, nor effective as a means of limiting the rate of growth of banks' assets and liabilities, the reserve asset ratio is to be phased out. Its main purpose was to ensure that banks maintained a prudent level of liquid assets. This objective can still be achieved by introducing liquidity requirements for all banks. Currently, the proposals are that the banking system should hold a significant amount of primary liquidity, consisting of all assets that are a ready source of cash to the banking system as a whole. Primary liquidity is thus cash, money market securities which the Bank of England normally buys in its open market operations, and assets which represent claims on discount houses that have lender of last resort facilities with the Bank. Primary liquidity thus represents claims on both the private and the public sectors. The amount of primary liquidity that banks should maintain is as yet unspecified, although the amount will probably be expressed as a norm rather than a daily minimum. Individual banks may then temporarily deviate from the norm in certain circumstances without incurring penalties.

Interest rate policy

The major means by which interest rates are controlled is through the Bank of England's minimum lending rate (MLR), which is the minimum rate of interest at which the Bank will lend to the discount houses, and thus indirectly to the banking system. Since May 1978, MLR has been a fully administered rate determined directly by the government. Prior to that date, and since 1971, MLR had depended on supply and demand in the money market and was linked, by a formula, to the weekly treasury bill tender rate.

The government uses MLR to maintain or change particular levels of interest rates in the market and thus indirectly to influence the expansion of credit. The authorities monitor the money supply figures, such as sterling M3 expansion in bank lending and the public sector borrowing requirement. These measurements are all interrelated, as shown at the end of this section.

The government sets target rates of growth for sterling M3. If growth is in excess of the target, the government will increase MLR or maintain it at a high level in order to constrain bank lending. If growth is within the target, MLR will be lowered or maintained at low levels. This interest rate policy is made effective by the complementary use of special deposits, debt management and open market operations.

Proposed revisions

According to new proposals the government aims to move towards a system of monetary base control. MLR would then cease to be an administered rate but would fluctuate according to the demand and supply of liquidity—the banking system. Less emphasis will be placed on supplying liquidity to the market through the discount window and more emphasis placed on open market operations. The Bank of England will aim to keep short-term interest rates within an unpublished band, to be determined by the authorities while borrowing at the discount window will be made available (equivalent to MLR) but at higher rates than prevailing money market rates.

Debt management and open market operations

The government finances its short-term requirements through the sale of treasury bills and its longer-term requirements—known as the Public Sector Borrowing Requirement (PSBR)—through the sale of gilts. The government can influence liquidity and interest rates in the money market and banking system by controlling both the quantity of the securities it sells and, to some extent, the price at which they are sold. Treasury bills are underwritten by the discount houses and gilts by the Bank of England, which ensures that the full quantity will be sold. Government securities bought by the banking sector reduce the amount of advances the banks are able to make, while government securities bought by the non-bank sector reduce the level of deposits placed with the banks, which are used by them for on-lending.

Apart from making new issues to fund government debt, the Bank of England also carries out open market operations by buying and selling government securities (usually treasury bills) in the open market. By such a mechanism the Bank buys or sells securities, depending on whether it wishes to increase or decrease liquidity in the banking system as a whole and whether it wishes to exert a downward or upward pressure on interest rates.

To the extent that liquidity and interest rates are also affected by the external value of sterling and the inward and outward flows of capital, the Bank also undertakes open market operations in the foreign exchange market in order to maintain or influence the exchange value of sterling. The US dollar is normally the currency of intervention and the Bank sells sterling for dollars if it wishes to exert a downward pressure on the exchange value of sterling. This indirectly reduces inward capital flows, and thus internal liquidity, which again indirectly has a firming effect on domestic interest rates. Conversely, the Bank buys sterling with dollars in order to exert an upward pressure on the exchange value of sterling.

The government proposes that increasing emphasis should be placed on open market operations, to be conducted mainly in the treasury bill market. By such intervention the government hopes to maintain short-term interest rates within a predetermined (though unpublished) band thus replacing the previous policy which depended on a fixed administered MLR. Since the monetary base will be controlled, short-term interest rates will fluctuate according to short-term changes in liquidity. The Bank of England will attempt to stabilize volatility by injecting or absorbing liquidity into or from the financial system through the use of open market operations which will continue to be conducted with the discount houses rather than in the interbank market. *Proposed revisions*

Economic indicators

Economic indicators which influence monetary policy, and thus conditions in the money and capital markets, are as follows:

Retail price index	second Friday of each month
Trade figures	third Monday of each month
Balance of payments	quarterly
Earnings (wages)	third Wednesday of each month
Money supply	end of third week in each month
Reserves	first Monday or Tuesday of each month
GDP	quarterly

Money supply is measured by adding liabilities in the financial system as follows:

Notes and coins in circulation
+ UK private sector sight deposits = sterling M1
+ UK private sector sterling time deposits and CDs
+ UK public sector sterling time deposits = sterling M3
+ UK residents' deposits in foreign currencies = M3

Alternatively, money supply is measured by adding assets in the financial system as follows:

Public sector borrowing requirement (PSBR)
+ purchase of public sector debt by UK non-bank
    private sector
+ sterling lending to UK private sector
+ sterling lending to overseas sector = domestic credit
    expansion
+ external and foreign currency borrowing by
    all sectors
+ non-deposit liabilities of banking sector = sterling M3

387

Withholding taxes

Interest

Tax is withheld from interest earnings at the standard rate of 30 per cent except where this is reduced by tax treaties as shown in Table 17.12.

Dividends

Corporations are normally required to pay advance corporation tax (ACT) on dividends, which are therefore normally paid net of the 52 per cent corporation tax. Thus, in Table 17.12 the additional withholding tax is shown as nil. In the case of

Table 17.12   Withholding taxes

Country of residence	Interest, %	Dividends, %
Non-treaty countries	30	0
Tax treaty countries		
Antigua	30	0
Australia	10	0
Austria	0	0
Barbados	15	0
Belgium	15	0
Belize	30	*
Botswana	15	0
Brunei	30	*
Burma	30	0
Canada	15	0
Cyprus	10	*
Denmark	0	*
Dominica	30	0
Egypt	15	0
Falkland Islands	30	*
Faroe Islands	0	*
Fiji	10	*
Finland	0	*
France	10	*
Gambia	30	0
Germany	0	0
Ghana	15	0
Gilbert and Tuvalu Islands	30	*
Greece	0	0
Grenada	30	0
Guernsey	0	0
Hungary	0	0
Indonesia	15	*
Ireland	0	*
Isle of Man	30	0
Israel	15	0
Italy	30	0

Table 17.12 (*continued*)

Country of residence	Interest, %	Dividends, %
Jamaica	12.5	*
Japan	10	0
Jersey	30	0
Kenya	15	*
Korea	15 or 10	*
Lesotho	30	0
Luxembourg	0	0
Malawi	0	*
Malaysia	15	*
Malta	30	*
Mauritius	30	0
Montserrat	30	0
Netherlands	0	*
Netherlands Antilles	0	0
New Zealand	30	0
Norway	0	*
Pakistan	30	0
Philippines	15	*
Poland	0	*
Portugal	10	0
Rumania	10	*
St. Christopher and Nevis	30	0
St. Lucia	30	0
St. Vincent	30	0
Seychelles	30	*
Sierra Leone	30	0
Singapore	15	*
Solomon Islands	30	*
South Africa	10	0
South West Africa	30	0
Spain	12	*
Sudan	15	*
Swaziland	30	0
Sweden	0	*
Switzerland	0	*
Tanzania	30	0
Trinidad and Tobago	10	0
Uganda	30	0
United States of America	0	*
Zambia	10	0
Zimbabwe	0	0

* See note on dividends at beginning of section.

some countries having tax treaties with the UK, residents of those countries may claim a tax credit for the amount of ACT paid, less a withholding tax of 15 per cent. Those countries qualifying for the tax credit are marked by an asterisk in the table.

Exemptions

The income deriving from the following securities is free of withholding tax:

Certain gilt-edged securities (see Table 17.6);
Government and local authority securities, if held for more than one year;
Unit and investment trusts.

Exchange controls

In October 1979 all forms of exchange controls were completely abolished, so ending a period of 40 years of controls.

Both residents and non-residents now have complete freedom regarding the inward and outward flow of capital in any currency. Non-residents may freely open and hold accounts with UK banks, there being no distinction made between resident and non-resident accounts. Non-residents are free to invest in any UK and sterling denominated securities. Repatriation of interest, profit and dividends is completely unrestricted. Gold and foreign currencies may be bought and sold and exported and forward contracts may be made in the foreign exchange markets.

The currency is the pound sterling. It is allowed to float freely on the world foreign exchanges, although the authorities intervene in the spot foreign exchange market, using the US dollar as the currency of intervention, in order to smooth out excessive fluctuations in the value of sterling.

Although the UK is a member of the EEC it is not also a member of the European Monetary System (EMS). Sterling floats freely in the foreign exchange markets against the EMS currencies and against all other currencies. The only other EEC member which is also not a member of the EMS is Greece—the most recent EEC member that joined after the EMS was established.

18.   South Africa

General market environment

South Africa has a sophisticated financial system, with many of the country's institutions modelled on the British system. There is a comprehensive range of instruments available to the investor and, during the last three to four years, both money and capital markets have been extremely active.

A number of restrictions are, however, presented to the non-resident investor. While the authorities would like to facilitate a more active role taken by foreign investors and would like to remove all exchange controls with respect to non-residents, such steps are being taken only cautiously. At present, South Africa operates a two-tier currency divided between the commercial rand, which floats against other currencies, and the financial rand, which stands at a discount to the commercial rand, the size of which depending on demand and supply. Investment

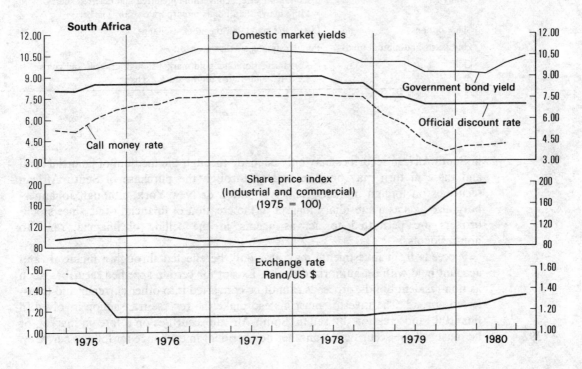

Table 18.1   Summary of instruments

Instrument	Characteristics
MONEY MARKET	
Deposits	
call deposits	Highly active and volatile market. Large volume
time deposits	Deposit of less than R250000 subject to maximum interest rate rate controls
certificate of deposit	Popular alternative to time deposits
Treasury bills	Fairly small but very active market. Weekly tenders
Trade bills	Mostly traded in interbank market
Bankers' acceptances	Trade bills which have been accepted by a bank. Good secondary market
CAPITAL MARKET	
Gilts	Government bonds. Irregular issues. Active secondary market
Semigilts	Bonds issued by municipalities, local authorities and public utilities. Reasonably good secondary market
Non-resident bonds	Issued monthly by government. Denominated in financial rands. Proceeds transferable in any currency
Foreign bonds	Bonds issued by some foreign governments are listed and traded on South African capital market
Debentures	Bonds issued by corporations. The majority carry an option to convert into common shares
Equity shares	Common preferred, convertible preferred and deferred shares. More active than bonds in corporate sector market
Share options	Listed and traded on the stock exchange
Unit trusts and mutual funds	Popular among smaller investors
Gold	No organized domestic gold market though kruggerrand coins are listed and traded on the stock exchange

in South African securities may only be made through the medium of financial rand and these in turn may only be created through the purchase of South African securities on foreign markets, namely London or New York, although Johannesburg also acts as a subsidiary market in the creation of financial rand, since stockbrokers are permitted to act as agents in the selling of financial rand to non-residents.

Proceeds from investments may also only be effected through a financial rand account held with an authorized dealer. Except for certain specified securities, such as non-resident bonds, proceeds cannot be converted into other currency and transferred abroad. The investor must instead make the reverse transaction involved in financial rand creation, by selling South African securities on a foreign market, or he must sell the securities to another non-resident in exchange for foreign currency.

The money market

Deposits

Call deposits

The market in call deposits is the most active part of the South African money market. It involves all banks, of which there are a wide variety, all large companies and the part-publicly owned National Financial Corporation of South Africa.

The volume of call money available within the financial system is highly volatile. It depends on many factors including the structure of interest rates in the domestic money market and the interest rate differentials between what have been persistently low rates in South Africa and the high rates obtainable in the US and European markets. These differentials sometimes precipitate a heavy flow of capital out of the country.

This volatility affects all other areas of the money market. It determines the level of treasury bills, trade bills and bankers' acceptances held by the discount houses and other accepting houses who finance the investments in such securities from the call deposits placed with them. The discount houses have to make use of the Reserve Bank discounting facility frequently and in large amounts. Non-resident investors place large sums of temporarily liquid funds in the call money market since the proceeds of sales of other investments are not freely transferable out of the country. These liquid funds may be held in the call market as financial rand balances.

Call money terms are for overnight call, two or seven days' notice, accepted usually in minimum amounts of R100 000. Yields are volatile depending on liquidity in the banking system but, since 1977, they have been on average low at about three or four per cent. This is several points lower than bank rate, which between mid-1979 and autumn 1980 was stable at seven per cent.

Time deposits

Time deposits may be placed with the commercial banks, savings banks, hire purchase banks and the general banks. As a rule, few fixed short-term time deposits are placed, primarily because time deposits in amounts of less than R250 000 are subject to maximum interest rate controls as imposed by the central bank on the banking system. The maximum deposit rate is fixed in relation to bank rate but is often less competitive than yields obtainable on alternative money market investments, or marketable time deposits in the form of CDs.

The majority of time deposits are made for medium terms of between one and three years, though rates of interest are still subject to controls. These controls affect the banking system's liquidity, particularly when domestic demand for money is high and when there are large foreign outflows of funds. These market controls (see p. 409) are a major factor contributing to the high volatility of funds in the call money market.

393

Certificate of deposit

Three- and six-month CDs are issued by the commercial banks and the general banks. They are marketable bearer deposit certificates which enjoy an active secondary market among domestic investors, particularly since they are not subject to interest rate controls that are imposed on time deposits. They are a less attractive investment for the non-resident investor because of the two per cent marketable securities tax that applies to non-resident purchases. Call deposits which are not subject to this tax, and where yields are normally comparable with CD yields, may offer a better net return to the foreign investor.

The yield on 90-day CDs is greater than the yield on 91-day treasury bills by an amount which depends on the liquidity in the banking system. In 1976, when liquidity was tight, treasury bills were yielding approximately seven per cent per annum, while CD yields fluctuated between 10 and 15 per cent per annum. During 1979, liquidity was easy and money market interest rates were falling. Despite bank rate at seven per cent, treasury bills fell to a yield of about 3.9 per cent per annum while CD yields reached a low of four per cent—only 10 basis points higher than treasury bills in November 1979.

Treasury bills

Ninety-one-day treasury bills are auctioned by weekly tender every Friday. The amount of each issue is announced in advance, usually at the close of the previous week's issue. The Treasury may vary the issue amount as a means of indirectly influencing the discount rate of interest attaching to the bills, which is otherwise determined by market conditions.

In the primary market, tenders are submitted by the discount houses, commercial banks, the Reserve Bank and the National Finance Corporation. Non-bank subscribers may bid via a commercial bank. Applications may be made in minimum amounts of R100 000 and above in multiples of R25 000.

The bills are issued at a discount from par, which is determined by the average of the bids received. All subscriptions made at above the resultant discount price are fully allotted, those bids at the resultant discount are proportionately allotted and those bids at lower than the resultant discount price are unallocated.

Treasury bills account for only about 12 per cent of total short-term fixed interest securities issued by the government, but they enjoy an active secondary market which is maintained primarily by the discount houses, though much dealing takes place with the banking system. For the banks, treasury bills are classified as liquid assets, and may be included in their statutory reserves, as well as being classified as securities eligible for rediscount with the central bank.

They are also traded in the secondary market by non-resident investors for whom treasury bills, along with other government securities, are free of withholding tax, though they are still subject to the marketable securities tax.

Yields on treasury bills are the lowest of all money market securities because of their high security and good marketability. Their yields depend on market conditions and not on the administered bank rate, as shown in Table 18.2.

Table 18.2 Yields on treasury bills and long-term government bonds compared with bank rate (period averages)

Year	Bank rate, %	Treasury bill rate, %	Long-term government bond yields, %
1972	6.00	5.30	8.35
1973	5.50	3.18	7.83
1974	8.00	5.43	8.96
1975	8.50	6.12	9.71
1976	9.00	7.44	10.38
1977	9.00	7.87	10.96
1978	8.80	7.81	10.49
1979	7.00	4.35	9.38
1980	7.00	4.65	9.70

Trade bills

Trade bills are bills of exchange drawn on one trader by another, usually to finance export transactions. The importer issues a bill to the South African exporter, promising to pay the latter a specified sum of money by a given date. Terms are normally for up to six months but may extend up to nine months. The bills are usually guaranteed by the bank of the issuer, i.e., the importing trader. The exporter in South Africa may then present the bill to a South African bank for discounting; that is, the bank will buy the bill from the trader, giving him immediate cash, at the bill's face value less a discount which represents a rate of interest commensurate with the terms of the bill and the level of money market interest rates.

The bill may then be traded in the secondary market. Most dealings take place within the banking system since banks may include trade bills in their liquid asset portfolios and also because trade bills normally carry greater yields than bankers' acceptances and CDs. Non-bank investors also purchase trade bills for similar reasons, but for non-residents the purchase of trade bills attracts the two per cent marketable securities tax and is subject to withholding tax.

Bankers' acceptances

Bankers' acceptances (BAs) are similar to trade bills except that they are drawn on, and accepted by, a bank; usually the South African correspondent bank of the importing foreign party. Payment of the bill's face value at maturity is thus the liability of the accepting bank. The bill, or BA, is offered to the exporting trader at a discount and he may sell it in the secondary market by offering it to the same, or any other, bank or dealer. He then receives immediate cash, at a discount determined by the term of the loan and the general level of interest rates ruling in the money market.

BAs are traded quite actively in the secondary market. Major participants are banks and discount houses, though they are also bought and sold by many non-bank investors.

Yields in the secondary market compare very closely with yields on CDs of a similar maturity. Original maturities of BAs are of fixed terms of usually three or six months and in the secondary market they may be dealt in minimum amounts of R50 000.

Non-residents are required to pay stamp duty on purchases of BAs and additional tax is withheld on the interest portion of their receipts.

The capital market

Government bonds (Gilts)

Bonds issued by the central government are registered securities known as gilt edged securities, or gilts, as in the case with British Government bonds.

Gilts are issued in par units of R100 each, though minimum trading denominations are R1000, and have fixed coupon rates of interest which is payable semi-annually. Most loans repay capital at maturity though some may be amortized by a sinking fund method.

They may be issued for short terms of a few years, for medium terms of 5 to 15 years, or for long terms of 15 to over 30 years.

They are not issued on a regular basis but as is necessitated by the government's borrowing requirement, thus resulting in seasonal patterns per quarter, these vary from year to year but are recently becoming more consistent. For the twelve months to March 1979, and for the following year to March 1980, there were fewer gilt issues than in previous years because of the government's policy to contain the growth of public expenditure. This resulted in a total value of outstanding gilt issues of R10 774 million for 1979 representing an increase of 14 per cent over the previous year—which was planned to be much the same for the year 1979–80—bringing the total outstanding value of gilts to about R12 250 million.

Semigilts (Municipal stocks)

Similar to gilts in all manners, except for source of issuer, are the bonds issued on behalf of municipalities and public utility corporations. They are not guaranteed directly by the government but are considered secure investments and command very similar yields and almost as good markets. Otherwise, their method of issue and the way in which they are traded are identical. Reference in the market to gilts also includes semigilts.

Primary market in gilts and semigilts

The sizes and terms of new issues are announced in advance together with a prospectus and tenders are invited, at the given terms, from subscribers up to a specified closing date. Any institutions or individuals may subscribe through a dealer or broker. Once the subscription has been closed, applications are allotted proportionately as determined by the treasury, although small subscriptions from individuals are normally allotted in full.

In the years to March 1979, there were 61 new gilt and semigilt stocks which amounted to 88.4 per cent of total (R5322 million) capital raised on the stock exchange. In the year to March 1980, there were 54 new issues of gilts and semigilts amounting to R2750 million representing 67.9 per cent of new capital raised. The number of gilts and semigilts outstanding was 815, up from 767 in the previous year.

While central government gilts dominated new issues of public sector stock for the years up to 1977–78, the proportion of capital raised by central government compared with the local authorities and public utilities has been insignificant in subsequent years (see Table 18.3).

Secondary market trading is transacted through a stockbroker. Activity in the secondary market has increased substantially largely due to a change in the method of dealing in gilts since June 1978. In order to foster a more active market in official securities, brokers have, since that date, been permitted to act not only as agents for gilt transactions on behalf of a client, but also as principals. This means that brokers, as well as carrying out client transactions on the stock exchange, may also deal on their own account and make their own books in gilts. Thus, the secondary market now comprises the stock exchange and an over-the-counter market made by brokers and other dealers including the banks. This new method of dealing applies not only to gilts and semigilts but also to stocks issued by the government of any other country and in shares and debentures issued by statutory corporations.

Secondary market in gilts and semigilts

Table 18.3 Net bonds issues in South Africa capital market

| | Issuer | | |
Year (Apr.–Mar.)	Central government, R million	Local authorities and public corporations, R million	Listed private sector companies, R million
1968–69	600	175	30
1969–70	160	160	80
1970–71	100	195	120
1971–72	590	220	80
1972–73	650	300	50
1973–74	100	400	120
1974–75	500	300	125
1975–76	800	300	180
1976–77	970	700	250
1977–78	1500	1000	180
1978–79	50	900	250

The new dealing method resulted in a gilt turnover of R940 million on the Johannesburg Stock Exchange for the year to March 1979, compared with R209 million for the preceding year. For the year to March 1980, turnover had quadrupled to R3888 million. This activity has resulted in the provision of a separate gilt trading floor on the Johannesburg Stock Exchange.

All types of investors participate in the gilt market though substantial purchasers are the large institutions such as banks, building societies, pension funds and insurance companies. For non-residents they present an attractive investment since interest is paid free of withholding tax, and transactions are also free of the two per cent marketable securities tax.

South African Government non-resident bonds

The Government issues—bi-monthly tender—treasury bonds which may be purchased with financial rand and which are specifically designed for non-resident investors. Issued at a substantial discount price, they carry no interest payments but are redeemed at par at maturity. They are issued with a fixed life of five years and in minimum denominations of R1000. They may be sold prior to maturity only to other non-residents. At redemption the proceeds are available in any transferable currency, and free of withholding tax.

Foreign bonds

Bonds of some foreign governments, particularly of other African countries, are listed on the South African Stock Exchange. These bonds enjoy some of the same privileges as do South African Government bonds in that they are exempt from the marketable securities tax but are, however, subject to stamp duty. Due to South African exchange control regulations and the operation of a two-tier currency, foreign corporations do not seek to issue bonds on the domestic South African market.

Eurobonds

For similar reasons that the corporate foreign bond market is not established, and because the government discourages an external market in rand-denominated securities, there is no market in rand Eurobonds.

Corporate bonds

Bonds issued by corporations are registered securities known as debentures. Issued with lives of from 5 up to 20 years, they are fixed interest, coupon bearing stock issued in minimum denominations of R100. Interest is payable semiannually and capital may either be repaid fully at maturity or amortized during the life of the loan. Straight bonds, however, are not as popular or as commonly issued as convertible debentures whereby the investor has the option to convert to ordinary shares of the issuing company. Terms are specified at issue, but several option dates for conversion are stated.

398

In the primary market, although there are also many private placements, the majority of corporate loans take the form of publicly issued debentures. New issues are announced in advance and subscriptions invited indirectly through any stockbroker or directly to the stockbroker or merchant bank chosen by the corporation concerned to manage the issue. Depending on the amount of applications received, the securities are allocated proportionately. If the issue is undersubscribed, the outstanding portion is taken up by the managing bank or broker who also underwrites the issue. In the year to March 1979, private sector companies raised R257 million by the issue of fixed interest debentures, compared with R180 million in the previous year. As at March 1980, there were 762 corporate fixed interest securities listed, to a value of about R275 billion, down from 766 in the year to March 1979. Bonds, however, account for only about five per cent of the private sector corporate capital market, most of the market comprising ordinary shares.

In the secondary market, debentures are listed and traded on the stock exchange, but since June 1978 brokers have also been allowed to maintain their own books in fixed interest stocks, thus creating an over-the-counter market. Trading volume is not as active as is the market either for gilts or for corporate shares. The major purchasers of debentures are the large financial institutions who tend to hold the stock in their portfolios because of their high yields, which are approximately two percentage points above gilt yields. For non-residents, interest earned from corporate debentures is subject to withholding tax.

Equity shares

The public issue of equity capital is the most common way in which South African companies raise required funds, while the equity share market represents good investment opportunities to both residents and non-residents. The latter additionally use the market for the creation of financial rands by purchasing South African securities that are quoted on foreign markets and then reselling those securities on the domestic market.

South Africa's economy is based on its mineral wealth and in particular its gold resources which represent three-quarters of all gold produced outside the communist bloc. Most of the equity shares quoted on the domestic capital market are shares of mineral related industries. Thus, South African shares may be classified into the following categories—collieries; diamonds; metals and minerals; gold; industrial companies and financial companies.

Shares are registered securities comprising:

Types of shares

- common or ordinary shares which have voting and dividend rights and a participation in the capital of the company subject to prior claims by debenture holders and preferred shareholders;
- preferred shares which do not normally have voting rights but have dividend rights subject to a fixed limit as specified in the issuing company's articles of association;

399

– convertible preferred shares which, at the option of the shareholder, may be converted to common shares at a specified future date;
– preferred shares, like common shares, carry both voting and dividend rights but rank for a dividend only after a stated minimum dividend has first been paid to the common shareholders.

Primary market

In the primary market, new share issues are managed by a merchant bank or a stockbroker. Amount, issue price and type of share are announced in advance and applicants are invited to subscribe through a broker or bank at the stated terms. Once the subscription is closed, shares are allotted either proportionately or alternatively on a first-come-first-served basis if the issue is oversubscribed, or in full if the issue is undersubscribed, while the outstanding amount of unsubscribed shares is underwritten by the issuing agent.

Secondary market

In the secondary market, shares are listed and traded on the stock exchange, although since June 1978 brokers have also been permitted to act as principals and to provide an over-the-counter market between themselves and other bank dealers in quoted shares. Certain shares of South African companies are also quoted on some foreign stock exchanges, notably London and New York, and it is by purchasing on these markets and reselling in the domestic market that non-residents are able to create financial rands. (See Exchange controls.)

There are approximately 1200 listed companies which account for 7791 million common shares and 278 million preferred shares, representing a market capitalization of R76 billion as at March 1980.

The number of listed companies has risen only slowly from 925 in the last 20 years, but the absolute number is deceptive since mergers and take-overs have caused many companies to be dropped from the listing. In contrast, the total nominal value of quoted shares has more than doubled in the last 10 years to R25

Table 18.4 Value of listed shares

Year (to March)	Nominal R000 m	Capitalized R000 m	No. of listed shares, million	No. of purchases, million
1971	11.0	19.5	1105	300
1972	11.0	23.0	....	350
1973	12.0	31.5	....	610
1974	13.0	38.5	....	550
1975	13.5	31.5	1010	350
1976	15.5	28.0	....	340
1977	16.0	24.0	....	310
1978	19.5	35.5	....	340
1979	22.0	52.0	....	430
1980	25.0	76.0	1220	725

billion while the capitalized value has more than trebled to R76 billion (see Table 18.4).

Turnover in shares has also been active, particularly since 1977, since when South Africa has been experiencing a strong bull market. This has been facilitated by the rise in the price of gold, which has benefited South Africa's balance of payments, and by South Africa's low dependence on imported oil. Unlike most industrialized countries, South Africa uses oil for only 20 per cent of her energy requirements.

Dividends paid by South African companies are declared gross and may be remitted to non-residents net of withholding tax, at the commercial rate of exchange. This sometimes results in a higher yield for non-residents as explained in the working of the financial rand in the section on exchange controls.

Share options

Both put and call options in certain specified corporate shares are listed on the stock exchange and may be dealt through a stockbroker. Particularly active options are those of gold or mining companies through which investors may speculate on the future price of gold or other metals. Most options have terms of three months but a few are also offered with a life of six months.

Unit trusts and mutual funds

Investors may participate in the equity market or the fixed interest market or a combination of both markets through the purchase of shares, or units, in trusts or funds. The former have a fixed capital structure while the latter do not. Investors may choose a particular type of trust or fund according to whether they require a return represented by income or capital growth. They are particularly attractive to smaller investors with limited resources and investment expertise. Units are commonly in minimum denominations of R100 although they may be of smaller size.

Trusts and funds are usually established and managed by a merchant bank or an insurance company. The units are not listed on the stock exchange, though they may be purchased through a stockbroker or through a bank.

The stock exchange

There is only one stock exchange, the Johannesburg Stock Exchange (JSE), which is regulated by a committee comprising 15 stockbrokers who are elected annually by members of the stock exchange. A government representative, the Registrar of Financial Institutions, also presides on the committee. Listing and trading regulations are enforced by statute according to the Stock Exchange Control Act of 1947. Members of the exchange are individuals who represent stockbroking firms and who may act as agent for clients or as principals for their firms.

Table 18.5 (*source: Johannesburg Stock Exchange*)

Market	Percentage change in market capitalization (January 1979 to March 1980)
South African golds	+110.0
South African industrials	+81.9
Hong Kong equities	+54.3
Australia equities	+45.0
Canada equities	+44.1
France equities	+18.7
Japan equities	+0.8
USA equities	-2.5
UK equities	-8.7
Germany	-16.5

A new stock exchange building was opened in April 1979 and, for the first time since the original stock exchange was established in 1886, all broking firms are now housed under the one roof.

The exchange is open between 9.30 and 4 p.m. and uses the open auction system of trading.

Securities listed and traded on the exchange comprise all publicly quoted capital market securities (except mutual funds and unit trusts), i.e., government and municipal stocks, statutory corporation loans, debentures and notes, corporation common and preferred shares, and gold kruggerrands.

The JSE ranks fifth of all world stock exchanges in terms of market capitalization but, for the year to March 1980, it was first in terms of market capitalization growth.

The year 1979–80 was a record year for the JSE. The total value of securities purchased, excluding gilts, was R2.6 billion, representing an increase of 141 per cent over the previous year. All sectors of the market performed well and the JSE actuaries index was up 63 per cent to 5655. This is a new index, introduced in November 1978. It is calculated and published daily by the research section of the JSE listing department and has been worked out back to 1960, which is an arbitrary date for the base of 1000.

Table 18.6 Turnover of securities on JSE (year to March)

Securities	1979, R million	1980, R million
Gilts and semigilts	940	2888
Corporate securities (shares and bonds)	1063	2563
Kruggerrands	....	25

On the basis of the JSE actuaries index, gold shares were up by 80 per cent in 1979–80, industrials up by 59 per cent, metals and minerals by 56 per cent and coal by 39 per cent. For the 15 months from January 1979 to March 1980, the South African market out-performed all other world markets as shown by Table 18.5. In the primary market, more than 80 per cent of new capital raised was by government and public sector stocks. New issues by the corporate sector represent a relatively small proportion of new issues for 1980 and R172 million was raised through rights issues by already quoted companies. There were 21 such rights issues in the year to March 1980 and, in addition, three capitalization or scrip issues.

Tables 18.7 and 18.8 illustrate the relative sizes of new issues made on the Johannesburg Stock Exchange.

Table 18.7 New capital raised on JSE (year to March)

	1979, R million	1980, R million
Gilts and semigilts		
new issues	2950	1768
additional issues	1513	952
Corporate shares		
by listed companies	519	395
by newly listed companies	91	708
Corporate debentures and notes	129	237
Total	4212	4062

Table 18.8 Value of new issues on JSE

Issuer	1976, R bil.	1977, R bil.	1978, R bil.	1979, R bil.	1980, R bil.
Banks, government, municipal and utility stocks	2.50	1.55	3.55	4.70	2.75
Industrial companies	0.10	0.30	0.10	0.25	1.20
Financial companies	0.30	0.20	0.30	0.10	0.10
Mining companies	0.20	0.25	0.15	0.40	0
Total	3.10	2.30	4.10	5.45	4.05

Gold

Despite the fact that South Africa is the world's largest gold producer, there is no organized domestic gold market for speculative investors. The only way in which gold can be purchased for investment is by the purchase of gold coins. Two gold coins are minted which, though legal tender, do not circulate in South Africa. One is the 2Rand which is 7.3 g of fine gold, and the other—much more commonly traded—is the kruggerrand. This is one ounce (31.1 g) of fine gold and has no face

403

value. Smaller kruggerrands, containing a half, a quarter and a tenth of an ounce of gold are now also available. The value of a coin at any time depends on the world price of gold, and the kruggerrand has the smallest premium, which is usually negligible, of all gold coins issued through the world. The majority of coins minted are sold abroad but, since April 1979, kruggerrands have been officially quoted on the Johannesburg Stock Exchange. For the year to March 1980, 54 923 coins were traded on the exchange, representing a value of R25.3 million. Activity was encouraged by the phenomenal rise in the world price of gold which rose from US$240.1 per ounce at the end of March 1979 to a high of US$850 in January 1980.

Dealing and fees

Money market

Money market securities are dealt through a bank or discount house. For purchases in the primary market, a small fee may be charged of R10 to R25 at the discretion of the dealer.

For secondary market transactions, the dealer's commission is included in the spread between his quoted bid and offer prices. Dealing spreads are $\frac{1}{16}$ to $\frac{1}{8}$ per cent for treasury bills and $\frac{1}{8}$ to $\frac{1}{4}$ per cent for CDs, bankers' acceptances and good quality trade bills. Delivery and settlement occurs on the same business day that the transaction is made.

Capital market

All capital market securities may be dealt through either a bank or a stockbroker. Both maintain an over-the-counter market in gilts though most gilt trading, as well

Table 18.9

Security	Percentage commission on purchases and sales
South Africa Government stock, stock of any foreign government, and municipal and local authority stocks	0.01% of yield to maturity × value of consideration
Debentures with no option or convertible rights	0.25% of nominal value (maximum R25) + 0.6% of consideration
Debentures with option or convertible rights	0.25% of nominal value (maximum R25) + 0.85% of consideration
Other fixed interest securities	0.25% of nominal value (maximum R25) + 0.60% of consideration
Shares and options	0.5 cents per share (maximum R25) + 0.85% of consideration
Unit trusts and mutual funds	0.5 cents per share (maximum R25) or 0.25% if nominal value of unit is R100, + 0.85% of consideration

as the majority of debenture and equity transactions, take place on the floor of the stock exchange.

Standard brokerage charges are shown in Table 18.9. All stock exchange transactions are settled within seven days, according to a weekly account basis. Dealings in shares normally take place in board lots of 100 shares.

Stamp duty

Stamp duty is payable by the purchaser on share transfer deeds at a rate of one and a half per cent provided that registration takes place within six months. Otherwise, a penalty rate of four and a half per cent is charged.

Stamp duty is exempted for the transfer of South Africa Government and municipal bonds and of bonds of the Rand Water Board, the South African Regional Water Supply Commission, the Electricity Supply Commission, the Land and Agricultural Bank of South Africa and the South African Broadcasting Association.

Marketable securities tax

A marketable securities tax (MST) is payable by brokers on behalf of clients on purchases only of all shares, options and debentures. Government securities of South African or of other country and municipal and utility stocks are exempt. The tax was reduced in 1979 from one and a half to one per cent but non-resident investors are charged an additional one per cent, resulting in an MST of two per cent.

Bank charges

If capital market transactions are made through a bank instead of through a broker, the following are typical of fees that may be charged.

Service	Fees and commissions
Purchase or sale of securities	0.2% of consideration—minimum R1.20 maximum R10.20
Registration in name of purchaser	R0.10 per 100 shares + R2.00 per security
Registration in name of bank nominees	R0.10 per 100 shares + R3.00 per security + 0.25% on dividends collected
Safe custody	R0.10 per certificate— minimum R4.

Financial and monetary systems

Financial institutions

South Africa has a well developed financial system and a wide range of financial institutions, most of which are similar in type to those existing in the British financial system.

405

The institutions comprise commercial banks, general banks, savings banks, hire purchase banks, merchant banks, discount houses, insurance companies, pension funds and building societies. All of these are privately owned but, in addition, there are a few public sector financial institutions.

The banks and discount houses deal in the money market, buying and selling bills and other short-term paper to match their assets against their deposit liabilities. The other institutions deal primarily in the capital market.

Commercial banks

There are nine commercial banks with over 7000 branches. The five largest are Barclays National Bank, the Standard Bank of South Africa, Nedbank, Volkskas Beperk and the Trust Bank of Africa. Together these banks control assets of over R22 billion. Although in terms of total asset size the largest group of financial institutions—the commercial banks—do not dominate the financial system because of strong competition from the other institutions. They now control only 40 per cent of banking assets compared with nearly 60 per cent in 1950. Many commercial banks, however, have subsidiaries which operate in competitive banking fields. The commercial banks provide mainly a retail service. They accept savings and time deposits and provide chequing account facilities, they provide short-term finance in the form of overdrafts and the discounting of trade bills; and provide spot foreign exchange to customers. The general banks, savings banks, and hire purchase banks are subject to the same banking regulations as are the commercial banks.

General banks

There are 19 general banks which provide corporate services not provided by the commercial banks, particularly in the field of medium- and long-term finance to industry. They accept time and savings deposits but, except for two banks, do not provide chequing account facilities. General banks also underwrite share issues and discount hire purchase paper. The largest is Bankorp with assets of R3 billion.

Savings banks

The eight savings banks collect individuals' savings in the form of savings deposits, but do not provide chequing account facilities. They provide medium-term finance in the form of loans, primarily to individuals.

Hire purchase banks

The two hire purchase banks collect time and savings deposits and provide instalment credit, leasing and factoring to business and individuals.

Merchant banks

There are 10 merchant banks, modelled on the British merchant banks; they are subject to the same banking controls as the commercial and other banks. They provide services which are more in the field of professional advice than of retail banking. They accept call and short-term time deposits and provide short-term finance to business in the form of acceptance credits such as bankers' acceptances and trade bills. They operate in the money market through the purchase and sale of bills and in the short-term end of the capital market through the purchase and sale of government and municipal bonds. They also operate in the foreign exchange market on behalf of clients and for their own accounts.

Otherwise they advise on, and act as, agent and underwriter for the issue of shares, bonds and private placements both in local and foreign markets. They advise companies on mergers and take-overs and also provide portfolio management services to clients.

Discount houses

There are three discount houses which again are modelled on the British system. They act as intermediaries between the banking system and the central bank, specializing in the mobilization of call money and facilitating an efficient market in treasury bills and other short-term instruments. They are able to rediscount treasury bills and other eligible short-term securities with the Reserve Bank or National Finance Corporation. When the banking system requires additional liquidity the banks sell such securities to the discount houses which in turn rediscount them with the Reserve Bank. Similarly, when the Reserve Bank wishes to influence liquidity or interest rates in the money market it may carry out open market operations through the discount houses or it may, through the National Finance Corporation, alter the rate at which it is willing to discount bills to the discount market.

National Finance Corporation

The National Finance Corporation of South Africa is a privately owned institution which is similar in function to the discount houses, except that it was established by an Act of Parliament in 1949 to act as lender of last resort to all financial institutions including the discount houses. It provides such facilities by discounting eligible securities such as treasury bills and short-dated government bonds.

Insurance companies, pension funds and building societies

The insurance companies accept savings in the form of premiums; pension funds accept savings in the form of savings deposits. The latter group provide almost all mortgage finance for house purchase. There are a large number of each type of institution and together they account for a major proportion of individual savings. They invest their funds mostly in the capital market. Government legislation requires that a fixed proportion of their funds should be invested in gilts or semigilts. This varies between 30 and 50 per cent according to the type of institution. The remainder may be invested in debentures, equities, mortgage bonds and lease-back agreements.

The insurance companies and building societies operate mainly in the gilt-edged and fixed interest markets while the pension funds, though also investing in gilts, hold large amount of equities.

407

Other institutions

Apart from the National Finance Corporation, there are a few other important public sector institutions. The Post Office Savings Bank operates in the same manner as the private savings banks but is the largest of such banks.

The Industrial Development Corporation of South Africa provides finance to specified industries at preferential rates of interest and raises finance through the issue of bonds and the acceptance of time deposits from companies.

Similarly, the Land and Agricultural Bank of South Africa provides finance to farmers at low rates of interest, and loans to agricultural co-operatives which in turn provide credit to farmers.

Central bank

The central bank is the South African Reserve Bank, which is wholly privately owned. Its shares are quoted on the Johannesburg Stock Exchange and it is structured as a limited liability company with a capital of R2 million and is required to hold gold and foreign reserves equivalent to 25 per cent of its cash holdings and liabilities. The bank is managed by a board of 12 directors. Half of the directors, including the governor and three deputy governors, are appointed by the government. The remaining six are appointed by the shareholders and are expected to represent the major fields of commerce, industry and agriculture.

The Reserve Bank provides all the functions of a central bank. It is the sole issuer of currency and, through the National Finance Corporation, offers lender of last resort facilities. It works closely with the Treasury and the Minister of Finance in the formulation of monetary policy but also has a high degree of authority in the control of credit. It manages the country's gold and foreign exchange reserves, acts as agent to the government in the issue of treasury bills and acts as a clearing house to the banking system. The only central bank function not performed by the Reserve Bank is the administration of the national debt.

Monetary policy

The system of monetary policy is currently under review by the de Kock 'Commission of inquiry into the South African Monetary System', headed by Dr Gerhard de Kock, senior deputy governor of the Reserve Bank. The stated objectives of the commission are '... the replacement of direct controls by market oriented policies. All measures or practices which directly or indirectly serve to keep interest rates below their natural market related levels, or which militate against the development of proper financial markets will therefore have to be substantially modified, if not abolished altogether'. The only progress has so far been the initial steps necessary for the establishment of a modern foreign exchange market.

At present monetary policy, as implemented by the Reserve Bank, is managed through the use of variable reserve and liquid asset requirements, direct control of the discount rate and certain other interest rates, quantitative restriction on bank credit and indirect moral suasion on the banking system. Only recently have open market operations been introduced, and as yet are not used as a major monetary instrument. The controls stipulated by the Reserve Bank apply to all commercial banks, general banks, savings banks and hire purchase banks.

Reserve requirements and liquid asset policy

Banks are required to hold eight per cent of their short-term liabilities as cash on interest-free deposit with the Reserve Bank, plus a further seven per cent of short-term liabilities as supplementary interest-free deposits with the National Finance Corporation. It is this supplementary reserve requirement which, of the two, is first subject to variation when a change in monetary policy is implemented. When first introduced in November 1972, the supplementary reserve ratio was 10 per cent, but as the Reserve Bank pursued moderately expansionary monetary policy, it was reduced to seven per cent in March 1973 where it has remained ever since.

The liquid assets requirements are subject to greater variability. In addition to the reserve ratios, banks are required to maintain a specified proportion of liabilities in the form of liquid assets comprising cash, gold coin or bullion, demand deposits with the National Finance Corporation and with other banks, callable loans to discount houses, treasury bills, government and Reserve Bank securities of less than three years' maturity, bills and short-term debentures of the Land Bank, notes and short-term debentures of the Industrial Development Corporation that have been issued for the financing of capital goods export and which are guaranteed by the government, and good quality bankers' acceptances, trade bills or promissory notes with less than 120 days' maturity. This wide range of liquid assets, it is argued, may sometimes cause monetary policy to lack effectiveness. The ratios are frequently revised. As at end 1980, banks must hold 55 per cent of liquid assets (which include the primary and supplementary cash reserve requirements) against their short-term liabilities, plus 10 per cent of the increase in their short-term liabilities, together with 29 per cent against their medium-term liabilities. These rates have held since September 1978 when they were reduced slightly from previous ratios set in September 1975 in a move by the Reserve Bank to cautiously expand bank liquidity. Returns showing each bank's liquid asset position must be filed with the Reserve Bank at the end of each month. In August 1978, a distinction was made and different ratios set for large banks—defined as those with assets of over R800 million—and small banks. Small banks are subject to lower liquid asset ratios to help them compete for medium-term deposits. In particular, the medium-term liquid asset ratio is 27 per cent instead of 29 per cent, while the liquid asset ratio for increases in medium-term liabilities by the small banks was abolished completely in March 1979.

Discount policy

It is currently the intention of the monetary authorities that the structure of interest rates in South Africa is determined by the 'bank rate', which is the rate at which the Reserve Bank will discount first-class bills to the discount houses. Time deposit maximum rates of interest are determined by the Reserve Bank for deposits of less than R250 000 in a fixed relationship to bank rate.

Overdraft rates also are determined by the Reserve Bank such that prime overdraft rate—the rate at which the banks may lend to its most credit-worthy customers, and thus the lowest lending rate—must be a minimum of 2.5 per cent and a maximum of 3.5 per cent above bank rate. As at mid-1980 bank rate was 7 per cent, having been reduced in a series of steps from its peak of $9\frac{1}{2}$ per cent which prevailed between mid-1976 and mid-1978.

Though these centrally imposed controls over interest rates influence the whole structure of interest rates, some money market rates tend to move independently of bank rate. In the corporate sector this leads to the use of the 'grey market' which, to some extent, bypasses the controlled system, in that companies can borrow in the form of acceptance credits at perhaps half the rate they would be charged on a bank overdraft. Many market rates are affected directly by demand and supply. This depends to some extent on bank rate and to some extent on the differential between domestic interest rates and those prevailing abroad, which influences the inflow or outflow of capital funds. Thus, in mid-1976 when liquidity was tight and bank rate was raised to $9\frac{1}{2}$ per cent, money market rates fluctuated between 10 and 17 per cent. Since 1978 and up to mid-1980, bank rate has been reduced to 7 per cent but money market rates dropped to 4–5 per cent. These money market rates include the treasury bill rate which is determined indirectly through the amount offered for weekly tender. In practice, movements in bank rate tend to follow trends in the money market, but with a considerable lag of 6 to 12 months. Direct control of the bank rate is obviously inadequate as a monetary policy tool and it is probable that the de Kock commission will recommend that the interest rate structure be more freely determined by the market.

Quantitive credit ceilings

The Reserve Bank may impose direct limits on the amount of credit extended by the banks to the private sector. These were first introduced in 1976 and, using 31 December 1975 as the base date, banks could only increase their discounts, loans and advances to the private sector and their investments in certain private sector securities by 1.5 per cent to 31 March 1976 and thereafter by 0.5 per cent per month.

In March 1979 the ceilings were raised by five per cent relative to the base figures although the monthly increase could still be only 0.5 per cent. This has the effect of raising the banks' maximum permissible lending to the private sector and their maximum holdings of private sector securities to 128 and 126 per cent respectively over their original levels at the end of 1975. The aggregate amount of credit to the private sector which banking institutions may not exceed without becoming subject to the ceiling requirements was raised from R10 million to R15 million in May 1978 and in March 1979 was raised again to R20 million.

Open market operations

Open market operations have only really been used since 1977 or 1978, but more to add to or subtract from the banking system's liquidity temporarily, rather than to have a direct lasting influence over interest rates and money supply growth. It is primarily because the Reserve Bank directly controls some rates of interest that open market operations are rendered less effective as an instrument of monetary policy.

Open market operations take the form of repurchase or sale of government securities by the central bank. For example, in open market operations between August 1978 and June 1979, the Reserve Bank sold more than R500 million of securities and bought R160 million. About 65 per cent of the sales were of government stock which was mostly taken up by the discount houses and banks. The purchases were made in periods of monetary tightness, specifically late August to early October 1978 and March, May and June 1979. In the earlier period, the bank bought short-dated government securities but in the later periods, as the investment climate changed, it bought medium-term stock of 3 to 10 years' life and long-term stock of more than 10 years' maturity.

Withholding taxes

Interest

Withholding taxes are deducted from interest where the 'true source'—the country in which the interest is made available—is South Africa. Thus, a British resident purchasing a South African government bond on the London Stock Exchange and receiving interest in London would not be liable to South African withholding tax. Where the true source of interest is South Africa, the recipient is liable to normal tax and any withholding tax paid may be credited against the normal tax. Normal tax paid by individuals ranges from 9 to 60 per cent on taxable income of between R1000 and R28 000 respectively. Normal tax paid by companies comprises corporation tax, a surcharge and a loan levy, as follows:

	To March		
	1979	*1980*	*1981*
Corporation tax	40%	40%	40%
Surcharge	2%	2%	2%
Loan Levy	6%	4%	0%

Dividends

Dividends that are paid out of profits derived from within South Africa are subject to withholding tax at the standard rate of 15 per cent. With few exceptions, this is not reduced by tax treaties. In the following table, where two rates are shown, the

411

lower rate applies if the recipient holds more than 25 per cent of the common shares of the distributing company.

Exemptions

The following securities are exempt from withholding tax on interest:

- South African Government treasury bills;
- South African Government bonds (gilts);
- South African municipality and public corporation bonds (semigilts);
- South African Government non-resident bonds;
- Foreign bonds listed on Johannesburg Stock Exchange;
- South African securities purchased in foreign markets.

Table 18.10   Withholding taxes

	Dividends, %	Interest, %
Residents of non-treaty countries		
non-residents not carrying on business in South Africa	15	10
non-residents also carrying on business in South Africa	0	10
South African branches of foreign companies	15	10
Residents of tax treaty countries		
Bophuthatswana	15	10
Botswana	15	10
Canada	15	10
Cyprus	15	10
Gambia	15	10
Germany	15 or 7.5	10
Grenada	15	10
Lesotho	15	10
Malawi	15	10
Mauritius	15	10
Netherlands	15 or 5	10
Seychelles	15	10
Sierra Leone	15	10
Swaziland	15	10
Sweden	15	10
Switzerland	7.5	10
Transkei	15	10
UK	15 or 5	10
USA	15	10
Zimbabwe	15	10

Exchange controls

The South African exchange territory includes South West Africa, Bophuthatswana, Lesotho, Swaziland and Transkei. The de Kock commission is currently examining the system of exchange controls with the intention of abolishing all controls as they relate to non-residents. This cannot be achieved until the two-tier currency is merged into a single currency and allowed to find its own level on the international exchange market. A first move towards this goal was taken in February 1979 when the new financial rand system replaced the old securities rand.

Authorities

The Treasury is responsible for exchange control legislation but the imposition of controls is managed by the Reserve Bank, although much regulatory authority is also delegated to the authorized dealers such as the commercial banks.

Currency

The currency is the South African rand which is subdivided into 100 cents and is quoted against the US dollar. Between the fourth quarter of 1975 and the fourth quarter of 1978 the rand was pegged at $1.15 but the weakness of the dollar has caused the authorities to make subsequent frequent revaluations of the rand *vis-à-vis* the US dollar. At the end of 1980 the rand was quoted at US$1.3402.

Financial rands

The rand is, however, a two-tier currency, divided between the commercial rand and the financial rand. Investment in South Africa by non-residents may only be made, and sales effected, through the medium of financial rands. The proceeds however are received at the same rate as commercial rand investments. Thus dividend and interest yields may be significantly different for non-residents relative to resident investors.

Financial rands can only be obtained from other non-residents or created through an arbitrage transaction involving the purchase of South African securities which are quoted on either the London or New York stock exchanges. The price of financial rands differs from the foreign exchange price of commercial rands. The latter is fixed by the monetary authorities, while the financial rand price depends on demand by non-residents wishing to invest in South African securities and supply by non-residents willing to sell South African securities. Non-resident demand is the most significant factor. The stronger the demand, the lower the financial rand discount and the narrower the differential between the financial and commercial rands. The financial rand discount therefore acts as a sensitive barometer of political and economic confidence in South Africa by the rest of the world. This influences the differential between share prices in Johannesburg and overseas markets *vis-à-vis* the commercial rand rate. The share price quoted on the London or New York exchanges is lower than the share price quoted on the Johannesburg Stock Exchange, the difference representing the financial rand discount. Stockbrokers and dealers on the Johannesburg exchange are able to buy and sell financial rands as agents for non-resident investors.

The following example illustrates the creation of financial rands. Although London is the major centre for the creation of financial rands, this example uses New York for ease of comparing currency conversions.

Share Price on JSE	R7.50
Share Price on NYSE	US$6.25

If the commercial rand rate of exchange is R1 = US$1.3115, then the JSE equivalent price in dollars is:

$$R7.50 \times 1.3115 = US\$9.86$$

Therefore the discount on the NYSE is:

$$\frac{9.86 - 6.25}{9.86} \times 100 = 36.6\%$$

Thus, compared to the price of commercial rands of US$1.3115, the price of the financial rand at a discount of 36.6% is:

$$1.3115 \times \frac{100 - 36.6}{100} = US\$0.8315$$

Since dividends paid by South African companies may be remitted at the commercial rate of exchange, this represents an advantage to non-resident investors. From the previous example:

Share price	= R7.50
Dividend at 10%	= R0.75
Share price to non-resident at financial rand discount of 36.6%	= $R7.5 \times \dfrac{100 - 36.6}{100}$
	= R4.755
Dividend at commercial rand rate	= R0.75
Dividend yield to non-resident	= 15.77%
Deduct non-resident withholding tax at 15%	= 2.37%
Net yield to non-resident	= 13.40%

Thus, the net yield to non-residents is 3.4 percentage points higher than the 10 per cent gross yield to residents. How much of this relative benefit can be realized by the non-resident investor depends on the financial rand discount when he wishes to repatriate the proceeds. Sales can only be effected through the medium of financial rands, which takes the form of selling the South African securities to other non-residents through a foreign stock market.

In the above example the financial rand discount is 36.6 per cent. During 1979 and 1980, the highest discount was about 41 per cent in January and February 1979. The lowest was about 16 per cent in January and February 1980 (the height of the gold boom).

Non-residents accounts

Non-residents may open financial rand accounts with South African banks and such accounts may be credited with the authorized payment by residents or other non-residents and with the proceeds of sales of specified currency to authorized dealers. They may be debited with similar transactions. Balances may not be remitted abroad except through a financial rand account, which must be maintained with an authorized dealer. They may be credited or debited with the sale and redemption proceeds of South African securities, or from other financial rand accounts. Balances on financial rand accounts may be converted to other foreign currency at the financial rand rate of exchange if the proceeds derive from the redemption of five-year non-resident bonds or certain other public sector bonds and thence remitted abroad. Alternatively, funds may be transferred either by exporting South African shares which have been bought on the Johannesburg Stock Exchange or by selling the rand to another non-resident in exchange for foreign currency.

Repatriation of profits and dividends

Repatriation of the proceeds of investment may only be effected through a financial rand account as detailed above.

Gold

There is no organized gold market in South Africa. Kruggerrands may be purchased on the stock exchange but proceeds may only be repatriated via financial rand accounts. Alternatively, kruggerrands may also be bought on foreign gold markets, in particular in Zurich or London.

19. Bahrain

General market environment

During the 1970s financial services have developed an increasingly important role in the Bahrain economy. In 1975 the Bahrain monetary agency, which is empowered with all the functions of a central bank, decided to create the conditions that would establish Bahrain as an alternative financial centre. Indeed, with the problems experienced in the Lebanon, Bahrain was well placed to attract much of the Middle East business lost from Beirut.

Bahrain has now deservedly earned the reputation of being the commercial and financial centre of the Gulf. This was brought about by positive policies of the government which has a long tradition of orderly administration—one of the best among the Gulf States. As a small country (only 230 square miles), the government determined in the mid-1960s, when Bahrain's oil output had maximized, that the future of its economy should be as a service industry centre. It created a free trade zone at the main port, Mina Sulman, and developed its air and telecommunications systems with the rest of the world. Excellent communications now exist in Bahrain thus enhancing the natural advantage which places Bahrain in an ideal time zone, linking the Far East and the rest of the Gulf States with financial centres in Europe and North America.

As a financial centre Bahrain offers the added attractions of being completely free of tax and of having no exchange controls. Thus, there are no restrictions on the retention of interest, profit or dividends, or on the transfer of funds into and out of the country.

The major advance, however, that has been mainly responsible for distinguishing Bahrain as a financial centre, has been the development of the offshore banking units (OBUs). The first of these was established in 1975 and their success has been such that there are now over 50 OBUs in Bahrain. Licences for these units are granted only to reputable international banks. They are not permitted to compete for local business but they transact considerable international business, such as interbank deposits and Eurobond secondary trading as well as providing a small over-the-counter market in shares of local Bahraini companies.

Following the success of the OBUs, exempt companies were subsequently allowed to be established which, although registered in Bahrain, must not carry on business in the country. The object is to develop Bahrain as a corporate business

416

Table 19.1 Summary of instruments

Instrument	Characteristics
MONEY MARKET	
Deposits	
call deposits	Active Eurocurrency market and smaller local currency market
time deposits	No restrictions, therefore a completely free market
certificates of deposit	Issued by a few banks. Poor secondary market
Promissory notes	Beginnings of commercial paper market. Small market at present
CAPITAL MARKET	
Government development bonds	Purchased mainly by local banks. Yields unattractive to other investors
Domestic bonds	Market in other domestic bonds not yet developed
Eurobonds	A number of issues in primary market denominated in dinars. Secondary market thin but good secondary market in other Eurobonds
Equities	Small OTC maintained by offshore banking units. Tendency for new issues to be greatly oversubscribed
Gold	All transactions are unrestricted. Beginnings of organized local market

centre although, in the same way that only banks of international standing are granted OBU licences, exempt companies must first demonstrate a high quality of financial creditability before they may be registered.

The money market

Although the development of Bahrain's financial market is very recent the Bahrain Monetary Agency is actively encouraging the growth of the money market and has initiated the introduction of CDs and promissory notes in order to assist its development.

Deposits

Both the local and offshore banks accept demand, time and savings deposits. Money may be placed either in Bahraini dinars or in any of the major convertible currencies. The best markets are available for US dollars, Swiss francs, deutsche-marks, sterling and yen. In addition to the banks, six international moneybrokers also service the market. Banks and brokers are competitive with their interest quotations but deposit rates depend entirely on demand and supply and on rates prevailing in the Eurocurrency markets. The Bahrain Monetary Agency does not attempt to influence domestic interest rates either through the use of discount policy or open market operations. It does, however, recommend an interest rate of between 6 and 8 per cent on Bahraini dinar deposits and a rate of 8 to 10 per cent on dinar loans. In general, banks tend to adhere to the Agency's recommendations except when monetary conditions are exceptionally easy or tight. Minimum acceptable sizes of deposits are US$250 000 for call deposits and US$50 000 for time deposits, or foreign currency equivalent.

Certificates of deposit

A few local and offshore banks issue three- and six-month negotiable certificates of deposit denominated in Bahraini dinars in unit sizes of BD 50 000. The primary market is still small and the secondary market is also not yet very liquid.

Monetary agency promissory notes

The government has little need to borrow in the short-term market because of Bahrain's high oil revenues, resulting in a large government surplus. The Bahrain Monetary Agency has facilitated the conditions for, as yet, only one major borrower—Aluminium Bahrain (ALBA)—to issue short-term promissory notes with maturities of between one and six months. The Monetary Agency hopes this will encourage the growth of the money market and eventually lead to a commercial paper market, once more borrowers seek to raise short-term capital in this way.

The notes are issued at par, carry a fixed coupon rate of interest, and are redeemed at par at maturity. The Monetary Agency stands ready to rediscount the notes to the local banks thus acting as lender of last resort and extending credit to the banking system.

Most of the notes issued in the primary market are taken up by the local banks, though non-bank investors may also apply through one of the banks or may purchase the notes in the secondary market.

The capital market

Bahrain has a very small domestic capital market. As an oil exporting country the government has little need to raise capital through bond issues while companies have ready access to the Euromarkets for borrowing. Nearly all bond trading activity is in the Eurobond market which was the principal reason for the establishment of OBUs.

Government development bonds

There have been a few issues of domestic government bonds. In 1977 the government issued BD 13 million of development bonds with a maturity of five years and a coupon of eight per cent payable semiannually. In 1978 a similar issue was made for an amount of BD 7 million with a seven and three-quarter per cent coupon. The bonds are in registered form, registered with the Bahrain Monetary Agency, and are transferable in minimum denominations of BD 1000. Non-residents may purchase these government development bonds but the secondary market is very inactive, principally because the returns available on these bonds are insufficient to attract the local wealthy individual investor who is able to obtain returns of three or four times these yields through speculation in local property deals. Most of the bonds tend to be held in the portfolios of the local banks which are able to borrow on a short-term basis from the Bahrain Monetary Agency against the security of development bonds.

Domestic bonds

Local companies tend not to issue bonds on the domestic market although public institutions are beginning to use the bond market to raise capital. The Housing Bank, formed in March 1979 is one such institution. Its objective is to help local people build their own homes by offering 25-year mortgages at interest rates of five or six per cent. Sums of up to BD 20000 may be made available to individuals and the bank is expected to turn over BD 74 million during its first three years of operation. To date, the bank has not made a public issue of bonds but has arranged short- and long-term loans from financial institutions on a private placement basis.

Eurobonds

A growing number of local banks are participating in and managing international bond issues denominated in Bahraini dinars. The Bahraini dinar Eurobond market was opened in 1977 and as at mid-1980 there have been some half-dozen internationally syndicated issues by foreign borrowers. The first issue, made in February 1977, was for BD 8 million issued at BD $99\frac{1}{2}$ with a coupon of nine per cent and a life of seven years. The other issues have been for amounts of between BD 6 million and BD 15 million, issued at par with coupons of $8\frac{1}{2}$ to $8\frac{3}{4}$ per cent and lives of 5 to 10 years. The primary market is supervised by the Bahrain Monetary Agency, but this is to ensure an orderly market, and in practice few restrictions are enforced.

Bahraini dinar Eurobonds are option bonds in the sense that subscribers are able to pay for the bonds in US dollars and may elect for payments of interest and/or principal to be made in US dollars. The reason for this is that the Bahraini dinar is not a widely held currency and it is anyway quoted on world foreign exchanges against the US dollar. All Bahraini dinar Eurobonds are bearer securities which pay interest annually, free of withholding tax. Secondary market turnover is low and is made mainly between the offshore banking units, although a small market does exist in London.

The offshore banking units also provide a secondary market in other Eurobond issues, particularly Kuwaiti dinar bonds and certain other well traded international bonds through interaction with the market in London.

Equities

A small equities market is developing in Bahrain. There is no physical market-place but new issues are managed and underwritten by one or a syndicate of offshore banks and an over-the-counter secondary market is thereafter maintained between the offshore banks and approximately 10 recognized stockbrokers. A temporary moratorium was imposed on the market in the fourth quarter of 1979 with respect

419

to the onshore issue of new shares by offshore exempt companies pending an inquiry into an issue made by the Gulf Investment Company (GIC). In that instance subscriptions were invited for a total issue of US$25 million but applications totalled US$30 billion, which was even more than the combined net worth of Bahraini offshore banks. The shares were oversubscribed 1263 times although the actual amount of cash advanced was considerably less because investors were required to put up initially only five per cent of the share price.

It was found that there had been 30 000 subscribers, all of whom were Kuwaiti citizens and individuals. Twenty-nine thousand had applied for the maximum quota of one million shares but were allotted only 858 each. Investors applying for 1000 shares received only one share each. The GIC incident was not untypical of new issues made on the Bahrain equity market. The first exempt company to make a public issue, Pearl Investment Company, was 106 times oversubscribed, again by Kuwaiti investors. The second issue made by the Gulf Union Insurance Company was 400 times oversubscribed, and an issue made in September 1979 by the Gulf Medical Projects Company of Dharjah of share capital of US$4 million was oversubscribed 2349 times.

In order to preserve Bahrain's reputation as a financial centre, the authorities are now enforcing stricter controls. The Monetary Agency must now be informed of the names of applicants for new share issues and must be able to ensure that bank lending for the purchase of shares is properly regulated.

A proper stock exchange is to be established at some stage with a view to it becoming an international trading floor. This is not yet imminent, however.

At the end of 1980 there were only about 20 local Bahraini companies with publicly issued shares. In order to protect the local market the new stock exchange may operate a two-tier trading system. The shares of Bahraini companies may possibly be permitted to be traded by Bahraini citizens only in order to prevent excessive demand from foreign sources. Non-residents, as well as nationals, would thus be permitted to trade in shares of offshore companies, certain regional companies and companies that already have listings on other foreign stock exchanges.

Some rules of this nature had previously existed but Kuwaiti investors were bypassing them by offering Bahraini citizens five Kuwaiti dinars to be able to use their names. Additionally, whole families were used in order that Kuwaiti investors could override the subscriptions limits for individuals.

Further proposals being examined by the Ministries of Commerce and Legal Affairs suggest that controls should be introduced to define the responsibilities of stockbrokers, to establish a finalized system of buying and selling shares and to ensure that closing prices and trading volumes are published daily in regional newspapers.

Exempt companies

Commercial companies that do not have Bahrain's majority shareholders may be registered in Bahrain as exempt companies provided they fulfil certain provisions. They must be companies with trading or commercial activities in the Gulf area although they may not trade in Bahrain itself. In order to obtain exempt status, companies must also comply with certain financial and reporting conditions. They must have a minimum capital of at least US$5 million, maintain an office and staff in Bahrain and hold board meetings at least once a year in Bahrain.

By these provisions, the authorities hope to prevent Bahrain from becoming just a tax haven but wish to attract the registration only of reputable and sound companies.

Exempt companies were first introduced in 1977 but only since 1979 have exempt companies been allowed to issue shares to the public. When first established, they had to be closely held companies and share transfers required the authorization of the Minister of Commerce.

Gold

Gold may be freely purchased, held, sold or exported, by both residents and non-residents although no organized market-place exists.

In October 1980, the Bank of Bahrain and Kuwait became the first bank to sell gold over the counter. The bank sells gold in the form of 24 carat ingots in sizes from one ounce up to one kilogram as well as the Austrian 100 crown and Mexican 50 peso gold coins. The bank will hold gold in safe custody on behalf of customers and transfer the rights if customers trade the gold but will not buy back the gold from customers who wish to sell.

Dealing and fees

Deposits

Demand or time deposits may be placed directly with a local bank, offshore bank or through a moneybroker. There are no fees since bid prices are net of commission.

CDs

Only a few local banks so far offer CDs. There are no fees for purchasing primary CDs. Because of a still poor secondary market, dealing spreads made by local or offshore banks for secondary CDs are $\frac{1}{4}$ to $\frac{3}{4}$ per cent.

Promissory notes

Dealt net. Dealer spread is $\frac{1}{8}$ to $\frac{3}{8}$ per cent.

Development bonds

Dealt through local banks. Dealing spreads are generally $\frac{1}{2}$ to $\frac{3}{4}$ per cent but may be greater because of the thin secondary market.

Eurobonds

Dealt through offshore banks. Dealing spreads are generally $\frac{1}{2}$ to $\frac{3}{4}$ per cent, but may be greater depending on activity in the secondary market.

Equities

Dealt through offshore banks. No standard brokerage is charged, but is at the discretion of the dealer. Depending on the size of transaction, brokerage may be up to one per cent of the consideration.

No stamp duty or additional taxes are charged.

Financial and monetary systems

Financial institutions

In order to foster the conditions necessary to create a financial centre in Bahrain, the authorities have encouraged the establishment of a number of financial institutions. Most important are the offshore banking units, though local banks, money-brokers, investment banks and merchant banks are now playing an increasingly important role.

There are now nearly 100 banking institutions in Bahrain which are all subject to supervision by the Bahrain Monetary Agency. These comprise 51 OBUs, 19 commercial banks, 34 representative offices and investment banks. All types of banks are subject to licence by the Monetary Agency which has become more selective since 1979. Major criteria for the granting of all types of licences are international reputation and creditability, financial management and expertise. More recently greater consideration has also been given to wider geographical representation by banks in Bahrain.

Offshore banking units (OBUs)

OBUs were first established in 1975, their purpose being to act as dealing intermediaries for Arab and foreign depositors to participate in the international wholesale money markets. They cannot compete for local business and do not provide chequing account facilities. OBUs are branches of international banks and, as intermediaries, they effect transactions between their clients, banks and other licensed dealers in Bahrain and other international financial centres. Most business consists of the acceptance and placement of call and time deposits in the Euro-currency markets, spot and forward foreign exchange transactions and dealings in Europaper, notes and bonds. They may accept large deposits from governments and from other banks, including the local banks, and provide large medium-term loans to foreign borrowers.

OBUs must first obtain a licence from the Bahrain Monetary Agency, and such licences are now quite expensive. In addition an annual fee of BD 1000 is charged to each bank. There are, however, a number of advantages for a bank establishing an OBU. In particular, there is no tax on profits, no personal or withholding taxes, negligible bureaucracy or government interference, and a time zone well placed between the Far East and Europe. At mid-1980 there were over 50 OBUs with combined total assets of US$23.5 billion. In these terms, Bahrain has become a

422

financial centre of a size equivalent to Singapore. The assets comprised US$14.5 billion held in dollar assets, US$7 billion held in local currencies and US$2 billion held in other currencies, mostly Swiss francs and Deutschemarks.

Local banks

The local banking systems, supervised by the Monetary Agency, is efficient and well developed. The local banks are commercial banks which provide mainly retail services and chequing account facilities to local individuals and businesses, although recently they have begun to participate in co-managing and lead managing Eurocurrency loans.

There are 34 local banks. Fifteen are foreign owned but the remainder are owned by majority Bahraini shareholders. The two major local banks are the National Bank of Bahrain and the Bank of Bahrain and Kuwait. The first is 49 per cent owned by the government and 51 per cent owned by Bahraini citizens. The second is 50 per cent owned by Bahraini citizens and 50 per cent owned by nine Kuwaiti banks.

Moneybrokers

There are six moneybrokers, all foreign owned, established in Bahrain who act as intermediaries between Bahrain based clients and the markets in Europe and the Far East. They accept call and short-term time deposits in Bahraini dinars and convertible currency or place clients' money in Euro CDs or other short-term paper.

Investment banks and merchant banks

A few foreign owned and some locally owned investment or merchant banks have been established in the last few years. They provide portfolio management services, advise corporate clients on share issues and acquisitions and accept call money from corporate clients. One such bank is the Bahrain Investment Company which was set up in 1977 and whose majority shareholders are Bahraini nationals.

Investment banks have only limited licences—Investment Banking Licences (IBL)—which cost BD 6000 each. Foreign banks with IBLs include Kleinwort Benson, a British Merchant bank and the first to be established in Bahrain, and Merril Lynch International, an American investment bank. Banks with IBLs are permitted to establish onshore subsidiaries with the purpose of improving the efficiency of the capital market. They may, however, only engage in a restricted range of banking activities.

Other institutions

Subject to licence, the Monetary Agency is also encouraging the establishment of other financial institutions, such as insurance companies, which should help to create a more efficient capital market since such institutions are large investors in medium- and long-term fixed-interest securities. There are now over 20 insurance companies, a state pension fund and a social insurance fund in Bahrain. One new financial institution, mentioned in the capital market section, is the Housing Bank, which was established in 1979 to provide long-term home loans and which may in the future seek to raise funds in the capital market. At present its capital is 37.5 per cent owned by the government and the remainder is financed by short- and long-term loans from financial institutions.

Bahrain Monetary Agency

The Bahrain Monetary Agency replaced the Bahrain Currency Board as the controller of the currency in December 1973 and since January 1975 has assumed the full powers of a central bank.

It is the sole issuer of notes and coins; it safeguards the value of the currency, and regulates the banking and financial system. The Agency is wholly owned by the government and together with the Minister of Commerce and Agriculture assists in the formulation of monetary policy.

Monetary policy

There is very little monetary intervention by the authorities. The Monetary Agency's main concern is to maintain the value of the currency which it does by intervention in the spot foreign exchange market using the US dollar as the currency of intervention.

Otherwise the Agency does not attempt to influence interest rates, the growth of credit or liquidity in the banking system. Reserve ratios are established for the local banks but these are not used as an instrument of monetary policy.

The Monetary Agency does have mandatory powers to regulate the banking system but so far has not implemented them. It continues to operate on the basis of direct consultation with the banking system which is now conducted through the newly formulated Bankers' Society. The Bahrain Monetary Agency advises the banking system of recommended interest rates on borrowing and lending in Bahraini dinars for the purpose of assisting Bahrain's residents rather than regulating liquidity or money supply. On the whole, the banks comply with these suggested rates. Other interest rates are determined purely by market forces.

Withholding taxes

Apart from taxes on oil companies, there are no taxes imposed in Bahrain on income, corporate profits or capital gains; nor are there any withholding taxes on interest or dividends from portfolio investments.

Exchange controls

There is no exchange control legislation in Bahrain. The Monetary Agency is the supervisory authority but, apart from maintaining stability in the value of the currency, it does not intervene in foreign transactions. Inward and outward invest-

424

ment is completely unrestricted and profits, interest and dividends may all be freely repatriated in any currency to anywhere in the world.

The currency is the Bahraini dinar which is divisible into 1000 fils. It is completely interchangeable with the UAE dirham and the Qatari ryal at the rate of ten to one Bahraini dinar.

The dinar is quoted against the US dollar, but the recent weakness of the dollar has led to frequent revaluations of the dinar against the dollar. Officially the dinar is pegged against the SDR at the rate of 1 SDR = BD 0.47619 with margins of fluctuations of 7.25 per cent. Daily quotes are also made by the Monetary Agency for spot exchange rates of the dinar against the pound sterling and the deutschemark, and the Agency attempts to ensure that the dinar maintains its value against both these currencies.

20. Kuwait

General market environment

Kuwait is one of the most advanced Gulf States in terms of its developed industrial infrastructure, the careful management of its financial resources, stable administration and its holdings of overseas reserves.

The financial sector plays an important role in Kuwait such that banking, insurance and other financial services produce about 20 per cent of the non-oil element of Kuwait's gross domestic product.

Kuwait's development as a financial centre was initially inhibited by controls over bank ownership and interest rates and the lack of a secondary market for Kuwaiti dinar denominated bonds and shares. However, banking regulations have recently been relaxed while a secondary market in securities is provided by a new stock exchange and also by the Arab Company for Trading Securities. This is a subsidiary of the Industrial Bank of Kuwait and the Kuwait International Investment Company. Technical assistance has been provided by two foreign banks, Credit Suisse and White Weld. In addition, the money market has been broadened by the introduction of CDs, floating rate notes and corporate promissory notes, though the secondary market in each of these instruments has yet to improve. Kuwait's financial markets are further aided by the growing number of banking, investment and insurance institutions which are establishing offices in Kuwait; this was encouraged by Kuwait's activity in the primary Eurobond market, for which it is now the leading centre in the Middle East.

Foreign capital is welcome in Kuwait and, except for equity investment, is afforded equal treatment with local capital. There are no exchange controls and no taxation is withheld on profits, interest or dividends. During 1979 and 1980, however, Kuwait's problem has been one of attracting foreign investment and of stemming the outward flow of capital which has resulted in acute domestic illiquidity. The major reason for this is a rigidly enforced structure of maximum interest rates based on Islamic religious principles which are not justified on economic grounds. A period of high interest rates prevailing in foreign markets has resulted in an exodus of capital from Kuwait to foreign markets.

The central bank has very little power to reverse this flow and to materially improve domestic liquidity since most traditional monetary instruments usually available to central banks necessarily require a compatible change in interest rate policy. Moral suasion to directly influence the course of bank lending has been the principal tool available but has not, to date, proved very effective.

Table 20.1 Summary of instruments

Instrument	Characteristics
MONEY MARKET	
Deposits	
call deposits	Reasonably active market for Kuwaiti dinars and other convertible currencies
time deposits	Convertible currencies placed through Eurocurrency markets. Dinar deposits subject to interest controls
CDs	Fixed and floating rate CDs, 3 months to 3 years. Issued by a few local banks. Poor secondary market
Central bank bills	Introduced in 1978 but no recent issues because of tight liquidity
Floating rate notes	Interest adjusted every 6 months. Issued in dinars by local banks. Poor secondary market
Promissory notes	Discount notes of 3 months to 4 years issued by companies. Thin secondary market
CAPITAL MARKET	
Domestic bonds	A few issues made by banks and property companies. Limited secondary market
Foreign bonds	Issued by international institutions, e.g., World Bank. Moderate secondary turnover
Eurobonds	Largest market in Middle East, but still too small to provide active secondary market
Equities	Small stock exchange on which 39 stocks are listed. Prices volatile because demand is greater than supply. Foreign participation restricted
Gold	No organized market but free trading permitted

The money market

Deposits

The local commercial banks accept all types of deposits, i.e., demand, time and savings deposits. Additionally, merchant and investment banks accept call deposits and time deposits for up to six months.

Call deposits may be placed in minimum amounts of KD 50 000 for periods of overnight call, two or seven days' notice. Time deposits may be placed in amounts of KD 10 000 or more for periods of from one week up to twelve months, or longer by negotiation.

Both call and time deposits may be placed in either Kuwaiti dinars or in any other convertible currency, since the local banks hold most of their assets in foreign currencies and are permanently in touch with banks and dealers in other financial centres in Europe, the Far East and the offshore banks in Bahrain.

Interest on currency deposits depends on supply and demand which determines interest levels prevailing in the Eurocurrency markets.

427

Interest on Kuwaiti dinar time deposits is subject to restrictions imposed by the central bank. The limits are intended to help domestic industry by keeping down the lending rates to industrial and manufacturing companies, although an additional but major reason is the Islamic aversion to high interest rates. The interest ceilings have been in force since 1977 and are shown in the section on monetary policy. The maximum interest rate payable on KD time deposits is 10 per cent per annum.

In contrast, call money is not subject to interest rate controls and, because Kuwaiti money markets suffer from acute illiquidity during periods when the level of international interest rates are high relative to those prevailing in Kuwait, rates offered for overnight call deposits may temporarily rise to extreme levels. Ignoring temporary volatility, two- and seven-day call deposit rates have in general fluctuated between 5 and 12 per cent during 1979 and 1980.

Certificates of deposit

Domestic banks issue bearer negotiable CDs denominated in Kuwaiti dinars in amounts of KD 50 000. Foreign owned banks with offices in Kuwait are not permitted to issue such securities.

Two types of CDs are issued, fixed rate and floating rate. Fixed-rate CDs have been available since 1977. They carry a fixed rate of interest and have maturities of between three months and three years. Usually they are issued on a tap basis, subject to demand by the borrower, and are available in both bearer and registered form.

A second type of CD was introduced in 1978. These are floating rate CDs, (FRCDs) with maturities of three years and bearing a rate of interest which is adjusted every three months to a rate of one-quarter per cent over the Kuwait interbank offered rate for three-month deposits, but subject to a minimum coupon specified at issue. FRCDs are available in bearer form only.

CDs are not subject to the same interest rate constraints as time deposits. Interest on both fixed- and floating-rate CDs is paid free of withholding tax.

A secondary market in CDs is maintained by the domestic banks and by investment and merchant banks, and by the Arab Company for Trading Securities (ACTS), but this has so far proved less active than was initially hoped for. At the end of 1979 there were KD 21.6 million CDs outstanding, representing a substantial reduction from the KD 70 million outstanding at the end of 1978.

Central bank bills

In 1978 the central banks issued short-term bills in order to absorb excess liquidity in the banking system. However, by the time that the bank had completed the necessary preparation in order to issue the bills, the banking system became extremely illiquid. Tight monetary conditions were caused by Kuwait's interest-rate structure being kept artificially low relative to interest levels in international markets, thus leading to a large outflow of capital. As a consequence, no secondary market in Central Bank bills developed and no new issues have been made recently.

428

Floating rate notes

Floating rate notes (FRNs) with maturities of up to four years are also issued by domestic banks, usually denominated in Kuwaiti dinars in minimum units of KD 1000. They are also sometimes issued in US dollars in minimum units of US$1000. They carry a rate of interest fixed at issue of one-quarter per cent over the Kuwait interbank offered rate for six months deposits, which is readjusted every six months. The notes are normally in bearer form, though they may also be available in registered form. Interest is paid free of withholding tax. A secondary market is made by the same dealers as for CDs but, as with the CD market, secondary trading in FRNs is thin.

Promissory notes

There is a developing market in promissory notes which were first issued by Kuwaiti companies in 1978. They are discount securities in bearer form with maturities of between three months and four years. They carry only one name—that of the issuing company—and are secured only against the general assets of the issuing company. A secondary market is made by the Arab Company for Trading Securities which has agreed to make its own book in promissory notes to help the development of the market, but as yet secondary trading is negligible.

The capital market

Domestic bonds

The Kuwaiti Government is the channel for the receipt of all oil revenues, amounting to almost KD 5 billion in 1979, and this revenue is reinvested in the basic infrastructure of the economy. The government has little need to raise additional capital through the issue of bonds on the domestic market, while domestic industry can obtain funds directly from the government, which is the primary source of local capital. The government owns and controls the major utility and welfare institutions and provides direct subsidies to the major industrial and agricultural sectors.

Nevertheless, there have been a few issues of domestic bonds by the Industrial Bank of Kuwait (for purposes of industrial development), and also some issues by real estate development companies. In 1979, there were twelve KD domestic bond issues which raised a total of KD 104 million. Issues have been made in sizes of between KD 5 million and KD 8 million for terms of three to five years. They carry fixed-rate coupons of between six and eight per cent with interest paid semiannually and are free of withholding tax to non-residents. Bonds are bearer securities with minimum denominations of KD 1000. In the primary market, new issues tend to be oversubscribed by Kuwaiti residents. About 80 per cent of issues are purchased by Kuwaiti residents while a further 18 per cent are purchased by Arab institutions in the Gulf. Secondary market trading is thin, however, as most securities remain tightly held. Liquidity has been improved since the Arab Company for Trading

Securities was established to maintain a secondary market in locally issued securities. Through this intermediary, it is possible to deal in amounts of up to KD 50000 depending on market conditions.

Foreign bonds

A number of World Bank bond issues, denominated in Kuwaiti dinars have been underwritten and placed entirely in the domestic Kuwaiti bond market. Six of these issues were managed by the Kuwait Foreign Trading Contracting and Investment Company (KFTCIC), which is 80 per cent owned by the state. Another 50 per cent state-owned company, the Kuwait Investment Company (KIC) has managed a further US$800 million worth of issues. The bonds carry maturities of up to five years and pay interest semiannually free of withholding tax. They are bearer securities, in minimum denominations of KD 1000.

As with domestic bonds, the secondary market is maintained by the Arab Company for Trading Securities, but turnover is moderate.

Eurobonds

The Kuwaiti Eurobond market is the most developed in the Middle East. Established in 1974, there have been approximately 60 Eurobond issues denominated in Kuwaiti dinars. The borrowers are, in general, large foreign companies, banks and government agencies from a wide range of countries. The lenders are mostly Kuwaiti residents or large Arab institutions in the Middle East.

In 1979 there were 13 issues totalling KD 106 million compared with 15 worth KD 22 million in 1978. At end September 1979 the government imposed a moratorium on further bond issues because of increasing illiquidity in the domestic short-term money markets. As at December 1980 this moratorium was still being enforced. Once lifted, certain controls will probably continue to apply and may limit issues to one per month.

Issues range in size up to KD 10 million and maturities vary between 5 and 10 years. A special feature of the Kuwaiti Eurobond market is that many issues may be redeemed at specified dates prior to maturity at the option of the bondholder. A further feature is that investors can subscribe to new issues in either Kuwaiti dinars or in US dollars and may opt for interest and/or redemption capital to be paid in US dollars instead of dinars. This concession exists because it is recognized that investors may not have sufficient dinars to purchase their required amounts of bonds and that to purchase sufficient quantities on the foreign exchange market may sometimes prove difficult. If dollar payment is elected, then the sum due is converted at the rate of exchange current at the time that payment is made.

Such issues are classified as option bonds in that the bondholder is given the option to receive interest and/or principal on redemption in either US dollars or Kuwaiti dinars. This option makes the bonds attractive to international leaders who want to invest in a strong currency like the KD, while the income is returned, at rates of exchange current at the time of payment, in another more usable currency such as the US dollar.

430

KD Eurobonds are bearer securities that pay interest annually free of with-holding tax. Minimum denominations are KD 1000 and coupons vary between six and nine per cent. In the primary market there are about 20 investment institutions participating in the underwriting and placing of new issues, which are nearly all by public offering, and now amount to approximately KD 100 million per annum. Issues outstanding total approximately KD 400 million.

The secondary market is maintained in Kuwait by the Arab Company for Trad-ing Securities; the Kuwaiti banks and investment companies together with the offshore banks in Bahrain also participate in the market. Some secondary trading is conducted in London. Turnover is now about KD 150 million per annum, which is inadequate to provide a good market. This is because the primary market is still fairly small. Most of the bonds are held in relatively few hands and there is very little demand for KD bonds outside the Gulf.

Equities

There is one stock exchange in Kuwait on which 39 shares of Kuwaiti companies are listed. All are Kuwaiti companies, 23 of which are private sector companies and 16 are jointly private and public sector companies.

However, only Kuwaiti nationals are allowed to hold shares, severely limiting the type of investor.

Despite the apparent small size, the Kuwaiti stock exchange is one of the most dynamic in the world. In terms of turnover, which on average is KD 4–5 million per day, it is the eighth largest of all world exchanges. There are as many as 18 000 shareholders of Kuwaiti shares, while about 400 are regular traders.

Nationals of Gulf States may purchase the shares of offshore companies which have recently been permitted to seek listings on the Kuwaiti exchange. The listing rules are so strict, however, that relatively few of the 37 Gulf companies will either be eligible or will wish to obtain a listing. It is likely, therefore, that their shares will continue to be traded in the unofficial over-the-counter market in Kuwait.

A somewhat primitive trading floor was opened in 1977 although an over-the-counter stock market has existed for 24 years. However, much trading continues to be effected in the over-the-counter market between brokers and dealers. Currently there are no dealing regulations and anyone may enter the exchange and make transactions directly, face to face.

There are 17 firms of stockbrokers but these operate as middle men only and do not provide ancillary services such as investment advice, portfolio management or custody of securities, nor do they accept any liability or guarantees on behalf of clients.

Kuwaiti company shares each has a nominal value of KD 1, and in order to be listed on the exchange each company must have capitalized market value in excess of KD 4.5 million. The majority pay a 10 per cent dividend. Most new issues are substantially oversubscribed by Kuwaiti residents since there are plenty of investors available with large amounts of surplus cash but only limited investment opportun-ities in Kuwaiti dinar denominated securities.

431

In addition to the listed shares, there are over 150 unlisted private companies, two of which are wholly owned by the government. These companies' shares have a very restricted secondary market with only about 20 transactions being made per year.

For both listed and unlisted companies, prices are subject to exaggerated fluctuations because the number of companies is small and, particularly in the case of the joint sector companies, the volume of shares available for primary trading is also small. Share prices are therefore high by international standards and the price of some bank shares may be as much as 90 times earnings.

There are 15 Bahrain offshore companies, owned by Kuwaitis. Their shares are not traded on the Kuwaiti stock exchange, however, but through the offshore banking units in Bahrain.

Demand for the shares by Kuwaiti residents has greatly outweighed supply and new issues have been oversubscribed by several thousand times. To encourage a more orderly market, the government attempted to stop all trading in offshore Gulf companies not registered in Kuwait in October 1979 and stipulated that Kuwaiti residents could only trade in shares registered in Kuwait. This has not, however, prevented such dealing since investors found means of circumventing the new regulations. This led to the new rules for listing of offshore companies but, being so stringent, they are not likely to encourage a shift in trading from the unofficial to the official market.

Gold

There is no organized gold market in Kuwait though both residents and non-residents may buy, sell, import or export gold in any form without restriction.

Dealing and fees

Deposits

May be placed with local banks, foreign banks or investment institutions. No charges made.

CDs

Purchased from local banks only. Dealt through the Arab Company for Trading Securities net of commission. Secondary dealing spreads $\frac{1}{16}$ per cent.

FRNs

Dealt through local banks and the Arab Company for Trading Securities net of commission. Dealing spreads about $\frac{1}{8}$ to $\frac{1}{4}$ per cent.

Promissory notes

Dealt through the Arab Company for Trading Securities net of commission. Dealing spreads $\frac{1}{2}$ per cent.

Domestic bonds and foreign bonds

Dealt through local banks or investment companies and the Arab Company for Trading Securities. Dealing spreads $\frac{1}{2}$ per cent.

Eurobonds

Dealt through the Arab Company for Trading Securities, local banks, investment companies, OBUs in Bahrain or London banks. Dealing spreads about $\frac{1}{2}$ per cent.

Equities

Dealt through local banks, broker or investment companies. Brokerage is 2 fils (KD 0.002) per share on all purchases or sales.

Financial and monetary systems

Financial institutions

Since the financial system is an important part of Kuwait's non-oil economy, a full range of financial institutions have developed to provide the necessary services. These include commercial banks, investment banks, special banks (some of which operate exclusively under Islamic principles) and other institutions of a specialized nature.

Commercial banks

Until recently, the government allowed only locally owned banks to operate in Kuwait. Changes in banking regulations now allow other Arab nationals to hold minority interests in domestic banking institutions. The authorities still limit the number of banks. Currently there are 10 commercial banks with about 105 branches throughout the country.

The oldest bank, established in 1952, is the privately owned National Bank of Kuwait; this is the largest commercial bank and is estimated to account for about one-third of banking business in Kuwait. Three other privately owned banks, the Gulf Bank, the al Ahli Bank of Kuwait, and the Commercial Bank of Kuwait, each have an approximate 15 per cent share of the market. Two other banks, having a much smaller share, and which are part owned by the government, are the Bank of Kuwait and the Middle East and Burgan Bank.

The commercial banks provide chequing account facilities, accept call, time and savings deposits, undertake foreign exchange transactions and deal in securities on behalf of clients.

The National Bank of Kuwait and the al Ahli Bank of Kuwait are also regular participants in Euromarket loan and bond issues.

433

Investment banks

There are approximately 30 investment banks which advise corporate clients on the issue of shares and manage and underwrite new share and international bond issues. They advise also on mergers and acquisitions and act as agents and advisers for corporate and individual clients on investment both within the Gulf States and in foreign markets.

The major investment banks, known as 'the three Ks', are the Kuwait Investment Company (KIC), the Kuwait International Investment Company (KIIC) and the Kuwait Foreign Trading Contracting and Investment Company (KFTCIC). KIC and KFTCIC are majority owned by the government which holds 50 and 80 per cent, respectively, of their issued share capital. KIIC is entirely privately owned and has a 65 per cent majority shareholding in ACTS (the Arab Company for Trading Securities). All are major participants in the Eurobond market.

Special banks

A few specialized banking institutions have been established to promote industrial development or investment in real estate or to offer banking services based on Islamic principles.

One such Islamic institution is the Kuwait Finance House which is based in Kuwait and owned 49 per cent by the state. Another Islamic bank recently established in Switzerland is the Kuwait Finance Bank. The bank has a capital of US$10 million provided by four Arab banks from both Dubai and Kuwait, one of which is the Kuwait Finance House.

To conform with Islamic principles, these banks neither charge nor pay interest on loans or deposits. Instead, borrowers are required to pay to the bank a part of the profit from the project which the loan finances, while depositors receive part of the bank's annual profits. The proportion of profits paid may correspond to a rate of interest in excess of the 10 per cent per annum maximum that is paid by the commercial banks. The Kuwait Finance House produced profits of about KD 12 million in 1980, which was more than a threefold increase from KD 3.5 million in 1979. The number of deposits doubled from 20 000 to 40 000 in the course of the year. The bank was consequently able to pay out profits at a rate in excess of 10 per cent of their deposits which approximates to about three per cent more than the interest being paid by commercial banks.

Other specialized banks, such as the Industrial Bank of Kuwait, which is partly state owned, are established specifically to help the banking sector to channel funds into the areas of real investment for the enhancement of Kuwait's industrial and manufacturing base. The Industrial Bank of Kuwait, which was set up in 1973 with a capital of KD 20 million, provides long-term loans for industrial projects and equity capital for new ventures.

Similarly the Kuwait Real Estate Bank, with a capital of KD 9.2 million and reserves of KD 10.7 million, was established in 1973 to finance real estate investments. It is also partly state owned.

Arab Company for Trading Securities

Perhaps one of the most important institutions as regards the efficient functioning of the domestic capital market is the Arab Company for Trading Securities (ACTS).

With an authorized capital of KD 3 million and paid-up share capital of KD 2 million, ACTS is 58 per cent owned by one of the local investment banks—the Kuwait International Investment Company. The Industrial Bank of Kuwait owns a further 12 per cent, and three other local commercial banks, the al Ahli Bank, Burgan Bank and the Commercial Bank of Kuwait are also shareholders.

Its specific function is to provide and maintain a secondary market in domestic money and capital market securities. It is the only institution that is committed to do so and acts as a dealing intermediary, buying and selling securities both on behalf of clients and for its own account. ACTS maintains its own books in all types of domestic securities and, without its existence, it probably would not have been possible to establish new markets in CDs or promissory notes. Nevertheless, many of the markets in Kuwaiti securities still lack depth, and while ACTS made a 23 per cent return on its capital in 1978, it made a loss during 1979 on a turnover of KD 94 million. The loss was incurred because ACTS is obliged to buy in securities that local investors wish to sell. During 1979, however, interest rates in foreign markets presented better investment opportunities and resulted in a net outflow of capital from the Kuwaiti markets. ACTS was consequently put in the unfavourable position of having to buy securities for which there was little demand and which it could only sell subsequently at a discount and thus a loss.

Central bank

The Central Bank of Kuwait is 100 per cent state owned and was established in 1969 to provide all the major functions of a central bank. It is charged with the responsibility of supervising the banking system, formulating and regulating credit policies, securing the stability of Kuwait's currency and ensuring its free convertibility into foreign currencies.

The Central Bank of Kuwait is the major channel through which financial statistics from banks and other financial institutions are directed and for which the central bank has recently assumed the role of monitoring the changes and growth in the financial system. It also handles all the clearing operations of the domestic commercial banks and acts as agent of the government in the issue of securities or the purchase and sale of securities in the market.

Monetary policy

The central bank is responsible for enforcing the government's monetary policies. The major features of domestic monetary policy is limits and direct controls on interest rates for both borrowing and lending. These controls are based on political and religious, rather than economic, considerations. According to strict Islamic law, usury is forbidden and the authorities therefore consider that 10 per cent is the maximum rate of interest permissible in an Islamic society. The structure of maximum rates of interest for loans in Kuwaiti dinars is as shown in Table 20.2, which

Table 20.2 Maximum interest rates for KD loans

Type of loan	Maximum interest rate
Short-term loans such as trade credit loans and loans to manufacturing and industry	7% per annum
All other short-term loans (excluding overnight call deposits)	8½% per annum
Time deposits (with a minimum of 4½% on savings deposits)	10% per annum
All other loans in KD	10% per annum

shows a somewhat rigid and artificial rate structure that renders most other tools of monetary policy virtually ineffective, particularly when residents have free access to foreign markets where rates obtainable may be at considerably higher levels. During 1979 and 1980, Kuwait's money market has suffered from a severe lack of liquidity, because residents borrow Kuwaiti dinars at low rates of interest and then invest abroad at considerably higher returns, and foreign investors have likewise not been attracted to Kuwaiti markets.

For 1979 the ratio of loans to deposits in the Kuwaiti banking sector was 130 per cent while the banking system's lending in Kuwaiti dinars to the domestic private sector exceeded its net foreign assets by a ratio of 161 per cent.

The central bank has limited means by which it can reverse the deteriorating liquidity problem. Reserve ratios and 25 per cent liquidity ratios are set for the commercial banks and, though these are maintained and ensure that depositors are protected, it is the shortage of liquidity outside these requirements that reduces the banks' profitability and affects conditions in the money market and the economy as a whole.

The central bank cannot use open market operations in order to influence liquidity because it refuses to lift the ceiling on interest rates and there are no exchange controls to prevent the outflow of capital.

The only courses of action open to the central bank are firstly, swap operations in the foreign exchange market, which can have only a temporary effect on domestic liquidity and alleviate problems only in the short-term money market and, secondly, to employ moral suasion with the banking system. The central bank has increased its swap facilities as well as its discount and rediscount facilities but still has had little success in increasing liquidity in the domestic banking system.

The banks tend to meet the high loan demand by increasing overdrafts and credit facilities. Since January 1980, through moral suasion the banks have been asked by the central bank to reduce the amount of their lending by overdraft in favour of term loans and to direct their loans towards investment in domestic productive enterprises rather than towards speculative portfolio investment, particularly if such investment is intended for foreign markets. The effects of both these directives should be to reduce both speculative and outward investment and to increase domestic longer-term investment.

To date, this policy has proved only partly successful, which is not surprising given that there are few real controls to support the banking system in trying to enforce such general guidelines.

Withholding taxes

Tax is charged only on the income of foreign corporations operating in Kuwait. There are no other taxes on interest, profits or dividends and no withholding taxes charged to non-resident investors in Kuwait securities.

Exchange controls

Authority

There are no exchange controls in Kuwait and thus no supervisory authority. Non-residents may freely buy or sell Kuwaiti securities (except equities) and repatriate the proceeds without restriction. Non-resident accounts, opened with a Kuwaiti bank, are treated identically with resident accounts.

Currency

The currency is the Kuwaiti dinar which is divisible by 1000 fils. The Central Bank of Kuwait is responsible for maintaining its value and stability on world foreign exchange markets and ensuring its free convertibility into foreign currency.

The dinar is maintained against a trade-weighted basket of six currencies, i.e., the pound sterling, the Netherlands guilder, the Swiss franc, the French franc, the Deutschemark and the yen. The Kuwaiti dinar is quoted daily against the US dollar, calculated according to the dollar quotation against each of the six currencies in the basket. The dinar's value on the foreign exchange markets is maintained by the central bank using the US dollar as the currency of intervention in the spot foreign exchange markets. No intervention takes place in the forward foreign exchange market.

21. Australia

General market environment

The whole of Australia's financial system is undergoing reform and is the subject of an independent inquiry into the workings of the system. The inquiry is being conducted by a government appointed committee headed by Mr Keith Campbell. The interim report of the committee was published in August 1980. The final report is to be published in mid-1981. The final report will contain recommendations for reform that are expected to be far-reaching and will affect almost every aspect of the Australian financial system. The role and operating methods of all financial institutions and intermediaries has been examined by the committee as have the workings of the money market, capital market and foreign exchange markets. The methods and implementation of monetary policy and the roles of the treasury and central bank are equally under review.

Australia already has, by comparison with many foreign markets, a sophisticated financial system. The object of the Campbell Committee is to recommend methods by which it can become yet more efficient and subject to fewer government controls and intervention. In the capital market, for example, all public sector loan issues must first be approved and are regulated by the Loan Council—a quasi-governmental body that includes each of the state premiers. The government bond market is one area in which innovations have already been made. Since 1980 new methods of issuing short-term treasury notes and longer-term commonwealth government bonds were introduced. Treasury notes are now issued on a weekly tender basis whereas previously they had been issued on a continuous tap basis. Government bonds are now issued on a tap basis instead of the previous periodic offering basis. The secondary markets in both types of securities have been consequently improved while greater stability, flexibility and efficiency has been introduced into both the money and the capital markets.

The Australian capital market is an interesting and exciting one for foreign investors. During 1980 about 15 per cent of the stock market turnover was represented by foreign investors. As a resource rich country, Australia is one of the world's major producers of many important minerals, as well as energy such as coal, uranium and natural gas. Approximately one-third of publicly quoted companies are mining companies and their share prices experience very high growth during upswings in commodity cycles. 1980 has been a boom period for Australian stock markets, with the share price index for major sectors of the market having

438

risen by well over 50 per cent during the year. The oil and gas sector increased by almost 100 per cent.

Share options markets are a popular method among local investors seeking a more highly geared investment to some growth stocks in the equity market. Other markets have been established recently in Australia. In particular, a futures market

Table 21.1 Summary of instruments

Instrument	Characteristics
MONEY MARKET	
Deposits	
Call deposits	Active interbank market
Time deposits	Maximum interest rates and minimum terms for deposits of less than $A 50 000. Larger amounts unregulated
Buy-backs	Method of lending money through exchange of securities
Certificates of deposit	Terms of 1 month to 4 years. Fairly good secondary market
Convertible deposit certificates	Same as CDs but in registered form. Can be converted to bearer
Treasury notes	13- and 26-week discount paper issued by government. Good market
Commercial bills	Bank bills with three signatures guaranteed by banks, or trade bills with two signatures only. Reasonable secondary market
Commercial paper	Corporate promissory notes with one name only. Reasonable secondary market
Finance company notes	Promissory discount notes issued by finance companies
CAPITAL MARKET	
Commonwealth government bonds	Short, medium and long maturities. Very good primary and secondary market
Australian government savings bonds	Designed for small investor. Maximum holding $A 150 000
Semigovernment bonds	Issued by state governments and public corporations. Less liquid market than government bond market
Eurobonds	Small market. Illiquid secondary market
Debentures	Bonds issued by companies. Reasonable secondary market
Unsecured notes	Promissory debt instruments which do not have charge over issuing company's assets
Convertible notes	Unsecured notes which may be converted to shares of the issuing company at given terms
Equities	Very active market. Preference and ordinary shares issued
Mutual funds and unit trusts	Growing number. Not quoted on stock exchange
Share options	Both put and call share options. Traded on stock exchange
Gold futures	New market established in Sydney in 1978
Commodity and financial futures	Sydney futures exchange provides a futures market for certain commodities, currencies and financial instruments

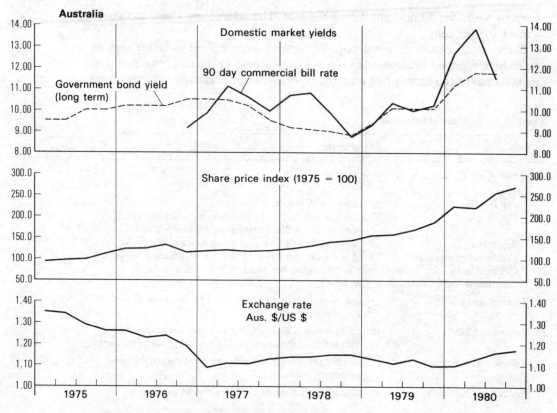

Australia

Domestic market yields

Government bond yield (long term)

90 day commercial bill rate

Share price index (1975 = 100)

Exchange rate Aus. $/US $

1975   1976   1977   1978   1979   1980

opened in Sydney in 1978 through which futures contracts in a few specific commodities, gold, currencies, and financial instruments can be traded.

The authorities are keen to encourage foreign investors, although they have certain apprehensions about their effect on the stability of domestic markets and on the exchange rate. The Campbell Committee is expected to make specific recommendations with respect to inward foreign investments which is likely to make access easier. As it is, the last of the inward exchange controls, which prohibited non-residents from investment in securities or bank deposits with less than six months to maturity, were abolished in 1978. Withholding tax on interest is 10 per cent and is not reduced by double taxation treaties. There is some lobbying from financial intermediaries in favour of abolishing this tax altogether in order to encourage foreign investors, particularly in the market for public sector instruments. The withholding tax on dividends is 30 per cent. This is reduced to 15 per cent by double taxation treaties but Australia has agreed treaties with only a relatively few countries.

The money market

Official market The money market is divided into two categories, the official market and the unofficial market. The official market which was established in 1959 is the market in short-term government securities, reserve bank credit, and cash secured by government securities. This market is maintained by nine officially backed money market dealers (authorized dealers) with the right to borrow substantial sums from the reserve bank through lender of last resort facilities. Total turnover in the official markets amounts to approximately $A 1.5 billion per month.

The unofficial market is the market in intercompany loans. It is known as an unofficial market because such loans are arranged and traded outside the market maintained by the nine authorized dealers. More importantly, the market in intercompany loans is not documented within bank credit figures and is thus outside the control of the authorities.

Unofficial market

The intercompany loan market exists because there is a wide spread between bank deposit and bank lending rates, particularly for overdrafts. Companies have developed a system of direct loans and borrowings between each other, (through the use of a financial intermediary such as a merchant bank), in short-term funds at rates of interest that are favourable to both parties. The market is known to be large but its actual size cannot be measured because the loans are from company to company and so do not show up in the credit figures of financial institutions. The authorities have attempted to discourage the market in intercompany loans mainly by introducing and fostering alternative markets in CDs, trade bills and commercial paper and by improvements in the existing markets. Expansion of the official market has proved successful in reducing the significance of the intercompany market.

Deposits

Call deposits

The call deposit market for short-term funds is mainly an interbank market made between the money market dealers, who have access to Reserve Bank discount facilities, and the banking system. Non-bank entities may also participate and are active lenders, and sometimes borrowers, of short-term funds. Most turnover however derives from transactions between the banks and authorized dealers. Deposits may be placed, usually in minimum amounts of $A 50 000 on overnight call or at seven days' notice, with either a commercial bank, building society, finance company, or through a money market dealer. If placed with one of the nine authorized dealers the depositor receives a certificate to the effect that the deposit is backed by a specific quantity of government securities. Call money placed with banks and building societies by contrast is not normally secured against specific securities.

Interest rates obtainable on call loans are influenced by the Reserve Bank discount rate, but the extent to which they are above or below the discount rate depends on liquidity in the banking system. Call rates are renegotiated on a daily basis. Call money placed with building societies or commercial banks may be up to 0.75 per cent higher than rates offered by money market dealers. This is because the dealers may borrow more cheaply from the discount window, to which banks and building societies do not have access.

Call deposit rates in the intercompany loan market may be 1.5 per cent or more above the rate offered by dealers, or approximately midway between call market deposit rates and overdraft lending rates.

Time deposits

For deposits of less than $A 50 000 the authorities impose a structured system of maximum interest rates that may be paid by the banking system. This is counterbalanced by a system of maximum overdraft rates that may be charged to borrowers of amounts of less than $A 50 000. These regulations are intended to aid small business and individuals. The minimum term for a deposit of less than $A 50 000 is three months. For deposits of more than $A 50 000 the banks are free to set their own interest rates, subject to a maximum rate determined by the authorities, which has been 10 per cent since July 1974.

The minimum term for deposits of $A 50 000 or more is 30 days. Other terms are available up to a maximum of four years. The principal acceptors of time deposits are the trading banks. Money market dealers accept time deposits of up to three months' term, in which case the deposit is guaranteed by government securities, but offered rates tend to be lower than those of the banks. The fringe banking system, comprising finance companies, merchant banks, building societies and some other non-bank deposit institutions, provides an important market for corporate leaders. Deposit interest rates are generally higher than the rates offered by the trading banks because of the different nature of their operations and because they are subject to less rigorous monetary controls. The building societies and savings associations, while taking call money, accept savings deposits rather than time deposits and are subject to interest rate regulations.

The buy-back market

This market developed during the 1950s at which time the Australian money market was inadequate to facilitate the efficient movement of short-term funds within the banking system. The nine money market dealers thus used the method of buy-back transactions. Buy-backs are equivalent to repurchase agreements in the US market. A borrower of funds, for example a money market dealer, borrows from a lender of funds, for example a bank or a company, by selling securities to the other party with a written agreement to buy back the securities on a given date.

The securities transferred are government or other short-term eligible securities. They are sold at face value and bought back at the same price plus an additional premium which represents an interest payment that is in line with other money market rates for loans of comparable maturity. The yield on buy-backs is, however, normally slightly lower than the discount rate, since the major borrowers are the money market dealers who have alternative access to central bank borrowing at the discount rate.

Buy-backs can be negotiated for any terms but are usually arranged for periods of a few days and up to three months.

Buy-backs are usually made in sums of $A 500 000 or more. $A 100 000 would usually be the minimum size. The size and the term is normally stipulated by the borrower rather than the lender as is the case with call and time deposits.

Reverse buy-backs are made when the lender initiates the transaction and stipulates the terms and amounts. That is, the lender agrees to buy securities with an agreement to sell them back at a specific date. This normally occurs between the Reserve Banks and the dealers as a part of the authorities' open market operations order to increase liquidity in the banking system and to ease credit expansion.

Certificates of deposit

Negotiable CDs were introduced in 1969, essentially to attract the liquid funds of companies and to offer an alternative to the intercompany loan market.

CDs are bearer securities issued by the trading banks, which have been free to establish their own rates of interest on the CDs they issue since 1973, prior to which a maximum rate was imposed by the government. CDs are thus frequently issued with yields higher than the maximum rate for fixed time deposits. They thus provide an attractive alternative to fixed time deposits and are additionally attractive because they are marketable. The issuing bank is prohibited by the Reserve Bank from repurchasing its own CDs in the secondary market, but can only repay at maturity. Nevertheless a good secondary market is made between the banks (who are permitted to purchase CDs issued by other banks) and the money market dealers who are also active participants. CD liquidity is not always good, however, depending on prevailing conditions in the money market.

CDs are issued in minimum denominations of $A 50 000 and above in multiples of $A 10 000. The maturity of CDs is stipulated by the issuer and may be a minimum of three months up to a maximum of four years.

Convertible deposit certificates

Convertible deposit certificates are issued on similar terms to negotiable CDs but are registered in the name of the depositor rather than in bearer form. At the option of the investor, they may be converted into a bearer negotiable CD or transferred in registered form to another named party.

Treasury notes

Treasury notes are short-term paper issued at a discount by the reserve bank on behalf of the government. They are a major money market instrument: the amount of the issues are determined by the monetary authorities based on the government short-term funding requirements. In normal weeks, the volume of notes issued varies between $A 50 million and $A 250 million. The method of issue has recently changed. Prior to December 1979, treasury notes were issued on a continuous daily tap basis. As a result the volume of notes on issue was subject to wide fluctuation and the notes were often unrealistically priced in relation to other money market securities. The market could only therefore be supported by captive investors—

443

mainly trading and savings banks, authorized dealers and certain government bodies. The secondary market was not particularly active and it provided little scope for the Reserve Bank to operate an effective monetary policy through this market. Notes had fixed maturities of either 13 or 26 weeks.

The primary market now operates very much like the British market in treasury bills. Since December 1979, treasury notes have been issued on the basis of tender applications, through auctions made weekly every Thursday. Two terms are issued at the weekly auctions—13- and 26-week notes. The discount rate of interest attaching to the issue is the adjusted average of the tender rates received. Previously, subscribers had to accept the predetermined rate of discount set by the Reserve Bank. The Reserve Bank makes its allotment of notes in ascending order of yield on the tenders submitted. It distributes notes pro rata at the highest yield necessary to complete the full amount of notes to be issued. The yields on treasury notes tend to be a few basis points lower than the Reserve Bank discount rate at which money market dealers may rediscount treasury notes and other short-term securities.

Treasury notes may be applied for directly by any investors provided they first register themselves with the Reserve Bank. The nine authorized money market dealers subscribe for about 40 per cent of notes issued but there is no formal provision that the note issues be underwritten by the dealers. They have, however, agreed in an informal way to cover in their tenders to the full amount being offered for both the three- and six-month issues.

The average bids accepted (see Table 21.2) do not always reflect the sometimes large spread between the highest and the lowest tenders accepted. Since the eventual yield on the notes is not now known in advance, subscribers may often submit a number of tenders at a series of stepped-up bids. The amount of notes offered and issued, the average and range of accepted bids and the percentage of bids allotted at the highest yield are announced later on the tender day. Successful applicants are not obliged to settle and take delivery of the notes on the same day but may settle any day from the current Thursday through to the next Wednesday, at the purchaser's option. Further, the purchaser does not have to specify in advance on which day he will take delivery.

As under the former system, treasury notes may be subscribed for in minimum amounts of $A 100 000 or above in multiples of $A 1000. They are normally issued in registered form although they may be in bearer form at the option of the investor. Interest, on a discount basis, is calculated according to a 365-day year. The notes are repaid at par at maturity. Treasury notes have a special feature which distinguishes them from other money market instruments, in that they can always be surrendered for cash at the Reserve Bank's rediscounting window. They are thus a highly liquid instrument but the rate of rediscount offered by the reserve bank is set below other money market rates and so reflects this fact.

The introduction of the tender system for treasury note issues has greatly enhanced the secondary market, which is largely maintained by the official dealers, but also participated in by the banks, financial institutions, corporations and individuals. Turnover has shown a marked increase during 1980. Under the old system yields were set by the authorities and changes in the rate were made sometimes in

444

Table 21.2 Yields on treasury notes issued under the tender system

Date	Amount offered and allotted ($A million)	13-week notes		Amount offered and allotted ($A million)	26-week notes	
		Yields accepted, %	Average accepted yield, %		Yields accepted, %	Average accepted yield, %
19 Dec. 1979	100	9.06–9.30	9.288			
21 Dec. 1979	300	9.20–9.37	9.311	50	9.80	9.800
2 Jan. 1980	350	9.18–9.29	9.242	100	9.55–9.84	9.800
9 Jan. 1980	350	9.02–9.09	9.059	50	9.60–9.73	9.656
16 Jan. 1980	250	8.98–9.24	9.179	100	9.63–9.75	9.693
23 Jan. 1980	50	9.20–9.35	9.268	50	9.70–9.77	9.738
30 Jan. 1980	300	9.23–9.38	9.329	50	9.71–9.76	9.731
6 Feb. 1980	50	9.15	9.150	50	9.67–9.68	9.678
13 Feb. 1980	150	9.15–9.27	9.240	100*	9.71–9.89	9.781
20 Feb. 1980	70	9.24–9.28	9.269	30	9.74–9.89	9.799
27 Feb. 1980	200	9.19–9.30	9.249	50	9.79–10.20	9.882
5 Mar. 1980	90†	9.27–9.80	9.455	30‡	9.90–10.50	10.268
12 Mar. 1980	50	9.48–9.58	9.520	25	10.40–10.60	10.489
19 Mar. 1980	30	9.50–10.00	9.938	20	10.50–10.88	10.711
26 Mar. 1980	30	10.30–10.64	10.438	20	10.95–11.48	11.193
9 Apr. 1980	30	10.75–10.85	10.767	20	11.55–12.05	11.825
23 Apr. 1980	30	10.75–11.00	10.937	30	11.45–11.50	11.474
30 Apr. 1980	20	10.64–10.70	10.670	20	10.94–11.04	11.015
7 May 1980	20	11.05–11.18	11.115	20	10.97	10.970
14 May 1980	40	10.90–11.00	10.950	80	10.48–10.87	10.751
21 May 1980	30	10.99–11.10	11.093	50	10.65–11.10	10.817
28 May 1980	40	10.90–11.00	10.919	60	10.95–11.18	11.045
4 Jun. 1980	20	10.75–11.05	10.953	20	10.60–10.84	10.720
11 Jun. 1980	20	10.70–10.89	10.833	50	10.60–10.89	10.751
18 Jun. 1980	40	10.90–10.97	10.926	40	10.57–10.69	10.635
25 Jun. 1980	20	10.84	10.840	20	10.55	10.550
2 Jul. 1980	60	10.69–10.84	10.787	40	10.59–10.80	10.753
9 Jul. 1980	90	10.50–10.78	10.735	60	10.50–10.74	10.686

* The amount allotted was $A 50.0 million.
† The amount allotted was $A 51.2 million.
‡ The amount allotted was $A 25.0 million.

intervals of several months. There was thus little need to trade in the secondary market because everyone could obtain the same yield by direct subscription. Since the introduction of the new system, yields are determined by market forces and this provides the investor with the potential of making a profit (or loss) in the secondary market. This fact has not only resulted in traditional investors making greater use of the secondary market but has also been gradually encouraging a wider range of investors into the market.

The success of the secondary market also provides for a more effective and efficient primary market, increasing demand for new issues and enabling the authorities to influence the money market through the amount of treasury notes sold.

Under the old system, it was possible for the authorities to influence the volume of sales through adjustments in the yield but the method was far less flexible or precise. The price of the notes under the old system was not necessarily in line with the rest of the market whereas the new system allows that the price is set by the market. This greater price flexibility assists the authorities in their open market operations for the purpose of smoothing out short-term and seasonal fluctuations in liquidity in the short-term money market.

Commercial bills

Like CDs, commercial bills are another money market instrument that were introduced in the 1960s in order to provide companies with an alternative to the intercompany loan market. Commercial bills are short-term notes which document an actual trade transaction, usually the import or export of goods. That is, they are bills of exchange secured against specific assets. Two trading parties are involved in such transactions but it is the seller, or exporter of goods, who must wait to be paid. He may, for example, negotiate to sell a shipment of wool to an importer in Japan. He will not be paid, however, until the shipment has been delivered at the earliest, which may be several months. He may therefore issue, using a bank or money market intermediary, short-term paper at a discount, to be repaid at par when the trade transaction is completed and he himself has been paid by the importer. He would only issue such paper, of course, if he needed the money to fund his working capital, and as an alternative to borrowing from his overdraft facility. The discount on commercial bills (which represents the interest charge to the issuer) is normally lower than the cost of an overdraft by up to as much as 2.5 per cent, provided that the amount involved is more than $A 50 000, below which lower overdraft rates apply.

Bank bills   Bank bills carry three names, or guarantors—those of the two parties involved in the transaction, the seller and the buyer, and the third the name of the bank that has accepted or endorsed the bill. Thus, in the unlikely event of default by both of the trading parties, the accepting bank stands ready to honour the repayment of principal to the holder of the bill at maturity.

Bank bills are issued with either 90- or 180-day maturity. A secondary market exists, maintained mainly between the banks and money market dealers.

The dealers are able to rediscount them with the Reserve Bank, or use them in buy-back transactions. The Sydney futures exchange also provide a futures market in 90-day bank-accepted bills of exchange.

Trade bills   Trade bills carry only two names, those of the two parties involved in the trade transaction. They do not carry the name or guarantee of a bank. Though as yet there has been no default, trade bills are considered less secure than bank bills and thus carry a higher yield, perhaps 0.75 per cent more than bank bills or prime trade bills. Prime trade bills are those that carry names of the highly rated, most credit-worthy companies.

446

Off-prime trade bills, carrying lesser names, command yet higher yields. Thus the interest cost to such issuing companies may often be higher than the overdraft costs. Companies will tend, therefore, to make use of this facility either when they are close to their overdraft limits or when they wish to set aside their own overdraft facility as a contingency reserve.

Like bank bills, trade bills are issued with maturities of 90 or 180 days. A secondary market exists in trade bills but it is not quite so liquid as the market for bank bills, primarily because they cannot be rediscounted by the money market dealers with the Reserve Bank. Commercial bills tend to be traded within the state in which they were issued since a stamp duty is payable on interstate secondary market transactions.

Commercial paper (promissory notes)

Commercial paper (also known as promissory notes) is, as both names suggest, a short-term promissory debt instrument issued at a discount by companies. Each issue carries but one name, that of the issuing company as guarantor, and is unsecured against specific assets. They carry only the promise of the issuer to repay principal and interest at maturity. As a money market instrument, they are thus similar to CDs but issued by companies instead of by banks.

Commercial paper was also introduced to the money market as an alternative source of finance, for companies, to the intercompany loan market. The amount of such paper issued is still relatively small. Development of the market may have been hampered by statutory restrictions which limit investment in 'one name' paper by certain groups.

Issue activity is higher when money market interest rates are low or falling, because borrowing is cheaper than using bank overdraft facilities, but only a few issues are made when rates are high or rising. Commercial paper is issued as discount notes with either 90 or 180 days' maturity. Being backed by the least security they yield the highest return of all money market instruments. Prime name notes, issued by the most creditworthy companies, may yield up to two per cent more than treasury notes and one per cent more than CDs.

A fairly good secondary market is maintained mainly by the commercial banks, though money market dealers are also major participants.

Finance company notes

Finance company notes are similar to CDs or commercial paper in that they are one name promissory notes, but issued by finance companies rather than by banks or industrial companies. Finance companies borrow short and lend long. They therefore have a continuous requirement for short-term funds. When they have insufficient deposits to finance their lending programmes they issue short-term promissory paper.

The notes are discount bearing and normally issued with a maturity of three months. They carry a lower risk than commercial paper and are of comparable security to CDs but, unlike CDs, they may be rediscounted at the reserve bank, by

447

Table 21.3 Yield differentials between 91-day treasury notes and other money market instruments

Instrument	Range of yield differential, %
3-month buy-backs	+0.25 to +0.45
Finance Company notes	+0.35 to +0.65
90-day bank bills	+0.85 to +1.50
90-day prime trade bills	+1.45 to +1.75
90-day prime commercial paper	+2.25 to +2.75

Table 21.4 Differential between overdraft and other short-term borrowing costs for companies

Instrument	Interest cost. Range of differential relative to overdraft rate,* %
Intercompany market	−2.25 to −2.75
90-day bank bills	−1.25 to −1.75
90-day trade bills	−0.50 to +0.50
From finance companies	+1.00 to +2.00

* For prime name companies borrowing $A 100 000 or more.

the money market dealers. Being slightly more marketable they yield between 20 and 30 basis points less than CDs and over 200 basis points less than prime commercial paper.

The secondary market is maintained by banks and money market dealers.

The capital market

The public sector bond market is regulated as to the amount which may be issued and the interest rates attaching to issues but the private sector bond and equities markets are self-regulated. The official regulatory body is the Australian Loan Council whose members include the Prime Minister and the premiers of each state. The Loan Council determines the total amount to be borrowed by the commonwealth government and by the states, the allocation between the government and the states and the rates and conditions of such borrowings. Borrowings by local and semigovernmental bodies are also reviewed and decided by the Loan Council. The Council also lays down rules and procedures under which borrowings on the domestic or overseas markets are made by authorities which are constituted under commonwealth or state legislation.

Commonwealth government bonds

Bonds are issued by the commonwealth government in order to assist its financing programmes and they are a major source of funds for this purpose. Fixed rate coupons are attached to the loans, the rate of interest being dependent on the term of the loan and on currently prevailing market levels of interest rates. Interest is paid semiannually and calculated on the basis of a 365-day year.

The previous system of issue was by raising periodic cash loans, usually one to three loan issues per year, incorporating short (2- to 3-year), medium (7- to 10-year) and long (up to 35-year) term investments.

At the same time that the loan council, which supervises the public sector bond issues, agreed to a change in the method of issuing treasury notes, it agreed to replace the previous system of periodic cash loans with a tap issue system, under which new commonwealth government securities would be available continuously.

Under the former system, once a cash loan issue was closed, which was usually within one week, the treasury would accept advance subscriptions for the next loan, and interest would accrue to the subscriber from the date that the funds were received by the treasury. Under the new system, bonds are available to subscribers every day up to a maximum amount per annum as decided by the government in its annual budget. The daily availability of commonwealth bonds, like the former system, incorporates short-, medium- and long-term securities.

The old system of periodic issues was inefficient for several reasons. Firstly, the yields at which the issues were made had an 'announcement effect' on the market, indicating the monetary authorities' desired direction of change in market trends and sometimes having a disturbing effect on the market.

Secondly, the dealers' requirements for securities did not always coincide with the issue periods although in practice the authorized dealers could obtain securities from the Reserve Bank at market prices at any time during the life of a loan issue. These would be sold out of the Reserve Bank's own portfolio.

Under the new top issue system, introduced in April 1980, new issues or open market operations in existing issues do not upset the market or result in market speculation as to the Reserve Bank's future operations in the market. Instead, the bank's intervention in the market can influence liquidity and interest rates more smoothly and efficiently without introducing an announcement effect. So as not to compete with the tap issues, the reserve bank no longer sells from its own portfolio securities which are close in maturity to other tap issues on offer.

The system of tap issues thus avoids the market instability which had sometimes been created by periodic loan issues and, while tap issues more easily satisfy the demands of investors, they also provide the authorities with greater control over the quantity of issues and the maturity spread.

The range of maturities of tap issues made since April 1980 until July 1980 (see Table 21.5) is 2 to 10 years. This is a small range due to the prevailing high level of interest rates. The yield range of unexpired taps as at July 1980 was 11.57 to 11.80 per cent, which constituted the official yield curve.

Commonwealth bonds are issued through the reserve bank of each state. Subscribers to the new loans are issued with bearer bonds, denominated in units of $A 20, $A 100, $A 1000 and $A 2000. Applications for new issues must be made in minimum subscriptions of $A 5000 or above in multiples of $A 1000. These bonds may, at the option of the investor, be taken in the form of registered stock, and be inscribed with the name of the stockholder on the ledgers kept by

449

Table 21.5 Commonwealth tap stocks issued between April and July 1980

Tap No.	Coupon % per annum	Maturity	Date opened (withdrawn)	Initial yield, % per annum	Closing yield, % per annum	Sub-scriptions, $A million	Indicative amount, $A million
1	11.5	April 1982	30 Apr. 1980 (27 Jun. 1980)	11.50	11.50	512.2	500
2	11.7	April 1985	30 Apr. 1980 (9 May 1980)	11.84	11.83	262.9	250
3	11.7	May 1986	2 Jun. 1980	11.79	....	142.5 (as at 8 July)	400
4	11.5	Nov. 1982	7 Jul. 1980	11.57	....	....	500
5	11.7	June 1990	7 Jul. 1980	11.80	....	....	250

the Commonwealth Government Inscribed Stock Registry held at the Reserve Bank. It is in registered form that treasury bonds are most usually traded in the secondary market. The secondary market is very active. Commonwealth loan stocks provide the maximum security and they have the status of trustees securities throughout Australia and the British Commonwealth. Thus, the banking sector and life assurance institutions (which have tax incentives for holding government stock) hold

Table 21.6 Commonwealth government securities on issue in Australia classified by holder as at 30th June

Holder	1969 $A mill.	%	1970 $A mill.	%	1971 $A mill.	%	1972 $A mill.	%	1973 $A mill.	%
Reserve bank	846	8	1190	10	910	8	501	4	611	5
Savings banks	2285	21	2229	19	2337	20	2397	19	2787	20
Trading and other banks	1379	13	1280	11	1412	12	1756	14	2304	17
Money market dealers	524	5	597	5	694	6	983	8	731	5
Life assurance offices	1150	11	1195	10	1325	11	1479	12	1632	12
Pension and provident funds	387	3	426	4	487	4	545	4	618	5
Insurance companies	263	2	277	2	274	2	277	2	318	2
Major common- wealth trust funds	2008	19	2518	22	2605	22	2545	20	2527	19
Public authorities	349	3	317	3	286	2	261	2	257	2
Others	1624	15	1596	14	1616	14	1848	15	1694	13
Total	10815	100	11625	100	11946	100	12592	100	13479	100

and trade more than half of the issued commonwealth stock which amounted to over $A 3 billion at the first quarter of 1980, while the local authorities, indirectly, account for a further 20 per cent or more. These securities are also held in company portfolios and used by authorized dealers, banks, brokers and companies in buy-back transactions.

Due to good relative yields (see Table 21.7), a large number of individuals also participate in the secondary market. In total there are an estimated 155000 holders of commonwealth government stock. There are about 100 separate series of treasury bonds outstanding, which are listed on the stock exchanges. Small transactions take place on the stock exchanges but the large turnover takes place in the market made by money market dealers and sharebrokers known as the *off 'change market*. Transactions in this market are often made in quantities of $A 250000 or more. The money market dealers are most active traders of treasury bonds which are within five years of maturity. They hold sizeable portfolios in these bonds and make frequent use of them in buy-back transactions.

Large quantities of short government bonds are also held by trading and savings banks. Through its open market operations the Reserve Bank often acquires a considerable quantity of maturing securities and has, on occasion, held about 80 per cent of all commonwealth government bonds that are near to redemption.

(*source: Government securities on issue*)

1974		1975		1976		1977		1978		(Est) 1979	
$A mill.	%	$A mill.	%	$A mill.	%	$A mill.	%	$A mill.	%	$A mill.	%
1143	10	1276	8	2739	14	4239	20	4392	19	5197	20
2943	21	2924	18	2845	15	2704	13	2671	12	3091	12
2227	16	3651	22	3802	20	3692	17	3711	15	4178	16
350	3	733	4	800	4	911	4	1200	5	1300	5
1786	13	1862	11	2054	11	2226	11	2447	11	2606	10
653	5	744	5	1034	6	1076	5	1294	5	1250	5
342	2	348	2	431	2	507	2	527	2	530	2
2497	16	2985	18	2398	13	2445	11	2966	13	3009	12
256	2	230	1	241	1	279	1	266	1	305	1
1777	12	1834	11	2669	14	3341	16	3813	17	4365	17
14274	100	16587	100	19013	100	21420	100	23287	100	25831	100

Table 21.7 Average annual treasury bond and note yields

Financial year July–June	91-day treasury notes yield, %	10-year treasury bonds yield, %
1970–71	4.75	5.75
1971–72	5.50	6.80
1972–73	5.25	5.90
1973–74	4.00	5.75
1974–75	7.25	8.00
1975–76	8.50	9.50
1976–77	7.00	9.90
1977–78	8.00	10.00
1978–79	8.20	9.20
1979–80 (to March)	9.25	10.00

Commonwealth government savings bonds

Savings bonds were introduced in 1976 to replace special bonds which had been issued since 1958. Savings bonds, like special bonds, are also issued by the commonwealth government but are designed principally to attract the small investors. They are issued two to three times a year with maturities of around seven years. Two special features are firstly that a maximum of $A 150 000 may be held by any one person (or company) and secondly that they may be redeemed by the holder at any time before maturity, subject to one month's notice. A lower rate of interest

Table 21.8 Changes in the amount of commonwealth government securities on issue ($A million)

Year to 30 June	Inscribed stock and bonds	Special bonds	Australian savings bonds	Total (net)*
1970	+4	+36	....	+41
1971	−137	+1	....	−136
1972	+18	+14	....	+32
1973	+67	+10	....	+78
1974	+453	−13	....	+440
1975	−73	−3	....	−77
1976	+1334	−50	+1178	+2462
1977	+547	−51	+459	+956
1978	+455	−35	+32	+452
1979	+796	−73	+367	+1090
1980 (Est)	−180*	−40*	+220*	Nil*

452   * Estimated figures.

applies if they are redeemed prior to the first interest payment date which is up to around nine months after the day of issue. Savings bonds are available either as bearer securities or as inscribed stock at the option of the investor.

Table 21.8 shows that there was a significant increase in government securities in 1976 which was due largely to the introduction of savings bonds. Holders of savings bonds fall into two categories, private individuals who hold the bonds because yields are higher than interest from savings banks or building societies, and professional investors who also are attracted by their relatively high yields and who purchase the maximum of $A 150 000.

Semigovernment bonds

Semigovernment authorities are the state and local authorities and the publicly owned state utility companies. These bodies issue their own securities which are short-, medium- and long-term bonds in the same form as commonwealth government bonds. They have specific redemption dates and may not be redeemed prior to those dates. The semigovernment authorities are required to submit their borrowing programmes to the Australian loan council for each financial year (April–March). The council determines the amounts which may be borrowed through loan issues to the public, and maximum coupon rates are set at a small margin (about 40–50 basis points) above the interest rates on commonwealth government bonds of comparable maturity.

So that an orderly market is maintained, no local authority or state loan can be made during a period seven days before, or concurrently with, a government bond issue. Nor may a state authority make an issue at the same time as another authority from the same state.

Interest is paid semiannually and calculated according to a 365-day year. Semigovernment bonds rank next in security to commonwealth government loans and are approved as trustee securities in certain states; often their interest and capital repayments are backed by the guarantee of the government of the state of issue. Interest and principal of semigovernment loan issues are fully guaranteed by the commonwealth government but loans of the local authorities are secured against the borrower's own revenues (e.g., municipal rates). Nevertheless, although higher yielding than commonwealth government securities, for reasons mentioned above, they enjoy a less active secondary market. For most issues the market is rather illiquid and narrow. The main investors are the same as for commonwealth government bonds (i.e., savings banks, life offices and superannuation funds). The market is made both on the local stock exchanges and off 'change between banks and brokers. Only the larger and better known authorities have their securities listed on a stock exchange outside their own state. Most transactions are, however, made in the off 'change market. Because there is a steady supply of new issues coming to the market, sellers in the secondary market usually have to offer a discount so that yields obtained by purchasing an existing security are marginally higher than those on new issues.

While new issues are normally in bearer form in denominations of between $A 20 and $A 2000, like commonwealth bonds they are normally converted into registered stock for secondary market trading. Transactions may be made in sizes up to $A 200 000.

Foreign bonds

No bonds of foreign institutions have been issued in the Australian market.

Eurobonds

The first Eurobonds denominated in Australian dollars were issued in 1976, since when a small market has developed but there are only some half dozen issues outstanding.

Eurobonds are issued by the federal government, public utilities, Australian state owned corporations and by foreign based companies holding interests in Australian companies which need to raise Australian dollars to finance Australian investment.

The guidelines of the Loan Council stipulate that the government and the authority concerned should do their best to obtain necessary funds in the Australian market. If, in exceptional cases, this is not possible on satisfactory terms, then the Loan Council grants approval for the funds to be obtained from overseas markets.

Issue sizes of Euro-Australian bonds are between $A 10 million and $A 15 million. Issues outstanding amount to about $A 70 million. Maturity terms range between five and seven years and principal is repaid in full at maturity. The bonds are bearer and carry fixed-rate coupons. Interest is paid annually, free of withholding tax.

Australian dollar Eurobonds are option bonds since they offer the investor the option to receive interest and redeem principal in US dollars converted at the spot exchange rate at the time of payment. Australian dollar Eurobonds are listed on the stock exchanges of London or Luxembourg but are mostly traded over the counter through Euromarket dealers. Secondary market activity is poor, partly because of the limited number of issues and partly because of Australian exchange controls which restrict dealers from financing their books in Australian dollars.

The Australian Reserve Bank maintains strict supervision over new issues and prohibits Australian residents from purchasing bonds denominated in external Australian dollars. The maximum transaction size that the market is normally able to handle is $A 50 000 and dealing spreads—the difference between a dealer's bid and offer prices—are commonly around two per cent.

Corporate bonds

Companies issue bonds, known as debentures, and other debt securities defined as unsecured notes and convertible notes. Much capital required by corporations is generated internally or borrowed from banks. When larger amounts of capital are required, equity issues are favoured though, not surprisingly, during periods of buoyant share prices. Over a long period, however, there has been a trend towards greater use of debt finance among Australian companies. Depending on the type of

454

company, the gearing or leverage ratio—that is the ratio of debt to equity capital—of Australian companies is now 25 to 45 per cent. Companies tend to maintain their preferred ratios: if too high, then new required capital is raised through equity issues; if too low, they are raised through debenture or note issues or bank borrowing. If the level of interest rates is high, convertible notes may be issued as a form of deferred equity issue.

One reason that debt issues have become a popular method of raising corporate finance is that interest payable is deductible for corporate tax purposes. Debentures are bonds that may be secured against either specific or general assets of the issuing company, and the interests of the debenture holders are represented by a trustee company or by a negative pledge (which specifies that no subsequent lender to the company may be granted a claim on the company's assets in preference to the debenture holder). *Debentures*

The debentures entitle the holder to a fixed rate of interest, paid semiannually and calculated on the basis of 365-day year, which must be paid irrespective of whether the company is making a profit.

Debentures are registered securities and in minimum denominations of $A 100. Original maturities are normally medium to long term, that is, in excess of seven years, and may extend up to 35 years. Debentures are not normally amortized but capital is repaid in full at maturity.

The corporate bond market is unregulated by the authorities in the sense that no restrictions are placed on the amounts that may be issued or on interest rates that may be paid. The amount of individual issues may range from $A 2 million up to $A 200 million depending on the type of company.

As at 30 June 1980 the nominal value of outstanding debentures was $A 2675 million and the market value $A 2423 million. This represented about 92 and 91 per cent respectively of the total corporate debt sector, but was only 12 per cent of the total bond market, including government and public sector debt issues.

The secondary market is reasonably active for the majority of debentures issues (depending on market conditions for debt instruments) and is maintained mainly through the stock exchanges, although most of the larger transactions take place in the off 'change market.

The major participants in the market are the life assurance companies, savings banks and pension funds. The latter group spend more than 50 per cent of their assets on company securities because of their higher yields relative to government bonds. Debentures of industrial companies yield an average of 75 to 150 basis points more than government bonds of comparable maturity while finance company debentures yield 100 to 200 basis points more.

Industrial and financial companies also issue notes that are similar in form to debentures but unsecured against the company's assets. They carry an entitlement to a fixed rate of interest, payable semiannually and independent of the company's profitability. The interests of the noteholders are specified by a trust deed and protected by trustees nominated by the issuing company. Maturities may be short, medium or long but few extend to longer than 15 years. *Unsecured notes*

455

As at 30 June 1980 there were 54 unsecured notes (including convertible notes) outstanding with a nominal value of $A 203 million and a market value of $A 237 million.

Because of their unsecured nature these notes bear a higher yield than ordinary debentures. In general they enjoy a good secondary market and are purchased mainly by pension funds, insurance companies and individuals requiring high-income stocks. Trading takes place mostly through the stock exchanges.

Convertible notes Some unsecured notes issued by companies may be converted to ordinary shares of the company at a specified conversion price and on a stated date or at stated periods, or they may be held until repaid by the issuing company at maturity. Similar to unsecured notes, interest is normally fixed during the life of the loan, though some may have special provision for coupon adjustments. They are issued at par ($A 100), and repaid at par at maturity unless converted to ordinary shares of the company. Convertible note issues must conform to special requirements in order that the interest paid is tax deductible for the issuing corporation.

These requirements are:

- that conversion be at the option of the noteholder and not the issuing company;
- that the first option date must arise within two years of issue and that the last option date is the maturity date, or within 10 years from issue if the note has an original life of more than 10 years;
- that companies having less than 75 per cent of their equity held by Australian residents may be subject to examination by the Reserve Bank in order to determine that the terms of the loan are fair and reasonable;
- that the conversion price must not be less than either the par value of the share or 90 per cent of the market value of the share six weeks before the note is offered for subscription—whichever is the greater;
- that the rights and obligations of the noteholder are not dependent on whether the conversion option is exercised.

Convertible notes are a popular form of investment for insurance companies, pension funds and individuals since they offer a guaranteed fixed income for the life of the loan and also offer investors the opportunity to participate in the growth of the issuing company if they choose to convert the notes into ordinary shares of the company.

Because of their convertibility, yields are in general marginally lower than the yields of non-convertible notes, with comparable maturities. They provide a higher yield, however, than do ordinary shares. Because they are convertible, the price of the notes generally moves in sympathy with the share price of the issuing company.

The conditions attaching to convertible note issues are designed to protect the noteholder and provide the issuer with a tax deductible debt financing instrument. The conditions have been in force since 1976, before which they were considerably more stringent and stifled the development of the market. The current, more relaxed legislation, together with a recently buoyant share market, have encouraged

456

a growing primary market in convertible note issues. An active secondary market is consequently hoped to develop.

In the year to 30 June 1980 there were 31 convertible note issues outstanding (an increase from the 25 issues in the year to 30 June 1979), with a total market value of over $A 100 million. In the secondary market the notes are traded on the stock exchanges where they are listed in the share section of the market rather than in the debt section. This is because they have most of the characteristics of ordinary shares. A particularly attractive feature of some recent issues is that noteholders participate in rights and bonus issues offered to ordinary shareholders. Rights may be exercised or sold by the noteholder at the time they are issued, whilst bonus issues are passed to the noteholder if and when he exercises the conversion option.

Equities

Companies issue both preference and ordinary shares. Preference shares entitle the investor to a dividend, but one that is restricted to a fixed amount of the capital value of the shares. Preference shares rank before ordinary shares for dividend payment, but not before interest payments due to debenture holders and other trade creditors. Preference shares may be either cumulative (which means that should a company not have sufficient resources to pay the fixed dividend in any particular year the deficiency must be made up in the following years), or they may be non-cumulative in which case the deficiency is not made up. They may also be participating preference shares in which case they are entitled to a share in profits after ordinary shareholders have been paid adequate profits, or they may be convertible (at prespecified terms) to ordinary shares. The rights attaching to preference shares are specified at issue.

Ordinary shares, which comprise the major proportion of the equity market, constitute the ownership of a company. Holders of ordinary shares are entitled to a share of the company's profits and its assets after other creditors' claims, including those claims by holders of debenture notes and preference shares.

Both types of shares are registered securities with pay values of either $A 0.5 or $A 1. Most shares carry one vote each though some companies, particularly life assurance and uranium companies, with the majority approval of their shareholders, may issue shares that carry more than one vote. New issues are managed by a stockbroker or an investment bank who recommend the shares to clients and who underwrite the issue. New issues of already public companies are made in the same manner as in the UK, which differs slightly from the US practice. In Australia now, shares are first offered to existing shareholders in the form of a 'rights issue'. Shareholders are given rights to purchase new shares in given ratios to the share they already hold. Thus a 1 to 4 rights issue would give each shareholder the right to apply for one new share for every four original shares held. By contrast, in the US shareholders are given the right to apply for new shares to an amount directly proportionate to those already held, that is on a one-to-one basis.

Nearly all shares of public companies are listed on the stock exchanges. It is not

457

mandatory that they be listed but if companies do seek a listing they must comply with requirements drawn up by the associated stock exchanges of Australia, and which apply uniformly to all exchanges.

The total market size in terms of market capitalization ($A 45 361 as at 30 June 1980) ranks seventh in the world. The market value of shares traded on the joint stock exchanges was $A 3600 million in the six months to 30 June 1980—an average of about $A 30 million per day.

Foreign investors represented about 15 per cent of this turnover. Practically all share transactions take place on the floor of the stock exchanges, though occasionally large deals may be made through the off 'change market. The major holders of equity shares are institutional investors, foreign investors and individuals.

Particular interest from foreign investors comes from Japan, the USA and Europe—mainly from the UK, France, Germany, Holland and Italy.

Although non-residents are restricted in investments in broadcasting and television, the major sectors are mining and energy, which are unrestrictive for foreign portfolio investors.

In a wide range of natural resources, Australia is one of the richest countries in the world. The mining industry has played an important role for over a century in the development of the economy. Australia has the world's largest reserves, in economic grades, of rutile (titanium dioxide); zircon (zirconium silicate) and bauxite (aluminium oxide). It has the world's second largest reserves of uranium and lead, and the world's third largest reserves of silver, zinc and iron ore. Additionally there are substantial reserves of other minerals, including, nickel, gold, coal and tin. Australia is also 70 per cent self-sufficient in petroleum but, unless new fields are found within a few years, far more will have to be imported. The mining industry is one of the most productive and efficient sectors of the economy. Although employing only about two per cent of the labour force, its contribution to exports has risen to 30 per cent from seven per cent 10 years ago. Although not expected to grow as rapidly in the next decade as in the last 10 years, growth of primary resource exports, especially coal, natural gas, aluminium and uranium is expected to be substantial.

There are approximately 850 industrial companies and 370 mining and oil companies listed on the associated stock exchanges.

On the Melbourne stock exchange, for example, 28 per cent of turnover by value was represented by shares of mining companies, 11 per cent by oil shares and 38 per cent by industrial shares. The remainder was fixed-interest securities. The biggest growth sectors during the decade 1970 to 1980 were oil and gas which averaged an annual share price growth of 17.55 per cent, developers and building contractors which averaged an annual growth of 12.82 per cent, and transport shares which averaged 12.19 per cent. These three sectors all out-performed the consumer price index which averaged an annual growth of 10.24 per cent over the same period.

Of the 20 largest companies by market capitalization, more than three-quarters are primary resources companies. The 20 most active resources companies had a turnover of $A 1014 million on the Melbourne stock exchange in the year to June 1980, compared to a turnover of $A 981 million for the 20 most active industrial shares. (NB. For traditional reasons two major resource companies, Broken Hill Propriety

Table 21.9 Australian stock exchange share price index (*source: The Stock Exchange of Melbourne Ltd and The Australian Stock Exchange Journal*)

Number of companies	Percentage of all ordinaries by market value	Aggregate market value as at 30 June 1980, $A million	Group name	Share price index (base = 500 at 1 Jan. 1980)		Accumulation index (base = 1000 at 1 Jan. 1980)	
				Index at 31 Oct. 1980	Percentage change since 1 Jan. 1980	Index at 31 Oct. 1980	Percentage change since 1 Jan. 1980
29	24.6	8 688	Metals	788.9	+ 57.8	1 641.8	+ 64.2
14	7.4	2 617	Solid fuels	942.6	+ 88.5	1 905.7	+ 90.6
17	8.8	3 093	Oil and gas	990.9	+ 98.2	1 988.1	+ 98.8
10	1.5	520	Developers and contractors	691.2	+ 38.2	1 443.2	+ 44.3
23	5.8	2 031	Building materials	687.9	+ 37.6	1 441.3	+ 44.1
7	0.8	272	Electrical, household durables	562.1	+ 12.4	1 191.7	+ 19.2
9	2.4	859	Alcohol and tobacco	522.2	+ 4.4	1 109.3	+ 10.9
22	2.8	987	Food, household goods	561.6	+ 12.3	1 196.2	+ 19.6
8	0.5	178	Textiles, clothing	559.6	+ 11.9	1 219.1	+ 21.9
8	0.9	336	Automative	584.7	+ 16.9	1 253.9	+ 25.4
6	2.1	738	Chemicals	656.9	+ 31.4	1 392.1	+ 39.2
11	1.4	511	Light engineering	584.2	+ 16.8	1 247.3	+ 24.7
16	2.5	876	Heavy engineering	749.0	+ 49.8	1 567.5	+ 56.8
8	1.9	664	Paper and packaging	620.0	+ 24.0	1 325.9	+ 32.6
10	6.1	2 144	Banks and finance	530.6	+ 6.1	1 109.4	+ 10.9
7	0.6	197	Insurance	527.0	+ 5.4	1 107.7	+ 10.8
10	3.1	1 087	Retail	551.1	+ 10.2	1 176.8	+ 17.7
5	1.0	359	Merchants, agents	601.1	+ 20.2	1 288.7	+ 28.9
5	1.8	644	Transport	803.0	+ 60.6	1 676.9	+ 67.7
9	1.9	662	Media	539.4	+ 7.9	1 120.4	+ 12.0
6	1.2	410	Property trusts	508.1	+ 1.6	1 099.6	+ 10.0
18	2.5	895	Other services	712.6	+ 42.5	1 491.1	+ 49.1
10	18.4	6 513	Diversified and miscellaneous				
43	32.0	11 304	All mineral and metal	815.5	+ 63.1	1 687.0	+ 68.7
60	57.6	20 326	All resources	828.5	+ 65.7	1 702.3	+ 70.2
198	42.4	14 949	All industrials	617.4	+ 23.5	1 302.6	+ 30.3
268	100.0	35 275	All ordinaries	731.7	+ 46.3	1 520.7	+ 52.1
50	68.5	24 167	50 leaders	749.5	+ 49.9	1 554.5	+ 55.5

Ltd and CSR Ltd, are included in the list of top industrial companies and not of top resource companies.)

The year to June 1980 was a particularly active one for Australian shares, and compares with the previous stock market boom of 1970. The total capitalization of all market stocks increased by over 30 per cent in the year 1979/80. Table 21.9 shows that the index for each category of shares increased during 1980 but the oil and gas sector showed the largest gains. In the 10 months from 1 January to 31 October 1980, the Australian stock exchange accumulation index showed an increase of 52.1 per cent for all ordinary shares. Oil and gas companies, which number 17 out of a total of 268 shares in the index, showed gains of 98.8 per cent. This was followed by companies in the solid fuels (i.e., coal) sector which showed a gain of 9.6 per cent, transport which was up by 67.7 per cent and metals which were up by 64.2 per cent. The worst performing sectors were property trusts, insurance, banking and finance, and alcohol and tobacco, which increased by 10.0, 10.8, 10.9 and 10.9 per cent, respectively.

The 50 leaders comprise the 50 companies with the largest market capitalization. This group recorded an increase of 55.5 per cent in its accumulation index. The sector includes mining companies, banks and industrials. The largest company is Broken Hill Proprietary with a market capitalization of about $A 4.5 billion. The largest bank in the group, the Bank of New South Wales, has a capitalization of about $A 400 million; the smallest company in the group has a market capitalization of about $A 200 million.

Companies balance their books and produce published full reports annually and interim reports half-yearly. The majority of companies have financial years that coincide with the tax year which runs from 1 July to 30 June. Reporting standards are detailed and uniform and accounts reliably disclose a company's financial position.

The stock exchanges

There is a stock exchange in each capital city of the six Australian states. The Melbourne and Sydney stock exchanges are the largest, together accounting for about 92 per cent of total Australian share trading volume. Plans are well developed for the establishment of a national stock exchange. This will be achieved by computer link up. Under the present system, all exchanges are members of the Australian Associated Stock Exchanges and are subject to the Securities Industry Act which regulates the major aspects of stock exchange operations. The exchanges are structured as companies limited by guarantee, and the day-to-day management of each exchange is supervised by autonomous committees elected by the members of each exchange.

A company may, if it chooses, be listed on more than one exchange. The major companies from all sectors are listed on both the Sydney and Melbourne exchanges. Listing requirements for companies are uniform across all exchanges, and are:

- that paid up capital exceeds $A 200 000;
- that the greater of $A 70 000 or 25 per cent of the capital of companies issuing up to $A 2 000 000, or $A 500 000 or 15 per cent of the capital of companies issuing over $A 2 000 000, be made available to the public.

The stock exchange also specifies requirements with respect to capital structure, reporting of results, payment of dividends and general financial conduct.

All capital market securities except unit trust and mutual funds may be traded on the floor of the stock exchanges, but there is no binding requirement to this effect.

Nearly all share transactions are made through the stock exchange as are also the majority of transactions in company debentures and unsecured notes. Government bonds, however, though listed on the exchanges are largely dealt in the off 'change market. This is the market maintained between banks and some stockbrokers. The savings banks and life assurance companies in particular hold large amounts of government bonds due to Reserve Bank regulations to the banking system and to the tax incentives for assurance companies to hold government bonds. These institutions deal in large amounts of bonds which can easily be effected through banks who themselves maintain large books for their own account.

Most smaller transactions of government bonds on behalf of individuals and small companies are, however, dealt on the stock exchange.

Since 1962 the trading post system has been the trading method used on the Australian exchange. Orders are placed through brokers, known as sharebrokers in Australia, who act as agents for their clients but do not deal for their own account. The brokers deal directly with each other at trading posts on the floor of the exchange. Each trading post is designated for the transaction of specific types of securities.

Apart from odd-lot specialists there are no specialists or jobbers on the Australian exchanges. There is no great necessity for these because most transactions may be easily completed between dealing agents. Substantial buying or selling orders in less active stocks may, however, take several days to complete.

Each of the stock exchanges publishes its own index of share prices but new indices, produced jointly by the stock exchanges of Sydney and Melbourne, were published for the first time on 2 January 1980. These indices have now replaced the former Sydney and Melbourne indices. It is envisaged that once all the exchanges are linked by computer, prices of shares quoted on other exchanges will be incorporated, thus ultimately giving rise to a national share price index. The new series of indices is known as the Australian stock exchange indices. They comprise two groups of indices, the share price indices and the accumulation indices. The share price indices are not adjusted for dividend payments and accruals. The accumulation indices notionally reinvest dividends on ex-dividend dates and thus provide a standard against which the total performance, including capital gains and income, of particular groups can be measured. Table 21.9 shows the two series of indices which each comprise 27 groups of companies and a total of 268 companies. The share price indices have a base of 500 as at 1 January 1980 while the accumulation indices have a base of 1000 as at the same date.

Stock exchange indices

Mutual funds and unit trusts

Mutual funds are funds that invest in specific types of securities and are subscribed to by investors and controlled by management companies. The investors' capital is invested in selected ordinary shares which exhibit high growth potential as well as solvency and, in the case of some funds, also in high-yielding fixed interest securities. The object of mutual funds is to produce long-term growth for their subscribers.

Unit trusts are identical except that they have an added tax advantage to the investor. The income and capital gains received by unit trusts are non-taxable and they are thus able to distribute the maximum amount of gross income to their unit holders.

Mutual funds and unit trusts have become increasingly popular in recent years, particularly among individual investors who wish to participate in the equity market but who have only small funds or who lack expertise. The units are not quoted or traded on the stock exchanges but may be purchased or sold on any business day through the controlling management company. Prices are quoted daily in the financial press and are calculated at stated regular intervals on the basis of the current market price of the investment portfolio of each fund or unit trust.

Share options

Both put and call options were introduced in Australia in 1960 and are now available and quoted on the Sydney and Melbourne stock exchanges.

A call option is the right to buy a particular share at a stated price within a specified period, which is normally one or six months. The investor has no commitment to exercise his option and if the share price does not realize that specified by the option he may allow the option to lapse.

A put option confers upon the investor the right to sell a particular share at a stated price within a defined period.

If the shares rise then he may allow his option to lapse. If they fall lower than the specified price in the option contract he may realize a profit by being able to sell above the prevailing market price. It is also possible to purchase put and call options in the same stock. These are known as straddles since the investor is hedging against both a rise or a fall in the price of a specified share but may make a small profit if the price moves significantly in either direction.

Table 21.10 Share options—monthly trading figures
(*source: Australian Stock Exchange Journal*)

Month	Number of contracts traded	Value of contracts traded $A 000's	Open positions
1981			
January	39 441	34 762	28 848
February	34 750	32 041	31 552
March	26 059	20 402	28 428
April	14 618	8 882	25 865
May	31 076	20 943	30 802
June	48 814	43 299	28 536
July	29 763	33 449	30 125
August	26 558	18 124	33 338
September	33 993	19 134	31 864
October	48 230	27 033	40 217

The market is a traded options market; that is, the options may be traded as securities in their own right. Thus the investor may choose to either exercise his option to allow it to lapse or to sell it before the final exercise date. If he chooses to sell the price of the option will be at a premium or discount to its original price, depending on whether the price of the relevant share has risen or fallen since the option was issued. The original option price at issue is usually around 10 per cent of the share price. A series of striking prices (prices at which the options may be exercised) is quoted for each of the final exercise dates, which may be up to twelve months forward.

As at October 1980, options trading had reached an all-time high in June 1980. Turnover was 48 814; contracts traded representing a value of $A 43.3 million.

Table 21.10 shows the volume and value of options traded during 1980 up to the end of October.

The largest number of options and those most actively traded are those of mining company shares.

Commodities

Although Australia is a major producer of many important commodities, particularly minerals, wool and beef, they are traded through the cash and futures commodity markets in London rather than in the local futures market. A few commodities are traded in the domestic futures exchange in Sydney (see Other futures markets below).

Gold

A market in gold futures was established in Sydney in April 1978. Since opening, the turnover had grown rapidly, encouraged largely by the high increase in the gold price in 1979/80. Futures contracts may be purchased for current month, one month forward or quarterly up to 12 months' forward delivery.

Contracts are traded in lots of 100 troy ounces of gold of 99.5 per cent fineness. Price movements are quoted in multiples of 10 US cents per troy ounce. The number of contracts traded averages about 7000 open contracts per month with a turnover of around 25000 contracts which is comparable with the level of activity in the Hong Kong gold futures market.

Other futures markets

The Sydney futures exchange, in addition to gold, provides futures markets in several commodities, currencies and financial instruments.

The commodities traded are fresh frozen boneless beef, live cattle and greasy wool.

Boneless beef is traded in contract sizes of 36000 lb and quoted in $A 0.001 per pound weight. Contracts are quoted for current month, one month forward, then two-monthly up to 14 months forward. The market is not very active.

Live cattle are traded in contract sizes of 10000 kg live weight and quoted in $A 0.001 per kilogram. Contracts may be traded for the current month, then monthly

463

up to 12 months forward. The market is fairly active with turnover in the region of 15 000 contracts per month.

Sydney greasy wool is traded in contract sizes of 15 000 kg and price quoted in multiples of $A 0.001 per kilogram. Contracts may be traded for the current month, then quarterly up to 18 months forward. This market is normally active with monthly trading of around 15 000 contracts.

Currency futures are traded in US dollars and Japanese yen. Contracts are available in sizes of US$100 000 and ¥20 million, respectively, and prices quoted in multiples of $A 0.01 per US dollar or per Japanese yen. Contracts may be traded for the current month or monthly up to 18 months forward. Some other currency contracts including the pound sterling are also available, but turnover is not normally active.

Activity in the currency futures market depends on relative interest-rate levels but is not as high as activity in live cattle or greasy wool futures. US dollar turnover is less than 1000 contracts per month while yen turnover is normally somewhat less.

Domestic interest rate futures are available in 90-day bank accepted bills of exchange in contract sizes of $A 100 000. These are available for the current month, then monthly up to 12 months forward, then quarterly up to two years forward. Unlike other futures contracts, bank bills are quoted on a yield basis (i.e., 100 minus percentage yield per annum) rather than as a price per unit size. The market is moderately active with a turnover of over 1000 contracts per month.

Dealing and fees

Money market

Buy-backs and CDs Buy-backs and CDs are both dealt on a 'net of commission' basis. They are dealt through a commercial bank and the quoted bid or offer price includes the return to the transacting bank. Delivery and settlement is three to four business days following the date of the transaction.

Treasury notes and short-term government paper Treasury notes, or securities issued by the commonwealth government or by semi-government institutions but which have less than one year to maturity, may be purchased through a commercial bank or a stockbroker.

Dealing commission is normally $\frac{1}{4}$ per cent on the first $A 10 000 and $\frac{1}{8}$ per cent on any amount exceeding $A 10 000. Settlement and delivery is three to four business days following the transaction.

Commercial bills commercial paper Finance company notes These securities are normally dealt through a commercial bank, net of commission. Dealing commission is represented by the spread between quoted bid and offer prices which is normally $\frac{1}{4}$ per cent on transactions of all sizes.

Capital market

All securities can be dealt through a sharebroker who, under stock exchange regulations, is required to provide information and advice free of charge, and may only charge commission for actual sales and purchases made on the client's instructions.

Transactions may be made on the floor of one of the stock exchanges through a stockbroker or, if a sizeable transaction, through a bank. Banks deal on a net basis with spreads of $\frac{1}{8}$ to $\frac{1}{4}$ per cent. Standard stock exchange commission rates charged by brokers are as follows:

Common-wealth government bonds special bonds

Securities with less than five years' maturity:

On first $A 10 000 of face value	0.25%
On that part exceeding $A 10 000 of face value	0.125%
Single transactions of over $A 25 000 face value	Discretionary

Securities with more than five years' maturity:

On first $A 50 000	0.25%
$A 50 000 to $A 100 000	0.125%
$A 100 000 to $A 200 000	0.05%
On amounts over $A 200 000	0.025%

Semi-government bonds

Securities of less than one year's maturity:

On first $A 10 000 face value	0.25%
On that part exceeding $A 10 000 face value	0.125%

Securities with more than one year's maturity

All transaction sizes (minimum $A 100)	0.25%

Settlement and delivery of government and semigovernment securities is normally three to four days following the date of the transaction.

Minimum rates for securities of under five years to maturity if face value is not less than $A 25 000:	Discretionary

Minimum rates for securities of over five years to maturity if face value is not less than $A 50 000:

5–10 years maturity	0.125%
Over 10 years maturity	0.25%

Shares, rights, convertible notes and convertible debentures

These securities are mainly traded on the associated stock exchanges and dealt through a broker. If securities are not listed on any of the exchanges the commission rates are double those shown. Dealings must be made in multiples of minimum sizes, known as marketable parcels.

Settlement and delivery for all stock exchange transactions is normally five business days following the transaction. Deals in difficult sizes or in less active stocks or shares take longer to be settled.

Brokerage commission is charged as follows:

On first $A 5 000	2.5% of consideration
On next $A 10 000	2.0% of consideration
On next $A 34 000	1.5% of consideration
On next $A 200 000	1.0% of consideration
On next $A 250 000	0.75% of consideration
On next amounts in excess of $A 500 000	0.5% of consideration

Marketable parcels

1. *Shares, options and convertibles*

Price range of security	Minimum number of securities
Less than 25¢	2000
More than 25¢ and less than 50¢	1000
More than 50¢ and less than $A 1	500
More than $A 1 and less than $A 10	100
More than $A 10	50

2. *On rights to new equity issues*

Price range of security	Minimum number of securities
Less than $A 5	100
More than $A 5 and less than $A 10	50
More than $A 10 and less than $A 25	20
More than $A 25 and less than $A 50	10
More than $A 50	5

3. *All fixed interest securities except convertible loan securities* — $A 100

In addition, minimum bids are accepted on all securities as follows:

Price range of security	Minimum number of securities
Less than 10¢	0.5 cent
More than 10¢ and less than $A 5	1 cent
More than $A 5 and less than $A 10	2 cents
More than $A 10 and less than $A 20	5 cents
More than $A 20 and less than $A 50	10 cents
More than $A 50	25 cents

Share options

For purchase of share options at issue the following brokerage fees are charged, one half payable on purchase, the other half when the option is exercised:

On first $A 5000 of consideration based on the exercise price	2.5% + $A 5
On next $A 10 000 of consideration based on the exercise price	2.0% + $A 5
On next $A 35 000 of consideration based on the exercise price	1.5% + $A 5
On amount that exceeds $A 50 000 of consideration, etc.	1.0% + $A 5

For transactions in options contracts traded in the options market, the following brokerage fees are charged:

1. On opening buying and selling transactions:

On first $A 5000 of premium,	2.5%
On next $A 10 000 of premium,	2.0%
On next $A 35 000 of premium	1.5%
On amount that exceeds $A 50 000 of premium	1.0%

2. On closing buying and selling transactions brokerage is charged at half the rates shown above, subject to a minimum of $A 10.

These are dealt on the stock exchange through a dealer. Minimum dealing sizes are $A 100. Commission rates are as follows:

Corporate debentures and non-convertible unsecured notes

Bonds with less than one year to maturity	0.25% paid up capital value of security
Bonds with more than one year but under three years to maturity:	
On first $A 10 000	1% of paid-up capital value of security
On next $A 40 000	0.5% of paid-up capital value of security
On next $A 50 000	0.25% of paid-up capital value of security
On amounts exceeding $A 100 000	0.25% of total consideration or $A 425, whichever is the greater
Bonds with more than three years to maturity:	
On first $A 10 000	1.0% of paid-up capital value of security
On next $A 40 000	0.5% of paid-up capital value of security
On amounts exceeding $A 50 000	0.5% of total consideration or $A 300, whichever is the greater

Stamp duty

In addition to commission fees a government stamp duty is payable on all securities transactions, by both buyers and sellers; it differs from state to state and according to whether the transaction has been made through one of the stock exchanges (market transaction) or in the off 'change market (non-market transactions). See Table 21.11.

Table 21.11

State	Transaction size	Stamp duty On market	Stamp duty Off market
Victoria	Up to $A 100	7¢ per $A 25 or part thereof	14¢ per $A 25 or part thereof
	Over $A 100	30¢ per $A 100 or part thereof	60¢ per $A 100 or part thereof
New South Wales	Up to $A 100	7¢ per $A 25 or part thereof	6¢ per $A 10 or part thereof plus contract note fee, or
	Over $A 100	30¢ per $A 100 or part thereof	6¢ per $A 100 or part thereof
South Australia	Up to $A 100	7¢ per $A 25 or part thereof	14¢ per $A 25 or part thereof
	Over $A 100	30¢ per $A 100 or part thereof	60¢ per $A 100 or part thereof
Tasmania	Up to $A 100	7¢ per $A 25 or part thereof	14¢ per $A 25 or part thereof
	Over $A 100	30¢ per $A 100 or part thereof	60¢ per $A 100 or part thereof
Queensland	Up to $A 100	7¢ per $A 25 or part thereof	14¢ per $A 25 or part thereof
	Over $A 100	30¢ per $A 100 or part thereof	60¢ per $A 100 or part thereof
Western Australia	Up to $A 25	8¢	15¢
	Over $A 25 but less than $A 50	15¢	30¢
	Over $A 50 but less than $A 75	23¢	46¢
	Over $A 75 but less than $A 100	30¢	60¢
	Over $A 100	30¢ per $A 100 or part thereof	60¢ per $A 100 or part thereof
Australian Capital Territory	Over $A 100	5¢ per $A 25 or part thereof	
	Over $A 100	20¢ per $A 100 or part thereof	

Financial and monetary systems

Every aspect of Australia's financial system, its institutions and methods of operating are subject to review by a government appointed Committee of Inquiry into the workings of the Australian financial system. The committee was established in January 1979 and is chaired by Mr Keith Campbell and thus also referred to as the 'Campbell Committee'. The interim report of the committee was published in August 1980. This did not contain any recommendations but, having received submissions from all sectors of the financial system, it provides the basis upon which recommendations can be framed. The final report is due to be published in mid-1981. The object of the final report is to recommend reforms in the financial system with the purpose of making financial markets there efficient while at the same time relaxing government controls over the system.

The new tap and tender methods of issuing government bonds and treasury notes, though not a result of the Campbell committee report, indicate that the government's attitude to more variable interest rates is relaxing, while one of the recommendations of the final report will almost certainly be that the banks be allowed greater flexibility in determining their own interest rates for lending and borrowing. Although the committee is covering all areas of the financial system the main issues under examination are:

- The conflict between macroeconomic policy objectives and the efficient working on the money and capital markets;
- Factors affecting the stability of financial markets;
- the efficient allocation of financial resources and the competitive structure of financial intermediaries;
- the decentralization and dispersion of control within the system;
- methods of raising public finance, the ways in which the marketability of government and public sector paper can be improved and the possibility of introducing new instruments to the market;
- the role of the Reserve Bank, its responsibilities in formulating and implementing monetary policy and its control over the banking system;
- the role and operating methods of banks and other financial institutions;
- the constraints on the granting of new bank licences, particularly with respect to foreign banks;
- the methods of domestic monetary policy;
- external monetary policy and whether the Australian dollar should become a freely floating currency;
- taxation of financial intermediaries and depositors, of companies and shareholders and of other specific transactions;
- the reporting and accounting standards of companies.

Within the current system there exists a wide range of financial intermediaries. The banking sector comprises mainly the trading banks and savings banks. The Reserve Bank and the authorized money market dealers both play important roles in the money and capital markets. Other non-bank financial institutions include

469

money market corporations, finance companies, building societies, life assurance companies, pension and superannuation funds. Some, but not all, financial institutions are subject to central bank control.

Trading banks

The trading banks perform a commercial banking function, that is they accept demand, time and sight deposits; issue certificates of deposits; provide chequing account facilities; grant credit and advances (mainly short-term) to businesses and individuals—which takes the form of short fixed-term loans, discounting of commercial bills, or of overdrafts (whereby a customer has access on demand to an advance up to a maximum, individually determined limit). They are participants in the short-term money market and may also act as agents for clients in money and capital market transactions in the off 'change market.

There are 10 trading banks with a total of almost 5000 branches throughout Australia. In addition trading banking is conducted by state banks in New South Wales, South Australia and Western Australia by banks which provide trading banking services within their own states.

Of the 10 nationwide trading banks, six handle about 90 per cent of all trading bank business in Australia. These six—five of which are public companies, and one other, the Commonwealth Trading Bank of Australia (established under Commonwealth statute)—are known as the major trading banks and are listed below. Three of these have head offices in Sydney and three in Melbourne.

The four smaller trading banks are known as prescribed banks. These comprise two banks owned by overseas governments and one small local bank, all of which have been established for a long time, and one new bank, established in 1980. The number of trading banks has been reduced since the war through a series of mergers and takeovers. The most recent of these was the takeover of one major trading bank by another in 1979 (reducing the number from seven to six); specifically the Australia and New Zealand Banking Group acquired the Bank of Adelaide and the enlarged group is known as the Australia and New Zealand Banking Group (ANZ).

The first application in 20 years for a new banking licence was made in 1980. This was a domestic bank, backed by Australian interests. It is a prescribed trading bank known as the Australian Bank and established in Western Australia. Foreign banks have not been granted licences since the war but the Campbell committee is examining the possibility of allowing foreign banks greater access to the Australian market. The six major trading banks each have savings bank subsidiaries. These banks with their subsidiaries comprise the Australian Bankers' Association (ABA). This, main association within the banking industry, provides an important link between banks and the Reserve Bank.

Trading banks are subject to the Banking Act of 1959 as administered by the Reserve Bank. The Banking Act distinguishes between the six major trading banks and the prescribed banks with respect to reserve requirements. The Act is also applied differently to savings and state banks.

470

1. *Major trading banks*

   The Australian and New Zealand Banking Group
   Bank of New South Wales
   Commonwealth Trading Bank of Australia
   The Commercial Bank of Australia
   The Commercial Banking Company of Sydney
   The National Bank of Australasia

2. *Prescribed banks*

   Bank of New Zealand
   Banque Nationale de Paris
   Bank of Queensland
   Australian Bank

In addition to the trading banks listed above there is a further category of trading banks owned by state governments and not subject to the Banking Act, namely,

3. *State trading banks*

   Rural Bank of New South Wales
   The Rural and Industries Bank of Western Australia
   The State Bank of South Australia

Savings banks

Savings banks collect deposits mainly from the household and personal sector and redirect these funds to provide loans for housing, either directly or through the building societies, personal loans, and loans to local institutions. They may not, however, provide cheque account facilities. They are also major investors in government and semigovernment securities.

There are 13 savings banks. The largest is the Government and Commonwealth Savings Bank which holds about 35 per cent of the assets in the savings bank sector. Five other savings banks are wholly owned subsidiaries of the five private sector major trading banks. A seventh is a subsidiary of one of the prescribed banks—the Bank of New Zealand. There are two savings banks in Tasmania. The remainder are state savings banks in Victoria, South Australia and Western Australia. The state savings banks are established by state governments and are subject to state legislation but not to the Banking Act. All other savings banks, including the Commonwealth Savings Bank, are subject to the Banking Act.

In total the savings banks have over 5600 branches and over 12 000 agencies throughout Australia.

1. *Savings banks (subject to Banking Act)*

   The Commonwealth Savings Bank of Australia
   The Australia and New Zealand Savings Bank
   The Bank of New South Wales Savings Bank

471

The CBC Savings Bank
The Commercial Savings Bank of Australia
The National Bank Savings Bank
Bank of New Zealand Savings Bank
The Hobart Savings Bank (also known as the Savings Bank of Tasmania)
The Launceston Bank for Savings

2. *State savings banks*

The Savings Bank of South Australia
State Savings Bank of Victoria
The Rural & Industries Bank of Western Australia

Other banks

In addition to the trading and savings banks, there are three others that provide specialist banking functions, and while they are all subject to the Banking Act, they do not fall into the category of either trading or savings banks. The Commonwealth Development Bank is wholly owned by the government; it provides short-term loans and hire purchase finance to mining and manufacturing industry and also provides development finance for new or developing industries where such finance cannot be obtained easily or at the right terms from other sources. It derives most of its funds from the Commonwealth Savings Bank, its own share capital and reserves, and from the issue of CDs.

The Australian Resources Development Bank is owned equally by the six major trading banks. It provides medium- to long-term loans to primary resource industries either directly or by refinancing loans made by the major trading banks, the Reserve Bank and some state savings banks. Most capital, however, is raised through the issue of negotiable certificates of deposit with maturities of between 5 and 10 years.

The Primary Industry Bank of Australia is owned by the major trading banks, the three state trading banks and the government. Most of its funds are raised through the issue of negotiable certificates of deposit and the remainder from its share capital and reserves and from commonwealth funds on deposit. It provides loans to the primary resource industries on terms of up to 30 years, which is longer than is normally available from other sources. All the loans are provided indirectly through the refinancing of other bank loans.

Authorized money market dealers

The money market dealers act as intermediaries between the trading banks and the central bank, and in this respect they are similar to the London discount houses. There are nine approved or authorized dealers who are given lender of last resort facilities at the central bank. This is granted in the form of advances against the security of commonwealth government bonds of less than five years' maturity. This also entitles them to rediscount specified securities, essentially treasury notes and commercial bills, as a source of borrowing from the central bank.

The commercial banks do not themselves have direct access to the central bank's discount facilities but may discount bills or sell short-term securities to the discount houses which in turn rediscount bills through the central bank, or borrow against the collateral of their short-term securities.

The dealers are thus able to improve liquidity in the banking system by buying and selling short-term securities, as traders, in the money market.

The central bank may also influence liquidity in the banking system through its transactions with the dealers. The rate at which it will discount bills or lend to the dealers affects interest rates in the money market, while buying from or selling securities to the dealers will respectively increase or absorb liquidity.

The major instruments in which the dealers trade are treasury notes and bonds, CDs and commercial bills.

The authorized dealers are the major market makers in government securities and in order to finance their large volume transactions they are substantial borrowers of short-term funds in the form of call and short-term time deposits (in minimum amounts of $A 50 000), buy-back loans and advances or discount loans from the Reserve Bank. The bulk of their assets consist of commonwealth government bonds of less than five years' maturity and treasury notes. In smaller amounts they also hold paper issued by public authorities and banks, non-bank commercial bills and some securities of more than five years' maturity. The authorities define the maximum holdings of each type of security in terms of gearing limits relative to the dealers' capital and reserves base.

The dealers are not subject to the Banking Act but are regulated under the Financial Corporations Act.

Money market corporations

Money market corporations are comparable to investment banks in the US and Europe and to merchant banks in the UK. Indeed some money market corporations are called merchant banks. They specialize in corporate financing, underwriting corporate securities and accepting commercial bills of exchange, advisory services to companies on mergers and takeovers, arranging loans on behalf of corporations and the placement of, and investment in, government and corporate paper. Apart from fee income, they obtain most of their funds from short-term borrowings in the form of call and short-term variable rate time deposits, principally from the corporate sector.

The money market corporations, like the authorized money market dealers, are registered under the Financial Corporations Act. Altogether there are 40 money market corporations, but the 10 largest account for over half of the total assets of the whole group, and the five largest for about one-third of the total assets.

Due to there being a relatively large number of these corporations and because they deal mainly with financially sophisticated customers there is a high degree of competition between them. Lending rates, deposit rates and fees are, therefore, fairly uniform although they can fluctuate in the short-term depending on the asset and liability mix of each particular corporation.

473

The corporations operate on a national scale but are located in the major cities and do not operate an extensive branch network.

About 62 per cent of the ownership of the money market corporations, as a group, is held by foreign interests—mainly foreign banks. About 12 per cent is owned by domestic banks. Since 1973 new foreign interests have been discouraged by the Reserve Bank. The existing dominance of foreign interests derives from the money market corporation's early developments in the 1960s when domestic banks were not permitted to hold more than minority shareholdings and when foreign shareholdings were not specifically prohibited.

Finance companies

Finance companies developed during the 1950s essentially to provide personal loans, mortgage and hire purchase finance to the household sector. During the 1960s they increasingly provided finance in the form of equity participation in the property market. These two aspects have become less significant during the 1970s and now a greater proportion of their business takes the form of leasing finance to the corporate sector. They derive most of the funds required to finance their operations in the form of call deposits, time deposits of less than two years maturities, and the issue of short-term promissory notes, debentures and unsecured notes. Only about 30 per cent of their liabilities take the form of deposits, or issued paper, of more than two years' maturity. The largest seven finance companies are owned either wholly or largely by Australian banks and the assets of these seven represent roughly half of the total assets of all finance companies. A further seven, accounting for about 14 per cent of total assets of the group, are owned by domestic corporations. In addition there are over 150 much smaller finance companies. The large companies operate extensive branch networks and provide a whole range of finance company services while the smaller finance companies tend to specialize in particular types of services and do not have large branch networks.

Other financial institutions

Other institutions include the life insurance companies, pension funds and building societies. All of these are large institutional investors in the government and public sector bond markets while pension funds in particular are large investors in the corporate securities markets. They raise funds by collecting small long-term savings from individuals. The building societies provide the major share of all Australian mortgage finance for house purchase. These, together with the life insurance companies, are geared to stimulate home ownership at the expense perhaps of a more efficient capital market structure.

Central bank

The central bank is the Reserve Bank of Australia which was established in 1960. The bank's head office is at Sydney, though it also has a branch in each state.

The bank is managed by the governor who is appointed by the Governor-General (Queen's representative) for a seven-year term, and by a deputy governor, also officially appointed, but subordinate to the governor.

The governor and deputy governor preside over the Reserve Bank board which also comprises the Secretary to the Treasury and seven other officially appointed members, each of whom serves on the board for a five-year term. At least five of these members must not be officers of the bank, public sector employees, or employees of other banking companies. Generally they represent a cross section of industrial, agricultural, labour and academic interest.

The board has autonomy in determining monetary policy, although it is required to inform the treasury of any potential change it intends to introduce. In addition the treasury has powers to advise the board on recommended policy changes. In practice the board and the treasury work closely together in determining monetary policy though the board, through the Reserve Bank, is the sole administrator of monetary policy.

The board is also required to provide the treasury, with copies to both Houses of Parliament, with annual reports of its operations and audited financial accounts for the year.

The Reserve Bank performs all the functions of a central bank. It is the sole issuer of notes and coins, banker and agent to the government, other governments, banks and certain financial institutions, regulator of the banking system and manager of monetary policy, manager of Australia's gold and foreign currency reserves, administrator of exchange controls, and is also charged with the responsibility for stabilizing the external value of the currency. In addition it maintains the stock register for commonwealth government securities, operates a substantial banking business and provides a wide range of services.

Monetary policy

The objectives of monetary policy as determined by the Reserve Bank board are to help provide conditions such as to achieve the stability of the currency, the maintenance of full employment, and economic growth subject to the welfare of the people of Australia.

The instruments used by the Reserve Bank for control over the money market and to effect monetary policy are reserve ratios, direct control over liquidity and credit, interest rate policy and open market operations. Since the development of the money market in the 1960s there has been a move towards greater use of the indirect market oriented policy of open market operations, but much reliance is still placed on direct controls, particularly on the banking sector, such as manipulation of liquidity and reserve ratios. With respect to bank regulations controls are applied differently to trading banks, savings banks and other banks.

Reserve and liquidity ratios (SRDS and LGS)

The major means by which the Reserve Bank regulates liquidity in the banking system is by the use of two direct measures: the Statutory Reserve Deposit (SRD) system and the Liquid Assets and Government Securities Convention (LGS).

475

The SRD system has been applied by statute since the Banking Act of 1959. Under the system trading banks (excluding state trading banks) are required to hold statutory reserves with the Reserve Bank. These reserves must be in the form of cash held on deposit at the Reserve Bank at a modest rate of interest (2.5 per cent since 1976). The amount of the SRD deposits is calculated as a percentage of each trading bank's total deposits in Australian dollars at a uniform rate for all major trading banks. The SRD requirement has varied between 3% and 10% between 1974 and 1980. The average for the period has been about 5.5%. It may, however, be increased to up to 25% of deposits with one day's notice or to over 25% with 45 days' notice. There is no minimum or maximum SRD ratio specified by the Banking Act.

The prescribed trading banks are set individual SRD ratios which cannot be higher than those set for the major trading banks. The Banque National de Paris (the only foreign trading bank) is usually set the same ratio as for the major trading banks. The other prescribed banks are generally set a ratio of 1 to 1.5 per cent below that of the major trading banks.

Used in conjunction with the SRD system is the Liquid Asset Ratio, or LGS. This is not backed by statute but is a convention that has been used since 1956 whereby the major trading banks agree to comply with the Reserve Bank in their minimum holdings of specified liquid assets. These liquid assets comprise cash held at the Reserve Bank, treasury notes, commonwealth government bonds and semi-government bonds. The minimum ratio, as a percentage of total Australian dollar deposits, is uniform for all major trading banks. The LGS ratio is not changed very often and, apart from a temporary increase to 23 per cent in 1976, has been 18 per cent since 1962. Commonly, the banks hold over 30 per cent of their deposit liabilities in the form of such assets since they provide a good return together with high security. By agreement with the Reserve Bank they may not allow their holdings of LGS assets to fall below the agreed minimum. The prescribed trading banks are not a party to the LGS convention but agree minimum holdings of selected assets with the Reserve Bank.

The purpose of the LGS convention is to increase the policy effect of changes in the SRD ratio on banking system liquidity and thus on interest rate trends and the expansion of credit.

It has been shown that the existence of the LGS convention allows an increase (or decrease) in the SRD to have a stronger and more immediate effect on bank lending to the private sector. If the SRD ratio is increased the banks can first run down their holdings of LGS assets to meet the extra call on their funds. If the SRD ratio is decreased, the banks can increase their overdraft lending and gradually build up their LGS assets. This use of the SRD ratio is thus likely to remain the major instrument of control for reducing or increasing domestic credit expansion.

Savings banks are (as at December 1980) subject to more stringent liquid asset requirements than are the major trading banks, although this requirement is being examined by the Campbell Committee. They are required to hold a minimum of 40 per cent of their assets in specified liquid and government securities. It is probable that this requirement will be replaced by a 15 per cent liquidity ratio which will be applied similarly to the SRD system for the trading bank sector.

Direct quantitive and qualitative credit controls

The Reserve Bank also has powers to apply direct quantitive and qualitative controls with respect to both the volume and direction of bank lending via loans and overdrafts. In the past, such controls have not proved very effective and have only occasionally been implemented in order to supplement the main instrument of a change in the SRD ratio. In practice the Reserve Bank relies on the co-operation of the trading banks to comply with the LGS convention in the expectation that the banks' lending policies will be adapted to conform with monetary policy objectives. The shift away from direct controls by the Reserve Bank indicates that, in the future, greater reliance will be placed on market oriented policies to influence the supply of bank credit.

Interest rate policy

The majority of interest rates prevailing in the money and capital markets are not administered rates but respond to market demand and supply conditions. The discount rate, the rate at which the Reserve Bank will rediscount bills to the money market dealers, tends to follow rather than determine other interest rates, while with the introduction of weekly treasury note tenders the treasury note rate has also become more market determined rather than government determined.

Maximum interest rates paid on deposits or charged on lending rates are set for the trading and savings banks from time to time. Since 1977 major trading banks have been free to set their own interest rates for large deposits or lending in excess of $A 100 000. The Reserve Bank sets a maximum interest rate for overdrafts and loans of less than $A 100 000; the rate was changed in December 1980 from 10 to 12.5 per cent. No limits on deposit interest rates apply but obviously the cost of bank loans influences the amount that banks can afford to pay on deposits. The objective is not so much to regulate credit and liquidity but more to help individuals and small businesses and particularly to encourage home-ownership for the majority of the population. Such controls do, however, hamper the development of a more efficient capital market since small savings tend to be directed towards non-bank financial institutions, which are not subject to the same controls. It results in a non-price rationing of bank lending and a misallocation of capital funds. The savings banks in particular cannot compete effectively in the market for funds, thus helping to sustain the dominance of the government bond market, since the yields obtainable in the latter are more attractive to the small investor than those obtainable in savings deposits. Consequently this is one of the major areas being examined by the Campbell Committee.

Open market operations

Increasing recourse is being made by the Reserve Bank to the use of open market operations to influence liquidity in the banking system and, indirectly, the levels of interest rates. This has been facilitated by changing attitudes of the monetary authorities and the growing sophistication of the domestic money market. Indeed, in recent years there has been a whole shift in emphasis towards market policies with the eventual intention of reducing or abolishing direct controls. The bank effects transactions in money market securities in the off 'change market through the nine authorized money market dealers, buying or selling treasury notes and short-term government securities either directly or through buy-back transactions. It buys securities if it wishes to increase liquidity and exert a downward influence on interest rates or sells when it wants to withdraw liquidity from the system. The bank also effects transactions in capital market government securities, through stock exchange brokers, also in the off 'change market, in order to augment its operations in the money market.

Open market operations are used in conjunction with changes in the SRD ratio when strong policy measures are required, or used separately in order to maintain stability or influence trends in bank credit and interest rate levels. Now that the new tender system for treasury notes has been introduced the Reserve Bank can operate in the market by varying the quantity of notes issued and the bids it accepts for new issues. In addition the Reserve Bank can vary the terms on which it will rediscount bills or extend advances (lender of last resort facilities) to the authorized dealers.

Withholding taxes

Withholding taxes apply to both interest and dividends at rates of 10 and 30 per cent respectively. For residents of those countries having double taxation treaties with Australia the rates are reduced to 15 per cent for dividends but remain at 10 per cent for interest payments. There is a fairly strong lobby of opinion in Australia in favour of the abolition of the 10 per cent interest tax in order to encourage greater foreign investment in Australian debt instruments.

Table 21.12   Withholding taxes

	Interest, %	Dividends, %
Residents of non-treaty countries	10	30
Residents of treaty countries		
Belgium	10	15
Canada	10	15
France	10	15
Germany	10	15
Japan	10	15
Netherlands	10	15
New Zealand	10	15
Papua New Guinea	10	15
Philippines	10	25
Singapore	10	15
Switzerland	10	15
UK	10	15
USA	10	15

Exchange controls

Authorities

The government, acting on the advice of the treasury department and the Reserve Bank, determines exchange control policy. Administration of controls with respect to foreign portfolio investment is delegated to the Reserve Bank.

Currency

The currency is the Australian dollar, which is also legal tender in the New Hebrides, Navru, the Gilbert Islands and Tuvalu. The exchange value of the dollar is maintained against a trade weighted basket of currencies, although the authorities do not disclose the exact composition of the basket. The largest components are the yen, US dollar and sterling. The authorities intervene in the spot foreign exchange market, using the US dollar as the currency of intervention in order to smooth out excessive fluctuations, but they do not attempt to maintain fixed margins with respect to the trade weighted index.

Banks are permitted to engage in spot foreign exchange transactions, within limits, for their uncovered positions and balances held abroad and in the forward market for covering trade transactions. In the forward market the Australian dollar is quoted at a premium or discount to the US dollar, rather than relative to any basket of currencies.

Non-resident accounts

Non-residents may freely hold accounts with Australian banks but credits to such accounts are subject to approval. This is normally a formality only for proceeds from portfolio investments. Transfers may be made freely between non-resident accounts except where such transfers are in excess of $A 250 000, in which case Reserve Bank approval is required; normally this is readily granted. Balances on non-resident accounts may be withdrawn freely in any other convertible currency. The restriction prohibiting non-resident deposits with Australian banks for periods of less than six months' maturity was discontinued in June 1978.

Purchase of securities and repatriation of proceeds

In theory all inward equity investment is first subject to approval from the Reserve Bank. These regulations are designed to control capital outflows. Capital inflows, for the purpose of portfolio investment, are monitored and supervised by the Foreign Investment Review Board (FIRB).

The banking, mining and media industries specifically are protected from foreign control but approval for inward foreign portfolio investment for these and all other sectors is automatic. Until 8 June 1978 non-residents were prohibited from purchasing fixed-interest securities with less than six months' maturity, which virtually excluded the money market to foreign investors. This regulation has now been abolished and non-residents (except banks dealing for their own accounts) are free

479

to purchase all types of fixed-interest securities. The proceeds from inward portfolio investment may be credited to a non-resident account, and may then be repatriated in any convertible currency.

Gold

Non-residents may purchase gold and export it subject to approval from the Reserve Bank. Non-residents are permitted to engage freely in gold transactions on the Sydney futures exchange.

22.   Hong Kong

General market environment

Hong Kong is perhaps the freest investment market in the world. Based completely on the principles of a free market economy, Hong Kong has no exchange controls and no distinction is made between resident and non-resident investors. Dealing costs are relatively low and no withholding taxes apply to dividends although a tax of 15 per cent on interest arising in or derived from Hong Kong is deducted at source.

This freedom in the investment market has provided a favourable environment for the development of a whole spread of financial, investment, management and advisory services, both domestically incorporated and representative of foreign entities. The institutions are virtually free of government controls although certain codes of practice exist regarding securities dealing. In particular, Hong Kong is unique in having no central bank, although the largest domestic bank, the Hongkong and Shanghai Bank, can, if necessary, assume some of the functions of a

Table 22.1 Summary of instruments

Instrument	Characteristics
MONEY MARKET	
Deposits	Large and active market in Hong Kong dollars, US dollars, yen, sterling and other Eurocurrencies
call deposits	Overnight, 2, 7 and 15 days through wide range of banks and institutions
time deposits	Terms of 15 days, one month and monthly up to six months placing available through a wide range of banks and institutions. One- to five-year terms available through finance companies
certificates of deposit	Fixed and floating rate CDs available, but poor secondary market
CAPITAL MARKET	
Bonds	No government bonds, very few corporate bonds either issued or traded
Equities	Highly active primary and secondary markets. Highly volatile. Seventy per cent of top traded shares are property companies
Unit trusts and mutual funds	A number of quoted funds. Tend to concentrate on Far Eastern equity markets
Commodities	Active gold and silver exchange. Less active commodities exchange dealing in gold futures and soya bean

481

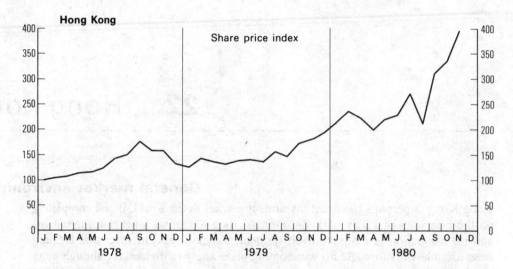

Hong Kong

Share price index

central bank. No monetary controls, except for a minimum liquidity ratio, are enforced on the banking system, and there is no government intervention in either the money or capital markets.

The range of investment instruments available in Hong Kong is, however, limited by comparison with other developed markets. Call and time deposits in Hong Kong dollars and Eurocurrencies constitute the major part of the money market. The government's conservative budgetary policy negates the need for any market in government securities issues in either the money or capital markets. In the main the domestic capital market comprises equity shares, there being very few fixed-interest securities either issued or traded. The Hong Kong stock market is exciting and highly volatile, and the potential for high capital gains is considerable. In addition, as an international market place Hong Kong is the major secondary market Euro-bond trading centre in Asia.

The money market

Deposits

Call deposits

The market for call deposits is an interbank market, with most transactions occurring between authorized banks. Money may be placed by the non-bank public in minimum amounts of HK$50000 for terms of overnight, 7- or 15-day call primarily with the commercial banks either directly or through the intermediary of a money-broker. There also exists a wide range of other financial institutions, including finance companies and merchant banks, with which call money may be deposited. Interest rates for Hong Kong dollars in the call money market now closely correlate to international Eurodollar interest rates, since the US is Hong Kong's largest trading partner and, in the absence of exchange controls, rates have to be broadly in line with US dollar rates to prevent excessive capital flows between US and Hong Kong dollars. Prior to 1971, when the Hong Kong dollar was linked to the pound sterling, domestic interest rates used to be largely influenced by the UK bank rate. Call money interest rates now act as a sensitive barometer indicating domestic economic conditions. Seasonally, however, short-term interest rates always rise substantially in the two months preceding the Chinese New Year in February and often rise well above US dollar interest rates.

Time deposits

Time deposits in local currency can be placed with the domestic commercial banks or with a large number of major international banks through their Hong Kong representatives. Interest rates for deposits in local currency with local banks are agreed from time to time by the Exchange Banks Association, which dominates the banking system because its membership includes the Hongkong and Shanghai Bank and the Chartered Bank. Market forces are however the major influence on interest rates. Subject to minimum deposits of HK$50 000, the deposit-taking companies have become a significant market factor over the past two years or so. Many deposit-taking companies are subsidiaries of major international banks but offer rates substantially in excess of the rates quoted by banks. They take deposits of up to two years' maturity. Finance companies, which specialize in short- to medium-term hire purchase and lease-lending to businesses, tend to accept deposits with maturities mostly of between one to five years.

Eurocurrency deposits

There is also an active market made by the local and international banks and deposit taking companies in Eurocurrency call and time deposits, which are subsequently placed through Singapore or other Euromarket centres.

In all cases, interest rates are determined by supply and demand conditions prevailing in the worldwide international currency markets. Maturities of Eurocurrency deposits are normally available for terms of from two days' call up to two years or beyond. There is no set minimum amount required.

Certificates of deposit

A market for Hong Kong dollar CDs has developed only recently—since 1977. They are the first marketable instruments of their kind to be introduced in Hong Kong. Deposit-taking companies such as Wardley (a subsidiary of the Hongkong and Shanghai Bank), and Sun Hung Kai Finance issue negotiable bearer CDs on a tap basis. These issues, however, have a low visibility in the market, tending to be held to maturity by primary market investors, and the volume of outstanding paper is insignificant.

Various banks, mostly the Hong Kong branches of foreign banks, have from time to time issued fixed amounts of negotiable floating rate CDs with maturities of from one to five years. The earlier issues carry coupons which are adjusted every six

483

months to the higher of a fixed minimum or Hong Kong dollar prime rate. The more recent issues bear interest at the higher of prime rate or $\frac{1}{4}$ per cent over average 30-day interbank deposit offer rate, determined monthly but paid quarterly in arrears. The total of outstanding CDs amounts to approximately HK$1000 million. Although marketability has improved, it is still lacking by international standards, mainly because competition between banks has been so fierce that customers have in practice been able to break deposits on demand. There is thus no advantage to the investor of receiving a lower yield if CDs are effectively no more liquid than an ordinary time deposit. The secondary market for CDs will thus remain inadequate as long as the effective liquidity of deposits is maintained. There are three main dealers, Wardley, Chase and Jardine Fleming in the secondary market for CDs, who make quotes with a spread between bid and offer prices of $\frac{1}{8}$ to $\frac{1}{2}$ per cent, depending on market conditions.

US$ CDs

Branches of some foreign banks in Hong Kong issue US dollar denominated CDs. Since 1980, the inland revenue has decreed that interest earned from US dollar CDs is not liable to interest tax. This ruling is likely to encourage an active market in US dollar CDs while the market in Hong Kong dollar CDs may continue to remain inactive.

Treasury bills

Due to the Hong Kong government's persistent budgetary surplus, there is no requirement for it to raise temporary finance through the issue of treasury bills. Furthermore, since the government does not intervene in the money market or use open market operations to control liquidity in the financial system, treasury bill issues are not required as a means of absorbing or supplying liquidity or of influencing interest rates. A few small issues have occasionally been made in the past, though none have been issued recently nor are any outstanding.

Commercial paper

There is a small market in commercial paper, which was started in 1979. Specifically, the Mass Transit Railway Corporation (MTRC) from time to time issues discount paper in amounts of about HK$25 million and denominations of HK$100 000 and HK$500 000. The paper is in the form of bills of exchange issued through a syndicate of seven financial institutions led by Trident International Finance Limited. The bills are bearer securities which represent an unsecured obligation of MTRC. They are 'accepted', but neither guaranteed nor underwritten by Trident. The bills may have a maturity of up to 360 days although usually they are issued with maturities of either 90 or 180 days. The value of bills outstanding at any one time may not exceed HK$270 million.

Most bills are held to maturity by investors although a secondary market is maintained by the managers comprising the syndicate. Prices are quoted on a yield basis, calculated according to a 365-day year, and the dealer's bid and offer spread includes the dealing commission. Settlement and delivery is the same or following business day depending on whether the transaction is made before or after midday. Since the bills are discount securities, the face value is paid to holders at maturity without deduction. If sold before maturity, however, any profit or loss is accountable for tax purposes.

The capital market

Government bonds

For the same reasons that no treasury bill market exists, there is a very small market in government bonds. The last issue was a HK$250 million issue redeemed in June 1980, but this must be regarded as an anomaly. The issue was almost entirely held by financial institutions in their own portfolios since it ranked as a liquid asset for the purposes of the Banking Ordinance. Though quoted on the stock exchange, it was never regularly traded.

Corporate bonds

Bond financing is not as favoured by Hong Kong companies as is equity financing, while investors also prefer the tax free capital gains available from shares to the taxable fixed income derived from bonds. There are a number of offshore Hong Kong dollar bonds in existence, which are not subject to tax. They were introduced in order to avoid the withholding tax problem. A more significant factor, perhaps, is the lack of local provident funds, insurance companies etc., with a need for long-term paper. The bond market has consequently remained fairly dormant since the second world war. A limited number of fixed-interest securities have been issued by local companies, including the Mass Transit Railway Corporation. In order to attract investors, some bonds have been issued by offshore subsidiaries of Hong Kong companies, thereby avoiding interest tax which is deducted at source for bonds of Hong Kong resident companies. Other issues have been offered to shareholders of Hong Kong companies originally in the form of a package with warrants as rights to purchase further shares at a predetermined price. These bonds are now traded separately from their warrants, but interest is paid subject to a 15 per cent tax deduction at source. The different tax status of domestic and offshore issues is reflected in their prices and redemption yields which, subject to the length of maturity and quality of borrower, are comparable on a net basis.

During a bull market, however, larger companies are able to float convertible loan stocks. They carry lower yields than straight bonds but give the holder the option to convert into shares of the issuing company at specified dates in the future and at predetermined prices. During times of a strongly rising equity market, the debenture holder stands to make a considerable profit by being able to convert into ordinary shares when the share price may stand at a more substantial premium than that fixed by the terms of the loan stock.

485

During 1980 several major companies issued convertible loan stock with warrants. Hutchinson Whampoa, Hongkong Electric and Jardine Matheson each issued stocks to the value of HK$600 million, HK$635 million and HK$1000 million, respectively. The total of loan stocks with warrants issued in 1980 (up to end November) was HK$1.3 billion. These securities have become very popular because the bonds provide a fixed-interest return to the investor—albeit at lower yields than straight bonds—while the warrant gives the holder the opportunity to purchase shares of the issuing company at a predetermined price. The warrants may be detached from the bonds and traded separately. If the value of the relevant share appreciates then the warrants may multiply to several times their original value and thus offer the investor the potential of a capital gain as well as a fixed-interest return from the bonds.

The nominal value of total bonds outstanding is about HK$4000 million, with a final maturity range of 2 to 13 years. Except for convertible bonds, their turnover is low and their marketability consequently poor.

Foreign bonds

Because of the insignificance of the domestic bond market, no foreign bonds have been issued in Hong Kong.

Eurobonds

A market for Hong Kong dollar Eurobonds (or offshore Hong Kong dollar bonds) was established in 1977. Four issues were readily floated with an aggregate nominal value of HK$750 million and maturities of five to eight years. The borrowers included Hongkong Land and the province of Manitoba in Canada. The bonds are in bearer form with interest payable annually in Kong Kong dollars and free of withholding tax. No further issues have been made, however, because of the subsequent weakness of the Hong Kong dollar.

The primary market is not regulated by any authority while secondary market turnover is constrained only by the limited volume of issues. The bonds are all listed on the London or Luxembourg stock exchanges and may also be dealt in any of the major international financial centres. A secondary market in other currency denominated Eurobonds is maintained in Hong Kong by financial institutions which include representatives of some of the world's leading Eurobond market makers. Hong Kong handles a far larger volume of Eurobond transactions than any other financial centre in Asia. Although Singapore is the major issuing centre in the area Hong Kong, because of its better developed financial infrastructure, attracts most of the secondary market transactions. Unlike domestic bonds, Eurobonds are not subject to 15 per cent withholding tax on interest.

Equity shares

The equity market in Hong Kong is well developed. An unusual aspect is the large presence of property companies, comprising 70 per cent of the top-traded shares, and which make continually increasing profits because of the high population

Table 22.2   Major Hong Kong companies

Company	Market capital- ization (Sept. 1980), HK$ billion	Pretax profits, HK$ million	Net assets, HK$ billion	Activity
Hongkong and Shanghai Bank	22.1	1760*	....	Banking
Hongkong Land	21.2	367	6.1	Property
Hongkong and Kowloon Wharf	14.1	219	1.8	Property, hotels, wharfage
Cheung Kong Holdings	9.2	308	1.3	Property
Jardine Matheson	8.3	608	2.6	Trading
Hutchinson Whampoa	7.3	519	2.5	Trading
Sun Hung Kai Properties	7.1	609	1.2	Property
New World Development	6.1	125	1.1	Property
Hongkong Electric	5.1	274	1.9	Electric utility
China Light and Power	3.9	204	1.6	Electric utility
Swire Pacific	3.2	620	3.1	Trading
World International	3.1	74	0.4	Shipping
Wheelock Marden	2.1	398	0.9	Trading

* Net profit to December 1980.

growth (augmented by refugees from China) and the scarcity of land. Property companies or financial companies with property interests together account for over 60 per cent at stock market capitalization. Many of the remaining listed companies are trading and shipping companies. Manufacturing companies are poorly represented partly because most local industries are labour intensive and seldom need to raise large amounts of capital. The major Hong Kong companies, ranked by market capitalization, are as shown in Table 22.2.

Although the standard of reporting by Hong Kong companies has improved in recent years there are few uniform auditing requirements. All publicly quoted companies are required to publish annual accounts although the degree of detail differs from company to company. Annual accounts must be published within one and six months of a company's year end and at least 14 days prior to the annual general meeting. Although there is no requirement to do so, a growing number of companies also publish unaudited interim accounts at the half-year stage.

The Hong Kong stock market has been one of the world's more volatile markets. The Hang Seng Index of stock prices (base of 31 July 1964 = 100) which represents 70 per cent of total market capitalization of local companies reached a peak of 1775 in the stock market boom of 1972/3 and collapsed to 150 in 1974. The index has again risen to a seven-year high of over 1500 in November 1980, and has doubled between March and November 1980. Much of the rise is justified, however, since equity shares in general have shown an above-average rate of capital appreciation if measured over a long period.

Stock exchanges

There are four stock exchanges in Hong Kong. The traditional one is the Hong Kong stock exchange, but the largest is now the Far East exchange. The other two are the Kam Ngan and Kowloon exchanges. Their relative shares of total 1979 stock exchange turnover are: Far East SE, 45.8 per cent; Hong Kong SE, 21.9 per cent; Kam Ngan SE, 32.1 per cent; and Kowloon SE, 0.2 per cent. The Hong Kong exchange was established in 1871 and existed as the only exchange until 1969 when, due to the exchange's reluctance to admit new members, the Far East stock exchange was set up by a group of Chinese business men. This stimulated business and attracted new money to the colony. It also inspired the establishment of the two other exchanges. The Kam Ngan exchange was set up in 1971 by members of the Chinese gold and silver exchange, and the Kowloon exchange was established by private entrepreneurs in 1972. The government then intervened to prevent the formation of further exchanges. Proposals to merge the four are currently under consideration, and the creation of a single stock exchange is scheduled to be effected in August 1983.

The exchanges are autonomous and self-regulating, but each is subject to the authority of the Securities Commission, which is headed by a government appointed commissioner. They are bound by listing procedures and a takeover code, similar to those of the London stock exchange, but modified according to local requirements. Additionally, a code on unit trusts and mutual funds was introduced in 1978 which bans unapproved trusts and requires approved trusts to file their trust documents with the Securities Commission.

There are over 1000 members of the four exchanges which comprise either individuals, or representatives of firms or limited liability companies. The larger firms of stockbrokers have one or more seats on each of the three major exchanges. The stock exchanges use the trading post system whereby buying and selling orders are matched by open outcry. Some of the larger brokers, however, make a market in the more popularly traded shares. The exchanges are open between 10 a.m. and 12.30 p.m. and between 2.30 and 3.30 p.m. from Mondays to Fridays. Settlement and delivery of securities transacted occurs on the following business day.

Apart from the Tokyo stock exchange Hong Kong provides the largest market capitalization and best market for shares in the Far East. Most activity in the new issues market, on all stock exchanges, occurs in share issues by property companies. Primary activity in the shares of other types of companies is not very active.

There are more than 300 companies quoted on the four exchanges. These are mainly domestic companies, although a few foreign companies, mostly Japanese, are also quoted.

In the stock market, marketability of the leading shares is excellent and the combined turnover on all four stock exchanges averages from HK$250 million to HK$500 million per day, but can reach over HK$1 billion a day.

Unit trusts and mutual funds

A number of unit trusts and mutual funds have been locally established. Some specialize in local companies, while others specialize in foreign markets, particularly Australian, Japanese and other Far East stock markets.

Commodities

A commodity exchange was established in Hong Kong in 1975. Initially, contracts in cotton and sugar were listed, but were only infrequently traded. The recent addition of gold futures contracts appears to have stimulated trading to some extent.

Gold and silver

Hong Kong has a well established gold and silver exchange. The exchange is essentially a forward market operating on a traditional Chinese system. This system deals in Chinese units known as taels which are a little over one ounce by weight and of slightly different purity than gold traded in London. A Loco London cash bullion market dealing in gold measured in ounces and of 99.5 per cent fineness also operates in Hong Kong. Turnover is reported to be huge even in times of a relatively stable world gold market. Though dealings by both residents and non-residents is unrestricted, it is unusual for non-residents other than specialized gold dealers to trade on the Hong Kong gold and silver exchange. No foreigners are allowed to be members of the local exchange, although of course they can deal through members.

Additionally, a gold coin with a face value of HK$1000 is in issue as legal tender, but does not circulate as such. These may be purchased through banks.

Dealing and fees

Over the past few years a very sophisticated network of financial services organizations has developed in Hong Kong. Major institutions comprise commercial and merchant banks from a number of countries, investment management organizations, stockbrokers, money and exchange brokers, commodity brokers, and Eurobond dealers.

A bank or other Hong Kong representative of a non-resident company or individual can therefore easily deal or arrange for transactions during normal Hong Kong office hours in respect of most, if not all, important investment instruments.

Deposits and CDs

For deposits and CDs no specific fee is charged, the relevant deposit-taking institution includes some return on CDs in the spread between their bid and offer quotes, usually about $\frac{1}{8}$ per cent.

Eurobonds

For Eurobonds, no fee is charged for dealing but the dealer's commission is included in the spread between his bid and offer prices—usually about $\frac{1}{4}$ to $\frac{3}{4}$ per cent.

Stock exchange transactions

For stock exchange dealings, stockbrokers charge a commission of 0.5 per cent of consideration (subject to a minimum of HK$25) on both purchases and sales, plus a stamp duty of 0.3 per cent on purchases and HK$5 per transfer deed on sales.

All Hong Kong shares and bonds are dealt in 'board lots' which vary according to the price of a share. Normally it is 1000 shares but board lots may range from 100 to 5000 shares or bonds. The higher the share price the lower the board lot. When the price of a share rises to a certain level the size of the board lot is reduced. Odd lots can be sold by negotiation, but this normally incurs a discount on the price of the security.

Settlement and delivery occurs on the business day following the transaction. Delivery takes the form of a transfer certificate but because registration of securities can take several weeks, shareholders usually keep securities with a bank or broker in unregistered, deliverable, form. The securities then need only be registered if a divided bonus or rights issue is due. Since registration can take up to six weeks, securities may not usually be sold during this period following a purchase.

As payment is due against delivery, within 24 hours it is essential for non-residents to have stock registered in the nominee companies of local banks. Charges made by banks for relevant services are as follows:

Bank charges

1. Receipt and delivery of stock against payment

Consideration of up to HK$4000	0.25% (minimum HK$5)
Consideration of HK$4000 to HK$8000	HK$10
Consideration of over HK$8000	0.125%

2. Safe custody of securities

Shares. Fee per account per stock, payable on deposit	HK$5 per board lot subject to a minimum fee of HK$10 and a maximum of HK$2500
Bonds	As with shares but payable per HK$1000 bond

3. Handling commission on scrip for registration and return — HK$20 per request and HK$5 for each certified transfer deed obtained

Financial and monetary systems

Financial institutions

The most remarkable aspect of the Hong Kong financial system is that it has no central bank, but yet has a highly sophisticated and efficient banking system.

The government-appointed Commissioner of Banking and the Hongkong and Shanghai Bank together play the role of the monetary authority. The latter, with government support, can act as lender of last resort in terms of crisis and indeed did so in 1965 in order to support a local Chinese bank. The bank does not, however, provide this facility to the banking system as a matter of automatic recourse.

Coins are issued by the Hong Kong government, but notes are issued jointly by the Hongkong and Shanghai Bank and by one of its subsidiaries, the Mercantile Bank, and also by the Chartered Bank.

Commercial banks

Hong Kong has 115 licensed, or authorized, banks. Thirty-four are locally incorporated and the remainder are branches of foreign banks. Between them they have over 950 branches in Hong Kong.

New licences are granted by the government but a moratorium on licences to foreign banks wishing to establish a branch in Hong Kong has been in effect during 1980 because of the government's concern about excessive credit expansion. New licences may be considered in 1981. New licences may sometimes be granted in reciprocation when a Hong Kong bank is given permission to open a new branch in a foreign country. Licensed banks are authorized to accept all forms of deposits in Hong Kong dollars, sterling and all other convertible currencies, and to grant overdrafts and loans to their customers. These banks are also very active in the foreign exchange markets.

All the commercial banks are privately owned joint stock companies. The largest is the Hongkong and Shanghai Bank which accounts for about 50 per cent of all domestic banking business.

Deposit-taking companies

There are approximately 300 registered deposit-taking companies (DTCs) which mainly accept call and time deposits, and make short- to medium-term loans to businesses. The main distinction between a DTC and a bank is that the minimum deposit that may be placed with a DTC is HK$50 000, and that DTCs are not allowed to issue cheque books. Many such companies are wholly owned subsidiaries of major international banks. About 70 per cent of DTCs are subsidiaries of licensed banks, others are used for offshore lending and some are inhouse financing vehicles which do not deal with the public at all. There is some concern over the activities of deposit-taking companies by both the licensed banks and by the government. The licensed banks are worried by the competition they present though the DTCs argue that they have been mainly instrumental in narrowing bid and offer spreads. Since the DTCs do not fall within the rules set out by the Banking Ordinance, the licensed banks also feel that they offer inadequate protection to depositors and may put at risk Hong Kong's reputation as a financial centre. This argument is perhaps one of sour grapes since DTCs are subject to prudential liquidity ratios similar to those applied to banks. Specified liquid assets totalling at least 30 per cent of short-term (up to 7 days) deposits and 15 per cent of other deposits must be held as liquidity cover. (The ratio for banks is 25 per cent.)

The government, however, is more concerned that the DTCs are largely responsible for the excessive domestic credit expansion (50 per cent in 1980) and that unregulated lending by the DTCs could jeopardize the stability of Hong Kong's financial system. Since many DTCs are now performing a number of retail banking functions, changes in the law are being considered to encompass the activities of DTCs. One likely amendment is that DTCs may no longer be allowed to accept deposits of less than three months' maturity which would not only reduce their competition with the licensed banks but would also reduce their ability to attract funds and, consequently, their ability to lend.

Finance companies

There are more than 1500 finance companies. They also grant short- to medium-term personal loans and hire purchase finance to individuals and businesses for mortgages and motor cars etc. Generally they accept time deposits in Hong Kong and US dollars for periods of one to five years.

Merchant banks

There are over 30 merchant banks which are wholesale banking companies specializing in loan syndication, financial restructuring of companies, underwriting of new security issues, and financial advisory services. In Chinese there is no distinction between merchant bank, finance company or deposit-taking company. So those 30 merchant banks are not necessarily separate banking entities. Wardley, for example, is a subsidiary of the Hongkong and Shanghai Banking Corporation and besides being the largest deposit-taking company, is also the largest merchant bank.

Others

Other financial services and institutions include investment management organizations, stockbrokers from a number of countries, money and foreign exchange brokers and commodity brokers. A major sector lacking in the local market is large savings/investment institutions such as insurance and assurance companies, pension funds and provident funds.

Monetary controls

Little official control is exercised over the financial market. The Banking Ordinance, supervised by the Commissioner of Banking, requires that banks and near-banks maintain a specified minimum percentage of their total deposit liabilities in the form of liquid assets. This ratio is legally 25 per cent, but in the last two years banks have in practice maintained liquidity of 45 per cent or so in their aggregate deposits. Some, e.g., those without a local deposits base, have been at the bottom of this range. Liquid assets are defined as gold, foreign exchange and demand deposits held with other banks or financial institutions.

Additionally, the banks' monthly average of primary liquid assets must not be less than 15 per cent of their demand deposit liabilities as at the last day of the previous month.

Liquidity in the banking system is affected by savers' high propensity to hoard liquid assets such as bullion and notes and coins. Changes in the amount of such hoarding influences both liquidity and interest rates.

Interest rates are influenced by the Exchange Banks Association (EBA) which is an interest-rate cartel operated by the licensed banks. The EBA is theoretically a voluntary organization but in practice requires all banks to join so that no one bank is able to compete for deposits by offering more competitive rates than those set by the EBA. The system evolved in the mid-1960s following a major banking crisis during which Hong Kong's largest Chinese bank nearly went into liquidation but was rescued by the Hongkong and Shanghai Bank in return for a controlling equity stake. The EBA interest rate agreement has been defended by its proponents as a safeguard preventing cutthroat competition and recurring bank crises. The constraints placed by the EBA on interest rate competition vary, but the power of the Hongkong and Shanghai Bank over its competitors (together with its subsidiary the Hang Seng Bank it accounts for over 70 per cent of all deposits) has resulted in arguments—mainly from US banks—that the EBA interest rate agreement has been working to the detriment of competition. In late 1978 and 1979 there was much agitation about the so-called interest-rate inversion, when interbank rates were substantially above prime lending rate. Prime rates are theoretically not subject to EBA regulations which only relates to deposit rates but are in practice determined by the rates set by the Hongkong and Shanghai Bank and the second largest bank, Chartered Bank. Other banks consequently complained that the interest-rate inversion (i.e., paying more for deposits than they were charging to lend) meant that (i) the Hongkong and Shanghai and Chartered Banks would collect cheap deposits, (ii) the two major banks would set a prime rate that suited them irrespective of its effect on the rest of the banking industry and (iii) charge above prime rate on interbank lending. These three factors would make it impossible for banks without large deposit bases to compete effectively with prime-based loan rates of the two major banks.

The government was also unhappy that the prime rate charged by the Hongkong and Shanghai and Chartered Banks was not high enough to discourage rapid credit expansion—which the authorities wished to do—in order to slow down inflation. Since the government has consistently abstained from controlling the money supply either directly or indirectly by exchange rate mechanisms or other controls, interest-rate policy has been its only available tool. The banks' commercial interests have, however, been at variance with the government's monetary objectives, and the government is now seeking to have a direct and openly recognized say in the setting of interest rates. The EBA is therefore to be incorporated as a statutory body, possibly with government representation, taking a direct participation in formulating interest-rate policy.

Withholding taxes

Interest

All interest arising from investments in Hong Kong is subject to a tax of 15 per cent which is deducted at source. This tax cannot be claimed back or offset by the non-resident investor since Hong Kong has no tax treaties with foreign countries.

Dividends

There is no withholding tax on dividends arising from investments in Hong Kong securities, but the absence of double taxation agreements means that any non-resident investor investing through Hong Kong would suffer from withholding tax on dividends from foreign equities, certain fixed-interest securities, and certain bank deposits that are levied in their respective countries of origin.

Profits

A 17 per cent profits tax is withheld on transactions in gold and silver, and also on transactions in commodities.

Capital gains arising from transactions in other securities are free of tax.

Exchange controls

Non-resident accounts. Repatriation of funds

Hong Kong is free from all forms of exchange control and there is no requirement to report transfers of funds into or out of Hong Kong. No distinction is made between resident and non-resident accounts. Any person or entity residing in Hong Kong or a non-resident investing in or through Hong Kong can, therefore, do so without any restriction.

Authorities

There being no exchange controls, there is no exchange control authority.

Currency

The currency is the Hong Kong dollar which is allowed to float freely against other currencies. There is no intervention on the part of the authorities in either the spot or forward foreign exchange markets. The Hongkong and Shanghai Bank may very occasionally intervene in the spot market, using the US dollar, in order to smooth out excessive fluctuations. Any bank, financial institution, company or individual may deal in the foreign exchange market with no constraints.

The Exchange Fund, a government department, used to regulate the currency when the Hong Kong dollar was fixed to the pound sterling. It still issues certificates of indebtedness (CIs) in exchange for Hong Kong dollar credits from the banks; these credits are then deposited in the government's accounts at the banks.

23. Japan

General market environment

Japan's short-term money markets, particularly those in call and time deposits, treasury bills and commercial paper, are very active. This is because there is high demand for short-term funds from both the central government and from the company sector. The banks, acting as intermediaries, hold large amounts of treasury bills and lend substantial sums to companies. As a result, they too need to borrow short-term funds in the form of call and time deposits, or through the market in repurchase agreements.

In the capital market, the bond market is the second largest in the world next to the US bond market. It is, however, principally a government and public sector

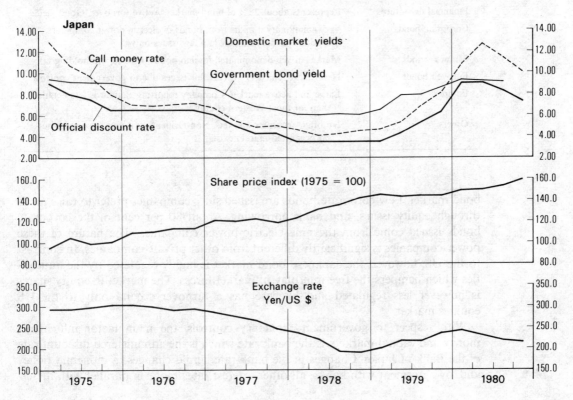

Table 23.1 Summary of instruments

Instrument	Characteristics
MONEY MARKET	
Deposits	
call deposits	Very active market. Yen only. Almost all deposits are made for overnight terms
time deposits	Smaller than call market, but also active
repurchase agreements	A major market between financial institutions. Corporate lenders may also participate
certificates of deposit	New market. First issue made in May 1979. Still underdeveloped but has been expanding rapidly
Treasury bills	Large primary market. Low secondary market turnover. Three types of bills issued
Commercial paper	Active market. Important source of borrowing for companies
CAPITAL MARKET	
Government bonds	Represents about 50% of outstanding bond issues. Very active secondary market
Local government bonds	Small market. Issued on irregular basis
Government guaranteed bonds	Small market compared to government bonds, but active turnover
Financial debentures	Represents about 25% of bond market. Active turnover. Good yields
Corporate bonds	Very small market apart from bonds of electric power companies. Good secondary market in a few issues only
Samurai bonds	Market in yen-denominated foreign bonds. Free of withholding tax
Euroyen bonds	New market since 1977. Very few issues due to government controls
Equities	Large and active market. Company reporting standards less detailed than for most Western countries
Others	No other securities markets. Non-residents may purchase gold, but no organized market exists

bond market. Few corporate bonds are issued since companies prefer to raise funds through equity issues, and bank borrowing. About 80 per cent of the corporate bonds issued come from the nine electric power companies. The nature of these power companies is significantly different from other private companies. In contrast to the US, however, the Japanese bond market is highly regulated by the authorities which hampers the free interplay of market forces. The market in equity shares is however less regulated and likewise has a turnover second only to the US equities market.

With respect to government monetary controls, the main factor influencing money and capital markets is the bank rate which is the administered discount rate of the Bank of Japan. Changes in the bank rate herald changes in monetary policy and, by agreement with banks, all other interest rates move in parallel with it.

The government's attitude to foreign investment in Japan is flexible. At times when the exchange rate is subject to strong upward pressure, non-resident portfolio investment is discouraged. Since the yen weakened during 1979, virtually no restrictions currently apply, but prior to February 1979 non-residents were prohibited from purchasing Japanese securities with maturities of less than five years and one month. Restrictions still exist with respect to the non-resident purchases of Japanese equities but these have been liberalized by new exchange control regulations that became effective on 1 December 1980.

Proceeds from investments may be freely repatriated, but interest and dividends are subject to a withholding tax of 20 per cent which may be reduced for residents of tax-treaty countries.

The money market

Deposits

Call deposits

The market in call money is similar to the US federal funds market in that it is a market in which short-term liquid funds are exchanged between financial institutions. Other non-bank entities, including non-residents, may also participate in the market.

Call money may be placed with a variety of Japanese banks and institutions, but the city banks are the major borrowers absorbing about 80 per cent of all call money.

The nature of the Japanese financial system, in which companies borrow heavily from the commercial banks, means that the banks are normally operating substantial short-term deficits, known as 'overloan'. The call money market is consequently very important in Japan as a means by which banks can borrow in order to balance their overloaned positions. The importance of the call market is indicated by the size of the market. The average daily balance of outstanding call deposits is approximately 3000 billion. Table 23.3 shows liabilities of financial institutions and it can be seen from this that the volume of call money represents about 20 per cent of the total deposits and savings of all banks. Changes in monetary policy and increasing liquidity during the 1970s due to balance of payments surpluses have, to some extent, reduced the banking system's demand for short-term funds. The banks still depend on external short-term financing from the call market, but the wide variety of terms that were once common are now not so readily available. Overnight call loans are the terms most commonly transacted.

Most business is first transacted through one of the six specialized call money dealers, who make two-way quotes and act as intermediaries in the interbank market, but may also deal for their own account.

Until revision of the foreign exchange laws in December 1980 there had been no Eurodollar market in Japan, so the call market is simply a yen market, though a

Table 23.2   Interest rates and yields in Japan's money and capital market, per cent (*source: OECD*)

	1979											
	Jan.	*Feb.*	*Mar.*	*Apr.*	*May*	*Jun.*	*Jul.*	*Aug.*	*Sep.*	*Oct.*	*Nov.*	*Dec.*
MONEY MARKET												
Bank rate	3.50	3.50	3.50	4.25	4.25	4.25	5.25	5.25	5.25	5.25	6.25	6.25
Call deposits	4.29	4.38	4.64	4.89	5.11	5.34	5.80	6.68	6.81	6.74	7.58	8.05
60-day treasury bills	3.39	3.39	3.39	4.15	4.15	4.15	4.15	5.17	5.17	5.17	5.17	5.68
CAPITAL MARKET												
Central government bonds	6.11	6.37	6.95	9.66	7.75	8.01	7.75	7.92	7.86	8.41	8.76	8.64
Public corporation bonds	6.26	6.29	6.79	7.33	7.35	7.85	7.62	7.71	7.79	8.18	8.64	8.67
Local government bonds	6.31	6.35	6.86	7.37	7.37	7.81	7.57	7.68	7.71	8.05	8.53	8.52
Nippon Telegraph & Telephone	6.61	6.78	6.95	7.47	7.49	8.01	7.12	7.67	7.78	8.38	8.73	8.61
Corporate bonds	7.25	7.28	7.65	8.04	8.07	8.35	8.11	8.08	8.08	8.30	8.63	8.57
Bank debentures	5.31	5.41	6.24	7.01	7.03	7.56	7.27	7.66	7.07	8.25	8.65	8.63
Equity shares yield	1.30	1.32	1.34	1.37	1.40	1.46	1.47	1.44	1.41	1.49	1.54	1.50

	1980											
	Jan.	*Feb.*	*Mar.*	*Apr.*	*May*	*Jun.*	*Jul.*	*Aug.*	*Sep.*	*Oct.*	*Nov.*	*Dec.*
MONEY MARKET												
Bank rate	6.25	7.25	9.00	9.00	9.00	9.00	9.00	8.25	8.25	8.25	7.25	7.25
Call deposits	8.06	8.74	10.73	12.21	12.56	12.64	12.70	12.09	11.40	11.04	9.50	9.49
60-day treasury bills	5.68	5.68	5.68	6.82	6.82	6.82	6.82	6.82	6.44	6.44	5.93	5.93
CAPITAL MARKET												
Central government bonds	8.50	9.32	10.00	10.30	8.75	8.61	8.88	9.09	9.21	8.99	9.52	9.41
Public corporation bonds	8.64	9.61	11.63	12.20	10.11	9.01	9.34	9.71	9.87	9.75	9.97	10.01
Local government bonds	8.43	9.33	11.15	11.78	9.92	8.89	9.22	9.56	9.73	9.57	9.77	9.84
Nippon Telegraph & Telephone	8.48	8.57	9.41	10.00	9.25	8.59	8.70	8.84	8.94	8.92	9.21	9.21
Corporate bonds	8.50	8.98	10.10	10.25	9.08	8.42	8.63	8.80	8.87	8.82	8.93	8.94
Bank debentures	8.48	9.63	11.73	11.99	9.66	8.78	9.30	9.67	9.91	9.59	9.77	9.80
Equity shares yield	1.47	1.47	1.53	1.53	1.55	1.49	1.50	1.48	1.46	1.46	1.46	1.46

highly active one. The new regulations allow Japanese securities houses and money-brokers to deal in foreign exchange and to bid for foreign currency deposits, but growth of a currency deposit market is proceeding with caution. Yen interest rates depend on liquidity in the banking system and although, in theory, they correlate with the discount rate set by the Bank of Japan, call rates are normally higher than the discount rate. They may fluctuate significantly from the official discount rate and when liquidity conditions are tight, may be higher even than long-term interest rates. The attractive returns to lenders of call money has to some extent hampered the development of the markets in treasury bills and bonds where yields are usually lower. The main reason for the establishment of the discount market was to limit the use of call money to short-term transactions. In the past, many investors left money on deposit for long periods in the form of unconditional loans which receive the overnight call interest rate but can be continued for indefinite periods. Table 23.2 shows interest rates and secondary market yields in the money and capital markets during 1978 and 1979. Although these figures are period averages and thus smooth out excessive fluctuations in the call rate, they clearly show that call rates are often higher than longer-term fixed interest yields. At one time there were five types of call loans:

Half-day loans	morning loans, repayable in the afternoon
Overnight loans	repayable the following day
Two- and seven-day loans	short loans of fixed maturity
Unconditional loans	unconditional for two days and thereafter subject to one day's notice at the call of either party
'Over-the-month' loans	subject to one day's notice as from a certain day of the following month

Since 1972 mostly overnight, two- and seven-day loans have been negotiated due partly to the banking system's recently improved liquidity and partly due to directives from the government in order to encourage the development of the treasury bill market.

Overnight loans are made for 24-hour periods and repaid before 1 p.m. the following day. Two- and seven-day loans are also repaid before 1 p.m. on the day of maturity.

Unconditional loans are still negotiated but the banks tend to recourse to this type of loan only when liquidity conditions are particularly tight and are likely to remain so for some time. Interest on all loans is calculated according to a 365-day year.

All call money is secured by specified collateral such as Government securities, local authority bonds and eligible bills. Normal transaction size is 500 million to 1000 million yen. Small local savings banks may accept deposits as small as 10 million yen, but large city banks may expect minimum sizes of 3000 million yen. In the interbank market, the spread between bid and offer rates (the turn made by dealers) is about $\frac{1}{4}$ per cent. Like the US Federal funds market, an increasing number of call loans are being made in the form of repurchase agreements.

Time deposits

The market for time deposits is active and the average outstanding balance of time deposits was approximately ¥90 000 billion in 1979. Deposits may be placed with commercial banks and other financial institutions such as savings banks and long-term credit banks. There are four types of time deposits accepted by commercial banks, for terms of three or six months and one or two years. Two years is the maximum term deposit that commercial banks are permitted to accept. Other institutions, such as the trust banks and long-term credit banks, accept deposits of longer maturity. However, six-month and one-year deposits are the most frequently placed terms. The city banks accept any size of time deposit but preferred minimum amounts are 100 000 yen. Time deposits are also secured against specified assets. Interest is calculated on the basis of a 365-day year and is normally two or three

499

points higher than the official discount rate, though they may often be lower than call market rates when liquidity is tight and banks are bidding competitively in the market for short-term funds.

Gensaki market (*repurchase agreements*)

Much call money is negotiated through the Gensaki market in the form of repurchase agreements (RPs), where a lender of funds buys securities from the borrower who agrees to repurchase them on a specified date at an agreed price. The price at which the securities are later repurchased is the price of the original transaction plus some consideration for interest commensurate with interest rates on time deposits of comparable maturity. Many RPs are made for as short a period as overnight but may be made for up to six months. The Bank of Japan undertakes RPs for one-month terms with the commercial banks. RPs are negotiated between the usual suppliers of funds on the one hand, namely companies, government, employees, mutual aid associations and postal life insurance, and the usual borrowers on the other hand, namely banks, securities companies and commercial companies.

Securities offered in repurchase agreements are normally government bonds and short-term paper. The volume of RP transactions is now so significant that it accounts for more than 50 per cent of total bond turnover. Consequently, it is an extremely important sector of the Japan money market.

The Japanese Securities Dealers Association publishes yields on RPs together with a Gensaki index, in accordance with a formula used for publication of quotes on representative issues in the over-the-counter market.

RP prices are fixed according to the median of the highest and lowest call money or time-deposit rates quoted on the day the RP is transacted.

Certificates of deposit

CDs represent a new market in Japan, the first issue having been made by city banks in May 1979. CDs are issued on a tap basis with three months maturity in minimum amounts of 25 million yen. The market has expanded rapidly during 1980, since when it has provided corporations with a useful additional instrument in which to invest their short-term surplus funds. The volume of issues outstanding has grown to about ¥1000 billion or more, so prospects for an active primary market are encouraging. During 1980 an active secondary market has likewise developed. Turnover is now sometimes quite substantial such that CDs are becoming a significant part of the short-term money market.

Treasury bills

Treasury bills are issued by the Bank of Japan on behalf of the treasury to fund its short-term debt requirements. The volume of new issues has risen substantially during the 1970s as the government has significantly increased its public spending programme. The bills are issued on a weekly subscription basis for terms of 60 days in denominations ranging from 1 million to 500 million yen. Treasury bills are registered securities and command yields below all other money market instruments, including call deposits and commercial bills, because of their greater security. This however has restricted the growth of the treasury bill market, as investor interest is concentrated in the higher-yield sectors of the short-term money market.

Funds raised through the issue of treasury bills are designated for specific purposes and in the government's annual budget (diet) a limit is announced for the maximum amount of each type of bill outstanding for the current fiscal year. Thus, treasury bills are issued to cover general short-term government expenditure; food bills are issued to pay for rice and are thus more prolific at harvest time in July; and foreign exchange bills are issued to cover temporary cash shortages in the foreign exchange special account that arise from net purchases of foreign exchange. Food bills and foreign exchange bills are classified as short-term government guaranteed bonds, but in method of issue and type of market they are identical to treasury bills.

Primary market

In the primary market, the government decides on the appropriate volume of issue for the week on the basis of the amount of funds demanded by the issuing account (e.g., food account). Details are then announced each Friday with respect to the type of bill to be issued, the amount, the discount rate attached to the bill, and the issue and redemption dates. The bills may be issued on Monday, Wednesday or Friday.

Subscriptions are then invited from the public who normally apply for between 5 and 12 per cent of the issue, while the Bank of Japan automatically subscribes to the remaining portion.

Subscribers are designated by the Bank of Japan. They include banks, credit associations, insurance companies, money dealers and securities companies.

Private companies and individuals may subscribe through one of the securities companies.

Secondary market

Due to their low yields, treasury bills do not enjoy an active turnover in the secondary market. Most are held to maturity by the original subscribers or used in repurchase agreements.

Commercial bills

Commercial bills are time drafts drawn on a bank by its customers and accepted by a bank, or drawn by banks themselves on customers' bills that have already been accepted. They are thus similar to US bankers' acceptances.

They were issued originally to finance trade or commerce, but since 1971 a secondary market has been established in commercial bills. This market is used as an alternative to the call money market and the participants are the same in both markets. The supply and demand relationships are similar and yields on bills (which are issued at a discount) are comparable with interest rates on call money.

The bill market is used by the Bank of Japan for its open market operations, and some bills are eligible for rediscounting by the commercial banks and discount houses with the Bank of Japan.

501

Eligible bills must be domestic paper only, which thus excludes import or export bills, and must relate to specific trade transactions which also excludes finance paper. In order to be eligible for discounting, the bills must also have a maturity of less than three months but more than two months. Bills are issued in varying amounts from a minimum of about 250 million yen and with maturities of up to six months.

Commercial paper

Commercial paper is short-term promissory notes issued by large corporations to provide them with additional temporary liquidity.

Issues of short-term paper, along with short-term bank borrowings, are an important source of finance for Japanese companies, which tend to be very highly geared. Commonly, more than 80 per cent of their capital comprises short- and long-term borrowing. Since the corporate bond market is subject to restrictive regulations, companies seek recourse to the short-term markets through bank borrowing or commercial paper issues. Such paper may be unsecured or secured by time deposits, bank guarantees, or other current or fixed assets. Credit may be extended for longer periods by repeated rollover of short-term debt.

Commercial paper is issued in amounts of about 2.5 billion yen for terms of 90 or 120 days. Interest, on a coupon basis, is calculated according to interbank time deposit rates and varies from a few basis points to several percentage points higher, depending on the credit rating of the issuing company and on the type of security

Table 23.3 Liabilities of financial institutions (*source: Fuji Bank Bulletin*)

Financial institution	Feb. 1979 ¥ billion	Feb. 1980 ¥ billion
All banks		
deposits and savings	127 283	137 905
CDs	....	1 526
bank debentures issued	17 473	18 641
trust accounts	34 087	38 158
Mutual loan and savings banks		
deposits and savings	21 687	24 053
CDs	....	66
Credit associations		
deposits and savings	27 324	30 706
CDs	....	10
Agricultural co-operatives		
deposits and savings	21 836	
Life insurance companies		
deposits and savings	19 065	
Trust fund bureau		
deposits and savings	72 556	84 015
Postal life insurance and annuity		
deposits and savings	11 084	12 938
Total all institutions		
deposits and savings	300 835	291 219
CDs		

by which the issue is backed. Commercial paper is purchased mainly by banks and companies which generally hold the notes to maturity. Secondary market trading is therefore thin.

The capital market

Next to the American bond market, in terms of new issue volume the Japanese market is the largest in the world. The majority of bonds are issued by the government, local governments (semi governmental organizations), municipalities and banks. Private placements comprise a fairly large share of the market (about 30 per cent), while corporate bonds represent but a small proportion—about five per cent.

The size of the market grew rapidly during the 1970s, due largely to the enormous increase in the central government's financing requirements. By the end of the decade, government bonds represented half of all new issues compared to about one-third at the beginning.

Central government, together with local government and the specialized long-term credit banks, account for about 92 per cent of new bond issues in the Tokyo market.

The secondary market is active, but closely regulated by the authorities, which inhibits the free play of market forces. About 50 per cent of the turnover is represented by the Gensaki market, or the market for repurchase agreements.

For non-residents, the attractiveness of the Japanese bond market is reduced by the 20 per cent withholding tax on interest for most types of bonds, except those issued at a discount from par.

Japanese yields are calculated on a different basis from that employed in most other financial markets (i.e. interest is not compounded in the same way) so for strict comparison it is advisable to recalculate a stated bond yield.

The following example shows how yield computations differ.

Assume a bond with seven years to maturity, a coupon of 6.1 per cent payable semiannually, a current price of 83.9 yen and a par value of 100 yen.

a. Japanese method

$$\text{Yield} = \text{annualized appreciation} + \text{current yield}$$

where

$$\text{Annualized appreciation} = \frac{\text{par} - \text{current price}}{\text{years to maturity}} \times \frac{100\%}{\text{current price}}$$

$$\text{Current yield} = \frac{\text{coupon rate}}{\text{current price}} \times 100\%$$

therefore

$$\text{Yield} = \left[\frac{100 - 83.9}{7} \times \frac{100\%}{83.9} \right] + \frac{6.1 \times 100\%}{83.9}$$

$$= 2.74\% + 7.27\%$$

$$= 10.01\%$$

b. Method used in other markets

The usual formula takes account of the accrued interest accumulated between coupon dates. The yield is found by solving the following formula for i using an iterative process.

$$P = A \times \left[\frac{1 - (1 + i)^{-n}}{i} \right] + \frac{100}{(1 + i)^n}$$

where P = current price
A = semiannual interest payments
n = number of coupon payment periods to redemption

From this formula, the yield i is found to be approximately 9.28 per cent.

Clearly the Japanese method results in a higher figure which the investor should be aware of when taking decisions on a yield basis.

Government bonds

Apart from the short-term government guaranteed bonds, which are issued by the same method and with the same terms as treasury bills, the state issues longer-term bonds with maturities of 1, 3, 5 and 10 years. The amount of bonds issued annually depends on the requirements for public works, public capital investments and government loans, but usually they represent about 50 per cent of total new issues and of bonds outstanding. Generally, individual issues may be for up to 1200 billion yen. Issues are made monthly in amounts determined in advance and announced in the government's annual budget.

Government bonds are issued in minimum denominations of ¥100 000 (though sometimes ¥1 000 000), and usually carry semiannual coupon dates, though some only pay interest annually. Most bonds are coupon bearing, but some with a life of less than five years may be issued at a discount. Interest is calculated according to a 365-day year. Yields on government bonds are comparable with yields obtainable on other bonds, including good quality corporate bonds.

Capital is generally repaid in full at maturity.

Local government bonds

Local government bonds are issued by prefectures, cities, towns and villages in amounts that are determined by their autonomous local budgets. They are thus not issued on a regular basis but as requirements for funds arise and represent only 4.3 per cent of bonds outstanding. If private placements are included the proportion of outstanding bonds is over 15 per cent. Like government bonds, they are issued with maturities of between 1 and 10 years, are normally coupon bearing, mostly pay interest semiannually, and redeem capital fully at maturity. Minimum denominations are 100 000 yen. Principal and interest are fully guaranteed by government. Yields are about 0.15 to 0.3 per cent above government bond yields.

Government guaranteed bonds

Bonds in this category are issued by the specialized long-term credit banks which grant loans of 5 to 15 years to industry, commerce and agriculture. Such banks are the Industrial Bank of Japan, Nippon Credit Bank, Bank of Tokyo, Norinchuki Bank (Central Bank for Agriculture and Forestry) and Shoko Chukin Bank (the Central Bank for Commerce and Industry).

These bonds are known as government guaranteed bonds since they are guaranteed as to principal and interest by the government but require the resolution of the local assembly and the approval of the Minister of Home Affairs prior to issue. They are issued on an irregular basis and constitute about 9.5 per cent of the market (or 21.8 per cent including private placements).

Government guaranteed bonds are coupon bearing with maturities of up to 10 years and in minimum denominations of ¥100 000 and upwards. Interest is paid both annually and semiannually and capital is redeemed in full at maturity. Yields are about 25 per cent greater than government bond yields.

Bonds issued by public corporations, semigovernmental corporations and special corporations are also government guaranteed to the amount specified annually in the government diet (budget). They are a subgroup of government-related organization bonds.

Financial debentures

Financial debentures are issued by long-term credit banks and certain other banks. The bonds are secured against the general assets of the issuing bank which must additionally meet certain minimum requirements. These bonds are known as financial debentures because they are borrowing for general funding purposes and not secured against specific assets. All debt instruments that are secured against specific assets are known as bonds. Financial debentures are, however, similar in all other respects to corporate bonds. They have maturities of from 1 to 10 years. Longer issues are coupon bearing while those of five years or less may be discount bearing. Most pay interest semiannually and repay capital at maturity. Denominations are in minimum amounts of ¥100 000 and upwards. Financial debentures comprise about 25 per cent of the bond market and yield approximately 0.45 per cent more than government bonds.

Corporate bonds

Corporate bonds, known as industrial bonds, comprise private placements and publicly issued, straight, or convertible bonds. Private placements constitute about 30 per cent of the total bond market but have very restricted marketability—most being held to maturity which is normally less than five years.

Of the publicly issued corporate bonds, straight bonds are more frequently issued and represent about 10 per cent of the total bond market, while convertible bonds account for only one per cent.

Corporate bonds, however, account for only about five per cent of new issues because bond market regulations allow companies to issue bonds only if secured

505

against mortgage collateral or bank guarantees. Since 1979 companies have been allowed to issue unsecured bonds, but only large, highly creditworthy companies may do so. Additionally, the bond market is closely monitored and controlled by the authorities. This not only restricts the interaction of market demand and supply necessary for an efficiently operating bond market, but also increases the costs charged to companies for bond issues. Consequently, companies more usually raise capital through the equity market, bank borrowing, or the issue of bonds in foreign capital markets.

The major corporate borrowers in the domestic bond market are the nine electric power companies, Japan Air Lines and Nippon Telegraph and Telephone. The latter two companies are both partly owned by the government. Bonds issued by Nippon Telegraph and Telephone, both in coupon bearing and discount form, are known as subscriber bonds and are the most actively traded of all bonds issued on the domestic capital market. Turnover is approximately ¥4000 billion a year in subscriber bonds, almost all of which is transacted in the over-the-counter market rather than on the stock exchange. By far the highest proportion of this turnover (some 95 per cent) was represented by coupon bearing, rather than discount bonds, although the same volume of each type is normally issued each year.

For some corporate bonds, in particular for Telegraph and Telephone bonds, the amount of the issue need not be specified but can depend on the amount actually taken up or subscribed for. For the majority of issues, however, it is more common that the amount to be issued is announced in advance, but if subscriptions fall short of this amount then the whole issue is invalidated, except if underwritten by a securities company.

Corporate bonds are issued for up to 12 years. Many bonds with maturities of less than five years are issued on a discount basis while longer bonds are issued on a coupon basis, except for Nippon Telegraph which issues discount securities with maturities of $11\frac{1}{2}$ years.

Discount bonds have two special features. Firstly, they do not pay interest at regular intervals but are issued with very large discounts to principal to be redeemed at par. The size of the discount depends, of course, on prevailing interest rate levels at the time of issue. Secondly, they are taxed at issue and are thereafter free of tax so that discount bonds bought in the secondary market are also free of the 20 per cent withholding tax normally payable on interest. Minimum denominations of corporate bonds, both coupon and discount, are ¥50 000 or ¥100 000.

Bond ratings Average yields of corporate bonds are about 0.45 per cent higher than yields on government bonds. However, corporate bonds are graded on a scale from double A to B (i.e., AA, A, BB, B). Gradings are calculated on the basis of a company's net assets, its financial condition and its earnings ratio. The gradings indicate the degree of security of corporate bond issues and result in a yield range of approximately +0.25 to −0.25 per cent of the average rate applicable to corporate bonds. Japanese investors, however, tend to ignore credit ratings, so bond prices may often not fully reflect the different creditability of issuers. It seems the investor considers that if a borrower has fulfilled all the requirements of issuing in the Japanese market then there is an implicit government guarantee behind the bond issue; this, of course, is not the case.

The secondary market in domestic bonds consists mainly of transactions in government and public sector bonds, but is active and very liquid such that it is possible to deal in amounts of up to 500 million yen without upsetting the market. Trading volume is high, mainly because of the thriving 'Gensaki' market whereby bonds, particularly government bonds and financial debentures are used in repurchase agreements. These types of transactions account for about 50 per cent of total bond turnover. Many transactions in the secondary market take place in the over-the-counter market through banks and brokers who maintain their own books and maintain a market in bonds. Most government bonds, Nippon Telegraph and Telephone bonds, and over 20 corporate bonds are also listed and traded on the Tokyo stock exchange, while convertible bonds, where deals are of a size less than 30 million yen, may be traded on the stock exchange only. Consequently, there are about 750 convertible bonds listed on the three major exchanges compared with only about 60 straight corporate bonds.

Traditionally, domestic bonds have been bought by banks and financial institutions, but increasingly individuals are participating in the market. Additionally, foreign corporations, financial institutions and individuals have entered the market since the abolishment in early 1979 of the rule that prohibited non-residents from purchasing domestic bonds with less than five years and one month remaining to maturity. Non-residents tend to favour the discount bonds issued by banks, government, and Nippon Telegraph and Telephone since they are free of withholding tax, having been taxed at issue, but which nevertheless provide attractive yields.

Foreign bonds (samurai bonds)

The market in bonds issued by foreign corporations, international institutions and sovereign states denominated in yen for trading in the domestic market is known as the samurai market. Samurai bonds represent less than 0.5 per cent of the total domestic traded bond market, but nevertheless, in terms of new issues, the samurai market is the fourth largest foreign bond market in the world after Switzerland, the US and West Germany.

International borrowers have been admitted to the domestic bond market since 1970. In the past few years the number of issues has been small and mostly comprised private placements. The market was twice closed completely for new issues. The first time was following the 1973 oil crisis when it was closed for twenty months to public issues and three years for private placement issuers. The second time was for a period of three months during the Japanese foreign exchange crises in 1978.

All issuers of samurai bonds have been international agencies such as the World Bank and Asian Development Bank or foreign governments. The first corporate samurai bond was issued in March 1979 by the American retail company Sears Roebuck. This represented a relaxation of policy on behalf of the regulatory authorities, particularly since this issue was unsecured—a unique situation not only for samurai but also for domestic bonds.

Samurai bonds are issued in both bearer and registered form, but can be freely converted from one form to the other. They are coupon bearing and pay interest semiannually free of withholding tax. Maturities range from 10 to 15 years though a few short-term, five-year issues, have been made.

New issues vary from about ¥350 billion to about ¥850 billion per annum, each individual issue being for ¥15 billion to ¥30 billion. The new issues calendar is closely controlled by the Ministry of Finance and the Bank of Japan to ensure that the issue of foreign bonds does not upset the domestic bond market.

In the primary market, new issues are made exclusively through one of four Japanese securities firms, Nomura, Nikko, Daiwa and Yamaichi. Non-resident investors in total are restricted to purchasing no more than 25 per cent of issued bonds in the primary market. This does not apply in the secondary market where non-residents average about 50 per cent of samurai bondholders. Some Japanese investors consequently are able to profit from taking up new bond issues in the primary market and selling them on to non-resident investors in the secondary market. There are outstanding more than 70 samurai bonds to a value of over ¥1000 billion.

The secondary market too is monitored by the Ministry of Finance, while the Bank of Japan requires that it be informed of all buyers and sellers in the market. The secondary market is an over-the-counter market and most transactions are made between dealers, but activity is not as good as that in domestic bonds. Unlike the domestic bond market, most dealers tend to be either buyers or sellers of samurai bonds and do not normally make two-way quotes. Bond denominations are ¥100 000, though sometimes they may be as high as ¥1 million. Transactions may be made in amounts of up to ¥50 million, or sometimes up to ¥100 million, but sizes larger than that are difficult to trade.

Eurobonds

Yen denominated bonds for trading in the international bond market (Euroyen bonds) were first issued in 1977, but as at December 1980 only some eleven issues have been made, three totalling ¥51.5 billion in 1977, one for ¥15 billion in 1978, two totalling ¥27 billion in 1979 and five in 1980 worth ¥60 billion. The authorities are reluctant to encourage the growth of the Euroyen market for fear of disrupting the domestic bond market on which central government is so reliant as a source of funds. Thus, Euroyen bond issues require the prior approval of the Ministry of Finance.

Primary issues are lead managed by a Japanese bank, but issued through the market in London or, latterly, the Asian dollar bond market in Singapore. Secondary market trading takes place in the major European centres such as London and Luxembourg and the Asian financial centres of Hong Kong and Singapore. Trading, however, is thin and usually in amounts of less than ¥50 billion.

Euroyen bonds have been issued in amounts of 10 to 20 billion yen, mostly at par and bearing annually paid coupons that are free of withholding tax. Maturities have been for 7 to 10 years. All bonds are bearer and triple A rated since issuers are international agencies or first-class corporations.

No market is made in Japan for secondary trading of Eurobonds denominated in other currencies. In contrast to the market in yen denominated Eurobonds, a substantial volume of bond issues have been made by Japanese companies in foreign bond markets, predominantly in Switzerland but also in the US Yankee bond market. Although they are denominated in the local currency of the foreign market many have the special feature of convertibility into shares of the issuing company, denominated in yen. The investor may thus have the benefit of a fixed interest security while having the option to participate in the Japanese equity market and perhaps also to benefit from exchange rate movements.

Equity shares

There is a thriving market in Japanese equity shares. Between one and three hundred companies come to the market each year to raise funds through the issue of shares, and this increases total paid-in capital of the market by between 1 and 10 billion yen per annum. The huge capital value of outstanding issues (about ¥66 000 billion) and the large trading turnover (¥36 498 billion on the Tokyo exchange in 1980) make the Japanese stock market the largest in the world after the New York stock exchange, though trading volume is about half that of New York.

Despite this, the majority of Japanese companies are extremely highly geared. Commonly, less than 20 per cent of their capital is represented by equity, the remainder being mainly in the form of short-term borrowing from the commercial city banks, which in turn often hold shares in the companies to which they lend. Bank lending to companies is a major feature of the Japanese financial system; this has repercussions in other markets, particularly the short-term money markets.

The banks tend to be heavily overloaned and consequently have to seek recourse to the Bank of Japan and to the money market for short-term funds to finance their lending deficits. Other means by which companies raise capital are through the issue of short-term paper (commercial paper) or by long-term borrowing from the long-term credit banks. Many Japanese companies have been reducing their gearing ratios in recent years—a rationalization due to conditions imposed by rising oil prices—and are replacing much of their liabilities by equity or corporate bond issues.

In addition, Japanese companies have only been required to report consolidated accounts since 1977, though accounting standards still remain below those of most other countries with developed financial markets. Reported earnings usually understate the true profitability of companies, and price earnings ratios (P/Es) are consequently apparently high. Cash earnings, defined as earnings plus depreciation, are sometimes used as a more reliable base from which to calculate P/Es that are more directly comparable with other markets. Dividends are paid gross, but are subject to withholding tax. Joint stock companies correspond in structure to, for example, American corporations. A Japanese joint stock company is denoted by the subscript KK (kabushiki kaisha).

Although the Tokyo stock exchange handles more than 80 per cent of trading volume, many shares are unlisted and both quoted and unquoted shares may be traded in the over-the-counter market.

Denominations and methods of trading vary according to type of shares and other factors (see Stock exchange and Dealing and fees sections). In general, shares have par values of 50 yen, and are traded in minimum units (board lots) of 1000 shares respectively. Non-residents are legally required to appoint a standing proxy in Japan to act as resident representative of the shareholder. Securities companies and banks provide this service for a fee.

Non-resident restrictions Although regulations regarding foreign investment in shares of Japanese companies have been significantly liberalized since new exchange controls were introduced on 1 December 1980, specific restrictions still exist. Previously foreign shareholdings in Japanese companies could not, in total, exceed 25 per cent of a company's equity capital. The new rules define Japanese companies according to two categories for foreign investment purposes. Companies may be classified as being in the 'national interest', or strategic, parties and their foreign shareholding thus limited to 25 per cent of their equity capital; or they may be classified as non-strategic companies and thus available to non-resident investors without a defined limit on foreign shareholding. Whichever category a company falls within, no individual foreigner (either private or corporate) is permitted to acquire more than a 10 per cent shareholding as a portfolio investment.

Eleven industries are defined as in the national interest which include traditional industries such as mining, agriculture and leather and others such as nuclear power, electric power, gas, railways, banks, aircraft companies, pharmaceutical industries and oil refineries. (The limit for foreign shareholdings in this last group is 50 per cent of equity capital.)

Other Japanese companies are open to foreign investors and 29 of these (whose foreign shareholding had reached the previous 25 per cent limit) have become newly available with the liberalization of exchange controls. These companies are listed below. The Ministry of Finance however reserves the right, at any time in the future, to designate companies as 'strategic' and to thus restrict foreign purchases.

Shares newly available to foreign investors

Asahi Diamond	Nihon Glass	Teikoku Oxygen
Fuji Machine	Nihon Light Metal	Tao Oil
Fujitsu Fanuc	Nippon Television (NTV)	Tokyo Aluminium
Hokusei Aluminium	Amron Tateishi	Tokyo Electric Engineering
Ikegami Tsushin	Oriental Chain	Tokyo Electron
Isuzu Motor	Osaka Titanium	Tsubakimoto Seiko
Kyowa Hakko	Shimura Kako	Ung Company
Marantz Japan	Sumitomo Cement	Uchida Oil Pressure
Max Company	Sumitomo Rubber	Yamatake Honeywell
Mori Seiki	Iamai Shipping	

Table 23.4 Gross new public issues of securities in Japan's capital market (¥ billion) (*source: Nippon Kangko Kakumaru Securities Co. Ltd, Tokyo Capital Market Report November 1980*)

Securities	1976	1977	1978	1979	Jan.–Oct. 1980
Government bonds	7 049	9 575	10 501	11 228	11 809
Discount government bonds	99	291	290	242	303
Municipal bonds	441	557	697	791	609
Government guaranteed bonds	804	1 035	1 373	1 465	1 268
Government associated organization bonds	160	185	180	105	100
Total government guaranteed bonds	8 553	11 643	13 041	13 831	14 089
Financial debentures	9 437	10 493	11 394	11 837	9 473
Corporate bonds					
Nine electric power companies	843	820	877	1 004	750
Industrial companies	323	421	437	243	134
Convertible bonds	567	163	277	372	71
Total corporate bonds	1 222	1 404	1 591	1 619	955
Foreign bonds (samurai bonds)	62	454	657	333	206
Total bonds	19 274	23 994	26 683	27 620	24 723
Shares					
Financial institutions	165	276	143	82	
Non-financial corporations	934	1 079	1 149	1 369	206
Total shares	1 099	1 355	1 292	1 450	206

* First quarter 1980

Investment trusts

Every type of investment trust is available to investors in the Japanese market. These provide for the spreading of risk by investing in a pool of funds which is reinvested in shares and/or bonds which, according to the type of fund, may be domestic or foreign. Lower-risk unit trusts specialize in bonds and provide income on an interest yield basis. Higher-risk trusts specialize in shares and provide capital growth, while other unit trusts, with a mix of both bonds and shares, offer a moderate share of both income and growth. Shares in the trust funds are quoted and traded on the stock exchange.

The non-resident however can also buy unit and investment trusts in foreign markets (e.g. London and New York) which specialize in Japanese equities.

The stock exchanges

There are stock exchanges in eight cities but the most important exchanges are in Tokyo, Osaka and Nagoya, which handle 83, 13 and 3 per cent respectively of all stock exchange business. The remaining five exchanges handle less than one per

511

cent of total turnover. Each is subject to the Securities and Exchange Law which is administered by the Minister of Finance. These regulations relate to the issue of securities and the operations of the securities companies. Since the war, the stock exchanges have been established as private, non-profit-making companies. Members of a stock exchange must be companies that conduct business in securities. Members are required to subscribe specified minimum amounts of capital.

There are two kinds of members. Regular members are companies whose main activity is the buying and selling of securities on the floor of an exchange, both for their customers and for their own account. Santoris are companies whose main activity as members is to act as intermediaries between the regular members. They have trading posts on the floors of the exchanges from which they deal in specific securities. Effectively, they are like specialists on the New York stock exchange, except that they may not trade for their own accounts.

Certain bonds, particularly government and public sector bonds, plus listed shares are traded on the stock exchanges while other bonds and shares (mostly unlisted shares) are traded on the over-the-counter market (OTC) made by banks and dealers.

First and second sections

Due to this division of market places, the Tokyo and Osaka stock exchanges have established two trading sections. The first trading section handles transactions in listed securities while the second section deals in securities that are newly quoted on an exchange or which are not listed but would otherwise be traded only on the OTC. About 1000 stocks are listed on the first section and over 400 are traded in the second section.

OTC securities are also defined by two categories, registered and subregistered securities. In 1976 Nihon Tento Securities (Japan OTC Trading Company) was established to foster and improve OTC trading in Tokyo.

In terms of volume, share transactions on the stock exchanges are 15 times greater than those through the OTC, while first-section trading is twice the size of second-section trading. In contrast, the volume of bonds traded on the stock exchanges is only one-twentieth of the volume traded on the over-the-counter market.

Two types of trading methods are used on the stock exchanges—the Itayose method, used mainly for bonds, and the Zaraba method, used for shares. The Itayose method is that by which selling orders are matched with buying orders. All orders reaching the floor before the opening of business are treated as simultaneous orders and may not be consummated until, in principle, the following could be executed:

1. all market orders;
2. all orders with price priority over the opening price; and
3. all buy or sell orders at the opening price.

The Zaraba method is an open auction method. Prices are first established at the opening of business by the Itayose method, but there will be many unmatched orders. Other investors then enter the market with further buy or sell orders that are matched as well as possible by open auction. Selling orders at the lowest prices and buying orders at the highest prices take precedence over other orders, and earlier orders take precedence over later orders. A special auction method is held to determine the opening and closing prices of specific shares, usually those of large companies that are widely traded, as designated by the stock exchange. This is the group auction method, whereby competitions are first held among the sellers and buyers and then between both buyers and sellers. Contracts are settled at a price which is close to the highest bid and the lowest offer prices.

Except for government bonds and other selected bonds which include government-guaranteed, local government and samurai bonds, trading is not restricted to the stock exchange. However, transactions in government bonds for deals to the value of more than 1 million yen and less than 10 million yen, plus other selected issues to the value of more than 100 000 yen and less than 10 million yen, must be dealt on the stock exchange. There are two trading sessions per day for these bonds. For all other bonds there is only one daily trading session. The trading sessions are 9 to 11 a.m. and 1 to 3 p.m. Transactions in convertible bonds to the value of less than 30 million yen must also be dealt on the stock exchange. For these the Zaraba method is used.

Government bonds are dealt in lots of ¥1 million and selected issues in lots of ¥100 000. Convertible bonds are dealt in lots of ¥100 000 or ¥500 000 and all other bonds in lots of ¥1 million.

Table 23.5 Stock exchange and over-the-counter transactions (Y billion)
(*source: Fuji Bank Report*)

	1978	1979
Over-the-counter market		
Government bonds—coupon-bearing	5 902	11 964
discount	165	301
Local government bonds	2 215	2 805
Government guaranteed bonds	839	943
Telegraph and telephone bonds	423	468
Bank debentures—coupon-bearing	4 256	3 160
Electric power bonds	521	382
Ordinary corporate bonds	142	113
Others	1 483	1 694
Total bonds	15 946	21 830
Tokyo stock exchange (first section)		
Listed bonds and shares		
volume (1000s of stock)	5 984 707	12 652 626
value (¥ billion)	1 972	3 537
All stock exchanges		
Listed bonds and shares		
volume (1000s of stock)	7 690 000	15 136 000
value (¥ billion)	2 582	4 265

513

Stock price indices

Two stock price indices are commonly used to measure share price movements. Perhaps the more frequently quoted is the Tokyo Stock Exchange (TSE) stock price average. This is calculated by a similar formula, created for the Dow Jones average as used in the United States. Indeed it was originally devised for the TSE by the Dow Jones Company. For this reason it is also referred to as the Nikkei-Dow Jones average. The calculation, made on a daily basis, uses the share prices of 255 companies listed on the first section of the exchange relative to a base of 4 January 1968 = 100. (The all-time high at 30 April 1981 was 7674.) Although the index is adjusted for rights issues and share splits it has several failings as a reliable indicator of total stock market movements. In particular it is only an arithmetic average, so small and large companies are given equal weighting. This means that volatile price movements in the share price of small companies, with a limited number of shares available for trading, can have a disproportionate effect on the index. Additionally, the index includes less than 25 per cent of total shares in the first section. A more recent index, the TSE stock price index, was devised to remedy the defects of the stock price average. This is a weighted average of all the shares listed on the first section of the Tokyo stock exchange. It has been calculated retroactively to have the same base as the stock price average—4 January = 100. It is revised to take account not only of rights and split issues but also of new listings. Subindices are also calculated for groups of small, medium and large companies defined by issued capital, for specified industrial groups and for 300 designated shares that are traded on the second section of the exchange.

Dealing and fees

All securities, whether money market or capital market issues, must be dealt through an authorized securities dealer, all of which are members of the Japan Securities Dealers Association. The four main dealers are Nomura, Nikko, Daiwa and Yamaichi. Dealers do not include the banks, except for transactions involving short-term money market securities. Non-residents may appoint banks to act on their behalf, but the banks must then trade through securities dealers. A non-resident dealing in Japanese shares is legally required to appoint a resident of Japan to act as standing proxy. This service is provided by banks and securities companies, who charge a small fee.

Money market

Deposits

There is no charge for accounts opened by non-residents with Japanese banks. The banks' spread between bid and offer rates for call or time loans and deposits in the interbank market is about $\frac{1}{4}$ per cent.

Certificate of deposits

CDs are issued at about $\frac{1}{4}$ per cent above the Tokyo interbank offer rate. The dealing spread in the secondary market is also about $\frac{1}{4}$ per cent.

Treasury bills

Dealt in discount form. New issue subscriptions must be made through one of the four main securities companies. Secondary market transactions may be made through other dealers, including banks. Dealing spreads are about 0.4 per cent.

Commercial bills

Primary issues are purchased directly from the issuing bank or broker who sells the bills at a discount from par inclusive of profit commission. Secondary transactions may be made through a bank or securities company. Dealing spreads are $\frac{1}{4}$ to $\frac{1}{2}$ per cent.

Commercial paper

Primary issues are subscribed for through a bank or securities company who charge a small fee.

Secondary transactions occur through the same dealers. Dealing spreads may be about $\frac{1}{2}$ per cent.

Capital market bonds

Euroyen bonds are traded in a separate market from domestic bonds. They may be dealt through banks in the major world financial Eurobond centres such as London, New York, Frankfurt, Hong Kong and Singapore. Dealing spreads are about $\frac{1}{2}$ per cent.

Table 23.6 Commission rate per ¥100 on sales and purchases

| Bonds | Value of transaction | | | |
	Up to ¥5 million	¥5 000 001 to ¥10 000 000	¥10 000 001 to ¥100 000 000	Over ¥100 000
Government bonds	0.4%	0.35%	0.3%	0.25%
Selected issues*	0.6%	0.50%	0.4%	0.3%
Other bonds	0.8%	0.65%	0.5%	0.35%

| | Value of transaction | | | | |
	Up to ¥1 million	¥1 million to ¥5 million	¥5 million to ¥10 million	¥10 million to ¥30 million	Over ¥30 million
Convertible bonds	1.2%	1%	0.8%	0.7%	0.6%

* Selected issues are government guaranteed bonds, local government bonds, samurai bonds and others designated by the stock exchange.

Transfer tax, on sale only = 0.3%

Samurai bonds are traded in the same way as domestic bonds. Domestic convertible bonds are dealt in the same way as equity shares, but in lots of either ¥100 000 or ¥500 000. Government bonds and selected issues are dealt in lots of ¥100 000.

All other bonds are dealt in lots of ¥1 million. Commission rates charged by securities companies for transactions on the Tokyo stock exchange are as shown in Table 23.6.

Custody fees

The fees charged by a bank or securities company for custody services are fixed by negotiation but are normally quite small, about 0.1 per cent per annum of the par value of the stock.

Settlement

Settlement and delivery is effected on the third business day after the transaction has taken place. Business days include Saturdays, except for the third Saturday of each month.

Shares

Shares of the major Japanese companies are quoted and dealt on the Tokyo stock exchange. Other shares may be dealt only in the over-the-counter market. Commissions may be slightly higher for OTC traded shares, but are based on stock exchange commission rates as shown in Table 23.7.

Shares traded in the first section on the stock exchange are dealt in lots of 1000 for shares of ¥50 par value and lots of 100 for shares of ¥500 par value.

Shares traded in the second section on the stock exchange are dealt in lots of 500 for shares of ¥50 par value and lots of 100 for shares of ¥500 par value.

Smaller amounts may be dealt on a renegotiated basis, but the transaction may take several days to complete.

Table 23.7 Commision on purchases and sales of shares

Value of transaction	Commission
Small transactions	(minimum) ¥2 500
Up to ¥1 000 000	1.25%
¥1 000 001 to ¥3 000 000	1.05% + ¥2 000
¥3 000 001 to ¥5 000 000	0.95% + ¥5 000
¥5 000 001 to ¥10 000 000	0.85% + ¥10 000
¥10 000 001 to ¥30 000 000	0.75% + ¥20 000
¥30 000 001 to ¥50 000 000	0.65% + ¥50 000
¥50 000 001 to ¥100 000 000	0.60% + ¥75 000
Over ¥100 000 000	0.55% + ¥125 000
Transfer tax on sale only of shares	0.45% of transaction value

Custody fees

Custody fees charged by a bank are by negotiation, but usually small, in the region of 0.1 per cent per annum of the par value of the shares held.

Standing proxy fees

Fees charged by a securities company for the services of standing proxy, which a non-resident is legally required to appoint, are ¥1000 per shareholding +¥0.1 per share, subject to a minimum of ¥5000 and a maximum of ¥100 000.

Fees charged by a bank for standing proxy services are likely to be higher than those charged by a securities company.

Settlement

Settlement and delivery may occur in one of four ways.

Regular way trans- actions

These are the terms on which the majority of transactions are settled. Orders are settled through the clearing department of the stock exchange with delivery and settlement occurring on the third business day following the transaction. Business days include Saturdays except for the third Saturday of each month.

Cash trans- actions

Some deals may be settled with delivery and cash payment made on the same day on which the transaction is made, or may be postponed to the following business day if agreed with both parties.

This type of settlement is made through the clearing department of the stock exchange, and also through the over-the-counter market.

Special agreement

This method is now seldom used. It is a facility originally provided for customers located in remote places, but modern communications negate the need for such a facility. Such transactions are settled on a fixed date, within 14 days from the contract.

When issued

This is the method used for new issues which are settled and delivered on a day designated by the stock exchange, usually the day after the issue is made.

Margin trans- actions

A further method of dealing was introduced in 1951, but is prohibited for non-residents. This is the method of margin transactions. Modelled on the US system, it is the method by which sales and purchases of shares and bonds may be made by putting up only a fraction of the full cost. Effectively, securities companies extend credit or lend shares to customers to enable them to settle the transaction. Securities so dealt must usually be listed as eligible for margin transactions. Minimum margin amounts are ¥300 000 to ¥500 000, but there are restrictions on short sales. Settlement and delivery occurs on the third business day following the transaction.

Financial and monetary systems

Financial institutions

Commercial banks

The major financial institutions in Japan are the commercial banks which play an important role in the finance of commerce and industry and rely heavily on the Bank of Japan and the money market as sources of finance.

The commercial banks, known as 'ordinary' banks, are classified into city banks and local banks. There are 13 city banks, so called because they are located in the large commercial cities, and these account for almost half of all banking business in Japan. One of the city banks, the Bank of Tokyo, specializes in foreign exchange transactions only, although other banks also deal in foreign exchange. All commercial banks operate in the foreign exchange market as part of their normal services. There are more than 60 local banks, each of which is located in a separate prefecture and which provides banking services to local business and commerce as well as to individuals.

The commercial banks are limited in their activities to the receipt of sight and time deposits (of two year maximum maturity), extension of loans and advances (both short and long term), the discounting of bills, foreign exchange transactions and certain other retail services.

Japanese companies rely to a significant degree on loans from the commercial banks. They borrow heavily from the banks, which in turn often hold equity participation in the companies to which they lend. Japanese companies are highly geared, having perhaps 80 per cent of their capital in the form of borrowing, a large proportion of which is short-term borrowing from commercial banks, principally the city banks.

As a result, the commercial banks carry substantially overextended credit, a position known as 'overloan'. This results in them similarly being dependent on external sources of funds, particularly from the money market and the Bank of Japan. This facilitates particularly active call money and Gensaki markets and also dictates the emphasis of monetary policy which is principally controlled by manipulation of the discount rate coupled with discount quotas.

Foreign banks

In addition to the domestic commercial banks, there are more than 40 foreign commercial banks. The Japanese banking regulations restrict their activities with respect to the number of branch offices they may establish and to the direction of their lending.

Long-term credit banks

Since the commercial banks are limited by regulation to the provision of mainly short-term loans and advances, three privately owned specialized institutions concentrate their activities on the provision of medium- and long-term loans of up to

20 years. These are the long-term credit banks. Their operations influence the capital market which they tap for funds through the issue of debentures, though they are also active in the market for call and time deposits.

Trust banks

In addition, seven trust banks, also privately owned, and three commercial banks with trust departments, provide financial and management services to industry as well as advancing long-term credit. They raise capital through the issue of trust certificates which are essentially non-marketable certificates of deposit with longer maturities than available from commercial banks.

Mutual loan, savings and credit banks

More than seventy privately owned mutual loan and savings banks exist to provide short- and longer-term finance to small businesses, raising most of their funds by accepting household savings deposits. They do not operate extensive branch networks but many of these banks are equivalent in size to local commercial banks and some also provide retail banking services. Also included in this category are a large number of credit associations, credit co-operatives and labour credit associations. The first two extend credit to small enterprises, which tend to be smaller business concerns than the customers of mutual loan and savings banks. The third group provide loans to labour organizations and their members. All three groups raise funds from savings deposits while some also offer chequing account facilities.

For each group, including mutual loan and savings banks, a central organization (federation) acts to coordinate their specialized operations.

One of the major federations in the semipublic Central Bank for Commercial and Industrial Co-operatives (Shoko Chukin Bank). The balance of shares not owned by the government are held by small co-operatives. The bank obtains funds by the acceptance of time deposits and by the issue of debentures, and relends money to its shareholders and to their members.

Additionally in the private sector, specialized credit institutions exist to finance agriculture, forestry and fishing. Each group likewise has a central federation. The superior federation for all three groups is the Central Co-operative Bank for Agriculture and Forestry (Norinchukin Bank) which acts as a source of finance to all co-operatives in this category, supplementary to finance derived from savings and sight deposits.

Public sector financial institutions

The government plays an important role in the collection of savings and the provision of finance to industry. Individual savings are collected through the postal savings companies and the government life insurance systems, and then passed on to several government owned credit institutions, particularly the Japan Development Bank, the Export-Import Bank of Japan and other public finance organizations for the provision of funds to small businesses, housing and overseas ventures.

519

These public institutions supplement this source of funds by the issue of bonds in the capital market. Such bonds are directly guaranteed by the government.

Bank of Japan

The central bank, the Bank of Japan, is a capital structured company which is wholly owned by the government. The Bank's board comprises the governor of the Bank, two non-voting government representatives, plus representatives from the city and local banks, industry, commerce and agriculture.

The Bank is the sole issuer of notes and coins, regulator of the banking system, enforcer of exchange control regulations and instrument of the government in the implementation of monetary policy.

With respect to this latter function, the Bank is not under the direct control of the government, but the two work in close co-operation. The Minister of Finance may issue general directives, but policy is determined principally by the board. The Bank is responsible for all policy instruments, except for changes in the reserve ratio for which approval from the Minister of Finance is first required.

Monetary policy

The objectives of the Bank of Japan's monetary policy are the regulation of the currency and the control of credit and finance pursuant to national policy. It is the government's intention to keep a tight rein on credit expansion to prevent fuelling inflation or depreciation of the yen. The major tools are informal controls over lending by the major commercial banks, supplemented by interest-rate manipulation through use of discount-rate policy. Reserve requirements are imposed, but while used as a flexible instrument are a somewhat ineffective tool. Credit ceilings (in conjunction with credit controls and discount policy) and open market operations are also used, but to limited effect.

Discount policy

Central bank lending assumes the form of the rediscounting of commercial bills and other eligible securities or advances against specified securities.

Three official discount rates are operated in Japan—the main rate, known as bank rate, is that at which the Bank of Japan will rediscount eligible commercial bills. The other two are advance rather than discount rates since they are charges made by the Bank of Japan for credit against specified securities: the second rate (normally the same as bank rate) is that at which the Bank of Japan will lend against the security of government bonds, bills of the same quality such as bank accepted commercial bills and other specially designated securities; the third rate (0.25 per cent higher than bank rate) is the one at which the Bank of Japan will lend against other securities not eligible for the second rate.

Banks and other financial institutions, including the mutual loan and savings associations, major credit institutions, Shoko Chukin and Norinchukin banks, securities finance companies, call loan dealers, large securities companies and foreign banks, are all provided the facility to borrow from the central bank. They are prescribed ceilings, however, on the amount of credit they may obtain from the Bank of Japan in this way. The bank will not normally lend in excess of these limits but when it does so, the borrowing bank or financial institution is charged a penal rate of interest of four per cent over bank rate on borrowings in excess of its ceiling.

Credit ceilings are not a very effective tool since they are not backed by legislation, and thus may only be enforced on those banks that are in debt to the Bank of Japan. These are normally the city banks and the long-term credit banks. If they are approaching their credit ceilings, they tend first to borrow in the call money or Gensaki markets, which has the effect of pushing up short-term interest rates.

By agreement between the banking system and the Bank of Japan, other short-term lending rates move in parallel with the official discount rate (bank rate). Changing bank rate is the most powerful policy tool available to the Bank of Japan. Central bank credit is a necessary source of funds for the commercial banks and long-term credit banks since they lend substantial funds to companies such that they are permanently in an overloaned position. If domestic credit is expanding too quickly, a rise in bank rate increases lending rates to businesses and effectively reduces loan demand. Because of tight liquidity in the banking system caused by 'overloan', this mechanism has traditionally been very responsive. During the early 1970s due to the persistent and large balance of payments surplus, money supply increased dramatically, and liquidity in the banking system eased considerably. Discount policy became less effective as existing liquidity reduced the banks' requirement to seek recourse to the Bank of Japan's discount window. From 1973 onward, discount policy was supplemented to a greater degree by the use of reserve policy and quantitive controls.

Since 1979, Japan's balance of payments surplus has been gradually eroded, primarily because of the country's total dependence on imported oil.

Liquidity in the banking system has consequently tightened and changes in bank rate once again are having a more immediate effect on credit expansion.

Qualitative and quantitive controls

The Bank of Japan uses moral suasion to impose quantitive controls on bank lending. This is a method known as 'window guidance' whereby the Bank of Japan grants credit facilities to the commercial banks, long-term credit banks and other financial institutions at the discount windows, provided that the banks in turn undertake to control their lending. Window guidance has been used since 1974 and is particularly designed to curb speculative lending. It is thus a qualitative control by which banks are requested to limit loans to specified purposes. Additionally, quantitive directives may be issued. These have greatest effect on the city banks who may be requested to contain the increase in their loans within specific limits. This may have the effect of raising interest rates in both the money and capital markets since companies either bid for short-term funds in the money market or sell securities in the capital market in order to raise required funds.

Since 1978, banks and other financial institutions have been required to submit their lending programmes to the Bank of Japan, which may intervene if necessary to reduce the volume of loans or change the direction of credit.

521

According to reports by the Bank of Japan, it appears probable that these methods of quantitive controls will assume greater importance and may succeed discount policy·as the major method of intervention, and it is assumed that direct controls on credit expansion will have greater effect in containing the growth of the money supply and consequently to slow the growth of inflation.

Reserve ratios

Although the Bank of Japan may recommend changes in the banks' ratios, it requires the prior approval of the Minister of Finance.

Traditionally reserve ratios have been used very little because of the banking system's tendency to 'overloan'. This means that the banks have very few matched assets. Consequently up until 1971, although the reserve requirement was set at 10 per cent, this limit was never approached but was on average about two per cent of deposits. Reserves were required to be held in cash, interest-free at the Bank of Japan, and they applied to commercial banks, long-term credit banks and trust banks.

In 1971 the reserve ratios widened to apply to a proportion of bank debentures and fiduciary accounts as well as to deposits, and the maximum ratio was increased to 20 per cent. Since then, minimum reserve ratios have been changed by the authorities, so as to be consistent with the rest of the government's monetary policy, but have had little influence on bank lending.

The reserve ratio was adjusted many times between 1973 and 1975 as a supplement to discount policy when the latter was proving less effective during a period of excessive monetary expansion. They did have the required effect of restricting credit expansion but as conditions eased, the authorities reverted to primary use of discount policy independent of reserve policy.

Open market operations

Open market operations are used but, by themselves, do not significantly influence credit expansion. This is because the capital market, being hampered by regulations, is not a perfect market.

Open market operations increased significantly during the 1970s, and take the form of government bond issues and sales or purchases of bonds through repurchase agreements.

The fact that the Gensaki market now accounts for about 50 per cent of bond turnover is due largely to the Bank of Japan's increasing use of open market operations. The Bank's main purpose is to smooth out excessive volatility in the money market and fluctuations in the banking system's liquidity when such movements are only temporary and do not require changes in bank rate.

Thus, when the Bank wishes to absorb funds from the system it arranges repurchase agreements, and when it wishes to add funds it transacts reverse RPs.

Withholding taxes

Withholding taxes applied to Japanese-source interest and dividends constitute a major factor that discourages greater foreign investment in Japanese securities.

The standard rate for both interest and dividends is 20 per cent, but tax treaties reduce this in most instances to 10 per cent for interest and 15 per cent for dividends.

Exemption

Interest on the following is paid free of withholding tax:

- Euroyen bonds;
- Yen foreign bonds (samurai bonds);
- all bills and bonds issued at a discount; i.e., mainly government bills and bonds and Nippon Telegraph and Telephone Company bonds.

Table 23.8   Withholding taxes

	Interest, %	Dividends, %
Residents of non-treaty countries	20	20
Residents of treaty countries		
Australia	10	15
Austria	10	20
Belgium	15	15
Brazil	12.5	12.5
Canada	15	15
Czechoslovakia	10	15
Denmark	10	15
Egypt	20	15
Finland	10	15
France	10	15
Germany	10	15
India	20	20
Ireland	10	15
Italy	10	15
Korea	12	12
Malaysia	10	15
Netherlands	10	15
New Zealand	20	15
Norway	10	15
Pakistan	20	20
Rumania	10	10
Singapore	15	15
South Korea	12	12
Spain	10	15
Sri Lanka	20	20
Sweden	10	15
Switzerland	10	15
Thailand	20	20
United Kingdom	10	15
United States of America	10	15
Zambia	10	0

Exchange controls

The system of exchange controls was revised as from 1 December 1980. The emphasis has been changed from most transactions being forbidden in principle but free in exceptional cases, to transactions being free in principle but forbidden in exceptional cases.

The Minister of Finance reserves the right to impose restrictions in the case of national emergency. An emergency may be described as one of three conditions: unusual movements in the foreign exchange rate; extraordinary swings in the balance of payments; and problems in the domestic economy. These definitions are all somewhat broad and the authorities do not define the severity of the conditions required in order that emergency restrictions be introduced. The foreign exchange banks will continue to report currency transactions and deposits so that the authorities can act in the event of an emergency. What constitutes an emergency will be decided by a 'Foreign Exchange Deliberate Council'.

Authorities

The Ministry of Finance is responsible for exchange control policy in co-operation with the Ministry of International Trade and Finance. The Bank of Japan is responsible for implementing and administering exchange policy.

Currency

The currency is the Japanese yen which floats freely with respect to all other currencies. The authorities intervene, using the US dollar in the spot foreign exchange market, only to smooth out excessive fluctuations in the yen's exchange value.

Residents and non-residents may freely carry out spot and forward foreign exchange transactions through an authorized bank (mainly city banks).

The new exchange regulations have now freed all foreign exchange transactions which were previously restricted in principle. Japanese commercial banks are now free to borrow and lend in foreign currencies and Japanese companies are now allowed to borrow directly overseas in, for example, the Eurodollar market. Previously they were required to operate only through a Japanese bank. Individual Japanese are still not permitted to hold foreign currency bank accounts abroad, though restrictions on foreign currency deposits by residents (of ¥3 million maximum) with domestic banks have been removed.

Non-resident accounts

Non-residents may freely open an account with any authorized bank in Japan. These accounts may be credited or debited with yen or any other foreign currency. Balances on accounts may be freely transferred abroad.

Short-term yen denominated loans to overseas clients have been liberalized but medium- and long-term loans must be registered with the Ministry of Finance in advance.

524

Purchase of securities

Since February 1979, non-residents have been freely permitted to purchase any Japanese domestic securities, including short- and long-term domestic bonds. There are however limits on the total amount of Japanese securities that may be purchased by foreign investors. Previous to February 1979 foreign shareholdings in Japanese companies could not exceed a total of 25 per cent of issued share capital (with a few exceptions). The new regulations allow unrestricted foreign investment in Japanese shares except in specially designated companies of strategic industries, where the 25 per cent limit still applies. There are eleven strategic industries:

Nuclear power	Banks
Electric power	Pharmaceutical companies
Gas	Mining
Oil refineries (limit of 50 per cent)	Agriculture
Aircraft companies	Leather
Railways	

Restrictions still apply to foreign purchases of samurai bond issues in the primary market which may not exceed a total of 25 per cent. No restrictions apply to secondary market purchases. Non-residents are free to purchase Japanese real estate and the new regulations remove the requirement to obtain approval from the Ministry of Finance and also allows local banks to lend to foreigners for such investments.

Profits and dividends from Japanese investments may be freely repatriated.

Gold

There is no major gold market in Japan but non-residents may freely purchase gold from residents of Japan and licensing is only required where the transaction is to the value of more than ¥3 million.

24. Malaysia

General market environment

Malaysia has a young financial market. The central bank, Bank Negara Malaysia, was established in 1959 but its present role emanates from the Banking Act of 1973. The Bank keeps cohesive control over the banking system and financial sector, yet has actively encouraged the development of the money and capital markets. It tends however to favour development of the domestic banking sector in preference to foreign banks which in the past have had a dominant presence in the local financial environment.

Modelled on the British financial system, the money market now has a broader range of instruments available to the investor than do those of some more

Table 24.1   Summary of instruments

Instrument	Characteristics
MONEY MARKET	
Deposits	
call	Interbank market. Overnight and eight-day call
time	Deposits for 3 to 12 months, but also up to five years. Also one month deposits in larger amounts are possible
currency	Time deposits accepted in other convertible currencies
CDs	Negotiable CDs issued with maturities of six months to three years in multiples of three months
Treasury bills	Issued weekly with maturities of 91, 182 and 364 days. Good secondary market
Bankers' acceptances	New market but very popular. Good yields
Repurchase agreements	Commercial banks will transact RPs in BAs and government securities
CAPITAL MARKET	
Government backed bonds	Three- to twenty-year maturities. Very marketable
Corporate bonds	Rarely issued. Thin market
Equities	Small but very active market
Commodities	New commodities exchange opened 1980
Gold	Market restricted to gold coins

developed countries. Two money market instruments were introduced as recently as 1979, specifically to add depth to the market.

The capital market is small but very active, particularly for government backed bonds and equities in which a lively interest is shown by resident individuals.

Withholding taxes are payable on both interest and dividends, but exchange controls are minimal with respect to portfolio investments.

The government welcomes inward foreign investment, particularly if funds are directed towards domestic industry and projects that will aid economic growth. Much of the government's domestic economic policy is directed towards these objectives.

The money market

The money market, like the whole of Malaysia's financial system, is relatively new but the central bank is actively encouraging its development. For example, two instruments, CDs and BAs, were introduced as recently as May 1979 in order to broaden the market.

Deposits

Call deposits

The market in call deposits is an interbank market, though the volume is not as large as the market for time deposits. Call deposits are particularly required by the discount houses for overnight terms or at eight days' notice. The rates of interest are influenced by yields on treasury bills and on government securities because the discount houses have to invest their funds entirely in such assets, which they can then readily rediscount with the central bank. Call rates are consequently slightly lower than treasury bill rate. Minimum denominations for deposits placed at call is M$25 000, although transactions are usually made in much larger amounts.

Time deposits

The time deposit market is also an interbank market. Time deposits may be placed with commercial banks for periods of 3, 6, 9 and 12 months. Deposits may in addition be made for periods of 24, 36 and 48 months, but the market in long-term deposits is not large. Interest rates are not regularly quoted for long-term money but determined by negotiations between the lender and the bank. Interest on loans made for more than three years is free of withholding tax. Interest earned on shorter deposits is subject to withholding tax. The minimum amount that will be accepted by the banks for such term deposits is M$1000. 'Short deposits' for periods of one month may be placed in minimum sums of M$25 000.

Interest is calculated on the basis of a civil year of 365 days. Due to deliberate government policy, for the last few years interest rates for Malaysian ringgit have been considerably lower than rates for other currencies in Asia, particularly when compared with deposits in Hong Kong and Singapore dollars.

Currency deposits

The banks will also accept time deposits in most other convertible currencies which are then placed in the Asian dollar market in Singapore. Two specific exceptions are the South African rand and the Israeli pound. The most easily placed currencies are US dollars, pounds sterling, Australian dollars, and the major Asian currencies—Japanese yen and Hong Kong and Singapore dollars. Interest rates on convertible currency deposits are in line with international Eurocurrency rates.

Negotiable certificates of deposit

With effect from 2 May 1979, commercial banks have been authorized to issue ringgit (M$) negotiable CDs in order to give companies and individuals greater flexibility in the use of their funds. The CDs are issued with a minimum maturity of six calendar months and a maximum maturity of three calendar years. The majority, however, are issued for less than one year. Minimum denominations of CDs are M$100 000. Some are issued in multiples of this amount, up to a maximum of M$1 000 000, but large CDs may be split for secondary market trading purposes into multiples of M$100 000 upon request from clients of the issuing bank.

The CDs are bearer securities and carry an interest coupon which is slightly lower than fixed time deposits of comparable terms. Interest is calculated on the basis of a civil year of 365 days, and paid in full at redemption, except where the CD is issued for a term of more than a year, in which case it is paid annually.

In the primary market, CDs are now issued by all the commercial banks. In the secondary market they may be purchased or sold through the commercial banks, discount houses, and dealers in securities.

CDs offer a suitable alternative to time deposits for investors who may require greater liquidity. The secondary market is developing with success. There is no problem in affecting a sale of CDs since dealers trade on their own accounts and make two-way books in CDs, acting as both buyers and sellers.

Treasury bills

Treasury bills are issued on a weekly basis by the central bank on behalf of the government. The bills are sold by auction in the primary market and applications are made by tender through a bank or a discount house. Applicants state the amount and the price at which they are willing to subscribe. The final issue price is the average of the tenders submitted.

All tenders received at above the issue price are allocated in full. Subscriptions at the issue price are allocated proportionately, while those bids below the issue price are unallocated.

Subscribers in the primary market are mainly the banks and the discount houses. Treasury bills are issued with original maturities of 91, 182 and 364 days. They are issued on a discount basis with a face value of M$100 for 100 units, though they are traded in minimum denominations of M$10 000. Yields are about two per cent below those on time deposits of comparable terms.

In the secondary market turnover is fairly active. The bills may be transacted through a bank, discount house or securities dealer.

Bankers' acceptances

BAs have been recently introduced as a money market instrument in Malaysia. The market has been established to provide firstly, an additional form of financing for domestic and foreign trade and secondly, an attractive investment medium for the short-term surpluses of companies, institutions and individuals.

BAs are bills drawn on, and accepted by, a commercial or a merchant bank to finance imports into, or exports out of, Malaysia, sales within Malaysia, or purchases within Malaysia of specified goods. They carry two signatures, those of the borrowing company or trader, and of the accepting bank.

BAs are issued in multiples of M$1000 in amounts of not less than M$30000 with original maturities of not less than 30 days and not more than 200 days. They are issued on a discount basis, the amount of the discount representing the interest portion which depends upon current interest levels, the financial standing and creditworthiness of the drawer (trader) and on the quality of other collateral given as security for the finance. The discount rate is calculated according to a 365-day year formula.

In the secondary market, BAs are bought by corporations, pension and provident funds and individuals. Yields vary in line with interbank interest rates but are, in general, higher than the rates applying to comparable time deposits or CDs. Trading hours for same day value are 9 to 11.30 a.m. from Monday to Friday. Settlement and delivery take place up to 2.30 p.m.

BAs are more marketable in the secondary market than are CDs, principally because the issuing bank stands ready at all times to repurchase their own or other BAs at prevailing market rates of interest. BAs are as secure as a CD or a fixed deposit placed with a bank since, having been accepted by a bank, the bank guarantees to pay the holder of the BA upon maturity. BAs however yield more than CDs, the size of the differential depending upon the financial standing of the company that has initiated the draft.

BAs are in theory readily discountable at the central bank. However the Bank (Bank Negara) has recently restricted the types of BAs that may be discounted because it feels that many large companies have been abusing the facilities and creating too many BAs in order to obtain cheap funds. Additionally, the Bank is unhappy about the financial standing of some of the companies issuing BAs. There are three types of BAs it will no longer rediscount, which may therefore not have quite as good a secondary market as others. These are BAs drawn by large and reputable companies which the Bank feels should be readily marketable and not need recourse to the discount facility, BAs drawn by companies of dubious financial standing, and BAs whose creation the Bank feels is artificial.

Repurchase agreements

A bank may sell both its own and other acceptable BAs with an undertaking to repurchase at an agreed price on a specified date. Conversely, a bank may contract a reverse repurchase (RP agreement) by buying BAs from a customer with an undertaking to resell them at an agreed price on a specified future date. Banks will also transact repurchase agreements in other securities, particularly treasury bills and government bonds. Where a bank sells and agrees to repurchase, the customer is lending to the bank. The advantage of this to the investor is that, firstly, his return is known exactly, the repurchase price being at a premium representing an interest payment; secondly, an RP is as secure as a time deposit with a bank; thirdly, RPs may be contracted for periods as short as one day or for odd periods not available in the time deposit market. They thus provide a suitable alternative method of placing very short-term money and sometimes at higher rates than obtainable in the call money market.

The capital market

Government backed bonds

Government backed bonds are issued both directly by the government and indirectly by local authorities or public sector institutions; these latter are guaranteed as to principal and interest by the full faith and credit of the government. In the primary market they are issues managed by the central bank. About two or three issues are made a year.

Purchase is made by subscription to the central bank. Usually both the amount of the issue and the price are known in advance. Issue price is normally at par—M$100 per unit. The main purchasers are the banks, discount houses, provident funds and larger companies.

The original life of government backed bonds may range from a minimum of three years to a maximum of 20 years. The issues carry a fixed coupon rate with interest paid semiannually, calculated on the basis of a 365-day year. Principal is redeemed in full at maturity.

The bonds are readily discountable to the central bank. A fairly active secondary market exists for these bonds since they are both secure and readily marketable instruments. They may be traded either over the counter through a bank, or on the Kuala Lumpur stock exchange. Many corporate investors, with short-term funds, purchase government backed bonds that are close to maturity as an alternative to other money market instruments.

Corporate bonds

Public sales of bonds by companies are rare. A few bonds and debentures are listed on the stock exchange but both the primary and secondary markets are limited. Private placements of corporate bond issues are more common than public bond sales.

Asian dollar bonds

There is no primary or secondary market for Asian dollar bonds in Malaysia. Such transactions are normally directed to the markets in Singapore and Hong Kong.

Equity shares and the stock exchange

In May 1973, Malaysia withdrew from the Joint Stock Exchange of Malaysia and Singapore. The new Malaysian stock exchange in Kuala Lumpur was inaugurated in June 1973, since when it has behaved actively compared to other markets in the region. For 1978 trading activity was double that in 1977, resulting in a turnover of over one million units traded at a value of M$2.5 billion. There is ample public interest in the purchase of shares and most new issues are oversubscribed.

As at July 1979 there were 255 equity stocks listed on Kuala Lumpur exchange which comprised quotations of 188 Malaysian, 55 Singaporean and 12 British companies. The industries represented in the listings include rubber plantations and manufacture, tin mines and processing, oil refining, as well as commercial companies and financial companies such as banks and provident funds.

New listings on the stock exchange are made through either merchant banks or, latterly, the commercial banks and are underwritten by the issuing bank or a syndicate of banks. New listings must first, however, be reviewed and agreed by the Capital Issues Committee, established in 1968.

For a quotation, a company must have a minimum issued share capital of M$2 million, a minimum of 500 shareholders, and a minimum of 200 000 shares held by the public to a minimum value of M$750 000 or 25 per cent of the issued capital, whichever is the greater.

Shares listed on the Kuala exchange may also be purchased or sold through the Singapore exchange.

Shares are traded in 'board lots' of 1000 shares. Residents of South Africa and Israel are specifically prohibited from operating in the market, but all other nationalities may freely make transactions in local shares. Transactions are made through one of the 30 or so firms of stockbrokers who are located in all the major cities.

The government has established a special foundation, the Bumiputra Investment Foundation (BIF), for the purpose of buying shares on behalf of Bumiputras (indigenous Malays). The foundation was formed in 1977, and in April 1978 the government allocated about M$200 million to the BIF to form the New Equity Corporation (NEC) to buy shares in companies offering new or special issues for Bumiputras.

In March 1979 the government allocated a further M$300 million for the same purpose. The NEC plans to form unit trusts once it has built up an adequate portfolio, and to sell participations in these mutual funds to Bumiputras.

Commodities

A commodity cash and futures exchange in Kuala Lumpur was established in October 1980 and is the first of its kind in South East Asia. The exchange is managed and supervised by the Commodities Trading Council which consists of up to 16 members appointed by the Minister of Finance. The members comprise a chairman, a representative of the Ministry of Primary Industries and representatives from the Treasury, the Ministry of Trade and Industry, the Ministry of Energy, Telecommunication and Posts, the central bank and other representatives from the banking and industrial sectors. The Minister of Finance attends the meetings of the council and has authority to give directives to it.

The exchange is constituted as a private company with the Commodities Trading Council acting as the management board in supervising the trading in commodity futures contracts and advising the Minister of Finance on all matters connected with the market. A commissioner and deputy commissioner are responsible for carrying out policy decisions of the council and for the general administration of the market.

Trading takes place through dealers specifically registered as members of the exchange. Members may deal both for clients and for their own account. Members of the exchange are also required to deposit M$15 000, and give an additional bank guarantee for a further M$15 000 for a compensation fund. The money is invested on their behalf in bank time deposits or specified securities and the fund used to pay claims in the event of death, disability or insolvency of a member.

Futures trading initially is available in local commodities such as rubber, tin, palm oil and timber, of which Malaysia is already established as one of the world's leading exporters. The futures market is thus a logical extension of Malaysia's existing export market. There is a possibility that contracts in other commodities may be introduced if the market develops successfully.

Gold

Gold may be purchased by authorized dealers, namely banks and bullion dealers, only. Several gold coins are minted which may be domestically traded by residents through a bank and some of which may be exported by residents and non-resident travellers. The coins and the regulations attaching to them are as shown in Table 24.2.

Table 24.2

Gold coin	Face value	Regulations
Tunka Abdul Rahman	M$100	Resident and non-resident travellers
Third Malaysia Plan	M$200	may take out one piece each of
Employees Provident Fund	M$250	these coins
Wildlife Conservation	M$500	Travellers may import one coin but export is prohibited
Ninth South East Asian Games	M$200	Import and export in any quantity is unrestricted

The trading value of each coin depends on its gold content and on the prevailing world price of gold, though they may stand at a premium at times of high demand.

Dealing and fees

Money market

Deposits

There is no charge to customers for opening accounts or for placing deposits denominated in either ringgit or convertible currencies.

CDs

Delivery and/or collection charges made by the issuing bank are M$10 per certificate, plus M$5 for every M$100 000 nominal value. When issued, CDs are delivered by the issuing bank to any depository of the original buyer's choice without charge. In the secondary market no specific fee is charged, but a small commission is included in the spread (about $\frac{1}{4}$ per cent) between bid and offer prices quoted by the bank or dealer.

Treasury bills

When making a subscription in the primary market for a new treasury bill issue, the bank or discount house through which the application is made may charge a small fee of a few Malaysian dollars, depending on the size of the subscription. In the secondary market, no specific fee is charged but commission is included in the dealer's spread between his bid and offer prices, usually about $\frac{1}{16}$ or $\frac{1}{32}$ percentage point.

Bankers' acceptances

BAs are dealt over the counter, through banks. Where the buyer is not a financial institution, settlement and delivery should take place not later than 11.30 a.m. for same day value on the date of transaction. The buyer must collect the BA from the bank with whom he has dealt. No specific fee is charged, but dealings are net—the bank's commission is included in its bid and offer prices, usually a difference of $\frac{1}{16}$ percentage point. BAs are also subject to stamp duty of M$5 per BA.

Capital market

Capital market securities are usually traded on the stock exchange, through a stockbroker. Standard commission fees are charged as shown in Table 24.3.

Bonds may also be traded through a bank. Banks do not charge commission but deal on a net basis. Dealing spreads between bid and offer prices are about $\frac{1}{2}$ per cent.

Table 24.3. Brokerage commission rates for dealing on Kuala Lumpur stock exchange

Securities	Transaction size or value	Brokerage
Government bonds, local authority bonds, public sector bonds	On first M$20 000	$\frac{3}{4}\%$ of consideration
	On amount in excess of M$20 000	$\frac{1}{4}\%$ of consideration
Corporation bonds and debentures	Less than M$50 000	1% of consideration
	M$50 000 to M$100 000	$\frac{1}{2}\%$ of consideration
	More than M$100 000	$\frac{1}{4}\%$ of consideration
Asian dollar	All transactions	$\frac{3}{8}\%$ of consideration
Ordinary shares, preferred shares, convertible debentures	Share price less than M$0.50	M$0.005 per share
	Share price more than M$0.50 but less than M$1.00	M$0.010 per share
	Share price more than M$1.00	1% of consideration

Brokerage at the above rates is payable by both buyer and seller. Minimum brokerage charges are M$2 on bond transactions and M$5 on transactions in shares and convertible debentures.

Stamp duty

Stamp duty is payable on transactions at rates as follows, payable by both buyer and seller:

Bonds	0.1% of consideration
Shares and convertible debentures	
contracts of under M$1000	M$1.50 per contract
contracts of over M$1000	M$3 per M$1000 or part thereof

Bank safe custody

The following are typical of charges made by a bank for the holding in safe custody of bonds and shares and for acting as agent in the transactions shown:

Service charge per holding (i.e., shares or stocks in one company regardless of quantity)	M$1
Registration in client's name	M$5
Registration in name of bank's nominee company	$\frac{1}{4}\%$ of market value
Subject to minimum of	M$5
maximum of	M$1000
Dividend claims	1% of market value
Subject to minimum of	M$5
maximum of	M$500

Withdrawal of scrip	$\frac{1}{8}\%$ of market value
Subject to minimum of	M$5
maximum of	M$1000
Receipt of scrip from broker	M$5
Collection of dividend warrants	M$2.5
Submission of application for new shares	M$1 per application

PLUS

Government transfer stamp duty on share transactions (payable by buyer only)	
If transferee's name is inserted on transfer note prior to transfer and endorsed by transferor	M$0.15 per M$100 or part thereof + M$1 per certificate
If transferee's name not inserted prior to transfer	M$0.30 per M$100 or part thereof + M$1 per certificate

Financial and monetary systems

Financial institutions

The financial and monetary systems are modelled on British traditions and concepts. The financial institutions include commercial banks, merchant banks and discount houses, all under the direction of the central bank.

Commercial banks

There are about 40 commercial banks, over half of which are domestic Malaysian banks with over 500 branches controlling 60 per cent of the total assets of the banking system. The commercial banks comprise the largest sector of the financial system and account for 70 per cent of total credit supply.

The three largest banks are the Bank Bumiputra, Malayan Banking and the United Malayan Banking Corporation. They are state owned and run by government nominees. The government is anxious to encourage the growth of the domestic banking system in preference to foreign banks, which still control 35 per cent of total deposits and retain some of the most lucrative clients. It also influences the direction of credit in favour of the indigenous Malay population (Bumiputras) in order to encourage their greater participation in domestic trade and industry, which has traditionally been dominated by the Chinese and British.

One means of achieving this objective has been for the government to establish, in 1977, the Bumiputra Investment Foundation to buy shares in Malaysian companies on behalf of Bumiputras and to sell them to Bumiputras in the form of unit trust shares. Another method is by qualitative directives to the commercial banks (see Monetary policy).

The commercial banks provide retail banking services. They accept savings, demand and time deposits, provide chequing account facilities, grant overdrafts and short-term loans to industry, trade and individuals, and will purchase (and hold in safe keeping) securities for their customers—though not for their own accounts—either through the interbank market or through stockbrokers.

Merchant banks

There are 12 merchant banks which provide an intermediary service to corporate clients. They accept time deposits, grant loans to companies, advise companies on capital restructuring, mergers and takeovers, float and underwrite new share and bond issues, and provide investment advisory and portfolio management services.

The merchant banks are now suffering from increased competition from the commercial banks whose range of operations have been expanded. The merchant banks have been directed by the central bank to achieve a target of 30 per cent of their income from fee-based activities by the end of 1981. Some may find this difficult to accomplish which could lead to mergers between some of them in the near future.

Discount houses

There are two discount houses which act as intermediaries between the commercial and merchant banks and the central bank. They lend to the banks by discounting bills and short-term government securities which they in turn can rediscount with the central bank.

They accept deposits—mostly call money—but may accept time deposits for up to 90 days to finance their purchases of treasury bills and government securities which they also sell on to the banks who hold such instruments in their asset portfolios.

Other financial institutions

Other financial institutions include the whole range of near-bank credit institutions. These include the post office savings bank and the national savings bank which are both government controlled and principally collect small individual savings and divert funds towards projects which promote the country's economic development.

In addition there are privately owned finance houses which are licensed to accept savings deposits and to grant credit, mostly in the form of hire purchase and leasing finance. Insurance companies and provident and mutual trust associations, also in the private sector, channel funds generally into the mortgage market and the long-term government bond market.

The central bank

The central bank is the Bank Negara Malaysia which was established in 1959 as a corporate body but wholly owned by the government. The Bank is managed by a 7-man board which includes the governor and a representative from the treasury. The board members are state appointed for terms of three to five years.

The Bank Negara has considerable power over the banking system and is responsible for determining and administrating monetary policy. It is required to keep the Minister of Finance informed of its activities. Bank Negara is also the sole issuer of currency, lender of last resort to the banking system, financial agent to the government, and the authority in charge of exchange controls.

Monetary policy

The main objectives of monetary policy are the controlled growth of credit such that it benefits the economic development of the country and the interests of the Bumiputra community while maintaining the external stability of the currency.

The main instruments used by the Bank Negara to effect this policy are variable minimum reserve requirements, liquidity ratios, interest rate policy and qualitative control of bank credit.

Reserve requirements

The central bank directs that commercial banks should keep a certain proportion of their total deposit liabilities as cash reserves held on interest-free deposit with Bank Negara. As an instrument of monetary policy this minimum reserve ratio is subject to alteration. When first introduced in 1958 it was four per cent of total deposits. The highest ratio applied was 10 per cent in 1974, but as at December 1980 it stood at six per cent.

A supplementary reserve requirement is that the commercial banks must hold an additional specified proportion of their total deposit liabilities in the form of liquid assets comprising cash in excess of reserves, balances with other banks, treasury bills, other eligible bills, and government securities. Not only the amount, but also the mix of these assets to be held by the banks is subject to variation by the central bank. Bank Negara may also differentiate its reserve ratio policy according to the size and location of banks.

The commercial banks must also maintain a minimum of 50 per cent of their savings deposits in long-term government securities and mortgages to individuals and financial intermediaries, and 10 per cent in small loans to the Credit Guarantee Corporation.

These somewhat stringent reserve requirements and their flexible use by the authorities enable the central bank to maintain a fairly tight control over the expansion of credit in the economy.

Liquidity ratio

Although the supplementary reserve requirement is effectively also a liquidity ratio, a further requirement is that the commercial banks maintain a certain proportion of their total non-savings deposits in the form of liquid assets, defined as cash in hand, with the central bank or as balances with other banks, treasury bills and other eligible commercial bills. This ratio currently, as at December 1980, stood at 25 per cent. The Bank Negara may raise or lower this ratio either to reduce or to increase the free reserves of the banking system and thus liquidity and the rate of credit expansion in the financial system.

537

Interest-rate policy

The banks, discount houses and other financial institutions have access to the discount facility provided by the central bank as lender of last resort. The Bank will discount treasury bills, other commercial bills, including specified types of BAs, and government backed bonds.

The discount rate is generally about two per cent below the commercial banks' prime rate, and as at December 1980 was 5.7 per cent. It is changed only infrequently and is not used as a major instrument of monetary policy. The Banks' discount rate for 91-day treasury bills is the best indicator of market interest rates and is the basis from which prime rates (the rates at which the commercial banks will lend to their most creditworthy customers) are established.

As at December 1980 prime rate had remained at 7.5 per cent since mid-1977 despite volatile interest rates in other parts of the world, including neighbouring countries. The Bank Negara's policies seemed to have succeeded in keeping interest rates low and this has helped its objectives of economic growth.

Qualitative and quantitive credit controls

The Bank Negara uses moral suasion to direct bank lending to specific sectors of the economy that it wishes to see developed.

For the 1980 financial year, commercial banks were required to lend 17 per cent of their loans to Bumiputras, 20 per cent to small-scale enterprises, 10 per cent for residential housing and five per cent for food production.

The domestic banks are well able to reach such targets, but the foreign banks have greater difficulty because most of their clients are the larger companies and foreign interests. The object of the controls is, however, to direct credit away from such sectors and into the Bumiputra sector. The relative proportions between sectors are subject to variations by the Bank Negara and, in addition, ceilings on the growth of particular types of credit are also imposed on the commercial banks.

Withholding taxes

Interest

Interest earned on deposits and other Malaysian securities by non-residents is subject to a withholding tax of 15 per cent, except for residents of Switzerland and Japan for whom it is 10 per cent. However, interest on overseas loans that exceed three years' duration and on loans granted for the purposes of assisting an approved project is exempt from tax. In addition, commercial banks and merchant banks are exempt from withholding tax on interest paid to non-resident banks.

Dividends

Dividends are already franked, i.e., paid net of the 40 per cent tax paid by the distributing corporation. This tax cannot be recovered through tax treaties except for Japanese nationals owning a majority shareholding of a Malaysian corporation. There is no additional withholding tax on dividends.

Table 24.4 Withholding taxes

Recipient	Interest	Dividends
Residents of non-treaty countries	15	0
Residents of treaty countries		0
Belgium	15	
Canada	15	
Denmark	15	
France	15	
West Germany	15	
India	15	
Japan	10	
New Zealand	15	
Norway	15	
Poland	15	
Singapore	15	
Sri Lanka	15	
Sweden	15	
Switzerland	10	
United Kingdom	15	

Exchange controls

Authority

Malaysian exchange control regulations are fairly liberal. The relevant authority is the Bank Negara, the governor of which is also the Comptroller of Foreign Exchange who administers controls on behalf of the government.

Currency

The Malaysian currency is the ringgit, otherwise known as the Malaysian dollar (M$). The Bank Negara intervenes in the spot foreign exchange market, usually using the US dollar as the currency of intervention, in order to maintain a stable exchange value of the ringgit against a trade-weighted basket of currencies. Commercial banks are permitted to operate freely in both the spot and forward foreign exchange markets.

Non-resident accounts

Non-residents may freely open an external account in ringgit. Balances may be transferred to any other account of residents or non-residents, or may be converted into any other currency apart from South African rand and Israeli pounds. There are no restrictions on debits from external accounts though credits to these accounts in excess of M$5000 require approval from an authorized bank, and credits in excess of M$2 million require approval from the Comptroller of Foreign Exchange.

539

Investment in securities

Non-residents, excepting nationals of South Africa and Israel, may freely purchase all types of Malaysian securities. Profits, dividends and principal resulting from liquidation of securities may be freely repatriated subject only to the completion of exchange control forms for transactions in excess of M$5000.

Gold

Only banks and authorized bullion dealers may purchase gold. A few gold coins may be purchased but may be exported in limited quantities only.

25. Singapore

General market environment

Singapore is now undisputed as a major financial centre of South East Asia and is rivalling Hong Kong in several aspects of the Far East market.

Regulations affecting the domestic money and capital markets have been considerably eased during the last decade. Exchange controls have been abolished and withholding taxes and stamp duty substantially reduced so as positively to encourage both foreign investment and the issue of securities by foreign interests in the Singapore markets.

By far the most important development, however, has been the growth of the Asian dollar market. This is the Asian equivalent of the Eurodollar market. It is an international money market for short-term loans and borrowings in any convertible currency, and an international capital market for the issue of medium- and long-term bonds in convertible currency. The Asian dollar market, though still much smaller than the Eurodollar market, is growing at a much faster rate.

This is encouraged by the Singapore government and facilitated by Singapore's ideal geographic position, placing it in a time zone that links the market of San Francisco, Japan and Hong Kong with those in the Middle East, Europe and New York. Thus, Singapore is successfully evolving from its role as a trade entrepôt into an important world financial centre.

The money market

Deposits

As the financial centre of South East Asia, Singapore now has a wide range of deposit-taking institutions. These include commercial banks with either full domestic or offshore licences, Asian currency units (ACUs), finance companies and discount houses. Merchant banks also accept deposits, but only from financial institutions. Deposits may be placed either in Singapore dollars or in other convertible currencies through the Asian dollar market. Since 1975, all banks have been free to establish their own interest rates on loans and deposits and the type of institution with which money is placed. For Singapore dollar deposits, the level of interest rates largely depends on the monetary policies of the Monetary Authority of Singapore. The banking system is, however, fiercely competitive and convertible

541

Table 25.1 Summary of instruments

Instrument	Characteristics
MONEY MARKET	
Deposits	
call deposits	In any currency through Asian dollar market or in Singapore dollars with variety of local institutions
time deposits	In any currency in Asian dollar market or locally in Singapore dollars. Amounts limited according to type of institution
certificates of deposit	Market improved since 1978. Secondary market still a little inadequate
Treasury bills	Ninety-day bills issued by weekly tender
Bankers' acceptances	No market yet, but may be established shortly
Commercial bills	Poor secondary market
Commercial paper	First issue made in Asian dollar market in 1980
CAPITAL MARKET	
Government bonds	Eighty per cent held by public institutions, therefore restricted secondary market
Corporate bonds	Uncommon in domestic market
Asian dollar bonds	Growing and active market. Primary market good, but secondary market better in Hong Kong. Still small, however, compared to other international markets
Equities	Market of reasonable size but turnover small because of tightly held interests. Government wants to encourage foreign companies to seek listings on the Singapore stock exchange
Options	A small number of call options quoted but market is virtually moribund
Commodities	New market established in 1980. Provides probably the largest rubber market in the world. Other local commodities traded. Markets are cash markets only
Gold	Active and free gold market for spot and forward contracts. The market is small compared to similar markets in other financial centres

currency interest rates are generally influenced by market forces in the international currency market.

The government may introduce a provision for banks to operate numbered accounts as in Switzerland so that anonymity of beneficial ownership may be preserved.

Call deposits

The call money market in domestic Singapore dollars is almost entirely an inter-bank market with restricted access to non-bank lenders of funds. The Asian dollar market provides a substantially better market to the non-resident investor. Domestic deposits of less than 90 days have a limited market because banks may only pay interest on fixed deposits of one month or longer which must be in minimum amounts of S$250 000 for deposits of one to three months maturity placed with offshore banking units (ACUs). Banks with full licences may accept call deposits in smaller amounts. The discount houses are allowed to pay interest on call money placed by non-bank depositors, but only in minimum amounts of S$50 000. On such deposits terms may be for either overnight or eight-day call. Interest payable by a discount house is however unlikely to compare favourably with other money market rates because the houses are required to invest 70 per cent of their assets in treasury bills which yield the lowest of all money market securities. It would thus be unprofitable for them to pay interest on call deposits in excess of treasury bill rate. Discount houses must offer collateral as security for all deposits.

Time deposits

Deposits may be placed with the commercial banks for fixed time periods of 1 month, 3 months, 6 months and less frequently 9 or 12 months. Minimum amounts are S$1000 for more than 3 months and S$100 000 for less than 3 months terms. Discount houses may accept time deposits, usually in short maturity of 3 to 6 months, in minimum amounts of S$50 000.

The finance companies will accept time deposits of generally longer maturity of up to three years in minimum amounts of S$1000. Rates of interest paid by finance companies are normally higher than those paid by commercial banks for deposits of comparable terms. This is so because finance companies are not subject to the reserve requirements imposed on the banks (although they are subject to liquidity requirements). Therefore, since they don't have to hold non-interest-earning cash balances against certain liabilities they can afford to pay more, while at the same time they hold fewer discountable bills and thus do not have access to cheap credit through the discount houses in the same way that the banks do, and thus are often obliged to bid above the banks for funds in the money market.

The Post Office Savings Bank (POSB), accepts time deposits in Singapore dollars. Interest is competitive with that paid by banks and finance companies. The POSB does not come under the Banking Act and is thus not subject to reserve requirements. Further, such interest is free of tax for deposits of up to S$100 000.

An investor would be advised to shop around for the best interest rates available. Commercial banks are generally prepared to give close to the interbank bid rate, with a profit margin (discount) of 0.5 or even as little as 0.125 per cent. Foreign banks with offshore licences only, and thus limited access to domestic funds, may often pay higher rates, the premium over interbank rate being dependent on the individual bank's demand for funds at the time. However, the minimum deposit of Singapore dollars that any offshore bank is allowed to accept is S$250 000.

Asian dollar market

Singapore is now undisputed as the centre of the Asian dollar market. Similar to the Eurodollar market in Europe the Asian dollar market is the market for loans

543

and deposits in convertible currencies—predominantly US dollars—and for foreign exchange transactions. The size of the Asian dollar market is, as at end 1980, some US$42 billion with a daily turnover of almost US$5 billion. This compares with the Eurodollar market of over US$1000 billion and a daily turnover of about US$75 billion.

About 30 to 40 per cent of Asian dollar market daily turnover is dollar/Deutschemark, 20 per cent is dollar/yen and 20 per cent sterling.

Much of the daily trading volume takes place between Singapore and Europe and Hong Kong.

Foreign exchange rates fluctuate freely according to market supply and demand. Transactions are made through the ACUs of authorized banks in both spot and, to a lesser degree, forward trading. Financial institutions may also make transactions through money/foreign exchange brokers, but these act as intermediary agents only, and may not deal directly with commercial customers. The market for deposits in all convertible currencies is the most important part of the Singapore money market. The ACUs of authorized banks accept both overnight and term deposits from a few days up to twelve months. About 80 per cent of such deposits are placed in US dollars, while the remainder is mainly Deutschemark, yen, Swiss francs, sterling and French francs. There is no fixed minimum amount for Asian dollar deposits, but the usually accepted minimum is US$25 000 per transaction or equivalent in other currencies. Up until 1979, individuals were subject to a maximum of US$250 000 per transaction, while companies were subject to a maximum of US$7.5 million. This has since been revised and now no maximum limits apply. The spread between borrowing and lending rates is smaller and rates more competitive in the Asian dollar market than in the domestic market, since the former is more international and thus open to more arbitrage between it and the Eurodollar market.

The Asian dollar market is continuing to grow in volume at a rate much faster than the Eurodollar market, though admittedly from a lower base. Current growth is about 20 to 30 per cent per annum.

The Singapore government has actively encouraged the growth of the Asian dollar market which was established by the initiative of the Bank of America in 1968. With the approval of the government, this bank set up the first Asian currency unit (ACU). There are now over a hundred such units, which are simply special departments within banks but which account separately and deal specifically in foreign exchange. The combined total assets of these ACUs amount to US$42 billion in 1980, which is a measure of the size of the market.

The success of the market is due partly to the natural advantages of Singapore's geographical position, and also to government incentives designed to encourage the local market. Its geographic position allowed the island's initial development as a trade entrepôt. This same feature has facilitated the subsequent stage of its economic evolution into that of a financial entrepôt. Not only is the proximity of the Asian dollar market a more useful haven than Europe for funds generated in the Far East and South East Asia, but Singapore also provides a vital link between the markets in Japan and San Francisco and those in Britain and Europe. Singapore's time zone means that at the start of its business day its dealers can do business with Japan and San Francisco, and with the Middle East a little later, while at the end of its day it can hand over to London, Frankfurt and Zurich, thus facilitating round-the-world 24-hour foreign exchange dealing.

The government has promoted this development by the liberalization of exchange controls in 1976 and by introducing the following fiscal measures.

Firstly, the government introduced a concessionary tax rate of 10 per cent to all offshore income of ACUs. This applies to interest received by ACUs from their loans to non-bank non-residents and to dividends paid up to their parent bank. This is a reduction from the 40 per cent withholding tax applied to interest earned from domestic sources. It was this measure that was primarily responsible for Singapore's current superiority to Hong Kong as an Asian dollar centre since the Hong Kong government refused to reduce its 15 per cent withholding tax on domestic interest earnings.

Secondly, non-residents were exempted from tax on interest earned on investments in Asian dollar bonds. Prior to the government budget of March 1980, this concession was in theory considered on a case-by-case basis. In practice it was anyway free but now it is statutorily given to all non-resident participants.

Thirdly, non-resident deposits with ACUs and capital profit on Asian dollar bonds are exempt from estate duty tax.

Lastly, the government has abolished stamp duty on Asian dollar bonds and loan agreements made by an ACU.

The result of these incentives has been to encourage many foreign banks to establish branches in Singapore and to set up their own ACUs. The presence of such facilities has consequently attracted considerable foreign funds.

Certificates of deposit

Banks have been authorized to issue negotiable CDs denominated in Singapore dollars since May 1975. The measure was introduced to encourage a shift into longer time deposits.

Singapore dollar CDs are issued with original maturities of 3, 6, 9 or 12 months, and in multiples of three months up to three years. Negotiable CDs are also issued denominated in US dollars with maturities from one month up to five years.

Minimum denominations are S$100 000 and US$50 000 in multiples of S$50 000 and US$50 000 respectively, but with maximum denominations of S$1 million for Singapore dollar CDs. Both types of CDs may carry either fixed- or floating-rate coupons, in each case generally calculated at $\frac{1}{4}$ per cent above Singapore interbank offered rate.

Initially, the Asian dollar CD market got off to a slow start, receiving very little support from investors and lacking an adequate secondary market. Fixed-rate issues were tried in 1970, but were rather unsuccessful. In 1978, the market was given a substantial impetus when new Japanese banking regulations required that Japanese banks must match, within specified limits, the maturities of their assets and liabilities. Thus, their longer-term lending had to be matched by longer-term

545

borrowing. Japanese banks consequently tapped the Singapore CD market by issuing 3-year floating-rate CDs, and using this market for reasons of convenience and proximity, and also to help the market to develop, which they saw to be in their own interest.

Primary market

Primary issues in 1978 amounted to some S$50 million, made mainly by US and Japanese banks. By 1980 the primary market has grown to a size of S$700 million, with total outstanding issues of about S$2 billion. Ninety per cent of primary issues are taken up by other banks. About 60 per cent of outstanding CDs are floating-rate issues. These floating-rate CDs (FRCDs) have largely facilitated the growth of the market. They enable Japanese banks to borrow on longer terms (up to 5 years), while offering attractive rates to lenders. Terms are usually 0.25 per cent above SIBOR (Singapore interbank offer rate), and revised every three months during the life of the CD.

Fixed-rate CDs are usually issued with maturities of between one and three months. Some are issued with three to six months maturities while fixed-rate CDs of more than six months are uncommon. ACUs of American banks are the largest issuers of fixed-rate US dollar CDs.

Next to London, Singapore now stands as the most important issuing centre for FRCDs in the world. The authorities have encouraged the market still further by abolishing the queuing system that required banks to issue FRCDs in a predetermined order and amount. Further, they are considering whether to allow foreign banks without branches in Singapore to issue CDs on the Asian dollar market.

Secondary market

The secondary market has grown commensurately more active with the growth of the primary market but the secondary market makers, comprising mostly commercial and merchant banks and US commission houses, consider that there is still scope for further improvement and development.

Treasury bills

The government issues 90-day treasury bills on a weekly tender basis. They may be subscribed to by non-bank entities including non-residents. Although in great general demand, they are purchased in the primary market and traded in the secondary market mainly by financial institutions, especially discount houses who are obliged to hold 70 per cent of their assets in the form of short-term Government securities. Also the lower yields make treasury bills less attractive than other market money instruments to the corporate or individual investor.

Since there is no official discount rate, the authorities use the issue of treasury bills to influence money market rates by varying both the discount attached to the bills and the amount issued. This indirectly influences call money rates, principally those paid by discount houses which are obliged to hold treasury bills. Consequently other short-term interest rates are ultimately affected.

Bankers' acceptances and commercial bills

There is no market as yet for bankers' acceptances. However, there is a domestic commercial bill market which is modelled along the same lines as the London market. Effectively such paper consists of bank bills, whereby a bank pays an exporter at a suitable discount and draws a bill on the importer for the value of the goods transacted. The bank may then rediscount the bills with the market, usually through a discount house. The secondary market is limited for the non-bank investor since the accepting bank or discount house either holds the bills to maturity or trades them mainly in the interbank market.

ASEAN (The Association of South East Asian Nations) is, however, currently considering the development of an acceptance market.

More specifically, ASEAN wants to harmonize its different financial systems so that trade financing instruments, such as bankers' acceptances, can be freely negotiable throughout the area. This would involve changes in the monetary systems of some of the other ASEAN countries, such that their central banks would stand ready to rediscount such bills.

It is doubted, however, whether an ASEAN-based acceptance market would be viable. Singapore may well decide to establish its own international acceptance market or to promote a cosmopolitan market aimed at financing trade outside the region as well as within ASEAN. Thus it would operate as an extension of the New York market in bankers' acceptances.

Commercial paper

Recent developments indicate that a commercial paper market is developing in the Asian dollar market. Effectively, like a CD, this is promissory paper offered by a company instead of a bank. The first issue of Asian dollar commercial paper was made in 1980 by the Singapore merchant bank DBS Daiwa on behalf of C. Itoh, a Japanese trading company. The total amount of the issue was US$10 million for terms of both three and six months at $\frac{1}{8}$ per cent over SIBOR. This is the beginning of what is hoped to be a fast expanding commercial paper market. This first issue was taken up mainly by banks and financial institutions. It is intended that corporations and individuals will eventually participate, and the commercial and investment banks are standing ready to make a secondary market in such paper.

The capital market

While the Singapore money market has become established as one of the most efficient of world markets, the capital market has yet to develop similar international status, though the authorities are keen to encourage such a development. The Asian dollar bond market is well evolved, but currently several factors as follow inhibit the domestic capital market's further expansion.

1. The CPF (Central Provident Fund) controls too large a share of domestic savings which are channelled into government securities rather than into private sector securities.

2. The government owns, or controls, a large portion of the corporate sector.
3. The marketability of companies listed on the stock exchange is too small to promote an active securities market. Although the number of shares listed is large enough for an adequate number the turnover is low and frequently there is an insufficient supply of available shares to provide an active market.

The authorities are considering moves to improve the market: handing over part of the CPF to private management; the public listing of government owned corporations; and encouraging foreign companies to seek quotations on the Singapore stock exchange.

These factors are more fully described in the following sections, as relevant.

Government bonds

At the end of 1979, total government debt was S$11.4 billion, S$9.7 billion of which was in the form of government bonds. Eighty per cent of these bonds are held by two institutions, the CPF and the Post Office Savings Bank (POSB). The balance is traded and held by discount houses, banks, insurance companies and trustee companies.

While non-bank companies and individuals, including non-residents, may purchase and trade government securities, clearly the secondary market is restricted to the approximate S$2 billion available to the market. The CPF, owning 10 times more than the POSB, is the main constraint on the development of a secondary market. Studies involving consultation between the Minister of Finance and the banking system have led to proposals that part of the CPF should be transferred to private sector management. The CPF is effectively a national insurance fund to which all employers and employees contribute an obligatory proportion of monthly wages. Part of this fund (standing at about S$8 billion) could, it is suggested, be managed by banks and financial institutions in the private sector. The danger is, however, that local management still lack certain practical skills and that the local stock market might not be able easily to absorb an additional S$8 billion of funds. On the other hand, the government does not want to encourage the investment of local funds in foreign markets. Additionally there is no guarantee that there would be adequate interest among private investors for the government bonds no longer purchased by the CPF. The government might then be obliged either to seek funds from external sources by foreign borrowing, or to pay more for its borrowing through higher yields on its bonds. The government is thus torn between the privatization of the CPF in order to foster the development of the local capital market or retaining the CPF within the public sector and obtaining cheap funds. The CPF is a superb machine for financing the government at below market costs. Members of the CPF are guaranteed an annual return of six per cent. Thus in 1980 the government was able to issue 15- to 20-year bonds at only 6.1 per cent, yields on government bonds, therefore, are lower than rates on other securities of comparable terms, but interest is paid free of tax. This makes then an attractive domestic investment, but of little interest to the non-resident investor. Additionally, current yields do not at present necessarily relate to market trends since the CPF, as the main investor, is more concerned with the long-term return. Government bonds are issued with minimum maturities of 1 year up to 20 years. New issues that are not taken up by the CPF and POSB are readily taken up by the banks and discount houses, leaving little in the way of a market for other investors.

Domestic corporate bonds

Bond issues are an uncommon source of financing for domestic Singaporean companies which prefer either to borrow from the banks or to issue equity share capital.

A few straight bonds and convertible debentures are listed on the Singapore stock exchange, but these enjoy a poor market compared to equities and represent only 0.1 to 0.2 per cent of stock exchange turnover. Local capital invested in domestic bonds derives from individuals, insurance companies, firms, units trusts, banks and investment companies.

Asian dollar bonds

Unlike the domestic bond market, the Asian dollar bond market is continuing to grow at a significant rate.

This market is the Asian equivalent of the Eurobond market. Companies wishing to raise money issue bonds—denominated usually in US dollars, although also in other currencies—through the Asian dollar bond market based in Singapore. Thus the Asian dollar bond market is really a local extension of the Eurobond market. There are very few genuine Asian issues, i.e., issues made in Asian currencies. Most are denominated in US dollars.

New issues are managed by a syndicate of banks through their ACUs, though lending and placement is managed by only one bank. Issues may be either for private placement or public offering. The latter are listed on the Singapore stock exchange.

The Asian dollar bond market began in 1971. By mid-1980 56 issues had been floated to a total nominal value of US$1.7 billion. Most issues were floated in US dollars though others have been offered in Australian dollars, yen, Deutschemark and SDRs. Some have also been jointly floated in the Eurobond market. Almost half of the issues have been fixed-coupon-rate issues, 40 per cent have been floating-rate issues and the remainder have been convertible bonds. The majority of recent issues have been floating-rate, with coupons being adjusted semiannually at $\frac{1}{4}$ to $\frac{3}{4}$ per cent above SIBOR for three- to six-months deposits, though bonds issued by non-prime names may carry a premium of two or three per cent over SIBOR.

Maturities of Asian dollar bonds range from under 5 years up to 15 years, though the majority have been issued for between 5 and 10 years.

The secondary market is not yet as active as the Eurobond secondary market in Europe because the primary market is smaller and liquidity is lower. Despite the fact that some international bond issues are lead managed by ACUs in Singapore and listed in the local market the major proportion of trading continues to take place in already established markets such as London, Zurich and New York. In recent uncertain market conditions, it has proved sometimes difficult for market makers to find buyers of the right size. Additionally, delivery costs are higher than in the Eurobond market.

The growth of the CD market and the government's continued encouragement for its development should help to attract more participants to the market. Currently, although the primary market is centred in Singapore, more secondary market trading in the area is conducted through the large stockbrokers and banks in Hong Kong rather than Singapore. The abolition of stamp duty by the government in its March 1980 budget is a further incentive for investors to use the Singapore market. In practical terms, however, the real impetus to the market will result from the development of Singapore's domestic capital market which is currently much smaller than Hong Kong's, and which does not yet generate or attract sufficient funds to fuel the international bond market. The government is planning methods of changing the institutional structure of the capital market and the role played by public sector institutions such as the CPF and Temasek Holdings (see Equities). Such moves should help the growth of financial intermediary and advisory services which currently are fewer and smaller than those in Hong Kong.

Equities

As at mid-1980 there were 264 companies listed on the Singapore stock exchange, 94 of which were Singapore incorporated companies, 159 were Malaysian, 8 British, 2 Japanese and 1 Hong Kong. The total market capitalization of these companies is approximately S$33 billion, only 35 per cent of which is represented by shares of Singaporean companies. The government wants to add depth to the market by encouraging multinational companies to seek quotations on the local capital market. This would only serve, however, to satisfy the demands of local investors and is unlikely to attract foreign investors who can deal in the same shares in their domestic market. Developments are likely to be slow since Hong Kong currently offers the better facilities of a larger and more active existing market, and the services of investment advisory expertise. Compared to Hong Kong, there are few foreign stockbrokers in Singapore and this compounds the relative lack of foreign interest in the Singapore market. Additionally, investors in the Singapore market are unable to reclaim tax deducted from dividends except under a few double taxation agreements, whereas no dividend tax applies to investments in Hong Kong. The Minister of Finance is looking into the possibility of establishing an over-the-counter market for the actively traded shares of major foreign companies which it has not yet been possible to attract for listing on the exchange. This may also prove unsuccessful. Certain foreign companies have had their shares listed on the Singapore stock exchange for several years but turnover has nevertheless been negligible. The real problems of the Singapore market concerning the non-resident investor are:

1. Most shares are held by existing shareholders and an inadequate quantity is sold in order to provide a sufficient supply to foster an active market.

2. The market is dominated by a relatively small number of local investors who, by the use of inside information and special relationships, are able to take advantage of the market and preclude satisfactory participation by other investors. Price/earnings ratios, if used at all, do not therefore reflect the true worth of a company.
3. Brokerage costs are high.
4. Settlement procedures are not sufficiently efficient and lengthy delays may occur.

The government controls some of the biggest and most successful companies through its holding company Temasek Holdings. Temasek has substantial shareholdings in several listed companies, i.e., the National Iron and Steel Mills, Development Bank of Singapore, Sembawang Shipyard, ACMA Electrical Industries, Keppeel, the United Industrial Corporation, Intraco, and Chemical Industries. Temasek in addition holds more than 50 per cent of the shareholding in 8 unquoted companies and substantial minority holdings in a further 18 companies. The government acknowledges that its holdings through Temasek is not conducive to the efficiency of the market. It therefore plans to seek listings of some of these companies on the stock exchange. Two such companies were to be floated in 1980. The government also plans the gradual selling off of its holding in already quoted companies, thus releasing more shares.

For local companies, many of which are family concerns, internal financing is often preferred, followed by borrowing from commercial banks. Equity financing is a less important method, but is still much preferred to bond financing when companies wish to tap the public capital market.

Despite its small size, local interest in the equity market is good and most new issues are oversubscribed, but this is not however indicative of an active market. The typical Singapore equity is usually held by, for example, family/friends over 50 per cent, another 10 per cent by foreign interests and yet a further 10 per cent by a local bank. Thus the volume of available shares remaining to be traded on the market is small.

Turnover in the secondary market, therefore, can only occur in the small proportion of shares that are not tightly held and which float freely on the market. Equity shares, however, account for virtually 100 per cent of stock exchange turnover to a value of approximately S$2 billion per annum.

The stock exchange

The Singapore stock exchange separated from the Joint Stock Exchange of Singapore and Malaysia in 1973. Many local companies are quoted on both exchanges; Singapore handles the larger turnover of transactions but its lead over the Kuala Lumpur stock exchange is diminishing.

The stock exchange is self-regulating, constituted as a joint stock limited company and managed by a five-man committee. Members of the exchange comprise both individual members and member companies. Company members have to show a minimum amount of liquid capital of S$100000 per member and S$50000

551

for each dealer's representative, together with bank guarantees of S$10 000 and S$20 000 respectively.

Member companies must at all times possess a seat, a condition of which is the subscription to one share in the Stock Exchange of Singapore Limited at a premium which is determined by the Committee.

New listings must first be approved by both the Stock Exchange Committee and the Securities Industry Council (SIC) which is established under the Companies Act but is an authority above the business community in general. Minimum listing requirements are that companies should have a paid-up capital of at least S$4 million and that at least 25 per cent of its issued and paid-up capital should be in the hands of not less than 500 shareholders. Bond issues must be a minimum of S$750 000 for a maximum of two loan securities of at least S$350 000 each. The bonds must be held by not less than 200 holders.

Most domestic quotations on the stock exchange are for ordinary shares and preference shares. Domestic corporate and straight bonds are rarely floated, though Asian dollar bonds comprise a large proportion of listed securities.

Listed shares are classified on the exchange according to eight categories:

Industry	Oil palm
Finance	Tin
Hotels	Dollar rubber
Property	Sterling rubber

On the exchange, the call-over system is used whereby trading is done by dealers calling out bids and offers. The highest and lowest bids for each share are recorded on a scoreboard.

Shares are traded in board lots of 1000 and in 'big board' lots of 5000 shares. Delivery and settlement for the latter occurs mid-month. Others are settled as below.

Table 25.2 Turnover in the Stock Exchange of Singapore (S$ million)

| Year | Total* | Corporate securities | | Government securities |
		Equities	Bonds	
1972	2155.6	2155.6	....	na
1973	2693.2	2573.1	....	120.1
1974	1319.3	1127.9	6.0	185.4
1975	2027.2	1818.0	9.6	199.6
1976	2361.1	1915.9	12.4	433.8
1977	1566.8	1157.6	3.9	405.3
1978	3950.6	3382.9	4.3	563.4
1979	2835.7	2308.9	2.6	524.2

* Prior to June 1973, turnover includes those executed in the Malaysia trading room.

For dealing purposes, shares are classified into two types, the first trading section and the second trading section. The first comprises companies having a share capital of more than S45 million dollars and which have paid dividends of at least five per cent of earnings for the preceding three years. All other shares fall within the second section.

First section shares may be traded for both spot and forward delivery, whereas second section may be traded for spot delivery only. Forward delivery is for the end of the account, each account running for one month closing at the end of each calendar month. In practice, about 95 per cent of all shares are traded on a spot basis so the forward market is relatively insignificant. Additionally, although the spot market is for cash there is no fixed settlement date and lengthy delays are common.

Options

Trading in call options began on 1 February 1977. The initial list of options comprised the shares of top rated companies such as Inchcape, United Overseas Bank and the Development Bank of Singapore. Since then, a further eight have been added to the options list which is now to be extended to companies that are listed on stock exchanges outside Singapore. In future, bond options may be introduced in order to broaden the market since activity is currently rather limited.

Transactions are made on the floor of the stock exchange on which option prices are quoted. Call options are made for three-month periods which expire in March, June, September and December.

The options market does not however allow trading in options but provides the investor with the possibility only of purchasing a call option, and then either to exercise the option or to allow it to lapse. The market has never really developed and the volume of options purchases is virtually negligible.

Commodities

There are two physical commodity trading places, the Rubber Association of Singapore (RAS) and the Chinese Produce Exchange. The rubber market is the largest in the world. Originally founded 65 years ago, the RAS was established as a corporate body in 1968 to give clearing facilities to European dealers. Members of the RAS comprise dealers, selling agents, manufacturers' buying agents and commodity brokers.

Dealing may be done on both a spot and a forward basis. Prices are fixed twice daily at 12 noon and 4.30 p.m. by a panel comprising brokers and dealers.

The Chinese Produce Exchange trades principally in coconut oil, copra, pepper and coffee. Transactions are made on a spot basis only, there being no forward market.

Other commodities produced in South East Asia such as palm oil, sugar, tin and other metals are traded on the London or New York exchanges. Most commodity dealing is done by traders and very few members of the public participate. Interest in commodity futures is, however, increasing.

Gold

The Singapore gold market was established in 1969. Since 1973 residents and non-residents alike have been free to trade in gold without restriction. The gold futures market (the Gold Exchange of Singapore), was established at the beginning of 1979. Since its inception, there has been substantial trading on the exchange, and turnover is continuing to grow rapidly. Average daily turnover is about 15 000 ounces, though during the rapid rise in the gold price in early 1980 turnover reached 50 000 ounces per day. However, this is tiny compared to the market in Hong Kong, and particularly so when compared to other markets in, for example, the United States.

Transactions may be made for spot delivery and settlement or for forward delivery in the futures market. Futures contracts may be made for the current month and for the subsequent four even months, i.e., for February, April, June, August, October and December. For example, on 23 June, contracts could be made for delivery for the next business day or for July, August, October, December and February.

Contracts made are cleared through the Singapore Gold Clearing House which is a separate institution owned by the four largest local banks. The clearing house also guarantees all gold contracts made on the exchange, and issues to buyers gold certificates which are valid for 12 months.

Gold is traded in lots of 100 troy ounces. Kilobar contract trading is expected to be introduced in the near future. The exchange accounts for probably only 10 per cent of all gold traded in Singapore, the major proportion being dealt by local bankers through the London or New York markets where, at present, fees are cheaper. Nonetheless, the government is attempting to attract more international interest in the Gold Exchange of Singapore and has already reduced the withholding tax on income derived from offshore gold transactions from 40 to 10 per cent.

Dealing and fees

Money market

Deposits

Call and time deposits may be placed in Singapore dollars in the domestic market with commercial banks, finance companies or other saving institutions. There is no charge for opening an account. Interest rates depend on domestic economic conditions, but vary between institutions.

Call and time deposits in Singapore dollars and other convertible currencies may be placed by non-residents with one of the hundred or so commercial banks that have ACUs. Interest rates depend on international supply and demand.

554

Certificates of deposit

CDs may be bought directly from an authorized bank or from discount houses which act as principals in the market. Dealing spreads are $\frac{1}{8}$ to $\frac{1}{4}$ per cent.

Treasury bills

Treasury bills may be dealt through a commercial bank or a discount house. Dealing spreads range from $\frac{1}{64}$ to $\frac{1}{8}$ per cent, depending on market conditions.

Commercial paper

Commercial paper is traded in the Asian dollar market through the ACU of an authorized bank. The market is not sufficiently established for dealing spreads to have been set, but are likely to be about $\frac{1}{8}$ per cent.

Capital market

Asian dollar bonds

Asian dollar bonds are traded through branches of foreign (particularly US) brokers and commission houses and through the ACUs of authorized banks.

Dealing spreads depend on the particular bond issue (bonds issued by prime names having a smaller spread than bonds of lesser names) and also to some extent on the liquidity and demand in the market.

The difference between bid and offer rates may, therefore, range from $\frac{1}{8}$ to 1 per cent. They may also be purchased on the stock exchange through a stockbroker, at commission rates shown below.

Domestic bonds

Domestic bonds are dealt on the floor of the stock exchange through a stockbroker. Orders may be made through a bank which will use its own broker. Commissions rates are as follows:

Asian dollar bonds	$\frac{3}{8}\%$ of consideration
Singapore government bonds	$\frac{1}{40}\%$ of consideration subject to minimum S$100
Other government bonds	$\frac{3}{8}\%$ on first S$20 000, $\frac{1}{4}\%$ on excess
Corporate bonds and non-convertible debentures	1% on consideration of less than S$50 000 $\frac{1}{2}\%$ on consideration of between S$50 000 to S$100 000 $\frac{1}{4}\%$ on consideration of over S$100 000

All bond transactions are subject to a minimum brokerage payable by both buyer and seller of S$2.

Equities

Equity shares are dealt through a stockbroker and traded only on the stock exchange.

First-section shares may be settled either on a cash basis or for delivery at the end of the month. Big board lots may be settled in the middle of each month.

In practice nearly all transactions are made on a cost basis, but settlement procedures are inefficient and may anyway take anything from a few days to several weeks to complete.

Different brokerages are charged for cash and forward settlement as follows:

Ordinary shares, preference shares and convertible debentures

(*a*) Cash settlement

Share price of under $0.50	0.5 cent per share
Share price of over $0.50 and under $1.00	1 cent per share
Share price of over $1	1% of consideration

(*b*) Forward settlement (N.B. minority of transactions only)

Share price of under $0.50	0.75 cent per share
Share price of over $0.50 and under $1	1.5 cents per share
Share price of over $1	1.5% of consideration

Options (Subject to a minimum commission of S$5)

Opening transaction	1.5% of premium value + $2.50
Closing transaction	1.5% of premium value

Stamp duty

Stamp duty is payable on all transactions apart from those in the Eurodollar market. Stamp duty is 0.1 per cent plus a government transfer charge of 0.3 per cent per contract.

Financial and monetary systems

Financial institutions

The whole range of financial institutions are represented in Singapore though the government would like to encourage the increase and further development of private sector and foreign intermediaries. Private intermediaries include commercial banks, merchant banks, discount houses, finance companies, building societies, stockbrokers, and money and foreign exchange brokers.

Public institutions comprise the Central Provident Fund, the Post Office Savings Bank, the Monetary Authority of Singapore and the Currency Board. The Development Bank of Singapore is also indirectly part of the public sector, being owned by the government participated Temasek Holdings Company.

Commercial banks

There are 103 commercial banks. Thirteen of these are local banks which in 1979 accounted for 41 per cent of total domestic banking assets and liabilities and 14 per cent of domestic ACU business. Their share of combined domestic and Asian currency business is 28.3 per cent of non-bank deposits and 20.6 per cent of loans and advances. These proportions have shown a steady decline during recent years because of competition from the growing number of foreign banks.

The 'big four' domestic banks in order of asset size are the United Overseas Bank (UOB), the Overseas Chinese Banking Corporation, the Development Bank of Singapore (DBS), and the Overseas Union Bank. The DBS is 49 per cent owned by the government and 51 per cent by the public. The other three are also publicly quoted but large shareholdings are owned by family interests.

The local banks all have full banking licences which means that they may have more than one branch and may engage in all banking operations without restriction. Such banks may accept savings, call and time deposits, provide chequing account facilities, finance exports and imports through acceptances, write commercial letters of credit, deal in securities on behalf of customers, provide investment advisory services, underwrite new security issues, operate an ACU and engage in foreign exchange transactions. Of the 90 foreign commercial banks, 24 have full banking licences. Of the remainder, some have restricted banking licences, some have offshore banking licences and some have representative offices only.

Banks with restricted licences may also operate more than one branch office in Singapore and may offer local currency savings account facilities and accept time deposits in sums of up to S$250000, but they operate mainly in the Asian dollar market.

As local banking requirements are satisfied by the banks with full and restricted licences, since the early 1970s most foreign banks have been granted offshore licences only. These banks operate mainly in the external Asian dollar market and do very little domestic banking business. They may not accept small local currency deposits, except from other banks, but attract funds from the interbank market or from the conversion of foreign currency from non-resident sources. They may accept call and time deposits in Singapore dollars, however, from either residents or non-resident lenders, but in minimum amounts of S$250000 only. They may lend to non-resident borrowers but not, in general, to domestic borrowers except in minimum amounts of S$1000000.

Asian currency units (ACUs)

An Asian currency unit is a separate department within a bank and which accounts separately and operates specifically in the Asian dollar market. That is, ACUs borrow and lend in foreign currencies but not in Singapore dollars because they may not compete for domestic business. They accept deposits from non-residents and also from residents but only up to specified limits. They also act as agents or managers in the public issue of foreign currency loans in the form of syndicated credits and Asian-dollar bonds. An ACU thus acts as an intermediary between borrowers and lenders of funds in the international market. The borrowers are mainly multinational corporations which need to finance capital projects or expansion, trading companies requiring foreign currency on a relatively short-term basis, and foreign or domestic commercial banks. The main lenders are domestic foreign multinational companies with short-term surplus liquidity, foreign commercial banks, including those which operate in the Eurodollar market, central banks, which hold large foreign currency reserves, and wealthy individuals. There are now 101 ACUs which are operated by local and foreign commercial banks, merchant banks and investment companies.

Merchant banks

There are over 36 merchant banks in Singapore. Some are foreign-incorporated while others have been set up as joint ventures between local banks or international foreign banks and foreign merchant banks. Their activities include the syndication of convertible currency financing; loans, guarantees and other forms of funding; underwriting of equities and bond private placements in all currencies; leasing; financial advisory services on mergers, acquisitions and capital restructuring; and investment management services. Merchant banks are subject to supervision by the Monetary Authority of Singapore. They may accept Singapore dollar deposits from financial institutions only.

Discount houses

There are four discount houses in Singapore, the first having been established in 1972. They act as intermediaries between the banking system and the Monetary Authority of Singapore and have aided the development of a more sophisticated money market than was operating at the beginning of the 1970s. They have recourse to the Monetary Authority of Singapore which provides a lender of last resort facility in the discounting of bills. They accept call deposits from banks and other lenders in minimum amounts of S$50 000 for which they must offer collateral, usually in the form of treasury bills and other short-term securities. They may trade in treasury bills, commercial bills of exchange and short-dated government securities and bonds only.

Finance companies

Finance companies provide near-banking facilities primarily in the domestic market. They accept deposits from the public either in the form of savings deposits or by the issue of CDs. They use the funds so obtained to lend to local individuals and companies through private loans or hire purchase. Surplus funds are often placed as redeposits with banks and other financial institutions.

Money brokers

There are several international money brokers in Singapore. They deal only in currencies, acting as intermediaries between financial institutions in Singapore and other world financial centres. They do not deal directly with commercial customers.

Central Provident Fund

The Central Provident Fund (CPF) is effectively a pension fund for Singapore employees. Its present methods of operation significantly affect the domestic capital market since it represents a 35 per cent share of domestic savings which are invested almost entirely in government securities. It is mandatory for both employers and employees to contribute 20.5 and 16.5 per cent respectively of an employee's monthly wages to the CPF. In 1980, the fund amounted to S$7.5 billion and is growing at a rate of S$2 billion per year. Almost all of the CPF's capital is invested in government bonds of which there were about S$10 billion outstanding. The CPF tends to hold these bonds to maturity rather than trading them in the market. Thus, effectively almost 75 per cent of government bonds are removed from the capital market.

The government is concerned about the inhibiting effects of the CPF monopoly and is reviewing the possibility of handing over part of the CPF fund to private management. In this way funds might be channelled into the private sector capital market (see Government bonds).

Post Office Savings Bank

The Post Office Savings Bank (POSB) is another public sector institution that influences the domestic capital market. It has 102 branches in Singapore and represents a substantial share of domestic savings. It attracts such savings by offering tax-free interest on deposits of up to S$100 000, and provides longer service hours to customers than do the commercial banks.

Though state run, the POSB is an independent statutory body; it does not come under the Banking Act so is exempt from the reserve requirement regulations.

Like to CPF, the POSB invests a large proportion of its funds in government bonds so that together they hold 80 per cent of government bonds.

Monetary Authority of Singapore

The Monetary Authority of Singapore (MAS) was founded in 1970. It performs all the functions of a central bank except for the issue of currency. Thus, the MAS administers monetary policies on behalf of the government; acts as fiscal agent for the government; issues treasury obligations and manages its overseas assets; supervises the banking system; administers exchange controls; supervises the stock exchange; provides clearing facilities for commercial banks; buys, sells, discounts and rediscounts treasury bills; buys and sells long-term government bonds.

The Currency Board

The Currency Board issues notes and coins and redeems Singapore currency in exchange for convertible currencies and gold. The currency is backed 100 per cent by external assets, mostly in US dollars, sterling and gold. The currency board maintains a currency fund into which is paid the US dollars and other convertible currencies against which Singapore dollars are issued. At least 30 per cent of the fund is held in liquid assets. The face value of the currency in calculation may not exceed the total value of the fund.

The monetary authority of Singapore maintains the exchange value of the Singapore dollar, relative to a trade weighted basket of currencies, by intervention in the spot foreign exchange market using the US dollar as the currency of intervention. It also acts as intermediary between the currency board and the financial system in the settlement of currency requirements by the banks.

Plans are currently in progress to merge the MAS and currency board so as to create a unified central bank.

Monetary policy

Monetary policy, along with fiscal policy, is determined by the Minister of Finance under the direction of the Prime Minister, but implemented by the monetary authority of Singapore and the currency board. The objects of monetary policy are the promotion of stable credit and exchange rate conditions conducive to the balanced and sustained growth of the economy. The main areas of development are improvement of the financial infrastructure and the growth of Singapore as a financial centre. The main instruments of control are reserve requirements, liquidity ratios, discount policy and open market operations. These primarily effect the domestic markets. Their effectiveness is measured by changes in monetary aggregates, principally the money supply. Certain constraints are imposed by the openness of the economy. Exchange rate stability is assisted by operations in the foreign exchange market but little intervention occurs in the Asian dollar market.

Reserve requirements

Commercial banks are required to maintain minimum reserves of six per cent of deposit liabilities on non-interest-earning deposit with the MAS. The reserve averaging period is fortnightly at the middle and end of each month. As a means of control over the banking system, in practice the reserve requirement is varied only infrequently. Although it has been as high as 9 per cent and as low as $3\frac{1}{2}$ per cent it has remained at 6 per cent since July 1975. The MAS has the authority to impose a supplementary special deposit, but this is currently zero. Offshore banks and ACUs are not subject to the reserve requirement. The effect of the six per cent reserve requirement is to ensure that a certain level of liquidity is maintained in the banking system. During the course of a day the banks' balances with the MAS are affected by the banks' financial transactions with the MAS; at the end of the day the banks are required to balance their books. If they find they have excess funds on account with the MAS, they may lend to other banks or the discount houses on an overnight or short-term basis. If, on the other hand, they have to make up their cash reserves, they may borrow from the discount houses by rediscounting treasury or commercial bills, or borrow in the foreign exchange market; alternatively they could issue CDs or sell securities.

Liquidity ratios

Liquidity ratios are used in addition to reserve requirements as a more flexible means of monetary control.

The overall liquidity ratio for banks and finance companies is 20 per cent of deposit liabilities. The MAS may vary the mix of assets which the banks must maintain. In 1980, half of the banks' liquidity was required to be in primary liquid assets, company notes and coins; excess balances with the MAS; money at call with discount houses; treasury bills and other government securities with a remaining life of less than one year. The other half of liquid assets, defined as secondary liquidity, had to be kept in other assets as directed by the MAS. These were government securities of more than one year; commercial bills of less than 90 days, discounted, purchased or receivable and payable in Singapore (up to a maximum of five per cent of their liability base). By such means the MAS can thus influence both the liquidity in the domestic banking system and the direction of funds towards particular sectors of the money and capital markets. Offshore banks and ACUs are not subject to these liquidity ratios.

Direct controls

The MAS restricts the expansion of credit also by requiring local commercial banks to limit their loans and advances, including guarantees, to some percentage of their capital funds. Such regulations are not varied as a flexible tool of monetary policy but are stipulated in the banking act and serve to ensure prudent lending activity by the domestic banks (foreign banks may apply for exemption from the controls). The regulations specify that, without specific approval from the MAS, a bank may not lend more than 60 per cent of its capital funds to any single borrower, and further that investments in non-banking activities, including property, may not exceed 40 per cent of its capital base. The domestic banks are also required to transfer 50 per cent of their profits each year into a reserve fund. This may be reduced to 25 per cent of profits if the reserve fund exceeds 50 per cent of their paid-up capital or 5 per cent of profits if it exceeds 100 per cent of capital.

From time to time, selective credit controls may be introduced by the MAS. These controls are designed to direct funds from the banking system to specific sectors of the economy, and are introduced during easy money conditions in order to curb inflation and speculative activities while, at the same time, ensuring a flow of funds to the productive sectors of the economy.

Discount policy

The discount rate in Singapore is not an administered rate, but is determined entirely by market forces as are other interest rates. Since 1975 all banks have been free to quote their own interest rates. The MAS can, however, influence the level of interest rates in the market by the discount rate on new treasury bills, by the size of new issues, and by changing the rate within limited parameters at which it is willing to rediscount bills to the discount houses. The MAS closely monitors money

561

market trends and intervenes in the market to smooth out interest-rate fluctuations; it provides discount facilities to the discount houses. The commercial banks in turn may rediscount bills through the discount houses.

The discount houses hold 70 per cent of their asset portfolios in treasury bills and the remainder in private sector paper, i.e., commercial bills and CDs. The MAS accepts both treasury bills and commercial bills from the discount houses for rediscounting. If the discount houses have insufficient quantities of such paper (within the constraints of their obligatory 70 per cent) then the MAS will provide lender of last resort facilities by advancing short-term credit to the discount houses against specific assets. However, these advances are granted at a penalty, in excess of the discount rate. The rediscount and lender of last resort facilities help to adjust liquidity in the whole of the banking system. The discount houses operate with the banks in the interbank market, whereby surplus short-term funds are borrowed and lent between financial institutions. When liquidity is tight, and the banks have temporary deficits, they may issue CDs or borrow from the discount houses by rediscounting bills through them. The discount houses in turn have recourse to MAS facilities. Liquidity is seasonally tight in December and during the Chinese New Year in February. The MAS assistance may have no immediate effect on interest rates, however, although the lack of assistance would certainly tend to increase interest rates. Greater influence over short-term interest rates is achieved through the use of open market operations.

When money conditions are easy, the MAS can absorb liquidity from the money market by issuing a larger quantity of treasury bills or by open market operations.

Open market operations

The MAS makes considerable daily use of open market operations to influence liquidity in domestic money and capital markets. Apart from its transactions with the discount houses the MAS operates also in the interbank and foreign exchange markets. Most of its interbank operations involve the borrowing or lending of short-term money but are conducted mainly through the discount houses. In the foreign exchange market the MAS intervenes in order to maintain a stable value of the currency and to adjust domestic liquidity caused by the inflow and outflow of external funds. One facility introduced in 1977 is swap arrangements to help the liquidity in the banking system, especially during the normally tight periods of the festive seasons (Christmas and Chinese New Year). Thus, banks with excess US dollars may swap them with the MAS for Singapore dollars, with an agreement that the swap will be reversed within a specified period of time.

Withholding taxes

Transactions in the Asian dollar market are not subject to withholding taxes on either interest or dividends.

For proceeds arising from investment in the domestic markets, interest is subject to a withholding tax of 40 per cent, which is reduced to 15 or 10 per cent for residents of tax-treaty countries. Dividends are paid net of the 40 per cent tax paid by corporations. There is no additional withholding tax in excess of this.

Table 25.3   Withholding taxes

	Interest, %	Dividends, %
Residents of non-treaty countries	40	40
Residents of treaty countries		
Australia	10	0
Belgium	15	0
Canada	15	
Denmark	15 or 10	0
France	10 or 0	0
Germany	10	0
Israel	15	0
Italy	12.5	
Japan	15 or 0	0
Malaysia	40	0
Netherlands	10	0
New Zealand	15	0
Norway	40	0
Philippines	15	0
Sweden	15 or 10	0
Switzerland	10	0
Thailand	25 or 10	0
United Kingdom	15	0

N.B. Where two rates are shown for withholding tax on interest, the lower rate applies for interest on approved industrial loan interest, except in the case of Thailand where the lower rate applies to financial institutions.

Exchange controls

Exchange authority

The Monetary Authority of Singapore is responsible for exchange control matters, although in 1978 exchange controls were abolished, so currently no formalities are imposed.

Currency

The currency is the Singapore dollar which is maintained against a trade weighted basket of currencies. The MAS intervenes using the US dollar in the spot foreign exchange market in order to maintain the stability of the currency.

All banks, companies and individuals, both resident and non-resident, may freely deal in the spot and forward foreign exchange markets.

Non-resident accounts
There is no distinction between resident and non-resident accounts.

Purchase and sale of securities
Non-residents may freely purchase or sell any Singapore securities, without limit and in any currency. Proceeds from investments may be repatriated freely or credited to any account.

26. International Markets

The international markets may be broadly defined as those markets that transcend national boundaries. Basically they are markets in which borrowers from one country may seek lenders of other countries and conduct transactions in currencies that need not be the domestic currency of either participant. Mostly the markets operate outside the legislation and regulations of any single domestic market.

Eurocurrencies

The largest, most important international market is the Eurocurrency market, a subset of which is the Eurobond market. A Eurocurrency is any currency that is on deposit in a bank outside the borders of the home country of that currency and thus beyond the control or jurisdiction of the monetary authorities of that country. A Eurocurrency is created when someone makes a transfer in the same currency from the country of origin to a bank in a foreign country either for the payment of goods or services, for transactions in the foreign exchange market, or just simply a straight transfer of deposits. Because the most important currency held externally in this way is the US dollar and since dollars account for some three-quarters of total Eurocurrencies, the market is commonly referred to as the Eurodollar market. Moreover, the prefix 'Euro' does not mean that the external currencies are necessarily held by a bank in Europe. They may be held on deposit in any bank which is external to the currency's country of origin. It is because the market first developed in Europe, primarily in London, that the prefix 'Euro' was adopted. In recent years, financial centres in other parts of the world have established markets in external currencies. Notably, the establishment of Asian Currency Units in Singapore has facilitated the development of the Asian dollar market. This is identical to the Eurodollar market but has centres in Asia rather than Europe. In practice the two markets are very much part of the same world-wide international market.

Similarly the Middle East has established offshore banking units (OBUs) in Bahrain, specifically for the purpose of transacting Eurocurrency business. These newer centres are providing essential time zone links which have enabled the market to become truly world-wide as well as international and ensure that the market may operate 24 hours a day.

In the same way that the terms Eurodollar market and Eurocurrency market may be used interchangeably, the terms international bonds and Eurobonds are

Table 26.1 Summary of instruments

Instrument	Characteristics
Deposits	
call deposits	US and Canadian dollars, sterling, and yen for overnight or longer. Other currencies—minimum of two days' notice
time deposits	All currencies for up to twelve months. Sterling and US dollars for up to five years. Some currencies may be negotiated for longer terms
certificates of deposit	Three types issued. Principally dollars though a few in sterling. Floating-rate issues have been made. First discount issue made in 1981
deposits in currency cocktails	Mainly SDRs and ECUs. Growing market for SDRs
Eurocommercial paper	New market. First issue 1980. Dollar denominated and available in coupon or discount form
Eurobonds	
straight Eurobonds	Fixed coupon. Maturity up to 25 years
floating-rate notes	Variable coupon adjusted semiannually or quarterly to a stated margin over LIBOR. Fixed maturity
convertible Eurobonds	Straight bonds with option to convert into equity shares of issuing company. Bonds and shares may be denominated in different currencies
Eurobonds with warrants	Warrant provides option to purchase shares of issuing company. May be traded separately from bonds
option Eurobonds	Straight bonds with option to receive interest and/or principal in different currency
Foreign bonds	Bonds issued in foreign domestic capital markets. Defined as international bonds but not as Eurobonds
Gold	Major internationally traded monetary commodity though not defined as a Euromarket instrument
gold bullion	Major markets in London and Zurich
gold bars	Available in smaller sizes than bullion
gold coins	Wide range of coins issued, kruggerrands provide most popular market
gold certificates	Issued by banks but representing specific quantity of gold. May be traded separately
gold savings accounts	Offered by some banks. Account balance linked to price of gold
gold linked securities	Securities issued in French market whose redemption values are linked to the price of gold
gold shares	Shares of gold mining companies whose prices are influenced by the price of gold
gold options	Options to purchase gold at predetermined prices. Available in a few markets
gold futures	Contracts in gold for future delivery. Large markets in US. Other markets developing in world financial centres

also used in the same manner, although there is a distinction. An international bond may refer to either a domestic foreign bond or a Eurobond. A foreign bond issue is one made by a borrower in a foreign domestic market. Foreign bonds issued and placed in the US market are commonly referred to as 'Yankee' bonds and foreign bonds issued and placed in the Japanese domestic market are known as 'samurai' bonds. A foreign bond issue is denominated in the currency of the market in which it is placed and is usually traded homogeneously with other domestic bonds. In contrast a Eurobond is an issue which is managed by a syndicate of international banks and placed with investors and lenders world-wide. It may be denominated in any of the Eurocurrencies for which exists a sufficiently liquid market. While it may be quoted and traded on particular domestic markets it never becomes homogeneous with other domestic bonds.

Eurobonds comprise the 'Euro' international capital market although a variety of short- and medium-term investment instruments exists within the definition of Eurobonds and innovation continues to take place such that the 'Euromarket' now encompasses a truly comprehensive international money and capital market.

History of the Euromarket

Although the first international bonds were issued in the early nineteenth century, the origin of the Euromarket as it is known today dates back to the late 1950s. At that time most European currencies became convertible into other currencies through the foreign exchange market but, more importantly, the US was running a large balance of payments deficit which was settled in US dollars rather than in gold. Since the US was importing, in value terms, more than it was exporting, it was paying out more than it was receiving in equivalent foreign currency. Foreign exporters who received those dollars tended to hold them on deposit with banks in Europe. The deteriorating balance of payments position and the resultant capital outflows from the US put pressure on the US dollar. In order to stem, or try to stem, further outflows the US government introduced interest equalization tax (IET), in July 1963 to be applied immediately. The tax was imposed on interest and other income from certain foreign securities. Although not the intention behind IET the main effect of the tax, together with additional subsequent controls, was to encourage US companies to retain funds abroad, and to borrow dollars from external sources in order to finance overseas expansion. Although the tax was abolished in 1974, it was IET that opened up the market for European banks to service borrowers who wished to issue bonds or borrow in the international bank syndicated loan market. These were financed by the Eurocurrency investor—in this case the holder of external dollars that were beyond the jurisdiction of US authorities such as the Federal Reserve or the Securities and Exchange Commission. Aided by IET, three things had happened during the 1960s which facilitated the growth of the Euromarket. Firstly, the volume of dollars held in foreign accounts with European banks had grown to a size substantial enough for the creation of a capital market. Secondly, a significant demand for dollar borrowing, principally by US corporations, developed outside the US. Thirdly, the restrictions imposed by the US authorities had led to an interest differential between domestic dollars and Eurodollars.

Interest rates on domestic dollars were determined by US domestic monetary policy while interest rates on Eurodollars were determined by the supply and demand for those dollars in the Euromarket. Restrictive monetary policy in the US meant that at times dollars could be borrowed more cheaply in Europe than in the domestic market. The growth of the Eurodollar market continued into the 1970s as the US balance of payment deficit persisted and there remained a surplus of dollars held outside the US in banks all over the world. At the same time there was a strong demand for these dollars from borrowers, particularly those from countries with poorly developed domestic capital markets or with tight credit conditions and low liquidity. Banks in Europe, meanwhile, were refining both their methods of issuing Euroloans and the range of deposit instruments in order to attract the lenders of dollars.

The oil crisis of 1973, when OPEC quadrupled the price of oil, resulted in further structural changes to the Euromarket. Initially the huge oil-backed surpluses of the OPEC countries (which was mainly in dollars, and much of which was held with banks in Europe) encouraged significant growth in the market as these funds sought suitable investment outlets. At the same time the US removed its previous restrictions on foreign investment (such as IET) in the hope that the OPEC funds would flow into the US domestic markets and help strengthen the dollar. The subsequent world recession that followed the oil price increases removed many corporate borrowers from the market but their place was taken by governments, state enterprises and international agencies such as the World Bank and the European Coal and Steel Community. The lesser developed countries (LDCs) were borrowing heavily as they became particular casualties of the world recession while the industrialized countries borrowed to help boost exports to finance the higher cost of oil imports. Many central banks also used the Euromarket to help support their own currencies by selling dollar reserves for other currencies, which contributed further to the weakness of the dollar.

By 1976, the weakness of the dollar and the comparative strength of other currencies, specifically the yen, Deutschemark and Swiss franc, had resulted in a diversification of currencies traded in the Euromarkets. Foreign exchange losses incurred by banks and other lenders of dollars forced borrowers to issue loans denominated in other currencies, thus broadening and deepening the market.

The quality of borrowers improved, in the sense that a higher proportion were sovereign states, or others that offered the highest security. Additionally, because there was an excess supply of dollars, lending margins narrowed. It became possible to borrow at margins as low as $\frac{1}{4}$ per cent over London interbank offered rate (LIBOR). Competition among banks for the management of Euro issues reduced management fees such that they became very low relative to the cost of issuing loan capital in any domestic capital market.

During 1979 and 1980 the Euromarket suffered a number of disturbances caused by high rates of inflation, rising and uncertain interest rates, and reverse yield curves. At the beginning of 1979 the outlook for the dollar was favourable and there was renewed activity in dollar borrowing by US corporations as well as by sovereign and international agency borrowers. By the summer of 1979, high inflationary expectations caused the US authorities to tighten monetary policy. Uncertainty about the dollar resulted in diversification by investors into Deutschemarks and Swiss francs but Germany and Switzerland subsequently also tightened their domestic monetary policies. High interest rates, particularly for US dollars, caused a phenomenal rise in Eurobond yields. At the end of 1979 and during the first quarter of 1980 bond prices slumped dramatically, new issue volume fell back substantially and secondary market turnover was low. By April, however, the US authorities had started to ease domestic monetary conditions and interest rates fell as dramatically as they had risen with the consequence that the Eurobond market recovered temporarily to show a healthy increase in primary new issue activity and secondary trading.

During the first half of 1981 monetary conditions in most markets have been tight but issue activity in the Euromarket has been relatively high. The main reason for this is that there are many borrowers needing funds who are able to tap the liquidity of the international market when finance from domestic markets is less freely available.

That the Euromarket, since its early beginnings in the 1950s, has not only survived but has also expanded enormously says much about its resilience. Economic conditions have not only changed significantly but have undergone dramatic swings not previously experienced. The Euromarket developed partly to meet the requirements of these changing economic conditions but still has managed to adapt to unanticipated changes in the world economic environment.

Current structure of the Euromarket

In order to summarize the current structure of the Euromarket this section examines first the range of investment instruments now available in the market, then the borrowers and lenders in the market and the methods by which new issues are made and summarized. Finally, the size of the markets, the secondary sector and the determination of interest rates are discussed.

The range of instruments falls broadly into two categories, those of deposits made in Eurocurrencies or in currency cocktails such as SDRs or ECUs and including promissory notes, and secondly Eurobonds which may take on a variety of different forms.

Deposits

Eurocurrency time deposits are by far the most important instrument in the Euromarkets in that they parallel the huge turnover on the foreign exchange markets for spot and forward transactions up to one year ahead. The outstanding volume in Eurocurrency time deposits is several times greater than, for example, all outstanding issues in the Eurobond and foreign bond markets.

569

An active interbank market exists for deposits in all the major Eurocurrencies. Specifically, these currencies are:

US dollar	(US$)
Deutschemark	(DM)
Japanese yen	(¥)
Swiss franc	(SFr)
Pound sterling	(£)
French franc	(Ff)
Belgian franc	(Bf)
Dutch guilder	(Dfl)
Italian lira	(Lit)
Canadian dollar	(C$)
Asian dollars	
Singapore dollar	(S$)
Hong Kong dollar	(HK$)
Bahrain dinar	(BD)
Kuwaiti dinar	(KD)
Saudi Arabian riyal	(SR)

Deposits may be placed at call or for fixed periods as time deposits. Call deposits may be made for overnight, two-day or seven-day notice for US dollars, Canadian dollars, sterling and Japanese yen. Minimum call periods for the other currencies are at two days' notice.

The size and liquidity of the markets in each of these currencies varies considerably as is discussed later. In general, the minimum size deposit that can be placed in the Eurocurrency market is $50 000 or foreign currency equivalent.

Time deposits may be placed for periods of 1, 3, 6 and 12 months for all the above currencies while US dollars and sterling may be placed for longer terms of up to five years. Such deposits may be placed with any commercial bank in any of the major financial centres or through banks that have branches in those centres. In Europe the principal centres are London, Frankfurt, Zurich and Geneva in Switzerland, Luxembourg, Paris and Amsterdam. As previously mentioned, the Euromarket operates outside the boundaries of Europe, and other major centres throughout the world include New York, Tokyo, Singapore and the offshore banking units in Bahrain.

It should be remembered, however, that a currency deposited with a bank situated within the home country of that currency ceases to be a Eurocurrency.

Thus US dollars deposited with a bank in London, whether that bank is British, American or other foreign bank, are Eurodollars. US dollars deposited with a bank in New York however, represent a domestic dollar deposit subject to domestic interest rates and Federal Reserve System banking requirements. In 1980, it was proposed to establish 'offshore' international banking zones within several cities in the United States, partly to meet competition from the truly offshore centres.

Certificates of deposit

Banks in London issue CDs denominated in US dollars. Since these CDs are issued outside the US domestic market, they are Eurodollar CDs. At present there are no markets in CDs denominated in other currencies apart from sterling and yen although it is highly probable that markets will develop for other major currencies. The volume of dollar CDs handled in the London market is substantial. Approximately US$40 billion are issued annually. Three different types of CDs are made available.

Straight CDs

The most common are tap, or straight, CDs which are issued at the instigation of the borrowing bank when it wishes to 'tap' the market. These bear a fixed rate of interest and have a fixed maturity date of 1 to 12 months. Interest is normally established at $\frac{1}{8}$ per cent below LIBOR at the time of issue, but also depends on the issuing bank's credit standing and need for funds.

Floating-rate CDs

Floating-rate CDs (FRCDs) are issued with maturities of up to three years. Interest is calculated and paid semiannually and adjusted to $\frac{1}{4}$ per cent over LIBOR which makes them more attractive to an investor than a six-month tap CD rolled over for three years. FRCDs are mostly issued by Japanese and European banks and denominated in US dollars, although there have been issues of sterling denominated FRCDs.

Tranche CDs

Tranche CDs are issued with maturities of up to five years with a fixed rate of interest. A tranche CD represents a share in a programme of CD issues by a bank up to a predetermined limit (usually US$100 million or more). Each tranche CD carries the same maturity date and rate of interest. Usually they are placed directly with investors rather than offered publicly to the market. In many respects they are, therefore, more like a short-term private placement Eurobond than a CD.

Discount CDs

Discount CDs were first issued in the Euromarket, through London, by Chemical Bank in May 1981. Unlike all other forms of CDs, which are issued at face value and receive interest at redemption or roll-over date, these were issued at a discount to their par value. The interest calculation is similar to that for treasury bills or bankers' acceptances. This first issue was denominated in US dollars, though other currencies are possible if this form of issue becomes popular. Investor interest was high and the first issue was rapidly taken up, which indicates good potential for further development of the discount CD market. Maturities were for one or two months at the option of the lender, but longer maturities (of perhaps up to six months) will probably be offered.

For all types of CDs the minimum denomination is often US$50 000, but frequently more. Until November 1980 it was often cheaper for US banks to issue dollar denominated CDs in the Euromarket rather than in the domestic US market. This was because reserve requirements were imposed on US banks' domestic CD issues but not on Euro CD issues. Thus the cost to a US bank of issuing

571

domestic CDs was greater than for issuing a Euro CD despite the interest rate differential between Euro and domestic CDs. In late 1979 the US Federal Reserve System introduced a supplementary eight per cent reserve requirement on the domestic liabilities of US banks, which made Euro CD issues an even more attractive method of borrowing.

The eight per cent supplementary reserve requirement was subsequently abolished but, effective from 1 November 1980 a new reserve requirement of three per cent was applied, across the board, on all US banks' issues of domestic and foreign, dollar denominated, CDs. Thus there is no longer a cost advantage for a US bank to issue CDs in the Euromarket in preference to the domestic US market. The interest-rate differential between domestic and Euro CD's has consequently narrowed as US banks have reverted to borrowing in the domestic market.

Deposits in currency cocktails

For investors operating a diversified currency portfolio it is possible to place deposits denominated in a basket of currencies that is designed to offer both the borrower and investor a reasonable degree of protection from exchange rate movements. Currency cocktails may be devised in various combinations to suit the investor or the borrower, but the two most successful have been the SDR and the ECU.

The SDR (special drawing rights) is a composite currency which has been used for many years for transactions between governments and the IMF. Until this year, however, it was a clumsy instrument which could not be used very easily as a transactions currency (i.e. a medium for the exchange of goods and services). It used to comprise 16 currencies with different weights according to their share of world trade. Several of these currencies (e.g. the Iranian rial, Italian lira) were not very marketable and consequently the composite instrument, the SDR, was also not very marketable.

Since 1 January 1981, however, the SDR has been simplified so that it now contains only five currencies, each of which is actively traded on the world's foreign exchanges (see Table 26.2). The SDR is now very marketable and can be quoted against any other convertible currency. As a result of the revision, a new market has rapidly developed both in London and in other financial centres. Within just a few weeks of the SDR revision, more than 15 banks in London were accepting deposits denominated in SDRs, and a number also issue SDR CDs. The number of banks participating in the market is growing and within a short time is likely to include all major commercial banks in London.

Apart from being marketable, the new SDR is more stable than any single currency. Since it is composed of the five major currencies its value is the weighted mean of those currencies. It is not highly volatile. If, for example, the US dollar falls (or rises) sharply relative to sterling the SDR, which contains both currencies, will remain close to its original level. In addition, the SDR, if placed on deposit with a bank, earns a rate of interest that is a weighted average of the three-month Euromarket interest rates for each of the composite currencies. Thus, the SDR interest

Table 26.2 Special drawing rights

Component currencies	Amounts of each currency per SDR	Approximate percentage weighting of each country	Exchange rate per SDR as at 23 Jan. 1981
US dollar	0.54 cents	42%	1.2653
Deutschemark	0.46 pfennigs	19%	2.5591
Japanese yen	34 yen	13%	254.96
French franc	0.74 centimes	13%	5.9153
Pound sterling	7.1 pence	13%	0.5258
SDR	1 SDR	100%	1.000

	Interest rates at 23 Jan. 1981			
	1 month	2 months	3 months	6 months
US dollar	19.25	19.0	18.8	17.5
Deutschemark	9.0	9.1	9.125	9.125
Japanese yen	8.2	8.3	8.4	8.5
French franc	10.6	10.75	10.9	11.0
Pound sterling	14.5	14.4	14.4	13.7
SDR	14.7	14.43	14.14	13.56

rate remains more stable than, for example, the US dollar interest rate. The interest rates used for calculating the SDR interest rate, as quoted in the international currency market, differs from the rates used by the IMF to calculate the official SDR interest rate. The IMF uses domestic interest rates on which to calculate the weighted two- or three-month average SDR interest rate.

The official interest rate and the official exchange rate for all convertible currencies is quoted once per day by the IMF in Washington DC. Banks operating in the international financial markets, however, quote the commercial rates at any time during business hours, at the request of clients.

The composition of the SDR and the units of each currency per SDR is normally reviewed every five years by the IMF. The last revision was made in 1978 and, therefore, no new revision was expected until 1983. This early change has occurred because the IMF recognizes a real need in the international markets for a widely accepted, more stable medium for international transactions. The SDR market already shows signs of developing into a large and major market. A number of multinational companies have begun to hold their assets in SDRs in order to match their mixed currency liabilities.

International agencies such as the IMF and the World Bank are expected to issue Eurobonds denominated in SDRs. There is a possibility that OPEC countries may price oil in terms of SDRs and even that international insurance contracts, placed through the London market, may be made in terms of SDRs. The component

Table 26.3   SDR and ECU currency baskets

Currencies	No. of units of each currency per SDR or ECU	Percentage weighting based on exchange rates as at	
	December 1980	December 1980	January 1981
SDR			
US dollar	0.40	33.0	42.0
Deutschemark	0.32	12.5	19.0
Japanese yen	21.00	7.5	13.0
French franc	0.42	7.5	13.0
Pound sterling	0.05	7.5	13.0
Italian lira	52.00	5.0	
Netherlands guilder	0.14	5.0	
Canadian dollar	0.07	5.0	
Belgian franc	1.60	4.0	
Saudi riyal	0.13	3.0	
Swedish krone	0.11	2.0	
Iranian riyal	1.70	2.0	
Australian dollar	0.017	1.5	
Spanish peseta	1.50	1.5	
Norwegian krone	0.10	1.5	
Austrian schilling	0.21	1.5	
		100.0	100.0
ECU			
Deutschemark	0.828	32.22	
Pound sterling	0.0885	13.12	
French franc	1.15	20.29	
Italian lira	109.00	10.28	
Netherlands guilder	0.286	10.39	
Belgian franc	3.66	} 9.44	
Luxembourg franc	0.14		
Danish krone	0.217	3.13	
Irish punt	0.00759	1.12	
		100.0	

currencies, their relative weights and the units of each which comprise the SDR are shown in Table 26.3.

Table 26.3 also shows the composition of the ECU (European Currency Unit). This is a basket of the nine currencies of the EEC, each weighted according to their relative shares of the combined gross national product of the community. The ECU includes pounds sterling although the UK is not currently a member of the European Monetary System which bases some of its currency intervention policy on movements against the ECU. As with the currencies comprising the SDR, the ECU may be quoted in terms of any other convertible currency on the world foreign exchanges, according to the weighted average exchange rates of the currencies in the ECU. Thus, for example, the ECU can be quoted in terms of the US dollar. The ECU is defined by the EEC central banks and became effective as from 13 March 1979, replacing the previous European unit of account.

Major commercial banks in London, New York and the other major financial centres in Europe will quote rates of interest for deposits denominated in SDR or ECU equivalents. The deposit would be made in a single currency, for example the US dollar, since the SDR and ECU do not exist as an actual medium of exchange. Thus, if the investor wished to deposit dollars in SDR equivalent the bank would quote him a rate of exchange for the dollar relative to the SDR. The deposit is denominated in SDRs and the investor would have to advance the equivalent number of dollars according to the exchange rate quoted. The rate of interest is calculated according to a weighted average, of the Eurocurrency deposit rates of the component currencies. Because the overall interest rate is a weighted average, currency baskets offer more stable rates of return. The investor specifies the size of the deposit in terms of SDRs (or ECUs) he wishes to deposit. The minimum size of deposit accepted by most banks is three million ECUs, or 500 000 SDRs.

When the deposit matures, a new rate of exchange is quoted for the transaction currency (US dollars in this example) and the SDR (or ECU) equivalent. The proceeds of the deposit are then returned to the investor at the prevailing rates of exchange.

The advantages to the borrower of SDRs or ECUs is that banks hold reserve assets in a mixture of the most commonly traded currencies. By taking deposits, and thus holding liabilities, in a similar basket of currencies, a bank is able to reduce the degree of risk borne by its asset portfolio. On the other hand a corporate investor, with liabilities (future payments) in a broad spread of widely traded currencies, can reduce his risk by holding assets denominated in a basket of currencies which approximates to the currency risk of his liabilities.

Eurocommercial paper

Commercial paper represents a bearer promissory note which may be likened to a CD but which is issued by a commercial company rather than by a bank.

The first issue of Eurocommercial paper was made in June 1980, lead managed by Merril Lynch, on behalf of IC Industries Inc., a good quality borrower with an A rating in the US bond market. Although US commercial paper has been made available to Eurodollar investors since the early 1970s this issue differed in size, type, and method of issue and is more suited to the specific requirements of the Euromarket.

The amount of the issue was a $100 million programme to be issued on a tap basis. Individual promissory notes may normally be purchased in minimum denominations of $250 000. The paper may be issued in either interest-bearing or discount form, at the option of the lender. In the case of interest-bearing paper, interest is payable on maturity of the notes, while for notes issued at a discount, the interest is discounted at issue. The investor therefore lends a lower principal amount equal to the present value which is determined by the rate of interest (or discount) and receives the par value at maturity. In both cases the yield is the same for paper of identical maturity. Interest (or discount) is calculated on the basis of a 360-day year and, for the first issue, at the rate of $\frac{1}{8}$ per cent over LIBOR for deposits of equivalent time periods. Margins over LIBOR will vary according to the quality of borrower, however, as further issues are made. The notes are available with maturities from 30 to 180 days, also for specific dates at the option of the lender. Eurocommercial paper is a bearer security and technically negotiable in the secondary market. Although such a secondary market has yet to develop it is likely that, similar to the US commercial paper market, turnover will be low relative to the issue volume since, having short maturities for periods chosen by the lender, most investors choose to hold the paper to maturity.

The primary market is expected to develop successfully while the majority of borrowers will probably be US and multinational corporations and most issues will be denominated in US dollars, though issues in other currencies are possible.

In effect, for the borrower and lender Eurocommercial paper is like a short-term Eurobond rather than a bank loan or negotiable deposit.

The advantage of a Eurocommercial paper market to borrowers is that it offers a large market to be tapped in order to raise short-term funds with which to finance current assets and at rates of interest that can be highly competitive with other forms of short-term borrowing.

For the investor the notes provide a flexible short-term investment instrument, with a range of maturities, being negotiable, discount or interest-bearing and yielding approximately $\frac{3}{8}$ per cent more than a CD of comparable maturity.

Eurobonds

A Eurobond is an international bond which is issued on behalf of a multinational corporation, international agency or sovereign state to investors from throughout the world. Eurobonds are normally issued as unsecured obligations of the borrower and in consequence only borrowers of good quality are able successfully to bring issues to the market. State enterprises and municipalities would normally require their government's guarantee unless their own financial status is undoubted. Normally, issues made by finance subsidiaries are also guaranteed by the parent company.

New issues are managed, underwritten and placed by a syndicate of international banks, although a single bank is usually responsible for assembling and co-ordinating the selling group of banks and for ensuring the efficient marketing of the issue. That bank is known as the 'lead managing bank'.

In the primary market there are two methods of issue—public issue and private placement. Public issues are managed by a large syndicate of banks in order that the issue may be introduced to a wide number of the investing public. Publicly issued Eurobonds, once issued, are quoted on one or more stock exchanges, usually London, Luxembourg or Zurich. They are fully negotiable and in general enjoy an active secondary market. Though listed on stock exchanges most trading takes place in the over-the-counter market made by banks in major financial centres.

Private placements are issued normally on behalf of prime borrowers, by a smaller syndicate of banks, and placed directly with a small group of major institutions. For this reason and because advertising is not required, the issuing costs tend to be lower. On the other hand, private placements are not normally quoted on any stock exchange and are not negotiable in the secondary market. Consequently they are often issued at a higher coupon than would apply to a public issue. The higher coupon can make them attractive investments, but they should only be bought by investors who are prepared to hold them to maturity because of the absence of a secondary market.

With public new issues the potential investor receives a prospectus showing the activities of the borrower, and in the case of a corporate borrower, a full financial history. The managing syndicate of banks assesses the creditworthiness or quality of the borrower, and this determines the coupon attaching to the bond relative to prevailing market rates of interest and current yields on comparable fixed interest securities. Once an issue has been completed, a tombstone advertisement is placed in the financial press. It is so called because the advert bears a resemblance to a tombstone stating the amount of the issue, the borrower, the lead managing bank and managing syndicate of banks followed by a long list of additional banks that assisted in the issue. This list can run to over 100 banks, all of international standing.

The size of a new issue generally varies between $10 million and $500 million, though the majority of issues are in the $50 million to $100 million range.

Maturities

Although up to 1974 the normal maturity for a fixed-rate Eurobond issue was 15 years, bond maturities have since then tended to be shorter as investors became more concerned about inflation and the currency risk resulting from exchange rate volatility. As a result it is now unusual for a fixed-rate Eurobond to have a 15-year

Table 26.4 Average maturities of Eurobond issues

	Total	Under 5 years, % of total	5–7 years, % of total	8–10 years, % of total	11–15 years, % of total	16–20 years, % of total	Over 20 years, % of total
1970	100	5	23	12	57	1	2
1971	100	2	18	4	74	2	0
1972	100	0	12	5	73	10	0
1973	100	2	16	6	67	9	0
1974	100	4	52	13	27	4	0
1975	100	1	66	27	5	1	0
1976	100	4	57	26	9	3	1
1977	100	2	33	25	30	10	0
1978	100	4	40	25	21	9	1
1979							

maturity and normal for any issue with a final maturity of more than 6 or 7 years to have a reduced average life.

A reduced average life may be achieved through a sinking fund, whereby the borrower agrees to redeem a certain number of bonds, either through purchase on the market or, if the market price of the bonds is above par, through drawings by lot at par during the life of the issue, according to a set schedule laid down in the offering prospectus. An alternative is to have a purchase fund through which the borrower agrees to buy bonds in accordance with a fixed schedule, but only if such purchases can be made at prices lower than par.

It is thus important for the investor to know the original terms in order to calculate the yield to maturity and the yield to average life which will differ if part of the issue amount is to be redeemed before final maturity.

For the borrower such maturity options provide the opportunity of refinancing his debt at lower interest costs. Normally, however, such advanced repayments are precluded for the first few years of the life of an issue.

Prices and yields As interest rates fluctuate, the price of fixed income bonds varies inversely to their yield. A rise in prevailing interest rates leads to a fall in bond prices while a fall in interest rates leads to capital gains on the principal amount of the bond. The sensitivity of market price to a given change in interest rates increases with the tenor or maturity of the bond. Thus, if a Eurobond of whatever currency has a 10 per cent coupon, a final maturity of 15 years and an average life also of 15 years (i.e., it is a 'bullet' issue with no sinking fund), its yield to maturity is 10 per cent if the bond is bought at par. If, after 12 months (when the long-term bond has 14 years to run), prevailing interest rates for an equivalent credit and equal period have moved up by 100 basis points to 11 per cent, the bond's market price will then be 93—a seven per cent capital loss to set against the 10 per cent interest income giving a total return, before currency gains or losses, of three per cent in one year. A shorter-dated bond, however, is less sensitive both on the upside and the downside to a given change in market interest rates. If the 10 per cent Eurobond had been bought at par as a seven-year intermediate term security and interest rates moved up 100 basis points to 11 per cent in a 12-month period the 10 per cent bond with another six years to run would carry a market price of $95\frac{3}{4}$, a capital loss of $4\frac{1}{4}$ per cent offset by interest income of 10 per cent to give a total return of $5\frac{3}{4}$ per cent per annum. Sensitivity to a given change in interest rates decreases as maturities are shortened and increases as they are lengthened. Unless bond prices are held to redemption there is scope for both capital gains and capital losses for the bond investor. As interest rates have become more volatile, the prices of bonds have also tended to go up and down in wider, more erratic, swings.

Any portfolio manager who holds fixed interest marketable securities is continually faced with the question of whether and when to realize capital gains if they occur, when to cut losses, and when to maintain a steady course in the comfort of high current returns or the expectation of capital recovery. Fixed income managers divided into two main schools: one subscribes to the 'buy and hold' philosophy which is combined with a ladder of maturities, which, as each rung is reached and a

578

security is redeemed, involves the reinvestment of principal at prevailing rates; the other maintains a very active presence in the market, constantly lengthening and shortening the average maturity of a portfolio according to interest rate expectations, swapping between different categories of credit or balances between coupon and price, depending on the relative attractiveness, after tax, of capital gains or current income.

Interest on most Eurobonds is payable annually, though it is paid semiannually on a number of older issues and on many convertible bonds. Where interest is paid semiannually, the effective yield to the investor is higher than that available on an identical coupon when the interest is paid annually. Interest is paid gross, free of all withholding taxes.

Currency

Most new issues are denominated in US dollars, though issues are also made in a number of other important Eurocurrencies as discussed later. At times, when the US dollar is weak, investors' interest turns to Eurobonds denominated in other currencies, the best established of which are the Deutschemark and the Dutch guilder.

Traded form

Eurobonds are bearer securities, normally in minimum denominations of 10 000 (i.e., US$10 000, DM 10 000 etc.). Occasionally units of five may be traded. In the secondary market prices are quoted as a percentage of par (US$100, DM 100 etc.) plus accrued interest.

In the secondary market (explained more fully later) Eurobonds are traded through major commercial and international banks who maintain the market, acting both as dealers and principals. Transactions are dealt net, with bid and offer spreads that vary according to types of issue, denomination and the state of the market. Settlement and delivery is normally on a seven-day basis.

There are four main types of Eurobonds issued, straight or fixed-rate bonds, floating-rate bonds, convertible bonds and option bonds.

Straight (*fixed-rate*) bonds

The majority of Eurobonds are straight or fixed-interest bonds, with a fixed coupon on which interest is normally paid annually, on the basis of a 360-day financial year. Some older issues may pay interest semiannually. Maturities may be as short as three years or as long as 25 years, though very few Eurobonds are issued for longer than 15 years and many have a reduced average life by way of either a sinking fund or a purchase fund.

Most Eurobonds (about 80 per cent) have been issued in this form, particularly when market conditions are relatively stable which is when the volume of new issues tends to be greatest.

Eurobonds with shorter maturities than five years are often known as notes. Bonds denominated in Netherlands guilders especially tend to be issued with short lives of less than five years and are thus known as Euroguilder notes.

Floating-rate bonds

As a result of rising inflation and consequently high and often volatile rates of interest in all major world markets, a growing number of Eurobonds are issued bearing variable coupons. The maturity range is the same as for straight Eurobonds, although the majority have an original maturity of five to seven years.

In 1979 FRN new issues amounted to just under US$3 billion. In the nine months to September 1980 FRN issues amounted to US$2.5 billion. As at September 1980 there had been 188 FRN issues to a value of about US$10 billion.

The special feature of floating-rate notes (FRNs) is that the coupon is set at some margin over LIBOR which is usually $\frac{1}{4}$ per cent. This can be as low as $\frac{1}{8}$ per cent if the borrower is of the highest quality and as high as $1\frac{1}{2}$ per cent for less than prime borrowers. The coupon applies for a predetermined period, which is normally six months, but may be three months, at the end of which time the coupon is re-established at the same margin over the prevailing London interbank rate. Thus if the London interbank offered rate for six-month dollar deposits is quoted at 10 per cent per annum, then for a semiannual Eurodollar FRN within a margin of $\frac{1}{4}$ per cent over six-month LIBOR, the coupon on the FRN is set at $10\frac{1}{4}$ per cent per annum.

Since interest is payable semiannually, and in some cases quarterly, it should be remembered that the effective yield to the investor is greater than that on a straight bond of identical coupon and maturity but which pays interest annually.

Drop locks In the terms established at issue, most FRNs state minimum rates of interest such that if LIBOR plus the predetermined margin falls below a certain level, the investor receives the stated minimum rate of interest. Some issues may include 'drop lock' clauses, whereby if, according to the LIBOR plus margin formula, market rates of interest fall below a specified minimum the rate of interest is fixed at that minimum and 'locked' in for the remaining life of the loan.

The amount of new issues made in FRN form is now approaching 10 per cent of new Eurobonds. The advantage to the borrower is that FRNs are more able to attract investors in periods of volatile interest rates, for whom the return is linked to short-term interest rates in the Euromarket. This guarantees respectable yields if interest trends generally are rising while also reducing the chance of capital loss since the price of FRNs remain at, or close to, par. To date, most issuers of FRNs have been banks.

Convertible Eurobonds

Convertible Eurobonds are similar to convertible bonds as issued in domestic capital markets since they give the investor the right to convert the fixed-interest bond into equity shares (or common stock) of the issuing company.

The bonds themselves have fixed rates of interest which, because of the conversion rights attached, are normally lower than coupons on straight bonds of comparable terms. They carry fixed redemption dates, the majority being issued with maturities of between 10 and 15 years.

The conversion rights stipulate that the bondholder may convert the bond into ordinary shares, either on a series of given dates or at any time between specified dates in the future. The price at which the shares may be purchased through such conversion provisions is specified at the time the convertible bond is issued. The conversion price is normally at a premium of 10 or 15 per cent over the share price prevailing at the time of issue.

Convertible bonds are attractive to the issuer because they provide a method of borrowing at below the cost of alternative fixed-interest debt instruments, while also receiving cash for a phased programme of newly issued shares when the investors exercise their options to convert. For the investor, convertible bonds offer the opportunity to participate in the capital growth of a company. He receives a fixed income from the bonds for as long as he holds them but stands to make a capital gain by converting the bonds to equity, provided that by the conversion date the price of the shares has risen higher than the fixed conversion price. On the other hand, if the share price fails to rise, or falls, the risk is limited by the income return available from the fixed interest feature of the bond.

Convertible bonds thus offer a mixture of the attributes of fixed interest and equity investments. They have a higher yield than equities but have the potential of capital gain while the risk of capital loss is limited by the ability to hold to maturity. They provide a fixed return coupled with possible capital appreciation although the price of convertible bonds is more volatile than for straight bonds, being influenced by the share price of the issuing company, as well as by yields in the international fixed interest market.

Convertible Eurobonds offer an additional advantage to the investor which is not available with convertible domestic bonds. They may be issued in a currency that differs from the currency in which the shares of the company are denominated. In the last three or four years Japanese companies, in particular, have issued convertible bonds denominated in US dollars and Deutschemark or Swiss francs but with options to convert into shares of the borrowing company, denominated in yen. Such issues give the bondholder the opportunity to participate in the Japanese stock market as well as the option to diversify currency risk. Japanese convertible bonds were particularly attractive during 1978 and 1979 when the Japanese equities market was booming and the yen was appreciating to a greater extent even than the Deutschemark and Swiss franc.

Convertible bonds are almost always issued with fixed exchange rate clauses specifying the rates at which the bonds may be converted into ordinary shares of the issuer. The investor's decision of whether to convert or hold convertible bonds is therefore greatly influenced by relative exchange rate movements.

Bonds with warrants

A variation on convertible bonds is Eurobonds issued with warrants attached which provide the bondholder with the option to purchase ordinary shares of the issuing company at a predetermined price. As with convertible bonds, the warrant

581

price of shares is normally 10 to 15 per cent above the share price at the time the bond is issued and the warrants are exercisable on or between specified dates.

Unlike convertible bonds, however, where the bonds must be exchanged for equities, warrants are physically separate from the bonds and may be detached and traded as securities in their own right. Also the warrants represent an option to purchase rather than convert into shares, so additional cash must be advanced if the warrants are exercised.

The value of the warrant is usually only a small fraction of the value of the equivalent share so warrants represent a highly geared (or leveraged) investment. Any significant rise in the share price may cause the value of the warrant to increase to several times its original value.

The advantage to the borrower of issuing Eurobonds with warrants is the same as for convertible bonds. The investor on the other hand has the advantage of two separately marketable instruments although the warrant may become worthless if the price of the shares falls rather than rises. The loss is limited however by continuing to hold the fixed interest bond, albeit at a lower yield than comparable straight bonds.

Option Eurobonds

Option Eurobonds are essentially straight Eurobonds that provide the bondholder with the option to receive interest and/or principal in a currency which differs from that in which the bond is denominated.

Some Eurobonds of this type are sterling Eurobonds, issued prior to the abolition of UK exchange controls in 1979, which pay interest either in US dollars or in Deutschemark as a way of complying with the exchange regulations. Additionally many Eurobonds denominated in Middle Eastern currencies such as Kuwaiti or Bahraini dinars have currency option clauses allowing the holder to receive interest and/or principal in US dollars. In this latter case, the reason is not one of exchange controls, which do not apply for most Middle Eastern countries, but because a limited market exists for their currencies. The supply of Middle Eastern currencies is small in the Euromarkets and the demand for them also restricted. For this reason some issues also offer the investor the opportunity to purchase the bonds with US dollars, which are then converted to the currency in which the bond is denominated. Currency option bonds are thus more flexible for the international investor than bonds purely denominated in Middle Eastern currencies.

The rate of exchange at which interest is paid on a currency option bond is, in the case of recent issues, determined according to the exchange rates ruling a few days before interest is due. Some early issues, particularly of sterling denominated bonds, carried fixed exchange rate clauses but, given the high volatility of foreign exchange markets during the 1970s, such bonds represented considerable exchange risks to either the borrower or the lender. Consequently option bonds with fixed exchange rate clauses are no longer issued.

Borrowers and lenders in the Euromarkets

Borrowers in the Euromarkets include large multinational companies, sovereign states, local governments, state enterprises and international agencies.

Of the corporate borrowers, most have already established international reputations for their products and most also have previously floated successful issues in their own domestic markets before seeking to borrow in the Euromarkets. Corporate borrowers also include banks, or their finance subsidiaries who borrow Eurocurrencies primarily to expand their direct lending to customers.

Sovereign states borrow principally to help their domestic balance of payments position. Although such borrowing may be designated for direct investment in specified projects, all foreign currency borrowings help to improve the balance of payments. Such assistance, however, proves only temporary. In the long run, borrowing fuels inflation which ultimately leads through to a deterioration of the balance of payments. Most frequent sovereign borrowers are the lesser developed countries (LDCs), of which Mexico and Brazil have been major participants. Industrial countries with persistent deficits, such as Norway, France and Italy also seek recourse to the market at times when their balance of payments position is particularly poor. Nevertheless, sovereign states are considered the highest quality and most secure of borrowers, and their bonds consequently reflect this by bearing the lowest of all Eurobond yields.

Local governments, municipalities and state owned utility companies or enterprises may borrow directly in the Euromarket rather than through their governments or domestic capital markets. Since these borrowers normally require the guarantee of their own governments, their bonds are also considered of the highest quality and thus similarly rank for low yields.

Some governments and state enterprises of developing countries receive money indirectly from the Euromarkets. International agencies such as the World Bank, the Inter-American Development Bank and the Asian Development Bank all borrow in the International Bond Market through the issue of Eurobonds and of foreign bonds in a number of domestic capital markets. The funds so raised are used for onlending to developing countries for specific projects. Not all international agencies, however, direct funds to the LDCs. Other agencies which are frequent borrowers in the market include the European Investment Bank and the European Coal and Steel Community (ECSC).

Eurocredits

Borrowing in the Euromarkets may take two forms, either by the issue of securities such as Eurobonds, or by borrowing Eurocurrencies directly from banks that operate in the Euromarkets. This latter method is the wholesale market for Eurocredits. Such loans are taken for short- to medium-term periods, but as for a standard bank loan, the rate of interest is variable according to prevailing market levels. As with Eurobond issues, Eurocredit borrowing is normally arranged by a syndicate of international banks. Borrowers of syndicated Eurocredits usually require larger amounts than can normally be raised by a Eurobond issue. Mostly such borrowers are sovereign states but at times the banks themselves can be major borrowers of Eurocredits. This was the case for US banks when in 1979, following the introduc-

583

Table 26.5 New issues of international bonds (US$ million) (*source: Bank for International Settlements*)

Years	Borrower's country of origin	Total all issues	Eurobonds				Foreign bonds			
			(1) Public issues	(2) Private placements	Amount of 1 and 2 issued in US$	Total	(3) Public issues	(4) Private placements	Amount of 3 and 4 issued in US$	Total
1977	Western Europe	14 070	7 150	1 860	5 740	9 010	2 150	2 910	1 280	5 060
1978		11 500	4 100	1 310	2 440	5 410	4 250	1 840	1 640	6 090
1979		12 780	5 840	1 280	3 730	7 120	3 220	2 440	970	5 660
1977	United States	1 520	870	430	1 190	1 300	220	200	....	220
1978		1 660	1 090	200	970	1 290	190	150	....	370
1979		2 730	2 440	130	2 480	2 570	160		....	160
1977	Other developed countries	2 810	3 640	390	2 440	4 030	2 540	2 340	3 650	4 880
1978		10 700	2 600	780	1 390	3 380	3 800	3 070	3 680	6 870
1979		9 470	2 850	280	1 560	3 130	2 900	3 440	2 140	6 340
1977	Developing countries and Eastern Europe	4 270	2 160	500	990	2 660	970	440	820	1 610
1978		5 190	2 240	750	1 080	2 990	1 370	830	440	2 200
1979		3 240	1 620	210	1 300	1 830	1 080	330	370	1 410
1977	International agencies	7 320	1 600	880	1 980	2 480	3 030	1 810	1 920	4 840
1978		8 710	1 640	1 230	1 810	2 170	2 770	3 070	600	5 840
1979		8 860	1 976	1 280	1 466	3 250	2 750	2 860	1 110	5 610
1977	Total—all borrowers	36 090	23 540	4 060	12 340	19 480	8 910	7 700	7 670	6 610
1978		37 320	11 670	4 270	7 690	15 940	12 420	8 960	6 390	21 380
1979		37 080	14 720	3 180	10 530	17 900	10 110	9 070	4 590	19 180

tion by the US Federal Reserve of a supplementary eight per cent reserve requirement on domestic liabilities, there developed a cost advantage to borrowing in the Euromarkets. Thus despite a premium on Eurodollar deposit rates compared with domestic dollar deposit rates, it was cheaper in many instances for US banks to borrow in the Euromarket rather than issue domestic dollar CDs.

The volume of Eurocredits and Eurobonds issued each year is roughly equal, together amounting to over US$200 billion outstanding.

Up to 1971 over 50 per cent of Eurobond borrowers were companies and 30 per cent were US corporations that sought recourse to the Euromarket facilities during the US domestic exchange restrictions enforced between 1963 and 1974. Since 1974, however, less than five per cent of Eurobonds have been issued on behalf of companies, the major borrowers now being sovereign states, international agencies and public sector enterprises from a wide range of countries. Of all forms of Euro-currency loans since 1974 approximately 36 per cent of borrowers have been from Western European countries, about eight per cent from the United States, 15 per cent from Canada, Japan and other developed countries, 7 per cent from Eastern European countries, 11 per cent from developing countries, 6 per cent from oil

Table 26.6 Eurobond issues breakdown by currency of issue (US$ million) (*source: OECD*)

Currency	1975	1976	1977	1978	1979	1980
Eurobonds						
US dollar	4922.1	9999.2	12336.4	2693.4	10214.5	13602.6
Deutschemark	3009.3	2821.4	5215.2	6531.2	4769.9	3604.4
Dutch guilder	627.4	467.4	362.7	384.3	307.5	545.9
Canadian dollar	566	1449.8	653.7	....	467.9	270.5
French franc	286	61.5	....	103.2	373.5	883.6
Japanese yen	....	....	111.3	78.9	115.1	298.2
Pound sterling	143.4	....	103.4	95.1	291.3	971.8
Kuwaiti dinar	164.8	304.4	129.9	480.5	383.7	26.1
Norwegian kroner	44.8	....	....	....	....	100.6
Danish kroner	....	....	....	....	....	7.4
Australian dollar	....	18.7	11.3	30.6	17.1	76.2
European units of account	387.6	102.7	33.5	202.8	305.8	76.4
SDR	172.9	....	....	32.1	106.6	19.6
Other currencies*	195.2	142.7	526.7	307.7		
Total	10519.5	15367.8	19484.1	15939.8	17352.9	20483.3

* Including Austrian schilling, Bahraini dinar, Hong Kong dollar, Luxembourg franc, Saudi riyal, Swedish kroner, UAE dirham, and Venezuelan bolivar.

exporting countries and the remainder from offshore banking centres and unallocated sources.

The lenders of funds in the Euromarkets are less easily identified than are the borrowers. It is a feature of unregistered Eurobond investments that, in most cases, anonymity of beneficial ownership can be preserved. Banks operating in the market tend not to disclose the names of their customers because of intense competition among bankers for valuable clients. It is estimated that over 50 per cent of Eurobond investors are individuals mainly from the US, South America, Western Europe and the Middle East attracted by the absence of withholding taxes and anonymity of beneficial ownership. The average size of individual investments is about US$15000, though some are considerably larger. Individuals and monetary agencies from the Middle East, as investors, play an important role of recycling OPEC surplus funds through the Euromarkets to countries suffering a balance of payments deficit largely caused by the high cost of oil imports.

Other major lenders are financial institutions, principally banks which are active as primary market issuers and as secondary market dealers of Eurobonds. Many also act as principals in the secondary market, holding and trading Eurobonds which form a significant proportion of their asset portfolios. To a smaller extent large corporations are also investors in Eurobonds but since, for the majority, their liquid funds are short-term reserve and transactions balances, they tend to favour Eurocurrency deposits or short-term Eurocurrency instruments such as CDs and FRNs.

Foreign bonds

Foreign bonds are loans issued by major corporations, sovereign states and international agencies on foreign domestic bond markets. They are denominated in the currency of the country in which they are issued.

They are similar to Eurobonds in respect of being issued and denominated in a foreign market and currency, and the types of borrowers are the same. They differ from Eurobonds in that they are issued and traded in a single specific foreign market. They are governed by the regulations affecting the capital market of the country in which they are issued and in many cases are traded homogeneously with other domestic bonds in that market.

Table 26.7 shows the foreign bond markets and the volume of new issues since 1975. The values have been converted to US dollars for comparative purposes but the bonds are all denominated in the local currency of the market of issue.

Until 1977 the US was the major market used by foreign borrowers in which to issue bonds. The Swiss domestic market has now moved into first place as the major market for foreign bond issues. This reflects the low issuing costs and low interest rates in the Swiss market, attractive to borrowers, and the strength of the currency which has made it easier to attract lenders.

Another factor is that US dollar denominated bonds may be issued in the Eurobond market whereas the Swiss authorities will not allow the issue of Swiss franc Eurobonds. The alternative means by which a borrower can tap the Swiss franc market is to issue a Swiss franc foreign bond.

Table 26.7 Foreign bond issues breakdown by currency of issue (US$ million) (*source: OECD*)

Market and currency of issue	1975	1976	1977	1978	1979	1980
Switzerland, Swiss franc	3 529.0	5 443.6	4 959.3	7 608.9	9 479.5	7 454.7
USA, US$	6 854.6	10 631.6	7 668.2	6 358.6	4 364.6	2 796.4
Japan, yen	341.5	287.3	1 393.5	4 686.0	2 655.3	1 164.6
Germany, Deutschemark	604.9	1 309.3	1 511.1	1 676.8	2 615.1	4 800.0
Netherlands, Dutch florin	235.4	692.4	182.1	351.5	162.8	321.9
France, French franc	56.6	76.4	61.8	230.9	197.7	261.3
Luxembourg, Luxembourg franc	45.7	37.3	80.3	206.8	208.3	198.3
Belgium, Belgian franc	....	38.0	....	29.0	136.7	62.1
Italy, lira	80.9	7.5	15.0			
Saudi Arabia, riyal	214.7	294.9	645.0	245.8	29.8	122.3
UK, pound sterling	32.8	....	....	....	....	174.8
Others*	304.7	125.0	93.9	147.8	129.8	102.5
Total	12 300.8	18 943.3	16 610.2	21 542.1	19 979.6	17 458.9

* Including Austria, Canada, Finland, Libya, Trinidad and Tobago, UAE, Venezuela and Yugoslavia.

For lenders, on the other hand, the Swiss franc foreign bond market is very much like the Eurobond market. There are no restrictions on investment or registration of interest, and principal and interest are paid gross, free of withholding taxes.

The Japanese and German foreign bond markets are the next most important markets, followed by Saudi Arabia, the Netherlands, France and Luxembourg. All other markets are of minor importance, with new issues made infrequently and in small amounts. The US and Japanese foreign bond markets are known by special names—the Yankee and samurai bond markets, respectively—the other markets are simply known as foreign bond markets, though the term 'bulldog' issue has been recently applied to foreign borrowing in the sterling bond market.

As Table 26.5 demonstrates, the volume of foreign bond issues each year usually exceeds the volume of Eurobond issues, though the volumes of each are of similar order.

The majority of borrowers originate from Western Europe although Japanese corporate borrowers are major issuers, particularly in the Swiss foreign bond market.

Yields attaching to foreign bonds will approximate closely to yields obtainable on good quality domestic bonds in the country of issue, and will fluctuate according to domestic interest rate levels. Maturities are in the same range as are generally available for domestic issues.

As with Eurobond issues foreign bond issues may be either public issue or by private placement. In the Swiss foreign bond market especially, approximately two thirds of annual new issues are made by private placement. For all markets, however, as shown by Table 26.5, less than 50 per cent of total issues are by private placement.

Size of the markets

The total size of the international money and capital market is difficult to estimate, primarily because the market is unregulated and dealers are not therefore required to report their operations in the market to any single authoritative body.

Upon breaking down the international market into its major components, it is possible to approximate the market size, although there is an element of double counting and overlapping between the components. They may be defined as:

1. The Eurocurrency market. This is the market in all deposits (including CDs) of currencies placed with banks outside their home country and is the broadest measure of the total international money and capital market.
2. The Eurocredit market. This is the market for syndicated loans advanced to major international borrowers by a group of international banks. The loans are made in a Eurocurrency as required by the borrower. They are normally medium- to long-term loans at variable rates of interest which change according to interest trends prevailing in the international capital market. Thus, apart from the fact that the lender is a syndicate of banks rather than a single bank, and that the loans are denominated in a Eurocurrency, Eurocredits are similar to a

587

bank loan or line of credit as extended to customers of a bank in most developed domestic capital markets.

3. The Eurobond market. This is the market in bonds (including notes and short-term debt instruments) issued outside the borrowers' country of residence and purchased by investors with Eurocurrencies. This market is thus a subset of the Eurocurrency market.

4. The foreign bond market. This is also the market in bonds issued outside the borrowers' country of residence but issued on foreign domestic capital markets. It encompasses markets such as the Yankee bond market in the US, the samurai market in Japan and the Swiss foreign bond market. Funds used to purchase foreign bonds may originate as Eurocurrencies but cease to be so once they enter the home country's domestic capital market.

In the above definitions, the prefix Euro has been used although all measures include similar international markets (such as the Asian-dollar market) that are centred outside Europe.

The best measure of the total size of the Eurocurrency market is the reported external liabilities of banks throughout the free world; in other words, all foreign currency deposits placed with banks in every country. This figure is, however, likely to exaggerate the market size because of interbank deposits which introduce a degree of double counting.

The Bank for International Settlements (BIS) estimates that, for the year to December 1979, the net (of interbank deposits) size of the Eurocurrency credit outstanding was US$475 billion, while the net volume of new funds for the year was US$98 billion.

The major part of this increase, some 35.3 per cent, was reported by banks in Europe, while banks in the US, Canada and Japan, and offshore banking centres, accounted for 12.1 and 12.3 per cent of the increase, respectively.

An alternative measure is that given by the IMF which shows deposit banks' foreign liabilities. The foreign currency deposits held by banks in all countries was US$1500 billion as at March 1980. This is considerably larger than the BIS esti-mate but probably includes a large amount of double counting and does not distinguish between interbank deposits and those made by the non-bank sector. Of the total US$1500 billion, US$1100 billion was held by banks resident in indus-trialized countries comprising North America, Europe, Japan and Australasia. The Middle East accounted for US$33 billion and Asia for US$72 billion.

The new issues of Eurobonds in 1980 totalled US$20.5 billion, representing an increase of 18 per cent over new issues in 1979, and higher than the previous record US$19.5 billion of new issues made during 1977. US$13.6 billion of new issues in 1980 were denominated in US dollars. Thirty-five per cent of all Eurobonds took the form of floating-rate notes reflecting both the continuing importance of the US dollar in the Eurocurrency market, despite its relative weakness and the uncertainty about interest rates resulting from world-wide, high inflation rates.

The market has grown considerably since 1963 when new Eurobond floatations amounted to less than US$1 billion for the year. Since that time, up to June 1980, over 2480 issues have been made to a total value of US$92 billion, and the estimated outstanding size of the Eurobond market at August 1980 was 1297 issues to the value of about US$65 billion.

The gross size of the international bond market increased by US$37.9 billion in 1980. This comprised the US$20.5 billion new Eurobond issues and US$17.4 billion of new foreign bond issues. US$3.0 billion of new foreign bonds were floated in the US Yankee bonds market, a smaller increase, by US$1.6 billion, than in 1979. Yen denominated samurai bonds also declined in new issue volume from US$3.1 billion to US$1.2 billion. Swiss franc foreign bond new issues decreased slightly from US$9.0 billion to US$7.5 billion.

The foreign bond markets thus reflected the weakness of the US dollar and the yen and the comparative strength of the Swiss franc coupled with lower Swiss interest rates. Up until 1970 the US Yankee bond market accounted for by far the larger proportion of new foreign bond issues, during the 1960s representing on average 150 per cent more than foreign bond issues in other financial centres. During the 1970s the importance of the US market and that of other centres has alternated. In 1977 they were roughly equal, new issues amounting to approximately US$7 billion each in the US and in other centres. Since 1978 other centres have dominated the market. The major foreign bond markets apart from the US are Switzerland, Japan, the Netherlands and West Germany.

The total size of foreign bonds outstanding is roughly equivalent to the outstanding size of the Eurobond market, roughly US$70 billion, although some estimates set the amounts of foreign bonds as slightly more than the amount of Eurobonds.

The following diagram illustrates the size of the international capital market and the overlap of its component markets. The diagram includes the market in Eurocredits, the bank syndicated lending of Eurocurrencies. Although not an investment instrument available to the public, syndicated credits represent direct on-lending by banks from the pool of Eurocurrencies deposited with them. The approximate size of the market is about US$665 billion outstanding as at December 1979, according to BIS estimates. The increase in Eurocredits for 1979, excluding interbank transactions, was US$130 billion.

Together with the Eurocurrency net deposits of US$770 billion, outstanding Eurobonds of about US$65 billion and the US$665 billion Eurocredits produce a combined Eurocurrency market in excess of US$1500 billion.

Table 26.5 shows the increase of issues in the international capital markets and of its major components.

The Venn diagram shown in Fig. 26.1 illustrates the total size of the international capital market.

A The large box A is the Eurocurrency market, using the IMF estimate of foreign currency deposits held by banks throughout the world. This volume (A) is approximately US$1500 billion.

B The Eurocredit market—the market in Eurocurrency syndicated bank loans to international borrowers. B is a subset of A and its approximate size is US$665 billion (BIS estimate).

589

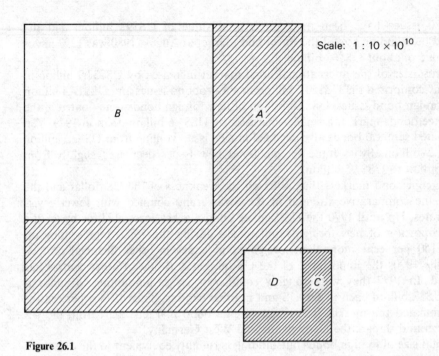

Figure 26.1

C represents the international bond market. *C* is the large box which includes *D*. The approximate size of *C* is US\$145 billion. The hatched part of *C* is the foreign bond market. Since foreign bonds are issued on domestic capital markets and denominated in local currency rather than Eurocurrency it is shown outside the larger box *A*.

D represents the market in Eurobonds. *D* is a subset of both *A* and *C*. The approximate size of *D* is US\$65 billion.

A − (B + D)   The hatched area of *A* [*A* − (*B* + *D*)] is a residual sum representing the approximate amount of Eurocurrency deposits that have not been on-lent by the banking system in the form of Eurocredits, nor have been invested in the Eurobond market. The approximate volume of deposits represented by the hatched area of *A* is US\$770 billion.

Currency composition of the international capital market

Table 26.5 shows that a large proportion of the international capital market is represented by US dollars. In 1980 US dollars accounted for 66 per cent of new Eurobond issues and 16 per cent of new foreign bond issues. As previously mentioned, the major foreign bond markets, and thus the currencies in which foreign bonds are denominated, in order of relative size are Switzerland, Germany, the USA, Japan and the Netherlands. In 1980, Swiss francs accounted for 43 per cent of new foreign bond issues, Germany for 18 per cent, Japan for seven per cent, while the Netherlands, together with foreign bonds issued in other markets, accounted for

16 per cent of new issues. Almost half of the issuers in the US foreign bond market are Canadian companies, while more than three-quarters of issuers in the Swiss market originate from Japan, Western Europe and other developed countries.

Of the total Eurocurrency market approximately 65 per cent of foreign currency assets are represented by US dollars, 21 per cent by Deutschemark, 6 per cent by Swiss francs and the remaining 8 per cent by other currencies. In the Eurobond market, the majority of existing Eurobonds are denominated in US dollars, as already noted, still the most important currency for new issues. At times, when the US dollar is weak, investor interest turns to bonds denominated in other currencies, the best established of which are the Deutschemark and the Dutch guilder. The Canadian dollar has only become important as a Eurobond currency since 1975 when changes in Canadian legislation allowed private sector Canadian borrowers to enter the market for the first time. The French franc sector operates sporadically as does the market for Eurosterling, depending on both the strength of the currency in the exchange market and the attitude of the government to Euro-issues. Other currencies introduced over the past few years to the Eurobond market include Euroyen, Hong Kong dollars, various Middle Eastern currencies and currency cocktails. These markets remain limited, however, both in the primary and secondary sectors.

Determination and behaviour of interest rates

Interest rates in the Eurocurrency market are determined by the present and expected demand and supply conditions with respect to the currency concerned. The absolute levels of supply and demand for a currency depend, to a large extent, on the volume of world trade transacted in that currency and thus on the amount of a currency that is physically produced and the requirements of foreigners to hold that currency in order to settle transactions. For this reason the US dollar continues to be the major Eurocurrency despite its weakness in foreign exchange markets during recent years. It is not, however, the absolute levels of supply and demand but changes in supply and demand that influence Eurocurrency interest rates.

The factors that influence supply and demand are domestic interest rates, domestic monetary policy and reserve requirements, domestic government regulations and relative strength of a currency in the foreign exchange markets.

Eurodollars are used here to illustrate how these factors affect Euro interest rates although the same applies for all Eurocurrencies.

In practice domestic interest rates act as a floor to Eurodollar interest rates since US banks will seek to borrow funds, in the form of deposits or CDs, in markets outside the US if the external dollars are cheaper than the cost of domestic dollar deposits. This pushes up demand and increases the Eurodollar rate until it equates with the domestic rate. Similarly lenders of dollars would deposit them in the US domestic market if such rates were higher than those available in the Euromarkets, thus increasing the supply to the domestic market and at the same time reducing the supply to the Euromarket. This reduces rates in the US domestic market relative to the Euromarket. In reality, the cost to US banks of borrowing in the domestic market is increased by Federal Reserve requirements.

591

If banks are required to set aside reserves of, say, eight per cent against increased deposit liabilities, the true cost of a deposit is higher than just the rate of interest, and it is this cost that should be regarded as the floor to Eurodollar rates. For example the true cost, including the cost of required reserves, to a bank of a six-month deposit at 10 per cent per annum interest would be about $10\frac{3}{4}$ per cent. Direct government controls may significantly alter the behaviour of particular participants in the Euromarkets and thus influence international interest rates. The imposition of IET (Interest Equalization Tax) by the US authorities in 1963 actually encouraged demand for Eurodollars rather than containing, as was intended, external dollar borrowing and lending. The three per cent reserve requirement on dollar CD issues by banks, in contrast, removes some of the attractions to US banks borrowing in the Euromarkets.

Exchange controls or central bank controls on foreign banks' holdings of foreign currency liabilities, as imposed by some governments, may affect the market for Eurodollars even though such controls are imposed by foreign governments.

One of the major influences that may cause very volatile fluctuations in the demand and supply of Eurodollars is exchange rate expectations. Forward market exchange rates are calculated according to a formula that equalizes interest rate differentials between currencies. Any change in expectations will not only cause a greater or lesser demand for certain currencies but will necessarily alter the relative interest rates. Central banks often operate in the foreign exchange markets to counteract expectations, but normally such intervention can only modify rather than reverse a trend.

Although the Eurocurrency market operates in a number of centres around the world, interest rates for a particular currency are consistent and any temporary geographical variations are quickly eliminated by international arbitrage. Since London is the major Euromarket centre, London interbank offered rates (LIBOR) for each currency are those normally quoted and used as the basis for most Eurocurrency transactions.

'Offered' rates are the rates at which banks in London will lend a currency to other banks for a given period of time. 'Bid' rates are the rates at which banks will pay for Eurocurrency deposits. Bid rates are lower than offered rates usually by $\frac{1}{8}$ to $\frac{1}{4}$ per cent.

Eurobond prices and yields are affected in the same way as are interest rates for Eurocurrency deposits, though they are also affected by additional factors. The most important is the credit standing of the borrower. The highest quality borrowers, such as sovereign states, will command yields of only a small margin over LIBOR, while bonds of the lowest quality among Eurobond issuers may carry margins of up to three per cent over LIBOR.

Location of the market place

Excluding foreign bonds the international capital market has earned the prefix Euro because it is largely maintained by banks in Europe. London is the major Euromarket trading centre; this is the principal contributor to the fact that London now accommodates more than 300 banks from all over the world.

In 1979 London accounted for 42 per cent of all European Eurocurrency business, which totalled approximately US$660 billion. Eurobonds to the value of approximately US$16 billion are quoted on the London stock exchange although most transactions take place in the over-the-counter market made between banks and brokers.

Luxembourg is another major European Euromarket trading centre and in 1979 accounted for just over 11 per cent of European business. Although this was less than France with a 14 per cent share of the market, Luxembourg is a considerably smaller country and Euromarket business contributes significantly to its GNP. Switzerland, although an active financial centre, particularly for foreign bonds, represented a less than five per cent market share of the Eurobond market. Germany, although a major Eurobond issuing centre, accounted for only about four per cent of the Eurocurrency market.

Outside Europe, the United States, principally New York, handled just under half the volume dealt with by London; Japan handled about one-sixth and Canada one-tenth of London's volume.

Other centres are mainly offshore centres. These include branches of US banks in locations such as the Bahamas, Cayman Islands and Panama, offshore banking units in Bahrain and Asian currency units (ACUs) in Singapore. This latter market, together with Hong Kong and Japan, comprise what is known as the Asian dollar market. This is a part of the Eurocurrency market but is so called because it is located in Asia. Such offshore centres together probably account for a little more than 13 per cent of total Eurocurrency business, or less than half that handled by London.

Eurocurrency deposits and CDs are traded through banks and brokers in much the same way as in domestic markets. Eurobonds are also traded in the same way, for although they are listed on a number of stock exchanges there is no single specific market-place for Eurobonds. The market is conducted as an over-the-counter market made by banks and brokers who are in constant communication with each other in both their local financial centres and in other centres all round the world.

The Association of International Bond Dealers (AIBD) comprises these market makers. Membership now totals some 550 institutions from about 30 countries. The major dealers are shown in Table 26.8.

Modern communications and clearing systems ensure that the market reacts quickly to demand and supply factors and, barring major world political disturbance, adjusts efficiently.

Dealing and fees

As already noted, the great majority of secondary market Eurobond deals are made by telephone or telex between banks and other financial institutions. A number of firms act as professional market makers, quoting both buying and selling prices, normally with an average $\frac{1}{4}$ to $\frac{1}{2}$ per cent spread, and are willing to buy or sell at the prices given.

Table 26.8 Major market makers in international bond market

Market	Dealers
PRIMARY MARKET—MAJOR ISSUERS OF NEW BONDS	
Listed in order of new issues brought to the market in last twenty years	Deutsche Bank
	Crédit Suisse—First Boston
	Union Bank of Switzerland
	Swiss Bank Corporation
	Westlandse Bank
	KB Luxembourg
	SG Warburg
	Paribas
	Dresdner Bank
	Amro Bank
	Banque Nationale de Paris
	Commerzbank
	Algemene Bank Nederland
	Société Générale
	Crédit Lyonnais
	Morgan Stanley International
	Bruxelles Lambert
	Crédit Commercial de France
	Banca Commerciale Italiana
SECONDARY MARKET—MAJOR EUROBOND DEALERS	
UK, listed alphabetically	Akroyd & Smithers Ltd
	Amex Bank
	Bank of America International
	Bankers Trust International
	Bondtrade
	Blyth Eastman Paine Webber Ltd
	Chase Manhattan Bank
	Chemical Bank International
	Citicorp International Bank
	Continental Illinois Ltd
	Crédit Commercial de France
	Crédit Suisse—First Boston
	Cresvale International
	Daiwa Bank
	Deltec Trading Co. Ltd
	Dillon, Read Overseas Corp.
	Dominion Securities Ltd
	European Banking Co. Ltd
	First Chicago Ltd
	Goldman Sachs International
	Hambros Bank
	IBJ International Ltd
	Kidder Peabody Securities Ltd
	Loeb, Rhoades, Shearson International
	London & Continental Bankers
	Kohn, Loeb Lehman Bros International
	Merril Lynch, Pierce, Fenner & Smith

Table 26.8—*Continued*

Market	*Dealers*
UK—*Continued*	Morgan Stanley International
	Nesbit Thomson Ltd
	New Japan Securities Europe Ltd
	Nikko Securities Co. (Europe) Ltd
	Nomura Europe NV
	Orion Bank Ltd
	Pinchin Denny & Co.
	Ross & Partners
	Robert Fleming & Co.
	Salomon Brothers International
	Samuel Montagu & Co.
	Scandinavian Bank Ltd
	Société Générale Straus Turnbull Ltd
	Sumitomo Finance International
	Vickers da Costa Ltd
	S. G. Warburg & Co. Ltd
	Wedd Durlacher Mordaunt & Co.
	Westdeutsche Landesbank Girozentrale
	White Weld Securities
	Wood Gundy Ltd
	Yamaichi International (Europe) Ltd
US, listed alphabetically	Arnhold & S. Bleichroeder Inc.
	Atlantic Capital Corporation
	Bear Stearns & Co.
	Drexel Burnham Lambert Inc.
	Kidder Peabody & Co. Inc.
	Lehman Bros Kuhn Loeb Inc.
	Lazard Freres & Co.
	Merrill Lynch, Pierce Fenner Smith Inc.
	Salomon Bros
Belgium	Dewaay, Sebille Servais & Co.
	Kredietbank NV
Luxembourg	Banque Générale du Luxembourg
	Banque Internationale du Luxembourg
	Bayerische Landesbank International
	Dewaay Luxembourg
	Kredietbank SA Luxembourgeoise
	Swiss Bank Corporation (Luxembourg)
Netherlands	H. Albert de Bary & Co.
	Algemene Bank Nederland
	Amsterdam—Rotterdam Bank (AMRO)
	Barclays Kol & Co.
	Central Rabobank Utrecht
	Bank van der Hoop, Offers
	Bank Morgan Labouchère
	F. Van Lanschot
	Nederlandsche Middenstandsbank

Continued over

Table 26.8—*Continued*

Market	Dealers
Netherlands (*continued*)	Nederlandse Credietbank Pierson Heldring & Pierson Slavenburg, Oyens & Van Eeghen
Germany/Austria	Commerzbank Creditanstalt Bankverein Deutsche Bank Dresdner Bank Girozentrale und Bank der Österreichischen Sparkassen Westdeutsche Landesbank Girozentrale
Switzerland	Bondpartners SA Crédit Suisse/Swiss Credit Bank Swiss Bank Corporation Union Bank of Switzerland
France	Banque Arabe et Internationale d'Investissement (BAII) Banque de l'Union Européenne Banque Nationale de Paris Crédit Lyonnais Interunion—Banque Smith Barney Harris, Upham & Co.
Italy	Banca Commerciale Italiana Banco Ambrosiano Banco di Roma Credito Italiano Istituto Bancario Italiano Istituto Bancario San Paolo di Torino
Scandinavia	Bank of Helsinki Ltd Bergen Bank Den Norske Creditbank Den Danske Bank af 1871 Aktieselskab R. Henriques jr Bank Aktieselskab Kansallis-Osake-Pankki Privatbanken Aktieselskab Skandinaviska Enskilda Banken Skopbank Sparekassen SDS Union Bank of Finland
Middle East	The Arab Company for Trading Securities (ACTS) National Bank of Abu Dhabi SAK

The dealing spread varies according to the quality of the bond and size of market for particular types of bonds. High-quality bonds with active markets may be quoted with spreads as low as $\frac{1}{8}$ per cent, though these are normally floating-rate notes. Lower quality, less active bonds may have dealing spreads of two to three per cent.

The average size of the individual deals on the secondary market depends both on the quality of the paper and the length of time elapsed since the date of issue. As a general rule, however, individual deals of around US$150 000 are possible for older issues and about twice that amount for newer issues without obviously affecting the market prices. It will be realized that this is still appreciably smaller than digestible transaction sizes in, for example, either US domestic bonds or UK gilts.

Prices quoted by dealers are net, the dealers' commission element being included in the quoted spread between their bid and offered prices. No additional fee or brokerage is charged. Eurobonds are dealt on a yield 'plus accrued' basis. That is, interest that has accumulated since the date of payment of the last interest coupon is not included in the dealing price. Thus if, for example, an investor buys a nine per cent Eurodollar bond at a price of 99 per cent (of par), the cost to him will be US$990 per US$1000 bond, plus accrued interest at a rate of nine per cent per annum times the number of days since the last interest payment, on the basis of a 360-day year consisting of 12 months of 30 days each.

For Eurocurrency deposits settlement occurs on the same day as the transaction. For most Eurobond secondary market transactions, settlement and delivery is for seven calendar days after the dealing date. Two exceptions to this are Euro-commercial paper and Euro-Deutschemark bonds, where in both cases settlement and delivery are two business days after the dealing date.

Two competing settlement systems currently exist—Cedel and Euroclear—both handle roughly equal volumes of business, that is, between one and two billion dollars per week of US dollar bonds and 250 to 500 million dollars per week of Eurobonds transactions.

A full list of Eurobonds available in the secondary market is printed in the British *Financial Times* every month. The information is provided by the Association of International Bond Dealers and lists Eurobonds by currency, country and type of borrower, the current issued and outstanding amount and the issue price, along with recent quotations and yields.

In addition the *Financial Times* prints a daily list of the latest 200 most widely traded bonds. This shows the amount issued, the previous day's closing bid and offer prices and yields.

Taxation

One of the attractive features of Euromarket investments is that they are free from all forms of taxation. Since they are part of the international market and not under the jurisdiction of any national authorities, Eurobonds and Euro deposits and CDs are free from any domestic taxation including withholding tax. All interest and capital is paid gross. Of course, once proceeds of Euro investments are repatriated they become subject to the local tax regulations of the country to which the funds are repatriated.

Regulation of the market and exchange controls

The international capital market, excepting foreign bonds issued in domestic markets, is not subject to regulation by any national authorities or international institution. Various governments may control the number and amount of new issues of bonds denominated in their domestic currency but the secondary sector is a completely free market, maintained by the commercial and investment banks of many domiciles who act as principals, dealers and managing agents in the market.

Since the principal operators are all major banks in their country of residence and subject to local banking regulations, it may be assumed that each manages its Euromarket business with the same commercial prudence as they use in conducting domestic business. Concern has been expressed by a number of governments and central banks that since banks' Euromarket operations are not constrained by reserve requirements, liquidity ratios or other methods, it is possible for the volume of 'stateless' money in the Euromarkets to grow at a rate far in excess of that acceptable for the money supply of any one country to grow. Indeed, during the 1970s the Euromoney supply has grown at an average rate of 25 per cent per annum while the banks' reserves have grown comparatively little. This Euro-currency 'multiplier', it is argued, is inflationary, particularly since a large proportion of loans are made to developing countries and others with balance of payments deficits, often to finance consumption rather than productive investment although, in favour of the market, it is contended that it plays a vital role in recycling the surpluses of the oil producing countries to deficit and developing countries. There are, however, no controls over the direction or purpose of lending. On the other hand, the market itself is the final arbiter in the sense that bonds issued by doubtful or lower-quality borrowers are difficult to float in the primary market and suffer from poor markets and high yields in the secondary sector.

A further worry is that the market's unconstrained growth and the banks' potentially inadequate reserves may prove to be destabilizing factors. So far, however, the Euromarket seems to have survived the type of international crises which would normally catalyse such instability. A prime example occurred in 1979 when the Iranians imprisoned US embassy staff causing an international political crisis that led certain US banks to suspend facilities on an Iranian loan while Iranian assets held in US banks were frozen. At the time it was felt that the market was imperfect and unduly risky if banks were empowered to freeze investors' assets or suspend facilities to borrowers for whatever reason. Activity in the market declined significantly and prices also dropped. The market did not, however, collapse but within a few months had returned to its previously active and buoyant state.

Because of severe criticism received by the US banks, it is unlikely that banks will again attempt to confiscate either borrowers' or lenders' funds.

A further concern is that the Euromarket encourages a distortion of exchange rate relationships. Non-US borrowers issuing bonds in dollars need to cover their dollar liability forward by selling their domestic currency against dollars. This has a tendency to weaken the domestic currency which, in all probability, is already weakened by a balance of payments deficit. Alternatively, an appreciating currency may suffer from further upward pressure through investor interest concertedly switching to bonds denominated in that strong currency.

Market advocates claim that currency hedging and speculation help, through international arbitrage, to adjust relative currency values to their true exchange values. Nevertheless, some governments choose to impose domestic exchange controls or banking regulations to restrict either the activity of their own residents in the Euromarkets or of foreign lenders in investing in Eurobonds denominated in their currencies.

The central banks of many countries, in whose currencies Eurobonds are denominated, control the primary market as for example, the West German Bundesbank does by regulating the new issues calendar. Some go farther by prohibiting entirely the issue of Eurobonds in their local currency. Switzerland is such an example. The Swiss authorities have been opposed to the Swiss franc becoming a major currency used in the international markets, and since 1963 have prevented the issue of Euroswiss franc bonds. Thus the only Swiss franc securities traded in the Euromarkets are dollar convertible bonds, issued in dollars and convertible into equity shares of the Swiss borrower. Swiss residents are, however, free to deal in the Euromarkets. By contrast, until the UK abolished exchange controls in 1979, British residents could only deal in the Euromarket by first purchasing investment currency at often a substantial premium, which effectively deterred UK lenders to the market. Other countries limit the amount of dollar and other foreign currencies which domestic residents can hold. This also has the effect of preventing their residents from investing in the Euromarkets.

Controls applied by governments to protect their domestic markets and currencies are not always permanent. A number introduce controls only when they consider their own markets to be under pressure, but then subsequently relax them. France is an example of a country which not only has a complex system of exchange regulations but which adjusts these frequently as a major instrument of economic policy. Up to 1972 the new issues volume of Eurofrench franc bonds ranked third behind Eurodollar and Euro-Deutschemark bonds. The weakness and volatility of the franc caused the French monetary authorities to restrict new issues between 1972 and 1976 and to close the market entirely during 1976/77. Since then the primary market has been re-established but remains closely controlled by the French central bank.

In summary, therefore, the primary Euromarket is or may be subject to a variety of controls imposed by national governments for the protection of their own economies. The secondary market remains entirely unrestricted and no controls are likely in the foreseeable future.

Gold

History

Gold is one of the oldest mediums of exchange and store of value. For thousands of years gold has been used, in many civilizations, to settle transactions in goods and services. As international trade developed it became cumbersome to ship gold bullion and coins around the world to settle payments. Paper money gained acceptance as legal tender merely because it was backed by gold. Britain was the first country in 1816 to link the pound sterling officially to the value of gold, though gold was still the main means of settling international debt. By 1870 Britain had adopted the full gold standard which meant that the pound sterling was not only fixed according to the value of an ounce of gold but was also fully convertible into gold. Other countries similarly adopted the gold standard and their currencies bore a fixed relationship to each other, linked by the value of gold.

The gold standard was abandoned in 1914 at the outbreak of the first world war. Adherence to the gold standard inevitably restricted money supply growth in proportion to the physical quantity of gold that a country held. European countries especially needed to increase their money supplies in order to pay for the war.

During the war gold had been again used as a medium of exchange. A certain amount of portfolio trading also developed in Europe and in 1919 the first London daily gold fixings commenced in the offices of N. M. Rothschilds and Son where they are still conducted today. The gold that was traded in this market was new gold, surplus to official reserve requirements of governments, which could be sold to the highest bidder.

Most countries, however, returned to the gold standard after the war and Britain readopted it in 1925. The London gold fixings ceased and there was a limited non-monetary market in gold. In the London market gold could only be held for monetary purposes although some trading continued in European centres—particularly in Zurich.

Many countries returning to the gold standard, including Britain, fixed their currencies at the same prewar value in relation to gold, despite the war's inflationary effects. This resulted in a disequilibrium of price levels between different countries and was one of the factors that contributed to the depressed economic conditions of the 1920s and 1930s. Britain in particular found that export prices were too high and import prices relatively low, due to the artificially high value for sterling. Terms of trade inevitably deteriorated and it became clear that the gold standard could no longer be maintained and it was consequently abandoned. The UK came off the gold standard in 1931; the US followed in 1933. In 1934 the US authorities increased the dollar price of gold from $20.62 to $35 an ounce—at which level it remained until 1968.

In place of the gold standard, the gold exchange standard was adopted. Under this system the pound sterling and US dollar were fully convertible into gold but the currencies themselves were used to settle international debt and were to be used by other countries as reserve currencies and held in their official reserves in lieu of gold.

Gold continued to be traded through Zurich and other European centres by non-monetary holders. The IMF ruling that it should only be traded in exchange for the settlement of official debt did not prove effective in constraining demand. The London daily fixing was re-established in 1954, and a wholesale market opened, but gold could only be sold through this market to holders of funds in the dollar exchange territories. By 1958, however, holders of funds outside the scheduled territories were allowed to deal through the London market. During the late 1950s a two-tier gold market was operating. Gold transferred between banks for debt settlement and held by central banks as official reserves was valued at $35 an ounce. The price of gold traded through financial markets such as London and Zurich was determined by demand and supply. London became established as the world's leading market in wholesale gold. The price was able to be controlled within fairly narrow limits because of the gold pool that was established by Western central banks in 1961. Transfers between banks were still maintained at $35 an ounce while the gold pool allowed the authorities in London to keep a close check on all flows and transactions in gold.

Demand for non-monetary gold continued to expand. Being unable to control the price within narrow limits the UK closed the London market for a few weeks in 1968. The operation of the gold pool was also ended. In the same year South Africa—the world's major supplier—ceased supplying further gold because of her large balance of payments surplus. Zurich took over from London as the main market centre but its supplies were almost entirely provided from private portfolio holdings. Though the London market reopened in 1968 and South Africa resumed supplies in 1969, Zurich retained its dominant position as a gold trading centre.

In 1971 the US authorities ended the convertibility of the dollar into gold (the UK had abolished the convertibility of sterling in the 1960s) and the US authorities began to sell gold from its official reserves in an attempt to support the value of the dollar. The price of gold thereafter ceased to be fixed in terms of any particular currency. Gold was then allowed to find its own value according to demand and supply in world markets. Supply is limited by the finite resources available and production capabilities. Demand initially came mainly from governments who hold gold as part of their official reserves. As the 1970s progressed, however, gold was sought increasingly by other participants in financial investment markets. It is now recognized by the investment community that gold has an intrinsic monetary value despite exchange rate fluctuations and inflation differentials between economies, and that during times of political crises the price of gold may even appreciate very rapidly as wealth is transferred into gold which retains its original role as the ultimate store of value. The price of gold has appreciated significantly during the 1970s. The upward trend has shown considerable volatility, peaking at almost $200 an ounce in December 1974 in the expectation of strong demand from US private investors who were once again allowed to hold gold as from 1975. This strong demand did not materialize and the price of gold then fell back to about $100 in August 1976.

The most phenomenal rise in the price of gold occurred in 1979. From a low of $193 an ounce in November 1978 it had increased 31 per cent within two months.

Political upheavals in Iran and further oil price increases had resulted in considerable anxiety in world financial markets. Rising inflation and worsening balance of payments positions in major economies were also exacerbating uncertainty in foreign exchange markets. Traditional investment markets became less secure and prices of fixed interest securities fell. Major investors switched funds from other markets into gold. It is thought that the surplus funds of OPEC countries significantly influenced the massive rise in gold prices which reached an all time high of $850 an ounce on 21 January 1980. A sharp downward reaction followed. The price fell to $650 in two days but the price rallied around $550 in mid-1980 and has since continued to move in a broad trading range around that level. International investors have become more aware of gold as an investment, as a store of value, as a hedge against economic and political uncertainty and also, at times, as a speculation for potential capital gains, and equally volatile losses.

As gold has been released from many of its earlier constraints a variety of markets developed during the 1970s to cater for the increased demand from a wide range of purchasers. Different markets are available around the world and trading can take place 24 hours a day.

History of gold market

Date

1816 UK fixed sterling in terms of gold.

1870 UK adopted full gold standard.

1914 Gold standard suspended.

1919 First London daily gold fixings by N. M. Rothschilds

1925 UK returned to gold standard.

1931 UK abandoned gold standard. Gold exchange standard introduced. London market closed.

1933 US dollar becomes part of gold exchange standard.

1934 US raises price of gold from $20.62 to $35 an ounce. Private US citizens no longer allowed to hold gold. Gold could only be sold for monetary purposes. Some trading still continued in European markets.

1954 London market reopened for limited trading to holders of funds in scheduled territories only.

1958 London market widened to include investors from non-scheduled territories.

1961 Western central banks established gold pool.

1968 London market closed for two weeks. South Africa temporarily halted supply. Zurich became major gold trading centre, dealing in portfolio holdings of gold.

1971 US authorities cease convertibility of dollar into gold. Gold no longer fixed at $35 an ounce for official transactions. Authorities supported currency by increasingly frequent auctions of gold.

1974 Gold reached high of nearly $200 an ounce.

1975   US private citizens allowed to buy gold. New York developed gold futures
       market.
1980   Gold reached high of $850 an ounce in January. Rallied at around $600 for
       rest of the year.

Supply

While the demand for gold fluctuates according to world economic and political
conditions, supply is fairly consistent—constrained by the finite availability of natural resources and by production capabilities.

South Africa is the world's major producer and supplies about three-quarters of
total gold produced in the non-communist world. Other major suppliers are
Canada and the USA which represent five and three per cent respectively of total
non-communist supply.

Gold production in the communist bloc countries is not known and supplies
from those countries are only made available when they require additional foreign
exchange or when prices in the free market are considered to be abnormally high.

Table 26.9   Gold: supply and demand in non-communist world (metric tons) (*source: Consolidated Gold Fields Ltd*)

	1970	1971	1972	1973	1974	1975	1976	1977	1978	1979	1980
ANNUAL PRODUCTION											
South Africa	1000.4	976.3	909.6	855.2	758.6	713.4	713.4	699.9	706.4	703.3	675.0
Canada	74.9	68.7	64.7	60.0	52.2	51.4	52.4	54.0	54.0	51.1	49.3
US	54.2	46.4	45.1	36.2	35.1	32.4	32.2	32.0	30.2	30.2	27.6
Latin America	35.4	34.1	34.8	35.2	36.9	41.8	55.0	55.9	62.7	66.6	85.5
Australasia	23.8	24.7	34.9	40.7	39.9	37.4	38.9	45.5	48.2	67.3	62.7
Other	84.9	85.4	90.0	93.6	83.9	77.5	77.2	84.5	78.8	42.8	42.9
Total	1273.6	1235.6	1183.6	1120.9	1006.6	953.9	969.1	971.8	980.3	961.3	943.0
South Africa as proportion of total, %	78.5	79.0	76.9	76.3	75.4	74.8	73.6	72.0	72.1	73.2	71.6
ANNUAL SUPPLY											
Total production	1273.6	1235.6	1183.6	1120.9	1006.6	953.9	969.1	971.8	980.3	961.3	943.0
Plus net sales from communist bloc	−3.0	54.0	213.0	275.0	220.0	149.0	412.0	401.0	410.0	199.0	90.0
Less net official purchases and sales	−236.0	96.0	−151.0	6.0	20.0	9.0	58.0	269.0	362.0	544.0	−230.0
Total net supply	1034.6	1385.6	1245.6	1401.9	1246.6	1111.9	1439.1	1641.8	1752.3	1704.3	803
ANNUAL DEMAND											
Jewellery	1066	1064	999	518	225	523	935	1003	1007	737	120
Other manufacturing	210	218	241	267	216	188	217	224	251	255	207
Medals etc.	54	52	41	21	7	21	47	47	50	33	15
Official coins	46	54	63	54	287	251	185	146	288	290	179
Net private bullion purchases	−341	−2	−98	542	512	129	55	222	156	389	282
Total net demand	1035	1386	1246	1402	1247	1112	1439	1642	1752	1704	803
Bullion purchases as proportion of total, %	....	....	....	38.7	41.0	11.6	3.8	13.5	8.9	22.8	35.1

Consolidated Gold Fields estimate that in 1980 sales from the Soviet Union amounted to 90 tonnes and 199 tonnes in 1979. This represented about 10 per cent of gold production in the non-communist world in 1980 and 24 per cent in 1979.

China produces a relatively small proportion of total world output, estimated by Consolidated Gold Fields to be between 30 and 60 tonnes per annum.

Table 26.9 shows the quantity of gold produced during the last decade and the different types of demand for gold. Clearly investment demand has grown significantly since 1971 and now represents a substantial proportion of total demand.

Gold markets

There are now a wide variety of ways to invest in gold, namely,

- fabricated gold, e.g., jewellery   - gold savings accounts
- gold bullion   - gold-linked securities
- gold bars   - gold shares
- gold coins   - gold options
- gold certificates   - gold futures

The markets are located in

- Switzerland   - Canada
- London   - Sydney
- US   - Tokyo
- Luxembourg   - Hong Kong
- Amsterdam   - Singapore

Gold bullion markets

In 1980 Consolidated Gold Fields estimated that net private sector bullion purchase in the non-communist world were 282 tonnes, or 35 per cent of the supply of gold to the private sector for the year. This is quite a significant increase compared with previous years but the figure is, however, calculated as a residual between total supply and gold used in fabrication. The estimate exaggerates the size of the investment market in bullion as it also encompasses other forms of trading such as gold certificate, savings accounts, futures and options.

The major bullion markets are located in Zurich and London, though it is possible to purchase gold bullion through major banks and bullion dealers in other financial centres such as Luxembourg, Frankfurt, Hong Kong, Sydney and New York. Of the two principal markets, Switzerland accounted for the largest turnover during the 1970s. This position may have been reversed in 1980 since the Swiss authorities introduced a sales tax of 5.6 per cent on all sales of gold bullion in January 1980. Although the volume of business handled through Switzerland has remained high, undoubtedly a greater proportion of dealing has switched to London where transactions are tax free for non-residents. It should be noted, however, that bullion transactions made by residents are subject to value added tax at 15 per cent.

Investors in bullion pay the spot price of gold for immediate settlement and delivery. While the purchaser may take physical delivery of the gold, in practice it is usually kept in safe custody with a bank and very often does not leave the country in which it has been purchased.

Bullion purchasers are large investors. Bullion is dealt in large units of one kilogram bars and 400 ounce bars (1 ounce = 31.1 g). The quality or fineness of bullion bars is 0.995% for 400-ounce bars and 0.999% for kilogram bars. The price range for gold during 1980 was $500 to $850 per ounce. The price of a 400-ounce bar therefore ranged between $200 000 and $340 000. Clearly the bullion market is a market for large investors only.

Banks and bullion dealers do not charge a commission but the dealer's profit is built into the price at which he is offering to sell, or bidding to buy, gold.

London gold fixing

Although Switzerland has dominated turnover in the bullion market London remains the principal international price fixing centre and prices at which gold is dealt in Zurich are based on those fixed in London.

The market in London is made by five firms comprising two merchant banks, one subsidiary of a merchant bank, one gold broker and one metallurgical company. Representatives of these firms meet twice daily in the offices of one of the merchant banks—N. M. Rothschild & Sons Ltd. The daily fixing of the gold price is made at these meetings by the five representatives who are in continuous communication with the trading rooms of their own firms and who between them match buying and selling orders at a price that equates the two. The price is always quoted in US dollars per ounce.

The trading rooms of the five member firms are also in direct communication with London banks, bullion dealers and gold trading centres throughout the world. Although foreign centres such as Zurich are active markets it is the London daily gold fix that determines the world price of gold.

The newer futures markets are however having a greater and greater influence over the prices fixed in London. The New York futures market, COMEX, is open after London has closed. When the London market reopens the following day the price reached on COMEX may be very different from the previous day's close in London. The price fixing takes this into account and normally takes its lead from the COMEX close rather than the London closing price of the previous day.

Gold bars

Bullion is mostly traded in bars of 400 ounces but smaller bars are also traded so as to be attractive to a wider range of investor. These bars are measured in grams rather than ounces. One troy ounce is equivalent to 31.1 grams and 1 kilogram is equivalent to 32.15 troy ounces.

The smallest gold bar has a weight of 5 grams (0.1608 ounces) of fine gold. Other bars are available in sizes of 10, 20, 100, 250 and 500 g and 1 kilogram. Consolidated Gold Fields estimated that about 30 tonnes of small gold bars of 5 to 50 g were sold in 1979. The bars are bought at the spot dollar price for immediate settlement and delivery. The price is determined by the London daily gold fix which in turn is determined by market demand and supply. The bars all have a gold content (fineness) of 999.9 grams per kilogram and there is therefore no premium on the price of a bar relative to the quoted price of gold that has a fineness of 99.5 per cent. It should also be noted that gold bars sold by the Soviet Union frequently have a slightly lower gold content than gold sold in other free markets. Depending on the amount purchased, dealers may charge a commission on purchases of bars, which may be up to five per cent of the consideration. The main markets for gold bars are made in Zurich and London, though some banks, commodity brokers and bullion dealers in other major financial centres also make a market in gold bars.

Gold coins

Many countries now mint gold coins which may have no additional numismatic value. They may have a nominal face value such as the British Sovereign (£1) or the American Eagle ($10) but their intrinsic value is determined solely by their gold content. Unlike that of gold bars, the market price of gold coins may stand at a premium over their gold content, sometimes because of a particular coin's relative rarity but also because they are usually sold in small quantities to small investors. Table 26.10 shows that demand for official gold coins has risen substantially since the mid-1970s and now represents about 15 per cent of total net supply.

Table 26.10 also lists all minted gold coins known to be available. The most popular is the South African kruggerrand. In 1980 3.2 million kruggerrands were sold, equivalent to 98 tonnes of gold representing about 50 per cent of all sales of gold coins. Over 3.0 million kruggerrands were sold in markets outside South Africa, and 40 per cent of these were sold in the US alone.

Gold coins are available in most financial centres but sales taxes are imposed on transactions in gold coins in a number of countries (see Table 26.10), and some countries forbid the export of gold coins.

Zurich and London are the major markets in which most types of minted gold coins are available. In Switzerland the major banks make a market in gold coins and prices quoted are competitive between banks.

In London major banks also supply gold coins but their prices tend not to be as competitive as those of the bullion dealers. Banks also tend to charge a commission on purchases while bullion dealers quote a buying and selling price, the spread between which represents their dealing commission. This spread is usually about one per cent for a single coin but falls as the consideration rises. In the London market premiums of gold coins over their gold content range from about $2\frac{1}{2}$ per cent for the kruggerrand up to 40 per cent for the Swiss and the French 20-franc gold coins. Similar premiums exist in other markets. There are no sales taxes on transactions in gold coins in either Zurich or London.

Whatever their face value or denomination, gold coins are nearly always traded at a dollar price according to the London gold fix dollar price. The markets in London and Zurich will also quote gold prices in pounds or Swiss francs respectively.

Table 26.10   Gold coins issued and local markets

Coin	Face value	Gold content* (fine gold)	Country of issue	Taxes in local market	Other restrictions
Kruggerrand	....	1 oz	South Africa	Nil	Exports controlled by reserve bank
2-Rand	R2	7.3 g			
Quarter rand	....	0.25 oz			
Edward VII sovereign	£1	7.3 g	Great Britain	Nil	None
George V sovereign	£1	7.3 g			
Elizabeth II sovereign	£1	7.3 g			
Elizabeth II coronet sovereign	£1	7.3 g			
Liberty double eagle	$20	30.1 g	US	Sales taxes in certain states	None
St Gavdentius double eagle	$20	30.1 g			
Liberty eagle	$10	15.05 g			
Vreneli	F20	5.8 g	Switzerland	Nil	None
Helvetia	F20	5.8 g			
Vreneli	F10	2.9 g			
Napoleon III with wreath	F20	5.8 g	France	None (capital gains tax charged on domestic transactions)	None
Third Republic angel	F20	5.8 g			
Cock	F20	5.8 g			
4-ducat Franz Joseph	d4	13.8 g	Austria	VAT of 18% on domestic sales	Export of coins subject to exchange controls
1-ducat Franz Joseph	d1	3.45 g			
100-Crown Franz Joseph	Cr100	30.49 g			
50-peso Eagle	p50	37.5 g	Mexico	Nil	None
20-peso Aztec Calender	p20	15.0 g			
10-peso	p10	7.59 g			
Maple leaf	....	1 oz	Canada	Nil	Exports to communist countries restricted
Bahamian dollar	B$10 B$20		Bahamas	Nil	None
Commemorative coin	B$50 B$100 B$150 B$200 B$2500				
$1000 coin	HK$1000		Hong Kong	Nil	None
Six commemorative coins			Indonesia	Nil	Exports allowed subject to maximum limits
Tanku Abdul Rahman	M$100		Malaysia	5% sales tax	Imports and exports restricted by exchange controls
Third Malaysian Plan	M$200				
Ninth South East Asian Games	M$250				
Wildlife Conservation	M$500				
Singapore currency coin	S$150		Singapore	Nil	None
₱1000 gold coin	₱1000		Philippines	Nil	Imports and exports require licences
₱1500 gold coin	₱1500				
Rs1000 gold coin	Sey Rs1000		Seychelles	Nil	None
Rs1500 gold coin	Sey Rs1500				
Chervonet	....	0.25 oz	Russia	....	Available in London and Zurich

* 1 ounce = 31.1 grams

Gold certificates

A gold certificate is a registered receipt held by the investor and represents a specific amount of gold bullion held in the vaults of a bank, to the account of the certificate holder.

Investment in gold certificates differs from investment in gold bullion in a number of ways. Certificates can be purchased in round money sums whereas bullion is purchased in specific quantities by weight. Purchasing a certificate does not require that the investor takes delivery of the gold and thus he does not have to arrange safe custody or pay sales taxes if applicable in local markets. Gold certificates have become increasingly popular in the Swiss market since the introduction in 1980 of a 5.6 per cent sales tax on bullion transactions. The certificate can be traded as a security in its own right and changes in value as the gold it represents rises or falls in value. It may be split down into smaller certificates if the investor wishes to sell off only part of his gold investments.

Banks, brokers and bullion dealers in the major markets such as Zurich, London, Frankfurt, Paris, Amsterdam, Luxembourg, New York, Japan, Hong Kong and Singapore may issue gold certificates but usually charge a commission on purchases which may be as high as five per cent depending on the size of the consideration.

Gold savings accounts

A number of larger banks in the major markets may also offer gold savings accounts. Effectively these are private bank accounts into which money may be deposited or from which money may be withdrawn at any time. The outstanding balance in the account is linked to the price of gold. Unlike gold certificates the amount invested is not represented by a specific quantity of gold but is related to a pool of gold held by the bank with which the account is held. The whole value of the balance is recalculated daily in proportion to the increase or decrease in the value of the pool of gold. No interest is earned on the balance in the account.

A new form of gold savings account offered, for example, by Standard Chartered Bank, does pay interest on balances provided they are kept on deposit for a minimum period of one year. The interest payment takes the form of a gold coin (or coins) that is paid to the depositor in advance, when the deposit is placed. The value of the coins paid reflects the size of the deposit and prevailing market interest rates. The investor is free to sell his coins at any time and is thus able to take advantage of any rise in the price of gold, though he cannot liquidate the balance on his account until the end of the minimum deposit term.

Gold-linked securities

At present, France is unique in issuing government fixed interest securities that are linked to the value of gold. These securities are the most popularly traded fixed interest stocks on the Paris Bourse and are available to both residents and non-residents.

There are two securities that are indexed in relation to gold—the 1973 ex-Pinay $4\frac{1}{2}\%$ state loan which is linked to the value of the 20-franc Napoleon III gold coin and the 7% 1973 state loan which is linked to the value of the gold bar in Paris.

The $4\frac{1}{2}\%$ stock has two semiannual payments comprising interest plus premium which is based on a formula that averages the value of the Napoleon coin over the preceding 100 stock exchange quotations. Since the Napoleon coin often stands at a volatile and high premium of up to 40 per cent over its gold content the yield can consequently be quite high. The 7% stock has a redemption value linked to the market value of the gold bar in Paris. It, too, has semiannual drawings that are calculated on the basis of the average gold value over the preceding six months.

The $4\frac{1}{2}\%$ stock is free from all taxes, including French withholding tax, though the 7% issue is not.

The advantage to the investor of this type of gold-linked security is that the bonds yield a semiannual interest return, regardless of the price of gold. Investment in physical gold or paper representing physical gold does not yield interest. Yet the bonds also offer the potential of substantial capital gains and are also readily marketable securities. The bonds are denominated in French francs and for a foreign investor the potential capital gain must be weighed in conjunction with the potential loss or gain on currency.

Gold shares

The shares of companies which mine or manufacture gold are price sensitive to changes in the value of gold.

Such companies are resident in those countries that supply gold to the non-communist world. The largest market, and thus the largest number of companies, are resident in South Africa. Other markets are Canada, the US and Australia.

South African gold shares can be purchased through the Johannesburg stock exchange by non-residents but only through the purchase of financial rand for which strict regulations apply (see South Africa). However, the shares are also listed on the New York and London stock exchanges, denominated respectively in US dollars and pounds sterling. A number of stockbrokers in each of these markets specialize in South African gold shares and provide advice to clients on the capital gains and dividend yield potential of each of the gold mining shares.

A London broker, L. Messel & Co. estimates that there are about 60 operating gold mines in South Africa but that only about two-thirds of these are major productive mines. In addition the major mines are owned by mining finance houses such as Anglo American Corporation of South Africa and Gold Fields of South Africa. Most South African gold mines have an estimated life of less than 20 years. It is expected that world production will fall during the next two decades and that not only the price of gold but the price of gold mining shares will rise.

Canada, being the second largest producer of gold (though a substantially smaller producer than South Africa) has about 20 operating gold mines. The mines are more varied in Canada than in South Africa and the ore more difficult and costly to extract. Their yields, both in terms of output to capital employed and in terms of dividends to shareholders, are consequently much lower than are yields on South African gold shares. Canadian mining shares are listed on the Canadian stock exchanges and are not in general quoted on other markets.

Australian shares are listed both in Australia and in London where they are quoted and traded in Australian dollars. The number of mines and output is relatively small although one mine—Bouginville (which is in New Guinea)—is currently the world's largest gold and copper mine.

Yields from Australian mines are relatively good and in general better than Canadian but not as good as South African mines. The number of shares and investment opportunities are smaller than those available in the Canadian and, of course, South African market.

In the US, the third largest producer in the free world, gold mining is not concentrated in a specific area but spread across the States. The different types of mines and varying costs of production make it difficult to generalize about returns on US gold shares. There are relatively few US gold mining shares available; they are listed on the New York stock exchange and are not quoted in foreign markets. The largest US gold mining company is Homestake Mining.

Gold options

The market in gold options is still relatively young. Futures exchanges in Chicago and New York have made applications to the US authorities to allow them to open trading in gold options, but these have so far been rejected by the Commodities Futures Trading Committee (CFTC).

For some years it has been possible to buy gold options privately through banks in Switzerland. Valeurs White Weld in Geneva is one such trader, dealing on average in about 300 000 ounces of gold options per day.

The first public gold option market to open was on the Winnipeg Commodity Exchange in Canada. Call options were first traded on 30 April 1979. Contract sizes were originally 100 troy ounces at striking prices in multiples of US$20. Small contracts of 20 troy ounces are now available as well as silver call options in contract sizes of 200 troy ounces.

The newest market opened in April 1981 on the European Options Exchange (EOE) in Amsterdam. The EOE already provides a traded options market in shares of US and European companies but the growth of that market has been slow. It is hoped that the introduction of a gold options market, together with a planned options market in fixed interest securities, will stimulate greater worldwide interest in the exchange.

The EOE offers both call and put options in gold contracts of 10 troy ounces. A call option is the right to purchase gold at a specified price (the exercise price). A put option is the right to sell gold at a specified exercise price. The option has a finite life of up to nine months. The investor may choose one of three specified expiration dates, each of which falls on the third Friday of the expiration months. The expiration months are February, May, August and November.

Market makers on the exchange (known as options writers) usually quote options prices for up to three expiration dates forward, e.g. February, May and August or August, November and February.

The price of an option, known as a premium, is quoted is US dollars per troy ounce. The premium depends on the exercise price and the expiration date. The premium is roughly four to five per cent of the contract value but, of course, is higher if the exercise price is low and the expiration date is farther away.

Once the premium is paid, the investor is not subject to any further margin calls.

He may exercise his option at any time up to and including the expiry date, or he may sell his option through the exchange to another third party. Alternatively he may allow his option to lapse, neither exercising nor selling it.

For example, if the price of gold is $600 per ounce and an investor expects the price to rise sharply in the near future he may choose to purchase a call option with a short expiry date: in November 1981 he may have purchased a call option contract for February 1982 at $630 per ounce. This would entitle the investor to purchase 10 ounces of gold at $630 per ounce at or before the third Friday (19th) of February. For this option he would have paid approximately $250 (i.e., about four per cent of $630 × 10 ounces). If, before the expiry date, the price of gold had risen to $660, he may have chosen to exercise his option to purchase the gold at $30 less than he would be able to resell it in the cash market. Alternatively he may have decided to sell his option which would be worth at least $300 (i.e., $30 × 10). If conversely an investor expected the price of gold to fall he would engage in a similar transaction but would purchase a put option entitling him to sell gold at a price he hoped would be higher than the future cash price.

Options trading thus enables investors to speculate in the price of gold while only having to put down a fraction of the contract value. There is potential for substantial capital gains, while the potential for loss is limited to the cost of the option. It should be remembered that the option premium is a foregone cost and does not represent part of the purchase price if the option to buy (or sell) is exercised.

Dealing may be arranged through any bank or stockbroker that is a member of the EOE. Members include about 90 banks and brokers from a number of European countries and the United States. They charge standard commission fees as shown in Table 26.11.

Table 26.11

Number of contracts	Commission fees (US dollars)		
	Opening orders	Closing orders	Combination orders
Less than 10 contracts	$15 per contract subject to minimum of $25	$4 per contract subject to minimum of $10	$15 per opening and $4 per closing contract subject to minimae of $25 and $10
10 contracts (one round lot)	$120	$30	$12 per opening contract and $3 per closing contract; less for more than 10 contracts at dealer's discretion
More than 10 contracts	$120 per round lot plus $12 per additional contract	$30 per round lot plus $3 per additional contract	

Gold futures

The gold futures market centres principally in the US, where there are five exchanges for public futures trading. These exchanges are:

Chicago Board of Trade (CBT)
International Monetary Market (IMM) also in Chicago
Commodity Exchange Inc (COMEX)
The New York Mercantile Exchange
Mid-America Commodity Exchange

Other markets have subsequently developed, namely,

Sydney Gold Futures Market
Hong Kong Gold Futures Market
Gold Exchange of Singapore
Winnipeg Commodity Exchange
London Gold Futures Market
Tokyo Gold Exchange

When an investor purchases a gold futures contract he pays a deposit on gold bullion which he contracts to purchase at a specific date in the future. In practice however most contracts are closed before the delivery date and less than one per cent of all futures contracts result in physical delivery of gold. Nevertheless, in theory the investor is undertaking to take delivery of the gold at the specified future date and must then pay the difference between his deposit and the price at which he has contracted to buy. If at the future date, the price of gold has risen above the price at which he contracted to buy, he has made a profit since he can sell the gold at a higher price than he has bought it. If the price of gold falls he makes a loss equivalent to the difference between the price he has contracted to pay and the current price of gold. He can however sell, or close, his contract through the exchange at any time prior to delivery date. The premium or discount at which he sells his contract will depend on the price of gold relative to the price of the contract. Futures trading differs from options trading in that the investor stands to lose all of his investment and more if the price moves against him. Unlike an options contract there is no striking price with a futures contract. The investor is under contract to purchase the gold at a future date and if the price moves against him he must put up a bigger and bigger margin deposit as a guarantee that he can make the purchase. While he may sell the contract on he may lose all of his original investment and perhaps more in the form of larger margin calls. On the other hand, if the price moves up the investor may make substantial gains. Since he has only been required to deposit a small proportion of the total value of the contract he may stand to gain a considerable profit of several times his original investment. Gold futures trading is thus a highly geared method of investment.

612

The deposit is usually known as a margin requirement. The original margin is the sum that the investor must initially put up when the contract is first negotiated. This is usually a minimum of $75 an ounce but more normally a broker will ask for $100 an ounce. Large and creditworthy clients may only be required to provide half of this amount. The minimum original margin amount is deposited with the clearing house, which is associated with the exchange. Variations in margins are assessed on a day-by-day basis. If the price of gold moves against the investor, he is required to put up a further margin to cover this loss. For example, assume an investor purchases a 100-ounce contract for October gold at $750 an ounce. The whole contract is worth $75 000. His original margin is a minimum of $7500 but the broker would probably ask for $10 000, the additional requirement being a form of performance bond. The current price is, say, $725 but the investor expects the price to rise. However, if the price falls to, say, $700 an ounce the investor will be running a loss of $50 an ounce. He will therefore be called on to make an additional margin payment of $100 \times \$50 = \$5000$. The margin is paid over to the clearing house which debits the investor's broker's account and credits the accounts of other brokers whose clients may have gained by selling gold short. By 'selling gold short' an investor contracts to sell gold at a future date even if he doesn't actually own the gold. If, at the future date, the price of gold has fallen, he can buy it in the spot market at a lower price than he has contracted to sell and thus make a profit.

The futures trading dates on the five US exchanges extend up to 30 months into the future. COMEX contracts may be for the current trading month, the next two months or to any even month (February, April, June, August, October, December) up to 30 months forward. Delivery on COMEX may take place at any time during the contracted month, at the option of the seller.

The IMM trades for current month or for quarter-end months (March, June, September, December) up to 21 months forward.

Contract sizes vary between exchanges. These are shown in the following table. The Chicago Board of Trade deals in contracts of 3 kg only while the smallest size contract is 33.2 oz, traded on the Mid-America commodity exchange.

On each exchange a forward price of gold is quoted for each future delivery month. The forward prices are determined by market forces. Forward prices will be higher than current prices if market sentiment feels that prices will move higher and is manifested by greater demand for forward contracts. Conversely, if a greater number of participants sell forward contracts because they believe that the price will fall, forward prices will be lower than current prices. These forward prices have a significant effect on current spot prices as cash buyers and holders of gold invest in or divest themselves of gold, influenced by the sentiment of the market. Thus while the US exchanges may open with the same spot quote as determined by the London daily gold fix, they may close with very different spot prices. When the London market reopens the following morning the price at which it fixes the spot quote for gold will be influenced by trading activity in the States the previous day.

Most exchanges, however, enforce a limit to the amount by which the price may vary in the course of a trading day. At the COMEX exchange, for example, price changes are registered in multiples of 10¢ per ounce ($10 per contract) and may not

613

Table 26.12 North American gold futures markets (*source: Consolidated Gold Fields and International Monetary Market (IMM)*)

Exchange	1972–1974	1975	1976	1977	1978	1979
No. of contracts						
COMEX	....	396 067	479 363	981 551	3 742 378	6 541 893
IMM	....	409 099	340 921	908 180	2 812 870	3 558 960
Mid-America	....	7 293	2 573	2 650	45 153	200 363
CBT	....	55 476	10 940	13 758	56 470	110 353
NY mercantile exchange	....	37 963	2 351	3 650	3 368	704
Total	....	905 898	836 148	1 909 789	6 660 239	10 412 273
Winnipeg	116 229					

	Forward contract dates	Minimum and maximum price fluctuations per ounce	Contract size	Fineness of gold traded, %	No. of ounces traded 1979	% of total US
COMEX	Even months up to 30 months forward	104 minimum $25 maximum	100 oz	99.5	654 189 300	63.7
IMM	Quarter and months up to 21 months forward	104 minimum $50 maximum	100 oz	99.9	355 896 000	34.6
Mid-America	....	....	33.2 oz	99.5	6 652 052	0.7
CBT	....	....	3 kg	99.5	10 643 546	1.0
NY mercantile exchange	....	....	1 kg	99.9	240 136	
			400 oz	99.9		

change by more than $10 per ounce in the course of a day. This helps to maintain an orderly market but applies only to prices for forward delivery and does not apply to spot or current month delivery contracts.

Of the five US exchanges COMEX and the IMM account for 97 per cent of all gold futures trading, with COMEX handling almost twice as much business as the IMM. The five exchanges all began trading on 31 December 1974. Since then their volume of business has grown dramatically and the COMEX exchange in New York is now a significant influence on all world gold markets. The COMEX exchange is also now reviewing the feasibility of trading futures in gold coins.

The American exchanges were not the first futures markets to be established—Winnipeg opened in 1972—but have established themselves as the major gold futures markets. Other markets have subsequently opened and provide important time links to facilitate round-the-clock trading. The newest market, which opened in London in 1981, has not yet had time to establish itself but is likely to develop as an important market. Even before the futures market opened it was possible to deal in bullion futures contracts in London. The market was very large and comparable in turnover with the Zurich bullion market. There was, however, no public trading floor and the market was made between banks, brokers and bullion dealers. Thus the investor was required to shop around for the best deal. A public market facilitates a common listed price for futures contracts and overall lower dealing costs.

In all futures trading brokers and dealers charge a commission on top of the quoted contract price. Depending on size this is about $90 round turn in COMEX (i.e., $45 for buying and $45 for selling). On the London market commission is $\frac{1}{8}$ per cent round turn.

The Sydney Gold Futures Market opened in April 1978. It operates in a manner similar to the New York COMEX exchange but as yet, relative to the US exchanges trading volume, is still comparatively small.

The fast growing Hong Kong Commodity Exchange, which opened in August 1980, is becoming important as an international market. It provides a vital time zone link between the markets in New York and Europe so that effectively gold trading can now take place 24 hours a day. However, compared to London and New York its volume is very small. The average number of contracts outstanding is about 3000 lots of 100 troy ounces. Daily trading volume is about 300 lots. Trading on the Hong Kong exchange is for the current month or for even months up to nine months forward. Apart from the gold futures market a previously existing cash market exchange—the Kam Ngan exchange—handles orders of about US$500 million a day. It operates on two different systems, one which is similar to dealing methods in London and the other which is based on the old Chinese system which trades gold in sizes and grades which differ from those traded on other western markets.

The Gold Exchange of Singapore which already had a cash market for delivery in either London or Singapore opened a futures market in November 1978. Like the Kam Ngan exchange, the spot market operates on both the Chinese system, in units known as taels, and on the London system in standard units and grades. The futures market operates in a similar fashion to the New York COMEX exchange. It is maintained by the four largest local banks and provides facilities for dealing futures contracts of 100-ounce lots for the current month and even months up to nine months forward. In 1980 the exchange opened trading in kilobar futures contracts (32.150742 troy ounces). This is the smallest contract size available on any market and is hoped to attract small investors to the exchange. The Singapore futures market is slowly growing in volume and also provides an important time zone link with Europe and the US. But turnover is nevertheless still small. The average number of contracts traded daily is 200 to 300 lots.

The Winnipeg commodity exchange was the first exchange to offer a public market in gold futures and opened in 1972. Contracts were available in sizes of 100 and 400 ounces. However, activity was not very high, and when three years later the US exchanges opened, most investor interest was attracted to those exchanges, and consequently further growth of the Winnipeg market has been limited.

The London gold futures market is the newest to open (Spring 1981). It is operated jointly by the members of the already established gold bullion market and the London Metal Exchange (LME) and is supervised by the Bank of England. It is subject to fewer restrictions than the American exchanges, which are supervised by the Commodities Futures Trading Committee (CFTC). For this reason London is likely to attract much business which has previously been transacted in the US. For example US brokers are required to disclose their clients and trading positions to

615

the CFTC but London business is handled on a much more confidential basis. The London exchange also fills a time zone gap since futures trading could previously only be transacted in the US or Far East. London is open for official trading between 8.30 a.m. and noon. This coincides with the close of the New York COMEX exchange and the IMM, both of which open between 9.30 a.m. and 2.30 p.m. Unofficial trading outside the LME ring continues in London in the afternoon.

Contracts are available on the LME in 100- and 400-ounce lots for which an initial margin or deposit of 10 per cent of the contract value is required. The future delivery dates, however, are more limited than on the US exchanges. Forward contracts may be made for spot delivery of six months forward whereas COMEX offers a wider variety of future dates up to 30 months forward. In practice, however, very few contracts are bought for longer than six months.

Finally, Tokyo plans to establish, in 1981, a private gold exchange which is to deal in spot and forward delivery contracts. The exchange is to be structured as a private joint stock company and will provide a dealing floor for members to arrange cash and future contracts.

Glossary

Acceptance credit facility. Where a bank agrees to accept bills of exchange for a customer on a regular basis up to a certain limit. Once the bills are 'accepted' they become bank bills and are readily discountable with a discount house so that the customer may receive the proceeds (less commission) immediately. The face amount of the bill is subsequently remitted to the accepting bank at the due date.

ACU (Asian Currency Unit). A department within some foreign banks with branches in Singapore, which is permitted to engage in specific international transactions but which is restricted in activities it may undertake in the Singapore domestic market.

Accrued interest. Interest due but not yet paid.

Amortization. 1. Where a loan is not repaid in one instalment but over a period of time, and by a number of instalments, the loan is said to be amortized.

2. The reduction of a debt through a 'sinking fund'.

Annuity. A series of payments at fixed intervals of time, for a fixed or determinable period. The payments may be uniform or may vary. They may be yearly or more frequently.

Arbitrage. The switching of funds between markets in order to maximize net gains on short-term investments. Arbitrage normally takes place in large volumes, when small differences in price or yield exist between markets, until such differences are eliminated.

Average life. Where a bond issue is amortized over the time to maturity, or repurchased in the market by means of a purchase fund, the average life is the period of years after issue when 50 per cent of the total loan remains outstanding.

Backwardation. Used sometimes in commodity markets to describe the position when the cash price is higher than the forward price. Used in stock exchange markets to describe the position taken by an investor where he has not yet acquired securities, and does not want to at prevailing rates, so does not take up delivery of securities but carries the delivery over to the next account period. A fee is payable for this facility. Backwardation is the opposite of contango.

Basis point. One hundredth of one per cent (i.e., 0.01 per cent). Used to define differences in interest or yield. For example 20 basis points is 0.20 per cent. Often abbreviated to '20 points'; 150 basis points (or points) is 1.50 per cent.

Bearer. Where the interest, dividends and capital are payable to the bearer, or holder, of the security. They may be readily transferred to another holder by hand. They carry coupons that may be detached and exchanged for interest or dividends when due.

Bear market. A market in which prices are falling. Sellers are more predominant than buyers. Usually refers to equity markets.

Bid. Price offered by a prospective borrower or purchaser for loans or securities.

Billion. One thousand million (1 000 000 000). In the terminology of financial markets, this definition of billion is always adopted.

Bond. A written, interest bearing, certificate of debt with the promise to repay the principal of the debt on a specific date.

Bond equivalent yield. See YIELD (1) YIELD ON DISCOUNT SECURITIES.

Book value. The value of a security as it is recorded in the holder's accounting records.

Bullion. Gold or silver of a standard purity in bars of a standard weight.

Bull market. A market in which prices are rising. Buyers are more predominant than sellers. Usually refers to equity markets.

Callable. A feature of some bonds that may be redeemed prior to maturity, at the option of the issuer, but according to terms specified prior to issue.

Call deposits. Deposits that can be called (or withdrawn) at the option of the lender (and in some cases the borrower) after a specified period. The period is short, usually one or two days. Interest is paid at prevailing short-term rates.

Call option. An option to purchase designated securities (i.e., shares, currencies or commodities) at a predetermined price and within a specified time limit.

Call-over system. Method of dealing used mainly on smaller stock exchanges. Bid and offer prices and amounts are matched by the dealers shouting out their orders by open outcry.

Capital market. The market for the purchase and sale of medium- and long-term financial instruments. The market includes bonds and notes, usually of more than one year maturity, equities and commodities.

Certificate of deposit (CD). A certificate evidencing an interest-bearing time deposit with a bank. The certificate is usually negotiable.

Civil year. Three hundred and sixty-five days (366 in leap years), used as the basis for interest calculations in many countries.

Commercial paper. A certificate evidencing in unsecured corporate debt of short maturity. The paper represents a promise by the borrowing company to repay the loan at a specified date. It is similar to a CD but is issued by a corporation instead of by a bank.

Contango. Used in commodity markets to describe the position when the cash price is lower than the forward price. Used in stock exchange markets to describe the fee paid by an investor for the privilege of carrying the settlement of a transaction over from one account period to another. Contango is the opposite of backwardation.

Convertible currency. A currency that is freely convertible into another currency. Currencies for which domestic exchange controls legislation specifically prohibits conversion into other currencies are non-convertible.

Convertible bond. A bond issued by a company and that confers on the holder the right to convert the bond into shares of the company at a predetermined price and at, or during, determinable dates.

Coupon. A slip attached to a bearer bond which can be detached and exchanged for an interest payment or dividend due at a specific date. The term 'coupon' is also generally applied to mean interest. Thus, a fixed coupon bond is one that bears a fixed rate of interest but need not necessarily be a bearer bond. The coupon date is the date to which interest is calculated and payable.

Currency exposure. Currency exposure exists if assets are held, or income earned, in one currency while liabilities are denominated in another currency. The position is exposed to changes in the relative values of the two currencies such that the cost of the liabilities may be increased or the value of the assets or earnings be decreased.

Currency swap. Where a currency is exchanged for another at current exchange rates and the transaction reverses at a specified future date at subsequently prevailing exchange rates. Currency swaps are undertaken by some central banks to help the domestic banking system when it is short of liquidity in a particular currency. They are also sometimes used to provide holders of one currency with deposits denominated in another currency.

Debenture. A document that sets out the terms of a loan. If the lenders are many members of the public, the debentures deed is held by trustees on behalf of the debenture stockholders. The stockholders receive a fixed rate of interest as stated by the debenture deed.

Demand deposits (Sight deposits). Deposits that may be withdrawn on demand by the depositor. Demand or sight deposits are normally placed for the safe-keeping facilities only and usually are not paid interest. They are current accounts against which cheques may be written and out of which current payments are made. They have no fixed maturity.

Deposits. Money placed with banks or similar financial institutions.

Deposits at notice. Deposits that remain placed unless called by the depositor at a specified period before the money is repaid. For example money at seven days' notice means the depositor must notify the borrower that he requires repayment at least seven days in advance. Interest on the deposit is recalculated every seven days.

Discount. A discount is the difference between the cost price of a security and its face value or value at maturity. Some securities (e.g., treasury bills) are issued at a discount. The annualized rate of discount represents the yield on the security. Securities that, shortly after issue, are selling at below their cost at issue, may also be described as being at a discount.

Discount rate. The annualized rate of discount attaching to debt securities that are issued below par (e.g., treasury bills and bankers' acceptances). For example, a sterling treasury bill issued at £97.50 has a price of £2.50 below par (£100). If the bill is of three months' maturity, it has a discount rate of 10 per cent, i.e. $(100 - 97.5) \times 4$. See also BOND EQUIVALENT YIELD. Alternatively, the annualized rate at which a central bank will purchase (at a discount) certain securities from the banking system.

Discount window. The rediscount facility offered by a central bank. The term derives from the days when a bank or authorized dealer could take securities to a special counter, or window, at the central bank where they would be purchased (or rediscounted) by the central bank in exchange for cash.

Dividend yield. Relates to the return on shares and is the ratio of the dividend per share to the market price of the share.

Double taxation treaty. A treaty between two contracting states to determine which of their two competing rights to tax certain income should be paramount. In the absence of such treaties, two states can tax the same income. For example, because

619

one taxes income from a source in their state and the other all income accruing to a resident of the state, double taxation will arise unless the domestic law of one of the states allows relief for tax levied by the other.

Earnings yield. Also known as income yield, relates to the return on shares and is the ratio of a company's net profit (or earnings) per share to the market price of the share. It is the reciprocal of price earnings ratio.

ECU. The European Currency Unit (ECU) is a basket of the currencies of the members of the European Economic Community (excluding the Greek drachma). It is valued according to specific amounts of the nine currencies of which it is composed. Its value is determined daily and published by the commission of the European Communities.

EMS. The European Monetary System (EMS) commenced on 13 March 1979 as a more broadly based successor to the 'snake' in an attempt to promote closer monetary co-operation and exchange rate stability between the members of the European Economic Community. The currencies of each member state (excluding those of the UK and of Greece, which is a new member of the EEC) participate in the monetary system. The system requires participating countries to maintain their currencies within margins of fluctuation relative to established central rates. These margins are 1.25 per cent either side of each currency's central rate (i.e., bands of 2.5 per cent fluctuation) except for the lira which may fluctuate within a six per cent band. The ECU, as the unit of account, against which each of the member currencies' central rates were established, is the denominator of the EMS.

Equity capital. That part of the capital of a company that belongs to the true owners of the company. Owners of a company's equity capital are entitled to all profits and reserves after the lenders of debt capital and other creditors have been paid their dues.

Eurobond. An international bond that is issued and traded outside the country of the borrower and also outside the constraints or regulations of any single country.

Eurocredit. Medium-term international credits provided by one or more syndicates of international banks, denominated in currencies that may not be those of the country of the borrower or of the banks.

Eurocurrency. A foreign currency deposited with a bank outside the country in which that currency is used as legal tender. The foreign currency may be used in transactions and remains a Eurocurrency unless it enters the boundaries of its home country. In brief it is any currency held by a non-resident.

Eurodollar. The US dollar is the major currency in the Euromarket. All dollars deposited with banks or used for transactions, outside the US, are Eurodollars.

Euromarket. The market for transactions in Eurocurrencies or financial instruments denominated in Eurocurrencies. The market is made by telephone between dealers in major financial centres around the world.

Factoring. The purchase of a trading company's invoiced debts at a discount by a factoring company in order to facilitate the efficient collection of the selling company's debts. The factor becomes responsible for the collection of the debt often without recourse to the selling company.

Fiscal policy. Controls determined by the government that take effect through the system of taxation.

Financial year. Three hundred and sixty

days comprising 12 months, each of 30 days. Used as the basis for interest calculations in many countries.

Fixed currency. A currency whose value is fixed relative to another currency or to a monetary unit. In order to maintain the fixed value of its currency, a country must intervene on the world foreign exchange markets and direct some of its domestic economic policy towards the same objective.

Fixed time deposits. Deposits that are placed for a specified period of time at a fixed rate of interest for the whole period. Early repayment at the request of the depositor normally incurs penalties in terms of interest lost.

Floating currency. A currency with no fixed value relative to other currencies or monetary units is said to be floating on the world foreign exchange markets. If the monetary authorities do not intervene in order to maintain the general value of a currency it is said to be freely floating, even when the authorities intervene to prevent excessive volatility. If the authorities do intervene in order to maintain a general value or a trend in value, the currency is said to be under a controlled float.

Floating rate note. Bonds on which the coupon is established periodically and calculated with reference to short-term interest rates.

Foreign bond. An international bond that is issued outside the country of the borrower but onto the domestic market of a foreign country where it is traded subject to that country's regulations.

Forward market. A market with no specialized trading floor for the buying and selling of currencies, financial instruments or commodities for future delivery. The market is conducted by telephone between customers and dealers. There are no specified contract sizes and the future delivery date is determined by the customer and not by specific set dates. No deposit or margin calls are paid when a position is opened. Most positions (about 90 per cent) result in actual delivery.

Forward position. A commitment to buy/sell a currency/commodity at some future date at a price agreed in advance.

Franked income. A technical UK tax term describing a dividend paid by a UK resident company together with its associated tax credit. This credit may be recoverable according to the country of residence and the status of the recipient.

Futures market. A market place with a specialized trading floor for the buying and selling of commodities, currencies or financial instruments for future delivery. Contracts are bought and sold in specific sizes for delivery at a specific future date. On purchase or sale a small proportion of the contract value is paid (see MARGIN). A very small number of contracts (about one per cent) are actually delivered since most positions are closed before the due delivery date.

Gold standard. A country on the gold standard has its currency backed entirely by gold which is held in the country's official reserves. The country also agrees to convert its currency into gold on demand from the bearer.

Gross new issues. The amount or value of new issues of securities excluding the amount or value of securities that have been redeemed.

Hedge. To guard against fluctuation of an exchange rate/interest rate/price of a currency/security/stock/commodity between two given dates. This is achieved by offsetting a present purchase sale by the sale or purchase of a similar or different security for delivery at some future date.

621

IMF. International Monetary Fund. An international agency founded in 1946 as a result of the Bretton Woods Agreement in 1944. Its object is to safeguard the foreign exchange markets and provide multi-lateral clearing systems. It provides advances to member countries, with balance of payments deficits and inadequate foreign currency reserves for transacting its foreign trade, with any currency in return for that country's currency repaid over a period of years.

Member countries contribute to the fund according to their economic size and have voting rights in proportion to the amount of their contributions.

Inscribed stock. Debt securities for which the names of the stock- or bondholders are registered in a record book. The same as registered securities.

Interbank market. A market for transactions exclusively or predominantly within the banking system. In many countries the market for short-term money is an interbank market since banks borrow and lend between each other in order to balance their books on a daily basis. Non-bank entities may or may not be permitted to participate.

International Monetary Fund. See IMF.

Issue. A sale of securities.

Jobber. Intermediary on the London stock exchange who stands ready at all times to make a market in specific securities.

Lead manager. A bank with the main responsibility for arranging a bond issue or international Eurocredit on behalf of the client, or borrower. It recruits other banks to help sell the issue to the public (or to lend if a Eurocredit). These other banks comprise the managing syndicate under the leadership of the lead managing bank which assesses the market and advises the client on rates and terms.

Leaseback. Where an asset is sold to a company which then hires (leases back) the same to the former owner normally for the duration of its economic life.

Lender of last resort. Term used for institutions, usually central banks, that provide original liquidity in a financial system and stand ready, at all times, to provide liquidity through the appropriate market mechanisms.

LIBOR. London Interbank Offered Rate. The interest rate at which banks in London lend (or offer) money to other banks or to substantial borrowers in the London interbank market. These offered rates are quoted by dealers in London and other financial centres for sterling and all other Eurocurrencies for all terms that are available in the market. Thus, three months Eurodollar LIBOR is the rate quoted in the London market for dollars lent for three months.

Liquidity. Cash or securities that are so marketable that they may be converted into cash at any time with minimal risk of capital loss.

Liquidity ratio. Proportion of the assets or liabilities of certain financial institutions that must be held in liquid assets as specified by the monetary authorities.

Listed company. A company whose shares are registered for trading on the stock exchange or share trading market.

London interbank offered rate. See LIBOR.

Long position. A long position signifies ownership of a financial instrument (see SHORT POSITION).

Making a market. Dealers who stand ready to buy and sell certain securities and quote bid and offer prices in these securities are said to be 'making a market' in those securities. If they stand ready at all times to buy and sell those securities they are said to be 'maintaining a market' for those securities.

Margin. Money or collateral deposited by both buyers and sellers of futures contracts. The original margin is the amount of money placed when the position is established. A margin call is additional money demanded by the brokerage house from the customer when the value of the contract has moved adversely. The margin call brings the customers equity in an account back to the minimum original margin level.

Marketability. A measure of the ease with which accounts can be sold in the secondary market.

Maturity. The date at which a loan becomes due for repayment or renewal.

Money market. The market for the purchase and sale of short-term financial instruments. The short term is usually defined as less than one year.

Monetary policy. Controls that are determined by the government and/or central bank and that take effect by influencing the workings of the financial and monetary system. Thus all controls that influence borrowing and lending flows and/or interest rates may be classified within the general term of monetary policy.

Negotiable. When used with respect to securities, it means that title to a security is transferable by delivery.

Net new issues. The amount or value of new issues of securities less the amount or value of securities redeemed.

Nominal value. The face value of a security. For debt instruments this is the par value (usually 100). For equity securities it is the fully paid-up issue price.

Nominal yield. The coupon rate of interest attaching to a debt security.

Offer. Price offered by a prospective lender or seller for loans or securities.

Offshore. Relates to locations outside the controls of domestic monetary, exchange and legislative authorities. Offshore may not necessarily be outside the national boundaries of a country. In some countries certain banks or other institutions may be granted offshore status and thus be exempt from all or specific controls or legislation (e.g., Offshore Banking Units and Asian Currency Units).

Offshore banking unit (OBU). A department within a bank that, in certain countries (e.g., Bahrain), is permitted to engage in specific transactions (usually Euromarket business) that, by local regulations, ordinary domestic banks are not allowed to undertake.

Open market operations. Dealings undertaken by the central bank in the financial market with the object of influencing overall liquidity and interest rates.

Option bond. A bond (usually a Eurobond) which confers on the lender the right to opt to receive interest and/or capital in a currency other than that in which the bond is denominated.

Overdraft. A permit to withdraw more money than is in a bank account but up to a specified limit.

Over-the-counter. The market made over the telephone by brokers and dealers. Transactions are made by negotiation rather than by general auction as otherwise occurs on the floor of an exchange market-place.

Par. The face value of a security exclusive of any premium or discount that may be inherent in the market value or current price. The par value is the value on which interest, in the case of loan securities, is calculated.

'Pass thru' securities. Securities usually mortgage backed, where part capital is repaid to the lender together with interest payments.

Point. One basis point (i.e., 0.01 per cent).

Portfolio. List of investments held by an individual or company, or a list of loans made by a bank or financial institution.

Preference shares. Shares that have preferential rights to dividends, usually a fixed sum, before dividends are paid out to

623

ordinary shareholders. They usually carry no voting rights. The rights of preference shareholders are established in a company's articles of association and may differ between companies in a variety of ways.

Premium. The difference between the market price of a security and its face value, or asset value, if that is lower than the market price. Alternatively, the price paid for the purchase of share or commodity options.

Primary market. The market relating to the original issue or first sale of new securities.

Prime rate. The rate at which a bank will lend to its prime or most creditworthy customers. Also known as bank rate in some countries.

Private company. A company whose shares are not available for purchase and sale by the general public.

Private placement. An issue of securities that is sold to a limited number of institutional investors, as compared with a public offering which is offered to the general investing public. Private placements are sometimes listed on the stock exchange in order to comply with certain formalities.

Privately owned. Owned by individuals or companies in the private sector.

Promissory note. A document, issued by a borrower, that represents an unconditional promise to the lender to repay a certain sum of money at either a fixed future time or on demand. The sum may be made payable to a specified person or to the bearer. The document, or note, carries the signature of the borrower. If it carries only the borrower's signature it is known as one name paper (e.g. CDs, commercial paper). If it is guaranteed by a bank and carries the signatures of the borrower and of the bank it is known as two name paper (e.g., bankers' acceptances). If it carries the signature of a third person it is known as three name paper (e.g., bill of exchange financing the export or import of goods). The lender's risk reduces as the number of signatures on the note increases.

Prospectus. A detailed financial statement issued by a company prior to the sale of new securities.

Public company. A company whose shares are available for purchase by the general public.

Publicly owned. Owned by the state or public sector.

Put option. An option to sell designated securities at a predetermined price and within a specified time limit.

Quoted company. Another term for listed company. Shares in the company are available for trading by the general public through a recognized stock exchange or share trading market.

Qualitative controls. Controls applied by the monetary authorities that influence the direction of lending or borrowing within specific sectors of the economy.

Quantitative controls. Controls applied by the monetary authorities that specify limits to specific types of lending or borrowing in the financial system.

Redemption. The liquidation of a debt by repayment by the borrower.

Redemption yield. See YIELD (4) YIELD TO MATURITY.

Rediscount. The resale of an instrument such as a bankers' acceptance or trade bill which, since it carries no coupon, has already been discounted by the lender. The resale is usually made with the central bank through its lender of last resort facilities, or with a discount house. The instrument is sold at a price which is less than its face value (i.e. at a discount).

Registered. Whereby the securities are not issued to the holders but the names of the holders are inscribed in a record book, or register. When the securities are transferred, certain formalities must be followed so that the name of one holder can be erased and the name of another be written in. The security holder receives a certificate stating the amount of his holding and interest or dividend payments are forwarded automatically.

Reserves. Assets set aside as security for liabilities or profits retained after all outgoings have been paid. The reserves of a company are retained profits. The reserves of banks are liquid assets held against a proportion of their liabilities represented by deposits and other borrowings. The official reserves of a country are gold and foreign currencies accumulated from foreign trade transactions.

Reserve ratio. The proportion of liabilities held by banks and, sometimes, other financial institutions that must be in the form of cash or liquid assets as specified by the monetary authorities.

Reverse yield curve. See YIELD CURVE.

Samurai bond. A bond denominated in Japanese yen and issued in the Japanese capital market by a foreign borrower.

Savings deposits. Accounts in which the depositor can place money at regular or irregular intervals. Money may also be withdrawn at any time by application. Such deposits usually earn a low rate of interest relative to other market rates. Interest rates are also more stable than other market rates and are usually changed only after a trend has been established.

SDR. Special Drawing Rights ('SDRs') were introduced as reserve assets for central banks in an amendment in 1969 to the Article of Agreement of the IMF. The value of the SDR is now defined as a weighted sum of the values of five major world currencies, the US dollar, Deutschemark, pound sterling, French franc and Japanese yen.

Secondary market. The market in the purchase and sale of outstanding or existing securities that have already been issued to and taken up by original holders and are subsequently being bought and sold for the second time or more.

Security. Strictly, paper given and guaranteed by a borrower as a safeguard for a loan. It is generally applied to bonds, shares, certificates of liability etc., but if used discriminatingly it should not be applied to shares that are not guaranteed by the borrowing company.

Settlement. The completion of an exchange of securities and the necessary payments. Accrued interest is calculated from the settlement date.

Share option. A right sold to an investor conferring on him the option to buy or sell shares of a particular company at a predetermined price and within a specified time limit.

Short position. In financial markets a short position normally means the sale of a security without ownership. Before or when delivery is due, the investor must purchase or borrow the securities in order that he can make the delivery and close his position. He makes a profit if the price at which he buys is lower than the price at which he has contracted to sell.

Short can also mean simply lack of ownership of a financial instrument.

Sight deposits. Deposits that may be withdrawn on demand by the depositor. Sight deposits are normally placed for the safekeeping facilities only and usually are not paid interest. They are current accounts against which cheques may be written and out of which current payments are made. They have no fixed maturity.

Sinking fund. In the case of a loan repaid by instalments, each instalment can be considered to consist of two parts, one portion of each instalment representing the interest payable on the loan, the other representing the capital repayment of the loan. The part that represents the repayment of capital is known as the 'sinking fund'. The sinking fund thus accumulated with interest over the period of the loan will equal the original loan.

Specialist. A dealer who specializes in the trading of specific securities, usually shares, on the floor of a stock exchange. He stands ready to buy or sell the securities in which he specializes at all times and thus maintains a market in these shares.

Spot. Cash or current, i.e., the spot price is the immediate cash price; the spot market is the market for current transactions.

Spread. The difference between the bid and offer price of securities.

Stag. Term applied to an investor who makes excessive purchases of a new issue in the hope that the price will rise quickly and that he can subsequently sell at a profit after only a short period.

Stamp duty. A tax payable to the state for transactions in certain types of securities. The securities concerned are stamped when transactions in them are made, signifying that the tax has been paid.

Stock. In some countries (e.g., US), the term applies to ordinary share capital of a company, i.e., common stock. In other countries (e.g., UK) stock may mean share capital that is issued in variable amounts instead of in fixed specified amounts, or it can describe government loans.

Stock dividends. Income from share capital paid in the form of additional share capital instead of in cash.

Striking price. The price which a particular share must reach before an option to purchase the shares can be exercised. Also known as the exercise price.

Tap. Tap stocks or securities 'issued on tap' are those that are continuously available and may be obtained on demand by the investor—as with water from a tap. The borrower may determine a maximum amount of a tap security to be issued. When this maximum limit has been reached, the tap is said to have 'run out'.

Tender. When securities are issued by tender, subscribers are invited to submit bids, in a similar manner to an auction. The securities are then allotted by one of two methods. They may be allotted to the highest bidders first and then in descending order of bids received, or they may be allotted at terms determined by the average bid price to all subscribers on a *pro rata* basis.

Tonnes. A metric ton equal to 2204.6 pounds or 100 kilograms.

Traded options. Options that may be bought and sold as securities in their own right.

Trading post system. Method of dealing used on many larger stock exchanges. Certain securities are traded at specific places, or posts, on the floor of the stock exchange. Dealers meet at these posts and make transactions either between each other or through specialists.

Underwriter. A financial institution that accepts the risk that a particular issue of securities is not fully subscribed in the market so that it then becomes responsible for taking up any amount not subscribed.

VAT. Value added tax. A tax calculated as a percentage of purchase price, payable on the purchase of goods and services in certain countries.

Warrant. Voucher evidencing the entitlement of the holder to purchase securities at a fixed price during a specified period.

Withholding tax. A retention on behalf of the tax authorities by the person paying over an amount that is taxable under the laws of the country, of which that person is a resident, to another person (resident in or outside that country) of a sum that represents part or all of the tax liability for that other person in respect of that income.

Writer. A dealer who makes a market in options by issuing options and who stands ready to honour the provisions of the options, should they be exercised by the holder.

Yankee bond. A bond denominated in US dollars and issued in the US market by a foreign borrower.

Yield. The return earned from an investment. In essence there are two main components to the yield or securities: the income from the investment and the principal invested. However, there are many different types of yields which are calculated in different ways according to how the return is to be measured and the type of security. The major yields are as follows:

(1) Yield on discount securities.

Securities such as treasury bills, trade bills or bankers' acceptances do not carry a coupon but are issued and traded at a discount to their par (or face) value. The difference between the purchase price and par value represents the return. The yield can be calculated on a simple basis or on a bond equivalent basis. The simple basis gives the annualized rate of discount. The bond equivalent yield gives the real return taking into account the principal invested and the face value of the security at redemption. The rate of discount is calculated as follows:

$$i = \frac{P \times d/y}{D}$$

where P = the face value
D = amount of discount
d = number of days per year (i.e., 360 or 365)
i = per annum rate of discount

For example, a discount security with a face value of 100 000 with a life of 91 days, purchased at 97 506.85 (i.e., a discount of 2 493.15)

$$i = \frac{100\,000 \times 91/365}{2\,493.15} = 10.0\%$$

(2) Bond equivalent yield.

This is the true yield available on discount securities and is always higher than the annualized rate of discount. The calculation is as follows:

$$\text{Yield} = \frac{i \times P}{A}$$

where i = per annum rate of discount
P = face value
A = amount paid at purchase

Thus, from the above example

$$\text{Yield} = \frac{10 \times 100\,000}{97\,506.85} = 10.256\%$$

Thus the true yield of 10.256 per cent is higher than the rate of discount of 10 per cent.

(3) Current yield; also known as **income yield, flat yield** or **running yield.**

This is a simple method of calculating the return on an investment but it does not take into account the profit on redemption nor does it compound interest payments due during the life of the loan. It is calculated as follows:

$$\frac{\text{Coupon rate}}{\text{Market price}} \times 100\%.$$

(4) Redemption yield; also known as **yield to maturity.**

It is used to calculate the return on bonds with a fixed redemption date and which carry a coupon rate of interest.

It takes account of the interest payments that are receivable from the date of calculation to maturity. In essence it gives the internal rate of return of an investment based on the current market price, the price at which it will be redeemed, the number of years to redemption and the income (or interest) payments between the time of purchase and redemption. The calculation involves an iterative process to solve the equation for i, which is the internal rate of return or yield to maturity. The general equation is:

$$P = A \times \left[\frac{1 - (1 + i)^{-n}}{i}\right] + \left[\frac{S}{(1 + i)^n}\right]$$

where P = price of security at purchase

A = amount of interest received in each period

S = the par value or value at maturity

n = the number of periods to redemption, i.e., if there are five years to redemption but interest is paid semiannually, then $n = 10$

i = internal rate of return or yield to maturity.

(5) **Yield to average life.**

This is the same as yield to maturity except the average life term is substituted in the number of periods to redemption.

Yield curve. A graphic illustration of the relationship between yield and maturity for the same type of security. In normal market conditions, yields should increase as maturity lengthens to compensate the lender for the loss of the use of his money for longer periods. In tight monetary conditions yields on short-term securities may be higher than on securities of longer maturity. This produces a downward sloping yield curve known as a reverse or inverse yield curve.

Index

compiled by K. G. B. Bakewell

The index is arranged 'letter by letter', spaces between words being ignored, so that 'United States' precedes 'Unit trusts'. Page references in italics indicate tables or diagrams.